A TEXT
FOURTH EDITION

PUBLIC ADMINISTRATION
i n   C a n a d a

Kenneth
Kernaghan

David
Siegel

Brock University

 I⊤P Nelson

an International Thomson Publishing company

Toronto • Albany • Bonn • Boston • Cincinnati • Detroit • London • Madrid • Melbourne
Mexico City • New York • Pacific Grove • Paris • San Francisco • Singapore • Tokyo • Washington

I(T)P® **International Thomson Publishing**
The ITP logo is a trademark under licence
www.thomson.com

Published in 1999 by
I(T)P® Nelson
A division of Thomson Canada Limited
1120 Birchmount Road
Scarborough, Ontario M1K 5G4
www.nelson.com

© ITP Nelson, 1999

Canadian Cataloguing in Publication Data

Kernaghan, Kenneth, 1940-
    Public administration in Canada

4th ed.
Includes bibliographical references and index.
ISBN 0-17-616653-X

1. Public administration - Canada.   2. Canada -
Politics and government.   I. Siegel, David.   II. Title.

JL108.K45   1999   351.71   C99-930272-8

Editorial Director	Michael Young
Marketing Manager	Kevin Smulan
Acquisitions Editor	Nicole Gnutzman
Project Editor	Jenny Anttila
Managing Production Coordinator	Brad Horning
Production Editor	Valerie Adams
Copy Editor	Marjan Farahbaksh
Interior Design	Suzanne Peden
Cover Design	Sylvia Vander Schee
Cover Illustration	Heather Holbrook
Composition	Alicja Jamorski

Printed and bound in Canada
1 2 3 4 (BG) 02 01 00 99

To Helgi, Kevin, Kelly, Scott, Kris, and Lisa
and
to Nancy and Sarah

About the Authors

Kenneth Kernaghan is Professor of Politics and Management at Brock University. He received his Honours B.A. in Economics and Political Science from McMaster University and his M.A. and Ph.D. in Political Science from Duke University. He is the author or editor of many books, monographs, and articles on public administration and public policy. He has served as President of the Institute of Public Administration of Canada, Editor of *Canadian Public Administration,* founding Director of the Case Program in Canadian Public Administration, Chairperson of the Academic Advisory Committee of the Ontario Council on University Affairs, and since 1989 Editor of the *International Review of Administrative Sciences.* He is a Research Fellow of the Canadian Centre for Management Development, a recipient of the Vanier Gold Medal for excellence in public administration, and a Fellow of the Royal Society of Canada.

David Siegel is Professor of Politics and Associate Vice-President, Academic, at Brock University. He received his undergraduate degree in accounting from the University of Louisville and is a Certified General Accountant. He has also received an M.A. in Public Administration from Carleton University and a Ph.D. in Political Science from the University of Toronto. He has written and edited several books about public administration and local government and has written articles for *Canadian Public Administration, Canadian Journal of Political Science, Municipal World, Optimum,* and *CGA Magazine.* He has served as Director of the Case Program in Canadian Public Administration, as a member of the National Executive of the Institute of Public Administration of Canada, as a member of the Board of Directors of the Ontario Municipal Management Institute, and as President of the Canadian Association of Programs in Public Administration.

Contents

Preface   vii
Introduction   ix

Part I: **Introduction to Public Administration**

   1. What Is Public Administration?   3
   2. What Is Public Bureaucracy?   23
   3. Public Administration and Organization Theory:
      The Structural Foundation   40
   4. Public Administration and Organization Theory:
      The Humanistic Response   62
   5. Communication, Leadership, and Motivation   89

Part II: **The Policy Dimension of Public Administration**

   6. Making Public Policy   125
   7. Implementing, Measuring, and Evaluating Public Policy   165

Part III: **Delivering Government Services**

   8. Government Departments and Central Agencies   199
   9. Public Enterprise and Privatization   224
  10. Regulatory Agencies and Deregulation   258
  11. Alternative Service Delivery   294

Part IV: **Politics, Values, and Public Administration**

  12. Institutional and Value Frameworks   319
  13. Power, Politics, and Bureaucracy   338
  14. Responsibility, Accountability, and Ethics   365

Part V: **The Bureaucracy in the Political System**

  15. The Executive and the Bureaucracy   389
  16. Interdepartmental and Intradepartmental Relations   406
  17. The Legislature and the Bureaucracy   424
  18. The Judiciary and the Bureaucracy   445
  19. Intergovernmental Administrative Relations   461
  20. Pressure Groups, Political Parties, and the Bureaucracy   483
  21. The Public, the Media, and the Bureaucracy   502

Part VI: **The Management of Organizational Resources**

  22. The Management of Government Programs   527
  23. The Management of Human Resources   554

24. Representative Bureaucracy, Employment Equity, and
    Managing Diversity   575
25. Collective Bargaining   596
26. The Budgetary Process   615
27. The Management of Financial Resources   643

Part VII: The Future of Public Administration

28. The Future of Public Administration in Canada   663

Appendix: How to Write a Research Paper in Public Administration   673

Glossary   677

Name Index   689

Subject Index   696

Preface

The response to the first three editions of this text has been very gratifying. In this fourth edition, we have made substantial changes to ensure that the book is as comprehensive and up-to-date as possible. We recognize that our text is already more comprehensive than most public administration texts, including the many texts published in the United States. We have, therefore, resisted pressures to extend the book's length. We have aimed for comprehensiveness in the dictionary sense of "covering much" rather than in the Thesaurus sense of "all-inclusive"; a single volume cannot cover every relevant topic in depth.

The organization of this fourth edition is the same as the third edition, with one major exception. The material in the old Chapter 11 has been integrated into other chapters and an entirely new Chapter 11 focuses on the important topic of alternative service delivery mechanisms. We have retained the popular features of the glossary, the advice on how to write a research paper, and the lengthy bibliographies.

Each chapter has been revised in content or updated, or both. The changes are a response to extensive and continuing reforms in the structures and processes of government in all spheres of Canadian government and to theoretical and conceptual advances. For example, material has been added to cover increasingly important areas of public administration, including the feminist critique of bureaucracy, new forms of organization and new approaches to management, policy communities and networks, and managing diversity.

The purpose of this book is to promote better understanding of the study and practice of public administration in Canada. We hope to enhance our readers' knowledge of the unique nature of administration in the public sector, and their appreciation of the challenges and opportunities of a career in the public service. The readership for the earlier editions of the book has included university and college students in public administration courses, public servants at all levels of government engaged in training and development courses, and knowledgeable lay readers.

We have tried to provide a balanced treatment of the diverse features of public administration by relating theoretical considerations to practical experience, by examining both the political and managerial dimensions of the field, and by covering both enduring and current issues. The book reflects the fact that writings on public administration in Canada have focused primarily on the federal government. Many of the ideas, issues, problems, and practices are, however, relevant to the provincial and municipal spheres of government as well.

Some of the material in this book appeared originally either in scholarly journals, in the fifth edition of *Public Administration in Canada: Selected Readings*, or in monographs published by the Institute of Public Administration of Canada. For permission to reprint sections of previous work, we are grateful to the Institute and to the journals *Canadian Public Administration, Canadian Public Policy, Public Administration (Britain),* and *The Australian Journal of Public Administration.*

For the scholarly foundation on which this book is based, we are indebted to the many academics and practitioners who have contributed to our understanding of the discipline and practice of public administration in Canada and elsewhere. The written contributions of most of these people are acknowledged in the book's endnotes and bibliography. However, we also wish to recognize the wealth of information and insights we have gained from formal and informal discussions with our academic colleagues and with public servants from all spheres of Canadian government. We express appreciation to students past and present who have shared—or endured—our fascination with the field of public administration.

In addition to the public servants and academic colleagues whose assistance we acknowledged in the preface to earlier editions, we wish to express warm appreciation to Ross Gibbins (King's College, University of Western Ontario) and Laurent Dobuzinskis (Simon Fraser University), whose reviews have been expecially helpful to this fourth edition.

Kenneth Kernaghan
David Siegel
February 1999

Introduction

This book is designed to cover the field of public administration in a logical, coherent fashion. The organization and content of the book are based on our conviction that the study of public administration requires the use of concepts and insights from several disciplines, especially political science and organization theory. "Organization analysis can provide a rigour and conceptual sophistication ... ; political science brings an awareness of political influences and environmental pressures upon public agencies that often seems slighted in organization theory and analysis; and public administration reminds us of the range of tasks and organizational problems of public agencies."[1]

Thus, Part I of this book deals with the importance of theories of bureaucracy, organization, and management for the study and practice of public administration. Chapter 1 examines the meaning of public administration, differences between public and private administration, the study of public administration, and the growth and environment of the public service. Chapter 2 reviews the evolution and major theories of public bureaucracy, with special emphasis on the relationship between bureaucracy and the state. Chapters 3 and 4 study the relationship between public administration and organization theory. While Chapter 3 focuses on the early structural and mechanistic theories of organization, Chapter 4 traces the evolution of humanistic theories from their beginnings to contemporary theories of employee participation and development. Chapter 5 draws on some of these theories to discuss the closely related management issues of motivation, leadership, and communication, and includes an examination of the concept and practice of empowerment. Part II deals with the policy dimension of public administration. Chapter 6 examines the primary models that have been developed to explain the making of public policy. Chapter 7 discusses on the two important phases of the policy cycle that follow policy making, namely policy implementation and policy evaluation.

Using the organization theories and principles discussed in Parts I and II as a foundation, Part III examines the major mechanisms used by contemporary governments to deliver services. We explain how the various mechanisms differ and why governments choose a particular mechanism for a particular responsibility. Chapter 8 focuses on central agencies and the most commonly used organizational mechanism—the operating department. Chapter 9 discusses public enterprises and privatization, and Chapter 10 deals with regulation, deregulation, and regulatory agencies. Chapter 11 examines a range of alternative service delivery mechanisms that have been developed or have received greater emphasis in recent years.

The insights provided in the first three parts of this book are used in Part IV to develop a frame of reference for examining interactions between public servants and other political actors. (These interactions are the focus of Part V.) Chapter 12 explains the institutional and value frameworks that provide the conceptual and organizational basis for the chapters in Part V. Chapters 13 and 14 examine in turn the enduring and interrelated themes of bureaucratic power and responsibility. Chapter 14 includes an examination of the increasingly significant issue of public service ethics.

The themes of values, power, and responsibility are pervasive in Part V, which deals with the role of the bureaucracy in the political system. The seven chapters in this part examine relationships between public servants, on the one hand, and political executives, legislators, courts, officials in other governments, pressure groups, political parties, the public, and the media, on the other. This Part contains broad coverage of the public servants' interaction with political actors found both within and outside government.

Part V provides an essential base of knowledge for the examination in Part VI of the management of organizational resources. Many of the public organizations and administrative values discussed in Parts III and IV appear again in Part VI. Chapter 22 describes several management issues which cut across the human resource and financial issues discussed later—the use of computers, strategic planning, performance measurement, and dealing with financial restraint. Human resource management, representative bureaucracy, and collective bargaining are studied in Chapters 23 to 25, and the budgetary process and financial management are covered in Chapters 26 and 27. Chapter 28—the concluding chapter—discusses the future of public administration; it examines alternative scenarios for the future public service and assesses the status of both traditional and new public service values.

Bibliographies at the end of each chapter contain valuable references for further reading.[2] A list of case studies that can be used to relate the theoretical and descriptive material in the text to actual administrative situations can be obtained from the Institute of Public Administration of Canada. Some readers may wish to use the chapters of this book in an order that suits their own purposes. We have, therefore, tried to make each chapter as self-contained as possible and to give cross-references to other chapters that elaborate on certain subjects. We have provided a definition and/or detailed explanation of new terms as they appear in the text. If the chapters are used in an order other than that presented, readers may wish to consult the Glossary at the end of the book for both definitions and page references for further discussion of key terms.

NOTES

1. Gary L. Wamsley and Mayer N. Zald, *The Political Economy of Public Organizations* (Bloomington, Ind.: Indiana University Press, 1976), 83.
2. For a comprehensive bibliography on Canadian public administration to 1985, readers should consult W.E. Grasham and Germain Julien, *Canadian Public Administration Bibliography:1972,* including supplements 1 to 4 dated 1974, 1977, 1980, and 1985 respectively. (Toronto: Institute of Public Administration of Canada).

I

Introduction to Public Administration

1

What Is Public Administration?

Several years ago, a professor of public administration wrote an article entitled "If You're So Damned Smart, Why Don't *You* Run Government like a Business?"[1] This article challenged the claim of many business people, journalists, politicians, and other taxpayers that government should be run like a business—a claim that is based on the notion that there isn't much difference between public administration and business administration, and therefore business people should run the government. This long-standing claim has been expressed much more strongly over the past decade and governments have responded by trying to incorporate business thinking and practices. However, recent experience suggests that this is not an easy undertaking, nor, in many respects, a desirable one.

A widely quoted rejoinder to the suggestion that government should be run like a business is that "business and government administration are alike in all *unimportant* respects."[2] And the argument is increasingly heard that government needs to be run not in a more businesslike fashion, but in a more government-like fashion because public administration is significantly different from private administration. Which side is right? What is public administration? How does it differ from private administration? Should public administration be taught as part of government and politics, as part of general administration, or separately from both? What are the major environmental influences on public administration? What is its scope? These are the questions that are dealt with in this chapter. The answers are important because the study and practice of public administration are central to effective governance.

This is an exciting period in the field of public administration, not only in Canada but in most other parts of the world. Governments in Canada are being challenged to respond effectively to such forces as the emergence of a global economy, startling advances in information technology, rapid social change, the need to provide more services with fewer resources, the public's insistence on a more open and participative policy-making process, and widespread criticism of government officials and institutions. However, some public servants use a less charitable term than "exciting" to describe this period because it is a very difficult one, characterized by tough challenges, painful resource reductions, and major restructuring.

Public servants are centrally involved in devising appropriate responses to these challenges, in part through efforts to reinvent, rethink, reshape, and revitalize government in general and the public service in particular. These efforts are discussed throughout this book, and we return to the theme of change and challenge in the final chapter on the future of the public service. Chapter 1 begins to lay a foundation for understanding the fascinating and complex world of public administration by examining its role and development in the Canadian context.

🏛 THE IMPORTANCE AND MEANING OF PUBLIC ADMINISTRATION

The Scope of Public Administration

During this century, and especially since the beginning of World War II, there has been an enormous expansion in the activities of Canadian governments. The growth of responsibilities in all spheres of Canadian government—federal, provincial, and municipal—has a great impact on the daily lives and future prospects of Canadian citizens. The degree of happiness and prosperity or misery and poverty experienced by Canadians is affected by the countless decisions made each day by our governments. The range of governmental activities includes the traditional functions of administration of justice, conduct of external relations, and defence of the country, as well as newer responsibilities such as medicare, environmental protection, and atomic energy research. Federal public servants control and inspect air traffic; protect coastal waterways against pollution and overfishing; guard prisoners in penitentiaries and rehabilitate offenders; protect our health and safety by inspecting food, water, air, and medicine; issue millions of cheques annually to seniors and needy Canadians; help unemployed Canadians find jobs; and support science, technology, and the delivery of foreign aid.

The two major areas of government activities are the provision of services and the enforcement of regulations. (Note that regulation is often treated as a form of government service.) The service functions include the delivery of mail, the maintenance of roads and highways, and the administration of grants and loans. Among the regulatory functions are the prevention and restraint of restrictive trade practices, and the enforcement of fair housing and employment regulations. In order to carry out these and other responsibilities as effectively as possible, governments are actively engaged in research on matters ranging from the inspection of food and drugs to scientific and medical concerns. Virtually every government department and agency is involved in research related to its service or regulatory functions. Research activities are a costly but essential component of the total responsibilities of government.

> The public sector makes a significant difference in the performance of nations. [It] contributes to competitiveness, provides countries with a comparative advantage in their competition for trade and investment, and contributes to citizens' quality of life and standard of living.
>
> Source: Jocelyn Bourgon, Clerk of the Privy Council and Secretary to the Cabinet, Canadian Student Leadership Conference[3]

Few Canadians are aware of the importance and the magnitude of their governments' operations. Canadians, like citizens of other countries, tend to be conscious of only those government activities that affect them directly and significantly, e.g., the collection of taxes, the provision of family allowances, or the payment of unemployment insurance benefits. Many important functions of government, such as the preservation of internal law and order or the administration of justice, are taken for granted unless the services are discontinued or disrupted for some reason. An excellent example is the sudden public concern about postal operations when normal service is disrupted by labour disputes.

The impact of government activities on the lives of Canadians during a typical working day is vividly demonstrated by the following example of government regulation:

> In the morning the clock radio awakens us with the sound of music subject to Canadian content regulations. The price, at the farm gate, of the eggs we eat for breakfast has been set by a government marketing board. We drive to work on tires that must meet federal minimum safety standards and in a car whose exhaust is subject to pollution emission regulations. At lunch, the restaurant in which we eat has been subject to the scrutiny of public health inspectors. The monthly rate for the telephone we use at the office is set by a federal or provincial regulatory agency. Shopping in the supermarket on the way home, we note the unpronounceable names of certain chemical preservatives that, by government regulation, are disclosed to us on a finely printed label.... Putting on our sleepwear, we are secure in our knowledge that it is not impregnated with a hazardous substance.... If we live in certain cities, we approach our rest reassured that the smoke detector we were required to install will stand on guard throughout the night.[4]

What do these extensive and pervasive activities of Canadian governments have to do with public administration? A great deal! Public administrators play a very large role in formulating and implementing policies to fulfil their government's service and regulatory responsibilities. These responsibilities are performed through what is known as the public bureaucracy, which is a system for achieving government objectives. Elected representatives, especially political executives (e.g., cabinet ministers, city mayors), are centrally involved in the making of public policies. However, we shall see in later chapters that public servants (also called civil servants, government employees, public employees, or bureaucrats) have considerable influence on the content of these policies and make most of the decisions required to implement them. Thus, while a recurring theme in this book is the importance of relations between the political and bureaucratic realms of government, the role of the bureaucracy is the major focus of attention.

The remainder of this chapter examines the meaning and the study of public administration and the environment in which it is set. The next chapter focuses on public bureaucracy.

The Meaning of Public Administration

Public administration is a term more easily explained than defined. This fact has not discouraged several scholars from trying to capture the meaning of the term in a single sentence. Some typical one-sentence definitions of public administration are:

The study and practice of the tasks associated with the conduct of the administrative state.[5]

The use of managerial, political, and legal theories and processes to fulfill legislative, executive, and judicial governmental mandates for the provision of regulatory and service functions for the society as a whole or for some segments of it.[6]

The coordination of individual and group efforts to carry out public policy.[7]

The application of organizational decision-making, and staffing theory and procedures to public problems.[8]

These brief definitions indicate the scope and purpose of public administration, but they are incomplete in their coverage and very general in their wording. The emphasis in these and most other definitions of public administration is on the implementation of policy; there is insufficient recognition of the role of bureaucrats in policy development. Moreover, these definitions contain abstract words and terms that tend to leave the reader with more questions than answers. For example, what are the *tasks* associated with the conduct of the administrative state? What are the *relationships* between bureaucrats and such institutions as legislatures, executives, and courts? Is public administration confined to the *carrying out* of public policy? What is distinctive about organization and management in *public* administration as opposed to *private* administration? This book provides answers to these and many other questions about public administration.

The terms public administration and public bureaucracy are often used interchangeably, but they do not mean the same thing. Public administration refers to a field of practice (or occupation) *and* to a field of study (or discipline). Public bureaucracy is the system of authority, people, offices, and methods that government uses to achieve its objectives. It is the means by which the practice of public administration is carried on; it is also the main focus of the study of public administration. We use the term public administration to refer to its practice unless we indicate otherwise by specific reference to its study. This book is devoted to studying the practice of public administration as that practice is conducted through the system known as public bureaucracy.

The scope of the practice and study of public administration is so broad that it is difficult to achieve agreement on where the boundaries of the field should be drawn. The size of the field could be demonstrated simply by listing the hundreds of departments and agencies at all levels of Canadian government that collectively carry out an enormous range of activities. It could also be demonstrated by showing the range of concerns shared by teachers and practitioners of public administration. Among the subjects covered during a recent two-year period in *Canadian Public Administration*, the learned journal of the Institute of Public Administration of Canada, are public service accountability, broadcasting policy, the budgetary process, contracting out local government services, employment equity, environmental lobbying, globalization, health care reform, local government autonomy, managing the policy process, the new public management movement, organizational design, policy networks, the senior public service, public service reform, and service quality management.

Public Administration versus Private Administration

The meaning of public administration can be clarified by comparing it with private (or business) administration. There is, in fact, much that is similar in the two sectors. Administration in all organizations involves cooperative group action. Moreover, all large organizations, whether they be government departments, hospitals, universities, labour unions, factories, or commercial enterprises, must provide for the performance of such functions of general management as planning, organizing, staffing, and budgeting. There are, however, many distinguishing factors in the administration of public sector organizations, and these differences have important implications for the study and practice of public administration.[9] At the very least, these differences suggest the need for caution in transferring practices and technologies from private sector organizations to public sector organizations.

In contemporary Canadian society, the line between public and private administration is somewhat blurred. Public and private sector organizations can be shown on a continuum running from typical operating departments of government to private sector corporations largely free from governmental control or assistance. In the middle of this continuum is a variety of organizations characterized by a mix of public and private elements. These organizations can be divided into three main categories. The first is public corporations (e.g., the Canadian Broadcasting Corporation [CBC]) which compete with, and operate much like, private corporations. The second category consists of mixed-enterprise corporations that are owned or controlled by different governments (e.g., the Saint John Harbour Bridge Authority) or by governments and private organizations (e.g., Canarctic Shipping). The final category is private sector organizations that are subject to close government regulation (e.g., pharmaceutical companies), companies that depend heavily on government financial assistance (e.g., textile firms), or those companies that conduct one hundered percent of their business with government (e.g., defence contractors).

As we shall see later, in Chapter 11 on program delivery mechanisms, this continuum has become more crowded as governments have become more involved in public-private partnerships and in new forms of organization. Despite the large and growing grey area in the middle of the continuum, for analytical purposes a broad distinction can be made between the public and private spheres of administration.

The first and most frequently cited difference is that the overall mission of public administration is service to the public, whereas the primary *raison d'être* of private administration is profit, or what is often described as "the bottom line." The service orientation of public administration results from the need for bureaucrats to assist elected politicians to respond to public demands and requirements for government services. Private administration is profit-oriented because the survival of private sector organizations ultimately depends on making a profit.

It is commonly argued that a second difference, following directly from the service-versus-profit distinction, is that public administration operates less effi-

[I]n government, we face an incredible onus to be fair and equal in the way we treat our customers and the way we run our operations. Our management decisions must be seen to give all Canadians, regardless of province, region, gender, or language, an equal shot at the benefits Canada has to offer. This can lead us to act in ways that business executives might find hard to swallow. For example:

It means that many government departments keep offices in every province whether they need them or not.... The onus of fairness means departments have to provide services of comparable quality to citizens of Kingston and Baker Lake, regardless of the differential in cost.

It was this same appeal to fairness which got government into employment equity, affirmative action, and equal pay for work of equal value long before the private sector. It's what comes from having to be government for all of the people in a country as large and diverse as Canada. And it affects not only the speed and quality of our operations, it also affects the cost.

Source: Jennifer McQueen, former federal deputy minister, Dialogue[10]

ciently than private administration. It is suggested that since government departments receive their funds largely through annual appropriations from the public treasury, they do not have to worry about profits; thus, they have less incentive to cut costs and operate efficiently. Business organizations are motivated to operate efficiently because they must compete in the marketplace; most government operations, however, are monopolistic (e.g., the police) so that the public does not have a choice among competing organizations for the delivery of services. It is argued that public organizations are less inclined to be efficient because they do not have to be as sensitive as private organizations to the preferences and grievances of their "consumers." Finally, many services are provided by government organizations because they would not produce sufficient profits to interest private sector organizations. Many people argue that when government activities produce a profit, such activities should be turned over to private enterprise.

Governments also provide what are called "public" goods; these are goods which, when provided at all, benefit all members of society. People cannot be charged for the services in the marketplace because no one can be excluded from benefiting from them. Examples of public goods include national defence and pollution controls, which are funded through the general tax system rather than on the "user-pay" principle that is characteristic of "private" goods (e.g., a carton of milk). The benefits of public goods are available to many people, and these benefits are not easily measured. Indeed, it is very difficult to measure the efficiency of many government expenditures (e.g., on health services).

Public administration does not have the measuring rods of prices and profits that are central to efficiency considerations in the private sector. Nevertheless, government departments and agencies do have incentives to operate efficiently. For example, the many administrative units within government compete with one another for public funds; this competition is especially vigorous during periods of financial restraint in government. Recently, treasury officials have paid much more attention to the economy, efficiency, and effectiveness of departmental operations, and an increasing number of government programs are operated on a cost-recovery basis. Another spur to efficiency in government is the threat of public criticism that may embarrass elected politicians and, in turn, damage the career prospects of the government employees involved.

The achievement of businesslike efficiency in government is greatly affected—and often hampered—by the demands of the political environment. In a study of productivity in the public sector, Canada's auditor general noted that departmental recommendations to cut operating costs are sometimes incompatible with political priorities. He observed that "private sector firms are not required, to the same extent as the public sector, to reconcile questions of productive management with concerns such as national unity, regional development, and national well-being."[11]

Another consideration is that politicians are concerned, first and foremost, with winning public support. The public judges politicians by their public personae and policy initiatives, not by how well they manage their departments. Thus, many politicians do not expend a great deal of effort in managing their departments well or in rewarding public service managers who do. Politicians want public servants who provide good policy advice and who keep them out of trouble.

In an effort to gain political support, governments frequently make decisions that are not efficient in the narrow economic sense. For example, many governments are systematically decentralizing their operations by moving organizational units out of the capital city. This imposes a significant one-time cost and probably increases annual operating costs, but it also demonstrates the government's commitment to regional development. Clearly, governments are not oriented toward a single goal such as profit maximization; rather, they typically must satisfy several goals simultaneously, some of which may conflict with one another, and some of which cannot even be stated openly. In this complex environment, it is not surprising that governments sometimes do things that would not stand the test of businesslike principles.

A third difference between public and private administration that hinders efficiency in government is the greater emphasis in the public sector on accountability. A major constraint on productive management "is the body of administrative regulations and the conflicting accountability requirements that limit managerial authority and autonomy."[12] The lines of authority and responsibility tend to be much clearer in private sector organizations. In government, such factors as the scale and complexity of operations, the desire for political control of the bureaucracy, and the search for consistency and coordination have resulted in a proliferation of accountability mechanisms that lengthen and complicate the decision-making process. For example, deputy ministers in the federal government are directly accountable to their minister, the prime minister, and several central agencies. Moreover, they are indirectly accountable through their minister to Parliament and to the public. While excessive and conflicting accountability requirements are most evident at the senior levels of the bureaucracy, the middle levels are also affected. The negative impact these requirements have on government efficiency is demonstrated by the auditor general's concern that "when constraints become a spider's web of rules, regulations, directives, prohibitions, and controls, managers lose sight of value-for-money concerns."[13] For example, the pursuit of efficiency through speedy program implementation may be hampered by numerous financial and human resource constraints. The auditor general has argued also that these strict procedures and accountability requirements mean that there are few incentives, but many disincentives, to good management.

A fourth difference between public and private administration is that the human resource management system is much more complicated and rigid in government than in private sector organizations. In general, it is harder both to hire and to fire government employees. In the public sector, the merit system of hiring and promoting employees includes several criteria that go well beyond the idea of technical proficiency. To promote sensitivity and responsiveness to the needs of a certain minority group, for example, the government may hire a person from that group who is not as well qualified as other candidates in terms of education and experience. The complexity and inflexibility of human resource management systems also result from the general emphasis on accountability. Of the top ten constraints on management productivity identified by federal public service managers, three lie squarely in the human resource field, in the areas of job classification, personnel rules, and staffing.[14]

Fifth, and finally, the "public" nature of public administration requires that much of it be conducted in a "fishbowl" of publicity. Many government deliberations are conducted behind closed doors but, compared to the private sector, many more government decisions are subjected to public scrutiny. Taxpayers insist on the right to know how much public money is being spent and for what purposes. Thus, a government decision to construct a new airport in a particular area will probably receive much more public and media examination than a decision by a major manufacturer to construct or close a plant in the same area, even if the latter decision has a greater economic or social impact on the community. The media will report on the effects of such private sector decisions, but they do not expect these decisions to be made in public. An important consequence of this public scrutiny is greater emphasis in the public sector on such considerations as responsiveness and accountability. This emphasis explains in part the presence of what is popularly described as bureaucratic "red tape" and the consequent slowness in decision making.

Two major characteristics of government account in large part for the differences between public and private administration: (1) the vast scope and complexity of government activities, and (2) the political environment within which these activities are conducted. Given these considerations, the issue of whether public or private administration is more efficient is not the most relevant concern. The critical question is whether public administration is conducted as efficiently as can reasonably be expected. We shall see at various points in this book that governments are actively engaged in reforms to increase their efficiency, effectiveness, and responsiveness by such means as improved service to the public and the reduction of rules and regulations.

It is important to avoid exaggerating the differences between public and private administration. In the private sector, many organizations are extremely large and complex, and most of them are influenced by the broad political environment that requires that they consider many factors other than the bottom line. Private sector organizations are being required to be much more open about their activities and to follow the public sector's lead in such areas as employment equity and pay equity.

> Public service is a special calling. It is not for everyone. Those who devote themselves to it find meaning and satisfaction that are not to be found elsewhere. But the rewards are not material. They are moral and psychological, perhaps even spiritual. They are the intangible rewards that proceed from the sense of devoting one's life to the service of the country, to the affairs of state, to public purposes, great or small, and to the public good.
>
> Source: Government of Canada, Discussion Paper on Values and Ethics in the Public Service[15]

🏛 THE STUDY OF PUBLIC ADMINISTRATION

The systematic study of public administration in North America is a relatively recent development. In the United States, the study of the field is generally acknowledged to date from 1887 with the publication of Woodrow Wilson's celebrated essay, "The Study of Administration."[16] Although no single date or publication marks the beginning of the study of public administration in Canada, there are several noteworthy developments in the evolution of the formal study of Canadian public administration.[17]

Several of the 23 volumes of *Canada and Its Provinces*, written by A. Shortt and A.G. Doherty and published in 1914, covered aspects of public administration and public bureaucracy in Canada. In 1918, the first work focusing on a particular problem in Canadian public administration was written by two scholars from the United States.[18] The earliest general work in the field was R. MacGregor Dawson's *The Civil Service of Canada*, published in 1929.[19] It was not until 1936 that Luther Richter and R.A. Mackay established the first degree program in Canadian public administration at Dalhousie University. Carleton College (now Carleton University) graduated students with a Bachelor of Public Administration degree in 1946, and the university's School of Public Administration was established in 1952. However, it was not until the early 1950s that a group of academic scholars[20] emerged and a more broad-based literature in public administration started to develop. *Canadian Public Administration*, the scholarly journal devoted to the study of the subject, commenced publication in 1958.

The academic study of public administration began to flourish in the late 1960s. Indeed, progress in the study of Canadian public administration since 1970, as measured by research, publications, teachers, and programs, has been greater than in all the preceding years combined. This increased attention to research and teaching in public administration is largely due to the growth of the operations, expenditures, and size of the federal, provincial, and municipal bureaucracies. It also coincided with the expansion of Canadian universities and colleges, which were thereby able to devote more resources to teaching and research in public administration.

The study of public administration is commonly described as a discipline, but it is not a discipline in the restrictive sense of an intellectual endeavour with a body of coherent and accepted theory. Even if the term discipline is defined less rigorously as a field of study with a nucleus of unifying beliefs, public administration has not yet achieved agreement on what those beliefs are. The matter is complicated by what has often been called the field's "crisis of identity," which arises from three developments: the evolution of public administration under the parentage of political science; the continually expanding dimensions of the field of public administration; and the increasingly interdisciplinary approach to its study and teaching. Should public administration be considered a subdiscipline (or subfield) of political science or of administrative science (i.e., organization theory and management science)?

Political Science or Administrative Science?

The two opposing positions on the appropriate theoretical base for the organization of studies in public administration have been succinctly expressed as follows:

> Any tendency for public administration to break away from the parent discipline must ultimately weaken both political science as a whole and the study of public administration. It will weaken political science by removing the part of it which brings the teacher into closest relationship with the practical business of government. It will weaken the study of public administration by divorcing it from political theory and the principles of government which underlie political and administrative institutions.[21]

> The greatest promise for study of public administration in the universities will be in association with the growth of an integrative, organizing, generic concept of administration. From the nucleus of general administrative studies, it may be possible to interrelate more meaningfully the study of administration to the various disciplines and professions. In the modern world, no clear line separates administration in government from the administrative processes of the total society. The organization of administrative studies in the university must ultimately correspond to this reality.[22]

There are sound theoretical grounds for teaching public administration as part of political science. Knowledge of the administrative structures of government and the political and legal environment in which the public administrator works is essential to an adequate understanding of the political system. In addition, the bureaucracy plays a central role in the political system through its active involvement in the development, enforcement, and adjudication of laws and regulations. Significant intellectual bonds lie between public administration and political science in their shared concern for inquiry into such key theoretical concepts as responsibility, authority, and the public interest. Political theorists who fail to explore the meaning of these themes in the particular milieu of public administration omit a perspective essential to adequate analysis. All these factors attest to the status of public administration as an integral part of the study of political science. The most productive approach for political scientists may be to treat public administration as a *subdiscipline* on the basis of existing organizational patterns and theoretical links between public administration and political science.

Those who view public administration as a part of administrative science contend that the study of administration can be most fruitfully pursued by dividing the general field of administration into public, business, health, educational, judicial, and other types of administration. To proponents of this view, the similarities among these forms of administration are greater than their differences. This belief has led to the establishment of "professional" schools or faculties of administrative studies. The administrative science approach involves considerable borrowing from such disciplines as economics, sociology, and psychology.

Some scholars favour the teaching of public administration—and other forms of administration—within a rigorous *discipline* of administrative studies. This approach is interdisciplinary and integrative in its subject content and teaching. It is characterized by combining the "academic" and "professional" streams in administrative studies for mutual enrichment. Discussion of the distinctive nature of "public" administration is generally founded on a solid base of knowledge about the concepts and techniques of administration. All students are required to take a group of "core subjects" in administration, regardless of the type of administration in which they are primarily interested (e.g., public, business, educational). The core subjects usually include organizational behaviour, accounting, economics, administrative law, and quantitative methods. Later specialization in a particular type of administration (e.g., public) or in the administration of a particular policy field (e.g., health care) is founded on this base of common knowledge.

Public Administration as Public Administration

A variety of structural arrangements exists for the Master's level education of current and aspiring public servants. Programs leading to a Master of Public Administration (M.P.A.) degree,[23] or to a degree in political science or public sector management, are available in departments of political science or in schools or faculties of administrative studies. However, the most common route to an M.P.A. degree is through one of the several specialized schools of public administration that have grown rapidly during the past 25 years. These schools offer an interdisciplinary approach with a professional emphasis. Programs are designed to accommodate students proceeding directly from their bachelor's degree as well as mid-career public servants. The schools require a similar group of core courses (e.g., government structure and organization, policy formulation, quantitative methods, applied economics, the management process in government, and public sector financial management and accounting) and a range of elective courses in specialized areas such as local government administration and intergovernmental relations.

Most of the schools have adopted a policy-management approach to program content that combines political science and administrative science with an examination of public policy. This approach focuses on public administration as a distinct field of study rather than as a subdiscipline or subfield of political science or administrative science.

🏛 THE ENVIRONMENT AND GROWTH OF PUBLIC ADMINISTRATION

Environmental Factors

Public administration is greatly influenced by the broad environment within which it is conducted. Aside from the political and legal environment of public administration, discussed in detail elsewhere in this book, the most important environmental influences are geography, technological change, culture, demography, and the economy.[24]

Geography

The influence of geography, manifested in large part by the need to disperse government operations and personnel across the country, or throughout a province, is discussed in Chapter 3. Canada's vast expanse also helps to explain the existence and nature of our federal system of government and the enduring impact of regionalism on politics and public administration—a subject to which we return later, notably in Chapter 19 on intergovernmental relations.

Technological Change

The environment within which contemporary governments work has also been greatly affected by technological developments. The widespread use of such inventions as the automobile, the airplane, and television have created difficult problems for government as transportation routes have become snarled, airports have become too small for huge jetliners, and intercontinental television transmission has become possible. The opportunities brought about by more recent technological developments involving automation, computers, and atomic energy have created such problems as unemployment due to technical advances, invasion of privacy, and possible misuse of atomic energy. Scientific and technical advances, such as increasing numbers of human tissue transplants, test-tube babies, and instruments of instant communication, also present challenging issues for government. The management and operations of the public service have been transformed by remarkable advances in information technology.

Culture

Cultural factors have also been influential in molding the public service. For example, the public service has been required to adapt to three extremely important cultural factors within Canada itself—the constitutional guarantees to the use of the English and French languages, the increasingly multicultural character of Canadian society,[25] and the large number of aboriginal peoples. In addition, the powerful influence of the United States on Canadian culture has led to such measures as "Canadian content" regulations in radio and television broadcasting. Both the United States and Britain have exercised significant influence on the organizational and administrative arrangements of the public service in Canada.

Demography

The impact of demographic factors on the public service is becoming increasingly important. Rapid population growth in Canada (from 5.4 million in 1901 to well over 29 million in 1998) was, until recently, accompanied by a movement of Canadians from rural-agricultural areas to urban-industrial centres. This urbanization of the Canadian population brought enormous problems for governments in such forms as air and water pollution and inadequate housing. The resolution of these problems continues to require large government expenditures and close cooperation between levels of government. It is notable that a counter-urbanization movement began in the early 1970s with more people moving to rural and fringe areas from urban areas than the reverse. If this trend continues, the population redistribution will require reconsideration of land development and environmental protection policies because increasing encroachments on rural areas will increase demand for the limited supply of arable land. Moreover, such people tend to bring with them "urban tastes" in the form of demands for improved services in such fields as transportation, recreation, and education.

Another demographic factor with significant implications for public administration is the changing age composition of the Canadian population. The percentage of Canadians over sixty-five years of age reached 12.2 percent in 1997 and is projected to rise rapidly after about 2012 when the first baby boomers turn 65.[26] As the number of seniors increases, so will their needs for health, housing, and community services. There will be a growing requirement for different orders of government and different administrative units within each order to find the financial and human resources to meet these needs.

A final demographic factor worthy of special mention is the greatly increased participation of women and minorities in the labour force. Women may soon become the majority in the work force; they are already the majority in the general population. It is anticipated that by the early years of the 21st century, most new additions to the work force will be women and members of visible minority groups. Some of the implications of these developments for the public service are discussed in Chapter 24, which deals in part with employment equity.

The Economy and Globalization

Among the most important economic factors affecting the public service has been the reliance of the Canadian economy on exploiting and marketing such staple products as fish, fur, wheat, timber, minerals, and pulpwood. Several of the original departments of the federal government (e.g., Agriculture, Marine and Fisheries) were created specifically to deal with problems connected with the production, transportation, and trade of staple products and several departments are still concerned with these problems.

Another important economic influence has been the growth during this century of large industrial and commercial organizations, e.g., multinational corporations such as General Motors and IBM, which are not totally Canadian-controlled, and of large labour organizations, such as the Canadian Automobile Workers (CAW) and the Canadian Labour Congress (CLC). Employer–employee disputes over such matters as wage levels and the effects of technological change on existing jobs can result in lengthy strikes. Such strikes may not only bring much personal strife and misfortune to those directly involved in the dispute but may also have an injurious impact on innocent third parties and on the economy as a whole. To protect the public interest, governments have been increasingly obliged to regulate the activities of business and labour organizations and to arbitrate disputes between them.

Over the past decade in particular, an extremely important economic influence has been *globalization*—the movement from a world of distinct national economies to a global economy characterized by world-wide markets for investment, production, distribution, and consumption; by the economic power of multinational business enterprises (MNEs); by the setting of rules for economic activity by international organizations such as the World Bank and the International Monetary Fund; and by the creation of regional trading blocs such as the European Union and the North American Free Trade Agreement (NAFTA). Since most policy issues now have international implications, governments must have the capacity to deal with public and private organizations outside Canada and to manage the domestic impacts of global forces.

This brief discussion of environmental factors shows that the operations of governments are extremely complex and that the demands on government are constantly changing. Governments must provide rapid solutions to urgent current problems while planning for the solution or avoidance of future problems. They must be conscious of the widespread ramifications of major governmental decisions on various sectors of Canadian society. For example, the federal government must assess the probable impact on Canada of changes in the economic policies of other nations. It must then decide how to counteract the potential adverse effects of these changes on the prosperity of businesses, on provincial and municipal governments, and on the level of employment in Canada. After an evaluation of the likely consequences, the government may have to alter existing plans and programs. Clearly, governments operate in a state of constant flux and must have the capacity and the inclination to adapt quickly to change.

The Growth of the Public Service

In Canada, as elsewhere, expansion in the scope and complexity of government activities since the end of World War II has been accompanied by substantial growth in expenditure and in the number of government employees.

During World War II, the federal government took control of the economy to promote the war effort with the result that by the end of the war, federal expenditure had risen to 82 percent of expenditure by all levels of government. During the postwar period, the total amount of money spent by governments has greatly increased. Figure 1.1 shows that government expenditure, expressed as a percentage of Gross Domestic Product (GDP),[27] rose from 21 percent in 1950 to 48 percent in 1995. The federal percentage of total expenditure, however, has declined steadily, while the provincial share has increased and the municipal share has remained relatively stable. The increase in expenditure by the ten provincial governments combined resulted from the increasing revenue available to the resource-rich provinces and the increased demand for provincially provided services, particularly in the areas of education, health care, and social services. Over the past seventy years, there has been a steady rise in the proportion of government spending devoted to these areas. However, expenditure on transportation and communications, natural resources, and international aid has risen much more slowly, and expenditure on defence has declined substantially since 1960.

Figure 1.2 illustrates the debt situation of the federal government. It shows how the gap between federal revenue and expenditure widened beginning in the 1970s, but has narrowed somewhat in the 1990s as expenditure has been reduced. In fact, in recent years federal revenue has exceeded its operating expenditure (all expenditure except debt service) so that if not for having to pay off previous debt, it would be operating at a significant surplus. The provinces have never had a deficit approaching the size of the federal deficit, but most provinces have also had serious deficit problems.

The increase in total expenditure at all levels of Canadian government has been accompanied by a related growth in the number of public employees required to carry out increased government responsibilities. Much public criticism has centred on the size and growth of public sector employment in Canada, especially at the federal level. Certainly, the absolute size of public sector employment has increased greatly since World War II. But, as a percentage of the total labour force, public sector employment was the same in 1982 as in 1960. And since the early 1980s and especially during the 1990s, reductions in government programs and expenditures have resulted in a substantial decline in the number of government employees. In the federal sphere, for example, employment declined from 240 000 to about 194 000 between 1986 and 1997.[28]

It is particularly notable that the federal public service constitutes a comparatively small portion of total public sector employment, and that since the mid-1960s growth has been slower in the federal government than in the provincial and municipal governments. In general, "it is clear that Canada does not have a large public sector presence. Total employment by all levels of government in Canada is far below that of most modern western democracies and very close to that of the United States."[29]

The variety and change in the occupational composition of the public service are related to the growth in the number of government employees. Virtually every occupation, trade, and skill can be found in the public service. Occupations in the federal public service range "from actuaries and anthro-

Figure 1.1
TRENDS IN GOVERNMENT EXPENDITURE

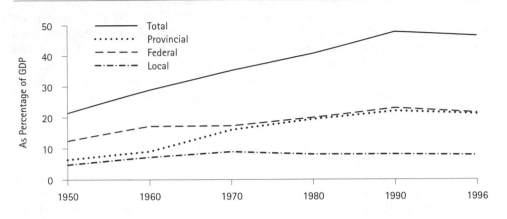

Figure 1.2
FEDERAL GOVERNMENT REVENUE AND EXPENDITURE

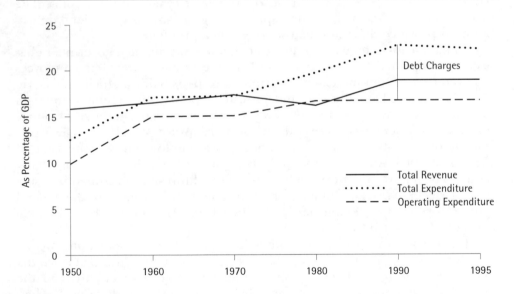

pologists through bee keepers, dry dock riggers, map compilers and pharma-cists, to veterinarians and X-ray operators. An element of mystery is created by the listing of such intriguing operations as insect sampling, ... receivers of wreck, ... strippers and layouters."[30] Clearly, a wide variety of job opportunities is available to those who aspire to become Canadian public servants.

The increasingly complex and technical nature of government operations has brought about a significant qualitative change in the public service. Especially over the past few decades, jobs in the managerial, professional, and technical occupational categories have increased while those in the traditional clerical and operational categories have declined. One result of this trend is that students must not only spend a longer time in school to obtain the education necessary for appointment to the public service, but they must also return to school in later years to keep informed about new developments affecting their jobs and to upgrade their skills.

To fulfil the growing responsibilities of government, additional administrative units were created in the form of new departments, new sections of existing departments, and new agencies, boards, and commissions. These units enjoy varying degrees of independence from political (i.e., cabinet and parliamentary) control. There are now 24 federal government departments, including, for example, the Departments of Finance, Justice, and National Defence. Among the large number of government agencies, boards, and commissions are such Crown corporations as the CBC and such regulatory agencies as the Canadian Radio-television and Telecommunications Commission (CRTC).

A variety of explanations has been offered for the growth of the public sector. The three main types of explanatory models suggested by Butler and Macnaughton are the socioeconomic, organizational, and political models.[31] *Socioeconomic* explanations for public sector growth focus on external social and economic influences such as inflation, population growth rates, demographic change, and the level of personal real disposable income. *Organizational* explanations emphasize pressures that emerge within the bureaucracy itself, including responsiveness to clientele demands, bureaucratic empire building, and incremental decision making. *Political* explanations stress the pressures to expand government expenditures, therefore increasing employment, that result from such factors as electoral competition, party ideology, and pressure group demands. It is difficult to determine with precision which of these explanatory models best accounts for growth in any particular government; usually, reference to factors from all three models is necessary for a full explanation.

Since the mid-1980s, pressures to expand the responsibilities and expenditures of government have run up against a severe financial crunch characterized by substantial accumulated debt and large annual deficits in both the federal and provincial spheres. Many governments have responded in part to this challenge by pursuing public service reforms designed to permit delivery of at least the current level of service despite declining resources. These reforms will be discussed in more detail later in this book.

NOTES

1. See C. Lloyd Brown-John, "If You're So Damned Smart, Why Don't *You* Run Government like a Business?" in Katherine A. Graham, ed., *How Ottawa Spends, 1990–1991: Tracking the Second Agenda* (Ottawa: Carleton University Press, 1990), 219–45. Emphasis added.

2. Wallace Sayre, quoted in Joseph L. Bowen, "Effective Public Management," *Harvard Business Review* 55 (March–April 1977): 132. Emphasis added.

3. Jocelyn Bourgon, Canadian Student Leadership Conference, Ottawa, 24 January, 1997.

4. Industry Canada, *Responsible Regulation* (Ottawa: Supply and Services, 1979), xi. Reproduced with the permission of the Minister of Public Works and Government Services Canada, 1998.

5. Ivan L. Richardson and Sidney Baldwin, *Public Administration: Government in Action* (Columbus, Ohio: Charles E. Merrill, 1976), 3.

6. David H. Rosenbloom, *Public Administration: Understanding Management, Politics, and Law in the Public Sector* (New York: Random House, 1986), 6.

7. John M. Pfiffner and Robert Presthus, *Public Administration*, 5th ed. (New York: Ronald Press, 1967), 7.

8. Thomas Vocino and Jack Rabin, *Contemporary Public Administration* (New York: Harcourt Brace Jovanovich, 1981), 4.

9. Brown-John, "If You're So Damned Smart Why Don't *You* Run Government like a Business?"

10. Jennifer McQueen, then Deputy Minister of Labour, *Dialogue (Public Service Commission of Canada)* 14 (October 1990): 21.

11. Auditor General of Canada, *Annual Report—1983* (Ottawa: Supply and Services, 1983), 57.

12. Ibid., 60.

13. Ibid.

14. Ibid., 62. See also Chapter 23 in this book.

15. Government of Canada, Deputy Ministers' Task Force, *Discussion Paper on Values and Ethics in the Public Service* (Ottawa: Privy Council Office, December 1996), 80.

16. Reprinted in Peter Woll, ed., *Public Administration and Policy* (New York: Harper and Row, 1966), 15–41.

17. For an account of the development of the study of public administration in Canada, see A. Paul Pross and V. Seymour Wilson, "Graduate Education in Canadian Public Administration: Antecedents, Present Trends and Portents," *Canadian Public Administration* 19 (winter 1976): 515–41.

18. H.S. Villard and W.W. Willoughby, *The Canadian Budgetary System* (New York: Appleton, 1918).

19. R. MacGregor Dawson, *The Civil Service of Canada* (Oxford: Oxford University Press, 1929). For a discussion of Dawson's views on the role of the public service, see Ken Rasmussen, "The Administrative Liberalism of R. MacGregor Dawson," *Canadian Public Administration* 33 (spring 1990): 37–51.

20. Prominent among these scholars were Albert Abel, Roch Bolduc, J.E. Hodgetts, J.R. Mallory, D.C. Rowat, and Malcom Taylor.

21. William Robson, *The University Teaching of Social Sciences: Political Science* (New York: UNESCO, 1954), 47.

22. Lynton Caldwell, "Public Administration and the Universities: A Half Century of Development," *Public Administration Review* 25 (March 1965): 60.

23. Carleton University's School of Public Administration and McMaster University's Department of Political Science each offer a Ph.D. program focusing on public policy, and the École d'administration publique du Québec (ENAP), which is part of the

University of Quebec, offers a Ph.D. program in public administration.

24. J.E. Hodgetts, *The Canadian Public Service: A Physiology of Government* (Toronto: University of Toronto Press, 1973), 17. See also, by the same author, "Challenge and Response: A Retrospective View of the Public Service of Canada," *Canadian Public Administration* 7 (December 1964): 409–21.

25. See the discussion in Chapter 24 of representative bureaucracy and employment equity.

26. Alanna Mitchell, "Greying of Canada Oversold Notion," *The Globe and Mail*, 30 July, 1997. For an examination of aging, see Auditor General of Canada, *Annual Report 1998*, Ch. 6 on "Population Aging and Information for Parliament: Understanding the Choices" available from http://www.oag-bvg.gc.ca.

27. GDP is the total value of goods and services produced in Canada; it is a measure of the total size of the Canadian economy.

28. Treasury Board, *Employment Equity in the Federal Public Service: 1996—97* (Ottawa: Treasury Board Secretariat, 1997), 49.

29. Sharon L. Sutherland, "Federal Bureaucracy: The Pinch Test," in Michael J. Prince, ed., *How Ottawa Spends, 1987–1988: Restraining the State* (Ottawa: School of Public Administration, Carleton University, 1987), 73.

30. Canada Report of the Royal Commission on Government Organization, vol. 1 (Ottawa: Queen's Printer, 1962–63), 21.

31. Dan Butler and Bruce Macnaughton, "More of Less for Whom? Debating Directions for the Public Sector," in Michael S. Whittington and Glen Williams, eds., *Canadian Politics in the 1980s*, 2nd ed. (Toronto: Methuen, 1984), 17–22.

BIBLIOGRAPHY

PUBLIC ADMINISTRATION—GENERAL

Barton, Rayburn, and William L. Chappell, Jr. *Public Administration: The Work of Government.* Glenview, Ill.: Scott, Foresman, 1985.

Fesler, James W., and Donald F. Kettl. *The Politics of the Administrative Process.* Chatham, N.J.: Chatham House, 1991.

Heady, Ferrel. *Public Administration: A Comparative Perspective,* 3rd ed. New York: Marcel Decker, 1984.

Henry, Nicholas. *Public Administration and Public Affairs,* 2nd ed. Englewood Cliffs, N.J.: Prentice-Hall, 1980.

Kramer, Fred A. *Dynamics of Public Bureaucracy,* 2nd ed. Cambridge, Mass.: Winthrop Publishers, 1981.

Lynn, Naomi B., and Aaron Wildavsky, eds. *Public Administration: The State of the Discipline.* Chatham, N.J.: Chatham House, 1989.

Mosher, Frederick C. *Democracy and the Public Service.* New York: Oxford University Press, 1968.

Nigro, Felix A., and Lloyd A. Nigro. *Modern Public Administration,* 6th ed. New York: Harper and Row, 1984.

Perry, James L., ed. *Handbook of Public Administration.* San Francisco: Jossey-Bass, 1989.

Peters, B. Guy, and Donald J. Savoie, eds. *Governance in a Changing Environment.* Ottawa: Canadian Centre for Management Development, 1995.

Pursley, Robert D., and Neil Snortland. *Managing Government Organizations.* Belmont, Calif.: Wadsworth, 1980.

Rabin, Jack, W. Bartley Hildreth, and Gerald J. Miller, eds. *Handbook of Public Administration.* New York: Marcel Dekker, 1989.

Rosenbloom, David. *Public Administration: Understanding Management, Politics and Law in the Public Sector.* New York: Random House, 1986.

Sharkansky, Ira. *Public Administration: Agencies, Politics and Policies.* San Francisco: W.H. Freeman, 1982.

Starling, Grover. *Managing the Public Sector,* 4th ed. Belmont, Calif.: Wadsworth, 1993.

Straussman, Jeffrey D. *Public Administration.* New York: Holt, Rinehart and Winston, 1985.

Vocino, Thomas, and Jack Rabin, eds. *Contemporary Public Administration.* New York: Harcourt Brace Jovanovich, 1981.

Wamsley, Gary L. et al. *Refounding Public Administration.* Newbury Park, Calif.: Sage Publications, 1990.

PUBLIC ADMINISTRATION—CANADA

Adie, Robert F., and Paul G. Thomas. *Canadian Public Administration: Problematical Perspectives,* 2nd ed. Scarborough, Ont.: Prentice-Hall, 1987.

Borgeat, Louis, René Dussault, and Lionel Ouellet. *L'administration Québecoise: organisation et fonctionnnement.* Québec: Presses de l'Université du Québec, 1984.

Bourgault, Jacques, Maurice Demers, and Cynthia Williams, eds. *Public Administration and Public Management: Experiences in Canada.* Québec.: Les Publications du Québec, 1997.

Charih, Mohamed, and Réjean Landry, eds. *La gestion publique sour le microscope.* (Québec.: Presses de l'Universite du Québec, 1997.

———, and Arthur Daniels, eds. *New Public Management and Public Administration in Canada.* Toronto: Institute of Public Administration of Canada, 1997.

Dawson, R. MacGregor. *The Civil Service of Canada.* Oxford: Oxford University Press, 1929.

Doerr, Audrey. *The Machinery of Government in Canada.* Toronto: Methuen, 1980.

Freeman, Laura, and Joseph Galimberti. "The Institute of Public Administration of Canada." *Canadian Public Administration* 40 (summer 1997): 375–80.

Hodgetts, J.E. *The Canadian Public Service: A Physiology of Government, 1867–1970.* Toronto: University of Toronto Press, 1973.

———, "The Intellectual Odyssey of Public Administration in English Canada." *Canadian Public Administration* 40 (summer 1997): 171–85.

Hodgetts, J.E., and D.C. Corbett, eds. *Canadian Public Administration.* Toronto: Macmillan, 1960.

Kernaghan, Kenneth, ed. *Bureaucracy in Canadian Government,* 2nd ed. Toronto: Methuen, 1973.

———. *Canadian Public Administration: Discipline and Profession.* Toronto: Butterworths, 1983.

———. *Public Administration in Canada: Selected Readings,* 5th ed. Toronto: Methuen, 1985.

Kernaghan, Kenneth, and Mohamed Charih. *Research in Public Administration: An Agenda for the Year 2000.* Québec: École nationale d'administration publique, 1996.

McReady, Douglas J. *The Canadian Public Sector.* Toronto: Butterworths, 1984.

Parenteau, R.E. "L'administration publique du Québec: a lorée du 21e siecle." *Canadian Public Administration* 40 (summer 1997): 186–203.

Sancton, Andrew. "Canada as a Highly Urbanized Nation: New Implications for Government." *Canadian Public Administration* 35 (winter 1992): 281–98.

Sutherland, Sharon L., and G. Bruce Doern. *Bureaucracy in Canada: Control and Reform.* Research Study no. 43 for the Royal Commission on the Economic Union and Development Prospects for Canada. Toronto: University of Toronto Press, 1985.

Wilson, V. Seymour. *Canadian Public Policy and Administration.* Toronto: McGraw-Hill Ryerson, 1981.

2

What Is Public Bureaucracy?

An unusual thing has happened on the way to the 21st century. People have begun to say nice things about the public bureaucracy. Even some of its primary critics, namely business people, journalists, and politicians, have recently acknowledged the significant achievements of government employees and the importance of their contributions to national and individual prosperity. According to Ted Newall, Chief Executive Officer of NOVA Corporation,

> [o]ne of Canada's assets—and a largely unrecognized asset—is the matchless integrity, the exceptional high quality and the extraordinary commitment of Canada's public service to the success of our nation.... To continue to be a winner it is not enough for Canada to create a competitive private sector. We must also have an outstanding public service. [And] a highly effective public service attracts some of the country's best and brightest, making the public service a career of choice.[1]

And in the 1997 Speech from the Throne, the Chrétien government said that it wished "to recognize the importance of a professional, non-partisan public service in a well-performing civil society. Canada is served well by its public service and the effort and dedication it exhibits in meeting the needs of citizens and building partnerships among governments and other sectors of society."[2] Even journalists have joined in. A *Toronto Star* editorial stated that "the public service is the nation's brain trust. It has been downsized and denigrated for years. It needs an injection of hope."[3] *The Globe and Mail* went so far as to title a column "Top Bureaucrats Deserve a Raise."[4]

What is this phenomenon called public bureaucracy? Should we side with its critics or its admirers? What can we learn about its nature and evolution from the writings of such great thinkers as Karl Marx and Max Weber? What is the relationship between bureaucracy and democracy? These are the major questions considered in this chapter.

In the previous chapter, public bureaucracy was distinguished from public administration and was defined as "the system of authority, people, offices, and methods that government uses to achieve its objectives." Large business and other non-governmental organizations are often described as bureaucracies, but the concept of bureaucracy is so closely associated with government that the terms "bureaucracy" and "public bureaucracy" are commonly used interchangeably. This chapter illustrates that the neutral definition provided above is not shared by all. The chapter begins with a review of the evolution and criticisms of public bureaucracy, which is followed by an explanation of theories concerning the relationship between bureaucracy and the state.

🏛 ORIGINS AND CRITICISMS OF PUBLIC BUREAUCRACY

Evolution of Public Bureaucracy

Many of the central features of contemporary public bureaucracy (e.g., chain of command, specialization, delegation of authority) were evident in the ancient civilizations of Egypt and China. In the West, many characteristics of present-day public bureaucracy existed during the period of the Roman Empire. After the fall of the Empire and the onset of the Dark Ages, some of the Roman achievements in administration were kept alive by the Roman Catholic Church. It is generally acknowledged, however, that the modern type of administrative system began in the 17th century after the emergence of nation-states from the feudal societies of Europe. It was not until the 1800s that Europe, Great Britain, the United States, and Canada developed their distinctive systems of public bureaucracy that have endured to the present.

Despite the long history of bureaucratic forms of administration, use of the word "bureaucracy" is comparatively recent. It appears to have been first used in 18th-century France by Vincent de Gournay to signify a form of government in which appointed officials play a central role. In France at the time, the word "bureau" referred not only to a writing table (or, according to some scholars, a cloth covering the desks of government officials); it also referred to a place where officials worked. A Greek word meaning "rule" was added as a suffix to "bureau" and by 1798 the *Dictionary of the French Academy* defined bureaucracy as: "power, influence of the heads and staff of governmental bureaux."[5] An indication of the subsequent pejorative interpretations of the term was provided by the Academy's approval of the term bureaucratic to signify "the influence of governmental bureaux, and also a regime where bureaux multiply without need."[6] Use of the term spread quickly to other European countries and eventually throughout the world.

During the past two centuries, the term bureaucracy has been interpreted in a wide variety of ways. For example, on the basis of an exhaustive study of interpretations and theories of bureaucracy, Martin Albrow identified seven "modern concepts of bureaucracy."[7] These are bureaucracy as rational organization, as organizational inefficiency, as rule by officials, as public administration, as administration by officials, as the organization, and as modern society.

Criticisms of Public Bureaucracy

Regardless of the neutral meaning assigned to bureaucracy at the beginning of this chapter, the most frequent usage of the term throughout history and in current conversation is a derogatory one. The word bureaucracy normally conjures up images of government employees and organizations characterized by unresponsiveness, inaccessibility, inflexibility, inefficiency, arbitrariness, and empire-building.

Among those groups whose negative views on bureaucracy have been most widely disseminated are novelists, journalists, politicians, business people, and academics. As early as 1836, in his novel *Les Employés*, Honoré de Balzac described bureaucracy as "the great power wielded by pygmies" and noted that bureaucracy was organized "under a constitutional government with a natural kindness for mediocrity, a predilection for categorical statements and reports, a government as fussy and meddlesome, in short, as a small shopkeeper's wife."[8] And in 1885, the English novelist Charles Dickens wrote in *Little Dorrit* about the Circumlocution Office where "numbers of people were lost." In this office, "unfortunates with wrongs, or with projects for the general welfare ... who in slow lapse of time and agony had passed safely through other public departments; who, according to rule, had been bullied in this, over-reached by that, and evaded by the other; got referred to the Circumlocution Office, and never reappeared in the light of day."[9]

Similar anti-bureaucratic sentiments have pervaded a great deal of fictional literature during the past century. Novelists have been joined by satirists whose works on bureaucracy include *Parkinson's Law, When in Doubt: Mumble,* and *Cover Your Ass.* In *The Completely Civil Servant*, a Canadian writing under the pseudonym of G. Arthur Sage describes his book as "the bible for survival, therapy and reform" for public servants and as a means by which "the taxpayer will get an insider's view of the practices that have mushroomed under the justification of improved service to a demanding citizenry."[10] Movies, popular magazines, professional journals, and public affairs shows on both television and radio all engage in the national sport of bashing bureaucrats.

Journalists make a major contribution to the bureaucracy's negative image through provocative headlines and reports that trumpet the bureaucracy's deficiencies and failures. Many of these headlines and stories reflect attacks on bureaucrats by politicians. An enduring theme of election campaigns at all levels of Canadian government is the need to control the bureaucracy, to make it more efficient, and to reduce its size. Journalists and politicians find a very receptive audience for anti-bureaucratic assertions among the general public and especially among business people. The kind of distorted picture of bureaucracy painted by some business publications is illustrated in an article in *Canadian Business* in which a writer is discussing the problems of running a restaurant:

> A restaurant ... is the natural prey of petty bureaucrats who will obstruct and complicate everything you do. All of them will hunt you down, and any of them, on a whim, can shut you down. A mouse in the house, you get a cat. A mouse in a restaurant, you get a visit, an hour's lecture and a warning notice (this time about the cat); and a series of visits and letters from the building inspector who wants to see the drawings for the cat box.[11]

In addition to these journalistic and popular accounts, there have been serious scholarly analyses of bureaucracy in which the bureaucracy has received mixed reviews from the academic community. Victor Thompson refers to "bureaupathic" behaviour in large-scale organizations that takes the form of "excessive aloofness, ritualistic attachment to routines and procedures, and resistance to change; and associated with these behaviour patterns is a petty insistence upon rights of authority and status."[12]

Other scholars sing bureaucracy's praises. Charles Perrow contends that "the sins generally attributed to bureaucracy are either not sins at all or are consequences of the failure to bureaucratize sufficiently."[13] For example, the impersonality and rigid adherence to rules found in bureaucracies are frequently criticized. However, it should be seen as a triumph of bureaucracy when a bureaucrat responds to people according to the objective merits of their case rather than to factors such as skin colour or religion. A bureaucratic response based on prejudice or other inappropriate considerations would, in Perrow's view, be evidence of "failure to bureaucratize sufficiently."

One of the strongest proponents of the positive elements of bureaucracy is Charles T. Goodsell. In his book, *The Case for Bureaucracy*,[14] he argues that bureaucracy in the United States has been the victim of unfortunate stereotyping and myth. He notes that while people rail against the evils of bureaucracy in the abstract, when they are asked how they have been treated by bureaucrats in specific situations, they tend to see the bureaucrats as being fair and helpful. After reviewing a great deal of evidence, he concludes that while bureaucracy is not perfect by any means, it does have an enviable record of providing services.

> [P]ublic servants have seriously exaggerated public hostility to [them] such that almost eighty per cent believe that their clients think of them as "lazy and uncaring." In fact, slightly less than one in five clients really hold this view. [T]he greatest anger and alienation from government is directed to politicians and the entire institution of government. In fact, trust in federal [and provincial] public servants is significantly higher than trust in politicians.
>
> *Source: Ekos Research Associates, Perception of Government Service Deliver*[15]

Goodsell's point about the contradictory nature of the public's perception of bureaucracy is supported by studies of Canadian attitudes toward the federal public service. Two early studies (in 1969 and 1978) demonstrated that despite favourable personal interactions with bureaucrats, many Canadians have a negative image of the bureaucracy as a whole.[16] And a 1996 study reported that members of the public "were more likely to describe specific transactions with federal public servants in more positive terms, compared to their *general* negative impression of government services and public servants."[17]

A 1990 study found that federal public servants, especially front-line employees, were strongly committed to serving the public; that there was substantial departmental support for such service; and that managers encouraged public consultation. However, the study also showed that departmental values regarding service were not always communicated effectively down the hierarchy: some public servants were confused about whom they were supposed to put first, the public or their minister and the government; there were no clear guidelines about how best to improve service; and the systems for evaluating service quality and client satisfaction were inadequate.[18] Many of the public service reforms in the 1990s, in all spheres of Canadian government, have been designed to improve service, in part to enhance the image of the public service.

The Feminist Critique of Bureaucracy

Since the mid-1970s, the role of women in bureaucracies has received much more attention than before. (However, most of the scholarly literature on this subject does not distinguish between public organizations and private organizations.) Several contributions to the literature are especially noteworthy. Rosabeth Kanter, a pioneer in this area, argued in 1977 that the values and behaviour of both men and women are a function of their location in the organization rather than of sex differences.[19] Since most organizations are male-dominated, women are relatively powerless and therefore occupy lower levels of the organization. To compete effectively with men, many women will adapt their behaviour to the dominant masculine culture, in part by repressing their real values.

In this connection, Kathy Ferguson observed in 1984 that "women entering the organization are usually required to put aside person-oriented values of women's traditional role in order to embrace the organization and prove themselves 'one of the boys.'"[20] She also distinguished between two components of the feminist movement: "those who are primarily interested in gaining access to established institutions and those who aim at the transformation of those institutions."[21] The first group, labelled liberal feminists, has called upon the state to integrate women into organizations by such means as affirmative action/employment equity programs. The second group, composed of radical feminists, "rejects the exclusive focus on integration because they see the existing institutional relationships themselves as fundamentally flawed."[22]

In 1994, Anneka Davidson made a related distinction between what she called the *feminine* and the *feminist* ethical perspectives. The feminine perspective emphasizes the importance in organizations of nurturing interpersonal relationships and of caring, cooperation, and concern for others. This perspective provides an alternative to the current ethical framework for administrative behaviour.

> Sadly, the voice of care is yet to be heard within mainstream public administration.... [W]omen who speak of cooperation, concern, or compassion are ridiculed; the feminine perspective is readily dismissed by scholars and practitioners alike.... It is time, I believe, for both men and women ... to listen with courtesy and thoughtfulness to the voice of feminine morality.
>
> *Source: Anneka Davidson, "Gender Differences in Administrative Ethics"[23]*

A prominent representative of this feminine perspective (also often called the *care* perspective) is Carol Gilligan. She challenged the application to women of the widely accepted view that moral maturity is based on respect for the dignity and freedom of the individual (the justice perspective). She argued that for women moral maturity is based on interpersonal responsibility manifested by caring, loving, and nurturing. Some theorists believe that traditional organizations can be transformed if they are populated by large numbers of women who are committed to such values. However, it is increasingly recognized that men too can base their moral reasoning on the care perspective and act in a loving and nurturing way.[24]

In contrast to the feminine perspective, the *feminist* perspective argues that the influence of feminine morality will not be felt in organizations unless there is a radical shift from the current hierarchical and competitive culture to one that emphasizes such values as cooperation, diversity, equality, and participation.[25] Furthermore, feminine values are suppressed in contemporary organizations because of men's dominance of the power structure: "[T]raditional power structures and hierarchies are fundamentally incompatible with feminine values.... Unless women create alternative organizations or obtain much greater power in traditional organizations, the feminine commitment to care and nurture will not be translated into new modes of behavior."[26] One way to enhance the power of women is to increase their numbers, especially at the senior levels. The subject of representative bureaucracy and employment equity will be further discussed in Chapter 24.

🏛 BUREAUCRACY AND THE STATE

This section reviews classical and modern theories of bureaucracy within the broad framework of theories of the role of the state.[27] The next two chapters cover, among other topics, theories of organization; these theories are more narrowly focused on the internal management of organizations.

Classical Theories of Bureaucracy

Karl Marx (1818–1883)

Marx's ideas on bureaucracy must be examined in the context of his theory of class conflict in capitalist societies and the advent of communism. According to Marxism, the state in capitalist societies does not represent the general interest but rather the interests of the dominant or ruling class. Marx regarded the state as "nothing more than the form of organization which the bourgeois necessarily adopt ... for the mutual guarantee of their property and interests."[28] The bureaucracy of the state is viewed as an instrument that the dominant class uses to exercise its power over other social classes. Bureaucracy is, in fact, one of the primary means for perpetuating class division and consolidating the power of the dominant class. The state becomes more oppressive as class conflict intensifies. For Marx, the increasing bureaucratization of the state under capitalism accompanied the intensification of the class struggle.

This class struggle eventually leads to a proletarian revolution and the gradual development of a classless society. With the advent of communism, the state and the exploitative elements of the bureaucracy will ultimately wither away. Administrative tasks will be everyone's concern and will involve the administration of things rather than of people.

In his early writings, Marx argued that bureaucracy contributes to the general process of alienation in society; it becomes an autonomous and oppressive force beyond the control of the people. He also asserted that bureaucracy is characterized by secrecy, incompetence, empire building, and self-interest. In his later writings, Marx downplayed the idea of bureaucracy as an autonomous social force by referring to bureaucracy as simply part of the state that would wither away with the state itself. Allowing for the possibility of bureaucracy exercising autonomous power would have been inconsistent with his later view that "nothing could prevent economic forces producing the polarization of society into bourgeoisie and proletariat."[29]

Classical Elite Theory

Gaetano Mosca (1885–1941) and Robert Michels (1876–1936)

Mosca and Michels belong to the elite school of classical theorists. Mosca, in his book *The Ruling Class*, contended that all societies are composed of two classes: a class that rules and a class that is ruled. The ruling class is a minority that rules the majority, not simply by coercion but through the ability to organize and by reference to such abstract principles as the sovereignty of the people or divine right.

Mosca divided states into two types, which he called the feudal and the bureaucratic. In the feudal state, any member of the ruling class can carry out all the functions of government, whether economic, judicial, administrative, or military. In the bureaucratic state, however, these functions are separated and become the exclusive territory of particular sections of the ruling class, including the bureaucracy and the military establishment. The government taxes a portion of the national wealth to support a large number of salaried administrative and military officials.

Mosca did not accept the Marxian notion of an identity of interests among persons in a similar class position. He proposed electing members of the ruling class to legislative bodies as a means of constraining bureaucratic power. He was, however, uncertain as to whether elected bodies would in practice be able to exercise adequate control over the bureaucracy.

Michels' major focus was not on the state bureaucracy but on the internal political structures of large-scale organizations. On the basis of his study of political parties and trade unions, he formulated his famous "iron law of oligarchy." According to this law, large-scale organizations are necessarily oligarchic because they tend to develop a bureaucratic structure that precludes internal democracy. In Michels' words, "who says organization, says oligarchy." Power becomes concentrated at the top of the organization and is wielded in a dictatorial manner by an organizational elite.

For Michels, the iron law of oligarchy has broad implications in that oligarchic bureaucratic structures undermine the democratic institutions of society. The eventual result is an oligarchic political regime that resists demands for change made by the general populace.

Michels viewed bureaucracy as inevitable in the modern state. Through bureaucracy, the politically dominant classes secure and preserve their power.

They use, indeed they expand, positions in the bureaucracy to provide security for middle-class intellectuals who, in turn, support the state. The bureaucracy tends to oppress the rest of society. Lower-level bureaucrats, in particular, suppress individual liberty and initiative.

Max Weber (1864–1920)

Max Weber, a German scholar, has had more influence on the study of bureaucracy than any other theorist. Weber did not agree with Marx that bureaucracy will eventually wither away. Indeed, he predicted that bureaucratic administration will pervade all forms of organization, in all spheres of life. He asserted that "the needs of mass administration make [bureaucratic administration] completely indispensable. The choice is only that between bureaucracy and dilettantism in the field of administration."[30] Weber also disagreed with Michels' view that bureaucratic domination of elected politicians is inevitable. But Weber was ambivalent about the power of the bureaucracy. Support can be found in his writings both for the view that in a democracy the bureaucracy must be subordinate to elected politicians, and for the view that, in certain circumstances, bureaucrats could dominate their political superiors.

Like Marx and Michels, Weber set his ideas on bureaucracy within the context of a study of the power structure of society. He examined the concept of bureaucracy within the broad and complex framework of political sociology. Unlike Marx and Michels, he treated bureaucracy as the central concept in his analysis and as a general phenomenon in modern society.

Weber related bureaucracy to his analysis of three sources of authority, which he distinguished on the basis of their claim to legitimacy. Under *traditional* authority, the right to rule is legitimated by such factors as heredity, religious beliefs, or divine right. *Charismatic* authority is based on the outstanding personal characteristics of an individual (e.g., Jesus, John F. Kennedy, Adolph Hitler). Finally, *legal* authority is legitimated by laws and regulations obeyed by both the rulers and the ruled. In this system, "obedience is owed not to a person—whether a traditional chief or charismatic leader—but to a set of impersonal principles."[31] Each authority type is associated with a different administrative arrangement; the usual administrative system under legal authority is bureaucracy.

From his knowledge of Western European bureaucracies, notably the German and the British, Weber developed his celebrated ideal type of bureaucracy, which is discussed in the next chapter.

Modern Theories of Bureaucracy

Pluralism

According to pluralist theory, political power in contemporary Western democracies is fragmented and diffused among many groups that check and balance one another. While certain groups have more influence on government than others, all have some influence. There is no power elite that dominates the decision-making process; rather there is a plurality of participants involved in the process. Success in influencing government decision making depends not only on access to such resources as money and expertise but also on a determination to have one's voice heard.

The structure of modern governments and, in particular, modern bureaucracies reflects and facilitates this pluralism because their complexity provides numerous points of access for groups wishing to influence government decision makers. In a pluralist political system, bureaucrats are influenced and constrained by a wide variety of political actors who pursue their interests by forming alliances with administrative agencies. Bureaucrats, in turn, influence and constrain these actors and welcome alliances that enable their agencies to achieve their objectives. This practice is especially characteristic of the United States, where administrative agencies act like pressure groups, mobilizing support from various groups to influence legislators and the public. In Canada, departments that operate in a similar fashion are often referred to as clientele departments; they include such departments as Agriculture (in alliance with farmers) and Veterans Affairs (in alliance with war veterans).

In addition, the bureaucracy itself, like the state, is a pluralist structure. It is composed of a large number of administrative agencies that are interdependent but that are also rivals for scarce government resources. Again, this is most easily demonstrated in the United States where administrative agencies use alliances within or outside the bureaucracy in competition with other agencies for resources and, in some instances, for survival.

Elitism and Technocracy

Modern elite theory draws on the contributions of such classical elite theorists as Mosca and Michels, who contended that societies consist of a class that rules and a class that is ruled. In contrast to the pluralists, modern elite theorists contend that public policy is decided by a small number of ruling elites who are drawn largely from the upper socioeconomic level of society, who agree on the basic values of the social system, and whose decisions are little influenced by the masses.[32]

C. Wright Mills,[33] a leading representative of this school of thought, argued in the mid-1950s that American society was dominated by a power elite occupying key posts in government, corporations, and the military.

Elite theorists view the bureaucratic-technocratic elites as only one element of the ruling elites. However, *technocratic* theory holds that the technocratic elite, or experts, in both public and private sector organizations, exercise the greatest influence on public policy. James Burnham[34] argued as early as 1942 that these experts would become the rulers of society. While contemporary proponents of the technocratic school of thought do not share this view, they are concerned that the power of technocrats, notably government bureaucrats, is a threat to democracy.

Several reasons for the increasing power of senior bureaucrats are offered: the scope and complexity of government activities require a greater number of bureaucrats with expert technical knowledge; political leaders are obliged to rely on bureaucrats for information and advice; since elected officials have limited time and little interest or expertise in certain areas, much is left for bureaucratic decision making; and finally, politicians come and go, but bureaucrats are permanent.[35]

It must be acknowledged that bureaucrats exercise substantial power in the political system and that much of this power is based on expertise. However, it can be argued that this expertise does not put the bureaucracy in a dominant position. Moreover, generalists, rather than experts, occupy the top posts in contemporary bureaucracies. It is notable that, while a powerful bureaucracy poses some danger to democracy, it can also constrain abuses of the democratic process by elected officials.

Corporatism

Corporatism can be defined as

> an institutional arrangement whereby public policy is worked out through an interaction between top state elites and the leadership of a limited number of corporate organizations (mainly business and industrial corporations on the one hand and labour unions on the other). Under this arrangement, the corporate organizations are granted a deliberate representational monopoly within their respective areas of interest in exchange for submitting themselves to certain constraints imposed by the state.[36]

There is, however, much debate among writers on corporatism about the exact meaning of the term, the countries where it exists, whether present trends are in the direction of its expansion, and its implications for relations between bureaucracy and the state.

While pluralist theory holds that government decisions are influenced by a considerable number of groups acting in a voluntary and competitive fashion, corporatist theory holds that these decisions are influenced by a small number of noncompetitive and functionally differentiated groups that are recognized or licensed by the state. Corporatist arrangements and tendencies are much less common in Canada[37] and the United States than in Western Europe (notably Austria, Denmark, West Germany, and the United Kingdom) where business organizations and trade unions are more integrated into economic policy-making through various consultative bodies and processes.

Some scholars contend that a corporatist state is less bureaucratic than other forms because the state can work through indirect and informal mechanisms to negotiate agreements with a small number of dominant groups. Other scholars argue, however, that in a corporatist state the government would require "an autonomous bureaucratic arm with independent access to information and capable of supervising the operations of capital."[38] Moreover, bureaucratic power is likely to be greater because of the close interaction between senior bureaucrats and the dominant groups.[39] It is notable that in a corporatist state, weaker groups and individuals would tend to be frozen out of the decision-making process.

Modern Marxist Theory

Modern Marxism is usually referred to as neo-Marxism. Contemporary Marxist scholars do not agree on a generally acceptable theory of the state. They do agree, however, that the state serves three major functions, namely, accumulating wealth and power for the capitalist class, legitimizing to workers the value of the capitalist state, and, if necessary, repressing or coercing workers to ensure social order. In Chapter 6, these functions will be elaborated in the examination of Marxist analysis as a model of public policy-making. The focus here is on the modern Marxist view of the role of bureaucracy in the power structure of society.

Like Marx, modern Marxists contend that state institutions, notably the bureaucracy, serve the interests of the capitalist ruling class. Ralph Miliband, a leading theorist on Marxism, offers several reasons for this.[40] First, members of the ruling class and senior officials in state institutions have personal ties of friendship, kinship, and experience because of their similar social origins. Indeed, members of the ruling class are direct participants in the bureaucracy and other state institutions. Second, the ruling class, because of its economic power, is the most influential pressure group in capitalist society. Third, the state operates in a capitalist system of production and is, therefore, constrained by structure to promote the capitalist economy. By doing so, it serves both its own interests and those of the capitalist class. According to Miliband, "a capitalist economy has its own 'rationality' to which any government and state must sooner or later submit, and usually sooner."[41] Nicos Poulantzas, another leading theorist, contends that the bureaucracy serves the capitalist class, not because of similar social origins, but because of Miliband's third point, namely that structural constraints mean that the interests of the bureaucracy and the ruling class coincide.[42]

Miliband and Poulantzas agree, however, that bureaucracy has become the dominant state institution. The power of the legislatures and, therefore, of those who elect them has declined; legislators have little direct contact with bureaucrats. Similarly, the accompanying decline in the power of political parties means that they no longer serve as mechanisms for channelling class interests to bureaucratic decision makers. The threat to democracy is aggravated in some countries by the politicization of the bureaucracy, which enables the government party to appoint its supporters to senior public service posts. The increased power of the bureaucracy is dangerous also because it tends to promote and sustain conservative forces.

Eva Etzioni-Halevy criticizes Marxists for turning into a dogma the idea that the state, and therefore the bureaucracy, promotes the interest of the capitalist ruling class.[43] She notes the Marxist argument that "if the state elite is conservative in its policies, then, obviously, it works in the interests of the ruling class." If, however, "it introduces reforms that benefit the lower classes ..., this too is interpreted ... as serving merely to co-opt those classes and make them more willing to accept the capitalist system." She contends that a more realistic approach would be to treat the state elites not as servants of the ruling class but "as two groups, each of which is intent on using the other to serve its own interests." She also criticizes the Marxists for arguing on the one hand that bureaucracy is simply a servant of the ruling class and on the other that bureaucracy is becoming too powerful in its own right.

Libertarian Theory

The school of thought represented by such thinkers as Frederich Hayek and Milton Friedman is called Libertarianism. In the tradition of Adam Smith and John Stuart Mill, the theories of Hayek and Friedman are concerned about the threat that the expansion of both government activities and bureaucracy pose for economic liberty. Indeed, they argue that this expansion threatens political as well as economic liberty.

Friedrich A. Hayek (1899–1992).   Hayek's best-known book, *The Road to Serfdom*, is based on principles of 19th-century economic liberalism. He argued that economic liberty is possible only in a capitalist system and that all forms of collectivism (e.g., socialism) are incompatible with democracy because the social planning involved in collectivism tends to destroy both political and economic freedom. Hayek did not oppose the idea of a welfare state but was concerned that even the moderate planning involved in creating a welfare state will have consequences, neither foreseen nor desired by the planners, that will put the state on the road to serfdom, i.e., totalitarianism. Moreover, the bureaucracy will play a critical role in putting the state on this path.

Hayek noted that economic planning and regulation in the welfare state lead to substantial growth in the size and power of the bureaucracy, some of whose members exercise extensive discretionary powers over individual citizens. In addition, the bureaucracy is composed of people whose careers depend significantly on the expansion of government services. According to Hayek, in the welfare state the rule of law is breached in that bureaucrats are delegated powers to make decisions that discriminate between individuals and against which appeal is very difficult. Efficiency is also reduced in that the welfare system doesn't really help those for whom it was designed; e.g., a progressive income tax benefits middle-income persons rather than the poor.

Milton Friedman (1912–).   Friedman's best-known books include *Capitalism and Freedom* and *Free to Choose*. Like Hayek, Friedman worries about the threat to economic and political liberty from the expansion of both government activities and bureaucracy. This expansion is the unavoidable result of the growth of the welfare state, which, in his view, diverts important economic resources from the private sector of the economy and creates a kind of government paternalism that undermines the very foundations of the capitalist system. Among government activities to which he objects are rent control, minimum-wage rates, legal maximum prices, detailed regulation of industries, and public housing.[44]

Friedman warns that the United States is moving in the same direction as other countries that have lost their economic and political liberty as a consequence of the expansion of the welfare state. He cites the examples of Chile and Britain (and New York City) to support his view that the expanded role of the state, the increased volume of government regulations, and the growth of government spending, no matter how well intended, threaten individual liberty. He contends that "the Welfare State's fundamental fallacy, which leads to both financial crisis and the destruction of freedom, is the attempt to do good at someone else's expense."[45] This happens because people do not spend someone else's money with as much care as they do their own. Moreover, to do good at someone else's expense, you have to take the money away from that person. Thus, the use of force and coercion, which destroy freedom, is necessary to do good at somebody else's expense.

Friedman distinguishes between the economic market, where you get what you vote for (by paying), and the political market, where there is very little relation between what you vote for and what you get. In the economic market, "each man can vote, as it were, for the color of the tie he wants and get it; he does not have to see what color the majority wants and then, if he is in the minority, to submit."[46] One of the myths about the political market is that a government bureaucrat can be distinguished from someone in private enterprise on the grounds that the bureaucrat serves a *public* interest rather than a *private* interest. Friedman contends that "a government bureaucrat is seeking to serve his private interest just as much as you or I or the ordinary businessman."[47] In the economic market, our self-interest motivates us to serve our customers' interests, but in a government bureaucracy the customers have nowhere else to go. Thus, the bureaucrats can serve their self-interest at their customers' expense by expanding their empire and reducing their workload.

The Libertarian school of thought has had a great deal of influence on the views of those associated with the contemporary neoconservative movement. The term neoconservatism[48] emerged in the mid-1970s to describe the views of a group of American intellectuals (e.g., Irving Kristol, Nathan Glazer, and Norman Podhoretz) who believe that big government is a threat to freedom and economic prosperity and who tend to ally themselves with business interests on many political and economic issues. Neoconservatism had a very significant influence on the Reagan and Bush administrations in the United States and on the Thatcher government in Britain. It also has followers in Canada (e.g., Michael Walker of the Fraser Institute in Vancouver, author David Frum, and John Bullock, former president of the Canadian Federation of Independent Business).

A practical application of neoconservative thinking can be seen in efforts beginning in the mid-1980s, in Canada and elsewhere, to reduce both government spending and the size and influence of the bureaucracy. In Canada, the Progressive Conservative government of Brian Mulroney pursued these objectives by such means as abolishing or cutting back government programs; privatizing government activities and ownership; deregulating industry;

emulating the management model provided by private enterprise; downsizing the public service; and increasing political control over the bureaucracy. It is notable that similar approaches have been taken in several countries by governments that are not ideologically neoconservative, including, in Canada, the Liberal government of Jean Chrétien.

🏛 BUREAUCRACY AND DEMOCRACY

The foregoing theories are concerned, in varying degrees, with one of the most central and enduring issues in public administration: the relationship between bureaucracy and democracy. Indeed, a pervasive theme in this book, and the primary concern of Chapters 12 to 14, is the nature of bureaucratic power and bureaucratic responsibility in the Canadian democracy. Etzioni-Halevy captures the essence of the problematic relationship between bureaucracy and democracy in three theses.[49] Her first thesis is that "bureaucracy generates a dilemma for democracy." She contends that bureaucracy threatens democratic political institutions because it is becoming increasingly powerful and independent, and because the rules affecting the exercise of its power are ill-defined. At the same time, however, a powerful, independent bureaucracy is required to prevent political corruption and to safeguard democratic procedures. "Bureaucracy is thus a threat to, but also indispensable for, democracy."

The second thesis is that "democracy generates a dilemma for bureaucracy." Because democracy's rules are self-contradictory, bureaucracy finds itself in a double bind. It "is expected to be both independent and subservient, both responsible for its own actions and subject to ministerial responsibility, both politicized and non-politicized at the same time." Public servants are centrally involved in policy development but are expected to be neutral in regard to party politics.

Etzioni-Halevy's third thesis is that "these dilemmas exacerbate strains and power struggles on the political scene," notably between senior bureaucrats and senior politicians. It is often unclear as to whether certain responsibilities belong to public servants or politicians. Thus, public servants and politicians, especially cabinet ministers, can become involved in serious disagreements over jurisdiction.

We shall see in subsequent chapters that the tensions resulting from these dilemmas explain a great deal about the organization and management of Canadian government in general and public bureaucracy in particular.

NOTES

1. Quoted in Huguette Labelle, "Pride and Recognition in the Public Service" (Presentation to Alberta Federal Council Workshop, 9 December 1997), 11–12.
2. *Debates*, House of Commons, 23 September 1997.
3. Carol Gore, *The Toronto Star*, 23 August 1997, E2.
4. Hugh Winsor, "Top Bureaucrats Deserve a Raise," *The Globe and Mail*, 13 February 1998, A7.

5. Martin Albrow, *Bureaucracy* (London: Macmillan, 1970), 12.

6. Ibid., 17–18.

7. Ibid.

8. Honoré de Balzac, *Les Employés,* translated by E. Marriage as *Bureaucracy* (1898), 84. Cited in ibid., 18.

9. Cited in E.N. Gladden, *The Essentials of Public Administration* (London: Staples Press, 1964), 66.

10. G. Arthur Sage, *The Completely Civil Servant* (n.p.: Eden Press, 1985).

11. James Barber, "Cordon Blues,"*Canadian Business* (June 1981): 116.

12. Victor Thompson, *Modern Organization* (New York: Knopf, 1961), 152–53.

13. Charles Perrow, *Complex Organizations: A Critical Essay,* 2nd ed. (Glenview, Ill.: Scott Foresman, 1979), 5.

14. Charles T. Goodsell, *The Case for Bureaucracy,* 3rd ed. (Chatham, N.J.: Chatham House, 1994).

15. Ekos Research Associates, *Perceptions of Government Service Delivery.* Study for Government of Canada, Deputy Ministers' Task Force on Alternative Service Delivery (Ottawa: Privy Council Office, 1996), 53.

16. Task Force on Government Information, *To Know and Be Known* (Ottawa: Queen's Printer, 1969); and Task Force on Service to the Public, *Surveys Among the Public on the Quality of Service to the Public from the Federal Government* (unpublished report, 1978).

17. Ekos Research Associates, *Perceptions of Government Service Delivery,* 24. Emphasis added.

18. Ekos Research Associates, *Survey of Public Perceptions of Service to the Public.* Study for Public Service 2000. Cited in ibid., 2.

19. Rosabeth Kanter, *Men and Women of the Corporation* (New York: Basic Books, 1977).

20. Kathy E. Ferguson, *The Feminist Case Against Bureaucracy* (Philadelphia: Temple University Press, 1984–94.

21. Ibid., 4.

22. Ibid.

23. Anneka M. Davidson, "Gender Differences in Administrative Ethics," in Terry L. Cooper, ed., *Handbook of Administrative Ethics* (New York: Marcel Dekker, 1994), 432.

24. Ibid., 431.

25. Ibid., 415–16.

26. Ibid., 426, 427.

27. For elaboration on these theories, see Eva Etzioni-Halevy, *Bureaucracy and Democracy* (London: Routledge and Kegan Paul, 1983); Nicos P. Mouzelis, *Organization and Bureaucracy* (Chicago: Aldine, 1967); and B.C. Smith, *Bureaucracy and Political Power* (Sussex: Wheatsheaf Books, 1988).

28. Karl Marx and Friedrich Engels, *The German Ideology* (1846), 78. Cited by Albrow, *Bureaucracy,* 70.

29. Ibid.

30. Max Weber, *Economy and Society* (New York: Bedminster Press, 1968), 223.

31. Peter Blau and Richard W. Scott, *Formal Organizations* (San Francisco: Chandler, 1962), 32.

32. See Thomas R. Dye and Harmon Ziegler, *The Irony of Democracy,* 6th ed. (Monterey, Calif.: Brooks/Cole, 1984), 6.

33. C. Wright Mills, *The Power Elite* (New York: Oxford University Press, 1956).

34. James Burnham, *The Managerial Revolution* (London: Putnam, 1942).

35. Eva Etzioni-Halevy, *Bureaucracy and Democracy* (London: Routledge and Kegan Paul, 1983), 57–59.

36. Ibid., 63.

37. For a discussion of the possible adoption of corporatist arrangements in Canada, see William D. Coleman, *Business and Politics* (Montreal and Kingston: McGill-Queen's University Press, 1988).

38. Leo Panitch, "Recent Theorizations of Corporatism: Reflections on a Growth Industry,"*British Journal of Sociology* 31 (1980): 165.
39. Alfred Diamant, "Bureaucracy and Public Policy in Neo-Corporatist Settings," *Comparative Politics* 14 (1981): 110.
40. Ralph Miliband, *The State in Capitalist Society* (London: Weidenfeld and Nicolson, 1969), 48–68.
41. Ralph Miliband, *Marxism and Politics* (Oxford: Oxford University Press, 1977), 72.
42. Nicos Poulantzas, *Political Power and Social Classes* (London: NLB and Sheed and Ward, 1975), 331–40.
43. Eva Etzioni-Halevy, *Bureaucracy and Democracy*, 82–84.
44. Milton Friedman, *Capitalism and Freedom* (Chicago: University of Chicago Press, 1962), 35–36.
45. Milton Friedman, "The Threat to Freedom in the Welfare State,"*Business and Society Review* (spring 1977): 8–16.
46. Ibid., 15.
47. Ibid., 12.
48. See Peter Steinfels, *The Neoconservatives* (New York: Simon and Schuster, 1979).
49. Eva Etzioni-Halevy, *Bureaucracy and Democracy*, 87.

BIBLIOGRAPHY

Albrow, Martin. *Bureaucracy*. London: Macmillan, 1970.

Blau, Peter M., and Marshall W. Meyer. *Bureaucracy in Modern Society*, 2nd ed. New York: Random House, 1971.

Blau, Peter M., and Richard W. Scott. *Formal Organizations*. San Francisco: Chandler, 1962.

Burnham, James. *The Managerial Revolution*. Middlesex: Penguin Books, 1962.

Crozier, Michael. *The Bureaucratic Phenomenon*. Chicago: University of Chicago Press, 1964.

Davidson, Anneka M. "Gender Differences in Administrative Ethics." In Terry L. Cooper, ed., *Handbook of Administrative Ethics*. New York: Marcel Dekker, 1994.

Downs, Anthony. *Inside Bureaucracy*. Boston: Little, Brown, 1967.

Etzioni-Halevy, Eva. *Bureaucracy and Democracy*. London: Routledge and Kegan Paul, 1983.

Ferguson, Kathy E. *The Feminist Case Against Bureaucracy*. Philadelphia: Temple University Press, 1984.

Friedman, Milton. *Capitalism and Freedom*. Chicago: University of Chicago Press, 1962.

_____. *Free to Choose*. New York: Harcourt Brace Jovanovich, 1980.

Fry, Brian R. *Mastering Public Administration: From Max Weber to Dwight Waldo*. Chatham, N.J.: Chatham House, 1989.

Goodsell, Charles T. *The Case for Bureaucracy*, 3rd ed. Chatham, N.J.: Chatham House, 1994.

Grant, Judith, and Peta Tancred. "A Feminist Perspective on State Bureaucracy". In Mills, Albert J., and Peta Tancred, eds., *Gendering Organizational Analysis*. Newbury Park, Calif.: Sage Publications, 1992.

Hayek, Frederich A. *The Road to Serfdom*. Chicago: University of Chicago Press, 1944.

Hummel, Ralph P. *The Bureaucratic Experience*. New York: St. Martin's Press, 1977.

Hynna, M. "Women in the Public Service—A Thirty-Year Perspective."*Canadian Public Administration* 40 (winter 1997): 618–25.

Kanter, R. *Men and Women of the Corporation*. New York: Basic Books, 1977.

Merton, Robert K. et al., eds. *Reader in Bureaucracy*. Glencoe, Ill.: Free Press, 1953.

Michels, Robert. *Political Parties*. Translated by E. and C. Paul. London: Jarrold, 1915.

Miliband, R. *The State in Capitalist Society*. London: Weidenfeld and Nicolson, 1969.

_____. *Marxism and Politics*. Oxford: Oxford University Press, 1977.

Morstein Marx, F. *The Administrative State*. Chicago: University of Chicago Press, 1957.

Mouzelis, Nicos P. *Organization and Bureaucracy: An Analysis of Modern Theories*. Chicago: Aldine, 1968.

Pal, Leslie A. *State, Class and Bureaucracy*. Montreal and Kingston: McGill-Queen's University Press, 1988.

Perrow, Charles. *Complex Organizations: A Critical Essay*, 2nd ed. Glenview, Ill.: Foresman, 1979.

Phillips, Susan D., Brian R. Little, and Laura A. Goodine. "Reconsidering Gender and Public Administration: Five Steps Beyond Conventional Research."*Canadian Public Administration* 40 (winter 1997): 563–81.

Poulantzas, N. *Political Power and Social Classes*. London: New Left Books and Sheed and Ward, 1975.

Smith, B.C. *Bureaucracy and Political Power*. Sussex: Wheatsheaf, 1988.

Stewart, Debra W. "Women in Public Administration." In Naomi B. Lynn and Aaron Wildavsky, eds., *Public Administration: The State of the Discipline*. Chatham, N.J.: Chatham House, 1990.

Thompson, Victor A. *Modern Organization*. New York: Knopf, 1961.

——. *Bureaucracy and the Modern World*. Morristown, N.J.: General Learning Press, 1976.

Weber, Max. *From Max Weber: Essays in Sociology*. Edited and translated by H.H. Gerth and C. Wright Mills. New York: Oxford University Press, 1946.

——. *The Theory of Social and Economic Organization*. Translated by A.M. Henderson and Talcott Parsons. Fair Lawn, N.J.: Oxford University Press, 1947.

——. *Economy and Society*. New York: Bedminster Press, 1968.

3

Public Administration and Organization Theory: The Structural Foundation

Bureaucracy! Everybody hates the word. It conjures up visions of red tape, needless rules, and heartless bureaucrats out to prevent people from accomplishing anything useful. Everyone has a favourite story about spending hours wandering around in a government office trying to complete a simple task, or being prevented from doing something totally innocuous because there was some obscure, senseless regulation against it. How can these stupid things happen?

It certainly seems that bureaucracy does not have a soul sometimes. How can these rules be used to kick sick people out of hospitals or make it difficult for homeowners to do simple renovations?

Or, is there a rationale for this apparent madness? Doesn't the presence of written rules and established procedures protect people from the foibles of individual bureaucrats, even though these rules and procedures can sometimes result in undesirable consequences? The set procedures can also improve the efficiency of operation of these organizations. It's true that jumping through the bureaucratic hoops can be bothersome, but it might be that the bureaucratic form of organization is the worst form of organization, except for all the others that modify Winston Churchill's famous statement on democracy.

Early cave dwellers who decided to join forces and divide responsibilities to improve their chances in hunting probably created the first organization. Given this lengthy history of organization, it is surprising that bureaucracy, as we know it today, has had a relatively short history. As noted in Chapter 2, bureaucratic forms existed in ancient China and in the medieval Roman Catholic Church. While these organizations had characteristics in common with modern forms of bureaucracy, they all lacked one or more of the essential features found in modern bureaucracies. The remaining chapters in this part of the book will discuss theories that have been used to explain bureaucracy or to attempt to improve its operation. The approach will be roughly chronological, beginning with the earliest theorists and moving, in the next chapter, to some contemporary writers.

The word bureaucracy has been saddled with a very negative connotation in recent years. In this book, the word is used in a nonpejorative sense. It will refer in a neutral way to a form of organization that has a particular structure which will be described in detail in this chapter. Thus, there is no negative connotation associated with the word; it is simply the term used to describe a particular form of organization.

It is useful to begin by explaining why something that sounds as dry and otherworldly as organization theory should be studied. Frequently, theory is contrasted with action and, not surprisingly, most managers seem to prefer the latter and disdain the former. This view is unfortunate because it ignores the fact that every member of society approaches organizations, other members of society, and tasks to be accomplished with a particular group of attitudes. Most people would not consider those attitudes as constituting a theory of organization, but they do. Whether we realize it or not, commonly held attitudes such as, "If I didn't watch my employees all the time, they'd just goof off," or "My boss treats me like a child—if she would just let me decide how to do the work, I could do it much better" are in fact parts of highly developed organizational theories. The problem with disparaging any systematic study of good theory is that members of organizations have attitudes that are theories, which they use in the operation of their organizations.

🏛 MAX WEBER AND CLASSICAL BUREAUCRATIC THEORY

It would be difficult to locate the first bureaucratic organization, but the first person who systematically studied the emerging phenomenon of bureaucracy was Max Weber (1864–1920). Weber was a brilliant scholar whose interests spanned many fields. Chapter 2 explained his views on the role of bureaucracy in society; this chapter will focus mainly on his discussion of the internal organization of bureaucracies.

The Characteristics of Weberian Bureaucracy

Weber's empirical study of the German bureaucracy suggested to him that the modern bureaucratic form consisted of a number of related characteristics. When these characteristics were combined in the same organization, the result was what he called the "ideal-type" bureaucracy.[1] The main components of this "ideal-type" bureaucracy were:[2]

- hierarchical structure;
- unity of command;
- specialization of labour;
- employment and promotion based on merit;
- full-time employment;
- decisions based on impersonal rules;
- importance of written files; and
- bureaucratic employment totally separate from the bureaucrat's private life.

Organization Chart

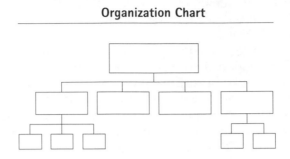

Hierarchical Structure.   A bureaucratic organization is arranged in a series of superior-subordinate relationships, at the pinnacle of which is one, and only one, superior. This can also be described as *unity of command*, which means that for each position in the hierarchy, there is one, and only one, supervisor. Thus, Weber identified what is now a commonplace characteristic of an organization chart.

The clear line of authority produced by unity of command was one reason Weber felt that bureaucracy was more efficient than previous forms of organization, but there were also other reasons for his belief.

Specialization of Labour.   The purpose of the hierarchical structure was to allocate responsibilities to subordinates in a clear and unambiguous fashion. This division of responsibilities was significant because a person could become very efficient when able to concentrate on a specific job. Specialization of labour, however, is not enough if the employees are not qualified to learn to perform the work.

Employment and Promotion Based on Merit.   In earlier times, people often obtained organizational positions through either heredity or outright purchase. Obviously, this method of staffing provided no guarantee that the person in a particular position was the best person for the job, or even a competent one. Without some assurance of competence, no organization could operate efficiently. In the German bureaucracy that Weber studied, employment and promotion based on an objective test of merit provided this assurance and, therefore, increased the efficiency of operation.

Full-Time Employment.   An important principle related to employment based on merit was that employment in the bureaucracy was the full-time activity and major source of income of the official. This ensured that the official would develop allegiance to the bureaucracy and that the bureaucrat's hierarchical superior could exercise real *control* over the day-to-day activities of the official. The superior needed effective control to force the subordinate to abide by organizational regulations in carrying out duties. This led to another important characteristic of modern bureaucracy.

Decisions Based on Impersonal Rules.   Bureaucrats are bound by certain rules in dealing with the public. These rules are "impersonal" in the sense that they apply equally to all clients in similar situations. Thus, bureaucrats cannot substitute their own set of rules for those legitimately proclaimed by superiors. If a particular benefit is to be provided without regard to race or religion, then a member of the bureaucracy would risk severe penalties if he or she allowed personal prejudice to affect the decision made. Reliance on impersonal rules in dealings between the bureaucracy and the general public increases confidence in the bureaucracy by establishing a regime of certainty in dealings.

Importance of Written Files.   The significance of these rules makes written files very important. If the bureaucrat must prove that he or she has abided by the rules in making decisions, then it is important to maintain written records, first, of the rules themselves, and second, of all decisions made and the rationale for those decisions. It is worth noting here that the bureaucrat's allegiance to the rules takes precedence over allegiance to her or his superior. A superior can exercise judgment in an area that is unclear under the rules, but he or she cannot order a subordinate to violate those rules.

Bureaucratic Employment Is Totally Separate from the Individual Bureaucrat's Private Life.   This is a recognition both of the autonomous nature of the bureaucracy as an organization and of the fact that the bureaucrat does not "own" his or her position and the rights that go with it. Bureaucrats possess a great deal of authority. In the case of members of a government bureaucracy, this could be highly coercive authority. However, it is always clear that the power is attached to the position rather than to the individual. This distinction was not always clear among members of the monarch's retinue in prebureaucratic times. An obvious result of this division is that the bureaucrat is not permitted to obtain any personal gain, other than a fixed salary, from his or her position.

Weber's Views on Bureaucracy

Weber seems to have had a rather difficult love-hate relationship with this new organizational form called bureaucracy. As a serious, objective scholar, he documented the characteristics of the German bureaucracy as he saw them without favourable or critical comment.

Beyond that, though, he seems to have been of two minds about bureaucracy. On the one hand, he argued that bureaucracy was the most efficient method of organization—a position that has been attacked by some contemporary critics. In fairness to Weber, he was likely suggesting that bureaucracy was more efficient than any *previous* system—an argument that would be difficult to refute. On the other hand, Weber foresaw many of the problems that contemporary critics find in bureaucracy:

> This passion for bureaucratization ... is enough to drive one to despair. It is ... as though we knowingly and willingly were *supposed* to become men who need

"order" and nothing but order, who become nervous and cowardly if this order shakes for a moment and helpless when they are torn from their exclusive adaptation to this order. That the world knows nothing more than such men of order—we are in any case caught up in this development, and the central question is not how we further and accelerate it but what we have to *set against* this machinery, in order to preserve a remnant of humanity from this parcelling-out of the soul, from this exclusive rule of bureaucratic life ideals.[3]

In this quotation, Weber touched upon the crucial aspects of bureaucracy that still confound us today. On the one hand, it seems to be the most efficient way of arranging a large number of offices and accomplishing complex, repetitive tasks. But, on the other hand, we condemn the impersonal, mind-numbing aspects of its operation.

Criticisms of Weber

The general criticism of Weber's work is that he dwelt too much on the structural aspects of bureaucracy and not enough on the human side of the organization. It is suggested that because Weber viewed bureaucrats as mere cogs in the mechanism, he overstated the impact of the organization on the worker and overlooked the impact of the worker on the organization.

Philip Selznick argued that the informal system of worker relationships could be just as important and influential as the formal system established in the rules of the organization.[4] To illustrate this point, he first distinguished between professed and operational goals. The professed goals are the original, overarching goals of the organization as a whole. The operational goals relate to the day-to-day functions and needs of the workers within the organization. He gave the example of a boys' reformatory that had adopted progressive ideals of rehabilitation as its professed goal but continually slipped into the use of such techniques as discipline, regimentation, and spying to solve its practical, day-to-day problems. Thus, operational goals can easily diverge from professed goals and so weaken the efficiency of the organization.

Warren G. Bennis and Philip E. Slater take a radical stance in arguing that bureaucracy is currently outmoded as a form of organization.[5] They suggest that modern trends such as rapid change and the increasing professionalization of the workforce make bureaucracy, with its emphasis on rigid rules and hierarchy of control, obsolete.

The next chapter examines contemporary theories of organization that purport to maintain the positive aspects of bureaucracy and circumvent its less desirable aspects. However, it is useful first to examine an American contemporary of Weber who was also very influential in the study of organizations.

🏛 FREDERICK W. TAYLOR AND SCIENTIFIC MANAGEMENT

Max Weber was a philosopher who could stand at arm's length from organizations and describe in broad terms their general characteristics. By contrast, Frederick Winslow Taylor (1856–1915) was a mechanical engineer who began his career working as a technician on the factory floor and spent much of his later life in either a supervisory or an advisory capacity dealing with problems of production management. His major concern was the proper arrangement of the human and mechanical resources of the factory so as to minimize waste, particularly waste of workers' time.

Taylor's experience in the factory showed him that a great deal of "soldiering," i.e., slacking off, was taking place, and that there were two reasons for this. One was what he regarded as the natural tendency of employees to do as little work as possible. The second was that work was sometimes arranged in such an awkward manner that no reasonable human being, regardless of how ambitious or honest, could physically perform what was expected by superiors. Since soldiering constituted the squandering of a resource, it was important for management to end it. Taylor argued that the resulting increased productivity would benefit both employers and employees.

The employee's natural tendency toward soldiering could be eliminated if the employer used scientific principles rather than informal calculations to determine an employee's appropriate workload. Some soldiering was caused by the employee's rational reaction to the method of piecework payment that was prevalent in Taylor's time. Employees knew that in the short run they could earn more by working hard and producing above standard, but they realized that in the long run this was counterproductive because employers simply raised the standard. Therefore, it was better to work at a steady pace and receive adequate pay than to be a "rate-buster." The problem was that employers had no idea what an employee *could* do in an average shift. Therefore, most employers used unscientific rules to establish standards and so did not have the confidence of their employees. The obvious solution to the problem was to establish *scientific standards* based on the proven physical capacities of workers and then refrain from adjusting those standards arbitrarily.

Taylor's usual approach to establishing these scientific standards was to select employees who performed a particular task exceptionally well (e.g., moving the most pig iron, shovelling the most coal). Then, a trained management employee would carefully scrutinize the actions of these employees, watching and timing their every movement. This was the beginning of the *time-and-motion study* that has stirred so much controversy on factory floors. The purpose of these studies was to learn the ideal method of performing a particular task from the most efficient employees. This is the "one best way" employed by Frank and Lillian Gilbreth and popularized with humorous effect by their children in the book and movie *Cheaper by the Dozen.*[6] When the best set of physical motions was determined, then it was the responsibility of managers to teach this technique to all employees.

The second cause of soldiering was the simple inability of workers to maintain the pace that was expected of them because of how the work was organized. Taylor pointed out that workers could be more productive if management took greater care in organizing the work. He put particular emphasis on such factors as determining the optimal working rhythm necessary to maximize output. The next time you are working in the garden or shovelling snow it might be useful to know that, according to Taylor, the greatest tonnage per day can be shovelled when the worker moves twenty-one pounds on each shovel-load.[7]

Taylor felt that it was important to have a clear division of duties between management and labour. It was the job of management to select employees for specific jobs in a scientific manner so that the physical and mental characteristics of the individual fit the job. It was then the role of management to teach labourers the optimum way to perform their duties. It was the job of labourers to supply strong backs, but since in Taylor's mind a strong back connoted a weak mind, it would be impossible for labourers to arrange their own duties.

Taylor also emphasized the importance of financial factors as a motivating force. However, he eschewed the crude principle of piecework, because he knew that workers could easily manipulate the standard. Instead, he singled out the best workers for the privilege of working in a higher-paid group. By examining their actions as described above, he was able to determine in a scientific manner how much work should be accomplished. In one experiment, workers who had met the standard in their previous day's work were given white slips at the beginning of their next shift, while those who had not were given yellow slips. Those receiving yellow slips obviously did not understand fully how their job should be done, so it was the responsibility of management to provide additional training. The consistent receipt of yellow slips would cause one's return to the lower-paid gang.[9] This was Taylor's method of using financial incentives without the drawbacks identified with piecework.

Some writers suggest that Taylor showed a lack of concern for the workers. It is clear that he viewed management as very enlightened and workers in a rather condescending manner. However, Taylor did strive for harmony between management and workers and was sensitive to the need to not alienate unions. He always argued that cooperation was the best way to maximize productivity—but one gets the impression that it would be cooperation on management's terms. Furthermore, he was strongly opposed to overworking

---

TAYLOR'S VIEWS ON A STRONG BACK AND A WEAK MIND

Now one of the very first requirements for a man who is fit to handle pig iron as a regular occupation is that he shall be so stupid and so phlegmatic that he more nearly resembles in his mental makeup the ox than any other type ... Therefore the workman who is best suited to handling pig iron is unable to understand the real science of doing this class of work. He is so stupid that the word "percentage" has no meaning to him, and he must consequently be trained by a man more intelligent than himself into the habit of working in accordance with the laws of this science before he can be successful.

Source: Frederick W. Taylor, The Principles of Scientific Management[8]

TAYLOR WANTED TO IMPROVE EVERYTHING HE TOUCHED

Taylor did not confine his emphasis on improvement and innovation to the factory floor. An avid tennis player, he and Clarence M. Clark won the first United States Lawn Tennis Association doubles championship in 1881. Not content to just play the game, he also invented an improved tennis net and the sprocket device that is still used to tighten the net. These changes were quickly accepted, but his spoon-shaped racket was just as quickly made the subject of ridicule.

employees in sweatshop conditions. Although this might well have been more for reasons of productivity than humanity, it was still a fairly radical idea for his time.

Taylor's main contribution to organization theory was his emphasis on the scientific approach to work management—the "one best way"—and his emphasis on the important role of management in organizing the work.

However, there were certain problems with how Taylor's ideas were implemented. In some cases, management used time-and-motion studies to attempt to extract the maximum possible production from workers. This led to worker resistance to the entire concept. The idea of the narrow subdivision of work into its smallest components created monotony, which led to further worker unrest.

The ideas of Weber and Taylor are significant because they had a great influence on management thinking at one time, and because their influence can still be detected in some mechanistic aspects of organization theory. However, their approaches have been replaced by newer forms of organization. Their ideas made sense when applied to large factories where workers assembled products manually. Contemporary knowledge-based organizations have made many of Weber's and Taylor's ideas obsolete. However, before these problems became evident, their ideas were tried in a number of places, including the Canadian federal government.

🏛 THE CANADIAN EXPERIENCE—FROM PATRONAGE TO MERIT

The Canadian federal government gradually began adopting some of Taylor's ideas to speed up the move from a patronage-based public service to a merit-based one, thus simultaneously moving toward the Weberian concept of bureaucracy.

The Civil Service Commission (CSC) was established in 1908 to act as guardian of the merit principle. The CSC was the outgrowth of a number of reports indicating that the prevalence of patronage appointments in the Canadian civil service was having a detrimental impact on its efficiency. The CSC began the process of entrenching the merit principle by administering competitive examinations to applicants for government positions. However, the CSC soon discovered that a serious problem existed because the duties of specific positions were not usually well defined. Without a clear description of duties, creating a meaningful competitive examination was somewhat problematic.

Gradually the powers and responsibilities of the CSC evolved, until in 1918 it was given the power to make appointments to positions and to reorganize departments, whether this was sought by the department or not. This legislation seemed to be influenced by officials of the CSC, who were in turn influenced by the principles of scientific management that were so prevalent at the time.[10]

The commissioners and the executive secretary of the CSC hired the American consulting firm of Arthur Young & Co. to introduce the principles of scientific management into the Canadian federal government. The exercise began with the systematic description and classification of 50 000 positions. The positions had to be described in great detail because this was the starting point for the mechanistic process of matching the person possessing the proper qualifications with the appropriate position. The next step was to be a sweeping reorganization of the entire governmental bureaucratic apparatus, streamlining and reducing the number of departments and agencies. Obviously, the idea of government reform is not as new and radical as some think.

Arthur Young & Co.'s involvement became bogged down in a series of problems and, as a result, the reorganization did not occur. The sole, but significant, result of the exercise was an extensive and systematic classification of all government positions. Not everyone was pleased with the result. The scientific management approach to job classification made it possible to match, in a mechanical fashion, the skills required in a particular job with the skills possessed by a particular person. When the match was complete, presumably the process would be like pushing a plug into a wall socket—an automatic perfect connection that would last until it was unplugged. Not everyone was impressed by the neatness of this arrangement. For example, R. MacGregor Dawson observed:

> [A]ll positions are deemed to call for special talents, and each is filled through an examination of its own designed to test those special qualifications. But therein lies its basic weakness. Some civil servants—a plumber, a chemist, a stenographer, an entomologist, an accountant, an engineer—should unquestionably be chosen because of the special knowledge or skill which they happen to possess at the moment of their candidature; but for others, such as a clerical or administrative official, the knowledge of their duties which they might have at entrance is comparatively unimportant. The really vital question is their inherent ability and what they will be capable of doing after they have been trained by years of experience in the department.[11]

These words could have been written as easily in 1999 as they were in 1936. The classification system has undergone a number of revisions since the original exercise, but most of these have been incremental changes still based on the original 1918 approach.

At roughly the same time that Taylor and consultants such as Arthur Young were concerned with the classification and arrangement of individual jobs, there was a movement afoot to consider broader questions of the appropriate overall structure of organizations.

🏛 GULICK AND URWICK AND THE SCIENTIFIC THEORY OF ORGANIZATION

In the United States in the 1930s, the President's Committee on Administrative Management spurred a great deal of interest by trying to develop a scientific theory of organization. Taylor's work dealt with how to organize work on the factory floor, but Luther Gulick and Lyndall Urwick were concerned with developing broader theories about the ideal structure for any organization. Their concerns were span of control and the proper alignment of related functions.

The Scientific Theory of Organization

Span of control refers to the number of subordinates who report to one supervisor. There has long been controversy about what that ideal number should be. For adequacy of supervision, the smaller the span of control the better. However, a span of control that is too narrow leads to too many supervisors and too much overhead.

This point is illustrated in Figure 3.1, which compares two different organizations, both of which have sixty-four production workers. In Figure 3.1a, the span of control in every case is four. This narrow span of control results in a total of eighty-five employees, with two levels of management between the chief executive and the workers. In Figure 3.1b, the span of control is eight. This results in a total of seventy-three employees and only one level of management between the chief executive and the workers. In the latter case, not only are there fewer total employees and therefore less cost, but the presence of only one intermediate level of management makes communication, both up and down, considerably easier. However, the intangible cost of using this system is that supervisors cannot supervise eight people as closely as they can four. This could lead to production problems. McLaren points out the nature of this dilemma quite well:

> Small spans of control may appear to tighten control for the superior-subordinate relationship, but they loosen the overall control of the organization by extending the number of levels and thereby making the top that much more removed from the bottom. To cut down on the number of levels will reduce the distance between

Figure 3.1
EXAMPLES OF DIFFERENT SPANS OF CONTROL

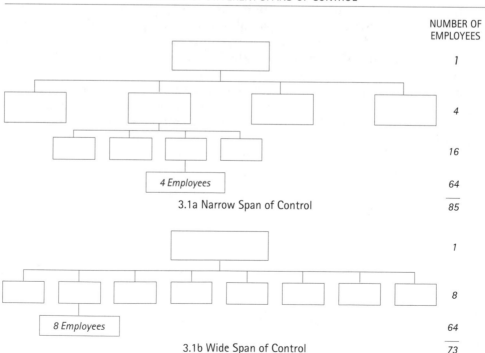

NUMBER OF EMPLOYEES

3.1a Narrow Span of Control

4 Employees

1
4
16
64
—
85

3.1b Wide Span of Control

8 Employees

1
8
64
—
73

top and bottom, but the resulting increase in the span of control at each level will lessen the control that each level can maintain.[12]

The question of the appropriate span of control is still answered much as it was in Gulick and Urwick's time. It depends on the interaction of several things:

- the nature of the work supervised (routine procedures allow for a broader span of control, but supervision of several heterogeneous activities requires a narrower span of control);
- the level of training of the subordinates;
- the extent of geographical decentralization of the work; and
- the overall stability of the organization.[13]

The recent catchphrases in organization structure are *flattening the hierarchy* and *removing layers of management*. A flatter hierarchy will lead to increased spans of control. In the current environment, this is a cost-saving move, but it is also justified on several other grounds. Reducing the number of levels between the top and the bottom of the organization decreases the isolation of those at the top and ensures that they will be more in touch with the organization's environment. It also reflects the fact that contemporary workers are much better trained than previous generations and workplaces are more mechanized. Both of these factors reduce the level of detailed supervision needed.

Aside from span of control, Gulick and Urwick were concerned with the problem of the ideal arrangement of duties within the organization. They argued that the process of organizational design should work simultaneously from the top down and from the bottom up.[14] When working from the top down, the primary criterion was to limit the span of control. Gulick reflected the conventional wisdom of the time that the senior executive should not have more than three direct subordinates. Working from the bottom up, the important factor was to combine homogeneous activities to facilitate coordination and supervision. The analyst then simply built in both directions until the two were joined.

When working from the bottom up it was important to have an appropriate definition of homogeneity. The definition suggests that people doing similar work ought to be grouped together, but on further analysis this idea is difficult to apply. Gulick suggested that each worker could be characterized in four different ways:

1. The major *purpose* he is serving, such as furnishing water, controlling crime, or conducting education;

2. The *process* he is using, such as engineering, medicine, carpentry, stenography, statistics, or accounting;

3. The *persons or things dealt with or served,* such as immigrants, veterans, Indians, forests, mines, parks, orphans, farmers, automobiles, or the poor;

4. The *place* where he renders his service, such as Hawaii, Boston, Washington, the Dust Bowl, Alabama, or Central High School.[15]

In designing an organization, employees who had all four things in common would be grouped together in the same organizational unit. If an employee was different in one category, for example, if he or she worked in a slightly different location, then that would suggest that he or she ought to be in another unit, but Gulick emphasized the importance of pragmatism and judgment applied to individual cases. Where employees had only one or two things in common, they would likely be in separate units. The question remains as to which of the four should be the dominant organizing principle.

> Each of the four basic systems of organization is intimately related with the other three, because in any enterprise all four elements are present in the doing of the work and are embodied in every individual workman. Each member of the enterprise is working for some major purpose, uses some process, deals with some person, and serves or works at some place.
>
> If an organization is erected about any one of these four characteristics of work, it becomes necessary to recognize the other characteristics in constructing the secondary and tertiary divisions of the work. For example, a government which is first divided on the basis of place will, in each geographical department, find it necessary to divide by purpose, by process, by clientele, or even again by place; and one divided in the first instance by purpose, may well be divided next by process and then by place. While the first or primary division of any enterprise is of very great significance, it must nonetheless be said that there is no one most effective pattern for determining the priority and order for the introduction of these interdependent principles. It will depend in any case upon the results which are desired at a given time and place.[16]

This problem occurs in a very practical way when deciding how to arrange the legal services function in a large, multi-function organization. Figure 3.2a illustrates an organization with one legal department containing all lawyers, who would then provide service to other departments. This is an example of an organization based on process. If, instead, the lawyers are divided and assigned to the units that handle the programs, as in Figure 3.2b, organization by purpose is being used. At first glance, one arrangement seems to have as many advantages and disadvantages as the other. Gulick admitted that the lack of empirical evidence made serious discussion difficult, but he did suggest some of the pros and cons of each method.[17]

It is difficult to resolve this question of the best method of organization. In general it can be said that provincial governments are organized by purpose, e.g., departments of health, education, social assistance, and so forth. However, some provinces also have departments with a special mandate to look after the unique problems of the northern areas of those provinces. In some cases, these "place" departments actually deliver services provided by the "purpose" departments in the south, and in others they act as coordinating bodies. There is usually some tension between this "place" department and the traditional "purpose" departments over their appropriate roles.

Figure 3.2
TYPES OF ORGANIZATION

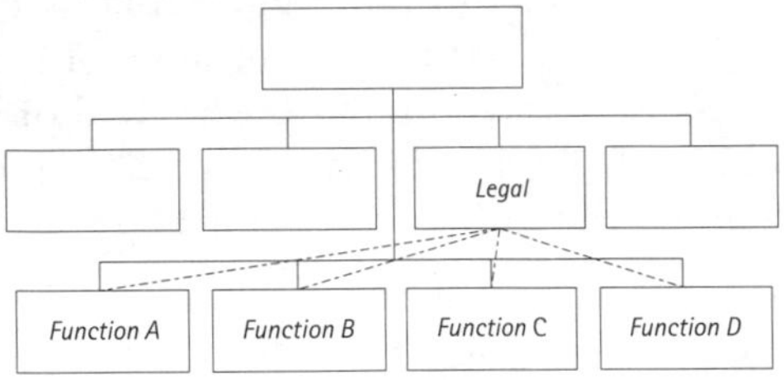

3.2a Organization by Process

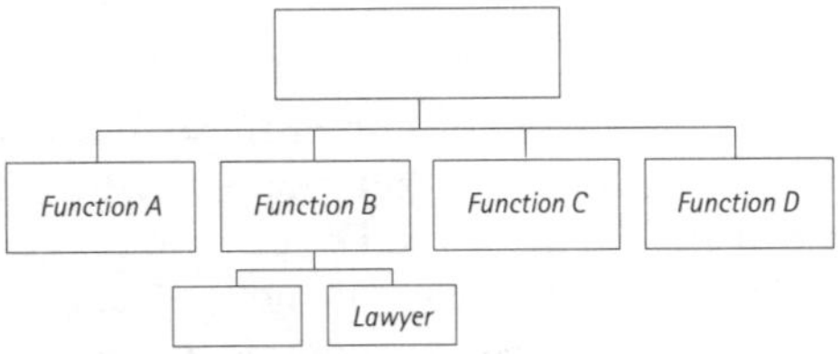

3.2b Organization by Purpose

Gulick also dealt with the activities of the executive. He argued that words like "administration" and "management" had lost their specific meaning. He felt that the job of the executive could be summed up by the acronym POSD-CORB,[18] which stood for the following activities:

- planning;
- organizing;
- staffing;
- directing;
- coordinating;
- reporting; and
- budgeting.

Carrying out all these functions as part of managing a complex organization became very difficult, particularly as each of these functions was becoming more complex in itself. Urwick noted that one way many organizations were dealing with this problem was by the use of separate line and staff functions.[19] A *line function* is directly involved in producing and distributing the goods or services provided by the organization. A classic example would be the manufacturing section of an industrial organization. Some typical examples in government would be public health nurses, social workers, or officers dealing directly with social assistance claimants.

A *staff function* is a function that aids, advises, and supports the employees providing the line function, usually without dealing directly with the clients or output of the organization. The obvious examples are human resource management, accounting, and legal services.

Some writers distinguish between three function categories—line, staff, and auxiliary.[20] Auxiliary is used to refer to such repetitive kinds of activities as human resource management and accounting, while staff refers to such nonrepetitive functions as policy advice and coordination. This distinction has some value, but it can be difficult to make these kinds of distinctions in practice, which explains why the twofold distinction is more common.

When organizations are structured in this typical line-staff manner, the organization chart resembles Figure 3.3. Ideally, the two functions work together closely to further the objectives of the organization. The staff units can provide specialized advice to the line units about handling unusual situations. This means

---

TYPICAL DISCUSSION BETWEEN LINE MANAGER AND STAFF PERSON

MANAGER: We're very busy right now. I need to find a replacement for Mary quickly. We have just the right person who knows how to do the work and is ready to start next week.

HUMAN RESOURCE ADVISOR: You can't hire people that way. It's not consistent with the merit system. If we hired people like that both the opposition parties and the unions would roast us. We'll need to establish a board and interview all the qualified applicants.

MANAGER: How long with that take?

HUMAN RESOURCE ADVISOR: About three months.

MANAGER: But the whole project has to be finished in two months.

Figure 3.3
LINE AND STAFF FUNCTIONS

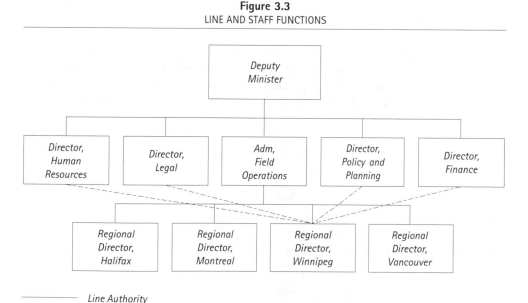

Line Authority
Staff Advisory Relationship

that line officers can concentrate on their standard repetitive tasks and do not have to be trained to cope with every eventuality. Another function frequently provided by staff employees is specialized record keeping. Again, this relieves the line officers of the responsibility for a specialized task and allows them to concentrate on their major function. Thus, one would expect a smooth, complementary relationship between these two functions, and this is the case in many organizations.

When problems do crop up in the line-staff relationship, they usually concern the question: Is the staff function a *service* or a *control* function? If the answer to the question is ambiguous, there can be serious problems. The organization chart in Figure 3.3 illustrates how the presence of the staff function could lead to a violation of the principle of unity of command. The Regional Director in Winnipeg is responsible to the Assistant Deputy Minister, Field Operations, for most things but may also be responsible to the various staff officers for a variety of different specialized activities. In some cases the staff department will render advice that the line department would rather not hear or act upon. Line officials argue that to carry out their duties appropriately, they cannot be constrained by the whims of some group that does not fully understand the operation of the organization. The line manager may point out the amount of profit or units of production that her or his unit has contributed to the organization and ask rhetorically how much the staff units have contributed.

The real problem for senior management arises from the fact that there are usually strong reasons why staff units should be involved in management decisions. The fictional conversation between the line manager and the human resource advisor illustrates this problem. There is no villain in this scenario; both people are right. The manager needs results quickly and is willing to cut administrative corners to get them. The human resource advisor is aware of the legal consequences of cutting those corners.

Organizations usually try to resolve this difficulty by establishing clear lines of authority and procedures to be followed in particular cases. These procedures seldom anticipate every circumstance. Obviously, both line and staff functions are important in an organization. How well they work together is frequently what separates good organizations from those that simply limp along from one crisis to the next.

Gulick and Urwick contributed to the theory of organizational behaviour by synthesizing and disseminating other people's ideas. Nevertheless, these two men made a valuable contribution both by forcing people to think about management in a systematic manner, and in beginning to set out certain principles—many of which are still seen as beneficial guides to action today. However, not everyone treated these scientific principles with reverence.

Herbert Simon and the Proverbs of Administration

Herbert Simon is a prolific writer on many topics of administration. One of his most widely quoted passages deals with the scientific principles of administration:

It is a fatal defect of the current principles of administration that, like proverbs, they occur in pairs. For almost every principle one can find an equally plausible and acceptable contradictory principle. Although the two principles of the pair will lead to exactly opposite organizational recommendations, there is nothing in the theory to indicate which is the proper one to apply.[21]

One example of this kind of problematic pair of proverbs is: "Look before you leap," and "He who hesitates is lost." If the so-called scientific principles of management could be seen to have similar flaws, then their validity would be in doubt.

Simon gives the juxtaposition of these two principles as an example:

Administrative efficiency is supposed to be enhanced by limiting the number of subordinates who report directly to any one administrator to a small number—say six ...

Administrative efficiency is enhanced by keeping at a minimum the number of organizational levels through which a matter must pass before it is acted upon.[22]

Obviously, an organization cannot be both ways. Earlier in this chapter, Figure 3.1 illustrated how a narrow span of control always results in a large number of layers in the organization. A truly scientific principle of management would not allow this dilemma. If one must exercise judgment and discretion in achieving a blend of the two rules, the rules are not very scientific.

Simon saves most of his attack for the idea of organizing by purpose, process, people, or place. He points out that not only is the overall idea contradictory in that one of the four must take precedence, but that the concepts themselves are somewhat fuzzier than Gulick had suggested, so that some of them shade into one another.

Presumably, the rebuttal could be made here that Simon is being too fussy. The principles are simply guides to action; they are considerations to be taken into account before acting, to be used to shape our judgment and guide our discretion. The rebuttal might be valid, but the crucial point is: If judgment and discretion are so important in applying these principles, then can they really be called "scientific"?

Simon's solution recognizes this point. He argues that these ideas should not be discarded because all have real value in certain cases. The trick is to find the proper combination of them to work in different cases. To accomplish this, he argues that good empirical work on the efficiency of existing organizations is needed more than additional theories.

🏛 CENTRALIZATION/DECENTRALIZATION

Gulick and Urwick's discussion of methods of organization opened the way for a serious discussion of decentralization of government services, which is a very important issue in a country as large and heterogeneous as Canada. The size and diversity of most provinces and even some of our larger cities make it an issue for provincial and municipal governments as well.

An important distinction must be made between decentralization and deconcentration. The difference between the two lies in the amount of *real decision-making authority* vested in the outlying unit. *Decentralization* suggests a vesting of *real discretionary authority* in the outlying unit. In some cases this might mean that the unit will also be physically removed from the centre to facilitate an understanding of local conditions, but physical dispersal is not a prerequisite for decentralization. *Deconcentration,* on the other hand, suggests a *physical dispersal* of members of the organization with only *very limited delegation of decision-making authority.*

Obviously, the line between the two is sometimes unclear. Even in deconcentration, there is virtually always some limited amount of discretion vested in field officials just as in decentralization there are always some kinds of decisions that can only be made after consultation with head office. Sometimes authority to deal with matters of an operational nature will be decentralized, while matters of a policy or program nature will be retained within the control of head office.

The large size and diversity of Canada causes Canadians to think of decentralization in terms of the physical dispersal of operating units. This is an appropriate use of the term, but it has a more general meaning as well. Geographic decentralization is decentralization by place, but decentralization can also be based on any of Gulick and Urwick's other classical methods of organization—process, purpose, or people.[23] Even an organization with all of its divisions located in the same building can be decentralized, if real decision-making authority is vested in each of the separate units.

More than two-thirds of federal employees in regular government departments work outside the national capital region (i.e., the Ottawa-Hull area). These employees are located across the vast expanse of Canada in field units that vary greatly in purpose, size, and organization.[24] This deconcentration of the federal government's operations is essential to the successful development and implementation of its policies and programs.

The present balance in each department or agency between the number and level of employees at headquarters and in the field is a culmination of more than a century of political, administrative, economic, and geographical factors. In the earliest days of the Canadian federation, it was necessary to establish outposts for such government services as the post office and customs. The subsequent geographical dispersal of the public service is a government response to the challenge of providing a broad range of services to a population that is spread across a large country. Virtually all government departments now have field units, although the size of these units varies enormously.

FEDERAL EMPLOYEES LOCATED OUTSIDE NATIONAL CAPITAL REGION MARCH 31, 1995	
Correctional services	95.6%
Human resource development	83.3
Fisheries & oceans	87.7
Finance	0.4
Treasury board	0.7
All Departments	68.3

Source: Barbara Wake Carroll and David Siegel, Service in the Field: The World of Front-Line Public Servants[25]

WHAT WOULD YOU DO?

It is a firm rule that applicants for social assistance must have a fixed address. This is a wise and important rule because it prevents abuse of the system.

You are a social worker who is well aware of this rule and the reasons behind it. One Friday afternoon at about 4 o'clock a young mother with a baby arrives in your office. She does not have a fixed address because she just moved into town to escape an abusive husband. She says she just needs a few dollars to buy food for herself and the baby over the weekend. You have a fund to provide money to existing clients with emergency needs, but this is not ordinarily used in cases where the person is not an ongoing client. The usual procedure in a case like this is to make an appointment for next week when a social worker can visit the mother and baby at their home.

What do you do?

Whether this dispersal represents decentralization or deconcentration, the problem remains the same. There must be a balance between accountability to rules specified in head office and responsiveness to regional needs. Officials in the field always feel pulled between the two. On the one hand, the rules and procedures set out by head office must be followed. On the other hand, field workers are sufficiently close to clientele in their everyday work to perceive situations in which an injustice is being done when the general rule is applied without sensitivity. The pressures to bend the rule are sometimes irresistible.

From the standpoint of head office, the problem is to maintain mechanisms to ensure that officials in the field are complying with head office rules and procedures without unnecessarily restricting the freedom of field officials to be responsive to local conditions. After all, it is these officials who are closest to the situation and are most knowledgeable about what should be done. However, they cannot be given carte blanche to do whatever they like without regard to the overall objectives of the department.

Specific approaches to departmental decentralization in Canada will be discussed in Chapter 8, but at this point it is important to consider the general form that decentralization or deconcentration can take. In any organization serving a large geographic area, there must be some form of decentralization. Oversimplifying somewhat, this decentralization can take one of two forms. Figure 3.4 illustrates the two possibilities for an organization carrying out three different functions across the country.[26]

Figure 3.4a illustrates decentralization by place. This style of decentralization is more likely to be true decentralization rather than deconcentration. In this case there is one main office in each region and that office is subdivided based on the three functions. This kind of structure will tend to improve coordination between the three functions within each region. Because of this ease of coordination and because of the orientation toward place, the regional office of this kind of organization is likely to be highly responsive to the needs of its geographic area.

In fact, with this kind of structure there is usually some concern that regional officials will become too sensitive to their geographic area and possibly deviate from the national objectives of their programs. For this reason, there is usually a group of staff advisors in head office who have some sort of functional authority over the people delivering the programs in the regional offices. This is illustrated by the dotted lines in Figure 3.4a. This group is necessary to ensure uniformity of the programs across the country. However, it can create the sort of line–staff problems discussed earlier.

The advantages of this form of organization include good coordination within each region and responsiveness to regional needs. The disadvantages include possible departures from national objectives and a complex form of organization.

Figure 3.4b illustrates decentralization based on purpose, although this same form could also apply to decentralization based on process or people. This form is more likely to result in deconcentration than decentralization. In this case, the primary division is by purpose, with the senior managers responsible for each function remaining in head office. Within each branch there is a subdivision by region, although the geographic areas covered by the regions are not necessarily the same for each branch. This reflects the fact that some programs might be more important in certain areas of the country than in others. Because each branch and each regional office specialize in providing only one function, it is relatively easy to ensure uniformity of administration across the entire country without the awkward organizational structure required in the case of decentralization by place.

The advantages of this style of organization are the simpler form of organization and the uniformity of program administration across the country. Its disadvantages are a lack of coordination of the programs at the regional level, and a weaker responsiveness to regional needs.

The optimum style of organization depends on the nature of the programs to be delivered and the need for regional responsiveness. If good coordination between programs at the regional level and a sensitivity to regional needs is important, then the preferable style is decentralization by place as illustrated in Figure 3.4a. An example of this kind of program would be one aimed at regional economic development. Uniform administration across the country is less important than responsiveness to local conditions.

However, if uniform administration of the program across the country is more important than regional sensitivity, then deconcentration by program as illustrated in Figure 3.4b would be preferable. The word deconcentration is used here because if there is uniformity of administration across the country, then, by definition, there will be little scope for decision making within each region. An example of this kind of organization would be a tax collection organization where fairness and equity demand that the same rules apply to everyone in the country.

🏛 CONCLUSION

Weber and Taylor, and even Gulick and Urwick later, viewed good management as devising an optimal organizational structure to maximize output. They took little account of the needs and desires of the workers themselves. In these

Figure 3.4
TWO TYPES OF ORGANIZATIONAL STRUCTURE

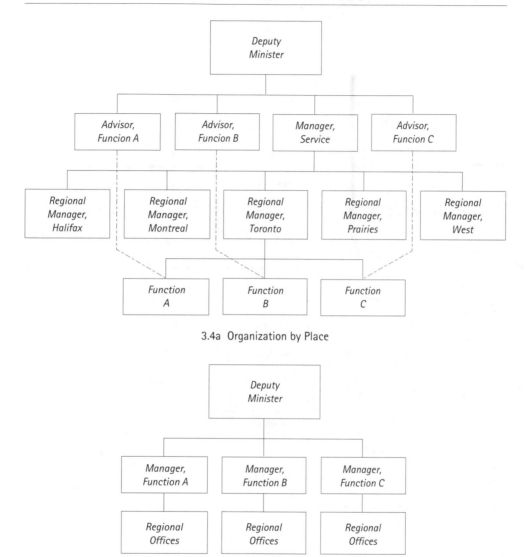

3.4a Organization by Place

3.4b Organization by Purpose

early theories, the worker is just like any other interchangeable machine part to be moved at the whim of management in order to create a better organizational chart. Taylor, in particular, seemed to view the worker as simply an extension of the machine. Gradually a different approach to management emerged—one that took a more human and humane view of the worker. This later approach will be the subject of the next chapter.

NOTES

1. The phrase "ideal-type" has a particular meaning in this context. It is not "ideal" in the sense of "perfect" or "cannot be improved upon"; rather, it suggests that Weber's characterization is a polar or extreme description that probably does not exist exactly in the real world. For a good explanation of this, see Michael M. Harmon and Richard T. Mayer, *Organization Theory for Public Administration* (Boston: Little, Brown, 1986), 71–74, 83.

2. Weber's famous discourse on bureaucracy, originally published in his *Wirtschaft und Gesellschaft*, has been translated and published in many places, but one of the most commonly cited references is *From Max Weber: Essays in Sociology*, eds. and trans. H.H. Gerth and C. Wright Mills (New York: Oxford University Press, 1946), 196–244.

3. Max Weber, *Gesammelte Aufsatze zur Sozial und Wissenschaftslehre*, as quoted in Arthur Mitzman, *The Iron Cage: A Historical Interpretation of Max Weber* (New York: Knopf, 1970), 178. (Emphasis in Mitzman.)

4. Philip Selznick, "An Approach to the Theory of Bureaucracy," *American Sociological Review* 8 (February 1943): 47–54.

5. Warren G. Bennis and Philip E. Slater, *The Temporary Society* (New York: Harper & Row, 1968), ch. 3.

6. Frank B. Gilbreth, Jr. and Ernestine Gilbreth Carey, *Cheaper by the Dozen* (New York: Thomas Y. Crowell, 1948).

7. Fredrick Winslow Taylor, *The Principles of Scientific Management* (New York: W.W. Norten. Norton, 1967), 65.

8. Ibid., 59.

9. Ibid., 67–68.

10. J.E. Hodgetts et al., *The Biography of an Institution* (Montreal: McGill-Queen's University Press, 1972), ch. 4.

11. R. MacGregor Dawson, "The Canadian Civil Service," *Canadian Journal of Economics and Political Science* 2 (August 1936): 293.

12. Robert I. McLaren, *Organizational Dilemmas* (Chichester, U.K.: John Wiley & Sons, 1982), 45–46.

13. Luther Gulick, "Notes on the Theory of Organization," in Luther Gulick and L. Urwick, eds., *Papers on the Science of Administration* (New York: Augustus M. Kelley, 1969), 7–9.

14. Ibid., 11–12.

15. Ibid., 15. (Emphasis in original.)

16. Ibid., 31–32.

17. Ibid., 21–30.

18. Ibid., 13.

19. Lyndall Urwick, "Organization as a Technical Problem," in ibid., 47–88.

20. J.E. Hodgetts, *The Canadian Public Service: A Physiology of Government, 1867–1970* (Toronto: University of Toronto Press, 1973), ch. 9.

21. Herbert Simon, *Administrative Behavior* (New York: The Free Press, 1957), 20.

22. Ibid., 26.

23. McLaren points out that decentralization can occur in several dimensions. *Organizational Dilemmas*, ch. 2.

24. One of the few systematic studies of field offices in government is contained in: Barbara Wake Carroll and David Siegel, *Service in the Field: The World of Front-Line Public Servants* (Montreal: McGill-Queen's University Press, 1998).

25. Ibid., Chapter 2.

26. McLaren's enlightening treatment takes a slightly different approach, but deals with the same issues. *Organizational Dilemmas*, 12–17.

BIBLIOGRAPHY

Bennis, Warren G., and Philip E. Slater. *The Temporary Society.* New York: Harper & Row, 1968.

Carroll, Barbara Wake, and David Siegel. *Service in the Field: The World of Front-Line Public Servants.* Montreal: McGill-Queen's University Press, 1999.

Copley, Frank Barkely. *Frederick W. Taylor: Father of Scientific Management.* 2 vols. New York: Augustus M. Kelley, 1969.

Dawson, R. MacGregor. "The Canadian Civil Service." *Canadian Journal of Economics and Political Science* 2 (August 1936): 288–300.

Gilbreth, Frank B., Jr., and Ernestine Gilbreth Carey. *Cheaper by the Dozen.* New York: Thomas Y. Crowell Company, 1948.

Gulick, Luther, and L. Urwick, eds. *Papers on the Science of Administration.* New York: Augustus M. Kelley, 1969.

Harmon, Michael M., and Richard T. Mayer. *Organization Theory for Public Administration.* Boston: Little, Brown, 1986.

Heffron, Florence. *Organization Theory and Public Organizations: The Political Connection.* Englewood Cliffs, N.J.: Prentice-Hall, 1989.

Hodgetts, J.E. *The Canadian Public Service: A Physiology of Government, 1867–1970.* Toronto: University of Toronto Press, 1973.

Hodgetts, J.E., William McCloskey, Reginald Whitaker, and V. Seymour Wilson. *The Biography of an Institution.* Montreal: McGill-Queen's University Press, 1972.

McLaren, Robert I. *Organizational Dilemmas.* Chichester, U.K.: John Wiley & Sons, 1982.

Merton, Robert K. "Bureaucratic Structure and Personality." *Social Forces* 18 (May 1940): 560–68.

Mitzman, Arthur. *The Iron Cage: A Historical Interpretation of Max Weber.* New York: Knopf, 1970.

Selznick, Philip. "An Approach to the Theory of Bureaucracy." *American Sociological Review* 8 (February 1943): 47–54.

———. *TVA and the Grass Roots.* New York: Harper & Row, 1966.

Simon, Herbert. *Administrative Behavior.* 2nd ed. New York: The Free Press, 1957.

Taylor, Frederick Winslow. *The Principles of Scientific Management.* New York: W.W. Norton, 1967.

Weber, Max. *From Max Weber: Essays in Sociology.* Edited and translated by H.H. Gerth and C. Wright Mills. New York: Oxford University Press, 1946.

4

Public Administration and Organization Theory: The Humanistic Response

Two recent university graduates get together after six months in the workplace. They compare notes on their working environments.

Rachel: I don't get any respect as a person at my job. The day I arrived my boss gave me a manual of standard operating procedures which covers every situation. He told me to read it and do what it says. He didn't say that I should never bother him again, but I'm sure he would be happy if I never had to ask him a question. Mind you, the manual is complete; it seems to cover every situation so that I never have to make any decision on my own. It even tells me how long it should take me to process each file. The problem is that I feel like a cog in a machine.

Michael: That sounds like an awful place to work. My office is just the opposite. We meet twice a month to discuss what we have been doing and where we should go in the future. The boss always attends the meetings, but she invites all of us to participate, and I feel like I have a real impact on where our organization is going. We really have a strong network at work. When an issue comes up between meetings, some of us get together informally to decide how to handle it. We can think back on what we discussed at our last meeting and make a decision which is in line with what we discussed then.

Rachel: Yeah, we have those informal meetings too, but we use them to get back at the boss. Last week, the boss sent us all a memo telling us that we had to increase the number of files we processed. Well, we got together at lunch and said "To hell with that." We know what we can do in a day, and that's all we're going to do. Of course, we all know that we could process a lot more forms if they just changed the procedure a little bit, but nobody has ever asked me about that, so why should I mention it? I'd probably get in trouble for speaking up. Oh well, I better get back to work in the salt mines. Two more days left until the weekend.

Michael: Yeah, I need to get back to work as well. The clients depend on us to get these files processed as quickly as we can and I don't want to let them down.

The two organizations described in this exchange illustrate the differences between the mechanistic view of work described in the previous chapter and the human relations approach to work described in this chapter. This chapter will trace the history of organization theory from the original humanistic, but still highly paternalistic, approach to some present-day theories that emphasize genuine worker participation in organizational decision-making.

🏛 ORGANIZATIONAL HUMANISM

Just as scientific management bore the imprint of production engineers such as Frederick Taylor, *organizational humanism,* or the *human relations school,* bore the imprint of the social psychologists who were its prime movers. Taylor focused on what *should* happen in the factory to maximize production. The organizational humanists focused instead on what *actually* happened on the factory floor. Their findings seem rather unspectacular now, but they totally upset scientific management theorists. They found that in addition to the formal system of authority through which management controlled workers, there was an informal system of worker control that was in some cases more powerful than the formal system. The informal system was characterized by the network of friendships, workplace banter, and informal sanctions that occur in every work setting. The devastating impact that this finding had on the scientific management theory was obvious. Of course, Taylor and his disciples could continue to set their standards, but workers would simply not comply with them if it meant the ostracism that is frequently accorded the "rate-buster." This meant that Taylor's emphasis on scientific principles to set the work pace and on financial incentives to improve productivity was somewhat misplaced. While these factors had some value, it was becoming clear that another route to increased productivity lay with the informal system.

Mary Parker Follett

One of the first people to understand the importance of the informal system was not a conventional researcher but a very perceptive student of human nature. Mary Parker Follett (1868–1933) did not study organizations systematically in the ordinary sense, but she did use every opportunity to discuss organizational questions with everyone from senior executives to factory workers. From these discussions, she developed a number of important ideas.

Her basic philosophy stemmed from the fact that she rejected the conventional use of raw power in organizations. She felt that its use was either futile or, in some cases, totally counterproductive. Instead, she focused on two related concepts—circular response and integration.

She rejected the biological concept of unidirectional stimulus-response relationships as inapplicable in the human setting. Instead, she emphasized shared interaction.[1] *Circular response* means no one unilaterally acts on someone else; rather, people interact with one another in ways that influence both parties. It was this view that caused her to reject the idea of power as a one-way street.

Integration referred to the need to combine diverse elements into a useful whole. In some ways, this could be seen as simply a restatement of the old idea of division of labour, but Follett realized that integration was a dynamic concept and not simply the static arrangement of slots on an organizational chart. She understood that conflict would inevitably develop in any organization because of the existence of circular response and the informal organization.

It was, however, the particular genius of Follett's contribution that she recognized and held fast to the notion that the process of change that generates conflict also provides the opportunity for the further changes necessary to resolve that conflict. Each solution contains the seeds of new differences, but these differences also contain the seeds of new solutions. What they need is freedom to grow within a milieu of intelligent and sympathetic cultivation.[2]

This latter point was a very important one for Follett. She frequently emphasized the importance of executives *exercising leadership* rather than *wielding power*. She felt that the way to motivate employees was through a rational appeal to a person's higher instincts rather than a reliance on fear or threats.

Follett was an important influence because she lectured widely and knew many of the senior business people of her time, but it is questionable whether her rather unscientific views had any influence on some of the more scientific researchers of her time. For this reason, her role in the development of the human relations school is sometimes overlooked.

Roethlisberger and Dickson and the Hawthorne Experiments

The beginnings of the human relations school are usually traced to an experiment conducted with workers at the Hawthorne Works (near Chicago) of Western Electric in 1924. The idea was to test the impact of different levels of lighting on employee productivity. The experiments were organized and conducted by an industrial psychologist from Harvard, F.J. Roethlisberger, and a Western Electric management employee, William J. Dickson. They were later joined by another Harvard professor, Elton Mayo.[3]

The experimenters assumed that improving physical working conditions by increasing levels of lighting would increase productivity. The research was poorly designed and the results inconclusive. One problem the researchers encountered was that production tended to move erratically up or down without much regard to changes in the level of lighting. The experimenters had to discard their original hypothesis because the ambiguity of the results indicated that the physical conditions surrounding work did not have the paramount influence assumed.

The Hawthorne experiment was followed by a series of experiments that tested many other changes in physical conditions in the workplace, to see which would produce changes in the level of output. Again, the results were ambiguous. This caused experimenters to think about a characteristic of the experiments that they had not considered previously. In every case, the tests were conducted using a group of people who were selected from the workroom, moved to a special place, and singled out for significant amounts of attention from researchers. This led experimenters to focus on the *Hawthorne* or *sympathetic observer effect*—the idea that workers singled out for special attention will experience an increase in morale, which will lead to greater productivity.

This finding has been criticized widely over the years.[4] Some critics have pointed to the poor design of the research, while others have argued that the research findings do not support the conclusions usually drawn from them. However, this did not seem to matter at the time. The human relations school grew and thrived over these years in both academic and business circles.

Chester Barnard and the Importance of Cooperation

Chester Barnard (1886–1961) was a career business executive who rose to become President of the New Jersey Bell Telephone Company. In 1938, after his retirement, he wrote his landmark work *The Functions of the Executive*. His crucial idea was that an organization is a cooperative system held together by a good communication system and by the continuing desire of individual members to see the organization thrive.[5]

Members of the organization make *contributions* to it, but only when they receive adequate *inducements* to encourage them to continue to do so. It is important to balance contributions and inducements. If inducements exceed contributions, business failure will result because the organization is too free with its resources. However, if inducements are inadequate, then workers will cease making contributions and business failure will result. The essence of good management is maintaining a balance between these two. The inducements offered to workers could be in the form of monetary rewards, but Barnard felt that other forms of inducement such as loyalty, good working conditions, and pride in both the work and the organization were probably more effective.

Barnard tried to be sensitive to the needs of workers, but his basic attitude to workers was somewhat patronizing. The title of his book, *The Functions of the Executive*, probably says it all. He felt that workers were rather docile, uninspired creatures who depended on leadership to accomplish anything. It was the responsibility of the executive to establish good communication systems that would, in turn, instil the appropriate company spirit in employees.

He recognized that there was an informal organization that could thwart the desires of management, but he argued that it was the responsibility of management to use the idea of cooperation to harness that informal system for the benefit of the organization. This idea is still found in the argument that job interviews are an important part of the hiring process, not particularly because they disclose specific job skills, but because they can indicate whether the prospective employee's personality fits with the organization's culture.[6]

Abraham Maslow's Hierarchy of Needs

Scientific management focused on the idea of monetary rewards as an incentive for good work performance. Maslow argued that this was too simplistic. He said that people are motivated by a hierarchy of five categories of needs ranging from the physiological to self-actualization. He believed that a person will first be motivated by a desire to satisfy the most basic physiological needs, but as these are satisfied, the person will strive to meet the next level of needs, and so on up the hierarchy. As an employee attains each succeeding level in the hierarchy, he or she will no longer be motivated by rewards directed at the more basic needs. The five levels in the *hierarchy of needs* are:

1. *Physiological*—food, shelter, clothing, sex, and sleep;

2. *Safety*—security, stability, freedom from fear;

3. *Belongingness and Love*—friendship, love, membership in some community;

4. *Esteem*—achievement, competence, independence, prestige, status; and

5. *Self-actualization*—self-fulfillment, attaining ultimate goals in life.[7]

Maslow's contention was that there is no "one best way" to motivate employees. Instead, management must be sensitive to the fact that workers have a variety of needs beyond the simple need for money. Thinking about employee needs such as self-esteem and self-actualization posed serious problems for managers who were accustomed to thinking in simple piecework terms.

A discussion of Maslow's complex theory of motivation appears in almost every management textbook, and it is the basis for most participative management philosophy. It also seems to strike a more responsive note than the simpler, one-dimensional approach of the scientific management school. It agrees with the usual observation that different people are motivated by different factors, and even the same person is motivated by different factors at different times.

In spite of the widespread repetition of Maslow's ideas, contemporary scholars have taken issue with it, as in this statement made by Florence Heffron:

> Since Maslow's theory appears in almost every textbook on business and public administration, frequently as uncontested truth, it deserves close scrutiny, and regrettably, much about the theory does not withstand this scrutiny. The evidence on which the theory was based was at best flimsy, primarily anecdotes drawn from the treatment of neurotic and psychotic individuals. Testing the theory has proven difficult, if not impossible.[8]

Heffron goes on to present a detailed critique suggesting that it is very difficult to substantiate Maslow's idea that there is a precise ordering of needs for all people. Even Maslow himself had some reservations about these ideas,[9] but they have been repeated so often that they have attained a life of their own.

Douglas McGregor's Theory X and Theory Y

In spite of Maslow's caveats, McGregor built on his ideas and related them to the attitudes of individual managers. He noted that some managers simply do not trust or respect their employees. He felt that this reflected a group of assumptions about human nature, which he called Theory X. Table 4.1 compares Theory X assumptions about workers with the more optimistic Theory Y, which McGregor advocated.[10]

McGregor's basic message was that employees react differently depending on how they are treated. If managers convey the impression that they believe their employees are Theory X types of workers, then the workers will likely meet those expectations. Conversely, managers who treat employees in a Theory Y manner will likely be more successful.

There are a number of similarities between Maslow's and McGregor's thinking. The most obvious is that they both have a very positive view of human nature. They argue that workers can be positively motivated without recourse to threats, but that this requires a certain amount of understanding and sensitivity on the part of managers.

Another major similarity they share is that both seem intuitively correct, but are difficult to subject to empirical testing. In fact, neither has been widely tested, although they are widely discussed in the management literature.

> **SUMMARY OF THE PRINCIPLES OF ORGANIZATIONAL HUMANISM**
>
> Respect for workers as complex human beings with diverse sets of needs.
>
> Distrust of simple, one-dimensional theories of motivation.
>
> Recognition that the informal organization can be as instrumental as the formal one in setting work rules.

Criticisms of Organizational Humanism

There have been many criticisms of the philosophy of the human relations school. The most significant are based on the idea that the presumed commu-

Table 4.1
A COMPARISON OF THEORY X AND THEORY

Theory X	Theory Y
It is a basic attribute of human nature to dislike work. All rational people will do as little work as possible.	Work is as natural as rest and recreation. All of these activities can be great sources of satisfaction, under the proper conditions.
Because of this dislike of work, average workers must be cajoled or threatened in order to persuade them to work.	Because work is a natural activity, workers do not need external threats. They will willingly perform work if they are committed to it. This commitment can be obtained by offering proper rewards which can be either monetary or intangible items such as ego gratification or self-actualization.
Most people are irresponsible and have little ambition. They must continuously be told what to do and supervised closely.	Most workers have a high degree of responsibility and creativity and, under the proper conditions, will enjoy taking on responsibility and will work well without direct controls. In fact, most workers have much greater potential than contemporary managers believe. If workers are just given more scope for action, they will respond positively.

nity of interest between workers and management does not exist and, therefore, the entire human relations concept is simply a method to manipulate employees to behave in the interests of management.

It is obviously in management's interest to extract as much work as possible from employees. This is the profit motive. However, it is in the employees' interest to restrict their output to what they can do in physical comfort. Employees are also aware that the amount of work to be done is usually finite and that their reward for working hard might be a layoff slip when the work is completed. When one views the workplace in this way, the cooperation treasured by the organizational humanists is somewhat elusive.

Critics charge that this is precisely the point where the theories developed by the organizational humanists become important. How does management convince workers to behave in the best interests of management rather than in their own best interests? The human relations response is to establish a feeling of caring and unity in the workplace that can then be used to manipulate employees. Critics like to point to one aspect of the work done at Hawthorne that involved hiring 300 employees to wander the factory floor and listen to complaints of other employees. Management never did anything about the complaints and never intended to do anything; the sole purpose of this action was to create the impression that management actually cared about workers.[11]

> In the end, therefore, the human relations approach to management proves to be simply another technique for managerial control. Although the human relations approach provides a recognition of the human factors in organizational life, it ultimately treats these as just another set of inducements to be manipulated in the pursuit of managerial control. Where conflicts arise between the individual and the organization, managers are admonished to resort to their hierarchical authority. Ultimately, this approach remains simplistic and unfulfilling and, in any case, hardly leads toward a true alternative to the rational model of administration. Though appearing humanistic, the human relations approach may simply be more subtle.[12]

The human relations approach was also criticized from the opposite perspective by production-conscious managers. They were concerned that this school was *too* employee-centred. Their criticism was that in its revulsion from scientific management, it tipped the balance too far in the other direction. Some derisively referred to human relations as "country club" management, meaning that the ideal workplace ought to resemble a country club. Others suggested that for human relations, the "one best way" was employee satisfaction rather than concern for production.

In the face of this criticism from both sides, organizational humanism had to evolve. The next step was a cluster of ideas that attempted to meet both kinds of criticisms. These varying concepts can be loosely grouped under the heading of participatory management.

🏛 PARTICIPATORY MANAGEMENT

Gradually it became accepted that there was an innate tension and conflict in the workplace. This tension could revolve around general issues such as rates of pay and speed of the production processes, or specific issues such as the attitude of a particular supervisor or the quality of food served in the lunchroom. Organizational humanism tried to cover over this tension by "bribing" employees to accept management views. The participatory theories held that the tension could be controlled and directed, but probably not totally eliminated, by allowing workers a *real decision-making role in the workplace.*

There are many approaches to *participatory management.* Peter Drucker is one of the early proponents of participatory management. His view of organizations stood Weber's views of bureaucracy on their head.[13] Drucker argued that the very characteristics that Weber saw as such powerful engines of *efficiency*—bureaucracy, hierarchical structures, and specialization—were, in fact, powerful forces for *misdirection.* Drucker felt that, in large organizations, managers and employees became too involved in their own specialty and had a tendency to emphasize this at the expense of the overall good of the organization. For example, if the purchasing department emphasizes buying at low prices rather than the high quality of the product or security of supply, then the production department can suffer precisely because the purchasing department is doing its job well—at least, in the view of people in that department. Thus, it frequently happens that inefficiency and misdirection occur *because* of hierarchy and specialization of labour. The problem is the inability to focus on the overall organizational goal; the solution is a more participatory form of management that would allow managers to have a broader view of the organization and a clearer understanding of its overall goals. Two recent and important approaches to participatory management are discussed here—organization development and total quality management.

Organization Development

Organization development is based on the idea that all organizations tend to become rigid or "frozen." While the organization remains rigid, the environment around the organization changes, and this has serious consequences. Usually, conditions gradually deteriorate until a serious crisis occurs, which causes either radical restructuring or even the collapse of the organization. The purpose of OD is to locate the barriers to change and to show the organization how to engage in planned, goal-directed change, not directionless evolution or radical revolution.

Organization development recognizes that all organizations have a history that creates an organizational culture.[14] In some cases this can be a good thing, but in many it is not. This history, or culture, develops as a result of the organization's past successes and failures. For example, when someone responds to a new proposal by saying: "We can't do that because we tried something like it ten years ago and it didn't work," history is at work. Of course, the fact that something similar was unsuccessful ten years earlier might or might not be relevant now, but in many cases this kind of argument will carry the day. When the culture or history of an organization has this kind of negative influence, it is referred to as "drag."

Practitioners of OD warn that the patterns and procedures that create drag are merely symptoms of a more serious underlying problem in the organization's culture. It is pointless to change these patterns and procedures—merely the manifestations of the basic problems—without also changing the underlying culture. Such changes would meet strong resistance, and inappropriate new patterns could possibly be imposed on an unfriendly environment.

There are many practitioners of OD, and each has a slightly different approach.[15] However, they all share a belief in a general three-phase approach—"unfreezing, moving, and freezing of group standards."[16] The unfreezing stage involves identifying current dysfunctional behaviour and helping the organization to "unlearn" that behaviour. In the second phase, the improvements needed are identified and implemented. The third stage involves refreezing the organization with its new behaviour in place so that the organization does not unconsciously revert to the old behaviour.

SOME VISIBLE SYMBOLS OF ORGANIZATIONAL CULTURE

- *Shared attitude toward client service,* e.g., the customer is always right

- *Common management style,* e.g., open door policy

- *Shared attitudes to new ideas,* e.g., it's OK to take risks to develop new ideas

- *Uniform style of dress,* e.g., formal, conservative attire

- *Shared extracurricular activities,* e.g., everybody goes to the fitness club at lunch

- *Common attitudes outside the workplace,* e.g., volunteering for local charities

---

There are many different definitions of OD.[17] The definition below captures the main elements of most of these. A better understanding of OD can be obtained by elaborating on each aspect of the definition.

Organization development is a process that uses a multi-disciplinary, behavioural science–based approach to examine the entire organizational unit as a system and to institute planned change in those aspects of the unit that are impediments to its health and efficiency. The exercise usually uses an outside change agent employing action-research techniques and involves all members of the organizational unit.

OD is a *multidisciplinary approach* to organizational change "in which theories, concepts, and practices from sociology, psychology, social psychology, education, economics, psychiatry, and management are brought to bear on real organizational problems."[18] This separates it from earlier approaches to organizational change that were based on only one discipline, frequently engineering or, later, psychology.

OD deals with the *entire organizational unit*, which is defined as all segments of the organization that interact closely on a regular basis. This could be the total organization or it could be a group of work units smaller than the full organization. The decision about the appropriate units to be covered is somewhat subjective, but it is important to understand that OD cannot be effective if it is confined to only one small unit.

OD views the entire *organization as a system*—a set of interacting parts. Any change in one aspect of the system will have repercussions for the entire system. Therefore, attempts to remedy only one aspect of a systemic problem will be futile, or even counterproductive.

One of the main tasks of OD is to *identify the impediments to the development of an efficient and healthy organization*—an organization that is concerned with both efficiency in production and ensuring that individuals in the organization have the maximum opportunity to realize their full potential.[19]

After the organization's problems are identified, the participants are then required to *plan the changes necessary to make the organization more efficient*. The changes specified could deal with any aspect of the organization—improved teamwork, the physical layout of the operation, the attitudes of workers or managers, the organizational structure, and so forth. Unlike earlier approaches, OD does not focus solely on one factor in the workplace and assume that all problems can be corrected by altering that one factor.

It is usually desirable to employ an *outside change agent* for three reasons. First, the size and complexity of an exercise of this sort normally require someone who is very knowledgeable about a range of behavioural science techniques. Second, the OD intervener might be the only person who can see, and is really concerned about, the whole organizational system. Members of the organization tend to be more concerned about their part of the organization than the organization as a whole.[20] Third, since OD can potentially involve major realignments of the organization's power structure, it is better that the project leader have no vested interest in the changes recommended.

The general approach of *action research* is to gather data about a client group, assist the client group in analyzing the data, and establish some action plan based on the findings of the data. Thus, action research combines research and action. It involves research not just to shed light on some academic hypothesis, but research undertaken for the purpose of stimulating action.

It is important that the exercise involve all employees in the unit because

> wider participation in goal setting leads to a greater utilization of an organization's resources, human and technical, and results in significantly better plans. In addition, the plans that have been the contribution of many people at all levels of the organization probably have more chance of being realistic and attainable and also have some built-in support for carrying them out.[21]

OD has been used fairly widely to effect organizational change. However, like many innovations which at first held great promise, some concerns have begun to develop about the benefits of OD.

Total Quality Management (TQM)

Total quality management was the next approach to participatory management. It was popularized in North America in the 1980s and early 1990s as a response to the Japanese approach to management, which will be discussed in more detail in the next chapter. Its leading proponent was the management guru who has been identified as one of the major architects of the Japanese breakthrough in productivity—W. Edwards Deming.[22]

Deming's work began before the Second World War in the United States with the development of statistical process control (SPC) to improve production quality. This involved using various statistical techniques to identify and correct deviations from the ideal quality production standard. After the war, he became disillusioned with the way American companies were using his philosophy because they tended to view the statistical techniques as an end in themselves and did not incorporate thinking about quality into their overall management and organizational culture. When he was given the opportunity to teach his technique to Japanese business leaders after the war he did not repeat this mistake. He emphasized to them that they must make quality the overall focus of their organizational culture.[23] The Japanese learned this lesson very well.

The basic difference in the American and Japanese approaches to quality can be illustrated by an example from the auto industry. The somewhat exaggerated stereotype suggests that the American auto industry focused on production rather than quality. This meant producing the maximum number of cars and then employing a separate quality control group to detect and repair problems after the cars were built. The Japanese approach was to place less emphasis on the raw speed of construction, but to make each employee responsible for quality control of her or his aspect of the work. Thus, the cars took longer and cost more to build in the first place, but there was greater assurance that the job was done properly the first time and less expense involved in the later correction of errors.[24] The guiding principle of TQM is to "get it right the first time."[25]

The basic tenet of TQM is the elimination of quality control as a separate function, and instead making each employee responsible for quality and giving each a role in designing production processes to ensure maximum quality.[26]

TQM has been defined as

> a broad-scale approach to changing an organization's entire culture to focus on establishing and maintaining high standards of quality, especially with respect to meeting "customer" expectations. The key of TQM is to serve the "customer," whether the "customer" is internal to the organization or someone outside. (Many government agencies serve citizens directly, but some serve other government agencies.)[27]

The important point of this definition is that TQM involves the creation of an entire organizational culture based on concern for both quality and production.

Contrary to conventional wisdom in the United States, quality and productivity were not to be traded off against each other. Rather, productivity was a by-product of quality and of doing the job right the first time ...[28]

As with most new management processes, there are a number of different ways in which this technique can be implemented.[29] One method of establishing TQM in the public sector focuses on three basic components:

1. Working with suppliers to ensure that the supplies utilized in the work processes are designed for your use.

2. Continuous employee analysis of work processes to improve their functioning and reduce process variation.

3. Close communication with customers to identify and understand what they want and how they define quality.[30]

An important aspect of TQM is that it focuses on how the organization relates to its environment. It recognizes that quality is largely a function of how well the organization works with its environment, i.e., with both suppliers and customers.

Working with Suppliers.   Quality organizations must be certain that the raw materials they purchase are of an appropriate quality and are produced in the most easily useable form. Thus, thinking about quality works its way through the entire production process. Many organizations, including Caterpillar Inc., have decided that they will only buy from suppliers who are also committed to quality management.[31] This maximizes the likelihood that the raw material that the production process uses will be of the proper quality.

Suppliers could refer to either external or internal suppliers. TQM sees the production process within an organization as a series of supplier-customer relationships.[32] Thus, work unit A becomes a supplier to work unit B. If workers in unit B are not satisfied with the product they are being supplied, they are encouraged to work with staff in unit A to improve the product. In this way, quality is built into the end product at every stage of the production process.

Continuous Staff Analysis of Work Processes.   This is the key part of the process. It ensures that all employees are actively involved in TQM. The previous chapter discussed Frederick Taylor's idea of time-and-motion studies. This approach involved hiring outside experts to come into the factory to tell workers how to do their work better.

TQM holds that the company already employs the best possible production experts it could have—the employees who are currently doing the work. The TQM approach is to ask workers to analyze their own work processes and find places for improvement. This is superior to Taylor's approach on several counts. First, workers know more about what they are doing and how to improve it than any outsider ever could. Second, TQM requires people from different parts of the organization to work together in teams to solve problems.[33] This increases group cohesion and improves communication throughout the organization. Third, workers are more likely to accept changes that they have initiated than those imposed from outside. Fourth, even if the actual changes are relatively minor, the worker involvement should create the "Hawthorne effect," i.e., the perception that management really cares about what workers think.

The most important aspect of this part of TQM is that it should instill an open and inquiring attitude on the part of all employees. Employees should not accept a weak point in the production process because "it's always been done this way." Instead, they should be encouraged to look at every aspect of their work and say: "Can this be done better? What must change for improvement to occur?" This requires senior management to be open and responsive to employee suggestions.

Working with Customers.   The third step is to work with customers to ensure that the organization really knows what customers want and that it is in fact delivering the desired product at the appropriate quality. This requires listening closely to customers and encouraging them to provide feedback.

> Successful organizations create an improvement system whereby their resources are aligned under the priorities of customers. The customers' concerns drive the improvement plans of the organization and of the separate groups within the organization.[34]

This customer feedback can be provided through a number of mechanisms. The British Columbia Parks Department has a very extensive evaluation system that uses customer-comment cards, annual surveys of visitors, and household surveys. It even consults customers in the planning of future park developments.[35]

TQM focuses on production processes, so it was first embraced by factory-type operations, but it can be applied very well in service organizations, including governments.[36] Governments do not ordinarily operate factories, but there are many other production processes involved in government operations, e.g., delivering health care, processing income tax returns, responding to complaints of criminal activity.

It is too early to pass definitive judgment about how successful TQM will be. It could be an important innovation, or just a passing fad. Some organizations have not obtained all the gains they had expected from TQM because it was not implemented properly. Poor implementation seems to be a major problem with TQM.[37] Some organizations have also seen TQM as a "quick fix" that they can attach to their existing organization with few changes. It is not surprising that an innovation such as TQM, which requires major changes in management culture, does not work well in this situation. In spite of these problems, many people have found TQM and the philosophy behind it to be of real value in reorienting their organizations.

It seems that all of these innovations leave some sort of mark on organizations, even when they are not completely successful. TQM emphasizes that product quality and customer satisfaction are paramount, and that each and every employee has a role in maintaining these values. This should encourage greater participation on the part of workers.

Criticisms of the Participative Approach

One of the criticisms frequently levelled at the participative approaches is that they require a huge commitment of resources on the part of the organization, and that they are so disruptive that they can lead to rather lengthy periods of turmoil. The basic principle of the approach is that virtually all employees of the organization must become involved and, in some cases, for fairly lengthy periods. This level of participation imposes a heavy internal cost on the organization, in addition to the usual fees charged by the outside consultants.

Moreover, there is usually a psychological cost to the organization from undergoing this kind of radical surgery. Even though the actual organizational changes themselves can be planned in an incremental and minimally disruptive manner, the rumour mill that always works full time in these situations can wreak havoc on morale.

The obvious response to this criticism is that the end result is worth the short-term trauma, and, in many cases, this has proven correct. However, given the cost and turmoil engendered in the short run, management's frequent reluctance to become fully involved in a participative management exercise is understandable.

Many of the criticisms of the concept of participative management echo those directed against the organizational humanists. There seems to be a lingering concern that the process is not really and truly participative but is guided—not to say manipulated—by management. "Frederick Taylor was satisfied if he could control the physical movements of the workers; OD wants their hearts, souls, and minds."[38]

While organizational humanism and participative management stress concern for the whole person, they both focus on "the person as a worker," with less concern for the nonwork-related aspects of the person's life. For example, it is not difficult to determine how they would view an employee who refused to work more than forty hours a week, even though it meant passing up a promotion, because the person wanted to spend more time with her or his family, or to take part in other activities.

As mentioned above, this stands more as a criticism of the manner in which the process has been applied in certain cases than a basic criticism of the process itself. However, it does raise a difficult conundrum. In a true hierarchical setting, those at the pinnacle of the hierarchy have authority over those at lower levels. Some things have not changed since Weber. Given this fact, is real participation possible?

Participative Management in the Public Sector

There is a particular set of problems with the use of participative management in the public sector. The most serious concern is whether a bottom-up participative approach to decision making is consistent with the principle of ministerial responsibility for the activities of her or his department.

A second concern arises when it is suggested that "participation" should extend beyond employees and allow clients who are affected by the agency to be involved in the decision-making process. Few would argue with the right of clients to have a voice in the consultation process. However, this must be limited because clients of a particular service constitute a special interest group whose perspective on an issue might be at odds with the broader public interest.

In practice, the concern for top-down accountability has won out over bottom-up participation. At the risk of generalizing, it seems that few government agencies give more than lip service to participatory management.

However, this does not preclude certain kinds of OD or TQM approaches that are geared more to operation of the agency than basic public policy decision making. Robert T. Golembiewski, a recognized expert on OD in the public sector, has argued that there are particular problems with the use of OD in the public sector, and that these problems result in a "lower batting average" in the success of OD in the public sector. After an extensive review of the literature on OD attempts, he arrives at the conclusion that "the 'lower batting average' is still pretty high."[39] The next section reviews the Canadian experience with participative management.

🏛 THE CANADIAN EXPERIENCE—FROM TAYLOR TO TQM TO NEW PUBLIC MANAGEMENT

Organizational Humanism

In the previous chapter, the status of scientific management in the federal government was considered. In this chapter, many other styles of management have been discussed, but there has been no comment on their impact on Canadian governments. The reason is quite simple—they seem to have had little impact. V.S. Wilson describes the impact that the organizational humanists had in the United States, and then addresses the Canadian situation in this manner:

> In Canada no developments of this sort surfaced in the public sector. The federal government, for example, continued in its well-established role as omnipotent employer. Institutions of employer-employee relationships created during this time ... had as their central focus "the problems of the government as employer and not those of the employees."[40]

It might be unfair to say that absolutely nothing of the organizational humanist school filtered into the Canadian public sector. Since the human relations school is, in large part, a prescription for changes in the actions of individual managers, it is possible that certain managers followed the advice of the organizational humanists without any system-wide documentation of the practice. But Wilson is surely correct in his overall assessment of the situation. Throughout the time of the organizational humanists, Canadian governments continued to exhibit rigid hierarchies, inflexible job classification structures, and the other trappings of scientific management.

Total Quality Management

When the participatory style of management came into full flower, it found easier acceptance. Many government organizations in Canada have espoused the TQM concept or similar participatory approaches under a variety of different names, such as service quality management.[41] TQM thinking underlies much of the federal government's PS2000 program and similar initiatives in several provinces. British Columbia has probably made the strongest effort in this regard.[42] TQM could become even more important as government organizations face resource restraint. It should enable government organizations to find ways of working smarter and ensuring that quality of service to clients does not drop even in times of restraint.

These various reforms have probably produced a higher quality of management, but they have also created problems. While new innovations have been implemented, few of the trappings of the older systems have been discarded. The entire arrangement is reminiscent of an old European building with a basic structure from one era and many additions, each bearing the architectural style of the era in which it was added. There is nothing wrong with each separate part, but the total building creates a rather unusual overall impression. For example, total quality management and team-building exercises that emphasize flexibility, empowerment, and cooperation have been combined with lengthy, complex job descriptions that emphasize rigidity and differentiation of duties. However, the next management innovation portends to bring a much more fundamental change.

New Public Management (NPM)

New Public Management is so new to Canada and amorphous that its exact parameters are not well established at this point, but it encompasses a variety of new ideas.[43] Its proponents view it as a paradigm shift or a complete change in culture rather than just the introduction of a few new techniques.

It arose from a critique of traditional public administration, seeing it as too inflexible and focused on control and not oriented enough toward satisfying the needs of citizens. Not surprisingly, it borrows heavily from private sector concepts of customer service, but it is much more than just a service improvement program. It requires a rethinking of the role of the state and of public servants. It suggests that public servants have been too heavily involved in policy making (which is the rightful preserve of the politician) and not concerned enough about service delivery. This has caused public servants to see themselves as policy advisors rather than as managers. New Public Management emphasizes the management side of the public servant's role.

Table 4.2 compares NPM to the traditional view of public administration. The tone of the difference can be seen in the contrast between NPM words like entrepreneurship, flexibility, and risk taking and traditional words like bureaucratic and process accountability.

Many governments have embraced the concepts of NPM as a way of breathing fresh air into a stale government bureaucracy. However, not everyone sees NPM in such a positive light. Donald Savoie argues that the private sector principles embedded in NPM do not travel well to the public sector.[44] He concedes that improvements could be made in government operations, but suggests that the major flaws are with representative institutions like Parliament and not with public servants. He is concerned that new values like entrepreneurship and flexibility will drive out important traditional values such as accountability and ministerial responsibility. Public servants should be concerned about improving the quality of government services, but they are not entrepreneurs. They are stewards of other people's money with an obligation to be accountable to elected officials about how they conduct their duties.

There is little question that "the New Public Management is here to stay," as Sandford Borins said in his rejoinder to Savoie.[45] The enthusiasm that it has generated for public servants about being more innovative has had a definite impact on the public service. However, Savoie's caveats must be heeded. Public servants certainly should be more innovative and concerned about service delivery, but they must do this in a framework that does not overlook the importance of maintaining accountability to elected officials.

While such practical changes as OD, TQM, and NPM were being imported into the Canadian scene, progress continued in the theoretical

Table 4.2
COMPARISON OF NEW PUBLIC MANAGEMENT AND TRADITIONAL PUBLIC ADMINISTRATION

Components	New Public Management	Traditional Public Administration
Focus	clients	citizens and communities
Principal Means	management	policy making
Characteristics of Public Servants	entrepreneur (acting)	analyst (thinking)
Values	entrepreneurship, freedom for managers, flexibility, creativity, enthusiasm, risk taking	ministerial responsibility, prudence, stability, ethics, probity, fairness, transparency
Vocabulary	service to clients, quality, skills, managerialism, empowerment, privatization	public interest, democracy, social equity, due process
Culture	private sector, innovation, business management, accountability by results, politics administration dichotomy	bureaucratic (hierarchicial), functionalism, stability, process accountability, politics-administration continuum
Structures	civil service as organizational units, simple and frugal government, introduction to quasi-market mechanism, decentralization	civil service as an institution, large departments, government-wide systems, central authority resource allocation

Source: Mohamed Charih and Lucie Rouillard, "The New Public Management," in Mohamed Charih and Arthur Daniels, eds., New Public Management and Public Administration in Canada (The Institute of Public Administration of Canada, 1997), p. 31.

study of organizations. Many of these new approaches were significant improvements in organizational theory but were still basically embellishments of ideas coming from the participatory approach.

🏛 KATZ AND KAHN'S OPEN SYSTEMS APPROACH

One such theory is *open systems theory*.[46] Some social psychologists such as Robert Merton, Talcott Parsons, Daniel Katz, and Robert L. Kahn became disenchanted with the earlier organizational theories because they placed too much emphasis on activities of individuals within organizations and on the activities of the organization as a monolithic body, without consideration of the environment within which the organization operated. They criticized this kind of thinking as the "closed system" approach because, in their eyes, it considered the organization only as a closed system and not as a part of its environment:

> The closed system metaphor depicts a self-contained entity in which the functioning of the component parts and their interrelations are the primary objects of inquiry. Any simple machine operating as a self-contained mechanism, such as a lawn mower or an automobile, is a prototypical closed system. Similarly, bureaucracy is often seen as an organizational equivalent of a closed system. Its relationship to its environment is regulated and stabilized in such a way that one can, analytically, ignore that environment when describing, dissecting, and manipulating the system. This is what Max Weber does, for instance, when describing the characteristics of ideal-typical bureaucracy. In the same way, Frederick Taylor's discussion of the functions of the planning department essentially assumes that the firm's environment is stable, calculable, and likely to have little impact, in the sense of changing the work of the department.[47]

Followers of the open systems approach were influenced by biological models that dealt with both the internal organization of organisms and how they interacted with their environment. Natural scientists did this by thinking in terms of inputs-throughputs-outputs-feedback. To continue to exist, any organism must receive certain inputs from its environment. It then converts these to outputs that, through feedback, help it to attain more inputs. In the case of simple, one-cell organisms, this means capturing some nourishment and converting it to energy, which it uses to move about to capture more nourishment. Human beings operate on the same principle, only with a more complex interaction system. They need nourishment, shelter, and psychic encouragement, which they convert to work effort that can be sold for cash or traded to satisfy such needs as food, shelter, and psychic encouragement.

The open systems theorists felt that organizations could be approached in the same manner. Organizations need inputs in the form of labour power, raw materials, and so forth. These are then converted to finished products, which are sold for cash so that more inputs can be purchased. Not-for-profit organizations do not follow exactly the same cycle in that their products are usually not sold, but they still must produce an acceptable level of output so that some organization, such as a government, will provide inputs to them.

Katz and Kahn argued that successful organizations arrange the input-throughput-output process so as to reverse the normal entropy to which living organisms are subject. Entropy is the process through which organisms are subject to deterioration. In complex physical systems, as the system becomes larger, the individual parts of the system become more disorganized until they are no longer able to sustain the organization as a whole. At this point, the system perishes.

A successful organization overcomes this process by developing *negative entropy*, which is the process of importing and storing more energy than it expends. This allows the organization to expand and to survive in difficult times by drawing on the stored reserve.[48] This stored reserve could take several forms. An obvious one is cash and other hard assets, but some other forms of stored energy could be the trust and goodwill of important people or a high-quality management team.

The crucial lesson for managers in open systems theory is that all organizations are a part of their environments. Earlier thinkers such as Frederick Taylor and, to a lesser extent, the organizational humanists attempted to see the organization as a closed system unaffected by its environment. The open system concept reminds managers that, in addition to managing the internal aspects of their organization, they must also be sensitive to the rapidly changing environment that affects such things as the acceptance of their product, their relationship with their clientele, and the attitudes of their employees.

The next theory we discuss continues the open system approach and focuses on how an organization must fit in with its environment.

🏛 CONTINGENCY THEORY

Contingency theory was first developed in a systematic fashion in the 1960s.[49] Its basic premise is "There is no one best way to organize," but "Any way of organizing is not equally effective."[50] Instead, contingency theory suggests that the best way to structure an organization is contingent on a number of factors affecting the organization.[51] The most commonly cited factors are "the task environment of the organization, the technology used within the organization, and the organization's size."[52]

> Enterprises with highly predictable tasks perform better with organizations characterized by the highly formalized procedures and management hierarchies of the classical approach. With highly uncertain tasks that require more extensive problem solving, on the other hand, organizations that are less formalized and emphasize self-control and member participation in decision making are more effective. In essence, according to these newer studies, managers must design and develop organizations so that the organizational characteristics *fit* the nature of the task to be done.[53]

The task environment of an organization consists of its clients or customers, competitors, suppliers, regulatory agencies, and, in the case of public organizations, the legislature that established it and provides its funding. Some organizations face a task environment that is uncertain and rapidly changing. These organizations must be very flexible and able to change as rapidly as their environment. Other task environments are considerably more stable and organizations operating in them can become a little complacent.

Technology refers to *"the process by which an organization converts inputs into outputs."*[54] In a manufacturing environment, this is the assembly line or other mechanism used to produce the finished product. However, service organizations and even organizations producing such ephemeral products as "policy advice" also have production processes.

Where a technology is very routine and repetitive, such as an assembly line, the organization can have a very broad span of control because problems are not likely to occur, and when they do, there is usually a prearranged solution. Where the production process is less highly specified, such as in a policy advice unit, the span of control must be considerably smaller because each new task is different from previous tasks, and superiors and subordinates must work closely together.

The size of the organization also has an impact on its organizational structure. In very small organizations, the chief executive is in daily contact with all her or his subordinates and everyone understands by tradition what is to be done. As organizations become larger, layers of hierarchy are established, and written job descriptions and standard operating procedures are required to delineate responsibilities.

The usual procedure to conduct empirical inquiries into the validity of contingency theory is to use survey research to compare a large number of organizations. Sometimes the investigator will select organizations engaging in the same activity but with varying degrees of success. In this case, the hypothesis is that successful organizations will possess congruence of the various factors and unsuccessful ones will not. Another approach is to choose organizations engaged in very different kinds of activity. In this case, the hypothesis is that organizations engaged in different kinds of activities will be structured differently and have different approaches to management.

In general, the results of these inquiries have been mixed. An early study conducted by Morse and Lorsch examined four firms—two engaged in predictable manufacturing tasks and two in unpredictable research and development tasks.[55] Their results strongly supported contingency theory in that for each pair, the one with congruence between the nature of its task and its organizational structure was the more effective performer. More recent studies employing larger samples have usually not produced such unambiguous results. Many have found, at most, moderate support for the linkages posited in contingency theory.[56]

Probably the safest thing to say is that the jury is still out on the value of contingency theory. Almost all the studies do find some kinds of linkages, although they seldom find all of those expected, and those found are sometimes weaker than expected. The authors of the studies usually conclude with a plea for more research in this area to search out other variables or refine measurement techniques. It is likely that contingency theory has some value, although it probably does not hold out the promise suspected initially.

One of the strengths of contingency theory is that, unlike many of the other theories that have been discussed, it is a dynamic approach to organization. Managers must be aware that there is no "one best way" to organize their operation. The structure that was highly successful last year might be a dismal failure with the changed conditions of the new year. The need to adjust to the rapidly changing environment is a challenge to all modern organizations.

🏛 THE EMERGENT PROCESS VIEW

The organization theories discussed to this point have been based on the idea that managers have a great deal of control in making decisions about organizational structure, and that they always exercise that control in a rational manner and after extensive evaluation of alternatives.

A newly developing view suggests that organization design should be seen "as an emergent process, partially under the manager's control and partially beyond control ... [Managers are] partly proactive and partly reactive, capable of influencing organization design but not being the dominant influence."[57] This idea recognizes that external constraints play an important role in influencing organizational design, but that there is a significant element of chance or luck involved in organizational design as well.

One of the first discussions of this idea was an article colourfully titled "A Garbage Can Model of Organizational Choice."[58] This article described organizations as "organized anarchies."

> The organization operates on the basis of inconsistent and ill-defined preferences. It can be described better as a loose collection of ideas than as a coherent structure; it discovers preferences through action more than it acts on the basis of preferences.[59]

The decision-making process can be viewed as a garbage can into which four items are thrown:

- problems looking for solutions;

- solutions looking for problems;

- participants, each having different interests and different amounts of time to devote to a situation; and

- choice opportunities, or occasions when organizations are forced to undertake some action.

These items are thrown into the garbage can on a random basis and stirred about. Thus, problems do not always precede solutions. In some cases, solutions that have not yet discovered a problem are available. In any particular situation, the decision made is a function not of cold, rational logic but of the arbitrary way these four elements are thrown into and stirred about in the garbage can. For example, decisions are frequently influenced by the particular people who attend a key meeting. Thus, a bout of the flu or a flat tire that prevents a particular person from attending a meeting can determine what decision is made.

However, one should not go too far in emphasizing the randomness of decision making. Clearly, managers have the legal and effective authority to make decisions and they do utilize rational processes in making those decisions. The significance of the *emergent process view* is that it recognizes that managers face certain uncontrollable factors in making decisions and that they do sometimes temper their rationality with impulse and irrational bias in making decisions.

🏛 CONCLUSION

The history of organizational theory begins with the mechanistic views of Weber and Taylor and progresses to the considerably more humanistic perspectives of the social psychologists and organizational development specialists.

> Organization theory has indeed come full circle, and the enduring conflicts that characterize the field remain unresolved: formal versus informal structure as the proper focus of analysis, rationality versus humanism as the proper approach, equity versus efficiency as the goal of organizations, and the responsibility or lack thereof of the organization for the development and satisfaction of its employees— ultimately, conflicting theories of human nature and personality. What becomes apparent is that organizations are far more complex and complicated than was initially believed; as important as it is to understand them, we are a long way from that understanding.[60]

The thread that runs through all of these theories is an emphasis on motivating employees to perform better. No organizational "quick fix" or even long-term structural reform can ever be effective if the most basic components of any organization—the people who make it work—do not carry out their duties in an efficient and effective manner. The next chapter will continue to focus on the behaviour of people in organizations by examining the related issues of motivation, leadership, and communication in organizations.

NOTES

1. Mary Parker Follett, *Creative Experience* (New York: Peter Smith, 1951), ch. 3; Mary Parker Follett, *The New State* (Gloucester, Mass.: Peter Smith, 1965), 25–26.

2. Mary Parker Follett, *Dynamic Administration: The Collected Papers of Mary Parker Follett*, eds. Elliot M. Fox and L. Urwick (London: Pitman, 1973), xxv.

3. Their work is described in great detail in Roethlisberger and Dickson's book, *Management and the Worker* (Cambridge, Mass.: Harvard University Press, 1964).

4. Two of the more trenchant critics are Charles Perrow, *Complex Organizations: A Critical Essay* (Glenview, Ill.: Scott, Foresman, 1972), 97–106; and Amitai Etzioni, *Modern Organizations* (Englewood Cliffs, N.J.: Prentice-Hall, 1964), 39–49. A good overview of many of the critical articles can be found in Michael M. Harmon and Richard T. Mayer, *Organization Theory for Public Administration* (Boston: Little, Brown, 1986), 96–102.

5. Chester Barnard, *The Functions of the Executive* (Cambridge, Mass.: Harvard University Press, 1962).

6. Glenn Bassett, "From Job Fit to Cultural Compatibility: Evaluating Worker Skills and Termperment in the '90s," *Optimum*, 25, no. 1 (summer 1994): 11–17.

7. Abraham H. Maslow, *Motivation and Personality* (New York: Harper & Row, 1970), ch. 4.

8. Florence Heffron, *Organization Theory and Public Organizations: The Political Connection* (Englewood Cliffs, N.J.: Prentice Hall, 1989), 242.

9. A.H. Maslow, *Eupsychian Management* (Homewood, Ill.: Dorsey Press, 1965), 55–56.

10. Douglas McGregor, *The Human Side of Enterprise* (New York: McGraw-Hill, 1960), chapters 3 and 4 and passim.

11. Perrow, *Complex Organizations*, 100.

12. Robert B. Denhardt, *Theories of Public Organization* (Pacific Grove, Calif.: Brooks/Cole, 1984), 97.

13. Peter F. Drucker, *The Practice of Management* (New York: Harper & Row, 1954).

14. A good, complete discussion of the concept of organizational culture is found in Heffron, *Organization Theory and Public Organization*, ch. 7.

15. Some interesting examples are Robert R. Blake and Jane S. Mouton, *The Managerial Grid III* (Houston: Gulf Publishing Company, 1985); Matthew B. Miles and Richard A. Shmuck, "The Nature of Organization Development," in Wendell L. French, Cecil H. Bell, Jr., and Robert A. Zawacki, eds., *Organization Development: Theory, Practice, and Research* (Dallas: Business Publications, Inc., 1978), 24 and passim; Samuel A. Culbert and Jerome Reisel, "Organization Development: An Applied Philosophy for Managers of Public Enterprise," in Robert T. Golembiewski and William B. Eddy, eds., *Organization Development in Public Administration 1* (New York: Marcel Dekker, 1978).

16. This terminology was first used by one of the founders of organization development, Kurt Lewin, in "Frontiers in Group Dynamics," *Human Relations* 1, no. 1 (1947): 34.

17. A good summary of some of these definitions is contained in Edgar F. Huse, *Organization Development and Change* (St. Paul, Minn.: West Publishing Company, 1980), 22–25; Wendell L. French, Cecil H. Bell, Jr., and Robert A. Zawacki, "Mapping the Territory", and Richard Beckhard, "What Is Organization Development?" both in French, Bell, and Zawacki, eds., *Organization Development*, 11.

18. Wendell L. French, Cecil H. Bell, Jr. and Robert A. Zawacki, "Mapping the Territory," in French, Bell, and Zawacki, eds., *Organization Development*, 11.

19. Richard Beckhard, *Organization Development: Strategies and Models* (Reading, Mass.: Addison-Wesley, 1969), 10–11.

20. Robert T. Golembiewski, *Humanizing Public Organizations* (Mt. Airy, Md.: Lomond Press, 1985), 303, 338, and ch. 8 passim.

21. Wendell L. French and Cecil H. Bell, Jr., *Organization Development: Behavioral Science Interventions for Organization Improvement* (Englewood Cliffs, N.J.: Prentice-Hall, 1978), 81.

22. Deming's simultaneously insightful and folksy approach to management improvement is well-illustrated in his major work: *Quality, Productivity, and Competitive Position* (Cambridge, Mass.: Massachusetts Institute of Technology, Center for Advanced Engineering Study, 1982).

23. Marshall Sashkin and Kenneth J. Kiser, *Putting Total Quality Management to Work* (San Francisco: Berrett-Koehler Publishers, 1993), ch. 1.

24. These statements are probably extreme caricatures of the reality, but hard data on the air conditioning industry indicate that there was a huge difference in quality in the two countries. David A. Garvin, "Quality on the Line," *Harvard Business Review*, (September–October 1983), 64–75.

25. Joseph R. Jablonski, *Implementing Total Quality Management: An Overview* (San Diego: Pfeiffer & Company, 1991), 7.

26. Armand V. Feigenbaum, "Linking Quality Processes to International Leadership," in Frank Caropreso, ed., *Making Total Quality Happen* (New York: The Conference Board, 1990), 4.

27. Robert B. Denhardt, *Public Administration: An Action Orientation* (Pacific Groves, Calif.: Brooks/Cole Publishing Company, 1991), 316.

28. David A. Garvin and Artemis March, "A Note on Quality: The Views of Deming, Juran, and Crosby," in *Unconditional Quality* (Boston, Mass.: Harvard Business School Press, 1991), 18. For a more complete discussion of this issue, see: Deming, *Quality, Productivity, and Competitive Position*, ch. 1.

29. A good overview of some of these approaches is provided in: Richard M. Hodgetts, *Blueprints for Continuous Improvement: Lessons from the Baldridge Winners* (New York: American Management Association, 1993).

30. Steven Cohen and Ronald Brand, *Total Quality Management in Government* (San Francisco: Jossey-Bass Publishers, 1993), 18.

31. Catharine G. Johnston and Mark J. Daniel, *The Integrated PDCA Approach to Continuous Improvement* (Ottawa: The Conference Board of Canada, 1993), 5.

32. Jon Chopin, *Quality Through People: A Blueprint for Proactive Total Quality Management* (San Diego: Pfeiffer & Company, 1991), ch. 13.

33. Ibid., 297 ff.

34. Ibid., xi.

35. Brian Marson, "Building Customer-Focused Organizations in British Columbia," *Public Administration Quarterly* (spring 1993), 37–38.

36. Jablonski, *Implementing Total Quality Management*, 3 and 33–37.

37. Sashkin and Kiser, *Putting Total Quality Management to Work*, ch. 1.

38. Heffron, *Organization Theory and Public Organizations*, 161.

39. Golembiewski, *Humanizing Public Organizations*, 61.

40. V. Seymour Wilson, "The Influence of Organization Theory in Canadian Public Administration," *Canadian Public Administration* 25 (winter 1982): 553–54. The quotation within the quotation is from J.E. Hodgetts et al., *The Biography of an Institution* (Montreal: McGill-Queen's University Press, 1972), 194.

41. Denis Martin, "Culture and Client Service at the Department of Fisheries and Oceans," *Optimum* 24, no. 3 (winter 1993), 99–104; "Un ministère qui se donne des airs de PME," *Le Devoir*, 2 October 1992; Tom Rankin and Archie Gardner, "New Forms of Work Organization in the Federal Public Service: The Case of CFB Shearwater/UNDE Local 80409," *Optimum* 24, no. 4 (spring 1994), 25–36.

42. Marson, "Building Customer-Focused Organizations in British Columbia," 30–47.

43. One of the best overviews is found in: Mohamed Charih and Arthur Daniels, eds., *New Public Management and Public Administration in Canada* (Toronto: The Institute of Public Administration of Canada, 1997).

44. Donald J. Savioe, "What Is Wrong with the New Public Management?" *Canadian Public Administration*, 38, no. 1 (spring 1995), 112–21.

45. Sandford Borins, "The New Public Management Is Here to Stay," *Canadian Public Administration*, 38, no. 1 (spring 1995), 122–32.

46. One of the best recent discussions of the open systems is: Saeed Rahnema, *Organization Structure: A Systemic Approach* (Toronto: McGraw-Hill Ryerson, 1992).

47. Harmon and Mayer, *Organization Theory for Public Administration*, 162.

48. Daniel Katz and Robert L. Kahn, *The Social Psychology of Organizations* (New York: John Wiley & Sons, 1966), ch. 2.

49. A good history of contingency theory is found in James L. Gibson, John M. Ivancevich, and James H. Donnelly, Jr., *Organizations: Behavior, Structure, Processes*, 5th ed. (Plano, Tex.: Business Publications, 1985), ch. 14; and John B. Miner, *Theories of Organizational Structure and Process* (Chicago: The Dryden Press, 1982), ch. 9.

50. Jay Galbraith, *Designing Complex Organizations* (Reading, Mass.: Addison-Wesley, 1973), 2.

51. A very thorough discussion of contingency theory is contained in Henry Mintzberg, *The Structuring of Organizations* (Englewood Cliffs, N.J.: Prentice-Hall, 1979), Part III and passim.

52. Daniel Robey, *Designing Organizations*, 3rd ed. (Homewood, Ill.: Richard D. Irwin, 1990), 26. See also: Saeed Rahnema, *Organization Structure: A Systemic Approach*

53. John J. Morse and Jay W. Lorsch, "Beyond Theory Y," *Harvard Business Review* (May–June, 1970): 62. (Emphasis in original.)

54. Robey, *Designing Organizations*, 28. (Emphasis in original.)

55. Morse and Lorsch, "Beyond Theory Y," *Harvard Business Review*, 61–68.
56. A good review of many of the studies that have been conducted can be found in: Claudia Bird Schoonhoven, "Problems with Contingency Theory: Testing Assumptions Hidden within the Language of Contingency Theory," *Administrative Science Quarterly* 26 (September 1981): 349–77.
57. Robey, *Designing Organizations*, 38.
58. Michael D. Cohen, James G. March, and John P. Olsen, *Administrative Science Quarterly* 17, no. 1 (March 1972): 1–25.
59. Ibid., 1.
60. Heffron, *Organization Theory and Public Organizations*, 8.

BIBLIOGRAPHY

Barnard, Chester. *The Functions of the Executive*. Cambridge, Mass.: Harvard University Press, 1962.

Bassett, Glenn "From Job Fit to Cultural Compatibility: Evaluating Worker Skills and Temperament in the '90s" *Optimum* 25, no. 1 (summer 1994): 11–17.

Beckhard, Richard. *Organization Development: Strategies and Models*. Reading, Mass.: Addison-Wesley, 1969.

Bennis, Warren G. *Organization Development: Its Nature, Origins, and Prospects*. Reading, Mass.: Addison-Wesley, 1969.

Blake, Robert R., and Jane S. Mouton. *The Managerial Grid III*. Houston: Gulf, 1985.

Borins, Sandford. "The New Public Management Is Here to Stay." *Canadian Public Administration* 38, no. 1 (spring 1995): 122–32.

Caropreso, Frank, ed. *Making Total Quality Happen*. New York: The Conference Board, 1990.

Charih, Mohamed, and Arthur Daniels, eds. *New Public Management and Public Administration in Canada*. Toronto: The Institute of Public Administration of Canada, 1997.

Chopin, Jon. *Quality Through People: A Blueprint for Proactive Total Quality Management*. San Diego: Pfeiffer & Company, 1991.

Cohen, Steven, and Ronald Brand. *Total Quality Management in Government*. San Francisco: Jossey-Bass Publishers, 1993.

Deming, W. Edwards. *Quality, Productivity, and Competitive Position*. Cambridge, Mass.: Massachusetts Institute of Technology, Center for Advanced Engineering Study, 1982.

Denhardt, Robert B. *Public Administration: An Action Orientation*. Pacific Groves, Calif.: Brooks/Cole Publishing Company, 1991.

Drucker, Peter F. *The Practice of Management*. New York: Harper & Row, 1954.

Etzioni, Amitai. *Modern Organizations*. Englewood Cliffs, N.J.: Prentice-Hall, 1964.

Follett, Mary Parker. *Creative Experience*. New York: Peter Smith, 1951.

_____. *The New State*. Gloucester, Mass.: Peter Smith, 1965.

_____. *Dynamic Administration: The Collected Papers of Mary Parker Follett*. Edited by Elliot M. Fox and L. Urwick. London: Pitman, 1973.

French, Wendell L., and Cecil H. Bell, Jr. *Organization Development: Behavioral Science Interventions for Organization Improvement*. 2nd ed. Englewood Cliffs, N.J.: Prentice-Hall, 1978.

French, Wendell L., Cecil H. Bell, Jr., and Robert A. Zawacki, eds. *Organization Development: Theory, Practice, and Research*. Dallas: Business Publications, Inc., 1978.

Galbraith, Jay. *Designing Complex Organizations*. Reading, Mass.: Addison-Wesley, 1973.

Garvin, David A. "Quality on the Line." *Harvard Business Review* (September–October 1983): 64–75.

Garvin, David A., and Artemis March. "A Note on Quality: The Views of Deming, Juran, and Crosby." In *Unconditional Quality*. Boston: Harvard Business School Press, 1991.

Golembiewski, Robert T. *Humanizing Public Organizations.* Mt. Airy, Md.: Lomond Press, 1985.

Golembiewski, Robert T., and William B. Eddy, eds. *Organization Development in Public Administration.* 2 vols. New York: Marcel Dekker, Inc., 1978.

Harmon, Michael M., and Richard T. Mayer. *Organization Theory for Public Administration.* Boston: Little, Brown, 1986.

Harvey, Donald F., and Donald R. Brown. *An Experiential Approach to Organization Development.* Englewood Cliffs, N.J.: Prentice-Hall, 1976.

Heffron, Florence. *Organization Theory and Public Organizations: The Political Connection.* Englewood Cliffs, N.J.: Prentice-Hall, 1989.

Hodgetts, J.E., William McCloskey, Reginald Whitaker, and V. Seymour Wilson. *The Biography of an Institution.* Montreal: McGill-Queen's University Press, 1972.

Hodgetts, Richard M. *Blueprints for Continuous Improvement: Lessons from the Baldridge Winners.* New York: American Management Association, 1993.

Hodgson, J.S. "Management by Objectives—The Experience of a Federal Government Department." *Canadian Public Administration* 16 (fall 1973): 422–31.

Huse, Edgar F. *Organization Development and Change.* 2nd ed. St. Paul, Minn.: West Publishing Company, 1980.

Jablonski, Joseph R. *Implementing Total Quality Management: An Overview.* San Diego: Pfeiffer & Company, 1991.

Johnston, Catharine G., and Mark J. Daniel. *The Integrated PDCA Approach to Continuous Improvement.* Ottawa: The Conference Board of Canada, 1993.

Katz, Daniel, and Robert L. Kahn. *The Social Psychology of Organizations.* New York: John Wiley & Sons, 1966.

Laframboise, H.L. "Administrative Reform in the Federal Public Service: Signs of a Saturation Psychosis." *Canadian Public Administration* 14 (fall 1971): 303–25.

LGMP Team, The. *The LGMP Experience: Guidelines for Organizational Change in Local Government.* Toronto: Ministry of Treasury, Economics and Intergovernmental Affairs, 1977.

Marson, Brian. "Building Customer-Focused Organizations in British Columbia." *Public Administration Quarterly* (spring 1993): 30–47.

Martin, Denis. "Culture and Client Service at the Department of Fisheries and Oceans." *Optimum,* 24, no. 3 (winter 1993): 99–104.

Maslow, A.H. *Eupsychian Management.* Homewood, Ill.: Dorsey Press, 1965.

————. *Motivation and Personality.* New York: Harper & Row, 1970.

McGregor, Douglas. *The Human Side of Enterprise.* New York: McGraw-Hill, 1960.

McLaren, Robert I. *Organizational Dilemmas.* Chichester, U.K.: John Wiley & Sons, 1982.

Mintzberg, Henry. *The Structuring of Organizations.* Englewood Cliffs, N.J.: Prentice-Hall, 1979.

————. *Structure in Fives: Designing Effective Organizations.* Englewood Cliffs, N.J.: Prentice-Hall, 1983.

Morse, John J., and Jay W. Lorsch. "Beyond Theory Y." *Harvard Business Review* 48 (May–June, 1970): 61–68.

Odiorne, George S. *Management by Objectives.* New York: Pitman, 1965.

Ontario. The Management Board of Cabinet. *Manager's Guidelines to Managing by Results.* Toronto: The Management Board of Cabinet, 1982.

Perrow, Charles. *Complex Organizations: A Critical Essay.* Glenview, Ill.: Scott, Foresman, 1972.

Rahnema, Saeed. *Organization Structure: A Systemic Approach.* Toronto: McGraw-Hill Ryerson, 1992.

Roethlisberger, F.J., and William J. Dickson. *Management and the Worker.* Cambridge, Mass.: Harvard University Press, 1964.

Salancik, Gerard R., and Jeffrey Pfeffer. "An Examination of Need-Satisfaction Models of Job Attitudes." *Administrative Science Quarterly* 22 (September 1977): 427–56.

Sashkin, Marshall, and Kenneth J. Kiser. *Putting Total Quality Management to Work.* San Francisco: Berrett-Koehler Publishers, 1993.

Savoie, Donald J. "What Is Wrong with the New Public Management?" *Canadian Public Administration* 38, no. 1 (spring 1995): 112–21.

Schoonhoven, Claudia Bird. "Problems with Contingency Theory: Testing Assumptions Hidden within the Language of Contingency 'Theory'." *Administrative Science Quarterly* 26 (September 1981): 349–77.

Wilson, V. Seymour. "The Influence of Organization Theory in Canadian Public Administration." *Canadian Public Administration* 25 (winter 1982): 545–63.

5

Communication, Leadership, and Motivation

Martha and Jane are long-time friends who work for different departments of the same government. They get together for coffee about once a week on their way to work. Let's eavesdrop on a conversation between them.

Martha: I've gotta rush because I have an important meeting that I don't want to miss.

Jane: Well, I have an important meeting, too, but that's all the more reason why I don't want to rush to the office. All these meetings are the same. Somebody will stand up and drone on about the latest management fad without telling us anything about what's really happening in the department. Of course, maybe that's because nothing is happening. Ever since this new management team came in, I don't have a clear understanding of where our department is going. We just seem to drift from one crisis to the next.

Martha: We used to be like that, but our new deputy minister has really changed things. That's why I'm looking forward to this meeting. He's obviously really taken charge of the department and is working with the minister to establish a clear idea of where we should be heading. Then, they have these monthly meetings where we have an opportunity to discuss the latest proposed initiatives with them. They make sure that everyone has the opportunity for some input, and then they make sure that everyone understands what has been decided. It sure makes a difference in my personal motivation. When you feel personally involved and committed to an idea, it's a lot easier to produce results.

Jane: Well, I'm glad you feel so motivated. For me, I'm not motivated enough to get up off this chair and listen to another exhortation about how I should be excited about doing whatever it is I'm supposed to be doing.

Some organizations are better to work for than others. The reasons can be a little difficult to define sometimes. The bosses are more accessible. They seem to inspire people to do more and better work. The communication systems work well so all the employees feel comfortable and understand their role. In sum, everyone is highly motivated and the organization works well. Why is it that some organizations just work better than others? The reasons are not always clear, and not everyone agrees on all of them, but some general statements can be made.

The previous two chapters focused more on organizations as organizations than they did on the actions and motivations of the people within them. This chapter will focus on the individual members of the organization.

It is frequently said that the most important resource that any organization possesses is its human resource—its employees. Yet it is shocking to see how carefully some organizations preserve and protect their other resources but neglect their human resources. This chapter will first consider two important aspects of motivation—communication and leadership—and then tie these together with a discussion of some general theories concerning the motivation of employees.

Communication, leadership, and motivation are very closely related concepts. Good communication and sound leadership are important in producing highly motivated employees, and highly motivated employees can make the organization operate more efficiently.

🏛 COMMUNICATION

Communication is the lifeblood of any organization. One of the main purposes of communication is to effect coordination between the various units in an organization. If an organization is to function properly, people in any part of it must understand what is taking place in other parts. Communication takes place in several ways. At one extreme are the formal, written instructions found in an organization manual or on a list of standard operating procedures. At the other extreme, communication can be by example. When senior managers all dress very conservatively, work long hours, and take short breaks, they are communicating something very significant to those below them in the hierarchy—without saying a word.

Pursley and Snortland capture the full subtlety of the situation when they define communication as "the transfer and reception of information, emotions, ideas, and orders."[1] Notice that this definition considers communication as a two-part process; communication is not just the sending of a message, but the reception of that message as well. We are all aware of situations where the message that was sent was not the same message received—either accidentally or intentionally.

Different Kinds of Communications

In many ways, *formal and informal communications* parallel the formal and informal organizations discussed in Chapter 4. All organizations provide certain formal communications to members. These take such forms as the orientation package for new employees, training materials, and operating manuals. They set out the formal rules of the organization and tell employees what is expected of them. However, as new employees become socialized in an organization, they also receive many informal communications that modify the communications they have received through the formal channel. For example, the operating manual might say that employees are entitled to be paid at a premium rate for all overtime worked. However, the informal channel of communications might suggest that if you value your future in the organization and want to be seen as a "team player," you will simply work the overtime and not bother to ask for the extra pay. In many cases, the information conveyed through the informal communication system can be as important as that conveyed through the formal system.

Management should attempt to keep track of communication flowing through the informal system. It will frequently provide advance notice of employee dissatisfaction or other problems in lower levels of the organization. There is also much misinformation that is passed through the "grapevine." This can be a sign that the more formal methods of communication are not adequate. An "organization's informal communications network begins to hum whenever the formal channels are silent or ambiguous on subjects of importance to its members."[2] If, for example, the formal system communicated that there was soon to be a major reorganization and then was silent, the informal system might begin to buzz with rumours about imminent layoffs. However, if senior management used the formal system to keep employees informed about the reorganization, there would be less misinformation in the informal system. Therefore, management must be conscious of this tendency and head it off by providing a steady flow of accurate formal communications.

Downward communications involve the communication of official organizational pronouncements from the top levels of the hierarchy down to operating employees. Downward communication is used by senior management to coordinate the activities of low-level employees. This is usually done through formal communications such as policy directives, operating manuals, or notices on bulletin boards, but, as mentioned earlier, downward communication can also be informal.

Great care must be taken to ensure that the message sent by senior managers is the same message received by operating employees. This problem increases with the number of levels in the hierarchy and with functional specialization. One of the barriers to communication discussed below is caused because the language spoken varies at different levels in the organization, and in its different functional areas. A communication that begins at the top level of the organization as a one-page statement about the need for better safety in the factory will be "translated" as it passes down the chain of command. It will develop into lengthy statements about who must wear safety shoes, hard hats, and protective glasses, when they must be worn, and how they will be paid for. In this translation process, the policy as implemented on the factory floor might or might not be the same one articulated by senior management.

Upward communications, sometimes called *feedback*, are messages from lower levels of the organization to higher levels. This is the most unnatural form of communication in the organization because it runs counter to the normal chain of command, but it can also be the most important. Operating-level employees are in a much better position to know about problems as they are developing than are senior managers. Operating-level employees deal with clients on a daily basis and so get immediate feedback about client dissatisfaction; factory employees see how a product is being assembled and so can frequently point to quality control problems and bottlenecks in operations.

Senior managers should always encourage upward communication, but this is easier said than done. Lower-level employees are sometimes reluctant to discuss problems with senior employees because of either the social distance involved or the unnaturalness of upward communications, or for fear that managers will "kill the messenger bearing the bad news." The major inhibition on the upward flow of information is simply that lower-level employees do not want to pass upward information that can be used against them.

Thus, there is a natural tendency to pass upward positive information but not negative information. The cumulative impact of this tendency can be so severe that senior managers become totally out of touch with what is actually happening at the operating level. David Halberstam suggests that the American involvement in Vietnam in the 1960s was characterized by this attitude of telling superiors what they wanted to hear. He states that one journalist felt that senior officers in the military "had created an elaborate machine to lie to them, only to become prisoners of their own lies."[3] Wartime situations bring about extreme cases, but it is not unusual for senior managers to be forced to deal quickly with a crisis that could have been headed off easily if they had had some advance warning.

Some companies have formal programs such as suggestion boxes or plans that reward employees for ideas to improve productivity, but these plans frequently meet with mixed success. One interesting method of stimulating upward communication is "management by wandering around" (MBWA).[4] MBWA, also called "the technology of the obvious," urges managers to put aside computer printouts and marketing surveys periodically and escape from their offices to wander about and see their product or service as customers do and experience the work environment as their employees do. Some managers' findings when they attempted this were obvious, basic, and brilliant at the same time. One manager insisted on cleaner washrooms in the factory because he did not see how employees could have a sense of pride in their work when they had to put up with the stench from the washrooms at the assembly line.[5] Some of the things that have the greatest effect on working conditions never find their way into computer printouts.

Lateral communication "takes place among workers of the same level in the hierarchy, or among individuals of different levels who are not in a superior-subordinate relationship."[6] *Most* communication in organizations could well be of the lateral variety, although it is impossible to measure this precisely. Some kinds of lateral communication are encouraged by the formal organization, but some kinds are discouraged or even prohibited.

Lateral communication between employees within the same work team is usually encouraged because it promotes coordination. It is impossible for standard operating procedures to foresee every future working condition; lateral communication between employees fills this void by facilitating informal solutions to work problems.

However, lateral communication between employees in different organizational units is more problematic. Strictly speaking, all communication within an organization should flow "through channels." This means that people at the same level, but reporting to different supervisors, do not consult directly with one another. Figure 5.1 shows the proper formal communication route in a bureaucracy. If X desires to communicate with Y, X passes the communication up the hierarchy until it reaches someone who has line authority over both X and Y. This person then makes some decision and passes that decision down.

However, people working in organizations quickly discover the difficulties with this communication "through channels." Not only is it time-consuming, but there is also a risk that relatively small issues will be caught up in larger concerns of "office politics" or territoriality. Subordinates learn quickly that it is much faster and easier to resolve minor problems through informal lateral communication than through the hierarchy. Thus, the rigid standard operating procedures found in formal communications are frequently modified in practice because people at lower levels in the organization have found better ways to coordinate their activities.

There is some risk to subordinates in ignoring the chain of command. If it is really a small matter that does not affect others, then it will be acceptable to circumvent the normal channels, but if something larger goes awry as a result of these informal agreements, subordinates can get in trouble for not keeping their bosses informed.

Some organizations see real value in encouraging lateral communication. It can smooth out many problems quickly and be a source of innovation. Henri Fayol developed the idea of the "gang plank," which allows lateral communications to occur while still preserving the concept of the chain of command. He strongly argued that lateral communications were highly preferable to the roundabout method of following channels as long as the communicators' immediate supervisors were kept informed of what was happening.[7]

Figure 5.1
FLOW OF COMMUNICATIONS

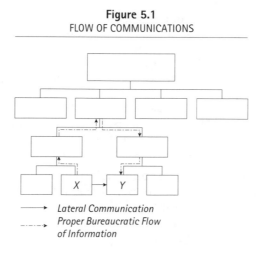

→ Lateral Communication
---→ Proper Bureaucratic Flow
of Information

Lateral communication can also occur between different organizations. This can be routine, such as when someone in a regional office communicates directly with a head office counterpart, or it can involve the transfer of major innovations from one organization to another. People performing the same function in different organizations frequently belong to associations that allow them to meet and discuss changes in their field. These can be as formal as the provincial engineers' or accountants' associations, or as informal as a periodic breakfast meeting of human resource directors employed in municipal governments in a certain area. These people engage in lateral communication about new activities in their organizations. This allows for the sharing of new ideas.

Lateral communications can have substantial value in certain cases. They aid problem solving and can foster innovation and the dissemination of new ideas. However, some organizations are fearful of this form of communication because it can appear to subvert the formal chain of command.

Obstacles to Communication

Good, clear lines of communication are important in coordinating activities and ensuring organizational effectiveness, but there are a number of factors that inhibit effective communication.

Territoriality and other organizational tensions occur in organizations where there is a climate that encourages managers to think solely about the furtherance of their own goals. In this environment, communication is discouraged because managers do not want to "tip their hands" too early and allow other departments to know what they are doing. This attitude is clearly dysfunctional to organizational health, but it is found all too often in organizations.

Language differences exacerbate problems that might already exist between various occupational specialties and organizational units. Andrew Dunsire compares a typical organization to a high-rise building that he calls the "Babel house." Each ascending floor is a higher level in the hierarchy, and the horizontal separation on each floor represents different functional specialties:

> The building is a Tower of Babel because a different tongue (concepts, vocabulary) is talked on each floor—amounting to a considerable linguistic disparity between top-floor speech and ground-floor speech—and different jargons and dialects are spoken on any one floor, in each of the corners and other areas. As between one floor and the next, or as between one office and its neighbour on the same floor, differences in language and habitual style of doing business can usually be noted, though it is quite easy for adjacent ranks, and denizens of adjacent offices, to understand one another. Messages from distant locations in any direction—from a faraway corner, or from a much higher or much lower floor—do not, by contrast, make much sense on first hearing or reading: the more distant, the less intelligible.[8]

These different languages and dialects come about as a result of professional and functional specialization. For example, both economists and accountants talk about "depreciation" and "rents," but the two groups have different meanings for those same terms, which are in turn different from their more common usage by members of the public. In a factory, a document that is clearly identified on its face as "Form No. C31–a" might be called a "requisition form" or "green sheet" in different parts of the plant.

Communications overload occurs when there are so many communications taking place that they overload the channels for processing them, causing organizational dysfunctions. In the popular novel and film *The Day of the Jackal*, the French authorities know that the Jackal has entered the country to assassinate President DeGaulle. And someplace in the elaborate French bureaucracy they have the information they need to find him. The problem is that they also have so much other information that they are unable to locate the relevant bits. This sort of thing is relatively frequent in large organizations. Senior executives are inundated with communications so that it is difficult for them to decide which are most relevant.

Noise or *distortion* occurs when messages are altered as they pass through the various steps in the hierarchy. Almost everyone has played the game that involves saying something to one person who, in turn, passes the information to someone else, and so forth until it has passed through many people. The message in its final form usually bears little resemblance to its original statement. This problem can be even more severe in large organizations when there is the possibility that territoriality or language differences can add to the distortion.

Organizations can attempt to minimize these distortions by relying on formal, written communications and hoping that the likelihood of misinterpretation of written documents is less than of word-of-mouth communication. However, even written documents can suffer from poor translation as information is passed from senior managers down the hierarchy.

The other factor that can be used to coordinate activities within any organization is good leadership. It can be used to supplement communications by putting unclear or distorted communications back into perspective.

🏛 LEADERSHIP

Leadership is an important factor in the motivation of employees. It is necessary to be a good leader in order to be a good manager, but the words are not synonymous. Managers possess power as a result of their organizational position; leaders possess power as a result of the concurrence of their followers. Some managers are leaders: their relationship with subordinates is such that subordinates comply with their requests not just out of fear for the consequences if they don't, but because they are willing followers. Katz and Kahn "consider the essence of organizational leadership to be the influential increment over and above the mechanical compliance with the routine directives of the organization."[9] Pursley and Snortland provide a more detailed distinction between a leader and a manager:

> Managers are appointed and have formal authority within an organization; leaders may be elected, appointed, or merely emerge from within a group. A manager has a formal position; a leader may or may not have a formal position. A manager usually can expect people to follow proper, official orders; leaders may be able to move people to do things far beyond the call of duty. Although every man-

ager should be a leader, not all leaders are managers. A manager is expected to be able to organize, plan, and evaluate; some leaders may not be able to perform these management tasks. A manager's formal authority provides the resources that the manager may be able to use to influence the behavior of people—in short, to lead. However, not every manager is a leader or even understands the importance of leadership.[10]

This raises the question of why a leader is even needed in a bureaucratic organization. After all, the rules are the rules and even totally uninspired managers can stand over workers and be certain that they follow the rules. Who needs a leader?

There is something to be said for this line of reasoning. Most people are familiar with organizations that stagger along without effective leadership—forms are processed, decisions are made, and so forth. However, such an organization is really only staggering along. Good leaders provide an atmosphere that allows organizations to develop and thrive rather than just stumble from one crisis to the next.

Leaders instil in subordinates the desire to excel. When you visit a store or office, it is very easy to distinguish an organization in which the employees are striving to do their job as well as possible from one where employees are simply going through the motions to get a paycheque. Usually, the difference will be the presence of a true leader rather than a "by the book" manager.

Leaders also help organizations survive crises. It is relatively easy to manage an organization in a stable situation, but a good leader is necessary when the organization is facing a threat to its continued existence, or must make a major change in its operations.[11]

In his compendium review of the literature on leadership, Ralph Stogdill clearly demonstrates the difficulty of defining leadership in an unequivocal manner: he devotes an entire chapter to definitions, in which he lists eleven different *categories* of definitions.[12] However, this lack of a precise definition has not restricted the amount of research undertaken in the area of leadership.

This voluminous research has yielded a number of different perspectives on the issue of leadership. One of the earliest approaches was to attempt to locate those *traits* that always seemed to be present in a successful leader. This was followed by a trend toward research to determine which *skills* were most likely to be of use to leaders. Traits are genetically a part of the individual, whereas skills can be learned and developed.

The switch to an emphasis on skills led to a concern for the development of an ideal leadership *style*—democratic, authoritarian, or laissez-faire. In recent years the trend has been toward the belief that there is no one ideal style, but that the most appropriate style is a function of the relationship between, on the one hand, the traits and skills of leaders and, on the other hand, the characteristics of followers and the environment of the organization. This is called the situational or *contingency* theory of leadership. Each of these approaches to the study of leadership will be discussed in this chapter.

Leadership Traits or Skills

One of the earliest approaches to the study of leadership was an analysis of a group of people who were commonly regarded as successful, or "natural leaders," to determine what traits these individuals had in common. The basis of this research was that there were certain inherited traits that would always mark a leader. Some studies suggested that leaders tended to be older, taller, weigh more, and have greater athletic and speaking ability than nonleaders.[13] However, this line of research fell out of favour when other studies did not produce consistent results.[14]

A second wave of research applied some of the same techniques used in the studies of "natural leaders" to locate the traits and skills common to successful leaders in the workplace—managers and supervisors. This focus was considerably more productive. Stogdill has summarized the findings of these studies:

> The leader is characterized by a strong drive for responsibility and task completion, vigor and persistence in pursuit of goals, venturesomeness and originality in problem solving, drive to exercise initiative in social situations, self-confidence and sense of personal identity, willingness to accept consequences of decision and action, readiness to absorb interpersonal stress, willingness to tolerate frustration and delay, ability to influence other persons' behavior, and capacity to structure social interaction systems to the purpose at hand.[15]

A more recent study of two thousand managers in twelve organizations identified several characteristics usually found in successful managers: efficiency orientation; proactivity; diagnostic use of concepts; concern with impact; self-confidence; use of oral presentations; conceptualization (middle-level managers and executives only); use of socialized power; managing group process (middle-level managers and executives only); perceptual objectivity; self-control; stamina; and adaptability.[16]

Some commentators see the situation more simply and suggest that management abilities can be identified in two or three clusters of skills. Katz's three-skills typology was first developed in 1955, but is still considered relevant:

> *Technical Skills*: "An understanding of, and proficiency in, a specific kind of activity, particularly one involving methods, processes, procedures, or techniques... Technical skill involves specialized knowledge, analytical ability within that specialty, and facility in the use of the tools and techniques of the specific discipline."[17]

> *Human Skills*: "The executive's ability to work effectively as a group member and to build cooperative effort within the team he leads. As *technical* skill is primarily concerned with working with 'things' (processes or physical objects), so *human* skill is primarily concerned with working with people."[18]

> *Conceptual Skills*: "The ability to see the enterprise as a whole; it includes recognizing how the various functions of the organization depend on one another, and how changes in any one part affect all the others; and it extends to visualizing the

relationship of the individual business to the industry, the community, and the political, social, and economic forces of the nation as a whole. Recognizing these relationships and perceiving the significant elements in any situation, the administrator should then be able to act in a way which advances the overall welfare of the total organization."[19]

All managers must possess these skills to some degree, but managers at different levels in the organization need different quantities of each.

The *first-line supervisor* must have high levels of technical skills because he or she must be able to advise workers on production problems. First-line supervisors must also possess human relations skills to maintain satisfaction and motivation among group members and direct them toward organizational goals. Conceptual skills are less necessary for first-line supervisors because the problems facing them are fairly well defined and recurring, and usually involve problems within the organization, rather than in its environment.

The skill needs of *senior managers* are reversed. Technical skills are considerably less important because there are large numbers of skilled operatives at lower levels to solve those kinds of problems. Conceptual skills are much more important for senior managers because they are constantly facing new and unstructured problems involving relationships among different units of the organization, or between the organization and its environment.

Thus, the study of leadership traits and skills led to a realization that leadership was not something contained only in the leader, but rather that leadership described a reciprocal relationship between the leader and followers. The next approach to leadership studied the exchange relationship between these two.

Styles of Leadership: Authoritarian, Democratic, and Laissez-Faire

There are probably as many different leadership styles as there are leaders. Recently developed situational theories of leadership stress this fact, but many earlier studies focused on three broad categories of leadership style—authoritarian, democratic, and laissez-faire. The *authoritarian* style involves the leader making all decisions and communicating work tasks to followers in a highly detailed manner so that followers have no role in making decisions or organizing their work. The *democratic* or *participative* style of leadership involves a more open relationship in which leaders encourage followers to work together in seeking and implementing solutions. Leaders guide the group by advising on different possibilities. The *laissez-faire* style allows followers to "do their own thing" with no direction or involvement on the part of the leader. This usually comes about as a corruption or a misapplication of the democratic style.[20]

The relative effectiveness of these different styles has been tested many times and the results have always been very similar. The laissez-faire style is universally rejected as having no redeeming value. It results in groups deteriorating into chaos, and produces neither organizational effectiveness nor member satisfaction. The democratic leadership style seems to further member satisfaction and group cohesion more than the other two. The evidence is less clear about the effect of leadership style on group productivity. Stogdill's comprehensive review of studies suggests that leadership style (authoritarian or democratic) had little impact on productivity.[21]

However, some researchers delved a little more deeply into this issue.[22] They found that authoritarian styles seemed to be more functional in cases where the task to be accomplished was clearly defined and could be well-structured, e.g., a factory assembly line. Democratic styles were more productive where tasks were ill-defined and nonrepetitive, e.g., a research laboratory. This was one of the findings that led to the idea that there was no "one best way" of establishing leadership, but that different leadership styles were more effective in different situations.

Situational or Contingency Theories

The contingency theory of organization, discussed in Chapter 4, holds that the ideal structure for an organization depends on a number of factors, such as the backgrounds of employees in the organization and the task to be accomplished. The situational theory of leadership borrows this concept in arguing that the best style of leadership is a product of a number of factors relating to:

- characteristics of the leader;
- characteristics of the members of the group;
- nature of the decision to be made; and
- the situation or environment.

A number of researchers have developed different forms of situational theories.[23] The Vroom-Yetton normative model will be discussed here as representative of this general approach.

Vroom and Yetton focus on how leaders *ought* to make decisions if they are to be perceived as good leaders.[24] This is a normative model, meaning that it suggests how decisions *ought* to be made. Vroom and Yetton are not saying that decisions are made this way, only that managers would be better leaders if they did make decisions this way. It is clear that their work is influenced by participative approaches to management, but they recognize that participation is not necessary, or even productive, in every decision.

Vroom and Yetton begin by identifying three categories of decision-making styles from the least participative to the most: autocratic, consultative, and group. Each of these methods of decision making is beneficial in certain circumstances. They then identify eight factors to be considered in choosing which method to use in each circumstance. Among the most significant factors are:[25]

- the importance of the decision for the health of the organization;
- the adequacy of knowledge possessed by the decision maker;
- the importance of subordinates' acceptance of the decision; and

- the likelihood that subordinates would make a decision based on the best interests of the organization.

Vroom and Yetton then use a fairly complex set of decision-trees to relate the circumstances facing the leader to the optimum leadership style.

Their approach serves as a reminder that leadership is not something to be valued in itself. Leadership must have some purpose; one of its main purposes is to improve organizational effectiveness by motivating employees. The next section reviews some theories of motivation.

🏛 MOTIVATION

Earlier ideas of motivation were rather simplistic. Bosses simply told workers what to do and they did it—or were fired. Henry Ford is purported to have said that the best incentive for an employee is the presence of unemployed workers outside the factory gate. Chapters 3 and 4 described how ideas of external motivation based on reward or fear of punishment have recently been replaced with ideas stressing the importance of internal motivators such as self-actualization or pride in accomplishment.

Traditional forms of motivation based on punishment have fallen into disuse for a number of reasons. The strength of unions and recent changes in labour laws to protect workers have reduced the unilateral power that employers once had to discipline employees. However, research indicates that motivation by fear of punishment is not very efficient anyway.[26] Negative forms of motivation might well motivate employees to do just enough to avoid being disciplined. The result could be a continual game of employees trying to find out how much they can "get away with" before they are disciplined. This could then lead to management continually imposing new controls and restrictions as employees find ways of circumventing them. Positive methods of motivating people are probably much more effective.

Chapters 3 and 4 discussed some of the motivating mechanisms employed in various schools of management. Table 5.1 summarizes the main points made in those chapters. This chapter will build on the general findings presented earlier and provide additional details on motivating mechanisms.

Chris Argyris' Maturity-Immaturity Theory

Chris Argyris points out that all social organizations are composed of individuals and a formal structure, but that tensions inevitably develop because there is a basic incongruence between the behaviour pattern of mature individuals and the needs of the formal organization. He suggests that the characteristics of a mature individual are:

- increasing activity or self-determination;

- independence rather than dependence;

- multifaceted behaviour;

Table 5.1
SUMMARY OF MOTIVATING MECHANISMS

Management School	Communication Style	Leadership Style	Motivating Mechanism
Weberian	formal; downward	authoritarian	commands; authority
Scientific Management (Taylor)	formal; downward	authoritarian	authority; financial rewards
Human Relations (Theory X–Theory Y; Hierarchy of Needs)	informal; upward; downward	democratic; potentially laissez faire	self-actualization
Participative (Organization Development)	upward; downward; lateral	democratic	self-actualization participation

- deepening interest in stimulating challenges;
- longer time perspective;
- feelings of equality with peers; and
- self-awareness.[27]

He goes on to point out that formal organizations are based on such principles as task or work specialization, chain of command, unity of direction, and span of control.[28] Most of these principles require not mature but immature behaviour on the part of the individual. For example, mature individuals capable of complex behaviour and interested in challenges are placed in jobs that require boring, repetitive actions. "[O]rganizations are willing to pay high wages and provide adequate seniority if mature adults will, for eight hours a day, behave in a less than mature manner!"[29]

It is quite rational for employees to react negatively when confronted with this situation. They could simply leave the organization. Or they could stay and become apathetic and/or establish an informal work group that could have a detrimental effect on production. Or they could resolve to work their way up the organizational ladder because the incongruity between personality and organizational demands is less pronounced at the higher levels.[30]

In a later work, Argyris presents some tentative suggestions for resolving this basic incongruity.[31] He suggests that organizations of the future will emphasize the pyramidal organizational structure less and recognize that there are other, less formal structures in place that are also important. He strongly supports a form of job enlargement (discussed in more detail later in this chapter) that would ensure that employees develop a greater understanding of, and concern for, the activities of the *entire* organization, rather than only their narrow portion of it. This should be supplemented by employees meeting in small groups to discuss problems and possibilities for improvement. He argued that autocratic leadership styles should be replaced by situational approaches to leadership—different types of employees and situations call for different leadership styles. Control mechanisms should be oriented less toward detecting transgressions and more toward helping individuals achieve greater "self-responsibility and psychological success."[32]

A standard criticism of Argyris' approach is that he views human nature as too homogeneous. His perspective that *everyone* is mature and wants interesting, challenging work is too simplistic. Robert Presthus argues that different personalities react differently to bureaucratic structures. He labels the three different bureaucratic personality types as "upwardmobiles," "indifferents," and "ambivalents."[33]

One might disagree with the specifics of Presthus' categories, but it does seem to be the case that different individuals behave differently in bureaucratic settings; most seem to hate the boredom, but some people can enjoy aspects of even the most boring job.[34]

Possibly it is the characterization of bureaucracy as homogeneous that misses the mark. The characteristics of particular jobs can vary quite widely; an employee's positive or negative feelings might have more to do with how he or she views the job than with how he or she relates to the overall bureaucracy.

Frederick Herzberg's Motivation-Hygiene Theory

People frequently assume that the factors that cause *satisfaction* in the work environment are simply the reverse of those that cause *dissatisfaction*. Frederick Herzberg tested this conventional wisdom by asking a number of employees to describe work occurrences that led to satisfaction and dissatisfaction. In many cases, the factors causing satisfaction were very different from those causing dissatisfaction.[35] For example, Table 5.2 indicates that a feeling of achievement tended to satisfy workers, but its absence did not make them dissatisfied; it simply reduced their satisfaction. Conversely, company policy and administration were a frequent source of dissatisfaction, but correcting problems in this area merely lessened dissatisfaction; it did not increase satisfaction.

Herzberg referred to the factors that led to dissatisfaction as *hygiene factors* because "they act in a manner analogous to the principles of medical hygiene. Hygiene operates to remove health hazards from the environment of man. It is not curative; it is, rather, a preventive."[36] Herzberg labelled the factors that led to satisfaction *motivators* because they had a highly positive effect on people's feelings about their job.

Herzberg noted a very interesting difference between the hygiene and motivating factors. The hygiene factors all relate to the general work environment, while the motivating factors are all intrinsic to the nature of the job itself. The implications of Herzberg's theory for management are clear: the general work environment should be pleasant enough to avoid dissatisfaction, but any major improvements in motivation can be made only through changes in the nature of the job itself.

Table 5.2
HERZBERG'S MOTIVATION AND HYGIENE FACTORS

Motivators	Hygiene
achievement	company policy and administration
recognition	supervision-technical
work itself	salary
responsibility	interpersonal relations
advancement	working conditions

The specific remedy suggested by Herzberg was job redesign or job enrichment.

Job Redesign

The theories of both Argyris and Herzberg focused on the ability to improve motivation through careful job design. However, two experts on job design, Richard Hackman and Greg Oldham, remind us that sometimes the problem is not with the nature of the job itself. They emphasize the need for proper selection and training techniques to ensure that there is a good fit between the person and the job.[37]

> When people are well matched with their jobs, it rarely is necessary to force, coerce, bribe, or trick them into working hard and trying to perform the job well. Instead, they try to do well because it is rewarding and satisfying to do so.[38]

However, the job itself must be reasonably attractive. A number of different approaches to improving job designs have been tried.

Job rotation involves keeping the job descriptions for all positions the same, but shifting the people who fill the position. This could be done for only a half-day at a time or for a few weeks. It adds some variety to an employee's workday and could increase an employee's sense of accomplishment and responsibility if he or she knows how to do several jobs instead of just one.

The rigidities introduced into the workplace by collective agreements and the merit system can limit the possibility of job rotation. Moving a person into a job temporarily could be seen as giving that person an advantage in any future competition for the job. When people try to perform too many tasks, they might not be properly trained, which could lead to mistakes or even serious accidents. Employees sometimes resist job rotation on the basis that it is no more interesting to do two boring jobs than to do one boring job.

Job enlargement tries to relieve the boredom in a job by expanding the size of the job. Instead of spending all day simply examining and filing forms, an employee might also be responsible for working at a counter and helping members of the public fill out forms. Having broader responsibilities and being able to see more of the total process should increase an employee's sense of belonging and accomplishment.

Job enlargement has been tried in many places and has been quite successful,[39] but, again, bureaucratic rigidities can cause problems. A job description with more duties probably means that the job will receive a higher rate of pay. If this is the case, management will likely resist job enlargement.

Job enrichment or *vertical job loading* is a variant of job enlargement proposed by Hackman and Oldham, Argyris, and Herzberg, among many others. Herzberg, in particular, emphasized the importance of expanding jobs not just by arbitrarily adding more duties but by considering the needs of the mature employee. He pointed out the difference between horizontal job loading, which means simply loading a person with more work, and vertical job loading, which means expanding the job through such means as:[40]

- removing some detailed controls and making the employee more responsible for her or his own work;

- carving out a "natural unit of work" for the person and granting her or him additional responsibility for dealing with all problems in that area; and

- introducing more specialized and difficult tasks.

Herzberg felt that these improvements in the job itself would increase an employee's satisfaction, but other theories argue that more extensive changes in the overall work environment are beneficial.

Expectancy Theory

Expectancy theory was originally developed by Victor Vroom in his 1964 book *Work and Motivation*,[41] and has been developed further by a number of other writers, most notably Edward Lawler and Lyman Porter. It is a fairly complex theory, but it has gained many followers in the last few years and is certainly a very influential theory now.

It is based on four assumptions:[42]

- An individual's behaviour is determined by the interaction of forces in the individual and in the environment.

- While there are some constraints on the behaviour of individuals within organizations, people still have significant scope to make their own decisions. In particular, they make decisions about joining and remaining within an organization, and about the amount of effort they will expend on particular activities.

- Different people have different needs, desires, and goals.

- People choose among alternative behaviours based on their expectations about the behaviour's impact on their ability to satisfy their needs, desires, and goals.

Expectancy theory has its own specialized vocabulary. *First-level outcomes* relate to the performance of the job itself (e.g., completing a report by a deadline). *Second-level outcomes* "are those events (rewards or punishments) that the first-level outcomes are likely to produce, such as merit pay increase, group acceptance or rejection, and promotion."[43] *Instrumentality* is the connection that the employee perceives between the first-order and second-order outcomes. For example, most people like to believe that there is a connection between satisfactory work performance and a positive performance appraisal.

A *valence* is the level of importance that a person attaches to specific first- and second-level outcomes. If an outcome is desired, it is positively valent; if it is not desired, it is negatively valent. Valences also have strengths associated with them to indicate the intensity of the person's feelings.

Figure 5.2 provides an illustration of the relationship between these various elements. An individual's performance will be determined by his or her level of motivation and ability. If a person has a great deal of ability to perform a particular task, then he or she would need little motivation; but a person must have a great deal of motivation to perform a task he or she finds difficult. The amount of motivation that a person will be able to muster will depend on the level of importance that he or she attaches to the first- and second-level outcomes (valences), and his or her perception of the strength of the linkages at points A and B (instrumentality).

This point is illustrated in Figure 5.3. The first-level outcome is the need to complete a report on time even though that will require extra effort. This worker envisions several second-level outcomes flowing from that need. They are arrayed here from the "highly positive" to the "highly negative." Not everyone would have the same list of second-level outcomes and not everyone would order them in the same manner.

There are a number of lessons that managers should learn from expectancy theory. The first is that not all people are motivated by the same factors and not all motivating factors have the same level of influence. Thus, one person will be strongly motivated by a sense of personal accomplishment, whereas someone else might be more interested in the praise of her or his supervisor.

The second lesson for managers is that linkages between performance and first-level outcomes must be clear and attainable. It is very difficult to motivate someone to attain a high level of performance when the first-level outcome is virtually unattainable. Some people attribute the high rate of burnout of social service workers to the fact that they realize very quickly that whatever their level of performance, they will never be able to eliminate various social problems. Maybe people in this line of work need to focus on some more easily attainable first-level outcomes.

The third lesson is that it is important to establish clear linkages between first and second-level outcomes, or, put more simply, *rewards are important*. A person will be highly motivated to produce a first-level outcome (completing a report on time) if it is clearly tied to a desirable second-level outcome (improving the possibility of obtaining a promotion). However, if an organization makes it clear that promotions will be based on seniority, then it is very

Figure 5.2
CONCEPTUAL DEPICTION OF EXPECTANCY THEORY

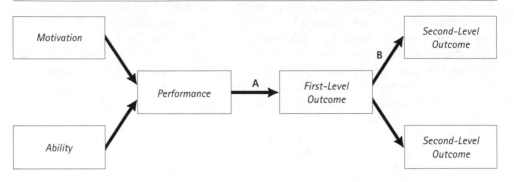

Figure 5.3
REAL-LIFE APPLICATION OF EXPECTANCY THEORY

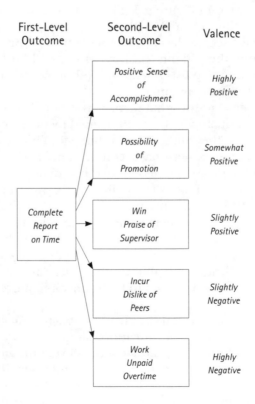

difficult to use promotion as a way to motivate someone to perform well. "Organizations usually get what they reward, not what they want."[44]

Expectancy theory is gaining a great deal of prominence in the literature on organizational behaviour. However, it also has its critics. Admittedly it is a very complex theory to understand and apply. Managers feel more comfortable with the more straightforward theories of Maslow and Herzberg. Some people have suggested that workers are not as coldly rational or as conscious about their motivation as this theory suggests. Most of us have only vague ideas of what really motivates us and some people seem highly motivated to do things that are clearly detrimental to their own welfare (e.g., abuse drugs, go over Niagara Falls in a barrel).

Expectancy theory also seems to pose an impossible task for managers. Is it really possible for a busy manager to understand the desired second-level outcomes of all employees and the valences that they attach to them? In many job situations, responding appropriately would be impossible anyway. The union would certainly frown on reducing someone's pay in exchange for greater praise from superiors, even if that is what the employee wanted.

However, expectancy theory principles cannot, and should not, be applied mechanistically. Maybe it is enough if expectancy theory reminds managers that people respond to different stimuli and that reward systems matter.

One important caveat about all of the theories discussed is that they have focused predominantly on employee motivation. Their only connection with productivity is their implicit assumption that a well-motivated worker will be a more productive worker. While this line of reasoning seems attractive, it is important to remember that it can be contentious. The linkage between a worker's satisfaction and productivity is not clearly established.

Theory Z — Japanese Management

One of the great success stories of recent years has been the performance of the Japanese economy. Japanese companies are both envied and feared by their North American competitors. Japan is a country with virtually no natural resources, but its companies have shown an ability to enter almost any market and produce very high quality products at competitive prices. This success is usually linked to the high productivity of the Japanese worker. This has produced an interest in Japanese management techniques to determine if they can be exported.[45] This section will discuss some of those techniques and some of the impediments to their use in Canada.

Lifetime Employment.   The large firms that employ approximately one-third of the labour force in Japan virtually guarantee lifetime employment to their management workforce. New employees are recruited once each year from that year's crop of university graduates. These people are not recruited to fill specific positions; rather, employers seek to hire a group of employees whose interests and temperament are compatible with the milieu of the firm. In some cases, there might not be a position available immediately for a new recruit, but this is not a concern because it is more important to hire good people for the long run than to fill specific positions in the short run.

After someone is hired, he (even today, Japanese firms tend not to hire women managers[46]) has a virtual guarantee that he will not be laid off or fired for anything short of a criminal offence. This is one of the factors that creates the system of trust on which much of Japanese management is based. William Ouchi points out a number of situations in which managers agree to do things that benefit the firm but leave them very vulnerable personally.[47] Canadian managers would be loathe to put themselves in this position, but in the Japanese system managers trust that their sacrifices for the firm will be remembered and rewarded in the long run. After all, if you know that you will be spending the rest of your working life with a person, it would not do to take advantage in the short term.

The fact that a person has lifetime tenure with an organization does not eliminate any sort of incentive to perform. On the contrary, good performance is very important to attain promotions and to maintain credibility with your life-long peer group.

Nonspecialized Career Paths.   The new recruit embarks on an orientation program that involves rotation through a number of different units in the company. In a Japanese firm, no one spends an entire career specializing in one function; people are systematically rotated through a number of different functions. There is a cost to doing this; Japanese firms do not have people with a high degree of specialization in particular functions. What they have instead is an entire workforce that understands the total operation of the organization, and the problems encountered in other organizational units, and one that is familiar with a great many of the people working in those units. This is another method of engendering the trust mentioned above, as well as of creating a concern for the total company rather than only one portion of it.

Slow Evaluation and Promotion.   After the new employee is hired, he moves through a number of different assignments, usually with progressively more responsibility, but he will not receive a formal evaluation or a promotion until he has been with the firm approximately ten years. This focus on the long term has a number of consequences.

Everyone has heard stories of the dysfunctional corporate "game playing" in Canadian companies—managers play tricks to make themselves look good in the short term and win a promotion. If evaluation is done only after ten years, there is simply no point in this kind of behaviour. Another consequence of this lengthy evaluation is that managers can take the risk of being innovative and experimenting with new ideas; they know that one project gone sour will not destroy a career.

The fact that a person does not receive a formal promotion does not mean that he is not given additional responsibilities. Canadians are sometimes confused in dealing with Japanese firms because titles—which are so important to Canadians—are frequently not commensurate with responsibility in Japanese firms. Promotions, once given, are seldom reversed. Therefore, aspiring senior managers are given great scope for decision making while still at apparently junior levels, in order to test their abilities before they are given the title to go with the responsibility.

Large Bonuses Based on Total Company Performance.   As much as one-third of a Japanese manager's annual pay can come in the form of a bonus. The most significant aspect of the bonus is that all employees receive the same percentage, which is based on *total company performance* and not personal, or even divisional, performance. This is another example of an incentive system that encourages managers to place the performance of the overall company ahead of their own personal good.

Slow, Collective Decision Making.   In Canadian companies, there is frequently a sense of individual responsibility for decisions. Managers take pride in saying: "The buck stops here." The Japanese system requires collective decision making, but a form of collective decision making that goes far beyond the standard prescriptions of participative management discussed in the previous chapter. A small team is assigned to prepare a report; its members must consult widely in the organization. The decision finally made reflects the needs and interests of a broad cross-section of employees. The system works well in Japanese firms because all employees are socialized to have a greater concern for the overall good of the company than for their own unit.

Canadians dealing with Japanese companies are frequently frustrated at the slow pace at which this kind of decision making proceeds. However, the slowness in decision making can be more than offset by the speed of implementation because everyone understands the aims of the decision and is in agreement with it.

A *quality circle* consists of a small group of employees who meet on a *voluntary* basis to discuss work-related concerns. Because of the title, there is usually an incorrect assumption that quality circles are concerned mainly with quality control. The group might discuss work factors that would improve quality control, but this is only one aspect of their concerns. Group discussions could involve "increasing output, improving work procedures, utilizing equipment better, and even improving product design. Quality circles also discuss ways to improve job satisfaction or morale."[48]

Can Theory Z Work in Canada?

Most of the reservations about adopting the Japanese management system in Canada revolve around the belief that it is culture-bound, i.e., it works in Japan because of certain aspects of its culture that are not present elsewhere.[49] For a variety of reasons, Japanese society is considered to be characterized by a high degree of trust among individuals and a concern for the collective good that does not seem to exist in other societies.[50] This is reflected in management techniques. The Japanese management system built on trust contrasts sharply with the Canadian one built on elaborate labour laws and collective agreements. Ouchi suggests that these obstacles can be overcome, but the distance to be traversed by labour and management is significant.

Certain aspects of the Japanese system might not sit well with other aspects of the Canadian value system. By Canadian standards, the Japanese system could be considered frankly exploitative. It works well for shareholders and, to a lesser extent, for (predominantly male) managers. It does not work so well for others. The fact that managers receive such a large portion of their incomes in the form of a bonus gives the company a nice cushion in difficult times. Bonuses are reduced so that managers, not shareholders, bear the risks. However, the male managers fare better than the female operating employees. The lifetime guarantee of employment security applies only to managers; operating employees are laid off and recalled very quickly in response to market demands.

The utility of quality circles in the North American context has also been questioned. The fact that they are based on Japanese systems of management means that they face the same cultural obstacles discussed above.[51] A review of the literature evaluating quality circles indicates that in many cases they have not improved the work environment.[52]

The Japanese system has worked very well—in Japan. There is also evidence that some of the best-managed American companies have adopted some of its ideas.[53] Canadians would be foolish not to examine it and consider the lessons it holds. However, it can be very difficult to adapt motivational techniques from other societies. It could well be that there are lessons to be learned from experiences closer to home.

Empowerment

One of the latest innovations in management techniques in Canada is empowerment. The term is used with varying degrees of specificity. At its broadest level, it can be viewed as a growing phenomenon involving demands by people all over the world to be recognized, consulted, and valued. It is also used more narrowly to describe a range of efforts to enhance the power and the efficacy of individuals, groups, and organizations in society. For example, it has been used since the 1960s by social activists seeking to enhance the political and personal power of members of disadvantaged groups, such as the poor and visible minorities. In this chapter, empowerment is used in the still narrower context of organization and management.

In the spheres of organization and management, empowerment has both external and internal dimensions. The external dimension involves an organization's efforts to empower its clients and customers[54] by involving them in its decision-making process. In the public sector, this involvement can be pursued through such means as partnership arrangements and various forms of community and client involvement. For example, in 1990 the Ontario Ministry of Natural Resources invited—and accepted—from local residents a strategy that turned a problematic waste disposal site into a model site and saved public money.[55] A side effect was the creation by local citizens of a group to organize a recycling program. This external aspect of empowerment is similar to higher-level forms of citizen participation, in which citizens exercise real power rather than being manipulated or being involved in merely token participation. While this chapter focuses on the *internal* dimensions of empowerment, it must be recognized that empowering individuals within organizations, especially those closest to the clients, is likely to lead to a greater measure of external empowerment.

The concept of empowerment, as it applies to managers and employees *inside* organizations, is a synthesis of several theories and practices in organizational behaviour and human resource management. It has been influenced by theories and techniques in such areas as participative management, quality circles, job enrichment, training, organizational design, and leadership, and it is closely related to the organizational development (OD) movement. There are obvious links between empowerment and such earlier innovations and emphases as Management by Objectives (MBO), Theory Z management, the search for excellence, and strategic planning. The newness of the concept of empowerment lies not in its component parts, but in the combination of its parts. The importance of the concept lies in large part in its integral relationship with the broad management movement known as total or service quality.

Even in the specific context of organization and management, empowerment is interpreted in different ways. For many managers and management theorists, it simply means the delegation of power to subordinates. To others, it is a more complicated concept that goes beyond delegation to the *enabling* of employees. To enable employees is to bring about conditions that will enhance their belief in their personal efficacy. Empowerment in this sense is "a process of enhancing feelings of self-efficacy among organizational members through the identification of conditions that foster powerlessness and through their removal by both formal organizational practices and informal techniques of providing efficacy information."[56]

The distinction between the concepts of delegation and empowerment was captured well by the Public Service 2000 Task Force on Service to the Public.

> In a command and control management culture, delegation is usually understood to involve handing over tasks to employees who follow guidelines, avoid taking risks and who carry out duties in traditional, sanctioned ways. Empowerment, by contrast, encourages managers, supervisors and employees to try new ways of achieving goals, motivating them to be creative and innovative in improving the service they deliver. Empowerment asks employees to assume responsibility for change and to be accountable for their actions within an environment which accepts a degree of risk-taking and acknowledges intent as well as results.[57]

Empowerment is not concerned with how managers can get employees to act as managers would like them to act; rather, it is concerned with what managers can do to foster individual and collective action by employees to the benefit of the organization, its managers, and its employees. The objective is to make the best possible use of the employees' knowledge and skills.

A critical aspect of empowerment is that it increases power in the organization by encouraging employees to share and work together.

It is an interactive process based on a synergistic, not zero-sum, assumption about power; that is, the process of empowerment enlarges the power in the situation as opposed to merely redistributing it....

Whereas most experts define power as A's ability to control or change B's *behavior*, the concept of empowerment implies that A can influence or affect B so that A and B's interaction produces more power or influence for both of them.[58]

An empowered organization has the following characteristics:

- Management uses innovative, effective approaches to increase employee involvement and teamwork; a high level of trust and respect exists between and among managers and employees.

- Cross-functional team cooperation occurs across the organization to meet customer/client needs more effectively.

- Trends toward team participation and other forms of employee participation include more employee suggestions being made and accepted.

- Employees have a strong feeling of empowerment; there is team ownership of work processes, employees exhibit personal pride in the quality of work, and union and management cooperate to achieve quality improvement.

- Power, rewards, information, and knowledge are moved to the lowest feasible levels; employee empowerment leads to substantial flattening of the organization.

- Improvements resulting from employee participation are clearly evident in systems, processes, products, and services.

- A regular formal survey process determines levels of employee satisfaction, follow-up actions are taken to improve human resource practices, and future plans address how to sustain momentum and enthusiasm.[59]

An empowered organizations is characterized not only by active employee participation, but also by team participation. Team-building initiatives can range from broad efforts to create a general commitment to working together, by such means as participative management, collegial decision making, and effective internal communications, to organizational restructuring based on the pervasive use of empowered workteams. These workteams are the most significant structural innovation in empowered organizations. "Quality teams, whether they are part of the formal organizational structure or temporary, are at *the heart of empowerment.*"[60]

An empowered workteam, often referred to as a self-managed or self-directed workteam, refers to a group of employees who come together, often on a voluntary basis, to work to improve the organization, both for their clients and for themselves. B.C. Hydro's strategy for empowered workteams is "to create a climate in which teams feel and use the freedom to act to achieve their goals in support of the corporate mission, objectives and climate goals."[61] These workteams are given decision making authority and resources and their manager alters her or his role from decision maker/controller to facilitator/coach. The arguments for empowering workteams are similar to those for empowering individuals, but team decision making has the added benefit of enhancing the quality of decisions by using the synergy created by people working together on a common problem. Empowered workteams can also provide a valuable mechanism for helping the organization to empower individuals.

Introducing empowerment in the workplace is a radical change. There are many obstacles to the introduction of a concept that involves such a basic change in organizational culture in most traditional organizations. The problems are particularly difficult in government organizations where long-standing conventions of ministerial responsibility and deeply ingrained ideas of agency control make the idea of workers making their own decisions and taking risks very problematic.[62]

At this point, empowerment is one of the latest management buzzwords. A relatively limited number of organizations have actually implemented it properly. In some cases, senior managers have been accused of using the word in a very hollow fashion in order to force more responsibilities on lower-level employees. The jury is still out on whether empowerment will actually catch on and produce a radical change in management style or whether it will be just another passing fancy.

🏛 THE CURRENT STATE OF COMMUNICATION, LEADERSHIP, AND MOTIVATION IN THE CANADIAN PUBLIC SERVICE

The general thrust of the theories of motivation discussed in this chapter is the need for better communication strategies and greater flexibility in leadership styles, organizational structures, and job design. There is substantial evidence that improved communication and more flexibility are highly conducive to achieving worker satisfaction, and there is weaker evidence that worker satisfaction is related to organizational effectiveness.

How do Canadian governments rate in terms of their use of the techniques mentioned in this chapter? The answer is mixed. Many governments are trying to improve communication and introduce the flexibility prescribed by most of the theories discussed, but the obstacles facing them are great. This does not bode well for attempts at job redesign, situational approaches to leadership, total quality management, or empowerment.

There is little hard evidence on this point, but there is a general feeling that morale has declined in most public service organizations in the last few years. One reason is the resource constraints that most of these organizations are facing, but the major reason is probably that public servants see the general public (including, in some cases, their political masters) engaging in an orgy of bureaucrat bashing.[63] At a time when public servants are being asked to do more with less, they are criticized for being excessively wasteful. At a time when public servants are being forced to cope with rapid changes, both within the public service and in the broader environment, they are criticized for being rigid and inflexible. At a time when public servants are being fired or laid off, they are criticized for having cushy, permanent sinecures. These events have an obvious impact on morale.

John L. Manion, a longtime public servant and astute observer of the Ottawa scene, summed up the situation this way:

> [I]f our public services are *perceived* to be second-rate at home, unfortunately they will become second-rate. We cannot continue to maintain the quality of the public service if we cannot continue to attract the best young Canadians to our ranks. *They will not devote their lives to serving people who demean them.*[64]

Two academics from the University of Ottawa, David Zussman and Jak Jabes, have done extensive surveys of senior managers in the federal government and compared their attitudes to senior managers in the private sector.[65] They do not paint a very positive picture of communication, leadership, or employee satisfaction[66] in the federal public service. Their book caused quite a stir in Ottawa when it was published because it clearly documented a malaise of which most people had been only dimly aware.

Their most significant finding is embodied in the title of their book—*The Vertical Solitude.* They found that there was no organizational culture or organizational perspective that was widely held, even among the senior managers within the service. By extension, if even the small cadre of senior managers do not possess a similar organizational view, then what hope is there for the large number of lower-level employees who receive their organizational culture through senior managers?

It is impossible to do justice to Zussman and Jabes' excellent work in a short summary, but a few quotations capture some of their findings. About communication:

> There appears to be a serious breakdown in the communication flow between the executive ranks and the managerial cadre in the federal public service. This breakdown suggests that it is unlikely that public servants working below the managerial level, and who are in constant contact with the public and client groups, will develop a valid understanding of the expectations of their ministers and the other people who set the tone and direction of their departments.[67]

About leadership:

> Comparing perceived leadership behaviour in the private and public sectors, we were struck by differences in perceived instances of leadership in the two sectors ... With regard to DM/CEO leadership, more than 80 per cent of private sector respondents reported that their most senior officer demonstrated leadership to a great or very great extent. The comparable figure for public sector managers was 51 per cent.[68]

About worker attitudes:

> We found, within the public service management cadre, divergent views among the five managerial levels with regard to almost all managerial practices. The differences were almost always dependent on where one worked in the management structure. This effect, which we have called "the vertical solitude", [sic] suggests that, as one moves down the bureaucratic hierarchy, managers are less satisfied and

less positive about managerial practices in their organization. As a counterpoint, we did not find this effect to any significant degree in the private sector.

> The data also revealed that levels of work satisfaction among the [lower levels of senior management] ... were substantially lower than those of their private sector counterparts and, in our opinion, were too low for managers occupying such pivotal positions in the organization.[69]

Given these negative findings, this comment that reflects on the morale of senior managers should not be surprising:

> Few managers in the private sector are contemplating career moves out of the private sector, whereas close to one-half of the most senior managers in the public service of Canada show a keen interest in working for the private sector.[70]

In fairness to governments, they face certain environmental constraints not present in the private sector. The most significant of these is the comparative openness of government. This openness makes governments hypersensitive about failure and gaps in their systems of control, since government failures are so public and are handled so brutally by the media. This sensitivity influences many characteristics of government organization. It creates a bias for *inaction* and constant study, and it gravitates away from autonomy and toward strong central control agencies. Because of government's basic concern about failure, it would be very difficult to establish management systems that provide for true employee participation and empowerment.

We should not conclude on a totally negative note. There seems to be a clear understanding that there is a problem, and there have been some attempts at correcting it by employing such techniques as empowerment.[71] Whatever problems our public service might be experiencing now, it is widely recognized on the international scene that Canada has a very high-quality and professional public service. This is clear from the requests that come from other countries for Canada's advice on issues in public administration. It is also clear to any Canadian who participates in international public administration associations. There are some initiatives, such as La Relève (discussed later in this book), that are system-wide attempts to show greater concern for motivation of employees. There are also many bright spots in government departments where individual managers have realized the importance of improving the system. It will be interesting to see how these initiatives fare in the face of a very long history of inflexibility.

NOTES

1. Robert D. Pursley and Neil Snortland, *Managing Government Organizations: An Introduction to Public Administration* (North Scituate, Mass.: Duxbury Press, 1980), 218.
2. Eugene Walton, "How Efficient Is the Grapevine?" *Personnel* 38 (March–April 1961): 45.
3. David Halberstam, *The Best and the Brightest* (Greenwich, Conn.: Fawcett, 1973), 771.
4. Tom Peters and Nancy Austin, *A Passion for Excellence: The Leadership Difference* (New York: Random House, 1985), ch. 2 and passim.
5. Ibid., 228–29.

6. Felix A. Nigro, *Modern Public Administration* (New York: Harper & Row, 1965), 197.

7. Henri Fayol, *General and Industrial Management*, trans. Constance Storrs (London: Pitman, 1971), 35–36.

8. Andrew Dunsire, *Implementation in a Bureaucracy* (Oxford: Martin Robertson, 1978), 176.

9. Daniel Katz and Robert L. Kahn, *The Social Psychology of Organizations*, 2nd. ed. (New York: John Wiley & Sons, 1978), 528.

10. Pursley and Snortland, *Managing Government Organizations*, 186. Reprinted by permission of Wadsworth Publishing Co.

11. D. Brian Marson has identified the characteristics necessary in a leader who is a catalyst for strategic change. D. Brian Marson, "Leading Strategic Change in the Public Sector," *The Public Manager*, (winter 1997-98), 6, 27–30.

12. Ralph M. Stogdill, *Handbook of Leadership: A Survey of Theory and Research* (New York: The Free Press, 1974), ch. 2.

13. Ibid., ch. 5.

14. Dorwin Cartwright and Alvin Zander, "Leadership and Performance of Group Functions: Introduction," in Dorwin Cartwright and Alvin Zander, eds., *Group Dynamics: Research and Theory*, 3rd ed. (New York: Harper & Row, 1968), 303; Gary A. Yukl, *Leadership in Organizations*, 2nd. ed. (Englewood Cliffs, N.J.: Prentice-Hall, 1989), 202.

15. Stogdill, *Handbook of Leadership*, 81.

16. Richard A. Boyatzis, *The Competent Manager: A Model for Effective Performance* (New York: John Wiley & Sons, 1982), 229.

17. Robert L. Katz, "Skills of an Effective Administrator," *Harvard Business Review* 33 (January–February 1955): 34.

18. Ibid. (Emphasis in original.)

19. Ibid., 35–36.

20. These depictions of the styles come from one of the earliest studies: Ronald Lippitt and Ralph K. White, "The 'Social Climate' of Children's Groups," in Robert G. Barker, Jacob S. Kounin, and Herbert F. Wright, eds., *Child Behavior and Development: A Course of Representative Study* (New York: McGraw-Hill, 1943), 485–508. See also the more widely cited Ralph K. White and Ronald Lippitt, *Autocracy and Democracy* (Westport, Conn.: Greenwood Press, 1972), 26–27.

21. Stogdill, *Handbook of Leadership*, ch. 32.

22. A good review of these different approaches is contained in J. D. Williams, *Public Administration: The People's Business* (Boston: Little, Brown, 1980), 147–48; Richard H. Hall, *Organizations: Structure and Process*, 3rd ed. (Englewood Cliffs, N.J.: Prentice-Hall, 1982), 163–66; Alan C. Filley and Robert J. House, *Managerial Process and Organizational Behavior* (Glenview, Ill.: Scott, Foresman and Company, 1969), 401–405. Some of the specific studies that support this view are Fred E. Fiedler, "Personality and Situational Determinants of Leadership Effectiveness," in Cartwright and Zander, eds., *Group Dynamics*, 3rd ed. (New York: Harper & Row, 1968); 362–80; and Kurt Lewin, Ronald Lippitt, and Ralph K. White, "Patterns of Aggressive Behaviour in Experimentally Created 'Social Climates,'" *Journal of Social Psychology* 10 (1939): 273.

23. A good review of the best-known theories is found in Yukl, *Leadership in Organizations*, ch. 6.

24. Victor H. Vroom and Philip W. Yetton, *Leadership and Decision Making* (Pittsburgh: University of Pittsburgh Press, 1973). The Vroom-Yetton model has been criticized and extended by Vroom and Arthur G. Jago. This model will not be discussed here because it is even more complex than Vroom and Yetton's original work, and the recent publication of the Vroom-Jago work means that it has not yet been subjected to serious review. *The New Leadership: Managing Participation in Organizations* (Englewood Cliffs, N.J.: Prentice-Hall, 1988).

25. Vroom and Yetton, *Leadership and Decision Making*, 21–31.

26. Leonard R. Sayles and George Strauss, *Managing Human Resources* (Englewood Cliffs, N.J.: Prentice-Hall, 1977), 132.

27. Chris Argyris, *Personality and Organization: The Conflict Between System and the Individual* (New York: Harper & Row, 1957), 50–51.

28. Ibid., ch. 3.

29. Ibid., 66.

30. Ibid., ch. 4.

31. Chris Argyris, *Integrating the Individual and the Organization* (New York: John Wiley & Sons, 1964).

32. Ibid., 275.

33. Robert Prethus, *The Organizational Society*, rev. ed. (New York: St. Martin's Press, 1978).

34. Henry Mintzberg, *Structure in Fives: Designing Effective Organizations* (Englewood Cliffs, N.J.: Prentice-Hall, 1983), 178–79.

35. The results of this research were reported in detail in Frederick Herzberg, Bernard Mausner, and Barbara Bloch Snyderman, *The Motivation to Work* (New York: John Wiley & Sons, 1959). A more elaborate discussion and further verification of the theory is contained in Frederick Herzberg, *Work and the Nature of Man* (Cleveland: The World Publishing Company, 1966).

36. Herzberg et al., *The Motivation to Work*, 113.

37. J. Richard Hackman and Greg R. Oldham, *Work Redesign* (Reading, Mass.: Addison-Wesley, 1980), ch. 2.

38. Ibid., 71.

39. Roy W. Walters, "Job Enrichment Isn't Easy," *Personnel Administration Review* (September–October 1972).

40. Frederick Herzberg, "One More Time: How Do You Motivate Employees?" *Harvard Business Review* 46 (January–February 1968): 59–62.

41. Victor Vroom, *Work and Motivation* (New York: John Wiley & Sons, 1964).

42. David A. Nadler and Edward E. Lawler, III, "Motivation: A Diagnostic Approach," in Patrick E. Connor, ed., *Organizations: Theory and Design* (Chicago: Science Research Associates, 1980), 212–13.

43. James L. Gibson, John M. Ivancevich, and James H. Donnelly, Jr., *Organizations: Behavior, Structure, Processes* (Plano, Tex.: Business Publications, 1985), 155.

44. Nadler and Lawler, "Motivation: A Diagnostic Approach," 216.

45. Most of the following commentary is derived from one of the most prolific writers on Theory Z: William G. Ouchi, *Theory Z: How American Business Can Meet the Japanese Challenge* (New York: Avon Books, 1981).

46. Ibid., 21.

47. Ibid., 5, 16–17, 40.

48. Jan P. Muczyk, Eleanor Brantley Schwartz, and Ephraim Smith, *Principles of Supervision: First- and Second-Line Management* (Columbus, Ohio: Charles E. Merrill, 1984), 206. See also Richard J. Schonberger, *Japanese Manufacturing Techniques* (New York: The Free Press, 1982), ch. 8; Edward E. Lawler, III, *High-Involvement Management* (San Francisco: Jossey-Bass Publishers, 1986).

49. Sandford F. Borins, "Management of the Public Sector in Japan," *Canadian Public Administration* 29, no. 2 (summer 1986): 175–96; Ouchi, *Theory Z*, 54–57.

50. S. Prakash Sethi, Nobuaki Namiki, and Carl L. Swanson, *The False Promise of the Japanese Miracle* (Boston: Pitman, 1984).

51. Gerald R. Ferris and John A. Wagner, III, "Quality Circles in the United States: A Conceptual Reevaluation," *The Journal of Applied Behavioral Science* 21, no. 2 (1985): 155–67.

52. Robert P. Steel and Gary S. Shane, "Evaluation Research on Quality Circles: Technical and Analytical Implications," *Human Relations* 39, no. 5 (1986): 449–68.

53. Ouchi, *Theory Z*, 57–59.

54. While the term "customers" is increasingly used in the public sector to emphasize the importance of service to the public, the more conventional term "clients" is used in this chapter.
55. Sharon B. Robbins, "Partnership, Politics and Public Administration: A Case Study of the Ontario Ministry of Natural Resources," Master's thesis (Brock University, 1994).
56. Jay A. Conger and Rabindra N. Kanungo, "The Empowerment Process: Integrating Theory and Practice," *Academy of Management Review* 13 (1988), 474.
57. Public Service 2000, *Service to the Public Task Force* (Ottawa: Privy Council Office, 1990), 51–2.
58. Judith F. Vogt and Kenneth L. Murrell, *Empowerment in Organizations* (San Diego: Pfeiffer & Company, 1990), 8–9.
59. Adapted from Federal Quality Institute, *Criteria and Scoring Guidelines for the President's Award for Quality and Productivity Improvement*, Federal Total Quality Management Handbook, June 1990, 24, 26–7.
60. Vogt and Murrell, *Empowerment in Organizations*, 96. (Emphasis added.)
61. Interview with Bruce Young, Manager, Team Effectiveness, B.C. Hydro, 27 August 1991.
62. Kenneth Kernaghan, "Empowerment and Public Administration: Revolutionary Advance or Passing Fancy?" *Canadian Public Administration*, vol. 35, no. 2 (summer 1992), 205–13.
63. The reaction of some public servants to the bureaucrat bashing is described in: Barbara Wake Carroll and David Siegel, *Service in the Field: The World of Front-Line Public Servants* (Montreal: McGill-Queen's University Press, 1999), ch. 8.
64. John L. Manion "New Challenges in Public Administration," *Canadian Public Administration* 31, no. 2 (summer 1988): 237. (Emphasis in last sentence added.)
65. David Zussman and Jak Jabes, *The Vertical Solitude: Managing in the Public Sector* (Halifax: The Institute for Research on Public Policy, 1989).
66. Zussman and Jabes were measuring "employee satisfaction" rather than motivation. The concepts are not identical, although they are closely related.
67. Ibid., 3.
68. Ibid., 62–63.
69. Ibid., 196.
70. Ibid., 128.
71. Government of Canada, Human Resources Development Council, *Strategies for People: An Integrated Approach to Changing Public Service Culture* (Treasury Board Secretariat, 1992).

BIBLIOGRAPHY

Argyris, Chris. *Personality and Organization: The Conflict Between System and the Individual.* New York: Harper & Row, 1957.

———. *Integrating the Individual and the Organization.* New York: John Wiley & Sons, 1964.

Argyris, Chris, with Roger Harrison. *Interpersonal Competence and Organizational Effectiveness.* Homewood, Ill.: Richard D. Irwin, 1962.

Blau, Peter M., and W. Richard Scott. *Formal Organizations: A Comparative Approach.* San Francisco: Chandler, 1962.

Borins, Sandford F. "Management of the Public Sector in Japan." *Canadian Public Administration* 29, no. 2 (summer 1986): 175–96.

Boyatzis, Richard A. *The Competent Manager: A Model for Effective Performance.* New York: John Wiley & Sons, 1982.

Cartwright, Dorwin, and Alvin Zander, eds. *Group Dynamics: Research and Theory.* 3rd ed. New York: Harper & Row, 1968.

Cohen, Michael D., James G. March, and Johan P. Olson. "A Garbage Can Model of Organizational Choice," *Administrative Science Quarterly* 17, no. 1 (March 1972): 1–25.

Conger, Jay A., and Rabindra N. Kanungo. "The Empowerment Process: Integrating Theory and Practice." *Academy of Management Review* 13 (1988): 471–82.

Cunningham, J.B., and T.H. White, eds. *Quality of Working Life: Contemporary Cases.* Ottawa: Minister of Supply and Services Canada, 1984.

Dubin, Robert, George C. Homans, Floyd C. Mann, and Delbert C. Miller. *Leadership and Productivity.* San Francisco: Chandler, 1965.

Dunsire, Andrew. *Implementation in a Bureaucracy.* Oxford: Martin Robertson, 1978.

Fayol, Henri. *General and Industrial Management.* Translated from the French by Constance Storrs. London: Pitman, 1971.

Federal Quality Institute. *Criteria and Scoring Guidelines for the President's Award for Quality and Productivity Improvement.* Federal Total Quality Management Handbook, June 1990.

Ferris, Gerald R., and John A. Wagner, III. "Quality Circles in the United States: A Conceptual Reevaluation." *The Journal of Applied Behavioral Science* 21, no. 2 (1985): 155–167.

Fiedler, Fred A. *A Theory of Leadership Effectiveness.* New York: McGraw-Hill, 1967.

Fiedler, Fred A., Martin M. Chemers, with Linda Mahar. *Improving Leadership Effectiveness: The Leader Match Concept.* Rev. ed. New York: John Wiley & Sons, 1977.

Filley, Alan C., and Robert J. House. *Managerial Process and Organizational Behavior.* Glenview, Ill.: Scott, Foresman, 1969.

Gibson, James L., John M. Ivancevich, and James H. Donnelly, Jr. *Organizations: Behavior, Structure, Processes.* Plano, Tex.: Business Publications, 1985.

Government of Canada, Human Resources Development Council. *Strategies for People: An Integrated Approach to Changing Public Service Culture.* Treasury Board Secretariat, 1992.

Hackman, J. Richard, and Greg R. Oldham. *Work Redesign.* Reading, Mass.: Addison-Wesley, 1980.

Hall, Richard H. *Organizations: Structure and Process.* 3rd ed. Englewood Cliffs, N. J.: Prentice-Hall, 1982.

Heffron, Florence. *Organization Theory and Public Organizations: The Political Connection.* Englewood Cliffs, N.J.: Prentice-Hall, 1989.

Hersey, Paul, and Kenneth H. Blanchard. *Management of Organizational Behavior: Utilizing Human Resources.* 3rd ed. Englewood Cliffs, N.J.: Prentice-Hall, 1977.

Herzberg, Frederick. *Work and the Nature of Man.* Cleveland, Ohio: The World Publishing Company, 1966.

———. "One More Time: How Do You Motivate Employees?" *Harvard Business Review* 46 (January–February 1968): 53–62.

Herzberg, Frederick, Bernard Mausner, and Barbara Bloch Snyderman. *The Motivation to Work.* New York: John Wiley & Sons, 1959.

Huck, James R. "Assessment Centres: A Review of the External and Internal Validities." *Personnel Psychology* 26 (summer 1973): 191–212.

Johnston, Carl P., Mark Alexander, and Jacquelin Robin. *Quality of Working Life: The Idea and its Application.* Ottawa: Minister of Supply and Services Canada, 1980.

Katz, Robert L. "Skills of an Effective Administrator." *Harvard Business Review* 33 (January–February 1955): 33–42.

Katz, Daniel, and Robert L. Kahn. *The Social Psychology of Organizations.* 2nd ed. New York: John Wiley & Sons, 1978.

Kernaghan, Kenneth. "Empowerment and Public Administration: Revolutionary Advance or Passing Fancy?" *Canadian Public Administration* 35, no. 2 (summer 1992): 194–214.

Lewin, Kurt, Ronald Lippitt, and Ralph K. White. "Patterns of Aggressive Behavior in Experimentally Created Social Climates." *Journal of Social Psychology* 10 (1939): 271–99.

Likert, Rensis. *New Patterns of Management.* New York: McGraw-Hill, 1961.

————. *The Human Organization.* New York: McGraw-Hill, 1967.

Lippitt, Ronald, and Ralph K. White. "The 'Social Climate' of Children's Groups." In Robert G. Barker, Jacob S. Kounin, and Herbert F. Wright, eds., *Child Behavior and Development: A Course of Representative Study.* New York: McGraw Hill, 1943, 485–508.

Manion, John L. "New Challenges in Public Administration," *Canadian Public Administration* 31, no. 2 (summer 1988): 234–46.

Marson, D. Brian. "Leading Strategic Change in the Public Sector." *The Public Manager* (winter 1997–98): 6, 27–30.

Mintzberg, Henry. *Structure in Fives: Designing Effective Organizations.* Englewood Cliffs, N.J.: Prentice-Hall, 1983.

Muczyk, Jan P., Eleanor Brantley Schwartz, and Ephraim Smith. *Principles of Supervision: First- and Second-Line Management.* Columbus, Ohio: Charles E. Merrill, 1984.

Nadler, David A., and Edward E. Lawler, III. "Motivation: A Diagnostic Approach." In Patrick E. Connor, ed., *Organizations: Theory and Design.* Chicago: Science Research Associates, Inc., 1980, pp. 212–18.

Nigro, Felix A. *Modern Public Administration.* New York: Harper & Row, 1965.

Ondrak, D.A., and M.G. Evans. *Quality of Working Life: Evaluation and Measurement.* Ottawa: Minister of Supply and Services Canada, 1981.

Ouchi, William G. *Theory Z: How American Business Can Meet the Japanese Challenge.* New York: Avon Books, 1981.

Peters, Thomas, and Robert H. Waverman, Jr. *In Search of Excellence.* New York: Warner Books, 1982.

Peters, Tom, and Nancy Austin. *A Passion for Excellence: The Leadership Difference.* New York: Random House, 1985.

Presthus, Robert. *The Organizational Society.* Rev. ed. New York: St. Martin's Press, 1978.

Public Service 2000. *Service to the Public Task Force.* Ottawa: Privy Council Office, 1990.

Pursley, Robert D., and Neil Snortland. *Managing Government Organizations: An Introduction to Public Administration.* North Scituate, Mass.: Duxbury Press, 1980.

Quality of Working Life: The Canadian Scene. (A periodical published by the federal Department of Labour from 1978 to 1986.)

Robbins, Sharon B. "Partnership, Politics and Public Administration: A Case Study of the Ontario Ministry of Natural Resources." Master's thesis, Brock University, 1994.

Sayles, Leonard R., and George Strauss. *Managing Human Resources.* Englewood Cliffs, N.J.: Prentice-Hall, 1977.

Schonberger, Richard J. *Japanese Manufacturing Techniques.* New York: The Free Press, 1982.

Scott, William G., Terence R. Mitchell, and Philip H. Birnbaum. *Organization Theory: A Structural and Behavioral Analysis.* 4th ed. Homewood, Ill.: Richard D. Irwin, 1981.

Sethi, S. Prakash, Nobuaki Namiki, and Carl L. Swanson. *The False Promise of the Japanese Miracle.* Boston: Pitman, 1984.

Steel, Robert P., and Gary S. Shane. "Evaluation Research on Quality Circles: Technical and Analytical Implications." *Human Relations* 39, no. 5 (1986): 449–68.

Stein, Barry A. *Quality of Work Life In Action: Managing for Effectiveness.* New York: American Management Association, 1983.

Stogdill, Ralph M. *Handbook of Leadership: A Survey of Theory and Research.* New York: The Free Press, 1974.

Tannenbaum, Robert T., and Warren H. Schmidt. "How to Choose a Leadership Style." *Harvard Business Review* 36 (March–April, 1958): 95–101.

Vogt, Judith, and Kenneth Murrell. *Empowerment in Organizations.* San Diego: University Associates, 1990.

Vroom, Victor H., and Arthur G. Jago. *The New Leadership: Managing Participation in Organizations.* Englewood Cliffs, N.J.: Prentice-Hall, 1988.

Vroom, Victor H., and Philip W. Yetton. *Leadership and Decision Making*. Pittsburgh: University of Pittsburgh Press, 1973.

Walters, Roy W. "Job Enrichment Isn't Easy." *Personnel Administration Review* (September–October 1972): 61–66.

Walton, Eugene. "How Efficient Is the Grapevine?" *Personnel* 38 (March–April 1961): 45–49.

White, Ralph K., and Ronald Lippitt. *Autocracy and Democracy*. Westport, Conn.: Greenwood Press, 1972.

Williams, J.D. *Public Administration: The People's Business*. Boston: Little, Brown, 1980.

Yukl, Gary A. *Leadership In Organizations*. 2nd ed. Englewood Cliffs, N.J.: Prentice-Hall, 1989.

Zussman, David, and Jak Jabes. *The Vertical Solitude: Managing in the Public Sector*. Halifax: The Institute for Research on Public Policy, 1989.

I I

The Policy Dimension of
Public Administration

6

Making Public Policy

Two people in a bar are having an animated discussion on the day after the election.

> **Chris:** I'm glad to see that the people finally came to their senses and threw out the old government. This new party has all sorts of really good ideas. They'll change all the old policies and it will make a real difference.

> **Pat:** Don't hold your breath. We see this all the time. A new broom sweeps out the old party with lots of plans for change, then nothing happens. Six months later the new party is doing everything the previous bunch was.

> **Chris:** No, no! You watch; this time it's going to be different.

> **Pat:** No, it won't. First of all, it takes forever to get agreement on changes. They'll appoint a Royal commission, then they'll produce a green paper and consult with interest groups, then they'll produce a white paper. And, of course, the whole time they're doing this, they have to remember that Canada is part of a global system. We can't do anything so extreme that it offends the international bankers. My guess is that by the time the whole process is finished, they will have wasted huge amounts of time to produce a policy which is only very slightly different from the status quo.

> **Chris:** Well, now that you mention it, there does seem to be some truth in what you're saying. We've had parties come to power before with great ideas for changing things, but nothing happens. I wish I understood why it's so difficult to change government policies.

This part of the book will examine the entire policy cycle. This chapter will examine a number of theories about how government policies are made and discuss several important instruments of policy making, such as Royal commissions, task forces, and coloured papers. Chapter 7 will discuss two relatively new areas of study in public administration—policy implementation and program evaluation.

In the past, the area of policy implementation was given very little attention because there seemed to be an assumption that once policy was articulated, implementation was automatic, with little friction or tension. In the last decade, there has been a growing awareness that the relationship between making and implementing policy is not always so smooth. There has also been greater concern in recent years about the systematic evaluation of public policy. Has the policy had the desired effect? Has it been worth the resources that have been spent to implement it? Program evaluation attempts to answer these questions.

Figure 6.1 illustrates one view of the total policy cycle. The first step is policy formulation. The cabinet and the legislature are dominant in this part of the process, but the public service also has an important advisory role. The next step is implementation. In this part of the process, the public service has the dominant role, but cabinet and the legislature have an important oversight role. The final step is evaluating the ultimate worth of the policy. This evaluation can be formal, employing sophisticated social science techniques, or it can be as informal as legislators responding to complaints of citizens.

Figure 6.1 conveys the impression that these three steps are totally separate and discrete processes. Figure 6.2 conveys a more realistic impression of the policy cycle as a dynamic process with a considerable degree of overlap between the three stages in the process. As will be discussed in this and the following chapter, implementation frequently begins before policies are firmly established, and evaluation frequently leads to changes in policies. In practice, policies are seldom carved in stone. Policies are always being revised. Most policies are subject to extensive revisions every few years as a result of major studies or initiatives, and to minor fine-tuning even more frequently.

🏛 WHAT IS PUBLIC POLICY?

There are a number of definitions of the term *public policy*. This book will use Thomas R. Dye's simple yet effective definition that "[p]ublic policy is whatever governments choose to do or not to do."[1] He explains that

Figure 6.1
SIMPLIFIED VERSION OF THE POLICY PROCESS

Figure 6.2
MORE REALISTIC VERSION OF THE POLICY PROCESS

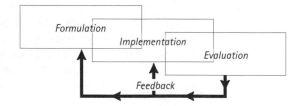

[g]overnments do many things. They regulate conflict within society; they organize society to carry on conflict with other societies; they distribute a great variety of symbolic rewards and material services to members of the society; and they extract money from society, most often in the form of taxes. Thus, public policies may regulate behavior, organize bureaucracies, distribute benefits, or extract taxes—or all of these things at once....

Public policies may deal with a wide variety of substantive areas—defense, energy, environment, foreign affairs, education, welfare, police, highways, taxation, housing, social security, health, economic opportunity, urban development, inflation and recession, and so on. They may range from the vital to the trivial—from the allocation of tens of billions of dollars for a mobile missile system to the designation of an official national bird.[2]

Several aspects of this definition are important. First, unlike some other definitions of public policy, there is no discussion of "goals" or "objectives." Policies are specific courses of action; the adoption of a policy does not imply that all those who agree on a specific policy share the same goals. In fact, some policies come about not because of an agreement on goals, but because several groups all favour a particular policy, although for totally different reasons. This phenomenon will be discussed in more detail later.

Second, Dye's definition recognizes that policies are reflected in choosing *not* to act, as well as in choosing to act. These "non-decisions" can be as important as decisions, especially for groups attempting to effect change. For example, the federal government has been discussing the need for universal day care for a number of years, but at this point the government's policy on this issue is to not have a policy. This is profoundly important for those interested in this service.

The other point about public policy that will be emphasized in this book is that policy is not merely a *statement* by a government about some problem; policy is also what actually *happens*. Thus, Dye's definition refers to what governments "do," not what they say they want to do or plan to do. Peter Aucoin takes this into account in his definition of public policy: "Public policy must be considered to encompass the actual activities undertaken by a government, whether or not a government's objectives and strategies are explicit, or are congruent with its activities." [3] As will be explained in Chapter 7, there can be significant slippage between policy statements and actual policy, and then further slippage between policy as adopted and policy as implemented.

This definition also suggests that a policy can be either a *specific action* by a government (e.g., the decision by a municipality to allow development in a particular area), or *the result of a series of diverse decisions* (e.g., environmental policy, which is really the combination of a large number of decisions—and non-decisions—by many governments). More usually, the word "policy" is used in the latter way—a policy is loosely made up of a series of decisions.

The policy-making process is very difficult to describe in a clear and simple manner. By its very nature, it is both continuous and messy.[4]

The process is *continuous* because government policies are virtually always in a state of change. Of course, some policies are subject to more frequent and more extensive change than others, but it is very difficult to identify a policy that has remained completely stable for any length of time. This means that it is impossible to find either the beginning or the end of most public policies. Policies should be seen as involving a relatively constant *flow* rather than ever being firmly established.[5] "Most policy-making involves making decisions about existing programs, rather than writing new policies on a *tabula rasa*."[6] For example, a consideration of health care policy in Canada might begin with the establishment of the national medicare program in 1968. However, this cannot be understood completely without referring back to the hospital insurance legislation passed in 1957, which had its roots in a Saskatchewan policy that began in the 1940s. A thorough search of the genealogy of health care policy in Canada would probably lead back to early treaties that the British signed with native people. This idea of public policy as a flow of decisions is well captured in the title and subtitle of Malcolm Taylor's book, *Health Insurance and Canadian Public Policy: The Seven Decisions That Created the Canadian Health Insurance System and Their Outcomes.*[7]

There is also no definite end to a policy because all policies are subject to continuing revision. In some cases, the revisions are minor adjustments in interpretation of regulations and have relatively minor consequences on the broad aspects of the policy. In other cases, the revisions are major changes in policies effected by extensive changes in the legislation.

Policy making is also *messy* because it is impossible to identify one single process that is always followed in the making or revising of established policies. The nature of the policy process is different in different policy fields and can change when such significant actors as the prime minister change.[8] Many influences converge to produce a policy.

Figure 6.3 illustrates the continuous and messy nature of the process. The overall line of the policy has numerous bends, some small and some much larger. This diagram illustrates the development of the policy over a period of time. However, the jagged end at the beginning of the diagram indicates that there is no clear beginning to the policy and the arrow at the end indicates that the policy will continue to evolve in the future.

The messy part of the policy-making process is indicated by the number of different factors that can influence policy development. One change in this particular policy resulted from media interest and public dissatisfaction, although the actual change in the policy was delayed for a considerable period after the initial concerns surfaced. This change activated an interest group, which led to the production of a white paper, which in turn resulted in some other minor changes in legislation. At a later point the policy was changed again as a result of such external and uncontrollable events as a natural disaster and international pressures. This is a reminder that not all influences on a policy can be controlled by the domestic pressure groups, which are concerned most directly with it. Many Canadian policies are strongly influenced by global pressures that force changes in domestic policy.[9]

Figure 6.3
THE CONTINUOUS AND MESSY NATURE OF THE POLICY PROCESS

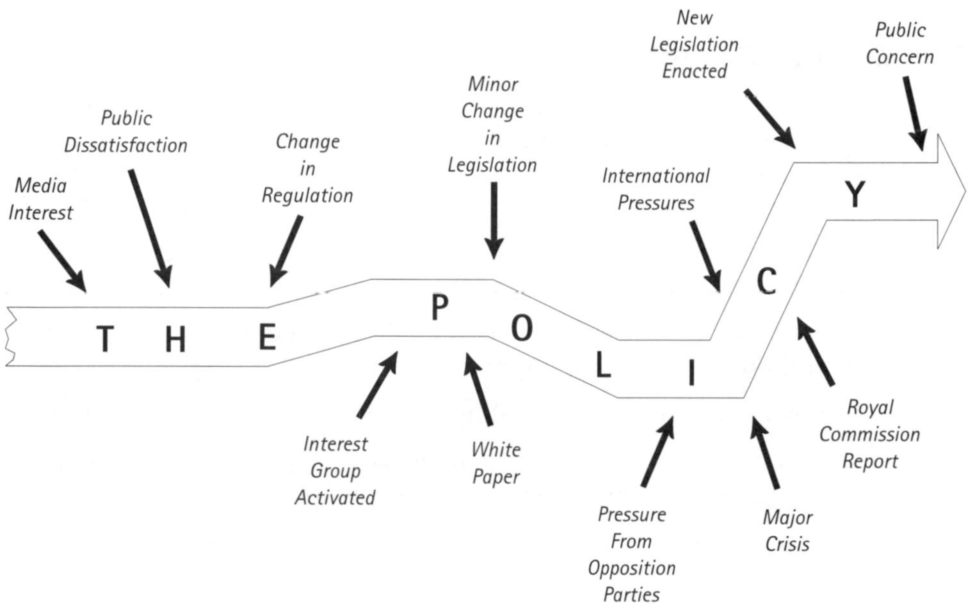

The figure depicts an arrow shape spelling out "THE POLICY" with various labels pointing to it: Media Interest, Public Dissatisfaction, Change in Regulation, Minor Change in Legislation, New Legislation Enacted, Public Concern, International Pressures, Interest Group Activated, White Paper, Pressure From Opposition Parties, Major Crisis, Royal Commission Report.

The point is that each action usually brings forth a reaction that prevents a policy from ever becoming totally set. The portion of the process illustrated in Figure 6.3 ends with an increase in public concern, which will likely result in another change in policy.

The idea that policy is a continuous, messy process poses a problem for students and others who want to identify exactly what the current government policy in some area is. There is ordinarily no one source to which one can turn for a clear and concise description of a policy. In practice, the government's *real* policy must ordinarily be pieced together from a variety of written sources and an analysis of specific decisions and actions.[10]

Political scientists and other students of public policy have developed several models of how public policies are made. However, policy makers usually do not consciously think about these models when they are making policy; the models have been developed by academics and others who analyze policy decisions after they have been made.

Models of public policy can be divided into two broad categories. *Normative models* prescribe how decisions *should* be made. Thus, a normative model is an ideal model of how a particular theorist feels the policy process ought to work. *Descriptive models* attempt to explain how decisions *are made in practice.* The formulation of a descriptive model involves the study of how a number of policies have been made and some generalization about how the system works. As discussed below, some models purport to be both normative and descriptive.

This section will consider different models of the policymaking process; most of the major models will be reviewed, but this review is not meant to be comprehensive.

🏛 COMPREHENSIVE RATIONALITY

The *comprehensive rationality model* suggests that policies are subjected to a multi-step analysis before a decision is made. Different writers list slightly different steps, but Anderson's list is typical:

1. The decision maker is confronted with a given problem that can be separated from other problems or at least considered meaningfully in comparison with them.

2. The goals, values, or objectives that guide the decision maker are clarified and ranked according to their importance.

3. The various alternatives for dealing with the problem are examined.

4. The consequences (costs and benefits, advantages and disadvantages) that would follow from the selection of each alternative are investigated.

5. Each alternative, and its attendant consequences, can be compared with the other alternatives.

6. The decision maker will choose that alternative, and its consequences, that maximizes the attainment of his or her goals, values, or objectives.[11]

The attractions of this style of decision making are obvious. It has an aura of careful forethought and scientific precision that contrasts with some of the more rudderless models of policy making that will be discussed below. Some of the techniques used in rational decision making are operations research, cost-effectiveness analysis, and cost-benefit analysis. Because comprehensive rationality involves careful analysis, it ought to provide a solution that produces the desired result with the most efficient use of resources.

However, there are many criticisms of this model. Most of them flow from the second step identified above—clarification and ranking of goals. In democratic, pluralistic societies, it is very difficult to rank "goals, values, or objectives" in order of priority. The question becomes whose goals and whose values will be reflected in the final decision. The best technical analysis available is useless if there is no agreement on this point, and there seldom is. Dunn points out this problem by suggesting that there are at least five different types of "rationality," which are frequently in conflict with one another.[12]

Even if there were agreement on goals, the requirement for *comprehensive* analysis would introduce severe complications. The model requires that the decision maker find and compare all potential solutions. At what point can the decision maker be confident that he or she has actually identified *all* possible solutions? And how far must one go in identifying *all* consequences (desirable and undesirable) of a decision? Because of these problems, comprehensive rationality is sometimes dismissed as "paralysis by analysis."

Given these difficulties, it is not surprising that the concept of comprehensive rationality is not applied very often in practice.

> With the possible exception of those few instances when there is the appearance of a full-scale review and analysis of policy alternatives, the empirical investigation of the making of a public policy usually tends to illustrate how logical procedures were overrun by a dominant political leader, a pressure group of some sort, or perhaps an influential section of the bureaucracy.[13]

It is difficult to think of examples of public policy decisions made in a purely rational manner, although most decisions are subjected to some limited form of rational analysis at some stage in the decision-making process. For example, in government purchasing decisions, the many alternatives available are frequently reduced to a smaller number on a fairly rational basis, e.g., minimum cost and security of supply, but "nonrational" elements, such as the number of jobs provided in particular areas of the country, frequently intrude on the final decision.

🏛 INCREMENTALISM

Charles E. Lindblom argued not only that comprehensive rationality is impossible, but also that policies are seldom changed radically as a result of extensive reviews.[14] In effect, he suggested that comprehensive rationality failed as both a normative and a descriptive model. Instead, he argued that, in the real world, policies are changed incrementally as a result of "successive limited comparisons" between the status quo and some very close alternatives. If some improvement on the status quo is desired, policy makers do not really search far and wide for the best possible alternative. Instead, they usually find some marginal improvement that makes the policy more acceptable to those affected by it.

Lindblom further argued that this "successive limited comparisons" approach, or *incrementalism*, was not only an accurate descriptive model, but also a normatively desirable one. He pointed out that comprehensive rationality tends to ignore the fact that new policies must be accepted by existing organizations and clientele groups. It might well be true that some radically different policy would be ideal if there were no ingrained ideological or institutional biases. However, these biases invariably exist. If a new policy recommendation is not acceptable to established players, then it will be very difficult to implement.

This is one of the reasons why Lindblom argues that the best test of the worth of a policy is its acceptance by most relevant actors, and not its rigid conformity to some preset objectives. It is difficult enough to implement policies when all are in agreement; if there is no consensus, then implementation problems are magnified greatly.

Incrementalism also recognizes that policy making is an ongoing process.[15] When a particular decision is made it will not be carved in stone to remain unchanged for the next hundred years. On the contrary, the policy-making process proceeds slowly by successive small iterations. This is sometimes referred to as "*serial decision making.*" Policy is developed as a series of decisions.

If certain groups lose as a result of one decision, then there will likely be an implicit understanding that the decision makers "owe them one" so that the next decision must provide some sort of recompense.

The incremental model also has its critics. Etzioni has expressed the fear that incrementalism goes too far in buttressing the established order.[16] If the status quo is satisfactory, then there is no point in searching widely for improvements. However, if the status quo is not acceptable to some groups in society, then incrementalism is a less suitable guide to action. It assigns too great a role to established and powerful interest groups and does not recognize the need to protect those who are unorganized.

Incrementalism also does not lend itself very well to some kinds of "all or nothing" decisions. If a society favours a system of state-run unemployment insurance, then incrementalism can provide a mechanism to determine such details of the plan as conditions for eligibility, amounts of payment, and so forth. Incrementalism does not work very well on such "all or nothing" decisions as going to war, instituting capital punishment, or legalizing abortion. Moreover, incrementalism does not work very well in dealing with new problems. For example, it does not help very much in dealing with new scientific breakthroughs in such areas as reproductive technology.

In practice, incrementalism explains some kinds of decisions better than others. Lindblom is right that *most* decisions are simply minor variations from previous decisions, but some *very important* decisions are not. It would be rather difficult to argue that the establishment of the Canada and Quebec Pension Plans or the founding of the Canadian Radio Broadcasting Commission and Trans-Canada Airlines were incremental decisions. It is true that only a small number of decisions fit in this category, but they are almost all very important decisions.

Yehezkel Dror is concerned about incrementalism because it provides a rationale for the inertia and lack of innovation that are too frequently found in large organizations. He argues that incrementalism acts

> as an ideological reinforcement of the pro-inertia and anti-innovation forces prevalent in all human organizations, administrative and policy making. The actual tendency of most organizations is to limit the search for alternatives to the minimum; there is little danger in real life, then, that administration will become bogged down in an exhaustive search for all alternatives and full enumeration of consequences, in order to achieve "rational-comprehensive" policy making. The "rational-comprehensive" model has at least the advantage of stimulating administrators to get a little outside their regular routine, while Lindblom's model justifies a policy of "no effort."[17]

Given the various shortcomings identified in both the rational-comprehensive and incremental approaches, it is not surprising that a number of attempts have been made to synthesize certain elements of the two into a better model.

🏛 BOUNDED RATIONALITY AND SATISFICING

Herbert Simon argued that, in practice, people do not really spend huge amounts of time searching for the *ideal* solution to a problem and that, even if they did, their attempts at rationality would fail because of the complexity of the problem.

> It is impossible for the behavior of a single, isolated individual to reach any high degree of rationality. The number of alternatives he must explore is so great, the information he would need to evaluate them so vast that even an approximation to objective rationality is hard to conceive. Individual choice takes place in an environment of "givens"—premises that are accepted by the subject as bases for his choice; and behavior is adaptive only within the limits set by these "givens."[18]

The presence of these "givens" and the innate limitations on human abilities provide boundaries that define the search for alternatives. In the real world, when people determine that the status quo is no longer working, they begin their search for alternatives by starting with solutions that are very similar to the status quo and gradually move further and further away, searching only until they find a *satisfactory*, not an ideal, solution. Simon coined the term "satisficing" to describe this type of behaviour.

> *Most human decision-making, whether individual or organizational, is concerned with the discovery and selection of satisfactory alternatives; only in exceptional cases is it concerned with the discovery and selection of optimal alternatives* ... To optimize requires processes several orders of magnitude more complex than those required to satisfice. An example is the difference between searching a haystack to find the sharpest needle in it and searching the haystack to find a needle sharp enough to sew with.[19]

Bounded rationality or optimal policy making uses the *process* identified with comprehensive rationality, but instead of searching for *all* possible alternatives, it searches for alternatives only within some limited range.[20] Also, it does not seek the *best* possible policy, but rather searches for an *optimal* policy. For example, when a politician says, "We must find a better solution to this problem, but we can't afford to increase our expenditure on it," that is a request for bounded rationality. Alternatively, the boundary could be a structural one in that a desire to improve the delivery of a service would be "bounded" by a need to retain the basic structure of the organization currently delivering the service. Many of the limitations on change in the current debate on health care are set by the fact that it is very difficult to disturb radically the existing delivery structures.

Bounded rationality is obviously considerably easier to accomplish than comprehensive rationality, and it does not simply give up any hope of furthering rationality as do some of the models to be discussed later. However, it does require the difficult and stressful agreement on goals and objectives mentioned as a problem with comprehensive rationality.

🏛 MIXED SCANNING

Amitai Etzioni has developed a different way of combining rationality and incrementalism. He argues that governments really make two different kinds of decisions—fundamental and incremental. Fundamental (or "contextuating") decisions are radical changes in policy, while incremental decisions are used either to pave the way for fundamental decisions or to fine-tune fundamental decisions after some of their consequences have been identified.

> Fundamental decisions are made by exploring the main alternatives the actor sees in view of his conception of his goals, but—unlike what rationalism would indicate—details and specifications are omitted so that an overview is feasible. Incremental decisions are made but within the contexts set by fundamental decisions (and fundamental reviews). Thus, each of the two elements in mixed-scanning helps to reduce the effects of the particular shortcomings of the other; incrementalism reduces the unrealistic aspects of rationalism by limiting the details required in fundamental decisions, and contextuating rationalism helps to overcome the conservative slant of incrementalism by exploring longer-run alternatives.[21]

Etzioni cites the history of the U.S. space program as an example of how this system operates.[22] First, the Congress made a *fundamental* decision to embark on a space program. Over the years, it has made a number of related *incremental* decisions to provide more or less funding, to proceed rapidly with some parts of the program, and to scrap other parts. This illustrates the interaction between fundamental and incremental decisions.

The framework of incremental and rational decisions and the many models in between are still used quite extensively, but there are some newer models of policy making that do not rely so heavily on these concepts.

🏛 PUBLIC CHOICE

Public choice is one of the newest models of public policy making and for this reason it seems to mean different things to different writers. The basic element of public choice is the application of economic styles of thinking to the analysis of political behaviour. "Public choice can be defined as the economic study of nonmarket decision making, or simply the application of economics to political science."[23] Public choice uses the concept of the market, except that, instead of seeing a market for tangible goods and services, public choice theorists think in terms of a market for votes and for specific public policies.[24]

In the public choice model, the basic building block of political action is the self-interested, utility-maximizing individual. The aim of the public choice model is "to explain collective decisions (about what are often thought to be political matters) in terms of the self-seeking behaviour of rational individuals."[25] The desire to maximize income, security, or, more generally, utility is the motivating force behind all actions—including voting. "Each citizen ... votes for the party he believes will provide him with a higher utility income than any other party during the coming election period."[26]

Of course, citizens can participate in the political process in ways other than voting. Breton suggests that individuals will begin to participate more actively in the political process when their perceived costs as a result of government policies exceed their benefits from them. The nature and intensity of their organizing efforts are a function of the distance between costs and benefits.[27]

This "market" for votes and other political activity leads politicians who want to be elected to espouse policies that will please voters—but not just any voters. Politicians would be advised to ignore committed voters—regardless of whether they are committed for or against the politician or party in question. It would be a better use of resources to try to sway undecided voters, since this is the group that normally determines electoral outcomes.[28] Thus, a study by Bruce Macnaughton and Conrad Winn indicated that federal spending on an economic development program flowed disproportionately into ridings that had a history of switching support for parties.[29] This was obviously a better use of funds than rewarding people who would never vote for the party or people who will vote for the party in any case.

Public choice can also explain the actions of public servants. Public servants will ordinarily attempt to increase their department's mandate and the size of its staff and budget because this will increase the individual public servant's income and status.[30]

This desire for increased status will also cause public servants to favour particular kinds of policies. For example, Breton and Wintrobe have argued that income and price controls are imposed by governments not because they are successful, and not because politicians or citizens want them, but because they make it easier for bureaucrats to obscure accountability and so take credit for successes and shift blame for failures.[31]

Public choice explains the behaviour of individual voters, politicians, and bureaucrats, but it can also be used to explain the interactions of these groups. Hartle discusses public policy making as a series of interacting games:

> Individuals involved in public policy decision making are self-seeking players ... engaged in sets of interrelated "games." Each of the several "games" (political, bureaucratic, lobbying, media) has its own set of unique rules including rules of entry and exit, rules of play, and rules of reward and punishment. In each "game" also, any one player makes decisions in the face of ubiquitous uncertainty concerning the actions and reactions of other players.[32]

The overall policy game consists of the interaction of these four games, because everyone in the system needs everyone else. Ministers and public servants need one another. Ministers need public servants to deliver programs well so that the government looks good. In exchange, public servants demand appropriate levels of funding so that they can keep interest groups satisfied and quiet. Media people need politicians to give them "scoops," but politicians also need media people to help establish their image. There are many games and many players. However, not all players in the game are equal; depending on the issue at stake and the resources (financial or other) of the various players, different outcomes can be expected. Thus, public policy is the result of the interaction of these games.

One of the problems with the public choice model is that it presents few testable hypotheses. People are presumed to act based on certain motivations, but since these are subjective motivations, they cannot be measured or tested.

What is developed is a logical progression based on untested and indeed unlikely hypotheses about how human beings actually behave. Norton Long makes this point sharply by concluding that public choice theorists "argue with elegant and impeccable logic about unicorns."[33]

For example, it is sometimes pointed out that many people do not act in the self-interested, rational manner posited by the model. Public choice theorists would suggest that such a person is, in fact, acting in some long-term self-interest or taking additional things into account.[34] This sounds suspiciously like "saving the hypothesis," but it is impossible to counter.

🏛 GOVERNMENTAL OR BUREAUCRATIC POLITICS

Public choice theory attempts to explain virtually all political actions in society as a result of the actions of various groups and their involvement in the making of major policy decisions. The governmental or bureaucratic politics model has some factors in common with public choice, but this model (hereafter referred to as the bureaucratic politics model) generally focuses on public policy as an outcome of the interaction of various groups within government.

Elements of this model have been the subject of much discussion, but these elements were drawn together and the model was given greater recognition as a fullblown theory of policy making by Graham Allison in his book *Essence of Decision*.[35]

In many ways, this model is the exact opposite of the rational model. The rational model sees "the government" as a monolithic actor guided by a dedication to efficiency, effectiveness, and rationality, however those concepts might be defined. The bureaucratic politics model sees government as composed of a number of different departments and agencies, each with its own goals and each trying to mould policy to further its own interests. Thus, government is a coalition of various interests, and government policies are the outcome of the interactions of these various entities. For that reason, this model is sometimes referred to as the *bargaining* model.

When a decision needs to be made, each department or agency within a government could well have a different perspective on it. For example, if Canada were called upon to act because one country had invaded another, there could be a number of different responses. The military might propose some sort of retaliation or other military solution. The Department of Foreign Affairs and International Trade might propose such diplomatic initiatives as international negotiations or actions through the United Nations, possibly including a trade embargo. Industrial development officials might propose that there be an embargo on food products, since Canadian manufacturers would not suffer. The Department of Agriculture might favour an embargo on manufactured goods so that Canadian farmers would not suffer. Each organization sees the problem and the solution in a different way depending on how its interests are affected. This gives rise to the maxim: "Where you stand depends on where you sit."[36]

There is no question of disloyalty to the public interest or the common good when different entities adopt different positions. All of these organizations are firmly committed to the public interest, but they all see that interest being served in a different manner.

The decision ultimately taken is the outcome of compromise and negotiation between the various interested parties and thus is heavily influenced by the relative power of the various organizations. In almost every policy area, there is a "lead ministry" that is most directly involved in the area, and whose opinions carry the greatest weight, but there are a number of other interested departments that also have some influence on the final policy.

> Government decisions are made, and government actions are taken, neither as the simple choice of a unified group, nor as a formal summary of leaders' preferences. Rather, the context of shared power but separate judgments about important choices means that politics is the mechanism of choice. Each player pulls and hauls with the power at his discretion for outcomes that will advance his conception of national, organizational, group, and personal interests.[37]

This theory is easier to see at work in the open presidential system of the United States than in the Canadian parliamentary system, where decisions tend to be made in cabinet behind closed doors and cabinet solidarity prevails after the decision has been made. However, this model has been used to describe the federal budgetary process,[38] and intergovernmental policy making in a number of areas.[39]

Cabinet secrecy and solidarity normally prevent us from actually seeing these kinds of tensions at work in the Canadian government, but a remarkably public example of this style of policy making occurred in the recent fight about generic drugs.[40] The issue is that Canadian manufacturers of generic drugs would like to be able to manufacture copies of expensive drugs in Canada and pay a relatively small royalty to the patent holder, usually a major multinational company. This would be good for consumers because it would reduce the price of prescription drugs. Therefore, the minister of health supported this initiative. However, the multinational drug companies cried foul and promised to provide more research jobs in Canada if their monopoly on production was maintained. The minister of industry, seeing more jobs on the table, opted to support the multinational companies. Here is a good example of "where you stand depends on where you sit." The job of the minister of health is to promote health care at reasonable cost; the job of the minister of industry is to encourage business investment and new job creation. Clearly, they are both concerned about the public interest, but they each see the public interest defined in a different way.

🏛 POLICY COMMUNITIES AND POLICY NETWORKS

The policy community approach is an expansion of the bureaucratic politics style of policy making. Bureaucratic politics emphasizes the prominence of government organizations in policy making. As policies have become more complex and decision processes more open, government organizations have lost their monopoly on policy making and policy implementation.[41] They have been forced to involve interests from outside government to obtain knowledge during the policy-making process and to foster acceptance of the adopted policy at the implementation stage.

A *policy community* consists of a cluster of interested groups organized around a particular policy. The exact content of the cluster varies depending on the issue at hand, but a typical cluster might include government organizations (from several governments, including foreign ones), interest groups, international agencies, interested companies and individuals, and journalists. These organizations constitute a *community*, and their interconnections are called a *network*.[42]

Policies are made through the interactions within this group, which Pross has referred to as a "subgovernment." The subgovernment group constitutes an inner ring that is surrounded by an outer ring, which Pross calls the "attentive public." This latter group is interested in the policy but is either not allowed to participate in the policy-making process by the members of the subgovernment or is not sufficiently interested in the outcome of the policy to expend significant resources to participate.[43] However, because this group is "attentive," there is always the possibility that something will motivate some of its members to move into the inner group. For example, if an interest group was reasonably satisfied with the existing policy, it would likely remain a member of the attentive public. However, if there was some pressure to change the policy, then the interest group might decide to attempt to move into the subgovernment to ensure that it could be influential.

The nature of the interaction, i.e., the network, can be characterized in several ways. One extreme is concertation, where one government agency works with one dominant interest group to make all the important decisions. At the opposite end of the spectrum is a much more complex system, where several government agencies and several interested parties, all with varying degrees of power, jockey for position and power. And, of course, the nature of the network in a particular policy area can change over time.[44]

Jeremy Wilson has used the policy communities framework to analyze wilderness policy making in British Columbia.[45] He sees the provincial Ministry of Forestry (MOF) as the most central actor, with the provincial Ministry of the Environment and the federal Department of Fisheries and Oceans playing weaker roles. He argues that before the rise of the environmental movement in the 1970s, the forest industry and the MOF acted in concert to set policies. Over time, environmental groups tried, with some success, to move from the outer, attentive public ring into the subgovernment ring. As this occurred, the policy-making process changed so that the concerns of the environmental groups began to carry some weight, although considerably less than those of the forest industry. This case study illustrates the nature of the policy community concept and shows how it can be used to explain changes in policy and in the policy-making process over time.

The concept can be viewed as an elitist theory—one has to be a member of the community to count in the process—but it is considerably more open than earlier styles of policy making because of the number of groups involved.

The theories discussed up to this point consider the various actors in the process to be influential. The theories discussed below suggest that policies are determined by broader factors, and individuals and groups have only limited influence.

🏛 SOCIO-ECONOMIC DETERMINANTS

The socioeconomic determinants model of public policy suggests that policies evolve in response to certain changes in the socioeconomic environment of a society. It does not suggest that individuals and groups are powerless in the policy process, but it says that their scope for autonomous action is severely limited by the environmental constraints that they face.

The conventional wisdom one reads in some political science textbooks and most popular journalism says that public policies are a product of the ideology of the political party in power, or possibly of the configuration of the present legislature, e.g., a weak minority government. Anyone who spends a great deal of time and energy studying the political system (such as political scientists and journalists) would like to believe that these political factors are highly influential. However, in the last twenty years the evidence has begun to mount in a number of jurisdictions that socioeconomic variables are more important determinants of public policy than are political ones.

Figure 6.4a illustrates the conventional wisdom about the central role of political factors in policy making. It suggests that there are certain socioeconomic factors that influence the decision of voters to support a particular political party. For example, union members vote for the NDP; wealthy business people vote for the Conservatives. The political party elected would then make policies that supported the political predispositions of those who supported it. Over time, these socioeconomic factors change, e.g., an increase in union membership, which could put a different political party in power and so bring about changes in public policy. Not only does this sound like the way a democratic system "ought" to work, but it coincides nicely with the legal arrangements of the situation.

Quantitative studies, first in the United States, then in a number of other countries, including Canada, indicate that in fact political variables may be less influential than previously thought. The general argument is that the model shown in Figure 6.4b is a more accurate depiction of the process than that in Figure 6.4a. Note that this refinement does not suggest that "politics doesn't matter," but it does suggest that political variables matter somewhat less than certain socioeconomic variables.

For example, the socioeconomic determinants approach to policymaking would suggest that the increasing size of government in the post–World War II period was not caused by some ideological motivation on the part of a particular political party. Instead, the more active role of government could be explained by the increasing urbanization of society, which destroyed the traditional safety nets of family and church, which formerly provided for people who were down on their luck. The fact that virtually all parties have, at one time or

Figure 6.4
ALTERNATE MODELS OF THE POLICY-MAKING PROCESS

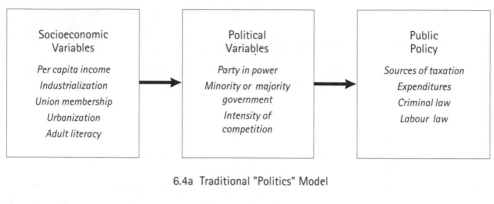

6.4a Traditional "Politics" Model

6.4b Socioeconomic Determinants Model

another, advocated the growth of certain aspects of the active state would support this approach.

Falcone and Whittington have conducted a comprehensive study of this question in Canada.[46] They tested the strength of such political variables as party in power, minority versus majority government, and social background of legislators. They found that such socioeconomic variables as income and urbanization had a greater influence on levels of public expenditure than did the political variables. In a similar study, Abizadeh and Gray found that changes in provincial expenditure were more heavily influenced by changes in Gross Domestic Product than by the ideological position of the political party in power.[47] A recent study at the municipal level contended that economic and demographic factors had a much greater impact on levels of revenue and expenditure than did changes in leadership.[48]

However, it is important to note that none of these studies has found that all changes in public policy can be explained by socioeconomic factors. As Richard Simeon has pointed out, the environment determines what issues will move to the forefront of the agenda, what constraints decision makers will face, and what resources will be available to them, but environment does not determine exactly what response they will make to an issue. "Urbanization generates the need to move people around, it does not tell us how the costs will be distributed."[49] *Politics does matter*, but probably not as much as some have believed in the past.

On further analysis, this should not be so surprising. In Canada, political parties seldom disagree on basic societal values. For example, all major parties believe in economic prosperity shared by all, lower inflation, lower unemployment, more equitable distribution of wealth, sunny weather in summer, and good snow on the ski slopes in winter. The strongest arguments at election times usually revolve around which party is more adept at furthering the basic societal values on which all agree. Richard Rose described this phenomenon in British politics:

> Parties can compete with each other by claiming to be more proficient in achieving goals generally valued by the electorate. For example, the Conservative and Labour parties do not compete by one party favouring full employment, and the other unemployment, or one favouring inflation and the other price stability. The parties compete by each claiming to be *better* qualified to achieve both full employment and stable prices. Instead of taking different positions, the parties take the same position, but differ in boasting of their competence in handling ... conditions commonly valued by the majority of the electorate.[50]

Therefore, it should not be surprising that *all* parties are more likely to be influenced by general societal trends than by rigid, historical ideological positions.

One reason for the similarity of policies is that all parties, once in power, face similar external constraints. In commenting on the British situation, Rose points out that whichever party is in power is so constrained when making economic policy by the power of big business and big labour, export policies of foreign governments, and the price of North Sea oil, that it has great difficulty engaging in a policy significantly different from its predecessor, which faced the same constraints. Thus, parties tend to arrive at the same policies regardless of their ideological differences.

> To emphasize the force of a relatively consensual electorate and powerful secular trends is *not* to assert that the beliefs and interests of Conservative and Labour politicians are identical. Similarity in behaviour need not imply an identity of values. It can occur in spite of underlying differences if the specifics of a given circumstance are sufficiently powerful to lead people with different perspectives to arrive at the same conclusion about what must be done. *Necessity more than ideological consensus is the explanation for similarities in behaviour.*[51]

For example, in the last few years, NDP governments have come to power in three provinces at a time when there has been general concern about high deficits and increasing levels of government spending. All three governments have used their mandate to restrain spending in the best conservative traditions. This has caused them a great deal of difficulty because many of the policies they are undertaking seem at variance with historical NDP positions. However, the socioeconomic situation that they faced as soon as they took office put severe limits on their abilities to implement the kinds of policies they discussed before they came to office.

In sum, the thrust of the socioeconomic determinants model of policy making is that variables relating to the stage of a society's socioeconomic development are more important in determining the types of policies formulated than are some of the political variables that are discussed so frequently. The Marxist theory of the state also emphasizes the significance of socioeconomic factors.

🏛 MARXIST ANALYSIS

Chapter 2 discussed the Marxist approach to the role of the state in society. Marxists see society as organized and divided on the basis of conflict between classes. The ultimate role of the capitalist state is to organize society in such a manner as to ensure that the economic elite will be able to exploit the working class. Neo-Marxists argue that the state has three roles—fostering accumulation, providing legitimation, and imposing social order.[52]

In the Marxist view, the overriding concern of the state is assisting capitalists in *accumulating* large amounts of wealth and power. The state can aid in accumulation directly through such means as the provision of industrial development grants to wealthy corporations; or it can act indirectly through labour laws that inhibit unionization; or it can act through "nondecisions" such as the refusal to enforce pollution or occupational health and safety laws aggressively. All of these policies result in what has been described as the privatization of profit and the socialization of costs, or private benefits and public costs.[53]

However, neo-Marxists argue that accumulation must be restrained somewhat, and capitalists must be saved from themselves, i.e., too much heavy-handed pure exploitation would incite armed rebellion or at least concerted action on the part of workers. The state could use its coercive force to prevent such action, but that would be dysfunctional.

> [T]he state must try to maintain or create the conditions in which profitable capital accumulation is possible. However, the state also must try to maintain or create the conditions for social harmony. A capitalist state that openly uses its coercive forces to help one class accumulate capital at the expense of other classes loses its legitimacy and hence undermines the basis of its loyalty and support.[54]

Therefore, the state also attempts to illustrate to workers the value of the present system by providing *legitimation*, which is, in a sense, the benevolent face of capitalism.

> Legitimation policies reduce inter-class conflict by providing subordinate classes with benefits that reduce their dissatisfaction with the inequalities generated by the capitalist economy. Social welfare policies and labour legislation are examples of state actions that promote social harmony by legitimizing the existing capitalist system in the eyes of those classes who, it is argued, benefit least from its operation.[55]

However, if workers cannot be kept in line through the persuasion inherent in legitimation, then the state stands ready to use *coercion* to impose the appropriate social order, such as legislation restricting union activity.

The role of the state, and by extension of public policy, is to mediate between the various conflicting interests present in society. However, this is not a neutral style of mediation. In the Marxist view, the state always acts in the long-term interests of the capitalist class. This might involve taking actions that have a short-term detrimental effect on accumulation and so are opposed by the capitalist class, e.g., extension of workers' compensation or unemployment insurance plans. However, these are necessary for legitimation and so benefit the capitalist class in the long run. In this sense, the role of the state is to maintain a relative autonomy[56] from *all* classes so that it can save the capitalist class from its own greed.

Evidence to support the Marxist model of the state can be seen in tax laws that provide generous benefits to people able to invest large sums while taxing wage earners on the basis of each dollar earned. Another example is the case of the legislators who have great difficulty passing legislation preventing business combinations that limit competition, but have no such difficulty passing legislation ordering the end of legal strikes and the jailing of union leaders. Not many Canadians accept this Marxist view of the state in its entirety, but it seems to be a valid explanation of certain actions of the state.

🏛 ROYAL COMMISSIONS AND TASK FORCES

The rest of this chapter will discuss important instruments of policy making. This section describes and analyzes the role of Royal commissions and task forces, and the next will discuss coloured papers. Frequently, governments face a problem that is so severe and far-reaching that they must study the situation carefully and seek policy advice widely before they act, so that they do not act unwisely. Cynics would argue that Royal commissions and coloured papers are really "nonresponses" geared to distracting people's attention and making government appear interested, when in fact the desire is simply to defer consideration of something until later, possibly after the next election. However,

> [e]ven where such comment has been perceptive, its implied criticism may have been misplaced. Institutionalized delay may have its merits where no adequate consensus for action exists. Grasping a nettle firmly is a fairly reliable formula for experiencing pain, but not necessarily for making progress. In any event, it is clear that in the case of a large majority of Royal commissions and task forces of recent years the object has been enlightenment, not evasion. Their aim has been to achieve more widespread public understanding of questions at issue and a more informed basis for policy choices by the decision-makers.[57]

Royal commissions and task forces have played a significant role in Canadian history.[58] In fact, it is almost possible to track the major events of Canadian history by reviewing the work of these commissions.

Most people who follow Canadian affairs remember a good many inquiries. They remember inquiries into dominion-provincial relations, pilotage, the place of firemen on diesel locomotives, price spreads in food products, the Canadian automobile in domestic markets, health services, the Gouzenko affair, freight rates, television broadcasting, government organization, taxation, bilingualism and biculturalism, the non-medical use of drugs, and innumerable other subjects, from the narrow and perhaps trivial to the general and (on the face of it) significant. Some inquiries have been controversial; others have been almost totally ignored. Some have had a substantial impact on government policy; the recommendations of others have been seemingly ignored, although they may have had indirect effects difficult to assess. But it is significant that much of the history of Canada could be interpreted through the work of commissions of inquiry.[59]

The federal Inquiries Act provides for three types of inquiries. Part II of the act allows a departmental minister to appoint a commissioner or commissioners for a departmental investigation. These kinds of commissions are more limited in scope and are less formal and public than the Royal commissions and task forces discussed in this chapter.

Part IV of the act empowers the Governor in Council to allow an international commission to carry on a portion of its work in Canada. This is a very specialized kind of arrangement and will not be discussed in this chapter.

Part I of the Inquiries Act governs those commissions with a much higher profile, such as Royal commissions and task forces. It stipulates that the Governor in Council, i.e., cabinet, may "cause inquiry to be made into and concerning any matter connected with the good government of Canada or the conduct of any part of the public business thereof."[60]

Royal commissions and *task forces* are temporary organizations created to investigate either specific incidents or general policy concerns and report to government. They are usually dismantled after the delivery of their report and so are not involved in the implementation of any of their recommendations.

There are more similarities than differences between task forces and Royal commissions. The Law Reform Commission of Canada has suggested that there is little reason to make a distinction between the two. "The adjective 'royal' is much abused, with some commissions technically entitled to its use not employing it, and others appropriating it when they have no business doing so. In our view, the term is best ignored."[61] In this chapter, this advice will be followed: commissions appointed under Part I of the Inquiries Act will be discussed without regard to the term used to describe any particular commission. However, there are some general statements that can be made about the two forms.[62]

Royal commissions tend to be more formal in their organization. For example, the members of the commission are appointed, and its mandate is assigned, by an order in council.[63] A task force might receive its mandate by a letter from the prime minister or another minister. Royal commissions tend to be used for major tasks requiring lengthy analysis; task forces emphasize speed of reply. Royal commissions tend to conduct most of their proceedings in public and produce public reports containing recommendations to the government. Task forces can report publicly but are sometimes asked to report privately. Public reports are more difficult for the government to ignore than private ones. As noted above, one should not make too much of these differences; there is wide variance in individual cases, and the general statements do not always apply.

Commissions have been a very popular policy-making device in Canada; between 1867 and 1979, 425 of them were established.[64] In the Trudeau era, more task forces were appointed under Parts I and II of the Inquiries Act than were full-blown Royal commissions, but Trudeau is responsible for appointing the largest ever Royal commission—the Royal Commission on the Economic Union and the Development Prospects for Canada (Macdonald Commission). Mulroney was less inclined to use Royal commissions, but he appointed some high-profile commissions such as the Dubin Commission of Inquiry into the Use of Drugs and Banned Practices Intended to Increase Athletic Performance; the Royal commissions on new reproductive technologies, electoral reform, and party financing; and the Commission of Inquiry on the Blood System in Canada.

Commissions can be appointed to delve into any area that the government desires, but Hodgetts has identified four major areas in which commissions have been active:[65]

- catastrophic incidents—train wrecks, air disasters, bridge collapses;

- social or cultural problems of national importance—broadcasting, arts and sciences, bilingualism and biculturalism;

- economic matters—transportation, banking and finance, corporate concentration, economic future of the country; and

- government organization—financial and personnel management, morale in the foreign service.

The purposes for which commissions are used have changed over time. Writing in 1964, John Courtney identified a trend that continues to this day:

> The trend, therefore, of recent royal [sic] commissions has been away from investigations important only to a limited number of people or a restricted geographic area and toward examinations of importance to the Canadian people as a whole. The changing pattern may be characterized as one away from "intensive" inquiries, of only limited significance, to one of "extensive" inquiries, of national significance. The effect of the changing pattern has been to turn the royal commission of inquiry into an investigatory technique suitable for publicizing group sentiments on a national basis and for formulating national objectives. The modern royal commission has become, in effect, a vehicle by which individuals, groups and governments are permitted to state their views on matters of concern to the nation as a whole.[66]

The Law Reform Commission has built on the distinction made by Courtney and has suggested that commissions be divided into two categories. *Investigatory* commissions "address themselves primarily to the facts of a particular alleged problem, generally a problem associated with the functioning of government."[67] *Advisory* commissions "address themselves to a broad issue of policy and gather information relevant to that issue."[68] Examples of investigatory commissions are those that investigated the suspicious deaths of babies at the Hospital for Sick Children in Toronto or Sinclair Stevens' alleged conflicts of interest when he was a cabinet minister. Advisory commissions have examined the health care system, electoral reform, and new reproductive technologies.

This distinction is important because it influences how the commission is organized; specifically, it determines how far the commission must go in following formal legal procedures that safeguard the "accused." An investigatory commission must operate on the basis of courtlike procedures to ensure that the reputation and the legal rights of the "accused" are protected, although commissions operate under relaxed rules with regard to hearing testimony and accepting evidence.[69] However, even these relaxed rules can restrict rather significantly how the commission can act. Policy-advisory commissions have much more latitude in organization and proceed much less formally.

Of course, few commissions fall squarely into one or the other camp. A good example was the Commission of Inquiry on the Blood System in Canada (Krever Commission). It addressed the investigatory questions of who knew what and when, but it also made policy recommendations to prevent similar tragedies from recurring. The commission was subject to legal challenge and was almost not allowed to name names in its report because of the potential that criminal charges would be laid against the people involved.[70]

The fact that commissions rarely fit neatly into either category means that most must proceed with a foot in both camps, i.e., with a reasonable amount of flexibility to speed up proceedings, but also with appropriate legal safeguards when they are needed.

Reasons for Use

There are several reasons why governments use the Royal commission or task force form of organization rather than some of the more permanent structures discussed in earlier chapters. All of the organizations and instruments discussed in this chapter have in common a concern with study and consultation rather than with implementation. As will be discussed later, this is both the strong and the weak point of the commission form.

Objective Policy Analysis.   Peter Aucoin provides three general reasons why commissions are very good instruments for policy analysis:

> First, their establishment enables decision-makers in government to delay or postpone decisions without being criticized for doing nothing at all. Policy analysis in this circumstance may be an excuse for a "non-decision", but at least it ensures that the issue at hand stays on the policy agenda in a certain fashion. Second, such commissions provide for a process whereby the views of special interest groups and the interested public can be presented in a forum that is not subject to direct government control ... Third, and perhaps most relevant, commissions of inquiry of this sort represent the most effective option available to government for policy analysis

undertaken by an independent and objective, and yet official, organization. Commissions are the most effective option in this regard because they have a greater capacity to be, and to be seen to be, independent and objective than other governmental instruments of public policy analysis.

Each of these characteristics is important to policy analysis as an activity of governance. The first provides time for analysis as an intellectual exercise; the second provides the opportunity to examine and assess demands and support for various policy options; and the third provides for analysts who are able to evaluate policy options free from the constraints of partisan controls or institutional limitations extant in other government organizations which conduct policy analysis.[71]

Identifying Innovative Approaches. Commissions usually employ people from outside the public service—both as commissioners and as staff advisors to commissioners. The hope is that they will be able to take a fresh look at some problem and propose innovative solutions. The Royal Commission on Financial Management and Accountability (Lambert Commission) was composed of a bank president, a political scientist, a former public servant, and an accountant with both business and public sector experience. In this case, the combination of members with public service experience and outsiders with a fresh view produced some innovative ideas about changes in government structures.

This positive point highlights a potential problem for the government. Governments do not have as much control over the activities or final conclusions of Part I commissions as they have over departmental, or Part II, task forces. Independent commissions report publicly, and their recommendations cannot be ignored by the government. Politicians are aware that they are unleashing a potentially powerful force by creating an independent commission, and so are reluctant to use this device in circumstances where they feel a need to control, or at least influence, the outcome.

However, where governments can make a valid case against the proposals of a commission, they are somewhat freer to reject advice from an independent commission than they would be from a body more closely related to the government.

This lack of accountability then preserves flexibility for the politician at the conclusion of the inquiry, in that at that point he is free either to embrace warmly the results or to indicate that he is not bound to accept the inquiry results. In contrast to this, in those situations where the inquiry is directly accountable to the politician, he is less able to disown the results.[72]

Fact Finding. Royal commissions and task forces are frequently established to investigate disasters or questionable activities, to determine exactly what happened and recommend measures to prevent their recurrence. The Commission of Inquiry on the Blood System in Canada, the Dubin Commission of Inquiry into the Use of Drugs and Banned Practices Intended to Increase Athletic Performance, and the Hughes Royal Commission on the Donald Marshall, Jr., Prosecution are examples of these kinds of Royal commissions.

Postponing an Embarrassing Problem.   It is sometimes suggested that governments have established commissions merely to ensure that a problem is temporarily placed on the back burner, and that, with luck, the problem might go away altogether. For example, the Royal Commission on Corporate Concentration was appointed when Paul Desmarais of Power Corporation was attempting to take over the giant Argus Corporation. The takeover bid was unsuccessful, but no action was ever taken on the recommendations of the Royal commission.

The delay caused by the use of the commission form is a frequent source of criticism:

> One can almost predict that nothing will be done without a Commission and in fact often not much is done with a Commission except to pass it on to the next Commission. It is a kind of commission chain letter process. Governments have been known to avoid a head-on collision with an issue for upwards of fifty years as was the case with the nationalization of wheat marketing.[73]

Stimulating Interaction with the Public.   Royal commissions are frequently established as a two-way communications link—both obtaining the views of members of the public on an issue and communicating important facts to them. Some commissions invite the participation of the public through the presentation of written briefs or appearances before the commission.[74] The Royal Commission on Aboriginal Peoples has been especially active in this regard.

> Its elaborate process of public hearings in four rounds is designed to do more than elicit public input. With its post-hearing summaries and discussion papers, the Commission committed itself to generating dialogues among Aboriginal peoples and others.[75]

It used toll-free telephone numbers to encourage interested people to call and voice their concerns in Chipewyan, Cree, English, French, Inuktitut, or Ojibwa.

Commissions also arrange for research to be done on the problem at hand and prepare interim reports in an attempt to improve the level of discussion of the issue. These reports are frequently used to start selling the ultimate conclusions of the commission to the public and politicians.

Low-Cost Way of Showing Concern.   Governments are frequently under great pressure to prove that they recognize a particular problem and are striving to resolve it. A full-scale attempt to solve the problem will likely be expensive. Commissions are often somewhat expensive, but the expense is almost certainly less than that of actually solving the problem.

> In sum, all public inquiries offer to politicians the opportunity to demonstrate concern about a policy issue and to indicate that action is being taken upon it, while deferring the need to expend substantial resources in response to a perceived policy concern ...[76]

Operation

The order in council that establishes a commission sets out the mandate of the commission, the names of the commissioners, and, sometimes, the date by which it must report.

In the past, it was common for commissions to be headed by a single commissioner, frequently a judge. This reflects the investigatory nature of some commissions. Even today, commissions with an investigative role are frequently headed by a judge, as is the case with the Commission of Inquiry on the Blood System in Canada. The benefits of the expertise and prestige of a judge as a commissioner are fairly clear, particularly where the major role of the commission is investigative. However, where the commission is delving into political matters, the involvement of judges is more problematic.[77] When Justice Willard Estey of the Supreme Court of Canada was appointed to investigate the causes of the collapse of the Canadian Commercial and Northland Banks, James Snell and Frederick Vaughan were strongly critical:

> The use of the judiciary, particularly members of the Supreme Court, to deal with political problems is a practice which should be ended for several reasons. First, it draws judges into political controversy. In taking advantage of the judicial reputation for nonpartisanship, governments are actually maintaining a practice which tarnishes that reputation. The judiciary itself can be, and certainly has been, brought into disrepute through this process.

> Second, inquiries such as Judge Estey's are essentially being asked to examine and comment upon the political judgment of a government ...

> Why should judges be asked to assess political decisions? Surely that is the job of the electorate or of its elected representatives.[78]

In recent years, the size of commissions has been expanding and there has been a tendency to appoint people with a diversity of backgrounds, including, but not limited to, law.[79] The members of the Royal Commission on Aboriginal Peoples included native leaders, judges, and academics.

Jane Jenson has argued very strongly that the composition of the commission will be very important because it will shape many aspects of the nature of the commission's work, including its ultimate conclusions. She identifies a number of controversies which have developed over the composition of commissions.

> A good part of the controversy over the practices of the Baird Commission [on new reproductive technology] involved the criticism that the concerns of the medical and scientific communities were being better represented than those of women, whose bodies were the intended terrain of such technologies. Objections were made, as well, to the choice of participants in the [Royal Commission on Electoral Reform and Party Financing]'s first symposium, on the Active Participation of Women in Politics. Invitations went to women active in electoral and party politics, but none to those whose activism was most associated with social movements through, for example, the National Action Committee on the Status of Women (NAC).[80]

Of course, there can be a negative side to appointing commissioners who come to the commission with a preconceived viewpoint.

> The proper place for special interests is in the witness box, not on the Commission. The generous representation accorded various interests in Britain has, it seems to me, unfortunate consequences. Most members have firmly rooted convictions which no amount of evidence is likely to shake. Unanimous reports for that reason are seldom obtained. But, what is more serious to my mind, minority reports can be used as vehicles for carrying to the public the prejudices of special interests (at the public's expense of course).[81]

The work of the Royal Commission on New Reproductive Technology was hampered by serious divisions among members, which led to dissension, public insults, and lawsuits, until the federal government eventually intervened and fired a group of commissioners to stop the fighting.[82] This had an obvious impact on the public's acceptance of the commission's recommendations.

The actual activities of the commissions vary considerably depending on their mandate, but they usually involve both public input and academic research components.

The public input aspect also varies widely, depending on the nature of the commission. Fact-finding commissions usually focus on input from the people involved in the incident and experts in the field. Commissions appointed under Part I of the Inquiries Act even have the power to compel reluctant witnesses to attend.[83] Sometimes, commissions will cast their net considerably wider to seek the views of a cross section of the public. The Commission of Inquiry on the Blood System in Canada travelled widely to hear heart-wrenching testimony about the effect of AIDS and other diseases transmitted through blood products.[84] The Royal Commission on Aboriginal Peoples established an intervenor participation program, which provides funding to certain groups to assist them in making representations to the commission. This is to ensure that even relatively small and less well-funded groups will have an opportunity to participate.[85]

Commissioners also usually arrange for academic research to provide them with some background on the issue under review, e.g., the history of the issue, how it is handled in other countries. This usually involves hiring academics or consultants to produce background papers, which may or may not be published and made available to the public. The Royal Commission on Electoral Reform and Party Financing generated twenty-three background reports on electoral systems in Canada and other countries. In spite of the money and time expended on research, there is some question about how much influence it has had on the conclusions of some commissions.[86]

EXAMPLES OF RESEARCH STUDIES OF THE ROYAL COMMISSION ON ELECTORAL REFORM

Aboriginal People and Electoral Reform in Canada

Drawing the Map

Polls and Media in Canadian Elections

Political Ethics

Reporting the Campaign

Rights and Electoral Reform in Canada

Women in Canadian Politics

Some commissions produce interim reports to advise the public of the direction of their thinking; this could incite some additional public participation. The commission always produces a final report containing its analysis of the situation and some recommendations. This report can sometimes be accompanied by a minority report, or a dissent from some part of the majority report, if all commissioners are not in full agreement.

The Provincial Scene

This section has focused mainly on federal Royal commissions and task forces, partly because these are the most widely known and partly because there has been little systematic study of provincial commissions.[87] However, provincial governments have legislation similar to the federal Inquiries Act that provides for the establishment of these kinds of bodies. Some of the areas investigated by provincial bodies seem very similar to those investigated by federal bodies, such as the Nova Scotia Royal Commission on Pensions (reported 1983) and Manitoba's Task Force on Government Organization and Economy (reported 1978).

Criticisms

The most common criticisms of the commission form of organization relate to cost, delay, and the lack of an implementation mechanism. For a device that was supposed to provide an ad hoc review of a specific problem, modern-day commissions can appear incredibly bureaucratic. Large numbers of people are hired and masses of literature are produced over the several-year life of the commission. When the commissioner is a high-profile person receiving a large per diem payment, the criticism can be even stronger.[88]

Delay can also be a problem in a situation where people want change quickly. They become very frustrated with yet another study about an issue that they regard as urgent.

These criticisms must be weighed against the quality of the recommendations and other output of the commission. Even the largest commissions cost considerably less than ordinary operating departments. Commissions have the further benefit of being finite; the costs incurred will continue for only a limited period. Even the delay caused by commissions is frequently beneficial. Government sometimes uses commissions to show its concern, while simultaneously marking time to see how a situation will develop. The Task Force on National Unity appointed shortly after the election of the Parti Québécois in 1976 is one example of this. Commissions are sometimes used to delay decisions, but it is better to delay and adopt a good solution than to act quickly and do the wrong thing.

The fact that there is usually no mechanism to ensure implementation of commission recommendations is a cause for some concern. This lack of responsibility for implementation could cause commissions to propose utopian recommendations that are effectively useless.

However, the opposite tendency is also possible. Wilson has argued that structural constraints make it very difficult for these commissions to do more than "administrative tinkering."

> Critics of staged inquiries into the policy process argue that these exercises must fall into two categories: (a) validating stamps of approval on changes already effected or sanctioned by the bureaucracy, and (b) reports that will never be implemented because they lack a powerful constituency. To attempt more is to ask for serious trouble. Tinkering with improving the inputs into the policy process is a very safe exercise. However, once task forces or other forms of inquiries start interfering or fundamentally questioning how resources are utilized, they challenge administrative competence. Should they be bold enough to question outputs, then they challenge political competence. Therefore, inquiries into the policy process in today's climate which construe their missions as being much wider than mere technical administrative exercises will end up as embarrassing political trials.[89]

Liora Salter refers to this as one of the contradictions of inquiries. On the one hand, these commissions can encourage radical debate about very innovative ideas, which raise the hopes of people dissatisfied with the status quo. On the other hand, when the commission actually makes its recommendations, it usually opts for incremental reforms because it knows that nothing else will be accepted.[90]

Another criticism of commissions has been that, even after all the resources that have been poured into the commissions' work, governments tend not to accept their recommendations if they do not fit their preconceived ideas. Sylvia Bashevkin found that Royal commissions and task forces that have dealt with issues of economic and cultural nationalism have not had much success in having their recommendations implemented. Her explanation is that usually these recommendations have had only lukewarm support from the general public and very little support from elites.[91] The lesson seems to be that the logical arguments made by Royal commissions do not carry much weight when they are out of line with public or, more important, elite, opinion.

However, it is very difficult to evaluate the real impact of a Royal commission. Some people have a scoreboard mentality about commission recommendations—they record the number of recommendations implemented versus the total number of recommendations.[92] By this measure, few commissions look good. However, a more thoughtful analysis of the general tone of commission recommendations suggests that governments have usually taken the recommendations very seriously and implemented at least some portion of them.[93] Also, certain commissions have set a tone for change that goes far beyond any specific recommendation.[94] The classic example of this is the Royal Commission on Bilingualism and Biculturalism, which operated in the late 1960s. There is no question that the status of the French language was considerably enhanced as a result of the attention devoted to the activities of the commission. Counting recommendations in this situation is meaningless.

One of the most serious problems that commissions will have to face in the Charter of Rights era is the clash between policy makers' values and lawyers' values.

The policy-maker sees commissions of inquiry as stepping-stones to policy. In this guise, inquiries serve several functions, of which the most important are the elucidation and education of public opinion, the discovery and exploration of policy options and the making of recommendations for action.[95]

Policy makers want a process that is relatively simple and allows all interested parties to have their say with a minimum of complication. Policy makers recognize, and are usually not bothered by the idea, that obtaining the ultimate "truth" is probably not possible. One simply listens to all sides of the issue and uses one's judgment to make a satisfactory decision.

Commissions that deal with general policy issues work very well this way, but there are some commissions in which people's actions will be discussed in such a way that their reputations could be tarnished or their right to a fair trial limited. In these cases, lawyers will want to intervene to ensure that their clients' rights are protected and proper procedures are followed by the commission.[96]

The problem is that this emphasis on procedure will undoubtedly slow down the workings of the commission and could shift the focus of debate to procedural rather than substantive questions, and thus defeat the purpose of appointing a commission. However, when people's names are thrown about in a public forum and serious accusations are made, some mechanisms for their protection must be introduced.

This has always been a problem, but it will become a more serious problem in the post-Charter era. If governments are not sensitive to this problem, it could destroy the benefits of the commission form of organization.

There is clearly a broader problem with the public perception of Royal commissions. If the public begins to dismiss all Royal commissions as expensive talk shops, then their value will be considerably diminished. Governments need to consider seriously the kind of issues they refer to Royal commissions, the specificity of the mandate they provide them, and a host of related issues if the credibility of these commissions is to be maintained.[97]

🏛 THE ROLE OF COLOURED PAPERS

Most policies are initiated within either political parties or operating departments. However, there are some other tools that can be instrumental in the policy-making process. One of these is coloured papers.

Coloured papers are documents prepared by government departments to communicate current government thinking on a particular issue to interested individuals or groups and to stimulate public discussion on the issue. One of Canada's foremost students of the use of coloured papers argues that they have three basic purposes:

- to provide information to interested parties;

- to involve Parliament and the public in decision making; and

- to stimulate federal-provincial consultation.[98]

Coloured papers are not always a part of the policymaking process, although they have become more common since the Trudeau era.[99] When both kinds of coloured papers are used, a green paper is followed by a white paper, although there is no set pattern, and sometimes one is used without the other.

A *green paper* is prepared fairly early in the policy-making process to stimulate discussion about the possibility of changing policy in a particular area. It is not a statement of government policy; rather, it usually attempts to set out a list of the options that the government is considering and the advantages and disadvantages of each. This is a signal to those interested in a particular policy area that the government is contemplating modifying a policy, and that they should make their views known to the government at this time.

The phrase "green paper" is used generically to describe all government communications of this sort. The actual colour of the covers of the papers varies widely; it is becoming more common to refer to specific documents by their actual colours such as the "blue paper" on Crown corporations[100] or the "orange paper" on social security[101] (sometimes irreverently called the "Halloween paper," after its rather garishly coloured cover).

A *white paper* is a statement of government policy that the government is attempting to establish in legislation. It usually provides a statement of policy in everyday, nonlegislative language, accompanied by an explanation and defence of the particular course of action chosen. It is the government's way of saying that it has reviewed the thinking in a particular area, possibly through the use of a green paper, and that this is its decision about how to proceed. This is the government's opportunity for the "hard sell." For example, the federal government's white paper titled *Enhancing the Safety and Soundness of the Canadian Financial System*[102] engendered a great deal of debate about the regulation of financial institutions.[103]

A white paper is less specific than draft legislation, and so groups still have an opportunity to effect some modifications in the government's approach to an issue. However, a white paper is meant to be government policy, and if the government is forced to make a major change after the white paper stage, the Opposition will use this opportunity to embarrass the government.

Coloured papers have been prepared on such wide-ranging topics as reform of the public service,[104] energy, immigration, social security, and the Constitution.[105] It is difficult to think of a major policy field that has not been the subject of a coloured paper.

Coloured papers are handled in a variety of ways after their release. They are frequently sent to parliamentary committees for formal discussion and review. This can sometimes lead to wide-ranging participation in the policy-making process:

> For example, the 1969 paper on tax reform was examined by two parliamentary committees. The Commons committee held a total of 146 meetings and heard 211 briefs presented by 820 individuals. Two subcommittees traveled across Canada and held 31 meetings to hear 68 briefs. In total, 524 briefs and 1,093 letters and other submissions were received by the Commons committee. The Senate committee received a total of 345 briefs from organized groups and individuals, of which it heard 118.[106]

This is an extreme case in terms of numbers of participants, but there is always great interest on the part of certain parties in the discussions on coloured papers.

Coloured papers play an important role in the policy development process because they encourage debate about a policy at a time when the government has that policy under review. Green papers provide a way for the government to gauge the depth and breadth of feelings about an issue without having to commit itself. White papers provide the government with the opportunity to state its case for a particular decision. Both devices encourage citizen participation in the policymaking process and help inform the public.

🏛 CONCLUSION

This chapter discussed some of the theories of policy making. The obvious question now is: Which one best describes reality? There is no easy answer. The discussion of each theory included examples of policies that seemed to fit that theory, so it seems clear that all of the theories discussed can be used to explain something. So, the answer to the question might be the admittedly vague idea that each theory has some value depending on the policy, the environment, the predispositions of the observer, and a whole series of other factors.

Is there any way of making these theories fit together? Richard Simeon suggests that different aspects of the policy process and different theories will be relevant at different points in the policy process. He describes what he calls a "funnel of causality."

> At the most general level, and most remote from the particular choice of alternative A or B, is the socioeconomic environment; next come the fundamental political variables, power, culture and ideology, and institutions; finally the most proximate source of decision is the operation of the decision-making process itself. To some extent, the more concerned one is with broad patterns of policy, and with international comparisons, the more one will concentrate on environmental, ideological, and structural variables; the more concerned with day-to-day shifts in policy, the more one will assume those prior factors as given and focus on the decision-makers themselves, though some environmental constraints may enter here too. Much of the literature has tended to focus on one end of the funnel without taking account of the other.[107]

This is a partial but reasonably representative explanation of the various theories. However, it is not enough for a government simply to make a policy; policies are only truly relevant when they are implemented. The next chapter discusses what happens during the implementation phase.

NOTES

1. Thomas R. Dye, *Understanding Public Policy,* 7th ed. (Englewood Cliffs, N.J.: Prentice-Hall, 1992), 2.
2. Ibid.
3. Peter Aucoin, "Public-Policy Theory and Analysis," in G. Bruce Doern and Peter Aucoin, eds., *Public Policy in Canada* (Toronto: Macmillan, 1979), 2.

4. Gilles Paquet, "Policy as Process: Tackling Wicked Problems," in Thomas J. Courchene and Arthur E. Stewart, eds., *Essays on Canadian Public Policy* (Kingston, Ont.: School of Policy Studies, Queen's University, 1989), 173.

5. This concept of policy being in constant flow is well-described in John W. Kingdon, *Agendas, Alternatives, and Public Policies* (Boston: Little, Brown, 1984).

6. B. Guy Peters, "The Policy Process: An Institutionalist Perspective," *Canadian Public Administration* 35, no. 2 (summer 1992), 165–66.

7. Malcolm Taylor, *Health Insurance and Canadian Public Policy: The Seven Decisions that Created the Canadian Health Insurance System and the Outcome* (Kingston, Ont.: McGill-Queen's University Press, 1987).

8. Arthur Kroeger, "A Retrospective on Policy Development in Ottawa," *Canadian Public Administration* 39, no. 4 (winter 1996), 457-68.

9. There are many illustrations of this. See, for example: Grace Skogstad, "Policy Under Siege: Supply Management in Agricultural Marketing," *Canadian Public Administration* 36, no. 1 (spring 1993), 1–23; Kathryn Harrison and George Hoberg, "Setting the Environmental Agenda in Canada and the United States: The Cases of Dioxin and Radon," *Canadian Journal of Political Science* 24, no. 1 (March 1991), 3–27.

10. A good example of how to assemble a policy from its constituent pieces is given in: Leslie A. Pal, *Public Policy Analysis: An Introduction*, 2nd ed. (Scarborough, Ont.: Nelson Canada, 1992), 3ff.

11. James R. Anderson, *Public Policy-Making*, 3rd ed. (New York: Holt, Rinehart and Winston, 1984), 8.

12. William N. Dunn, *Public Policy Analysis* (Englewood Cliffs, N.J.: Prentice-Hall, 1981), 225–26.

13. Peter Aucoin, "Theory and Research in the Study of Policy-Making," in G. Bruce Doern and Peter Aucoin, eds., *The Structures of Policy-Making in Canada* (Toronto: Macmillan of Canada, 1971), 24.

14. Lindblom's ideas on incrementalism have been elaborated in several places. The shortest and most succinct treatment is in "The Science of 'Muddling Through,'" *Public Administration Review* 19 (spring 1959): 79–88. Some of the other more thorough treatments are David Braybrooke and Charles Lindblom, *A Strategy of Decision* (New York: The Free Press, 1970); Charles Lindblom, *The Policy-Making Process* (Englewood Cliffs, N.J.: Prentice-Hall, 1968); and Robert A. Dahl and Charles E. Lindblom, *Politics, Economics, and Welfare* (New York: Harper & Row, 1953).

15. Braybrooke and Lindblom, *A Strategy of Decision*, 99–102.

16. Amitai Etzioni, "Mixed-Scanning: A 'Third' Approach to Decision-Making," *Public Administration Review* 27 (1967): 387.

17. Yehezkel Dror "Muddling Through 'Science' or Inertia?" *Public Administration Review* 24 (1964): 155.

18. Herbert Simon, *Administrative Behavior*, 2nd ed. (New York: The Free Press, 1957), 79.

19. James G. March and Herbert A. Simon, *Organizations* (New York: John Wiley & Sons, 1958), 140–41. (Emphasis in original.)

20. Yehezkel Dror, *Public Policymaking Reexamined* (Scranton, Pa.: Chandler Publishing Company, 1968), chs. 13–15 and passim.

21. Etzioni, "Mixed Scanning," 389–90.

22. Ibid., 388.

23. Dennis C. Mueller, *Public Choice* (Cambridge: Cambridge University Press, 1979), 1.

24. Some of the clearest statements of the public choice approach are found in: Stephen Brooks, *Public Policy in Canada: An Introduction*, 2nd ed. (Toronto: McClelland & Stewart, Inc., 1993), 35–9; M.H. Sproule-Jones, *Public Choice and Federalism in Australia and Canada* (Canberra: Centre for Research on Federal Financial Relations, The

Australian National University, 1975), ch. 2; Mark Sproule-Jones, "Institutions, Constitutions, and Public Policies: A Public-Choice Overview," in Michael M. Atkinson and Marsha A. Chandler, eds., *The Politics of Canadian Public Policy* (Toronto: University of Toronto Press, 1983), 127–50.

25. D.G. Hartle, *A Theory of the Expenditure Budgetary Process* (Toronto: University of Toronto Press, 1976), 12.

26. Anthony Downs, *An Economic Theory of Democracy* (New York: Harper & Row, 1957), 38–39.

27. Albert Breton, *The Economic Theory of Representative Government* (Chicago: Aldine, 1974), ch. 5 and passim. One of the most complete formulations of public choice theories of collective action is contained in Mancur Olson, *The Logic of Collective Action* (Cambridge: Harvard University Press, 1965).

28. Hartle, *A Theory of the Expenditure Budgetary Process*, 65.

29. Bruce Macnaughton and Conrad Winn, "Economic Policy and Electoral Self Interest: The Allocations of the Department of Regional Economic Expansion," *Canadian Public Policy* 7 (spring 1981), 318–27.

30. William A. Niskanen, Jr., *Bureaucracy and Representative Government* (Chicago: Aldine-Atherton, 1971), ch. 4. For a more recent assessment of this important work, see: André Blais and Stéphane Dion, eds., *The Budget-Maximizing Bureaucrat: Appraisals and Evidence* (Pittsburgh: University of Pittsburgh Press, 1991).

31. Albert Breton and Ronald Wintrobe, *The Logic of Bureaucratic Conduct* (Cambridge: Cambridge University Press, 1982), 146–54. For a similar point, see also Breton, *The Economic Theory of Representative Government*, 163.

32. Douglas G. Hartle, *The Expenditure Budget Process of the Government of Canada: A Public Choice—Rent-Seeking Perspective*, Canadian Tax Paper no. 81 (Toronto: Canadian Tax Foundation, 1988), 35. (Footnote omitted.)

33. Robert B. Denhardt, *Theories of Public Organization* (Pacific Grove, Calif.: Brooks/Cole, 1984), 146. (Footnote omitted.)

34. For a good general criticism of public choice which discusses this point, see: Sandford F. Borins, "Public Choice: 'Yes Minister' Made It Popular, but Does Winning the Nobel Prize Make It True?" *Canadian Public Administration* 31, no. 1 (spring 1988), 12–26.

35. Graham Allison, *Essence of Decision*, (Boston: Little, Brown, 1971), ch. 5.

36. Ibid., 176.

37. Ibid., 171.

38. Richard D. French, *How Ottawa Decides* (Toronto: James Lorimer, 1980), ch. 2 and passim.

39. Richard J. Schultz, *Federalism, Bureaucracy, and Public Policy* (Montreal: McGill-Queen's University Press, 1980); Simon McInnes, "Federal-Provincial Negotiation: Family Allowances 1970–1976" (Ph.D. diss., Carleton University, 1978); David Siegel, "Provincial-Municipal Relations in Ontario: A Case Study of Roads" (Ph.D. diss., University of Toronto, 1984). For a dissenting view about the explanatory value of bureaucratic politics, see: Gerard Boychuk, "Bureaucratic Politics Versus Institutional Norms: Alberta, FIGA, Social Services, 1973–79," *Canadian Public Administration* 37, no. 1 (spring 1994), 31–47.

40. Shawn McCarthy and Edward Greenspon, "PM Rejects Rock's Drug Prescription," *The Globe and Mail*, December 23, 1997; Tim Harper, "Drug Patent Battle Heating Up," *Toronto Star*, December 20, 1997.

41. Michael M. Atkinson and William D. Coleman, "Policy Networks, Policy Communities, and the Problem of Governance," in Laurent Dobuzinskis, Michael Howlett, and David Laycock, eds., *Policy Studies in Canada: The State of the Art* (Toronto: University of Toronto Press, 1996), 201.

42. One of the best overviews of the literature is contained in: Leslie A. Pal, *Beyond Policy Analysis: Public Issue Management in Turbulent Times* (Scarborough, Ont.: ITP Nelson, 1997), ch. 6.

43. A. Paul Pross, "Pressure Groups: Talking Chameleons," in Michael S. Whittington and Glen Williams, eds., *Canadian Politics in the 1990s* (Toronto: Nelson Canada, 1995), 263–68.

44. Michael Howlett and Jeremy Rayner, "Do Ideas Matter? Policy Network Configurations and Resistance to Policy Change in the Canadian Forest Sector," *Canadian Public Administration* 38, no. 3 (fall 1995), 382–410.

45. Jeremy Wilson, "Wilderness Politics in BC," in William D. Coleman and Grace Skogstad, eds., *Policy Communities and Public Policy in Canada: A Structural Approach* (Mississauga, Ont.: Copp Clark Pitman Ltd., 1990), 141–69.

46. David J. Falcone and Michael S. Whittington, "Output Change in Canada: A Preliminary Attempt to Open the 'Black Box'" (Paper presented to the Annual Meeting of the Canadian Political Science Association, Montreal, Quebec, 4 June 1972.)

47. Sohrab Abizadeh and John A. Gray, "Politics and Provincial Government Spending in Canada," *Canadian Public Administration* 35, no. 4 (winter 1992), 519–33.

48. Stephen Begadon and Carol Agócs, "Limits to Power: A Study of the Influence of Mayors and CAOs on Municipal Budgets in Ontario, 1977–1990," *Canadian Public Administration* 38, no. 1 (spring 1995), 39.

49. Richard Simeon, "Studying Public Policy," *Canadian Journal of Political Science* 9 (December 1976): 567.

50. Richard Rose, *Do Parties Make A Difference?* (London: Macmillan, 1980), 12. (Emphasis in original; footnote omitted.)

51. Ibid., 145. (Emphasis in original.)

52. Leo Panitch, "The Role and Nature of the Canadian State," in Leo Panitch, ed. *The Canadian State: Political Economy and Political Power* (Toronto: University of Toronto Press, 1977), 8 and passim.

53. Rick Deaton, "The Fiscal Crisis of the State and the Revolt of the Public Employees," *Our Generation* 8 (October 1972): 11–51.

54. James O'Connor, *The Fiscal Crisis of the State* (New York: St. Martin's Press, 1973), 6.

55. Brooks, *Public Policy in Canada*, 41.

56. Nicos Poulantzas, *Political Power and Social Classes* (London: Verso Editions, 1978), 255ff. and Part IV passim.

57. Ronald S. Ritchie, *An Institute for Research on Public Policy* (Ottawa: Information Canada, 1971), 8.

58. A good historical overview of the use of commissions is found in: Nick d'Ombrain, "Public Inquiries in Canada," *Canadian Public Administration*, 40, no. 1 (spring 1997), 86–107.

59. Law Reform Commission of Canada, *Commissions of Inquiry* (Ottawa: Minister of Supply and Services Canada, 1977), 10–1.

60. R.S.C. 1985, c. I-11, s. 2.

61. Law Reform Commission of Canada, *Commissions of Inquiry*, 5.

62. These differences in form and tone are discussed in M.J. Trebilcock et al., *The Choice of Governing Instrument* (Ottawa: Minister of Supply and Services Canada, 1982), 40; and V. Seymour Wilson, "The Role of Royal Commissions and Task Forces," in G. Bruce Doern and Peter Aucoin, eds., *The Structures of Policy-Making in Canada* (Toronto: Macmillan 1971), 115, 121–26.

63. An order in council is an official proclamation made by the governor general in council.

64. George Fletcher Henderson, *Federal Royal Commissions in Canada, 1867–1966: A Checklist* (Toronto: University of Toronto Press, 1967). This has been updated by Denise Ledoux,

Commissions of Inquiry Under the Inquiries Act, Part I: 1967 to Date (Ottawa: Library of Parliament, 1980). These figures are reasonably accurate, but exact numbers are virtually impossible to confirm. Law Reform Commission of Canada, *Commissions of Inquiry*, 10.

65. J.E. Hodgetts, "The Role of Royal Commissions in Canadian Government," in *Proceedings of the Third Annual Conference of the Institute of Public Administration of Canada* (1951), 354–55.

66. John Childs Courtney, "Canadian Royal Commissions of Inquiry, 1946 to 1962: An Investigation of an Executive Instrument of Inquiry," Ph.D. diss., Duke University, 1964, 121. J.E. Hodgetts makes a similar distinction in "Public Power and Ivory Tower," in Trevor Lloyd and Jack McLeod, eds., *Agenda 1970: Proposals for a Creative Politics* (Toronto: University of Toronto Press, 1968), 271–78.

67. Law Reform Commission of Canada, *Commissions of Inquiry*, 13.

68. Ibid.

69. A good discussion of the legal framework facing commissions is contained in: A. Wayne MacKay, "Mandates, Legal Foundations, Powers and Conduct of Commissions of Inquiry," in A. Paul Pross, Innis Christie, and John A. Yogis, eds., *Commissions of Inquiry* (Toronto: Carswell, 1990), 29–47; John Sopinka, "The Role of Commission Counsel," in ibid., 75–85.

70. André Picard, "Court Lets Krever Probe Proceed," *The Globe and Mail*, 28 June 1996; Rebecca Bragg and Donovan Vincent, "Krever Allowed to Name Names," *The Toronto Star*, 28 June 1996.

71. Aucoin, "Contributions of Commissions of Inquiry to Policy Analysis: An Evaluation," in Pross, Christie, and Yogis, eds., *Comissions of Inquiry*, 197–98. (Footnote omitted.) Reprinted by permission of Carswell, a division of Thomson Canada Limited.

72. Trebilcock, *The Choice of Governing Instrument*, 45.

73. Meyer Brownstone, "To Commission or not to Commission: As An Advisory Body," *Canadian Public Administration* 5 (fall 1962): 261.

74. For an analysis of the extent of this kind of participation, see Hugh Whalen, "Public Participation and, [sic] the Role of Canadian Royal Commissions and Task Forces: 1957–1969," Paper presented to the Annual Conference of the Institute of Public Administration of Canada (September 1981), 15.

75. Jane Jenson, "Commissioning Ideas: Representation and Royal Commissions," in Susan D. Phillips, ed., *How Ottawa Spends 1994–95: Making Change* (Ottawa: Carleton University Press, 1994), 52.

76. Trebilcock, *The Choice of Governing Instrument*, 44.

77. Law Reform Commission of Canada, *Advisory and Investigatory Commissions* (Ottawa: Minister of Supply and Services Canada, 1979), 32–3.

78. "Putting Judges in the Political Hot Seat," *The Globe and Mail*, 10 October 1985, A7.

79. Henderson, *Federal Royal Commissions in Canada, 1867–1966* and Ledoux, *Commissions of Inquiry Under the Inquiries Act, Part I: 1967 to Date.*

80. Jenson, "Commissioning Ideas ...," 52. (Footnote omitted from original.)

81. Hodgetts, "The Role of Royal Commissions in Canadian Government," 358.

82. Rod Mickleburgh, "Panel Was Mired in Controversy," *The Globe and Mail*, 30 November 1993.

83. R.S.C. 1985, c. I-11, s. 4.

84. André Picard, "Hearings to Mix Blood, Politics and Drama," *The Globe and Mail*, 14 February 1994; Rod Mickleburgh, "Blood Victims Will Have Their Say," *The Globe and Mail*, 15 February 1994.

85. Royal Commission on Aboriginal Peoples, *Project Description Abstracts* (April 1993).

86. Jenson, "Commissioning Ideas ...," 54–58.

87. For a listing of provincial Royal commissions, see Lise Maillet, *Provincial Royal Commissions and Commissions of Inquiry* (Ottawa: Minister of Supply and Services Canada, 1986).

88. Editorial, "A Royal Waste," *Vancouver Sun*, 9 September 1983; "Macdonald Commission Members Get $350 a Day," *Toronto Star*, 3 May 1983; "Macdonald Commission: Chairman Eager to Demonstrate He's Worth His Wages," *Calgary Herald*, 10 November 1983.

89. V. Seymour Wilson, "What Legacy? The Nielsen Task Force Program Review," in Katherine A. Graham, ed., *How Ottawa Spends—1988/89* (Ottawa: Carleton University Press, 1988), 25.

90. Wilson, "The Two Contradictions in Public Inquiries," in Pross, Christie, and Yogis, eds., *Commissions of Inquiry*, 177 and passim.

91. Sylvia Bashevkin "Does Public Opinion Matter? The Adoption of Federal Royal Commission and Task Force Recommendations on the National Question, 1951–1987," *Canadian Public Administration* 31, no. 3 (fall 1988): 390–407.

92. A good critique of this scoreboard mentality is found in: G. Bruce Doern and Richard W. Phidd, *Canadian Public Policy: Ideas, Structure, Process* (Toronto: Methuen, 1983), 543-44.

93. Courtney, "Canadian Royal Commissions of Inquiry," 140–55.

94. Doern and Phidd, *Canadian Public Policy*, 543–44.

95. Innis Christie and A. Paul Pross, "Introduction," in Pross, Christie, and Yogis, eds., *Commissions of Inquiry*, 4.

96. This issue is discussed very well in: Bryan Schwartz, "Public Inquiries," *Canadian Public Administration*, 40, no. 1 (spring 1997), 72–85.

97. Bryan Schwartz provides a good list of recommendations in "Public Inquiries," 82–83.

98. Audrey D. Doerr, "The Role of Coloured Papers," *Canadian Public Administration* 25 (fall 1982): 370–76.

99. For a good history of the process, see A.D. Doerr, "The Role of White Papers," in Doern and Aucoin, eds., *The Structures of Policy-Making in Canada*, 180–87.

100. Canada, Privy Council Office, *Crown Corporations: Direction-Accountability-Control* (Minister of Supply and Services Canada, 1977).

101. Marc Lalonde, Minister of National Health and Welfare, *Working Paper on Social Security in Canada*, 2nd ed. (1973).

102. Canada, Department of Finance, *Enhancing the Safety and Soundness of the Canadian Financial System* (Ottawa: Department of Finance, 1995).

103. Most of the entire June 1995 edition of the infulential periodical *Policy Options* was given over to conflicting articles on this topic.

104. Government of Canada, *Public Service 2000: The Renewal of the Public Service of Canada* (Ottawa: Minister of Supply and Services Canada, 1990).

105. A more complete list of recent coloured papers is contained in Doerr, "The Role of Coloured Papers," 378–79.

106. Ibid., 372.

107. "Studying Public Policy," 556.

BIBLIOGRAPHY

Abizadeh, Sohrab, and John A. Gray. "Politics and Provincial Government Spending in Canada." *Canadian Public Administration* 35, no. 4 (winter 1992), 519–33.

Allison, Graham. *Essence of Decision: Explaining the Cuban Missile Crisis.* Boston: Little, Brown, 1971.

Anderson, James R. *Public Policy-Making*. 3rd ed. New York: Holt, Rinehart and Winston, 1984.

Atkinson, Michael M., and Marsha A. Chandler, eds. *The Politics of Canadian Public Policy*. Toronto: University of Toronto Press, 1983.

Atkinson, Michael M., and William D. Coleman. "Policy Networks, Policy Communities, and the Problem of Governance." In Laurent Dobuzinskis, Michael Howlett, and David Laycock, eds. *Policy Studies in Canada: The State of the Art*. Toronto: University of Toronto Press, 1996, 193-218.

Bashevkin, Sylvia. "Does Public Opinion Matter? The Adoption of Federal Royal Commission and Task Force Recommendations on the National Question, 1951–1987." *Canadian Public Administration* 31, no. 3 (fall 1988): 390–407.

Beer, Samuel H. "Federalism, Nationalism and Democracy in America." *American Political Science Review* 72 (March 1978).

Begadon, Stephen, and Carol Agócs. "Limits to Power: A Study of the Influence of Mayors and CAOs on Municipal Budgets in Ontario, 1977-1990." *Canadian Public Administration*, 38, no. 1 (spring 1995), 29-44.

Blais, André, and Stéphane Dion, eds. *The Budget-Maximizing Bureaucrat: Appraisals and Evidence*. Pittsburgh: University of Pittsburgh Press, 1991.

Borins, Sandford F. "Public Choice: 'Yes Minister' Made It Popular, but Does Winning the Nobel Prize Make It True?' *Canadian Public Administration* 31, no. 1 (spring 1988), 12-26.

Boychuk, Gerard. "Bureaucratic Politics Versus Institutional Norms: Alberta, FIGA, Social Services, 1973-79" *Canadian Public Administration* 37, no. 1 (spring 1994), 31–47.

Braybrooke, David, and Charles Lindblom. *A Strategy of Decision*. New York: The Free Press, 1970.

Breton, Albert. *The Economic Theory of Representative Government*. Chicago: Aldine, 1974.

Breton, Albert, and Ronald Wintrobe. *The Logic of Bureaucratic Conduct*. Cambridge: Cambridge University Press, 1982.

Brooks, Stephen. *Public Policy in Canada: An Introduction*, 2nd ed. Toronto: McClelland & Stewart, Inc., 1993.

Brownstone, Meyer. "To Commission or not to Commission: As An Advisory Body." *Canadian Public Administration* 5 (fall 1962): 261–68.

Canada, Department of Finance, *Enhancing the Safety and Soundness of the Canadian Financial System*. Ottawa: Department of Finance, 1995.

Clokie, Hugh McDowell, and J. William Robinson. *Royal Commissions of Inquiry*. Stanford: Stanford University Press, 1937.

Courtney, John Childs. "Canadian Royal Commissions of Inquiry, 1946 to 1962: An Investigation of an Executive Instrument of Inquiry." Ph.D. diss., Duke University, 1964.

_____. "In Defense of Royal Commissions." *Canadian Public Administration* 12 (summer 1969): 198–212.

Dahl, Robert A., and Charles E. Lindblom. *Politics, Economics, and Welfare*. New York: Harper & Row, 1953.

Deaton, Rick. "The Fiscal Crisis of the State and the Revolt of the Public Employees." *Our Generation* 8 (October 1972): 11–51.

Denhardt, Robert B. *Theories of Public Organization*. Pacific Grove, Calif.: Brooks/Cole, 1984.

Doern, G. Bruce, and Peter Aucoin. *The Structures of Policy-Making in Canada*. Toronto: Macmillan, 1971.

_____. eds. *Public Policy in Canada*. Toronto: Macmillan, 1979.

Doern, G. Bruce, and Richard W. Phidd. *Canadian Public Policy: Ideas, Structure, Process*. Toronto: Methuen, 1983.

Doern, G. Bruce, and V. Seymour Wilson, eds. *Issues in Canadian Public Policy*. Macmillan, 1974.

Doerr, Audrey D. *The Machinery of Government in Canada*. Toronto: Methuen, 1981.

_____. "The Role of Coloured Papers." *Canadian Public Administration* 25 (fall 1982): 366–79.

d'Ombrain, Nick, "Public Inquiries in Canada," *Canadian Public Administration* 40, no. 1 (spring 1997), 86–107.

Downs, Anthony. *An Economic Theory of Democracy*. New York: Harper & Row, 1957.

Dror, Yehezkel. "Muddling Through 'Science' or Inertia?" *Public Administration Review* 24 (1964): 153–58.

_____. *Public Policymaking Reexamined*. Scranton, Pa.: Chandler, 1968.

Dunn, William N. *Public Policy Analysis*. Englewood Cliffs, N.J.: Prentice-Hall, 1981.

Dye, Thomas R. *Policy Analysis: What Governments Do, Why They Do It, and What Difference It Makes*. University, Ala.: The University of Alabama Press, 1976).

_____. *Understanding Public Policy*. 5th ed. Englewood Cliffs, N.J.: Prentice-Hall, 1984.

Etzioni, Amitai. "Mixed-Scanning: A 'Third' Approach to Decision-Making." *Public Administration Review* 27 (1967): 385–92.

Falcone, David J., and Michael S. Whittington. "Output Change in Canada: A Preliminary Attempt to Open the 'Black Box.'" Paper presented to the Annual Meeting of the Canadian Political Science Association, Montreal, Quebec, June 4, 1972.

French, Richard D. *How Ottawa Decides*. Toronto: James Lorimer, 1980.

Granatstein, J.L. *The Ottawa Men*. Toronto: Oxford University Press, 1982.

Hanson, Hugh. "Inside Royal Commissions." *Canadian Public Administration* 12 (fall 1969): 356–64.

Hartle, D. G. *A Theory of the Expenditure Budgetary Process*. Toronto: University of Toronto Press, 1976.

_____. *The Expenditure Budget Process of the Government of Canada: A Public Choice—Rent-Seeking Perspective*. Toronto: Canadian Tax Foundation, 1988.

Henderson, George Fletcher. *Federal Royal Commissions in Canada, 1867–1966: A Checklist*. Toronto: University of Toronto Press, 1967.

Hodgetts, J. E. "The Role of Royal Commissions in Canadian Government," in *Proceedings of the Third Annual Conference of the Institute of Public Administration of Canada* (1951): 351–67.

_____. "Should Canada Be DeCommissioned? A Commoner's View of Royal Commissions." *Queen's Quarterly* 70 (winter 1964): 475–90.

_____. "Public Power and Ivory Tower." In Trevor Lloyd and Jack McLeod, eds., *Agenda 1970: Proposals for a Creative Politics*. Toronto: University of Toronto Press, 1968, 256–80.

Howlett, Michael, and Jeremy Rayner, "Do Ideas Matter? Policy Network Configurations and Resistance to Policy Change in the Canadian Forest Sector," *Canadian Public Administration* 38, no. 3 (fall 1995), 382–410.

Jenson, Jane. "Commissioning Ideas: Representation and Royal Commissions," in Susan D. Phillips, ed., *How Ottawa Spends 1994–95: Making Change* (Ottawa: Carleton University Press, 1994), 39–69.

Kroeger, Arthur, "A Retrospective on Policy Development in Ottawa, *Canadian Public Administration* 39, no. 4 (winter 1996), 457–68.

Laframboise, H.L. "Moving a Proposal to a Positive Decision: A Case Study of the Invisible Process." *Optimum* 4, no. 3 (1973): 31–41.

Law Reform Commission of Canada. *Advisory and Investigatory Commissions*. Ottawa: Minister of Supply and Services Canada, 1979.

_____. *Commissions of Inquiry*. Ottawa: Minister of Supply and Services Canada, 1977.

Ledoux, Denise. *Commissions of Inquiry Under the Inquiries Act, Part I: 1967 to Date*. Ottawa: Library of Parliament, 1980.

Lindblom, Charles E. "The Science of 'Muddling Through.'" *Public Administration Review* 19 (spring 1959): 79–88.

_____. *The Policy-Making Process*. Englewood Cliffs, N.J.: Prentice-Hall, 1968.

Macnaughton, Bruce, and Conrad Winn. "Economic Policy and Electoral Self Interest: The Allocations of the Department of Regional Economic Expansion," *Canadian Public Policy* 7 (spring 1981), 318–27.

Maillet, Lise. *Provincial Royal Commissions and Commissions of Inquiry.* Ottawa: Minister of Supply and Services Canada, 1986.

Manzer, Ronald. *Public Policies and Political Development in Canada.* Toronto: University of Toronto Press, 1985.

March, James G., and Herbert A. Simon. *Organizations.* New York: John Wiley & Sons, 1958.

McInnes, Simon. "Federal-Provincial Negotiation: Family Allowances 1970–1976." Ph.D. diss., Carleton University, 1978.

Mueller, Dennis C. *Public Choice.* Cambridge: Cambridge University Press, 1979.

Niskanen, William A., Jr. *Bureaucracy and Representative Government.* Chicago: Aldine-Atherton, 1971.

Nossal, Kim Richard. "Allison through the (Ottawa) Looking Glass: Bureaucratic Politics and Foreign Policy in a Parliamentary System." *Canadian Public Administration* 22 (winter 1979): 610–26.

O'Connor, James. *The Fiscal Crisis of the State.* New York: St. Martin's Press, 1973.

Olson, Mancur. *The Logic of Collective Action.* Cambridge: Harvard University Press, 1965.

Pal, Lelsie A. *Beyond Policy Analysis: Public Issue Management in Turbulent Times.* Scarborough, Ont.: ITP Nelson, 1997.

_____. *Public Policy Analysis: An Introduction*, 2nd ed. Scarborough, Ont.: Nelson Canada, 1992.

Panitch, Leo. "The Role and Nature of the Canadian State." In Leo Panitch, ed., *The Canadian State: Political Economy and Political Power.* Toronto: University of Toronto Press, 1977.

Paquet, Gilles, "Policy as Process: Tackling Wicked Problems," in Thomas J. Courchene and Arthur E. Stewart, eds., *Essays on Canadian Public Policy* (Kingston, Ont.: School of Policy Studies, Queen's University, 1989), 171–86.

Phidd, Richard W., and G. Bruce Doern. *The Politics and Management of Canadian Economic Policy.* Toronto: Macmillan, 1978.

Poulantzas, Nicos. *Political Power and Social Classes.* London: Verso Editions, 1978.

Pross, A. Paul "Pressure Groups: Talking Chameleons," in Michael S. Whittington and Glen Williams, eds. *Canadian Politics in the 1990s.* Toronto: Nelson Canada, 1995, 252–75.

Pross, A. Paul, Innis Christie, and John A. Yogis, eds. *Commissions of Inquiry.* Toronto: Carswell, 1990.

Rose, Richard. *Do Parties Make A Difference?* London: The Macmillan Press, 1980.

Schultz, Richard J. *Federalism, Bureaucracy, and Public Policy.* Montreal: McGill-Queen's University Press, 1980.

Schwartz, Bryan, "Public Inquiries," *Canadian Public Administration* 40, no. 1 (spring 1997), 72–85.

Siegel, David. "Provincial-Municipal Relations in Ontario: A Case Study of Roads." Ph.D. diss., University of Toronto, 1984.

Simeon, Richard, "Inside the Macdonald Commission," *Studies in Political Economy* 22 (spring 1987), 167–79.

_____."Studying Public Policy." *Canadian Journal of Political Science* 9 (December 1976): 548–80.

Simon, Herbert. *Administrative Behavior.* 2nd ed. New York: The Free Press, 1957.

Sproule-Jones, M. H. *Public Choice and Federalism in Australia and Canada.* Canberra: Centre for Research on Federal Financial Relations, The Australian National University, 1975.

Taylor, Malcolm. *Health Insurance and Canadian Public Policy: The Seven Decisions That Created the Canadian Health Insurance System and Their Outcomes.* Kingston, Ont.: McGill-Queen's University Press, 1987.

Trebilcock, M.J., Douglas G. Hartle, J. Robert S. Prichard, and Donald N. Dewees. *The Choice of Governing Instrument.* Ottawa: Minister of Supply and Services Canada, 1982.

Whalen, Hugh. "Public Participation and, [sic] the Role of Canadian Royal Commissions and Task Forces: 1957–1969." Paper presented to the Annual Conference of the Institute of Public Administration of Canada, September 1981.

Wilson, Jeremy. "Wilderness Politics in BC," in William D. Coleman and Grace Skogstad, eds. *Policy Communities and Public Policy in Canada: A Structural Approach.* Mississauga, Ont.: Copp Clark Pitman Ltd., 1990, 141–69.

Wilson, V. Seymour. "What Legacy? The Nielsen Task Force Program Review," in Katherine A. Graham, ed., *How Ottawa Spends—1988/89.* Don Mills, Ont.: Oxford University Press Canada, 1988, 23–47.

Windfield, Mark. "The Ultimate Horizontal Issue: The Environmental Policy Experiences of Alberta and Ontario, 1971–1993," *Canadian Journal of Political Science* 27, no. 1 (march 1994), 129–52.

7

Implementing, Measuring, and Evaluating Public Policy

The Health-Care Crisis! How many stories have you read or heard recently that begin with those ominous words? The health-care system is in crisis and why doesn't the government fix it? Governments have huge amounts of money and a great deal of power, so why can't the government simply solve the problem. Many issues are more complicated on deeper inspection than they seem initially.

Not everyone agrees that the system is in crisis, or sees the crisis in the same way. For example, some argue that the system is under-funded, while others say that there is enough money in the system, but it is being spent in the wrong ways. Therefore, the first task is to measure the outputs and outcomes of the existing system so that we can evaluate exactly where we stand now.

After that, we might decide that we need to implement some changes in the current system. Making changes in the health care system is not a unilateral government initiative. There are many players in the system. Governments have direct control over some of these players, but many must be coaxed or persuaded to change their method of operation.

Implementation is never as easy up close as it looks like it's going to be from a distance. In the first place, the government must find the money and the political will to initiate the change. In a time when many problems are competing for the attention of the government, this is not easy. Second, other players must be brought on side. In many cases, this involves persuading an organization to change the way it has done business for many years.

There are many obstacles to proper implementation of government policies—some deliberately placed, some accidental. This chapter will examine some of these obstacles and look at ways of overcoming them.

As discussed at the beginning of Chapter 6, the formulation of public policy is only one part of the overall policy process. This chapter will examine what happens after the initial decision about the adoption of a policy is made. It will examine how the policy is implemented, how its outputs are measured, and how it is evaluated to determine its ultimate worth.

🏛 IMPLEMENTATION

Traditionally, political scientists were predominantly concerned with the study of political institutions, e.g., cabinets or legislatures, and their impact on policy making. The general implication was that after policy decisions were made, they were simply automatically carried out, so that there was nothing of interest to political scientists in the implementation process. At best, there were a few questions of organization and motivation, which were considered to be more properly in the realm of those who study administration than of those who study important things like political science.

This attitude began to change in the 1970s, at least partly as a result of an increasing interest in policy-impact studies. These studies found that public policies frequently did not have the impacts that were envisaged when they were first formulated by the executive or legislature. For example, it was discovered that children were not learning as much in school as some thought they should be, that poverty was no closer to elimination in spite of the expenditure of significant amounts of money, and that courts were experiencing such a backlog that justice was seriously delayed. This led to a clear understanding that there was some slippage between policy making and policy impact; this, in turn, led to the realization that implementation is an integral part of the political process.

> [T]he bargaining and maneuvering [sic], the pulling and hauling, of the policy-adoption process carries over into the policy-implementation process. Diehard opponents of the policy who lost out in the adoption stage seek, and find, means to continue their opposition when, say, administrative regulations and guidelines are being written. Many who supported the original policy proposal did so only because they expected to be able to twist it in the implementation phase to suit purposes never contemplated or desired by others who formed part of the original coalition.[1]

Clausewitz wrote that war is simply the conduct of foreign relations by other means; on the domestic scene, implementation can be seen as the conduct of politics by other means.

The Implementation Process

Successful implementation is very difficult. Ripley and Franklin explain why:

> Implementation processes involve *many important actors* holding *diffuse and competing goals and expectations* who work within a *context of an increasingly large and complex mix of government programs* that require *participation from numerous layers and units of government* and who are affected by *powerful factors beyond their control.*[2]

They go on to describe implementation as a game. However:

> [t]he game does not resemble some nicely ordered sport with small team size and well-defined rules like basketball. Rather it resembles lacrosse in its original form—played between two tribes with the number of players, the boundaries, the duration, and other important aspects of the game all somewhat nebulous.[3]

One of the keys to understanding the implementation process is a better grasp of the complex relationship between those who make policy and those who implement it. Nakamura and Smallwood suggested that there could be five different styles of linkage between them.[4]

The *"classical" technocratic* linkage closely approximates the Weberian ideal-type. It assumes that formulators state goals clearly and unequivocally and delegate the technical responsibility for carrying out those goals to implementers, and that implementers automatically carry out those duties in the desired manner.

The *instructed delegate* approach is similar to the classical technocratic approach in that formulators specify goals and implementers agree with those goals, but it differs in that formulators delegate a somewhat broader area of discretion to the implementers. Implementers are not simply automatons; they have limited authority to make decisions about programs during the implementation process.

In the *bargaining* approach, the formulators and implementers do not agree on policy goals. However, since each needs the cooperation of the other in order to carry out any program, bargaining occurs. "The final outcome of bargaining between policy makers and implementers is determined by the distribution of relative power resources (actual or perceived) among the two groups."[5] This plays havoc with the traditional Weberian notion of bureaucracy in that it suggests that implementers could have some influence over formulators.[6]

The *discretionary experimenter* approach occurs when formulators can decide on broad general goals but do not have enough knowledge to specify precise goals or directions. In this case, formulators have little choice but to convey general goals to implementers and to provide them with wide discretionary powers to carry out these general abstract goals.

The *bureaucratic entrepreneur* approach turns the traditional relationship between formulators and implementers on its head. In this style of interaction, implementers begin by formulating their goals and then marshalling support for those goals among various significant groups. After this is done, the implementers approach the formulators to obtain the necessary resources, including legitimation, to undertake the program. This is the most radical approach, but it is also a very common one. Samuel H. Beer had this sort of relationship in mind when he made this comment on the political process in the United States:

> I would remark how rarely additions to the public sector have been initiated by the demands of voters or the advocacy of pressure groups or the platforms of political parties. On the contrary, in the fields of health, housing, urban renewal, transportation, welfare, education, poverty, and energy it has been, in very great measure, people in government service, or very closely associated with it, acting on the basis of their specialized and technical knowledge, who first perceived the problem, conceived the program, initially urged it on the President and Congress, went on to help lobby it through to enactment, and then saw to its administration.[7]

The closed nature of the parliamentary system makes it difficult to see this process at work in Canada, but cases can be cited where implementers have, in fact, had a major role in formulating policies.[8]

The "classical" technocratic approach is the approach that most closely corresponds with traditional democratic theory. The opposite extremes—the discretionary experimenter and bureaucratic entrepreneur approaches—seem to be at odds with the classic idea of "politicians on top, experts on tap." However, there are frequently situations where some slippage between the policy as originally stipulated and as implemented is necessary or even beneficial.

Paul Berman has identified what he calls *adaptive implementation*. He defines this as "processes that enable initial plans to be adapted to unfolding events and decisions."[9] He argues that the traditional style of implementation, which he calls *programmed implementation*, is frequently insensitive to the existing bureaucratic culture and so can result in symbolic implementation that amounts to no real change in how things are done.

He recognizes that adaptive implementation is at variance with traditional ideas of political control of implementation. However, he argues that for certain kinds of new programs, it is not only an accurate description of what generally happens, but it is actually preferable.

> Implementation problems arise because of the over-specification and rigidity of goals, the failure to engage relevant actors in decision-making, and the excessive control of deliverers. The ideal of adaptive implementation is the establishment of a process that allows policy to be modified, specified, and revised—in a word, adapted—according to the unfolding interaction of the policy with its institutional setting. Its outcomes would be neither automatic nor assured, and it would look more like a disorderly learning process than a predictable procedure.[10]

In particular, he feels that where policies involve radical changes in the status quo, where the technology to be employed is uncertain, where there is high conflict over the policy, and where there is an unstable environment, adaptive implementation might be the most beneficial approach.[11]

One of the keys to good implementation is understanding what conditions will improve the possibility of implementation, and what problems stand in the way of implementation. The next two sections of this chapter focus on those two points.

Making Implementation Easier

Two long-time students of implementation, Sabatier and Mazmanian, list five conditions that they feel are necessary for effective implementation.[12]

"*Condition 1. The program is based on a sound theory relating changes in target group behavior to the achievement of the desired end-state (objectives.)*" It must be clear that acting on the target group will actually cause progress toward the desired goal. For example, imposing stringent environmental standards on one group will not have much overall impact on pollution if that group is not a major contributor to pollution. In fact, such a policy could be very expensive to enforce if it incited resentment on the part of the target group.

"*Condition 2. The statute (or other basic policy decision) contains unambiguous policy directives, and structures the implementation process so as to maximize the likelihood that target groups will perform as desired.*" Clear guidance from legislators allows implementers to stay on track and helps them resist forces that would try to deflect or change the policy as it is being implemented. It is also important that responsibility for implementation is assigned to an organization that is supportive of the program and that adequate resources are allocated to that agency to carry out its responsibilities.

"*Condition 3. The leaders of the implementing agencies possess substantial managerial and political skills and are committed to statutory objectives.*" Usually, there are a number of agencies that could be assigned the responsibility for implementation. Legislators must exercise care in assigning a policy to an organization whose management is both competent and committed to the policy.

"*Condition 4. The program is actively supported by organized constituency groups and by a few key legislators (or the chief executive) throughout the implementation process, with the courts being neutral or supportive.*" This seems quite straightforward, but it can be more difficult to achieve than it might seem at first. The problem is the very short attention span of individuals and groups that causes them to lose interest in a cause quickly after initial legislation has been passed.

Sabatier and Mazmanian suggest that two factors should be present to achieve this condition. First, they recommend an individual whom they call a "fixer," but who might be called a "champion" by others. This is someone who will make it her or his mission to push for or "champion" a particular policy. This person will not allow others to forget commitments that they made in the heat of the moment. Second, there is a need for a supportive interest group that will monitor the activities of the implementing agency and ensure that it is making progress in the desired direction.[13] Consumers' and women's groups have carried out this function very well in some policy areas.

"*Condition 5. The relative priority of statutory objectives is not significantly undermined over time by the emergence of conflicting public policies or by changes in relevant socioeconomic conditions that undermine the statute's 'technical' theory or political support.*" The importance of specific policies can ebb and flow over time. In recent years, concerns about improving social programs have run head-on into concerns for reducing the deficit. When this happens, it is very difficult to maintain the interests of legislators in the policy that is falling out of fashion.

Difficulties of Implementation

Implementation is frequently much more difficult than it is perceived to be. All sorts of problems develop during implementation that were only dimly seen when the original policies were made.

Communications Problems. Chapter 3 discussed the Weberian idea of bureaucracy, which held that senior officials give orders and subordinates simply carry them out. Chapters 4 and 5 went on to suggest that it is not quite that simple. Subordinates are not programmed automatons; they have minds of their own and are capable of misunderstanding or misinterpreting (either accidentally or intentionally) the desires of senior officials. The need for communication between policy formulators and policy implementers presents problems.

[C]ommunications linkages within any policy system can be replete with potential pitfalls. Mishaps can occur because of (1) garbled messages from the senders; (2) misinterpretation by the receivers; or (3) system failure in terms of transmission breakdowns, overload, "noise," and inadequate follow-though or compliance mechanisms.[14]

These possible problems can be magnified by the presence of organizational and other kinds of systematic bias on the part of implementers.

Organizational Rigidities.   These communication difficulties raise the possibility of some sort of selective perception on the part of implementers. There are situations where this is deliberate and malicious, but that need not be the case. Most people have a strong predisposition to handle new problems using techniques with which they are familiar. This creates a tendency to respond to new initiatives using past techniques. For example, most professions possess what has been described as a "trained incapacity." Professional training teaches people one specific way to deal with a problem and so makes them unable to develop new approaches.

Policy makers frequently ignore the existence of these organizational biases when they are deciding on new policies. This means that policies are produced under the assumption that organizations will change to fit the needs of the policies; in fact, it is more likely that policies will be changed to fit the needs of the organization.

Insufficient Resources.   Even when people are willing and able to implement policies, there can still be difficulties if adequate resources are unavailable. This problem is sometimes compounded when policy makers who are instrumental in the adoption of a policy deliberately underestimate the resources needed to implement it in order to facilitate adoption of the policy. Implementers then suffer a shortage of funds, but this is not the only resource necessary to implement some policies. In the case of scientific programs in particular, there are sometimes not enough people with appropriate training to carry out a project, regardless of the funds available to pay them.

Implementers also complain that they do not receive enough political support at key points in the implementation phase. Frequently, politicians lose interest in a policy after it has been approved; they simply assume it will be implemented properly. However, implementers can have difficulty battling inertia or even hostile forces in the environment. Without continuing political support, implementers can be left, like the proverbial explorers, up the creek without a paddle. Political support is particularly necessary when there are a number of different organizations involved in implementation.

Interorganizational Complexity.   The problem of implementing programs that have intergovernmental or interorganizational implications is given a special place in the literature on implementation because of the great difficulties encountered.[15] These problems arise because of the number of different organizations involved, and because each of these organizations has different goals. At times, the numbers alone can be devastating. Pressman and Wildavsky's analysis of an economic development program found that it was necessary to arrive at seventy different agreements involving fifteen different organizations. They calculate that with this number of agreements needed, if each has an 80 percent probability of success, then the probability that all seventy would be arrived at successfully is 0.000000125. One would have to assume a 99 percent probability of success for each contract to come close to a 50 percent chance of having all seventy contracts completed successfully.[16] They also point out the importance of speed in arriving at agreements because once made, agreements can still be abrogated if later decisions are not made promptly.

> It could be said that the EDA public works program was characterized by the slow dissolution of agreement. As one delay succeeded another, the major individual participants changed and so did the understandings they had with one another. Agreements were reached, eroded, and remade. The frequent calls for coordination reflected the inability of the machinery for implementation to move fast enough to capture the agreements while they lasted. Allow enough time to elapse in a rapidly changing external world and it is hard to imagine any set of agreements remaining firm.[17]

Fullness of Time.   An important aspect of implementation that many people do not understand can be shown by the analogy that one cannot produce a child in one month by impregnating nine women. When a large organization with many accumulated organizational structures and biases is asked to accept a new idea, it takes time for that idea to sink in. This is particularly important because in "the implementation process ... politics appears primarily *defensive.* Actors seem more concerned with what they in particular might lose than with what all in general might gain."[18]

Many times the best implementation strategy is a very low-key one that involves simply mentioning a new idea that is currently being considered, without activating defence mechanisms by suggesting it be adopted. Then, after there has been some discussion of it, the idea begins to seem more palatable. Finally, it comes to be accepted by most people in the organization, and the time is ripe for implementation. This entire process might take months or even years. A great deal of damage can be done by trying to ram through a new idea without taking time to let people feel comfortable with it. In spite of the old saying, the shortest distance between two points is not necessarily a straight line.

Inadequate Participation.   The importance of participation was discussed in Chapters 4 and 5, but it is important to realize that participation is not just therapeutic for the individual; there is some evidence that it can have real benefits for the organization. Some studies have indicated that when people have the opportunity to participate in the early stages of policy design, the implementation process works much more smoothly.[19] There are at least two reasons for this. First, people who have been consulted about a policy will feel that they own a part of the policy and will feel comfortable with it during the implementation phase; the defence mechanisms mentioned above will never be activated. Second, early consultation with administrators will allow them to identify certain problems that can be corrected sooner rather than later.

The discussion in this and the preceding section makes it clear that a great deal of care must be exercised in choosing the means of implementing a policy. A unique Canadian contribution to this discussion has been the development of theories about how governments choose these instruments of implementation.

Choice of Governing Instrument

The concept of the "choice of governing instrument" recognizes that policy making is not simply the choice of a policy objective; rather, it also involves a decision about *how* the policy will be implemented. Doern and Phidd define governing instruments as "the major ways in which governments seek to ensure compliance, support and implementation of public policy."[20]

When most people think of government policy, they think of the more visible aspects of government activity, usually government expenditure or regulation. However, in attempting to implement some policies, governments have a number of techniques, or instruments, at their disposal. Doern and Phidd categorize these under a number of headings:

- exhortation and symbolic policy outputs;

- expenditure;

- taxation;

- regulation; and

- public enterprise.[21]

This section will discuss three theories of how governments select which instrument or mechanism they will employ to implement a policy. All three operate on the somewhat questionable assumption that governments have free rein to make more or less conscious decisions about which instrument to use. Kenneth Woodside has argued that this apparent breadth of choice is frequently limited by such factors as legislation, tradition, or level of experience with particular instruments.[22] For example, Atkinson and Nigol argue that one of the reasons why Ontario chose to regulate auto insurance rates, rather than establish a government-run insurance corporation, is that the ministry responsible for dealing with this issue had more experience in using regulation than in operating Crown corporations.[23]

Doern and Wilson have developed the *coercion theory*, which holds that in choosing governing instruments, governments will move from the least coercive instruments to more coercive ones. Note that the order in which the instruments were listed above moves from the least to the most coercive. Doern and Wilson have suggested that the choice of governing instrument is made with a keen eye on public acceptability and that the public will more easily accept persuasive than coercive measures:

This hypothesis would suggest that politicians (especially the collective cabinet) have a strong tendency to respond to policy issues (any issue) by moving successively from the *least coercive* governing instruments to the *most coercive.* Thus they tend to respond first in the least coercive fashion by creating a study, or by creating a new or reorganized unit of government, or merely by uttering a broad statement of intent. The next least coercive governing instrument would be to use a distributive spending approach in which the resources could be handed out to various constituencies in such a way that the least attention is given as to which taxpayers' pockets the resources are being drawn from. At the more coercive end of the continuum of governing instruments would be a larger redistributive programme, in which resources would be more visibly extracted from the more advantaged classes and redistributed to the less advantaged classes. Also at the more coercive end of the governing continuum would be direct regulation in which the sanctions or threat of sanctions would have to be directly applied. It is, of course, obvious that once a policy issue has matured and been on the public agenda for many years, all or most of the basic instruments could be utilized.[24]

Examples of the movement from less coercive policies to more coercive ones can be seen in a number of areas. The issue of equality for women was dealt with first by the use of a Royal commission to highlight the fact that there was a problem. Next, governments took action to improve the ability of women to compete in the labour force by providing innovative kinds of job training and *encouraging* employers not to discriminate against women. These kinds of policies benefited women without imposing an obvious cost on anyone. Next, legislation was passed to force employers to provide equal pay to women. This confers a benefit on women and imposes an obvious cost on only one limited group—employers. To this point, Canadian policy makers have generally stopped short of employment quotas that would be the most coercive form of policy, in that they would clearly benefit women and impose a cost on men.

Thus, we see a movement along Doern and Phidd's hierarchy from exhortation to expenditure to regulation. Similar examples could be found in the approach to bilingualism, inflation, and foreign ownership, although the handling of the issue of foreign ownership indicates that one can move both ways on the continuum. During the 1970s, successively stronger actions were taken to limit foreign ownership, but in the 1990s, as economic stagnation has become a concern, governments have been acting in a less coercive manner with regard to foreign ownership.

Nicolas Baxter-Moore has developed a *neo-Marxist approach* to choosing governing instruments. He argues that the state will choose different types of instruments, depending on whether it is attempting to influence dominant or subordinate classes, or whether it is implementing a policy aimed at accumulation or legitimation.[25] He has developed two specific hypotheses.

> From the neo-Marxist perspective, we may hypothesize first that the state will generally use less intrusive instruments when seeking the compliance of the dominant capitalist class and deploy more intrusive measures to direct or control the behaviour of subordinate classes.

> But the performance of the (sometimes contradictory) accumulation and legitimation functions often requires the state to disguise its activities on behalf of cap-

ital and to emphasize policies orientated towards subordinate groups. Therefore, we may also hypothesize that the state will tend to use less intrusive (or less visible) measures to foster capital accumulation and more intrusive (or more obvious) instruments when pursuing policies aimed primarily at legitimizing its rule.[26]

Woodside, too, argues that this perspective could explain government actions better than the coercion theory.

> [E]xperience suggests that governments do not always seek to avoid coercive solutions but, indeed, may at times seem to revel in taking a hard line from the start. While there are undoubtedly many reasons for these more heavy-handed responses, surely some of the most important ones include the constituency or group at which the policy is aimed, the circumstances in which the problem has appeared, and the nature of the problem involved.[27]

The example he gives is that the coercive mechanisms available to fight welfare fraud are much harsher than those for tax evasion. He suggests that these offenses are treated differently because of the differences in the type of person likely to commit them.

Michael Trebilcock et al. have developed a *public choice* theory about the use of governing instruments. This employs the public choice theory discussed in Chapter 6. They argue that politicians choose governing instruments not on the basis of policy rationality or efficiency but rather to improve their electoral position. For example, they point out that there is a tendency for politicians to assign the administration of programs that impose significant costs on voters to "independent" agencies, so that the actions of these agencies are not directly associated with politicians.[28]

Another general rule that they suggest will be followed by politicians is that benefits will be conferred on a concentrated group of uncommitted voters, while costs will be spread as widely as possible. This strategy could be supplemented by control of information, so that the benefit side could be emphasized and the cost side obscured.[29]

This approach would explain the growing use of tax expenditures as policy instruments. Tax expenditures are benefits in the form of reduced taxes to taxpayers who do (or refrain from doing) something desired by government. Their obvious attraction is that they provide low-visibility benefits while spreading the cost (in increased taxes to others) so widely that people do not feel coerced.[30]

It is clear that the choice of governing instruments approach has a great deal of value in illuminating certain characteristics of public policy. First, it emphasizes that policy making is not simply choosing a desired end; rather, it also involves a selection of means to accomplish that end—implementation. Second, it points out that there is a substitutability between the various instruments. Several instruments could potentially be used to accomplish the same ends; if one does not succeed, then policy makers might try another.

In Part III, we borrow this concept of choice of governing instrument and apply it to the choices that governments make about how services will be delivered. When confronted with a particular task, governments must choose the appropriate mechanism for accomplishing the task. They have available such traditional forms as operating departments, Crown corporations, and regulatory agencies, as well as an entire range of alternative service-delivery mechanisms. We will discuss the various characteristics of these delivery mechanisms, with particular reference to why governments would choose one form over the others to deal with a particular problem.

🏛 PERFORMANCE MEASUREMENT

Performance measurement is the process of determining how well a government service has been provided. Implicit in this statement is the idea that the performance will be measured against some standard to determine if the level of service provided meets that standard or is at least improving. This process can be defined as narrowly as ensuring that the floors in the office are clean, or as broadly as improving the well being of citizens. Ideally, policies would have performance measures already defined when they are adopted so that their success can be measured and evaluated and corrective action taken if they are not achieving the desired outcomes. However, this is seldom done. Implementers, working after the fact, must frequently divine the objectives desired by policy makers and establish performance measures accordingly.

In recent years, there has been increasing pressure to measure the performance of public policies. The first serious attempts at performance measurement occurred in the 1970s.[31] Governments were becoming more active and moving beyond providing pure public goods such as national defence, which are very difficult to measure qualitatively, and beginning to provide more services directly to citizens, such as job training and social assistance. In the 1980s, the concern about performance measurement was fuelled by expenditure restraints, which have increased the pressure to measure whether the policy is actually delivering the promised outputs.

This has become even more important in recent years as governments have begun to rely more on nongovernmental organizations for the delivery of government services. This trend will be discussed in more detail in Chapter 11, but the idea is that governments now frequently pay private sector or other type of organizations to deliver a service. The government must have some way of ensuring that it has received value for its payment. This need has spawned a much greater interest in measuring the real effects of policies. Some examples of performance indicators are illustrated in Table 7.1.

The idea of performance measurement is contentious. People providing funds such as legislators and the general public want performance measures because they want to see the funds accounted for. Service providers frequently resist the use of performance measures for a variety of reasons—some valid and some more questionable.

Table 7.1
EXAMPLES OF PERFORMANCE INDICATORS

Policy	Performance Indicator
university education	number of students enrolled
	graduation rate
	placement rate of graduates
highway system	volume of traffic carried
	accident rate
police service	arrest rate
	enforcement activity
food inspection	number of plants inspected
	incidents of dangerous food products found

Service providers often argue that the performance indicators are not appropriate or that they are beyond the control of the service deliverer. The indicators of university performance in Table 7.1 are good examples. University administrators generally accept that the number of students enrolled is a valid measure, although one must consider the fact that educating large numbers of engineering or medical students will cost more than educating liberal arts students. Universities have somewhat less control over graduation rates of students. They can hardly be blamed if students choose to work in income-producing jobs or just "goof off" and therefore not complete their program within the normal time. Placement rates are the most problematic because universities do not want to be held responsible if poor economic conditions make it hard for graduates to obtain jobs.

Performance Measurement in Practice

The Canadian International Development Agency's (CIDA) *Results-Based Management* is a good example of a performance measurement technique. CIDA has been strongly criticized by the auditor general for providing funding to international development projects but not knowing what value has been generated by those projects.[32] In response to those criticisms, CIDA has developed the Results-Based Management approach, illustrated in Table 7.2, to evaluating projects.

This table illustrates the linkages between the inputs needed for the project and the impacts expected as a result. The box on page 178 provides definitions of the various terms. Basically, the proponents of the project should identify exactly what resources they will need in terms of personnel and other expenses. These inputs are used to undertake certain activities (e.g., development of training courses), which produce outputs (e.g., trained workers and instructors). The

Table 7.2
RESULTS-BASED MANAGEMENT APPROACH TO AN INTERNATIONAL DEVELOPMENT PROJECT—
ECONOMIC DEVELOPMENT AND ENVIRONMENTAL MANAGEMENT IN THE EASTERN SEABOARD OF THAILAND

Inputs	Activities	Outputs	Outcomes	Impacts
Time of Canadian and Thai educators	Develop ten new courses to train workers in:	Train 800 workers in these courses	Workforce skilled in latest production techniques	Assist in the economic development in the eastern seaboard of Thailand with proper attention to environmental concerns
Time of Canadian and Thai educational development specialists	• Hazardous materials handling	Develop twenty highly qualified instructors to deliver courses	Educational institutions able to plan curricula and develop and deliver additional courses in the future	
Travel costs for mutual visits to Canadian and Thai educational institutions	• Environmental management • Total quality management	Develop five highly qualified course developers who can develop additional courses in the future		
Computer time to develop course material	Establish analytical chemistry laboratory	Develop Thai educational institutions as centres for environmental testing	Assist local industry in meeting ISO 14000 environmental protection standards	
Books and other course material	Train ten chemists and technicians in analytical chemistry			

CIDA'S RESULTS-BASED MANAGEMENT

Inputs — Direct or indirect human, organizational, or material contributions to implementation of the project/program.

Activities — Management, coordination, technical assistance, and training organized and carried out by the personnel assigned to a project/program.

Outputs — *Short-term* developmental changes that logically result from the implementation of project/program activities.

Outcomes — *Medium-term* development changes that logically result from the production of project/program outputs.

Results of this type involve changes in partner institutions and must be defined so as to materialize within the project/program cycle.

Impacts — *Long-term* development changes that logically result from the production of project/program outputs and outcomes.

Expected results of this type involve changes in the living conditions of populations in developing countries. It is not normally possible to achieve results of this type within the project/program cycle.

Source: Canadian International Development Agency, Results-Based Management: A Guide for UPCD Partners
(Autumn 1997), 3–4. (Emphasis in original.)

---

activities to be undertaken and outcomes expected are defined precisely in terms of number of courses developed and number of workers trained. The outcomes and impacts expected from them are described but not quantified, because the farther one moves to the right of the table, the more difficult it is to determine the precise causal connection between inputs and impacts.

In fact, this is one of the problems with performance measurement. It is relatively easy to establish linkages between inputs and outputs, but it is less easy to establish the relationship between inputs and impacts because so many other factors are influencing impacts. In this example, the Thai government has determined that the eastern seaboard will be the major target for future economic development. This will occur with or without the presence of this particular project; the hope is that this project will assist in the development in some way. The same problem can occur with job training programs. If the program experiences a very high placement rate for graduating students just at the point when the economy is improving, was the program successful? Or would these people have found jobs anyway, even without training, because of the improved economy? Nobody can really determine the answer to that question.

The federal government's *Report on Plans and Priorities (RPP)* is another example of performance measurement. This document is produced by each department and agency of the federal government. It sets out the department's objectives and planned results. Table 7.3 is an example of this report for Transport Canada. On the left it lists the services Transport Canada will provide to Canadians (e.g., "safe and secure national transportation system"), and on the right it describes how they will be measured (e.g., "reduced accident and fatality statistics"). Some of the measures are easily quantifiable whereas others are more abstract (e.g., "effective and harmonized legislation").

These documents are prepared for each federal department and agency and are tabled in the House of Commons each February as a part of the budget process. The companion document is the *Departmental Performance Report,* which is tabled in November and sets out how the department is doing with

Table 7.3
REPORT ON PLANS AND PRIORITIES FOR TRANSPORT CANADA

Transport Canada

Plans to Provide Canadians With:	To Be Demonstrated By:
A safe and secure national transportation system.	• reduced accident and fatality statistics in the aviation, marine, rail, and road modes, including the transportation of dangerous goods;
	• a simplified and more modern and effective regulatory regime;
	• effective and harmonized legislation, standards, and regulations in all transportation modes;
	• public awareness about safety; and
	• transportation industry awareness and compliance with regulations.
A competitive, efficient, and effective transportation system.	• cost effectiveness, commercial/financial viability, and levels of competition in transportation services;
	• devolution and commercialization of most remaining operations;
	• effective operation of remote airports, harbours, and ports;
	• removing institutional and legislative barriers to transportation operations;
	• shifting costs from taxpayers to users; and
	• fair and service-oriented fee structures.
Stewardship and environmental awareness.	• an effective sustainable transportation strategy;
	• an environmental management system for Transport Canada operations; and
	• effective administration of leases for airports and navigation sites.

regard to its objectives. This process is a fairly new innovation so it is too early to assess if it will deliver the results hoped for it.

Both of these examples of performance measurement are in the formative stages. If they deliver what they promise, they should be very beneficial for the governing process because they will help legislators and citizens determine how well government is doing in delivering on its promises.

Performance measurement is, or should be, an ongoing activity throughout the life of a policy. At times during its life, there will also be major reviews of the efficiency and effectiveness of the policy called *evaluations*.

🏛 EVALUATION

Evaluation is one of those unfortunate words that has different meanings at different levels. At the most basic level, government programs have always been evaluated.[33]

> It could be argued that program evaluations had been conducted virtually from Confederation. Parliamentary committees, central agencies, line departments, and the cabinet had examined and reviewed policies and programs over the years. Royal commissions and, more recently, "colored" papers and task forces were used frequently to examine and evaluate the effectiveness of various government policies and programs ... [I]t is clear ... that such efforts were sporadic and of uneven quality.[34]

This kind of rough-and-ready evaluation still goes on and its value should not be minimized.

> Assessment takes place constantly, even if it is only carried out on the basis of the intuitive feel of policy makers and even if the criteria are exclusively political in the narrowest sense of "what's in it for me?"[35]

Definitions of Evaluation

Beginning roughly in the 1960s, the word evaluation began to take on a more rigorous and sophisticated meaning.

> *Program evaluation* is the periodic, independent and objective assessment of a program to determine, in light of present circumstances, the adequacy of its objectives, its design and its results both intended and unintended. Evaluations will call into question the very existence of the program. Matters such as the rationale of the program, its impact on the public, and its cost effectiveness as compared with alternative means of program delivery are also reviewed.[36]

The Treasury Board of Canada has defined five roles for program evaluation:

- to foster or *support policy development*;

- to *modify programs* to meet strategic demands to increase productivity, to recover costs, or to increase service without additional resources;

- to *define, measure, demonstrate, and document program performance* for both internal use and external reporting;

- to *determine client satisfaction* with program delivery; and

- to *improve programs* by helping line managers determine deficiencies in their programs.[37]

The basic idea is that evaluation should provide information on three questions about a program. It should determine whether a program is:

- Relevant: continues to be consistent with department and government-wide priorities and to address realistically an actual need.

- Successful: is effective in meeting its objectives, within budget, and without significant unwanted outcomes.

- Cost-effective: is the most appropriate and efficient means for achieving the objectives, relative to alternative design and delivery approaches.[38]

Evaluations run the gamut from rough, seat-of-the-pants judgments to highly sophisticated, heavily quantitative research documents. Governments spend a significant amount of money on evaluations. In 1992–93, federal government departments spent $28.5 million on program evaluations. This included both the internal costs of evaluations performed by government employees and evaluations contracted out to the growing industry of evaluation consultants.[39] Most accounting/consulting firms have the capacity to perform evaluations, and there are even consulting firms that specialize in performing evaluations.[40] There is also a professional association of evaluators—the Canadian Evaluation Society—and a journal—the *Canadian Journal of Program Evaluation*. And there is some evidence that evaluators are adopting more of the trappings of a full-fledged profession by moving toward the formulation of professional standards.[41]

The more sophisticated, quantitative evaluations can take several forms.[42] Some compare output measures before and after the implementation of a program, e.g., student test scores before and after introduction of a new teaching program. Others survey participants in a program to determine how they perceive its worth.

There are also less quantitative approaches based on expert judgment of the status of a program. The "professional review" approach to evaluation involves a group of established experts reviewing a program and providing their best professional judgment on its value.[43] This is a common way to evaluate university programs or accredit professional programs. This approach is less objective than the previous types, but if the panel is chosen wisely, and its members have professional credibility, its results will be taken seriously.

There can be some confusion between policy analysis and program evaluation because they both tend to use the same kinds of analytical tools. Most writers make the distinction that policy analysis is a prospective, or before the fact, consideration of the likely future impacts of a policy if it is implemented. Program evaluation is a retrospective consideration of how a policy has functioned in the past. While this is a good general distinction, Ray Rist reminds us that the policy process is a bit too dynamic to make these kinds of firm distinctions.

[W]hat appears at first glance as a clear dichotomy—retrospective and prospective—becomes with closer scrutiny two stages of an interactive process: decisions are made, information is gathered about the effects of those decisions, further decisions are made with data available on the results of previous decisions, etc., etc., etc.[44]

This point raises the question of whether the evaluation is focused on the policy or on the program. Sometimes the terms "policy evaluation" and "program evaluation" are used interchangeably. While neither "policy" nor "program" is amenable to precise definition, ordinarily the word "policy" carries a much broader and amorphous connotation than the word "program." For this reason, it is more common to evaluate programs than it is to evaluate policies. For example, an evaluation of environment policy would be an impossible task, whereas, the evaluation of a program designed to stimulate environmental awareness among schoolchildren is quite manageable.

This chapter will not deal with the mechanics of how to conduct an evaluation because that can become quite complicated and is described well in other books.[45] This chapter will discuss the political issues surrounding evaluation. First, however, it will be helpful to present an example of what an evaluation looks like.

An Example: Community Policing in Edmonton

In 1988, the Edmonton Police Service initiated the Neighbourhood Foot Patrol (NFP) program. This was a limited program to replace the traditional form of policing with community policing in twenty-one areas of the city. The difference between traditional and community policing is that the former is based on "a professionally autonomous, police-controlled crime control organization," while community policing is "driven by the community as client and partner in the joint enterprise of managing local crime and disorder problems."[46] The idea of community policing is for officers to become closer to the community and to deal with crime by working with members of the community for prevention rather than by responding to incidents after they occur. For example, traditional forms of policing would handle barroom violence by responding to incidents, apprehending suspects, and dealing with other violations of the law. Community policing would identify repeated calls to the same location and work with staff in the bar to prevent these incidents from occurring.

The Edmonton NFP has three goals:

1. To prevent crime and create a better community;

2. To provide proactive policing services that involve solving problems rather than simply reporting incidents; and

3. To provide a service that is community based rather than criminal justice based; that is, one that involves the community in identifying and solving problems.[47]

With these objectives, the evaluators can now determine the extent to which the program as implemented actually meets these objectives. There are two types of evaluations, and this study included both. An *outcome evaluation* or *impact evaluation* "is concerned with examining the extent to which a policy causes a change in the intended direction."[48] This kind of evaluation focuses on what the outcome or impact of the policy was supposed to be and compares that to what has, in fact, happened.

A *process evaluation* is

> concerned with the extent to which a particular policy or program is implemented according to its stated guidelines. The content of a particular public policy and its impact on those affected may be substantially modified, elaborated, or even negated during its implementation.[49]

It is important to do both kinds of evaluations, particularly if it appears that the policy is not working well. Some policies do not produce the desired result because they were flawed from the outset; other policies do not produce the desired result because they were never implemented as intended. Performing both kinds of evaluation at the same time helps determine where the problem lies.

This evaluation employed several techniques to measure the characteristics of the program. The general idea was to compare pre- and post-test information in areas of the city where NFP was implemented and to compare NFP and motor patrol (MP) figures for the same time period in different areas of the city. A number of measures were employed:

- time-budget study—how officers spent their time;

- travel-time analysis—amount of time needed to arrive at the scene of an incident;

- survey of service users—how members of the public reacted to police service;

- personnel survey—how police officers felt about their work;

- analysis of repeat calls—change in the number of repeat calls at same location;

Figure 7.1
TYPES OF EVALUATIONS

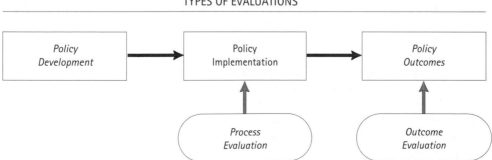

- interviews with NFP constables—identify attitudes of NFP officers to their work; and

- problem-solving case studies—telephone interviews to identify successful ways of solving problems.

This indicates the multidisciplinary approach of evaluation. The methods employed range from the strictly quantitative (e.g., time-budget study, travel-time analysis) to much softer forms of analysis (e.g., interviews and case studies).

The *process evaluation* indicated that the program had been implemented as planned. For example, the time-budget study indicated that NFP officers actually operated in a manner different from an MP officer. For example, NFP officers had more contact with "general citizens" and "business people" than did their MP counterparts.

The *impact evaluation* also indicated positive results. For example, the number of repeat calls in several NFP areas declined, and NFP officers became more satisfied with their jobs than were MP officers.

The evaluation also resulted in a number of recommendations for continuing improvement in policing:

1. The NFP program should be extended to include additional areas with high crime rates.

2. The Program should remain flexible to permit constables to have the autonomy necessary to deal with special problems in each area.

3. Attempts should be made to keep the store-fronts open longer each day by staffing them with volunteers.

4. Constables should be provided with training and/or management resources for the organization and use of volunteers.

Impediments to Good Evaluation[50]

While there are significant pressures to perform evaluations, there are also problems encountered in doing good evaluations. This section reviews some of those before considering some of the Canadian experiences with evaluation.

Many of the obstacles to good evaluation are the same *methodological problems* that one encounters in any social science research. These will not be reviewed in detail here, because there are many good, comprehensive reviews of these problems.[51] However, it is worth mentioning just a few to convey the general idea.

Measuring some kinds of intangible outputs of programs is a standard problem. For example, how would one measure the worth of a program designed to improve people's self-confidence and self-esteem?

The establishment of experimental and control groups is always a problem with government programs because it is politically very difficult to tell some people that, for the good of science, they will not be allowed to benefit from a new program.

Establishing the causal link between a new program and some change is also very difficult in a dynamic world. In the evaluation of community policing discussed earlier, the evaluators noted that repeat calls to the same location declined. However, proving that this decline was a direct result of community policing is difficult. The statistical trend suggests that there could be a causal link between the two, but statistical evidence can never *prove* a linkage of this sort.

The list can go on and on. Walter Williams has used the phrase "the iron law of absolute evaluation flaws" to suggest that no real-life evaluation could ever match the methodological rigour demanded by some social scientists, particularly since it seems that there are always some people who want to attack programs on political grounds, anyway.[52] However, there are a number of other problems more specific to public policy evaluations.

Government programs frequently have *multiple and/or unclear goals*. In order to evaluate a program, there must be a clear understanding of what the program was supposed to accomplish. If a program has several objectives, some of which politicians refuse to acknowledge openly, then it is very difficult to determine how successful the program has been.[53] For example, if the purpose of a regional economic development program is to create permanent jobs in an area, then it might not appear to be successful. However, if the real purpose of the program is to ensure that politicians have the discretion to throw money at selected ridings immediately before an election, it might be highly successful.

There are some things that governments do not want to know. When a government is firmly committed to a particular program for political, historical, or ideological reasons, it is unlikely to change that program, regardless of the findings of an evaluation. And if it is unlikely to change the program, then it does not want to know whether it has been successful; the answer might be negative. Therefore, what purpose would an evaluation serve? "Governments concerned with their popular support are unlikely to take unpopular decisions simply because of the weight of intellectual argument that backs up such proposals."[54]

The best example might be the federal government's policy with regard to a bilingual public service. Over several years, all previous governments have been committed to the policy. If an evaluation were performed that indicated that, in strict economic terms, a unilingual public service would function better, no change in the status quo would occur. The only use of such an evaluation would be to provide a tool for certain groups to attack bilingualism, and in the current environment, the federal government is unlikely to fund such an effort.

A dog will not bring the stick with which it will be beaten. Douglas Hartle coined this picturesque phrase when writing about budgetary systems, but it is equally applicable to evaluation. Public servants resist evaluations, in the first place, because they cost too much and take up too much time that could be spent actually administering the program. However, they also fear the results of the evaluation. If the conclusions are negative, it could result in media coverage that could jeopardize the future of the program and therefore their jobs. The fears of the public servant are compounded by a concern that the evaluator (or readers of the evaluation) will misunderstand or overlook some aspect of the program, and provide a negative evaluation based on faulty perceptions. The media, in particular, are notorious for searching for, and magnifying, the one negative comment in an otherwise positive report.

The Current State of Evaluation in the Government of Canada

In 1977, the federal government instituted a policy requiring that departments evaluate their programs on a regular basis. Responsibility for evaluation was divided. The Treasury Board,[55] a central agency whose role will be discussed in more detail in the next chapter, has government-wide responsibility to encourage departments to undertake evaluations and to set standards for their quality. Departments that deliver the programs are responsible for performing the evaluation, which could involve hiring outside consultants to do the actual work.

Responsibility for conducting evaluations was situated within the department because the government wanted to emphasize that evaluation is an integral part of the policy-management process, and not a separate process imposed by an outside agency that visits periodically yet does not really understand the operation of the program. It was hoped that the evaluation process would be more acceptable to managers if it was clear that it was to be used as a management tool.

The deputy head of the department, i.e., the administrative, not the political, head of the department, is viewed as the client for the study. This means that the evaluation will be performed to the deputy head's specifications and will be geared to meeting her or his needs. Of course, the terms of the evaluation must also meet guidelines determined by the Treasury Board. In identifying the client, the government could have cast its net a bit wider and said that the client would be the minister, the full cabinet, the legislature, the clients of the program, or even society as a whole. The choice of the client will influence the scope of the evaluation.

A *formative evaluation* is targeted at senior management, i.e., the deputy head. Therefore, it focuses on how well the delivery of the program is managed rather than the ultimate value of the program. It involves "monitoring and feedback activities which enable managers to improve performance by adjusting operations and redesigning programs."[56] A formative evaluation does not deal with the overall value of the policy because that is a matter for politicians, not administrators.

A *summative evaluation* is targeted at the minister, full cabinet, or even the entire community. These evaluations are "comprehensive assessments of the degree of success achieved by programs."[57] This kind of evaluation is directed at the efficacy of the policy itself and could result in a modification of the underlying policy. This would be of more concern to the minister than the deputy minister.

In sum, a formative evaluation measures how well a program is managed, while a summative evaluation measures whether the policy is attaining its desired end. Both types of evaluation have their uses.

It can be difficult to draw firm lines between formative and summative evaluations, but the federal government's decision to make the deputy head the client for all evaluations has meant that most evaluations have tended to be formative rather than summative. Formative evaluations obviously have value as a management tool, but viewing evaluation strictly as a tool to improve management risks that it could sink

> into the soft folds of the bureaucratic underbelly, and become an information source of managers to improve programs rather than a real tool of accountability and comparison. In itself, there is nothing objectionable to the use of program evaluation for management purposes, but its almost exclusive dedication to this end falls short of its potential.[58]

This point is supported by Segsworth's lament that Parliament has not made extensive use of evaluation studies.[59]

The public distribution of evaluations has been a contentious issue for the Canadian government. At first, most evaluations were regarded as confidential, and so were available only within the department and the Treasury Board. Gradually, this policy has been loosened, so that now all evaluations are available to the public, except those involving sensitive areas such as national security.

Given that a policy evaluation is a very important document in promoting accountability and responsibility in government, it would seem rather extraordinary to keep it confidential. However, this is a more complex issue than it seems at first. The knowledge that an evaluation will be made public can have an impact on which programs will be evaluated, what issues the evaluator will address, and how much cooperation the evaluator will receive from program managers. When a report is to be made public, there could be a tendency to focus on the most positive aspects of the program and cover up any problems. This is clearly not in the best long-term interests of the program, the program managers, or the general public. Paradoxically, the desire to make the maximum use of evaluations could result in reducing both the number of evaluations performed and the scope of those that are performed.[60]

Evaluating Evaluation

The obvious questions that arise from all this discussion of evaluation are: Does any of this matter? Are evaluations ever actually used for anything? Keeping in

Table 7.4
A COMPARISON OF FORMATIVE AND SUMMATIVE EVALUATIONS

	Formative	Summative
Client	deputy minister, senior management	Parliament, public
Focus	economy and efficiency of program management	effectiveness of program
Objective	improve management	improve or terminate policy

mind the powerful coalitions that frequently grow up in support of programs, do these data have any real impact?

The answers to these questions are mixed. Rick Linden has argued that the weight of numerous evaluations over the years has caused significant changes in the way police forces operate.[61] Other researchers have argued that evaluators can adopt particular strategies to maximize the possibility that their findings will be used.[62] However, most commentators have not been so sanguine. Stephen Brooks has argued that there "is an impressive consensus that [evaluation's] impact has been marginal."[63] Many other critics of the process have noted the very low profile of these evaluations in the media and the fact that there are virtually no well-known cases of programs being terminated as a result of negative evaluations.

Timothy Plumptre, who has done an extensive review of management in the federal government, provides a similar assessment.

> Is program evaluation in Ottawa "working"? Evaluation is like chastity: people support it in principle, but in practice they prefer if it is mandatory for others and optional for them ... [I]t is clear that some useful work is being done. However, the results are a good deal less than what was originally hoped for: evaluation has not, at time of writing, become a key element in the resource allocation process, and major studies still tend to take place outside the system. In the mid-1980s, five deputy ministers, questioned on the usefulness of the program evaluation system, agreed that there should be more rigorous reviews of program performance, but their assessment of the system in place at that time was broadly consistent: "The jury is out."[64]

The auditor general performed a major review of the government's system of evaluation. His findings indicated that the system has not been working as well as it could. "[O]ur audit found that the story of program evaluation in the Government of Canada is one of high expectations and great potential that have been only partly fulfilled."[65] The report identified several problems.

The resources devoted to evaluation have been declining[66] and, not surprisingly, the number of evaluations performed has also declined. In fiscal year 1991–92, only eighty evaluations were performed.[67] Since there are approximately 1500 components that are subject to evaluation, it would require almost twenty years to evaluate them all, compared to the five-to-seven-year cycle that was planned.[68]

The auditor general was also concerned that the evaluations tended to be too narrow in focus. In 1993, and, using almost the same words again in 1996, he complained that evaluations were generally "directed to smaller activities and toward operational questions ..."[69] While this level of focus made them useful to management, it provided only limited information of value to Parliament and restricted their value as accountability devices.

The auditor general found it difficult to find specific examples of cases where evaluations had resulted in cost savings.[70] Table 7.5 illustrates the primary use of 168 evaluations reviewed by the auditor general. It indicates that 47 percent of the evaluations were not used for any of the four purposes listed. If one adds to that the 23 percent of evaluations that were used for the nebulous purpose of understanding the program better, over two-thirds of evaluations were not used to modify the existing program.

Table 7.5
PRIMARY USE OF A SAMPLE OF EVALUATIONS

	%
Terminate program	1
Reform program	9
Modify program	20
Understand program better	23
Percent of evaluations used	53
Number of evaluations reviewed	168

Source: Auditor General of Canada, Report of the Auditor General of Canada to the House of Commons—1993 (Ottawa: Ministry of Supply and Services Canada, 1993), 253.

To put this discussion in perspective, it might be that some commentators have expected too much of program evaluation. Evaluation should not be considered as the final word on the value of a program; rather; they should be seen as one element to be used in a very complex decision-making process.

> Program evaluation is one means of providing relevant, timely, and objective findings—information, evidence and conclusions—and recommendations on the performance of government programs, thereby improving the information base on which decisions are taken. In this view, program evaluation, as part of this decision making and management process, should not be seen as an exercise in scientific research aimed at producing definitive "scientific" conclusions about programs and their results. Rather it should be seen as input to the complex, interactive process that is government decision making, with the aim of producing objective but not necessarily conclusive evidence on the results of programs.[71]

🏛 CONCLUSION

This chapter has reviewed what happens after a policy has been formulated. The main point was to show that the frequently unseen mechanisms that implement and evaluate policies can have as great an impact on the success of those policies as the high-profile legislators who formulated the policy. The next section of this book looks at the organizational units that implement polices and deliver services—operating departments, public enterprises, and regulatory agencies.

NOTES

1. Eugene Bardach, *The Implementation Game: What Happens After a Bill Becomes Law* (Cambridge, Mass.: The MIT Press, 1977), 38.
2. Randall B. Ripley and Grace A. Franklin, *Policy Implementation and Bureaucracy*, 3rd ed. (Chicago: The Dorsey Press, 1986), 11. (Emphasis in original.)

3. Ibid., 13.
4. Robert T. Nakamura and Frank Smallwood, *The Politics of Policy Implementation* (New York: St. Martin's Press, 1980), ch. 7.
5. Ibid., 122.
6. This phenomenon of subordinates' power over superiors is also considered in Donald S. Van Meter and Carl E. Van Horn, "The Policy Implementation Process: A Conceptual Framework," *Administration & Society* 6 (February 1975): 454–58.
7. Samuel H. Beer, "Federalism, Nationalism and Democracy in America," *American Political Science Review* 72 (March 1978): 17. (Emphasis in original.)
8. H.L. Laframboise, "Moving a Proposal to a Positive Decision: A Case Study of the Invisible Process," *Optimum* 4, no. 3 (1973): 31–41; J.L. Granatstein, *The Ottawa Men* (Toronto: Oxford University Press, 1982); Kenneth Kernaghan and T.H. McLeod, "Mandarins and Ministers in the Canadian Administrative State," in O.P. Dwivedi, ed., *The Administrative State in Canada* (Toronto: University of Toronto Press, 1982), 17–30.
9. Paul Berman, "Thinking about Programmed and Adaptive Implementation: Matching Strategies to Situations," in Helen M. Ingram and Dean E. Mann, eds., *Why Policies Succeed or Fail* (Beverly Hills, Calif.: Sage, 1980), 205–206. (Footnote omitted.) A book of case studies influenced by this approach is: Dennis J. Palumbo and Marvin A. Harder, eds., *Implementing Public Policy* (Lexington, Mass.: Lexington Books, 1981).
10. Berman, "Thinking about Programmed and Adaptive Implementation," 210–11.
11. Ibid., 214.
12. Paul Sabatier and Daniel Mazmanian, "The Conditions of Effective Implementation: A Guide to Accomplishing Policy Objectives," *Policy Analysis* 5 (fall 1979): 481–504. (Emphasis in original.)
13. Malcolm L. Goggin, Ann O'M. Bowman, James P. Lester, and Laurence J. O'Toole, Jr., *Implementation Theory and Practice: Toward a Third Generation* (Harper Collins Publishers, 1990), ch. 4.
14. Nakamura and Smallwood, *The Politics of Policy Implementation*, 24.
15. Goggin et al., *Implementation Theory and Practice*.
16. Jeffrey L. Pressman and Aaron B. Wildavsky, *Implementation* (Berkeley and Los Angeles: University of California Press, 1974), 92.
17. Ibid.
18. Bardach, *The Implementation Game*, 42.
19. In spite of many pious protestations about the positive value of participation, the hard evidence is not clear on this point. For a good review of this literature, see Neal Gross, Joseph B. Giacquinta, and Marilyn Bernstein, *Implementing Organizational Innovations: A Sociological Analysis of Planned Educational Change* (New York: Basic Books, 1971), 25–29.
20. G. Bruce Doern and Richard W. Phidd, *Canadian Public Policy: Ideas, Structure, Process* (Toronto: Methuen, 1983), 110.
21. Ibid.
22. Kenneth Woodside, "Policy Instruments and the Study of Public Policy," *Canadian Journal of Political Science* 19, no. 4 (December 1986): 787.
23. Michael M. Atkinson and Robert A. Nigol, "Selecting Policy Instruments: Neo-Institutional and Rational Choice Interpretations of Automobile Insurance in Ontario," *Canadian Journal of Political Science* 22, no. 1 (March 1989): 131–32.
24. G. Bruce Doern and V. Seymour Wilson, "Conclusions and Observations," in G. Bruce Doern and V. Seymour Wilson, eds., *Issues in Canadian Public Policy* (Toronto: Macmillan, 1974), 339.
25. Nicolas Baxter-Moore, "Policy Implementation and the Role of the State: A Revised Approach to the Study of Policy Instruments," in Robert J. Jackson, Doreen Jackson, and Nicolas Baxter-Moore, eds., *Contemporary Canadian Politics* (Scarborough, Ont.: Prentice-Hall, 1987), 336–55.

26. Ibid., 346.

27. Woodside, "Policy Instruments and the Study of Public Policy," 786. (Footnote omitted.)

28. M.J. Trebilcok et al., *The Choice of Governing Instrument* (Ottawa: Minister of Supply and Services Canada, 1982), 33.

29. Ibid.

30. Kenneth Woodside, "The Political Economy of Policy Instruments: Tax Expenditures and Subsidies in Canada," in Michael M. Atkinson and Marsha A. Chandler, eds., *The Politics of Canadian Public Policy* (Toronto: University of Toronto Press, 1983), 175–76 and passim.

31. Treasury Board, *Operational Performance Measurement* (Ottawa: Information Canada, 1974); D.G. Hartle, "Operational Performance Measurement in the Federal Government," *Optimum* 3, no. 4 (1972), 5-18.

32. *Report of the Auditor General of Canada to the House of Commons (November 1996)*, (Ottawa: Minister of Public Works and Government Services, 1996), ch. 29.

33. One review of evaluation in the federal government begins with confederation. See: Werner J. Müller-Clemm and Maria Paulette Barnes, "A Historical Perspective on Federal Program Evaluation in Canada," *The Canadian Journal of Program Evaluation* 12, no. 1 (1997), 47-70.

34. R.V. Segsworth, "Policy and Program Evaluation in the Government of Canada," in Ray C. Rist, ed., *Program Evaluation and the Management of Government* (New Brunswick, N.J.: Transaction Publishers, 1990), 21. (Footnote omitted.)

35. Ripley and Franklin, *Policy Implementation and Bureaucracy*, 9.

36. Office of the Comptroller General, *Guide on the Program Evaluation Function* (Ottawa: Minister of Supply and Services Canada, 1981), 19. (Emphasis in original.)

37. Treasury Board of Canada and Comptroller General, *Into the 90s: Government Program Evaluation Perspectives* (Ottawa: Minister of Supply and Services Canada, 1991), 40. (Emphasis in original.)

38. Auditor General of Canada, *Report of the Auditor General of Canada to the House of Commons—1993* (Ottawa: Minister of Supply and Services Canada, 1993), 223-34. These concepts are explained more fully in: Treasury Board and Comptroller General, *Into the 90s*, 26 and *passim.*

39. Auditor General of Canada, *Report of the Auditor General ... —1993*, 222.

40. The development of the policy analysis industry is described well in Leslie A. Pal, *Public Policy Analysis*, 2nd ed. (Scarborough: Nelson Canada, 1991), ch. 4.

41. Canadian Evaluation Society, Standards Development Committee, "Standards for Program Evaluation in Canada: A Discussion Paper," *The Canadian Journal of Program Evaluation* 7, no. 1 (April/May 1992), 157-70.

42. Thomas R. Dye, *Understanding Public Policy*, 7th ed. (Englewood Cliffs, N.J.: Prentice-Hall, 1992), 358-62.

43. Ernest R. House, *Evaluating with Validity* (Beverly Hills Calif.: Sage Publications, 1980), 34 ff. For a good example of this type of evaluation, see: W. Moore and R. Newstead, "Evaluation of Research and Development Accomplishments: Northern Forestry Centre," *The Canadian Journal of Program Evaluation* 7, no. 1 (April/May 1992), 41-51.

44. Ray Rist "Managing of Evaluations or Managing by Evaluations: Choices and Consequences," in Rist, ed., *Program Evaluation and the Management of Government*, 4.

45. Office of the Comptroller General, *Principles for the Evaluation of Programs by Federal Departments and Agencies* (Ottawa: Minister of Supply and Services Canada, 1981); David Nachmias, *Public Policy Evaluation: Approaches and Methods* (New York: St. Martin's Press, 1979); Arlene Fink and Jacqueline Kosecoff, *An Evaluation Primer* (Beverly Hills, Calif.: Sage Publications, 1978).

46. The material in this section is adapted from: Joseph P. Hornick, Barry N. Leighton, and Barbara A. Burrows, "Evaluating Community Policing: The Edmonton Project," in Joe

Hudson and Julian Roberts, eds., *Evaluating Justice* (Toronto: Thompson Educational Publishing, Inc., 1993), 61.

47. Ibid., 75.
48. Nachmias, *Public Policy Evaluation*, 5.
49. Ibid.
50. One of the best general critiques of evaluation is found in W. Irwin Gillespie, "Fools' Gold: The Quest for a Method of Evaluating Government Spending," in G. Bruce Doern and Allan M. Maslove, eds., *The Public Evaluation of Government Spending* (Toronto: Institute for Research on Public Policy, 1979), 39–59.
51. Felix A. Nigro and Lloyd G. Nigro, *Modern Public Administration*, 7th ed. (New York: Harper & Row, Publishers, 1989), ch. 10.
52. *Social Policy Research and Analysis* (New York: Elsevier, 1971), ch. 7.
53. Shawna L. Mercer and Vivek Goal, "Program Evaluation in the Absence of Goals: A Comprehensive Approach to the Evaluation of a Population-Based Cancer Screening Program," *Canadian Journal of Program Evaluation* 9, no. 1 (1994), 97-112.
54. Stephen Brooks, *Public Policy in Canada* (Toronto: McClelland & Stewart, 1989), 83.
55. At one point, an agency called the Office of the Comptroller General (OCG) was created by splitting off certain responsibilities, including evaluation, from the Treasury Board. In 1993 these two organizations were consolidated. Treasury Board now has full responsibility for evaluation, but some documents still refer to the OCG.
56. Rodney Dobell and David Zussman, "An Evaluation System for Government: If Politics Is Theatre, Then Evaluation Is (Mostly) Art," *Canadian Public Administration* 24, no. 3 (fall 1981): 415–16.
57. Ibid., 416.
58. Leslie A. Pal, *Beyond Policy Analysis: Public Issue Management in Turbulent Times* (Scarborough, Ont.: ITP Nelson, 1997), 250.
59. R.V. Segsworth, "Public Access to Evaluation in Canada," in J. Mayne, J. Hudson, M.L. Bemelmans-Videc, and R. Conner, eds., *Advancing Public Policy Evaluation: Learning from International Experiences* (Amsterdam: North Holland, 1992), 308.
60. Michael Hicks, "Evaluating Evaluation in Today's Government: Summary of Discussions," *Canadian Public Administration* 24, no. 3 (fall 1981): 357.
61. "The Impact of Evaluation Research on Policing Policy in Canada and the United States," *The Canadian Journal of Program Evaluation* 6, no. 1 (April/May 1991), 83-96.
62. Alan G. Ryan and Caroline Krentz, "All Pulling Together: Working Toward a Successful Evaluation," *Canadian Journal of Program Evaluation* 9, no. 2 (1994), 131–149; Vicki Strang and Jean Pearson, "Factors Influencing the Utilization of Results: A Case Study of an Evaluation of an Adult Day Care Program," *Canadian Journal of Program Evaluation* 10, no. 1 (1995), 73–87.
63. Stephen Brooks, *Public Policy in Canada* (Toronto: McClelland & Stewart, 1989), 83.
64. Timothy Plumptre, *Beyond the Bottom Line: Management in Government* (Halifax: The Institute for Research on Public Policy, 1988), 267.
65. Auditor General of Canada, *Report ... 1993*, 222.
66. Ibid., 244. The auditor general in his 1996 report said that the decline was continuing, but at a slower rate. *Report of the Auditor General of Canada to the House of Commons*, ch. 3, Evaluation in the Federal Government (May 1996), 3-21.
67. Auditor General of Canada, *Report ... 1993*, 247.
68. Admittedly, this somewhat overstates the problem since some of those 1500 components are quite small and some could be evaluated as a group. However, this does provide a rough idea of the order of magnitude of the deficiency.
69. Auditor General of Canada, *Report ... 1993*, 229. See also, 248-50. *Report of the Auditor General of Canada to the House of Commons*, ch. 3, Evaluation in the Federal Government (May 1996), 3-13.
70. Ibid., 253.
71. *Guide on the Program Evaluation Function*, 4.

BIBLIOGRAPHY

Adie, Robert F., and Paul Thomas. *Canadian Public Administration: Problematic Perspectives.* 2nd ed. Scarborough, Ont.: Prentice-Hall Canada, 1987.

Atkinson, Michael M., and Marsha A. Chandler, eds. *The Politics of Canadian Public Policy.* Toronto: University of Toronto Press, 1983.

Atkinson, Michael M., and Robert A. Nigol. "Selecting Policy Instruments: Neo-Institutional and Rational Choice Interpretations of Automobile Insurance in Ontario." *Canadian Journal of Political Science* 22, no. 1 (March 1989): 107–35.

Auditor General of Canada. *Report of the Auditor General of Canada to the House of Commons— 1993.* Ottawa: Minister of Supply and Services Canada, 1993.

Bardach, Eugene. *The Implementation Game: What Happens After a Bill Becomes a Law.* Cambridge, Mass.: The MIT Press, 1977.

Baxter-Moore, Nicolas. "Policy Implementation and the Role of the State." In Robert Jackson, Doreen Jackson, and Nicolas Baxter-Moore, eds., *Contemporary Canadian Politics.* Scarborough, Ont.: Prentice-Hall Canada, 1987, 336–55.

Berman, Paul. "Thinking about Programmed and Adaptive Implementation: Matching Strategies to Situations." In Helen M. Ingram and Dean Mann, eds., *Why Policies Succeed or Fail.* Beverly Hills, Calif.: Sage Publications, 1980, 205–27.

Canadian Evaluation Society, Standards Development Committee. "Standards for Program Evaluation in Canada: A Discussion Paper," *The Canadian Journal of Program Evaluation* 7, no. 1 (April/May 1992): 57–70.

Dobell, Rodney, and David Zussman. "An Evaluation System for Government: If Politics Is Theatre, Then Evaluation Is (Mostly) Art." *Canadian Public Administration* 24, no. 3 (fall 1981): 40427.

Doern, G. Bruce, and Peter Aucoin, eds. *Public Policy in Canada.* Toronto: Macmillan, 1979.
————. *The Structures of Policy-Making in Canada.* Toronto: Macmillan Canada, 1971.

Doern, G. Bruce, and Allan M. Maslove, eds. *The Public Evaluation of Government Spending.* Toronto: Institute for Research on Public Policy, 1979.

Doern, G. Bruce, and Richard W. Phidd. *Canadian Public Policy: Ideas, Structure, Process.* Toronto: Methuen, 1983.

Dunn, William N. *Public Policy Analysis.* Englewood Cliffs, N.J.: Prentice-Hall, 1981.

Dunsire, Andrew. *Implementation in a Bureaucracy.* Oxford: Martin Robertson, 1978.

Dye, Thomas R. *Policy Analysis: What Governments Do, Why They Do It, and What Difference It Makes.* University, Ala.: The University of Alabama Press, 1976.

Fink, Arlene, and Jacqueline Kosecoff. *An Evaluation Primer.* Beverly Hills, Calif.: Sage Publications, 1978.

Goggin, Malcolm L., Ann O'M. Bowman, James P. Lester, and Laurence J. O'Toole, Jr. *Implementation Theory and Practice: Toward a Third Generation.* Harper Collins Publishers, 1990.

Gross, Neal, Joseph B. Giacquinta, and Marilyn Bernstein. *Implementing Organizational Innovations: A Sociological Analysis of Planned Educational Change.* New York: Basic Books, 1971.

Hartle, D.G. "Operational Performance Measurement in the Federal Government." *Optimum* 3, no. 4 (1972): 5–18.

Hicks, Michael. "Evaluating Evaluation in Today's Government: Summary of Discussions." *Canadian Public Administration* 24, no. 3 (fall 1981): 350–58.

Hornick, Joseph P., Barry N. Leighton, and Barbara A. Burrows. "Evaluating Community Policing: The Edmonton Project." In Joe Hudson and Julian Roberts, eds., *Evaluating Justice.* Toronto: Thompson Educational Publishing, Inc., 1993, 61–94.

House, Ernest R. *Evaluating with Validity.* Beverly Hills, Calif.: Sage Publications, 1980.

Kernaghan, Kenneth, and T.H. McLeod. "Mandarins and Ministers in the Canadian Administrative State." In O.P. Dwivedi, ed., *The Administrative State in Canada.* Toronto: University of Toronto Press, 1982, 17–30.

Laframboise, H.L. "Moving a Proposal to a Positive Decision: A Case Study of the Invisible Process." *Optimum* 4, no. 3 (1973): 31–41.

March, James G., and Herbert A. Simon. *Organizations.* New York: John Wiley & Sons, 1958.

McInnes, Simon. "Federal-Provincial Negotiation: Family Allowances 1970–1976." Ph.D. diss., Carleton University, 1978.

Mercer, Shawna L., and Vivek Goal. "Program Evaluation in the Absence of Goals: A Comprehensive Approach to the Evaluation of a Population-Based Cancer Screening Program." *Canadian Journal of Program Evaluation* 9, no. 1 (1994): 97-112.

Müller-Clemm, Werner J., and Maria Paulette Barnes. "A Historical Perspective on Federal Program Evaluation in Canada," *Canadian Journal of Program Evaluation* 12, no. 1 (1997): 47–70.

Nachmias, David. *Public Policy Evaluation: Approaches and Methods.* New York: St. Martin's Press, 1979.

Nakamura, Robert T., and Frank Smallwood. *The Politics of Policy Implementation.* New York: St. Martin's Press, 1980.

Nigro, Felix A., and Lloyd G. Nigro. *Modern Public Administration.* 4th ed. New York: Harper & Row, 1977.

Office of the Comptroller General. *Guide on the Program Evaluation Function.* Ottawa: Minister of Supply and Services Canada, 1981.

Pal, Leslie A. *Beyond Policy Analysis: Public Issue Management in Turbulent Times.* Scarborough, Ont.: ITP Nelson, 1997.

Palumbo, Dennis J., and Marvin A. Harder, eds. *Implementing Public Policy.* Lexington, Mass.: Lexington Books, 1981.

Plumptre, Timothy. *Beyond the Bottom Line: Management in Government.* Halifax: The Institute for Research on Public Policy, 1988.

Pressman, Jeffrey L., and Aaron B. Wildavsky. *Implementation.* Berkeley and Los Angeles: University of California Press, 1974.

Rayner, Michael H. "Using Evaluation In the Federal Government." *The Canadian Journal of Program Evaluation* 1, no. 1 (April 1986): 1–10.

Ripley, Randall B., and Grace A. Franklin. *Policy Implementation and Bureaucracy.* 3rd ed. Chicago: The Dorsey Press, 1986.

Rist, Ray C., ed. *Program Evaluation and the Management of Government.* New Brunswick, N.J.: Transaction Publishers, 1990.

Ryan, Alan G., and Caroline Krentz. "All Pulling Together: Working Toward a Successful Evaluation." *Canadian Journal of Program Evaluation,* 9, no. 2 (1994): 131–49.

Sabatier, Paul, and Daniel Mazmanian. "The Conditions of Effective Implementation: A Guide to Accomplishing Policy Objectives." *Policy Analysis,* 5 (fall 1979): 481–504.

Schultz, Richard J. *Federalism, Bureaucracy, and Public Policy.* Montreal: McGill-Queen's University Press, 1980.

Segsworth, R.V. "Public Access to Evaluation in Canada." In J. Mayne, J. Hudson, M.L. Bemelmans-Videc, and R. Conner, eds., *Advancing Public Policy Evaluation: Learning from International Experiences.* Amsterdam: North Holland, 1992, 301–12.

Siegel, David. "Provincial-Municipal Relations in Ontario: A Case Study of Roads." Ph.D. diss., University of Toronto, 1984.

Simon, Herbert. *Administrative Behavior.* 2nd ed. New York: The Free Press, 1957.

Strang, Vicki, and Jean Pearson. "Factors Influencing the Utilization of Results: A Case Study of an Evaluation of an Adult Day Care Program." *Canadian Journal of Program Evaluation,* 10, no. 1 (1995): 73–87.

Treasury Board. *Operational Performance Measurement.* Ottawa: Information Canada, 1974.

Treasury Board of Canada and Comptroller General. *Into the 90s: Government Program Evaluation Perspectives.* Ottawa; Minister of Supply and Services Canada, 1991.

Trebilcock, M.J., R.S. Prichard, D.G. Hartle, and D.N. Dewees. *The Choice of Governing Instrument.* Ottawa: Minister of Supply and Services Canada, 1982.

Van Meter, Donald S., and Carl E. Van Horn. "The Policy Implementation Process: A Conceptual Framework." *Administration & Society* 6 (February 1975): 445–88.

Woodside, Kenneth, "Policy Instruments and the Study of Public Policy." *Canadian Journal of Political Science* 19, no. 4 (December 1986): 775–93.

III

Delivering Government Services

Government Departments and Central Agencies

Agriculture and Agri-Food Canada, Treasury Board, National Transportation Agency, Petro-Canada, Consulting and Audit Canada. Government organizations seem to come in a bewildering array of different names and organizational structures. Some are directly controlled by a minister; others are deliberately kept at arm's length so that there is limited ministerial control. Why does there need to be such a huge variety of organizations? The answer is that form follows function. Governments deliver a variety of different services, and they need to be organized in such a way as to facilitate the delivery of those services. You would not expect a company that sells gasoline to be organized in the same way as an agency that regulates airline safety.

In the 1960s and 1970s when governments were expanding, they adopted or extended the use of a number of organizational forms. Crown corporations were one of the most popular. They were created very quickly to solve all sorts of problems, but many other forms were the subject of some experimentation as well.

The more recent contraction of government has seen experimentation with a number of other innovative forms of organization. Part III will review this great variety of different organizational forms.

🏛 AN INCREASING VARIETY OF SERVICE DELIVERY MECHANISMS

In the first two parts of this book, the emphasis was on how certain general principles or theories developed. The major purpose of this part is to build on those general ideas and discuss how they apply in the Canadian context. It will describe how government services are delivered to citizens. In this book, the phrase government services will be used in its broadest sense to include more than just tangible products delivered by governments. It is true that governments build roads and deliver mail, but they also provide a service when they ensure that food products are safe or that cable TV is delivered at a fair price. Therefore, the term government services includes both tangible products and government regulation.

Each of the first three chapters in this section covers the structure and standard method of operation of one of the main organizational forms employed in delivering government services—government departments and central agencies (Chapter 8), Crown corporations (Chapter 9), and regulatory agencies

(Chapter 10). Chapter 11 changes the focus by discussing the broad range of alternative service-delivery mechanisms that have emerged in recent years.

Until recently, most government services were delivered directly by government through one of the traditional organizational forms discussed in Chapters 8, 9, and 10. In the last few years, there has been an explosion in the number of different delivery mechanisms that governments employ. This innovation in service-delivery mechanisms has been a response to both financial constraints and citizen demands for improved service delivery. In some cases, the innovation has resulted in government's adopting new structures that are variations of the structures to be discussed in Chapters 8 to 10. In other cases, governments have employed nontraditional means of service delivery, such as partnerships with nongovernmental organizations to share the cost and responsibility for delivering services. These innovative arrangements will be discussed more fully in Chapter 11.

The theme that ties these chapters together is the *choice of service-delivery mechanism.* That is, how do the various means of service delivery differ from one another, and why do governments choose a particular method to carry out a particular responsibility?

Chapter 7 pointed out that when a government is confronted with a problem, it has a number of ways of dealing with that problem. The main instruments that government could employ were summarized as:

- exhortation,
- expenditure,
- taxation,
- regulation, and
- public ownership.[1]

In some cases, the instrument to be employed is fairly obvious. For example, taxation is likely to work better than exhortation in raising revenue. However, in many cases there is a variety of instruments that could be used to accomplish a particular end.

> If a government wishes to promote indigenous cultural activity, it can engage in public ownership, as in the case of the Canadian Broadcasting Corporation or the National Film Board; provide direct subsidies to theatre groups; finance granting institutions (e.g. the Canada Council); provide tax incentives, such as capital cost allowance on films or an expense allowance for advertising; and engage in regulation (e.g. through the Canadian Radio-Television [sic] Telecommunications Commission's broadcasting content rules).[2]

Governments have available to them a broad range of delivery mechanisms. When governments organize, or reorganize, they are not simply deciding to carry out a particular function, they are also making a strategic choice about *how* that function ought to be carried out and *by whom.* In most cases, the choice of delivery mechanism and the strategy for implementation can be key determinants of how well the government's objective will be met.

One of the key choices that a government makes is choosing the method—operating department, Crown corporation, regulatory agency, partnership, or other arrangement—which will be employed to deliver the service. A number of factors could influence governments in choosing a particular arrangement. This decision is not always made according to the tenets of comprehensive rationality. In many cases, governments simply "follow the leader" by adopting the kind of structure that is already employed, for the same or similar purposes, in other jurisdictions.

However, in some cases, governments make conscious decisions about delivery mechanisms. For example, if a particular function is very much like a commercial operation, such as operating an airline or oil company, then the Crown corporation form is likely to be chosen. If a function requires an arm's-length relationship with government, such as regulating broadcasting, then the regulatory agency will likely be the preferred form. Each chapter in this section will consider the unique purposes and characteristics of each of the delivery mechanisms.

This chapter starts that examination by considering the departmental form of organization. It begins with a discussion of the legal foundations of departments, which requires an examination of interactions between departments, the legislature, and the political executive (that is, the cabinet).[3] Then, the role of central agencies such as the Prime Minister's Office and the Privy Council Office will be discussed.

🏛 THE LEGISLATURE, THE EXECUTIVE, AND DEPARTMENTS

It is customary to speak of three branches of government—legislative, executive, and judicial. The judicial branch, which consists of the law courts and related institutions, is not discussed in this chapter, but is considered in detail in Chapter 18. In Canada, the legislative branch of the federal government consists of the Queen and two houses or chambers—the House of Commons and the Senate. Each of the provincial legislatures has only one house (e.g., the National Assembly in Quebec, and the Legislative Assembly in several western provinces).

As illustrated in Figure 8.1, the executive branch is technically headed by the Queen, represented in Canada by the g*overnor general* and the *lieutenant governors* of the provinces. In practice, neither the Queen nor any of her vice-regal representatives ever acts except on the advice of the government of the day as embodied in the prime minister (or provincial premier) and the cabinet. This means that the responsibilities of the executive branch are carried out collectively by cabinet or what is commonly called "the government." All public servants act under the direction and control of the cabinet and are included, therefore, as part of the executive branch. Thus, in this book, the practical, working definition of the executive is the cabinet and the public service.

One sometimes hears that something is done by the *Governor General in Council* or the *Lieutenant Governor in Council*. This means that the governor general or the lieutenant governor has taken some legal action after consultation with the cabinet. It actually means that the cabinet has taken some action; the governor general's or lieutenant governor's signature is a formality.

Figure 8.1
THREE BRANCHES OF GOVERNMENT

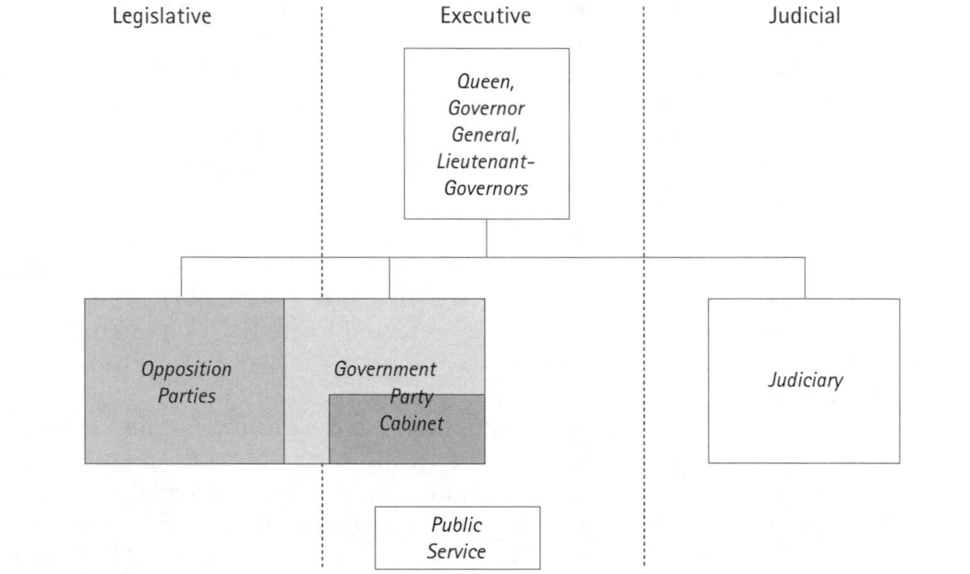

The congressional system of government in the United States is character-ized by a balance of powers between the three branches so that no one branch has authority over any other. In parliamentary systems, like Canada's, it is an important principle that the executive branch is accountable to the legislative branch (i.e., the branch most directly responsible to the general public). Figure 8.1 shows that the two branches are, in fact, joined because cabinet ministers are almost invariably members of the legislative branch. This institutional arrange-ment helps the legislature to hold the executive accountable for its actions.

Definition of a Department

It is difficult to establish a precise, working definition of an *operating department.* Legal definitions can be found in both the Financial Administration Act[4] and the Public Service Employment Act,[5] but these two legislative definitions differ somewhat. However, since their purpose is to determine which organizations will be subject to a particular regime of financial or personnel administration, they do not capture the essence of a department anyway.

The definition used in this book is that of J.E. Hodgetts, who states that

> [A] department is an administrative unit comprising one or more organizational components over which a minister has direct management and control. This defi-nition restricts our terms of reference to major ministerial portfolios ... Since we are also concerned with the ways in which programs are allocated to these units, we can disregard cabinet portfolios to which no duties are assigned: thus the cus-tomary minister without portfolio will be excluded from the list.[6]

One characteristic that should be emphasized in distinguishing operating departments from regulatory agencies and Crown corporations is that of direct management and control by the minister. It is a constitutional convention that the minister should very closely and directly control the actions of an operating department. This differs from the minister's relationship with regulatory agencies and Crown corporations in which there are certain understood limits on the minister's direct involvement in the specifics of their day-to-day management.

Classification Systems for Departments

There are so many departments with so many specialized responsibilities that a number of writers have tried to facilitate understanding of their roles by grouping them in some way. Hodgetts's classification system is based on the *general policy fields* addressed, or functions carried out by the department, such as "public works, communications, and transportation" and "conservation, development, and promotion of physical resources."[7]

Doern focuses on the *relative power* of different departments by developing a classification system that considers size of budget, responsibility for coordination, and knowledge or research capability.[8] He argues that all three of these factors are sources of power, although of different types. Thus, it is very difficult to compare the importance of a department with a large budget, such as Human Resources Development, with one that has a small budget but a broad coordinating role, such as Treasury Board. He identified four types of departments, but one was an experimental structure that is no longer in use. The three remaining types are horizontal policy coordinative, administrative coordinative, and vertical constituency. A contemporary application of Doern's classification scheme results in the grouping of departments shown in Table 8.1.

The *horizontal policy coordinative* departments tend to be the most politically influential:

> They have inherent high policy influence because of the formal authority they possess and because they afford their occupants the highest number of strategic opportunities to intervene in almost any policy issue if the occupant wishes. They each deal respectively with the traditionally most basic horizontal or crosscutting dimensions of government policy, namely overall political leadership and strategy, foreign policy and the foreign implications of domestic policy fields, aggregate economic and fiscal policy, the basic legal and judicial concepts and values of the state, and the overall management of government spending programmes.[9]

These departments tend to be small in terms of number of employees and size of budget, but very strong in terms of responsibility for coordination and knowledge or research capability. Because of this responsibility for coordination across the activities of other departments, some of these departments are also called *central agencies*, as will be discussed later in this chapter.

The *horizontal administrative coordinative* departments are usually felt to be the least influential, in that they are assumed to be the "nuts and bolts" departments that provide the wherewithal for other departments to operate. However, even these departments have some political and policymaking significance. The Department of National Revenue has caused a stir in the past because of its

Table 8.1

CLASSIFICATION OF FEDERAL GOVERNMENT DEPARTMENTS

Horizontal Policy Coordinative

   Finance
   Foreign Affairs and International Trade
   Justice
   Privy Council
   Treasury Board

Vertical Constituency

   Agriculture and Agri-Food
   Canadian Heritage
   Citizenship and Immigration
   Environment
   Fisheries and Oceans
   Forestry
   Health
   Human Resources Development
   Indians Affairs and Northern Development
   Industry
   Multiculturalism and Citizenship
   National Defence
   Natural Resources
   Solicitor General
   Transport
   Veterans Affairs
   Western Economic Diversification

Horizontal Administrative Coordinative

   National Revenue
   Public Works and Government Services

Source: Based on G. Bruce Doern, "Horizontal and Vertical Portfolios in Government," in G. Bruce Doern and V. Seymour Wilson (eds.), Issues in Canadian Public Policy (Toronto: Macmillan, 1974), pp. 315–16, but updated to reflect changes since the earlier tables were originally prepared.

assessment and collection practices, and it is sometimes suggested that the purchasing policy of the Department of Public Works and Government Services could be used as a tool for economic development.

The *vertical constituency departments* are generally involved in providing services directly to the public. These are high-profile departments in that they have the largest budgets and deal with a large constituency. In general, they lack the power to intervene in the affairs of other departments, which only comes with the responsibility to coordinate, but their large budget and vocal constituency give these departments a significant amount of power. It is difficult for the horizontal coordinative portfolios to intervene too much in the affairs of these departments without raising the ire of the large number of constituents who are dependent on the departments for service.

While it is possible to group departments according to characteristics, it is considerably more difficult to rank these portfolios, or the ministers who hold them, in order of importance. A minister's relative position in cabinet is determined in part by her or his portfolio, but also in large part by such other factors as regional power base, personal diplomatic and judgmental skills, and relationship with the prime minister. In short, no portfolio can be deemed unimportant. All portfolios have significant roles, and they can all lead to substantial embarrassment for the government if the occupant of a portfolio is careless or incompetent.

The structure of departments outlined in Table 8.1 is the product of a very substantial reshuffling of responsibilities made by Prime Minister Campbell in June 1993, and largely retained by Prime Minister Chrétien when he came to office. These changes constitute a significant change in the ministry structure.

Over the years cabinets had become larger until Mulroney cabinets had approximately forty members. This posed a number of problems. A cabinet this size cannot really function as an integrated decision-making body, and so most decisions were made in a very large and complicated committee system. A second problem was that a large number of cabinet ministers requires a large number of operating departments. The number was becoming so large that it was difficult to coordinate actions among all the departments[10] and the budget process of allocating funds to such a large number of units was becoming very cumbersome. Finally, the size of cabinet was becoming a political issue. The public was increasingly concerned about the size of government and a large cabinet was a high-profile target for this concern. In reality, the size of cabinet has little impact on the cost of government, but the symbolism of a large number of ministers drawing salaries and having cars and drivers was an easy target for reformers.

Plans had been in the works for some time to reform both cabinet and the system of operating departments by consolidating departments so that there would be fewer ministers. Prime Minister Campbell implemented these changes when she took office in June 1993. Prime Minister Chrétien made a few small changes, but generally he accepted the direction of the change established by his predecessor.

It is too early to assess the impact of these changes,[11] but Peter Aucoin and Herman Bakvis have analyzed a similar change in the Australian system and offered some lessons for Canada.[12] They suggest that these changes could be beneficial in several ways. The decreased size of cabinet should allow it to operate more effectively as an integrated decision-making body. The larger size of departments will improve policy coordination by allowing more policy decisions to be made within departments and reducing the need for cumbersome interdepartmental coordination. Finally, the budget process should be simplified because there are fewer departments, and more budget allocation decisions can be made within departments. Their major caveat is that it will be more difficult for ministers to manage their larger departments. Therefore, they suggest the increased use of parliamentary secretaries to assist ministers in ensuring appropriate political control over their departments.

The organization structure of the government is the personal prerogative of the prime minister. While most changes must ultimately be approved by Parliament, the Public Service Rearrangement and Transfer of Duties Act[13] gives the prime minister a great deal of power to transfer duties among departments and even create new departments. These changes could be made immediately through orders in council, even if the legislation dealing with this is not passed for some time.

It is obviously tempting for each new prime minister to reorganize ministries to suit her or his style of governing, and virtually every prime minister has made certain changes. However, these shifts must be made with care because major organizational shifts, such as those made in June 1993, impose significant tangible and intangible costs on government. The tangible costs arise from the time spent on finding new accommodation, drawing up new organizational structures, preparing new job descriptions, and so forth.[14] The intangible costs are the personal costs that people feel when their long service in an organization with a particular kind of culture is interrupted by having to integrate into a new department with a vastly different culture.

> Organizing is not a free lunch. Adding new organizations or ministerial portfolios adds complexity, and reorganizing existing ones causes disruption. Neither of these costs should be taken lightly. At a minimum, it can take three years to implement a major organizational change—in many cases five years. Where major adjustments in organizational culture are necessary, even more time may be required. During the time these adjustments are taking place, the time and energy of politicians and officials is occupied with organizational issues, at the expense of the policy and program issues that the organization was meant to address.[15]

Jean Chrétien has appointed secretaries of sate in addition to the cabinet ministers who head departments.[16] These secretaries have been assigned specific responsibilities to assist a minister. They are in an intermediate position in that they are members of the ministry and so are bound by collective responsibility, but they are not cabinet ministers. These positions will be used to indicate the government's concern about certain issues, and so their titles have changed over time. These posi-

---

SECRETARIES OF STATE AS OF JUNE 1998

Agriculture and Agri-Food

Asia-Pacific

Atlantic Canada Opportunities Agency

Children and Youth

Economic Development Agency of Canada for the Regions of Quebec

Fisheries and Oceans

International Financial Institutions

Latin America and Africa

Multiculturalism

Parks

Science, Research and Development

Status of Women

Western Economic Diversification

The number of positions does not equal the number of ministers because some ministers hold more than one position.

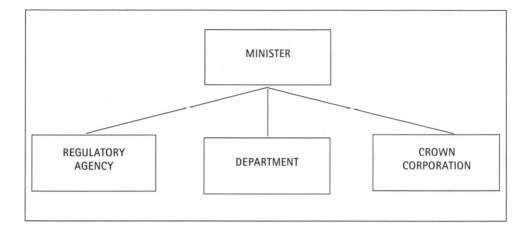

tions are also used to develop and evaluate certain "cabinet-ministers-in-waiting." This sort of position has been used in other governments to address specific important issues that do not respect traditional departmental boundaries. For example, when Frank McKenna was Premier of New Brunswick, he appointed a minister of state for the information highway to signal the importance he attached to this issue.[17]

Departments are the most closely controlled of all government agencies. Other entities such as regulatory agencies and Crown corporations are deliberately insulated, to some extent, from direct control by the legislature and the executive, but departments have no such insulation. It is important to consider some of those avenues of legislative and executive control.

The Legislature and Government Departments

This section will discuss the various methods used by the legislature to control government departments. (A more complete description of the interactions between the legislature and the bureaucracy is contained in Chapter 17.) This control begins at the time of the creation of a new department because a new department can be created only by an Act of Parliament. This enabling legislation sets out the responsibilities of the department and the limits of its authority. The statute establishing the federal Department of Veterans Affairs is typical in that it is only five pages long, and its very general wording imposes only broad conditions on the department's operation. The statute provides in part that:

2. (1) There is hereby established a department of the Government of Canada called the Department of Veterans Affairs over which the Minister of Veterans Affairs appointed by commission under the Great Seal shall preside.

(2) The Minister holds office during pleasure and has the management and direction of the Department ...

4. The powers, duties and functions of the Minister extend and apply to

(a) the administration of such Acts of Parliament, and of such orders of the Governor in Council, as are not by law assigned to any other department of the Government of Canada or any Minister thereof, relating to the care, treatment, training or re-establishment in civil life of any person who served in the Canadian Forces or in the naval, army or air forces of Her Majesty, of any person who has otherwise engaged in pursuits relating to war, and of any other person designated by the Governor in Council, and to the care of the dependants of any such person; and

(b) all such other matters and such boards and other bodies, subjects, services and properties of the Crown as may be designated, or assigned to the Minister, by the Governor in Council.[18]

In some provinces, this kind of legislation is considerably longer and more detailed and restrictive. In any case, the executive has fairly broad prerogatives to arrange the internal structure of departments. Under the federal Public Service Rearrangement and Transfer of Duties Act, the executive also has the power to transfer responsibilities between departments, which can involve some major changes.

In addition to the initial, enabling legislation, Parliament sometimes passes other legislation affecting departments. This includes both specific legislation, such as setting up a new program and assigning it to a department, and general legislation, such as the Financial Administration Act or the Public Service Employment Act, that binds all departments in certain matters. Thus, Parliament can specify a department's mandate as loosely or as tightly as it wants, although the usual practice is to provide a broad mandate that allows maximum flexibility to the executive.

Another important element of Parliament's relationship to the executive is the annual budget. Each year the executive must seek parliamentary approval to spend funds in the upcoming year. At a minimum, the members of Parliament, particularly Opposition members, use this opportunity to question ministers and public servants about the operation of their departments and programs. In extreme cases, Parliament could decide to reduce, or even entirely eliminate, an appropriation for a department.

While these methods by which the legislature can affect departmental operations are, legally speaking, correct, reality requires some modification in practice. When the government party holds a majority of seats in the legislature, the government has fairly effective control over the legislation passed. Members of the Opposition can introduce amendments to proposed legislation, including reductions of appropriations, but these are unlikely to be passed. In the case of a minority government, the situation is more complex, but the government usually finds some method of exercising a certain amount of control over activities in the legislature.[19] Obviously, if it cannot exert sufficient control, it will not govern long.

However, this should not be taken to mean that the government can totally dominate the legislature. Opposition members have certain tools at their disposal to thwart arbitrary government actions. The legislature is a highly public forum, and the government is very sensitive to the embarrassment that it can suffer when the Opposition rallies public opinion against some unpopular action of the government. The government, particularly in a majority situation, has a strong position, but not an absolutely commanding one. Opposition parties still have means of holding a government accountable for its actions.

This is where the doctrine of *individual ministerial responsibility* becomes important.[20] This principle holds that a minister is responsible for all actions carried out by her or his department. This means that, even if the minister did not approve an action in advance or had no knowledge of it, he or she still must accept responsibility for the action. This principle is an important element in a system of responsible government because the minister is the only link between the legislature and the operating department. If the minister could avoid responsibility for the actions of her or his department, then the legislature would have no effective way of holding the executive accountable for its actions. Since the minister is accountable for the actions of her or his department, it is important that there are adequate methods available for the minister to control the department.

The Executive and Government Departments

The minister is the political head of the department and so has line authority over all public servants in the department. Within the provisions of relevant legislation, he or she has full authority to assign duties to departmental employees and supervise their activities. In Chapters 3, 4, and 5, there was some discussion of the difficulties of administrative superiors holding subordinates truly accountable for their actions. The large size and geographical decentralization of most departments, and the incredible demands made on ministers' time in the legislature and in constituency work, make the enforcement of real accountability problematic. However, ministers have a number of tools to assist them in controlling the activities of operating departments.

All ministers have a small personal staff. The members of this staff are selected personally by the minister and are not considered to be public servants; rather, they are the minister's political assistants. They are selected partly for their administrative competence, but unlike public servants, they are also selected for their partisan affiliation. Their roles are difficult to define because each minister uses them in somewhat different ways; however, one role they have in common is assisting the minister to exercise political control over the bureaucracy.[21]

Ministers also have more formal, legal means of controlling their departments. The legislation establishing departments and programs seldom specifies in precise detail how all activities are to be carried out, in large part because the legislature is simply unable to foresee every future possibility. There is usually a clause in this kind of legislation that allows either the minister or the governor in council (that is, the cabinet) to make certain regulations as long as they are consistent with the terms of the enabling legislation. In some cases, this is done in strict legal form through an *order in council*. This is a formal regulation approved by the governor in council and, in the case of the federal government, published in the *Canada Gazette*, which is a biweekly listing of official announcements prepared by the government. Provincial governments have similar official publications.

These orders in council frequently establish the ground rules governing relationships between public servants and members of the public who are affected by their actions and decisions. For example, there are lengthy orders in council specifying the rules about access to information and privacy. They describe the sorts of information that are not available to the public, but they also restrict public servants by specifying those items that must be released. In this sense, regulations are an important means of controlling the actions of public servants.

In a less formal manner, ministers frequently issue internal departmental regulations. These are also binding on all departmental officials, provided that the regulations are within the terms of the enabling legislation. It is these regulations—covering such matters as which form is to be completed in a particular case and how a particular situation is to be treated—that are the lifeblood of most large organizations. Over the years, these regulations can accumulate to several volumes.

Organization of a Typical Operating Department[22]

Figure 8.2 is an organization chart of the federal Department of Transport.[23] The minister is at the top of the pyramid. The minister has a political staff reporting directly to her or him. These people are not permanent public servants but are appointed on a political basis to work directly and personally for the minister. When the minister leaves or the government changes, these people are replaced. Their role is to provide the minister with overtly political advice. They do not have direct line authority within the department. They advise the minister and frequently consult on the minister's behalf with public servants, but they must always act through the minister in seeking action by public servants.

Most ministers have a variety of Crown corporations and agencies reporting to them in addition to their department. These organizations report directly to the minister, not through the department or deputy minister. This reporting relationship can sometimes make it difficult for the minister to coordinate her or his entire portfolio.

The next link in the chain of accountability is the *deputy minister*. Deputy ministers are the administrative (as distinct from political) heads of departments. They are permanent heads of departments in that they do not usually leave when governments change. Unlike ministers, who are politicians, deputy ministers usually work their way up through the ranks of the public service, although, in some cases, they are brought in directly from other governments or the private sector.

In some senses, deputy ministers have the most difficult position in the entire system because they must act as a link between the political desires of the minister and the administrative concerns of the public servants in the department. Of course, ministers are not totally insensitive to administrative concerns, any more

Figure 8.2
ORGANIZATION CHART OF THE DEPARTMENT OF TRANSPORT

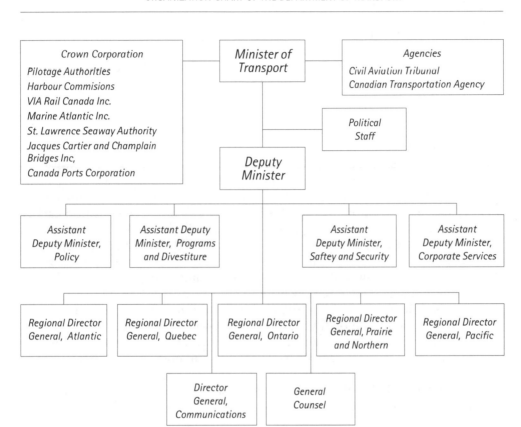

than public servants are totally insensitive to political ones, but each side brings a different dimension to the issue at hand. Ministers, particularly if they represent a new government, often feel under pressure from colleagues to make changes in programs and activities. It would not be appropriate for public servants to oppose these changes, but public servants are frequently more attuned to the administrative problems posed by change than to its political benefits.

Good deputy ministers must stand between these two concerns and not be afraid either to impose change on a reluctant department or to advise ministers fully and frankly if their actions will lead to serious administrative problems. However, if this advice is not delivered in a very sensitive and diplomatic manner, it can be taken for disloyalty. Because the role of the deputy minister is so important, it is described in greater detail in Chapter 16.

The relationship between the minister's political staff and the deputy minister requires some explanation. In principle, the system should work very well when the minister is receiving two streams of advice—political advice from her or his staff, and administrative advice from the deputy. The minister will then be able to come to a decision after weighing these two types of advice. In practice, the relationship can be rather difficult. Some deputies have complained that political staff have functioned as gatekeepers preventing them from taking important information to the minister. The role of political staff will be discussed more fully in Chapter 16.

A word of caution about terminology is necessary. The term "deputy minister" is not used consistently throughout departments. For example, in the Treasury Board where the minister is called the "president," the senior public servant is called the "secretary." Confused? In most government publications, the term "deputy head" is used to cover all of these senior people. In normal discussion around government offices, one frequently hears reference to "the deputy."

Beneath the level of deputy minister (DM), the nomenclature can become even more confusing. Usually, there will be several "assistant deputy ministers" (ADMs) reporting to the DM. Sometimes the superior status of one of these positions will be established by designating it as "associate deputy minister" or "senior assistant deputy minister." This is usually a sign that the position carries a heavier weight of duties or responsibilities than the other ADM positions.

Also, in the Department of Transport, there is a director general reporting directly to the DM. These positions have almost the same status as the ADM in that they report directly to the DM, but their title indicates that their ranking is slightly lower, usually because they have less weighty responsibilities.

At this point, it is useful to relate this organization chart to some of the material about organizational behaviour covered in Chapter 3. In terms of the line-staff distinction, the line units are the regional directors general, while the staff functions are the ADMs in charge of policy and corporate services and the general counsel who is responsible for legal services. A more complete organization chart would also illustrate the functional lines of authority between the line and staff functions.

🏛 CENTRAL AGENCIES

Rationale for Central Agencies

The discussion in Chapter 3 of span of control drew attention to the fact that as the number of units reporting to the same person increases, that person has more difficulty maintaining control of the units and coordinating their activities. The organization of the government of Canada demonstrates a very broad span of control with thirty or forty[24] departments, agencies, and so forth coming under the direct control of cabinet. Even though the number of departments was reduced by Prime Minister Campbell, the numbers are still quite formidable. This broad organizational structure requires some method of coordinating the activities of the separate departments to prevent overlap and working at cross-purposes. One of the methods employed in Canada is the central agency.

There are other ways of dealing with this problem. In Britain, there are many departments headed by ministers who are not members of cabinet.

Ministers heading related departments are then grouped under a senior minister who is a member of cabinet. This creates a situation where the span of control is reasonable both for cabinet, with a relatively small number of senior ministers, and for the senior ministers, each of whom has a reasonable number of noncabinet ministers reporting to her or him. It provides for both reasonable spans of control and a relatively small cabinet.

It is this latter characteristic that precludes the use of this system in Canada. In Canada, the concept of the *representative cabinet* is very important. This principle means that many diverse interests must be represented in the federal cabinet. It requires the selection of cabinet members to provide an appropriate balance of geographic, religious, ethnic, linguistic, gender, and other criteria. As a result, the cabinet must be fairly large to ensure that all groups are represented adequately.

The principle of a representative cabinet also requires adherence to the concept that all cabinet ministers are equal. If there were a distinction between cabinet and noncabinet ministers, it would be impossible to achieve the appropriate representative balance with a limited number of senior ministers. The Clark government of 1979–80 had a small, powerful "inner cabinet," but opposition members delighted in pointing out to residents of certain provinces that they had no representative within the important "inner cabinet." The practice has not been resurrected by subsequent governments.

These conventions of representative cabinet and equality of cabinet ministers require the wide span of control discussed above, which requires the presence of some mechanism to coordinate and control the activities of the operating departments. This is the role of the central agencies.

Definition of a Central Agency

A *central agency* (previously also called a horizontal policy coordinative department) is any agency that has a substantial amount of continuing, legitimate authority to direct and intervene in the activities of departments. The application of any definition, particularly one that contains words such as "substantial" and "continuing," is somewhat arbitrary, but it is widely acknowledged in the 1990s that there are four full-fledged central agencies in the government of Canada—the Prime Minister's Office, the Privy Council Office, the Treasury Board Secretariat, and the Department of Finance.[25]

Central agencies obtain their power either from legislative authority to operate in a particular area or from proximity to someone with legitimate authority, such as the prime minister. They usually do not have a large number of employees, although most of the staff employed are relatively high-level, professional people. Table 8.2 shows the number of people employed in these four agencies, and some of the largest and smallest departments in the fiscal year ending March 31, 1999. Even the smallest departments have more employees than the central agencies, and the largest departments completely dwarf them.

All four agencies discussed in this section have either been created, or experienced significant change, as a result of the style of government brought to office by Prime Minister Trudeau in 1968.[26] Trudeau's predecessor, Prime Minister Pearson, never had a majority government, and so had to be concerned with conciliation and fire fighting. Trudeau, with a majority government in his first term, had the luxury of focusing on specific goals he wanted to accomplish and using such newly fashionable rational tools as cost-effectiveness and systems analysis to attain those goals. His limited experience in working in large organizations could have made him somewhat uncomfortable in a bureaucratic environment. As a result, Trudeau wanted *competing sources of information* so that he did not have to rely solely on the traditional information sources of the operating departments. This was not evidence of distrust of the traditional organizational structures; rather, it was the understandable desire to obtain more than one point of view on an issue before acting. Thus, another major role for central agencies developed in addition to the coordinating role discussed above. Trudeau began to use these agencies as competing sources of information.

It is important to understand that each prime minister has placed her or his own personal stamp on the government bureaucracy, but there has been enough consistency that it is still possible to generalize about the duties of the central agencies. They have two related roles. They are responsible for coordinating both the political and the administrative activities of line departments. They are also involved in advising the prime minister and cabinet on policy initiatives and shepherding these initiatives through the decision-making and implementation processes. Van Loon argues that the ascendancy of central agencies

Table 8.2
NUMBER OF FULL-TIME EQUIVALENT EMPLOYEES IN
CENTRAL AGENCIES AND SELECTED DEPARTMENTS
1998–99

Central Agency or Department	Number of Employees
Finance	706
Prime Minister's Office	85
Privy Council Office	348
Treasury Board Secretariat	781
National Defence (civilian and military combined)	81 417
Human Resources Development	20 074
Public Works and Government Services	11 408
Justice	2 254
National Archives	593

Source: *Minister of Public Works and Government Services, 1998-99 Estimates: Part III.*

derives from the continuing attempt within the federal government to impose financial and qualitative discipline and a notion of collective responsibility on what was hitherto a rather undisciplined policy process.[27]

These roles and responsibilities can be illustrated best by a discussion of the activities of each of these four agencies.

The Prime Minister's Office

The *Prime Minister's Office (PMO)* works directly for the prime minister and has an overtly partisan political role.[28] Its major responsibilities are to serve the prime minister by providing advice on how policy initiatives will be viewed politically in the country, and to assist in other ways that will cast the prime minister in the best political light. Specifically, these responsibilities include planning and coordinating major new policy initiatives, providing liaison with the party machinery across the country, maintaining good relations with the media, writing speeches, advising on appointments and nominations, and briefing the prime minister concerning issues that could come up during daily question period and debate.

Because these functions are all overtly political activities, Prime Minister Trudeau began the tradition of making the small number of people in the PMO overtly partisan appointees. This means that they are there to serve unabashedly the prime minister's political needs and that they hold their positions at the pleasure of the prime minister and always resign when there is a change of government.

Trudeau's former principal secretary (head of the PMO) has argued that the PMO's role should be to establish a "strategic prime ministership."[29] By this, he means that the PMO must assist the prime minister in keeping new policy initiatives on track and avoid being sidetracked. He describes how the prime minister and PMO are continually being confronted with urgent crises. It is imperative, but very difficult, to prevent the urgent from overwhelming the important. Axworthy feels that the role of the PMO is to assist the prime minister in identifying the five or six major initiatives that he or she wants to accomplish during a term of office, and then making sure that the prime minister's energies are expended in this direction rather than on small matters.

The PMO has other important activities of a "housekeeping" nature, such as making travel arrangements and responding to the huge volume of mail sent to the prime minister. The largest number of employees in the PMO are involved in the latter function. The growth in the size of the office has been severely criticized, but much of that growth has occurred in this correspondence function.

It is difficult to generalize about the relationship between the PMO and operating departments. The PMO has no statutory authority of its own; it derives its power from the fact that it is headed by the prime minister, through whom it must act in taking initiatives with departments. Its contact with departments is largely limited to consulting about new policy initiatives or dealing with political problems. There is some idea that the PMO would like to become more involved in policy matters, but its small size and other responsibilities prevent it from doing so to a great extent. In sum, the PMO usually chooses not to become too involved with the activities of operating departments, but it has a significant amount of power that it can exercise on the authority of the prime minister.

The Privy Council Office

The *Privy Council Office (PCO)* is a relatively small organization that provides policy advice and administrative support to the prime minister, cabinet, and cabinet committees. The title of the office comes from the fact that the formal name for cabinet is the Queen's Privy Council.[30] The status of the PCO is illustrated by the fact that the senior public servant in the agency, who is called the Clerk (ordinarily pronounced "clark," in the British tradition) of the Privy Council and the secretary to the cabinet, is officially recognized as the "Head of the Public Service."[31]

Unlike the PMO, the PCO is staffed by career public servants rather than political appointees. However, the kind of advice provided by the PCO, while not overtly political in the partisan sense, is certainly sensitive to the political pulse of the nation. A former clerk of the privy council described the roles of the PMO and the PCO in this manner:

> The Prime Minister's Office is partisan, politically oriented, yet operationally sensitive. The Privy Council Office is nonpartisan, operationally oriented yet politically sensitive.[32]

The Privy Council Office has a number of different roles, including some that are assigned to it by the prime minister on a temporary basis. However, the major, continuing activities of the PCO fall into the three categories of support for the cabinet and its committees, monitoring of federal-provincial relations, and advice on machinery of government.[33]

The PCO provides several different kinds of support for cabinet committees. Organizationally, the office is divided so that there is a small secretariat attached to each cabinet committee, except Treasury Board, which has its own secretarial arm. Each secretariat monitors the general policy environment in the area for which its committee is responsible. The secretariat advises on new policy initiatives or responses to ongoing problems and ensures that all proposals that go before a cabinet committee are in good order. Among other things, this means that the interdepartmental aspects have been discussed and any problems resolved. This aspect of the PCO has prompted some to refer to it as a "gatekeeper," although this might be something of an overstatement. The PCO also assists in the preparation of the agenda of cabinet committee meetings, and in briefing the chairperson of the committee. At the housekeeping level, the PCO arranges for meeting space and maintains the minutes of the meetings.

The PCO also has a role in ensuring that the relationship between the federal government and the provinces progresses smoothly. While individual departments take a lead role in developing programs with the provinces, the PCO maintains an active liaison with officials of these departments to ensure that relationships are operating well and the position of the federal government is not compromised. The PCO is most concerned with policy issues and the overall operation of the federal-provincial structure, and not as concerned about the details of individual programs.

The group responsible for the machinery of government advises the prime minister on the reallocation of programs between departments, and the reorganization of government departments and agencies. This also involves the handling of jurisdictional disputes between ministers or departments and an analysis of the operation of the cabinet committee system.

The machinery of government section also advises the prime minister and cabinet about senior appointments within the federal bureaucracy. It is concerned with moving highly competent public servants through senior postings so that they are always employed in a capacity where their talents can be best used and can gain experience for their next position. The PCO is involved in advising only about employment of public servants; advice about more political kinds of appointments comes from the PMO.

The PCO provides a good example of central agency activities and the general position of central agencies in the organizational structure. The duties of the PCO give it the legitimate right to become involved in the activities of every other department of government. It does not have line authority over those departments, but its position as "gatekeeper" and its proximity to cabinet mean that operating departments always consider advice offered by the PCO very carefully. This helps to explain the complex love-hate relationship that operating departments usually have with central agencies.

Treasury Board

Treasury Board (TB) is a cabinet committee consisting of the president of treasury board, the minister of finance, and four other ministers appointed by the prime minister. TB differs from other cabinet committees in two respects. It is the only cabinet committee that is enshrined in legislation—the Financial Administration Act—and it is the only cabinet committee that has a large bureaucracy reporting to it—Treasury Board Secretariat (TBS).[34] A former secretary of the Treasury Board has written that the board is one committee, but it has a dual role. It functions as both the cabinet's committee on the expenditure budget and the cabinet's committee on management.[35] The Treasury Board itself considers these matters in the final analysis, but in practice most of the preparatory work is done by TBS.[36]

TBS has gradually accumulated many seemingly diverse responsibilities.[37] The one factor that ties them together is that they all relate to ensuring the efficient and effective use of government resources, both human and financial.

TBS is responsible for the preparation of the expenditure budget that the government proposes in the House of Commons each year. It receives general guidelines from the cabinet and the Department of Finance, which allow it, in turn, to set guidelines for expenditure by operating departments. This requires TBS to negotiate with departments about starting new programs, or cutting back or eliminating existing ones. The budget process will be described in greater detail in Chapter 26.

TBS is also responsible for certain aspects of human resource administration. When it was established as a separate organization in 1966, this was a very minor part of its activities, but it had grown so much that by 1988

> nearly 50 per cent of the Treasury Board Secretariat's staff currently works on human resource management functions. The Treasury Board is responsible for the development of personnel policies, the classification of positions, the application of the Official Languages Act, the coordination of the government's human resource planning process and for conducting negotiations and consultations with the unions.[38]

The introduction of collective bargaining in 1967 and the progressive establishment of a truly bilingual public service since the 1960s have imposed a tremendous workload on TBS. Societal and legislative changes in the 1980s have also made its responsibilities considerably more complicated. For example, Treasury Board policies have been affected by the application of the Charter of Rights to employment and union activity, human rights legislation, pay equity legislation, and access to information and privacy legislation.

On top of this, TBS has a special concern for reducing the deficit, which has caused it to, among other things, take the "lead role in defining the government's workforce adjustment policy."[39] "Workforce adjustment policy" is a government euphemism for layoffs—how they will be made, what rights to other government jobs people have, and so forth. It is a very complex and difficult chore to ensure that these adjustments occur at the rate promised by the government and that employees affected by them are treated fairly.

TBS is also responsible for ensuring that sound administrative principles are followed in all government activities. It is responsible for making regulations dealing with administrative matters such as purchasing, entering into contracts, and receiving and spending public funds. The general thrust of these duties is to ensure that proper controls are in effect concerning government assets and that adequate safeguards are in place before funds are spent.

TBS also has a special interest in ensuring the quality of all departmental financial officers and the integrity of the internal audit function to help improve departmental management. As discussed in Chapter 7, evaluations are actually done by departments, but TBS is responsible for providing the guidance and direction under which the evaluations are undertaken. It is then responsible for discussing the results of the evaluation with the department to help it improve its management.

In sum, Treasury Board has numerous responsibilities, but they all relate to ensuring the wise use of resources—both human and financial—within federal government departments. This involves determining that prudence and probity are always observed in government transactions and attempting to ensure uniformity across all government departments in areas such as levels of pay.

From the standpoint of operating departments, Treasury Board is easily the most active—some might say, intrusive—of the central agencies, simply because there are so many points of contact and so many specific activities for which TB clearance must be obtained. Treasury Board officials are aware that

> program managers see uniform, government-wide rules and regulations as obstacles to efficient program delivery. Treasury Board fully recognizes that such rules can inhibit efficient program delivery.[40]

However, Veilleux and Savoie go on to say that this concern must be balanced against other, possibly more important, concerns. Because departments are dependent on public revenue, and because cabinet is collectively responsible for actions of individual ministers, it is impossible to allow department officials a totally free hand in the use of assets and the implementation of policies. It is clear Treasury Board recognizes the need to move away from the detailed, intrusive controls and toward more general guidelines that will allow for a reasonable level of control without stifling departmental initiatives.[41]

Department of Finance

The *Department of Finance* is responsible for advising cabinet on matters of economic policy. Thus, the department has an exceedingly broad mandate. It advises on questions of fiscal policy, international trade policy (including tariffs), domestic industrial policy, taxation policy, and the preparation of the revenue and expenditure budgets.[42]

The Department of Finance could potentially intervene in the activities of any department involved in policies that touch upon any of the above areas. And, given the breadth of those areas, it is difficult to think of a department that does not. The role of the department does not bring it into the same kind of obtrusive, day-to-day contact with operating departments as that of TBS, but its concern with economic policy allows it to intervene at strategic points in the policy development process. Its role in the preparation of the expenditure budget helps determine whether the upcoming year will be a lean or a fat one for government agencies. Finance also has a role as the budgetary gatekeeper. Indeed, it has traditionally provided the strongest opposition to new spending programs.[43] This brings the Department of Finance into fairly frequent conflict with operating departments.

Central Agencies in the Provinces

It is obvious that the functions performed by central agencies in the federal government will also be necessary in provincial governments. However, the smaller size of the provincial governments usually means that organizational structures are less complex and differentiated.[44] In most provinces, the functions of the PMO, the PCO, and sometimes the TB are all carried out in the premier's office. However, there is a general movement toward the establishment of what is commonly described as an institutionalized cabinet, i.e., a cabinet with a formal committee structure and supporting agencies.[45] Several provinces have a separate organization with duties similar to those carried out by Treasury Board at the federal level.[46] For example, the duties of the Management Board of Cabinet in Ontario are very similar to those of TB. The functions of the Department of Finance are carried out in most provinces by a Treasury Department headed by the provincial treasurer.

🏛 CONCLUSION

This chapter has described the main characteristics of the departmental form of organization. This form is usually preferred when the situation calls for strong ministerial control. There are other cases in which it is better for an agency to function at arm's length from the direct control of the minister. The next two chapters will deal with two organizational forms that ensure this distance—the Crown corporation and the regulatory agency.

NOTES

1. G. Bruce Doern and Richard W. Phidd, *Canadian Public Policy: Ideas, Structures, Process*, 2nd ed. (Scarborough, Ont.: Nelson Canada, 1992), 97, 191–92.
2. Michael J. Trebilcock et al., *The Choice of Governing Instrument* (Ottawa: Minister of Supply and Services Canada, 1982), 1.
3. A more detailed treatment of these interactions is contained in ch. 15–17.
4. R.S.C. 1985, c. F-11, s. 2.
5. R.S.C. 1985, c. P-33, s. 2.
6. J.E. Hodgetts, *The Canadian Public Service: A Physiology of Government* (Toronto: University of Toronto Press, 1973), 89.
7. Ibid., ch. 5.
8. G. Bruce Doern, "Horizontal and Vertical Portfolios in Government," in G. Bruce Doern and V. Seymour Wilson, eds., *Issues in Canadian Public Policy* (Toronto: Macmillan, 1974), 310–29. This same idea is also developed in Doern and Phidd, *Canadian Public Policy*, ch. 8.
9. Doern, "Horizontal and Vertical Portfolios in Government," 316–17.
10. Peter Aucoin and Herman Bakvis, *The Centralization-Decentralization Conundrum: Organization and Management in the Canadian Government* (Halifax: The Institute for Research on Public Policy, 1988), 63.
11. Bruce Doern anticipated some of the changes and provided an interesting analysis of some of their consequences: "Efficiency-Democracy Bargains in the Reinvention of Federal Government Organization," in Susan D. Phillips, ed., *How Ottawa Spends: A More Democratic Canada ...? 1993–1994* (Ottawa: Carleton University Press, 1993), 203–29.
12. "Consolidating Cabinet Portfolios: Australian Lessons for Canada," *Canadian Public Administration* 36, no. 3 (fall 1993), 392–420.
13. R.S.C. 1985, c. P-34. A good critique of the use of this legislation is contained in: Gordon F. Osbaldeston, *Organizing to Govern* (Toronto: McGraw-Hill Ryerson, 1992), 24–25, 110–13, 134, and passim.
14. Osbaldeston, *Organizing to Govern*, ch. 7.
15. Ibid., 144.
16. Office of the Prime Minister, "Release," 4 November, 1993.
17. Edward Greenspon, "N.B. Makes a Beeline for the Information Highway," *The Globe and Mail*, 21 January, 1994.
18. R.S.C. 1985, c. V-1.

19. For a description of how the Ontario Progressive Conservative Party managed this, see: Vaughan Lyon, "Minority Government in Ontario, 1975–1981: An Assessment," *Canadian Journal of Political Science* 17 (December 1984): 685–705.

20. For a more complete discussion of ministerial responsibility, see Chapter 17.

21. The general role of these staff members is discussed in more detail in Chapter 16.

22. Surprisingly little is written about the internal organization of government departments. Some of the best references are: Aucoin and Bakvis, *The Centralization-Decentralization Conundrum*, ch. 3, 4, and *passim.;* Hodgctts, *The Canadian Public Service,* Osbaldeston, *Organizing to Govern*; Saeed Rahnema, *Organization Structure: A Systemic Approach* (Toronto: McGraw-Hill Ryerson, 1992).

23. Adapted from: *1998–99 Estimates: Transport Canada: Part III—Report on Plans and Priorities* (Minister of Public Works and Government Services Canada, 1998), 40.

24. It is difficult to pin down the precise number because some organizations have very ambiguous reporting relationships.

25. This list coincides with the list used in the most recent comprehensive study of central agencies, except that some agencies have been combined since then. See: Colin Campbell and George J. Szablowski, *The Superbureaucrats* (Toronto: Macmillan, 1979).

26. G. Bruce Doern, "Recent Changes in the Philosophy of Policymaking in Canada," *Canadian Journal of Political Science* 4 (June 1971): 243–66.

27. R. Van Loon, "Stop the Music: The Current Policy and Expenditure Management System in Ottawa," *Canadian Public Administration* 24 (summer 1981): 176.

28. Marc Lalonde, "The Changing Role of the Prime Minister's Office," *Canadian Public Administration* 14 (winter 1971): 509–37.

29. Thomas S. Axworthy, "Of Secretaries to Princes," *Canadian Public Administration* 31, no. 2 (summer 1988): 247–64.

30. Technically, the Queen's Privy Council consists of all previous and present federal cabinet ministers plus a limited number of others on whom the honour has been bestowed.

31. S.C. 1992, c. 54, s.26.

32. Gordon Robertson, "The Changing Role of the Privy Council Office," *Canadian Public Administration* 14 (winter 1971): 506.

33. For a good discussion of the role of PCO, see Audrey D. Doerr, *The Machinery of Government in Canada* (Toronto: Methuen, 1981), 30–34, and Richard D. French, "The Privy Council Office: Support for Cabinet Decision Making," in Richard Schultz, Orest Kruhlak, and John C. Terry, eds., *The Canadian Political Process* (Toronto: Holt, Rinehart and Winston, 1979), 363–94.

34. For a time, Treasury Board had a second administrative arm—the Office of the Comptroller General. This was abolished as a separate organization in 1993 and its duties were transferred to the Treasury Board Secretariat.

35. A.W. Johnson, "The Treasury Board of Canada and the Machinery of Government of the 1970's," *Canadian Journal of Political Science* 4 (September 1971): 346.

36. The duties of the Treasury Board and the secretariat will be discussed in more detail in Chapters 25, 26, and 27.

37. For a good discussion of the full range of responsibilities currently vested in Treasury Board, see: Evert A. Lindquist, "On the Cutting Edge: Program Review, Government Restructuring and the Treasury Board of Canada," in Gene Swimmer, ed., *How Ottawa Spends 1996–97* (Ottawa: Carleton University Press, 1996), 205–52.

38. Gérard Veilleux and Donald J. Savoie, "Kafka's Castle: The Treasury Board of Canada Revisited," *Canadian Public Administration* 31, no. 4 (winter 1988): 527.

39. Ibid., 529.

40. Ibid., 532.

41. A good discussion of how Treasury Board sees its changing role is found in: Ian D. Clark, "Restraint, Renewal and the Treasury Board Secretariat," *Canadian Public*

Administration. 37, no. 2 (summer 1994), 209–48; Treasury Board of Canada Secretariat, *Treasury Board Secretariat Initiatives in Support of Good Governance* (March 26, 1998), 1. For a discussion of some of the specific initiatives which Treasury Board has taken to revise its relationships with departments, see: Peter Harder and Evert Lindquist, "Expenditure Management and Reporting in the Government of Canada: Recent Developments and Backgrounds," in Jacques Bougault, Maurice Demers, and Cynthia Williams, eds., *Public Administration and Public Management Experiences in Canada* (Quebec: Les Publications du Québec, 1997), 80–82, and passim; Lindquist, "On the Cutting Edge," 227 ff.

42. For a more detailed description of the responsibilities of the Department of Finance, see Richard W. Phidd and G. Bruce Doern, *The Politics and Management of Canadian Economic Policy* (Toronto: Macmillan, 1979), ch. 7.

43. Ibid., 224.

44. Graham White, "Big Is Different from Little: On Taking Size Seriously in the Analysis of Canadian Governmental Institutions," *Canadian Public Administration* 33, no. 4 (1990), 526–50.

45. Christopher Dunn, "Changing the Design: Cabinet Decision-Making in Three Provincial Governments." *Canadian Public Administration* 34, no. 4 (winter 1991), 621–40.

46. Marsha A. Chandler and William M. Chandler, *Public Policy and Provincial Politics* (Toronto: McGraw-Hill Ryerson, 1979), 101–05.

BIBLIOGRAPHY

Aucoin, Peter, and Herman Bakvis. *The Centralization-Decentralization Conundrum: Organization and Management in the Canadian Government.* Halifax: The Institute for Research on Public Policy, 1988.

_____. "Consolidating Cabinet Portfolios: Australian Lessons for Canada." *Canadian Public Administration* 36, no. 3 (fall 1993), 392–420.

Axworthy, Thomas S. "Of Secretaries to Princes." *Canadian Public Administration* 31, no. 2 (summer 1988): 247–64.

Borgeat, Louis, René Dussault, Lionel Ouellet avec la collaboration de Patrick Moran, Marcel Proulx. *L'administration québécoise: Organisation et fonctionnement.* Presses de l'Université du Québec, 1984.

Campbell, Colin. *Governments Under Stress.* Toronto: University of Toronto Press, 1983.

Campbell, Colin, and George J. Szablowski. *The Superbureaucrats.* Toronto: Macmillan, 1979.

Chandler, Marsha A., and William M. Chandler. *Public Policy and Provincial Politics.* Toronto: McGraw-Hill Ryerson, 1979.

Chenier, John A. "Ministers of State to Assist: Weighing the Costs and the Benefits." *Canadian Public Administration* 28 (fall 1985): 397–412.

Clark, Ian D. "Restraint, Renewal and the Treasury Board Secetariat." *Canadian Public Administration.* 37, no. 2 (summer 1994), 209–48.

Doern, G. Bruce. "Efficiency-Democracy Bargains in the Reinvention of Federal Government Organization." In Susan D. Phillips, ed., *How Ottawa Spends: A More Democratic Canada ...? 1993–1994.* Ottawa: Carleton University Press, 1993, 203–29.

Doern, G. Bruce, and Richard W. Phidd. *Canadian Public Policy: Ideas, Structures, Process.* 2nd ed. Scarborough, Ont.: Nelson Canada, 1992.

_____. "Horizontal and Vertical Portfolios in Government." In G. Bruce Doern and V. Seymour Wilson, eds., *Issues in Canadian Public Policy.* Toronto: Macmillan, 1974, 310–36.

Doerr, Audrey D. *The Machinery of Government in Canada.* Toronto: Methuen, 1981.

Dunn, Christopher. "Changing the Design: Cabinet Decision-Making in Three Provincial Governments," *Canadian Public Administration* 34, no. 4 (winter 1991), 621–40.

French, Richard D. "The Privy Council Office: Support for Cabinet Decision Making." In Richard Schultz, Orest Kruhlak, and John C. Terry, eds., *The Canadian Political Process.* Toronto: Holt, Rinehart and Winston, 1979, 363–94.

Harder, Peter, and Evert Lindquist, "Expenditure Management and Reporting in the Government of Canada: Recent Developments and Backgrounds." In Jacques Bougault, Maurice Demers, and Cynthia Williams, eds., *Public Administration and Public Management Experiences in Canada.* Quebec: Les Publications du Québec, 1997, 71–89.

Hodgetts, J.E. *The Canadian Public Service: A Physiology of Government.* Toronto: University of Toronto Press, 1973.

Jackson, Robert J., Doreen Jackson, and Nicolas Baxter-Moore. *Politics in Canada: Culture, Institutions, Behaviour and Public Policy.* Scarborough, Ont.: Prentice-Hall Canada, 1986.

Johnson, A.W. "The Treasury Board of Canada and the Machinery of Government of the 1970's." *Canadian Journal of Political Science* 4 (September 1971): 346–66.

Lalonde, Marc. "The Changing Role of the Prime Minister's Office." *Canadian Public Administration* 14 (winter 1971): 509–37.

Lindquist, Evert A.. "On the Cutting Edge: Program Review, Government Restructuring and the Treasury Board of Canada." In Gene Swimmer, ed. *How Ottawa Spends 1996–97.* Ottawa: Carleton University Press, 1996, 205–52.

Loreto, Richard A. "The Structure of the Ontario Political System." In Donald C. MacDonald, ed., *The Government and Politics of Ontario.* 3rd ed. Scarborough, Ont.: Nelson Canada, 1985, 17–47.

Lyon, Vaughan. "Minority Government in Ontario, 1975–1981: An Assessment." *Canadian Journal of Political Science* 17 (December 1984): 685–705.

Osbaldeston, Gordon F. *Organizing to Govern.* Toronto: McGraw-Hill Ryerson, 1992.

Phidd, Richard W., and G. Bruce Doern. *The Politics and Management of Canadian Economic Policy.* Toronto: Macmillan, 1978.

Rahnema, Saeed. *Organization Structure: A Systemic Approach.* Toronto: McGraw-Hill Ryerson, 1992.

Robertson, Gordon. "The Changing Role of the Privy Council Office." *Canadian Public Administration* 14 (winter 1971): 506.

Tellier, Paul M. *Public Service 2000: First Annual Report to the Prime Minister on the Public Service of Canada.* Ottawa: Minister of Supply and Services Canada, 1992.

Treasury Board of Canada Secretariat. *Treasury Board Secretariat Initiatives in Support of Good Governance* (26 March, 1998).

Trebilcock, Michael J., Douglas G. Hartle, J. Robert S. Prichard, and Donald N. Dewees. *The Choice of Governing Instrument.* Ottawa: Minister of Supply and Services Canada, 1982.

Van Loon, Richard J., and Michael S. Whittington. *The Canadian Political System: Environment, Structure, and Process.* 3rd ed. Toronto: McGraw-Hill Ryerson, 1981.

Veilleux, Gérard, and Donald J. Savoie. "Kafka's Castle: The Treasury Board of Canada Revisited." *Canadian Public Administration* 31, no. 4 (winter 1988): 517–38.

White, Graham. "Big Is Different from Little: On Taking Size Seriously in the Analysis of Canadian Governmental Institutions." *Canadian Public Administration.* 33, no. 4 (1990): 526–50.

9

Public Enterprise and Privatization

Why can't the CBC make a profit? Private television networks make money. What's wrong with this Crown corporation that it can't make any money? Wouldn't we all be better off if it were privatized and sold to the same people who run the private networks? By some criteria, we would be, but by other criteria, we might be considerably worse off. This is one of those issues that is quite a bit more complicated than it seems at first glance.

The problem is that Crown corporations have an ambivalent role. Because the CBC is a government entity, it is expected to carry out a public policy role in maximizing Canadian content and providing regional programming. However, because it is called a corporation, there is also an expectation that it should make a profit like private-sector corporations. The conflict is that it is difficult to make a profit by producing and showing Canadian and regional shows. The CBC provides a valuable service by linking us together as Canadians, and informing us of what is happening in all areas of our huge country, but when Canadians vote with their fingers, it seems like they would rather watch American television.

This is the dilemma faced by the CBC. It can be true to its public policy purpose and continue to provide Canadian content, or it could do what other Canadian networks do and provide more American shows and probably make money. It seems impossible to do both.

So, can we privatize the CBC? Of course. It has a huge amount of valuable assets which many investors would love to have. Would the private investors make money? They wouldn't buy it if they couldn't make money. However, you should expect a different kind of CBC. The private investors can make more money by showing "Baywatch" than Canadian programs. If you live in the far north or other sparsely populated areas, you might not have any television because you don't generate enough revenue. Don't expect a private investor to continue to subsidize a region that's not paying for itself.

In sum, the CBC can be privatized, and it can make money, but it will be a very different kind of organization.

This chapter will focus on the form of government organization traditionally known as the Crown corporation or public enterprise. This organizational form is commonly used by government to deliver commercial types of services. Crown corporations affect us virtually every day; for example, when we receive our mail, use electricity in our homes, or ride to work in a public transit vehicle operated or manufactured by a public enterprise.

This chapter first defines public enterprise and then discusses trends in the use of this organizational form. In keeping with the theme of this part of the book—the choice of service-delivery mechanisms—there will be an analysis of why the corporate form of organization is chosen over other methods. Then, concerns such as methods of control of the corporation and its internal structure and method of operation will be considered. Finally, some of the criticisms of the corporate form and related proposals for reform will be discussed.

🏛 DEFINITION OF PUBLIC ENTERPRISE

A number of different terms are used to denote the corporate form. The most common are "Crown corporation," "mixed enterprise," "joint enterprise," and "public enterprise." Sometimes, these terms are used interchangeably, but this section will provide different definitions for each.

Separating the corporate form from other forms of government organization is relatively easy.[1] Crown corporations are established either through their own legislation, or through incorporation under the federal or provincial companies legislation in exactly the same way as any private sector corporation. Determining what constitutes a corporate form, as distinct from other organizational forms, is not difficult; the difficult part is determining what constitutes a Crown corporation.

Patrice Garant suggests that

> Crown corporations are companies in the ordinary sense of the term, whose mandate relates to industrial, commercial or financial activities but which also belong to the state, are owned by the government or the Crown or whose sole shareholder is the government or the Crown. This also includes wholly owned subsidiaries. Such companies must be considered part of the governmental public sector: they belong to the state and are exclusively controlled by it.

> On the other hand, institutions that are really administrative bodies rather than companies should be excluded from the family of Crown corporations: for example, organizations concerned with economic or social regulation, administrative management and consultation. On the other hand, semipublic companies, that is, majority or even minority subsidiaries in which there is coparticipation of public and private capital, are not Crown corporations, although they are often similar to them.[2]

This definition leaves out certain noncommercial entities that are defined as Crown corporations in the federal Financial Administration Act; these include the Canada Employment and Immigration Commission and the Agricultural Stabilization Board. While there are valid financial and political reasons for separating these organizations from their related departments, they are excluded from this definition because their *method of operation* is much more like an operating department than a corporation.

The federal government classifies its corporate holdings in a number of different categories.[3] *Parent corporations* are corporations that are one hundred percent owned by the federal government. There are three classes of subsidiaries of a parent corporation—*wholly-owned subsidiaries,* and *other subsidiaries* and *associates,* held at less than 50 percent.

There are four other types of corporations that are less directly controlled by the federal government.

Mixed enterprises are corporations whose shares are partially owned by the government of Canada with the balance owned by *private sector parties.* These can be corporations that have been partially privatized (Petro-Canada), or corporations that have been specifically created to work with a private sector corporation for a particular purpose (National Sea Products Limited).

Joint enterprises are similar to mixed enterprises except that the other shareholder is *another level of government.* Currently, all of these are in the field of economic development—Lower Churchill Development Corporation Limited, North Portage Development Corporation, and Société du parc industriel et portuaire Québec-sud.

Other entities are

> corporate entities in which Canada holds no shares but, either directly or through a Crown corporation, has a right pursuant to statute, articles of incorporation, letters patent or by-law, to appoint or nominate one or more members to the board of directors or similar governing body.[4]

Some examples of these organizations are the Canadian Centre for Swine Improvement, the Canadian Sport and Fitness Administration Centre, and the Maritime Forestry Complex Corporation.

International enterprises are "corporate entities created pursuant to international agreements by which Canada has a right to appoint or elect members to a governing body."[5] Some examples are the International Monetary Fund, the Commonwealth War Graves Commission, and the International Porcupine Caribou Board.

Public enterprise is the most general term and is usually used to encompass all the above terms. This chapter will focus predominantly on parent corporations, although there will be some discussion of the various other types of organizations as well.

🏛 CHANGING TRENDS IN PUBLIC ENTERPRISE

Governments grew very rapidly in the 1960s and 1970s, and it is not surprising that public enterprise followed suit.[6] In more recent times, the growth of government has slowed considerably, and the size of the corporate sector has declined as a result of a growing trend toward privatization.

The Federal Scene

Table 9.1 shows the number of Crown corporations currently held by the federal government and illustrates the trend over the last fifteen years. The clear trend is toward a reduction in the number of corporate entities.[7] This has been effected both by high profile activities, such as major privatizations, and by

Table 9.1
FEDERAL CROWN CORPORATIONS BY METHOD OF OWNERSHIP

	1997	1982
Parent Crown Corporations	47	72
Wholly-Owned Subsidiaries	25	114
Other Subsidiaries and Associates	23	89
Mixed Enterprises	3	17*
Joint Enterprises	3	*
International Organizations	20	*
Other Entities	86	23
Corporations Under the Terms of the *Bankruptcy and Insolvency Act*	6	*

* Some changes have occurred as a result of differences in reporting methods.

Source: Treasurey Board of Canada Secretariat, Crown Corporations and Other Corporate Interests of Canada —1997 and the comparable report for December 1982. Reproduced with the permission of the Minister of Public Works and Government Services Canada, 1998.

simply winding up some inactive corporations and consolidating others. During the rapid growth of the 1960s and 1970s, the federal government almost lost control of all the various corporate entities in which it had some stake. New corporations were being created and subsidiaries added to existing corporations in a manner that made it difficult for the federal government to keep track of all these organizations.[8] In recent times, it has made a conscious effort to maintain better control.

Table 9.2 provides an idea of the size of the largest federal Crown corporations. Obviously, federal Crown corporations are major employers. The number of employees and levels of assets controlled have declined over the last few years, mostly as a result of privatizations, but a number of Crown corporations have followed their private sector counterparts by streamlining their workforces.

The activities in which federal Crown corporations have been involved have changed over the years. In the years immediately after Confederation, the federal government was most concerned with nation building, and so focused on transportation undertakings that would unify the diverse parts of the country. During World War II, the major theme of public policy changed from national unity to national defence, with the creation of many new corporations to supply the war effort.[9] Since the end of the war, federal Crown corporations have become more involved in the areas of finance, insurance, and real estate.

It is clear that Crown corporations no longer play as major a role in the economy as they once did. For example, with the sale of Air Canada and

Table 9.2
SIZE OF SELECTED LARGER CROWN CORPORATIONS AND TOTAL CORPORATE SECTOR—1997

	Employees	Assets ($ millions)
Canada Post Corporation	43 831	2 725.8
Canadian Broadcasting Corporation	7 311	1 664.7
Atomic Energy of Canada	3 675	1 040.5
VIA Rail	3 000	712.5
Canada Mortgage and Housing	2 565	17 646.2
Marine Atlantic	2 011	326.1
Cape Breton Development Corporation	1 894	252.6
Bank of Canada	1 600	*
Business Development Bank of Canada	1 066	4 029.8
Export Development Corporation	512	9 706.0
Canadian Wheat Board	454	8 281.2
Farm Credit Corporation	800	5 022.5
Total Corporate Sector	75 074	56 661.2

* Financial information excluded because of the unique nature of its operations.

Source: Treasury Board of Canada Secretariat, Crown Corporations and Other Corporate Interests of Canada—1997, pp. 24–25.
Reproduced with the permission of the Minister of Public Works and Government Services Canada, 1998.

Canadian National Railways, the federal involvement in transportation is more strategic and regional than predominant.

The question of which political party has employed the corporate form more frequently has always been contentious. Langford and Huffman point out that the federal Liberals have created an average of two corporations for each year they have been in power, which is more than twice the average of the Conservatives.[10] And the Liberal years of the 1960s and 1970s certainly saw the creation of a large *number* of Crown corporations. However, the Conservatives have created such major corporations as the Canadian Broadcasting Corporation, the Bank of Canada, Canadian National Railways, and the Canadian Wheat Board. This topic is likely to remain a subject of lively partisan debate.

The Provincial Scene

Defining the public enterprise sector in the provincial sphere is even more difficult than in the federal one. The ten jurisdictions each have slightly different definitions of Crown corporations, so that the data collection and comparability problems are significantly multiplied. However, it is usually suggested that provincial Crown corporations are both considerably larger and have grown more rapidly in recent years than federal Crown corporations.[11]

Provinces have adopted the Crown corporation form in a number of different functional areas. Industrial development, liquor sales, housing, power generation,[12] and research and development are the most popular, in terms of the number of provinces employing them. As measured by the total value of assets controlled, the two major fields are electrical power and banking, followed by housing, education, and telephone and communications. These five functions account for just over 80 percent of total assets.[13]

The major activities in which provincial Crown corporations have been involved have changed over the years. In the early years, one function was dominant—power generation.[14] This gave way to diversification into the trade, finance, insurance, and real estate sectors. More recently, provincial Crown corporations have become involved in industrial and resource development areas, with the newest area being insurance.[15] One of the recent trends is the privatization of portions of the electrical corporations in most provinces. It is likely that the next review of provincial Crown corporations will indicate considerably less involvement in this field.

Marsha Chandler suggests that this growth was the result of the presence of more left-wing (NDP and Parti Québécois) governments in provincial capitals. Her data indicate that left-wing governments not only use the corporate form more often, but they also use it for different purposes from those of their right-wing counterparts. "[N]on-socialist governments have used public ownership almost exclusively to facilitate economic development,"[16] e.g., hydroelectric and industrial development corporations. Left-wing governments have been more likely to use the corporate form for redistributive ends and to supplant private sector corporations, e.g., insurance and natural resources.

🏛 THE RATIONALE FOR THE CREATION OF PUBLIC ENTERPRISES

This section will examine some of the reasons why governments use the corporate form to accomplish certain goals.[17]

There is one important factor that distinguishes Crown corporations in Canada from similar entities in many other countries. In some countries, public enterprises are referred to as "nationalized industries" because they were at one time private sector corporations that have been taken over as a result of some degree of coercion by the state. The phrase "nationalized industries" is not usually employed in Canada because this has not been the ordinary mode of establishing Crown corporations.

In most cases, Crown corporations have been started from scratch. In some recent cases, governments have taken over existing entities, but seldom with any overt coercion. Takeovers have sometimes involved picking up the pieces of a failed or near-failed company and continuing to operate it to provide jobs, or purchasing a publicly traded company on the open market, such as Alberta's purchase of Pacific Western Airlines[18] or the numerous purchases made by Petro-Canada.[19]

Corporations have been created for many different reasons. "It cannot be said that any unifying philosophy underlies the use of the public corporation in Canada: the whole development has been piecemeal and pragmatic."[20] However, several attempts have been made to categorize a few of the diverse reasons for employing the corporate form.[21]

Nation Building (or Province Building) and Community and Economic Development.

Trebilcock and Prichard suggest that this is the most common rationale for the creation of public enterprises. They suggest that it usually involves two components:

1. integrating the country by making infrastructure investments and providing essential services, which private business is unable or unwilling to provide; and

2. promoting Canadian nationalism, i.e., developing a national identity and preserving Canadian control over certain services and sectors of the economy.[22]

Some Crown corporations have been created partly out of cultural nationalism. Canada's proximity to the overwhelming magnetism of the United States has prompted a conscious desire to maintain a unique Canadian culture, but has simultaneously raised doubts about the ability of the private sector alone to accomplish this. The Canadian Broadcasting Corporation and some more recent initiatives in the film industry are examples of corporations geared to developing a national identity.

Regional Development and Job Preservation.

A different kind of economic development is the increasing number of cases that involve rescuing failed or floundering private companies to preserve jobs. This has been referred to as "hospitalization," because the theory is that these organizations have temporarily become ill and that with some nurture provided by government funds, they will be on their feet again and supporting themselves. The problem is that some of the corporations that have been rescued under this rationale are more in need of a hospice than a hospital.

Enhancing Global Competitiveness.

Laux and Molot build on this economic development theme and identify a worldwide trend to larger scale, even global, production and marketing units. Countries like the United States and Japan have adapted to this trend well, but they argue that certain factors limited Canada's ability to join the fray.[23] Thus, Canadian governments invested heavily in large commercial corporations because this was the only way there would be a Canadian presence in these fields.

Separation from Political Control. It is important that an organization that carries out government policy is closely controlled by the political executive. However, when an organization has a predominantly commercial mandate, it is possible that political concerns could interfere with that mandate. The Crown corporation form places the organization under the control of a board and at arm's length from government control. This is beneficial from the standpoint of assisting the corporation in furthering its commercial activities, but one of the problems, as discussed later, is that Crown corporations can become too independent of legislative and government control.

Diverse Representation on the Board. Crown corporations are headed by boards of directors that allow for the presence of geographic, consumer, ethnic, language, and other types of representation. This differs from an operating department headed by a single minister. In the Crown corporation form, a number of people representing interested groups are actively involved in the decision-making process, thus ensuring that these diverse interests are considered in the making of important decisions. For example, it is traditional that the Board of Directors of the Canadian Broadcasting Corporation contain balanced representation from the various geographic areas of the country.

Attracting Business People to Management. One of the most important keys to success for any organization is attracting good people as directors and managers. Successful business people frequently have much to offer to government organizations, but they are sometimes uncomfortable coming into an unfamiliar management structure such as an operating department with a political head, with central agency controls and the other trappings of government. These people feel more comfortable in a more familiar setting, such as the corporate form. Therefore, it is sometimes suggested that one of the benefits of the Crown corporation is an increased ability to attract successful business people as managers.

Providing a "Window" on the Private Sector. Some kinds of activities are usually carried out by the private sector but are still immensely important to the overall public well being. In these cases, governments sometimes feel a need to use the corporate form to obtain a "window" on this particular industry, so that the government can ensure that the industry will act in the national interest.

Freedom from Central Agency and Other Controls. Operating departments frequently complain that they experience difficulties in fulfilling their mandate because of the strict financial and personnel regulations imposed by organizations such as the Treasury Board and the Public Service Commission. The argument is frequently made that entities engaging in commercial activities would be at a competitive disadvantage if they were subject to the same regulations. Thus, the corporate form is frequently employed in cases where competitive pressures require more flexibility than is provided in other organizational forms.

Low Visibility Taxation.   Crown corporations pay dividends to their share-holders, i.e., government, in the same manner as private sector corporations. In some cases, governments use Crown corporations as sources of income, which might be considered a form of scarcely concealed taxation. For example, the provincial liquor sales agencies make significant profits, which are passed along to provincial governments. As discussed later in this chapter, some provinces have or are considering privatizing liquor sales. Depending on the financial arrangements made, this could have a significant impact on provincial revenue.

Joint Undertakings.   Governments frequently engage in joint ventures. These could be between governments within Canada, such as the North Portage Development Corporation, or internationally, such as the Asian Development Bank, or they could be between governments and private sector organizations, such as Canartic Shipping Company Limited or NPM Nuclear Project Managers Canada Inc. The corporate form is the obvious one to employ in these cases because it creates an autonomous entity separate from any of the governments involved.

This is not a comprehensive list of the reasons for the use of the Crown cor-poration form. However, it does provide the major rationales that are usually put forward when a new corporation is being formed. Given the many different reasons for the creation of Crown corporations, it is not surprising that they exhibit many different characteristics. Therefore, not all Crown corporations are treated the same way for purposes of political accountability.

🏛 CLASSIFICATION OF FEDERAL CROWN CORPORATIONS

Most governments have a classification system that determines the type and amount of political control to which particular groups of corporations will be subject. For example, the federal Financial Administration Act has four sched-ules that define the accountability regime of federal organizations.[24] *Schedule I* lists the operating departments. *Schedule II* lists those entities that have separate corporate status but that perform "administrative, research, supervisory, advi-sory or regulatory functions of a governmental nature."[25] These organizations, such as the Canada Employment and Immigration Commission and the National Research Council, do not meet the criteria of a Crown corporation specified at the beginning of this chapter. Some of the Schedule II organiza-tions function in a manner almost identical to departments, and some are advi-sory councils that were discussed in more detail in Chapter 6.

Schedule III-Part II lists the names of each corporation that

(i)   operates in a competitive environment,

(ii)   is not ordinarily dependent on appropriations for operating purposes, and

(iii)   ordinarily earns a return on equity ...[26]

These are the high-profile corporations, such as Canada Post Corporation, Canada Development Investment Corporation, and Petro-Canada.

Schedule III-Part I lists those corporations that do not meet one of the three criteria mentioned above. Some of these are not commercially oriented, e.g., National Capital Commission; most fail to meet the second criterion—financial independence, e.g., VIA Rail Canada Inc.

The purpose of the classification system is to establish different accountability regimes for corporations in the different schedules. Moving from Schedule I to Schedule III-Part II is moving from the least to the most autonomous type of entity.

🏛 POLITICAL CONTROL OF CROWN CORPORATIONS

The Accountability-Autonomy Conundrum

One of the reasons for the use of the Crown corporation form of organization is to separate the corporation from direct political control. However, a Crown corporation is a creature of the government, carries out government objectives, and, in many cases, uses government funds. Therefore, a Crown corporation cannot behave in a totally autonomous manner, but the precise method of political control is awkward because of the need for some limited amount of autonomy. This section will examine how the current system of political control of Crown corporations operates.

Establishing the appropriate amount of control over the activities of a Crown corporation is an awkward problem. On the one hand, the corporation is an emanation of government and uses government funds, and so cannot be allowed to operate completely outside government control. On the other hand, too much control defeats the purpose of using the corporate form.

> Parliament and even the responsible Minister must show confidence in the corporation by refraining from breathing down the neck of management. On the other hand, the Canadian system of parliamentary government can impose responsibility only on the Ministers of the Crown. Hence the public corporation cannot be used as a means of evading ultimate responsibility. Where to draw the line between the claims of managerial autonomy and the claims of parliamentary responsibility remains for Canada a problem that has been seriously posed rather than solved by contemporary use of the public corporation.[27]

Establishing the Crown Corporation

Public enterprises can be established in three ways: by separate enabling legislation, under the relevant companies legislation, and through the purchase of the shares of a going concern.[28]

The first method provides the greatest legislative control and accountability. The legislature passes a separate law for each new corporation, specifying the mandate of the corporation, i.e., the activities in which it can engage, and its accountability regime to the legislature (e.g., annual reports and method of financing). Thus, the accountability relationship can be as tight or as loose as members of the legislature desire. In most cases, the corporations created in this manner do not have any share capital because they are controlled directly by the government. Some of the federal corporations that have been established by separate legislation are the Canadian Broadcasting Corporation[29] and the Canada Post Corporation.[30]

Alternatively, governments can incorporate companies under the relevant federal or provincial companies legislation in the same manner as any private citizen. A minister, or even a public servant, simply prepares the necessary documentation and, in due course, the Crown corporation is in business. These companies have share capital that is legally vested in either the minister or the Crown. At one point, this method was relatively common, but now it requires Cabinet approval[31] and so is used very seldom.

Finally, the government can enter into any sort of contract, which means that it may decide to purchase the shares of a company on the open market or through a private arrangement. The shares so obtained are then vested in either the minister or the Crown. This same heading covers those relatively rare situations in which governments have forcibly nationalized companies against the will of the previous shareholders. This requires enabling legislation and usually provokes a court challenge. The most recent examples are the actions of the Quebec government with regard to the asbestos industry[32] and of the Saskatchewan government with regard to the potash industry.[33]

The Financial Administration Act

This act establishes a general framework for the allowable activities and the accountability of Crown corporations. The purposes of the act are to provide for enhanced accountability and some uniformity in the treatment of Crown corporations, but this uniformity is tempered by the provisions of the various acts that created the corporations.

The specific provisions of the act will be discussed at various points in this chapter. The general thrust of the legislation is to stipulate what types of approvals corporations need before they undertake certain activities and what reports they must file at the end of their year. The Financial Administration Act is generally seen as the keystone of formal, legal accountability requirements, but there are a number of other accountability mechanisms based on constitutional conventions.

Ministerial Responsibility

All corporations report to Parliament through a minister. The concept of ministerial responsibility was discussed in the chapter on government departments, Chapter 8, because the ability to hold the minister accountable for bureaucratic actions is a very important control mechanism over operating departments. The concept of ministerial responsibility is not as strong with regard to the Crown corporation form of organization as it is for departments. It is clear that ministers are not accountable for the day-to-day activities of corporations that report to them; but when a Crown corporation has been created by the government, crucial appointments have been made by government, and subsidies are provided by government, then the government cannot escape some measure of responsibility for the actions of that corporation.[34]

This dilemma could present itself regarding almost any Crown corporation, but some examples from the Canadian Broadcasting Corporation highlight the nature of the problem. Most would agree that the government should not interfere with the operations of the CBC; this would smack of censorship or news management. Not only would it destroy the credibility of the CBC, but it would also open the government to severe criticism.

However, should the government step in when the CBC crosses over the boundaries of appropriate morality or good taste? Members of the Opposition have raised questions in the House of Commons concerning such matters as inappropriate conduct on a news show,[35] cancellation of a popular television series,[36] and even the broadcasting of the World Series in northern areas.[37] For the minister, choosing a position in all of these cases is very difficult. On the one hand, the CBC cannot take public money and engage in activity that is repugnant to the general public. On the other hand, if the minister becomes too deeply involved in the activities of the CBC, he or she will be open to the charge of political interference, or even censorship. There is no obvious solution to this problem; ministers must simply learn to walk a tightrope on each issue.

Scrutiny of Corporate Plans and Annual Reports

Federal Crown corporations are required to submit an annual corporate plan for the minister's approval. This plan must include a statement of:

(a) the objects or purposes for which the corporation is incorporated ...

(b) the corporation's objectives for the period ...

(c) the corporation's expected performance for the year ... as compared to its objectives for that year ...[38]

After the plan is approved by the minister, it is tabled in Parliament in summary form for information purposes.

All Crown corporations are also required to submit year-end annual reports of their operations. These reports must include:

(a) the financial statements of the corporation ...

(b) the annual auditor's report ...

(c) a statement on the extent to which the corporation has met its objectives for the financial year,

(d) such quantitative information respecting the performance of the corporation, ... relative to the corporation's objectives as the Treasury Board may require to be included in the annual report, and

(e) such other information as is required by this or any other Act of Parliament, or by the appropriate Minister, the President of the Treasury Board or the Minister of Finance, to be included in the annual report ...[39]

The presence of a plan filed at the beginning of the year and a year-end reca-pitulation of the level of performance should close the circle on accountability. If these reports are prepared in a meaningful manner, they should provide leg-islators with enough information to assess the performance of Crown corpora-tions. The auditor general's assessment of the quality of these reports will be discussed below.

Power to Issue Directives

A directive issued to a corporation would require it to do something even if its board of directors and/or management was opposed. The governor in council may issue *public* directives to any Crown corporation covered by the act, after consultation with the board.[40] The requirement that the directive be public ensures that these directives will be tested in the court of public opinion and so will not be used for any nefarious purpose.

If the directive approach were used frequently and in anger, it would indi-cate heightened tension between the corporation and the government and would likely provoke resignations from the board of directors and/or senior management of the corporation. The Lambert Commission suggests that the directive function will more likely be used in a friendly manner in two situa-tions.[41] If the government wanted the corporation to act against its own eco-nomic interests for some political reason, the board might request that the government issue a directive to this effect so that the board would be absolved of any guilt for the consequences.[42] The second way a directive could be used would be to clarify details of the corporation's mandate.

Method of Funding

Crown corporations receive their funding in a wide variety of ways.[43] In some cases, a corporation will need only a lump sum at its inception, similar to the amount provided by shareholders at the creation of a private corporation. In other cases, corporations will need start-up funds as well as periodic infusions of additional funds. These infusions could come directly from government, in the form of grants or loans, from the private sector in the form of loans guar-anteed by the government, or from nonguaranteed loans.

The classification system of Crown corporations discussed earlier usually determines the type of financial control that the government and legislature have over particular Crown corporations. By way of illustration, Table 9.3 com-pares the accountability regime of Schedule III-Part I and Part II corporations, but the factor that probably has the greatest impact on a corporation's autonomy is whether it is self-financing. If the corporation must return to the public treasury on an annual basis and steer its request for funding through the surveillance of an operating department, the Treasury Board, a legislative com-mittee, and ultimately the legislature, then it has little more autonomy than an operating department. On the other hand, if a corporation is self-funding, it has a much greater degree of autonomy.

Table 9.3
FINANCIAL ACCOUNTABILITY OF SCHEDULE III CROWN CORPORATIONS

	Part I	Part II
Corporate Plan	approved by minister and governor general in council; summary tabled in Parliament	same as Part I
Operating Budget	approved by minister and Treasury Board; summary tabled in Parliament	not required by legislation
Capital Budget	approved by minister and Treasury Board; summary tabled in Parliament	same as Part I
Borrowing	approval of minister and minister of finance required	same as Part I
Audit	audit required by auditor general	audit required (not necessarily by the auditor general)

Appointment and Removal of Directors

Like private sector corporations, a Crown corporation is under the control of a board of directors, which determines the general direction of the corporation. The board of a Crown corporation has a particular responsibility to act as a buffer between the corporation's management and the political concerns of the shareholder, i.e., the minister.

These directors are appointed (and removed) by the minister, after consultation with cabinet.[44] There is no recent comprehensive analysis of the backgrounds of board members, but they seem to be mainly business and professional people. Public servants and, in some provinces, ministers also serve as board members.

These positions have been used for purposes of political patronage. Directors appointed in this manner might lack expertise in the company's operation and might be so politically sensitive that they become unduly passive.[45] This situation also diminishes the status of the board and limits its credibility in policy making.[46]

There is a dilemma concerning the advisability of appointing public servants or ministers to be members of boards. The appointment of a public servant to a board could improve coordination between the corporation and the public servant's department, but it could also place the public servant in a conflict situation.[47] For example, should the public servant advise the corporation if her or his department is considering regulatory changes that will affect it?

However, even at best there can be problems with the operation of these boards. Just as in the private sector, there is some question about whether these part-time directors really effectively control the full-time, professional management of the corporation.[48] The auditor general has suggested that steps need to be taken to ensure that directors have a better understanding of their roles.[49] In the case of Crown corporations, this difficulty in determining the role of the board is exacerbated by the role of the minister. The minister (or full cabinet) usually retains some of the powers that the board of directors in a private sector corporation would have. Chief among these are the power to issue directives and the power to appoint senior management.

Figure 9.1 illustrates the messy relationship involved in the management of a Crown corporation.[50] In the first place, the minister is not totally autonomous even though he or she nominally controls all the corporation's shares. The minister is responsible to her or his colleagues in cabinet and must be sensitive to the position of central agencies. The minister must also be mindful of the provisions of the legislation that created the corporation as well as other relevant legislation.

Then both the board of directors and the chief executive officer are in a difficult position because the minister can deal directly with the chief executive officer if the minister feels the need to do so. In sum, this can be a very difficult and confusing relationship for all the various actors.

Scrutiny by Legislative Committees

Crown corporations are subject to the same kind of scrutiny by the various legislative committees as are the operating departments. Hearings are sometimes instituted as a result of information generated by the auditor general or by public concerns about some controversial actions. This is an important element

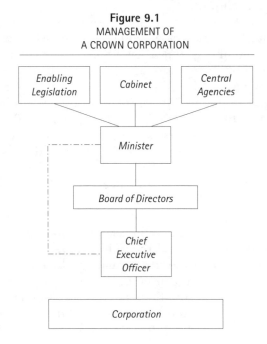

Figure 9.1
MANAGEMENT OF
A CROWN CORPORATION

of control, but its usefulness is somewhat limited. Elected members have many responsibilities and little assistance in meeting them. This makes it very difficult for them to use the committee system in an optimal manner. This situation is exacerbated in the case of Crown corporations because they see themselves as somewhat removed from detailed political control anyway. Furthermore, unless a corporation needs additional funding or a change in its legislation, there is no automatic mechanism to bring its affairs before a committee and no incentive on the part of the corporation to be totally forthcoming.

Centralized Cabinet Control of Crown Corporations — Crown Investments Corporation of Saskatchewan

In the federal government, there is a fairly clear understanding that ministers are responsible for the operation of corporations within their portfolio, subject to the minister's continuing responsibility to cabinet. However, the Crown Investments Corporation (CIC) of Saskatchewan provides for more direct cabinet control over the operation of corporations and greater coordination of the activities of all corporations. The CIC is a holding company that owns all the shares of eleven active companies (as of December 31, 1996) including the Saskatchewan Power Corporation, Saskatchewan Government Insurance, and the Saskatchewan Forest Products Corporation, and also has investments in a number of other companies such as HARO Financial Corporation (and its subsidiary Crown Life), Bi-Provincial Upgrader Joint Venture, and IPSCO Inc.[51]

The role of the CIC and its predecessors has been to enhance the *accountability* of Crown corporations to cabinet through three mechanisms. First, cabinet ministers serve as chairpersons or vice-chairpersons of the boards of directors of Crown corporations. This has provided a direct link between the corporation on the one hand and the cabinet and legislature on the other. Second, the board of directors of CIC is composed entirely of cabinet ministers, so that it functions as a cabinet committee or as a kind of central agency concerned with Crown corporations, as well as having a great deal of influence over the operation of the Crown corporations. Third, there is a Crown Corporations Committee of the legislature that reviews the annual reports and financial statements of all Crown corporations.

If this system works well, it should provide for greater cabinet involvement in the management of Crown corporations and better coordination between operating departments and corporations, as well as among the corporations themselves. The difficulty in this type of structure is its complexity. There are a large number of actors and almost all of them have the legitimate right to become involved in the activities of others. Thus, the minister is responsible for the corporation, but the Crown Management Board could legitimately approach the board of directors of a corporation and/or its chief executive officer about certain matters. If one also adds other actors such as the provincial treasurer and the minister's department, the entire picture becomes even more complex.

🏛 STRUCTURE AND OPERATION OF CROWN CORPORATIONS

The internal structure and operation of Crown corporations resemble those of private sector corporations so much that little elaboration is necessary. As discussed above, the role of the minister and/or Cabinet complicates the picture somewhat, but the general direction of the corporation is the responsibility of the board of directors and the senior officials of the corporation. The members of the board, except sometimes the chairperson, serve on a part-time basis and their main involvement is attending meetings several times a year at which important policy issues are considered. The governor in council, i.e., cabinet, appoints (and can remove) the chief executive officer after consultation with the board, but all other senior appointments are the responsibility of the board and senior management. The senior officials of the corporation then carry on the activities of the corporation on a day-to-day basis. These day-to-day activities of the corporation are so similar to the operation of private sector corporations that many of the theories developed to describe the operation of private sector corporations can be applied directly to public sector corporations. However, there are enough differences in the incentives that apply to managers that there needs to be some variation of these theories.[52]

🏛 SOME CRITICISMS OF CROWN CORPORATIONS

Over the years there have been a number of criticisms of the operation of Crown corporations. This section will assess some of the main problems identified.

Proliferation of New Corporations and Subsidiaries

One of the most basic criticisms of the existing arrangement is that there are simply too many corporations, and many of them constitute a questionable use of the corporate form.[53] The trend toward privatization, which will be discussed later in this chapter, has changed this situation somewhat, but there still remain a large number of Crown corporations, frequently in fields that could be explained more easily by history or accident than logic.

Inefficiency of Crown Corporations

There are frequent allegations that Crown corporations are less efficient than their private sector counterparts. Critics suggest that where Crown corporations have a monopoly position, there is no incentive for them to be efficient or innovative. Even when Crown corporations must compete in the marketplace, financial and political factors tend to limit that competition.

While there is some evidence of efficiency problems in Crown corporations, some of these criticisms have more to do with ideology than fact. Most broad assessments of this topic find that the evidence is mixed at best.[54] Some criticisms are based on a single isolated incident, e.g., cost overrun on a project. Others flow from forgetting that Crown corporations have a public policy objective that frequently prevents them from maximizing efficiency. For example, the CBC might make as much money as the other networks if it did not have more stringent rules about Canadian content. Other criticisms are simply unfair: why can't Canada Post deliver a letter as fast as a courier that charges twenty-five times more for the service?

Empirical evidence on this point is very difficult to find. First, there are not many sectors in which private and public corporations co-exist. Second, establishing comparability is difficult when the public corporation also has some public policy objective. Borins and Boothman reviewed a number of sectoral studies that compared private and public sector corporations. Their conclusions were:

1. *There is no consistent evidence demonstrating that public enterprise is inherently less efficient than private enterprise.* At least in mature industries, the overwhelming bulk of the published research conducted in Canada and abroad, particularly the more sophisticated studies of productivity and cost efficiency, suggests that public and private firms have comparable performance levels when examined on an industry-by-industry basis ...

2. *Environment appears to be a stronger determinant of efficiency than form of ownership.* A consistent pattern which has emerged in the case studies is that performance is conditional upon the intensity and form of competition ...[55]

Unfair Competition with the Private Sector

Crown corporations receive financial support from government to become established, and, in some cases, to meet operating deficits. In other cases, the support is less direct; for example, the government may provide loan guarantees so that money can be borrowed at a lower interest rate or the Crown corporation could be the beneficiary of some regulatory preference. Any or all of these factors could make Crown corporations less susceptible to the discipline of the marketplace. For example, CTV has argued that CBC made an unreasonably high bid to broadcast the 1996 Olympics from Atlanta because it was out of touch with the market.[56] This kind of situation can be very frustrating for independent entrepreneurs who see their funds being used to subsidize a Crown corporation that is competing with them.

Increasing Financial Power of Crown Corporations

The trend on the part of Crown corporations to be more involved in financial activities was discussed earlier. In some cases, the effect of this has been to create a very large pool of capital that could be used in any number of ways, some controversial.

Quebec's Caisse de dépôt et placement and the Alberta Heritage Savings Trust Fund are two examples of these kinds of corporations. The size and power of the Caisse in particular has raised concern on the part of some businesses that it could become a political tool of the Quebec government so that it would be forced to make decisions based on political, rather than business, considerations.[57] When the owners of the Montreal Expos wanted to sell the team in 1990, there was some discussion that the Caisse should buy it so that it would definitely stay in Montreal. It did not go ahead with that purchase, but the Caisse has been criticised for putting its concern with building the Quebec economy ahead of sound investment decisions.[58] However, its 1993 rate of return of 19.7 percent and its ten-year return of 11.9 percent is about average compared to similar investment funds.[59] There is little evidence that the Caisse has used its power as a political tool,[60] and its chairman has denied that it would,[61] but it is clear that it and similar organizations in other provinces *could* wield significant power if they chose to do so.

Profits or Public Purpose? Problems of Accountability

One of the most basic problems facing a Crown corporation is whether it ought to function to make a profit or to serve a public purpose. There can easily be conflicts between these two objectives. For example, VIA Rail can maximize profit by terminating long-distance runs and reducing services to smaller towns and instead focusing on high-volume routes, e.g., the Quebec-Windsor corridor. However, whenever it proposes this, various interests point out VIA's requirement to serve the public interest.

Determining the amount of control that the government should have over the activities of a Crown corporation is not an easy task.

> In the context of responsible government, the most telling questions turn around the problem of establishing a balance between the autonomy that the Crown corporation requires as an organizational form to perform the task it has been given, on the one hand, and the government's need to control and direct the corporation and Parliament's need to oversee or scrutinize it, on the other. This problem of balance runs through every aspect of the complex interrelationships between Parliament, government, and the Crown corporations.[62]

This problem engenders a number of difficulties. It is sometimes suggested that the managers of Crown corporations engage in activities that are contrary to the desires of politicians and that later cause political embarrassment. This situation is frustrating to politicians who must bear criticism, even though they feel that in some cases they have very little control over these corporations. The managers of Crown corporations are also placed in a difficult position because they are frequently ridiculed in the media for their inability to make a profit, or to operate more efficiently, when the problem is sometimes that profit and efficiency have been sacrificed deliberately to political concerns. Of course, when they sacrifice political sensitivity to the profit motive, they suffer for that as well. Premier Ralph Klein had to bear a great deal of criticism when Gainers, a provincial Crown corporation, decided to save $10 000 by providing a jamboree with steak imported from New Zealand.[63]

Accountability to Whom?

Not only is there this division between a concern for profits and public purpose, but there is also some concern that accountability is divided among a confusing number of different organizations.

Earlier in this chapter, it was suggested that Parliament has a number of ways of exerting its control, but a sober assessment of the role of Parliament would have to admit that its control is rather weak and sporadic. More effective control resides with the government, but even here there is significant division.

Legally, the shares of a Crown corporation are held by the minister, in trust for the Crown, but that does not mean that the minister can make unilateral decisions about Crown corporations. Members of the board of directors and the chief executive officer can be appointed by the minister only after consultation with cabinet. Then the roles are reversed, so that directives can only be given by cabinet after consultation with the appropriate minister.

> [I]n attempting to respond to the demands for increased accountability, the government has resorted to building a complex web of multiple bureaucratic approvals which attempt to make Crown corporations accountable to everyone in sight. Parliament, Treasury Board, Department of Finance, various ministers, committees, officials and others now monitor Crown corporations. Although Crown corporations are nominally accountable to many people in Ottawa, they are, in fact, truly accountable to no one. At the same time, making the accountability process more bureaucratic threatens to stifle the very characteristic of Crown corporations that made them the chosen instrument in the first place: freedom from departmental bureaucracy.[64]

Problems of Mandate and Reporting

A part of the problem of ensuring accountability is the difficulty of specifying a mandate for the corporation. Cabinet and legislature are frequently reluctant to specify a corporation's mandate so narrowly that it could not engage in innovative behaviour to take advantage of a changing environment. After all, one reason for choosing the corporate form is to allow it to be more flexible and innovative. However, there have been allegations that some corporations have used this broad mandate to move into areas of activity that were not envisaged for them when they were created. Langford uses the phrase "mandate creep" to describe this phenomenon.[65]

This problem has been exacerbated by the uneven quality of reports that corporations provide to the government and legislature. These reports ought to make it possible to determine if the corporation actually followed the plan that was approved at the beginning of the year, but due to lack of information it is often difficult to do this. The auditor general has reviewed this situation and provided this assessment.

Most annual reports do not explicitly state performance information on all approved objectives. Though we noticed considerable improvements in the reporting of performance (with 65 percent of corporations now providing some disclosure of information on objectives), 60 percent of those reporting do not report on all objectives. Furthermore, in those corporations that do report some information, performance reporting still requires improvement.[66]

Recent Improvements

A discussion of problems should not close without a review of how much the situation has improved in recent years. Twenty years ago the auditor general and others would produce stinging indictments suggesting that the federal government had virtually lost control of this entire sector. However, great strides have been made since then. The Financial Administration Act has been tightened to provide a better accountability regime. Treasury Board now produces an annual publication entitled *Crown Corporations and Other Interests of Canada,* which provides an overview of the Crown corporation sector with detailed financial reports of all Crown corporations. Recent reports of the auditor general have a much less alarmist tone and tend to focus on deficiencies in strategic planning and communications between board and management[67]—the kinds of problems that most organizations experience on a fairly regular basis.

🏛 PROPOSALS FOR REFORM

The problems mentioned above cover a very wide range, but the most serious problems have been identified in the area of accountability. Thus most of the reforms discussed below will be geared to improving accountability. Patrice Garant, for one, applauds this trend, but he also sounds a note of caution:

> This awakening [to the need for better accountability] was necessary because Crown corporations are neither private companies nor "states within the state." But beware the pendulum! Some reform proposals, while well intended, are dangerous because they contradict both the raison d'être of the Crown corporation network and certain objectives inherent in this choice of instrument designed to ensure adequate intervention by the public authority.[68]

Single Window Approach

The main problem identified with the current accountability regime is that it is too complex and involves too many different agents to whom corporations are supposed to be accountable. The single-window approach would streamline this system by making corporations accountable to only one body. Each corporation would be accountable only to its own minister, or all corporations would be accountable to the same body.

While this idea seems to be beneficial, the likelihood of its adoption is fairly slim. Central agencies are well entrenched in Ottawa and departments like finance and Treasury Board jealously guard their prerogatives to control spending. These agencies feel that a weakening of control over Crown corporations would provide ministers with a loophole to do things through their corporations that they would not be allowed to do through their departments.

Privatization

Privatization has a number of meanings.

> In its narrowest sense privatization encompasses the whole or partial sale of state-owned companies but more broadly and importantly it also embraces actions to reduce the role of government and enhance market forces to produce a more competitive economy. In this larger sense, privatization includes deregulation, trade liberalization, and the increased contracting out of government services.[69]

This section will only discuss privatization in its narrow meaning. The broader aspects of alternative service delivery will be discussed in Chapter 11.

Privatization is a worldwide trend[70] and Table 9.4 indicates the extent of federal government activity in this area. Most provinces have also considered this idea, but some have espoused it more whole-heartedly than others.[71] The Nova Scotia government has sold the Sydney Steel Corp. to Chinese interests;[72] Alberta has privatized its liquor stores (not without a certain amount of controversy);[73] and Quebec is also running into some difficulty in attempting to privatize its liquor stores.[74] The Saskatchewan government had a significant pri-

Table 9.4
MAJOR FEDERAL GOVERNMENT PRIVATIZATIONS

Corporation	Method of Disposal
Canada Communications Group	Sold to St. Joseph Corporation in a competitive sales process
Canadian National Railway Company	Sale of shares to public for $2.1 billion
Air Canada	Sale of shares to general public
Teleglobe	Sale by tender to Memotec
deHavilland	Sale by tender to Boeing
Petro-Canada	Shares are being sold to the public on a continuing basis. The number of shares sold at any given time is limited so as not to reduce the price.
Hotel and truck transport portions of CN Rail	Sale by tender to related companies
Canada Development Corporation	Sale of shares to general public
Canadair	Sold by tender to Bombardier

vatization program that was proceeding well but was halted abruptly when it moved too quickly and attempted to privatize SaskEnergy Incorporated.[75] Even municipalities are joining the trend as the City of Edmonton is contemplating selling its telephone company—the eighth largest in the country.[76]

In the federal government, privatization was pursued fairly aggressively by the previous Progressive Conservative government, and a number of major corporations were privatized. The current Liberal government has not been pursuing this goal quite as aggressively partly because the Liberals are less ideologically disposed to privatization, but also because there are simply fewer remaining attractive candidates for privatization.

Privatization is usually seen as fulfilling a number of different goals.[77] At the forefront of many arguments in favour of privatization is a desire to *reduce the size of the public sector*. This is sometimes also stated as a need either to reduce the amount of the budget consumed by Crown corporations or to limit the managerial time that governments must devote to Crown corporations. This argument carries considerable weight when a corporation needs a significant infusion of funds to remain viable. One of the main reasons that Air Canada was privatized was its need for a major cash inflow to upgrade its fleet.[78] This money was provided by the sale of shares to private investors instead of from an already cash-strapped federal government.

This argument should be seen as having a value-driven component, since it is difficult to prescribe an objectively determinable optimum size for the public sector. Still, it is clear that this approach is in line with the thinking of the 1990s. This argument is usually supplemented by the idea that certain corporations *no longer serve a public policy purpose*. For example, Air Canada was at one time an important tool of nation building and economic development. As the airline industry has matured in Canada, it is now clear the country is reasonably well served by a network of airlines and no one particular airline serves a more central role than any other.

It is frequently suggested that converting a Crown corporation to the private sector will *improve the efficiency of the privatized company*. This argument can be presented in several ways. Some argue that public sector organizations are innately less efficient than those in the private sector. There seems to be little evidence to support this argument,[79] but it does not stop people from making it. A more enlightened form of this argument suggests that Crown corporations are continually being drawn into serving some public policy objective, which limits their ability to make a profit.

At a highly practical level some governments seem to want to sell some of their more profitable Crown corporations because the inflow of funds will *reduce their outstanding debt*. The attraction of this argument is obvious, but it can be shortsighted. Profitable corporations can produce a major inflow of funds each year. A government choosing to sell such a corporation should ensure that its one-time cash inflow is greater than the value of the annual cash flows foregone. Unfortunately, the immediate pressure to reduce the debt sometimes overwhelms this logic.

Finally, many commentators have argued that some governments, particularly the previous federal Conservative government, have an *ideological predisposition to favour the private sector* at the expense of the public, which drives them to privatize corporations even when there are no other sound reasons to do so. Baxter-Moore has criticized the sale of Teleglobe on these grounds.[80] Teleglobe was the Crown corporation that had a monopoly on the provision of long-distance telephone service between Canada and all points outside North America. It was making a significant profit and operating autonomously from government control. The manner in which it was sold has increased the level of corporate concentration in the communications industry. In spite of government statements to the contrary, the only rationales Baxter-Moore can find for the privatization are the ideological commitment and the need for a cash inflow.

When the federal government first began its privatization efforts, there was some criticism that the process was disorganized and inefficient.[81] However, over time it has established a more orderly approach to the privatization process. This approach has been the product of a conscious plan, because a careful approach is needed if the government is going to maximize its return on the sale.

The first step is *initial assessment.* At this stage the following questions are asked:

- Does the corporation play a continuing role in support of national and regional public policy objectives?

- Does the company have the potential to be commercially viable?

- Is it ready to operate in the private sector?

- Will privatization be compatible with other federal government policies, such as bilingualism, competition, foreign investment and trade?

- What will be the effect on the employees, competitors, suppliers, or customers of the corporation?[82]

When this initial review identifies a potential candidate for privatization, the second step is an *in-depth review* by a variety of government officials examining different aspects of the potential privatization. These groups study not simply whether or not to privatize, but also what steps would need to be taken to get a corporation ready for privatization, if that is the decision made. Their recommendations might involve either winding up an unprofitable part of the operations, changing the company's industrial relations policy, or any number of other actions that would make the corporation more attractive to purchasers. These teams also consider any conditions that could be put on the sale, such as location of head office, restrictions on nonresident ownership of shares, and continuity of pension plans.

The next step is the *passage of divestiture legislation* that defines how the transaction will take place, including any conditions that are to be imposed on purchasers.

After this legislative approval, the company is *prepared for sale*. This involves making the company more attractive to potential investors by following the recommendations of the earlier study teams.

The final stage is the *actual sale*. This can involve a competitive bidding process that is likely to result in one buyer taking over all shares of the company, e.g., Boeing's purchase of deHavilland Aircraft, or engaging underwriters to sell the shares to the general public, e.g., Air Canada.

The funds generated by the sale can be used in two ways. They can go into federal government coffers as payment for the shares, or they can go to the company for use in future expansion. In some cases, funds have been divided between the two uses. The direction of the cash flow will obviously have a major impact on the attractiveness of the share issue.

A number of commentators have evaluated the privatization effort to this point. Tupper and Doern described the Mulroney government's record on privatization as

> one of slow and deliberate movement but with an approach that is very conscious of the pitfalls and of the underlying fact that Canadian public opinion is not overly critical of the current level and form of public enterprise.[83]

However, even this cautious approach has incited a number of criticisms.

Canadian nationalists have objected to sales of corporations to foreign purchasers. The most publicized case was the sale of deHavilland Aircraft (the manufacturer of the very popular Dash-7 and Dash-8 aircraft) to Boeing. This caused some concern about a reduction in the number of jobs in Canada, but it "raised a political storm as much for the loss of Canadian hopes as for the loss of taxpayers' investment."[84]

Jeanne Kirk Laux has suggested that the federal government's privatizations have not been all that they seem on the surface.[85] She identified four different categories of privatizations, all of which fall short of true privatizations.

In some cases, the federal government *privatized to the public sector*. For example, the Northern Canada Power Commission was sold to the territorial governments. While this reduces the number of federal Crown corporations, it does nothing about the overall size of the public sector.

Some privatizations have actually *increased market concentration* in some fields—not exactly an affirmation of the free market system. For example, the giant companies Bombardier, Canadian Pacific Ltd., and Bell Canada Enterprises have all significantly increased their market share by acquiring privatized corporations. Borins and Boothman's review (mentioned earlier) indicated that intensity of competition in a sector is a better spur to efficiency than locus of ownership, i.e., private or public.[86] If privatization leads to greater concentration in certain sectors, then it might result in less, rather than more, efficiency.

Political barriers to entry have been erected around some privatizations. In response to the furor around the foreign purchase of deHavilland, the government has generally limited concentrations of ownership and particularly foreign ownership. For example, when Air Canada was sold, no individual could hold more than 10 percent of the shares, and all foreign investors collectively could not hold more than 25 percent of shares. These kinds of limitations obviously limit the price that can obtained for the shares by making it impossible for anyone to buy a controlling interest, even though this might be the most effective way to improve the efficiency of operation.[87]

Many privatizations involve only *conditional freedoms* for the corporations to make decisions. Air Canada must maintain its head office in the Montreal area, and must maintain overhaul facilities in Winnipeg and the Montreal and Toronto metropolitan areas. Governments frequently find it difficult to make a clean break from privatized corporations. For example, in order to sell the Urban Transportation Development Corporation, the Ontario government has to agree to take over certain contingent liabilities of the pre-privatization company.[88] If the government's desire was to limit public expenditure, it was only partially successful.

Another criticism is that the government is "selling off the family silver to pay the rent." Critics have pointed out that many corporations pay regular dividends to the government. It could be very shortsighted to sell those companies for a one-time deficit reduction.

The reality is considerably more complex than either side states. When the government privatizes a profitable corporation it receives an immediate lump sum payment in exchange for the right to receive a steady flow of annual payments in future years. Whether the government receives full value depends on how one estimates the future flow of incomes, which requires making some very difficult assumptions. Such a transaction can benefit both parties. The government will receive a large one-time payment for an entity that, as long as it was restricted by government policies, could never earn much money anyway. The purchaser receives an entity that will be a good money maker when it is no longer constrained by government policies.

Compensation Principle

One of the major irritants to managers of Crown corporations is that they are frequently criticized for failure to make a profit when this failure comes about not as a result of their mismanagement, but because the government demands that the corporation work in the broader national interest, which is not necessarily in the corporation's economic interest. It has sometimes been suggested that when a corporation incurs expenses in this situation, it should be compensated out of general tax funds. This would allow the corporation to act in the national interest without suffering financially as a result.

A good example of this principle is the subsidy that the federal government pays to CNRail to transport western grain to eastern Canada. For years, CN was simply expected to haul this grain at less than cost as a part of its public policy mandate, but the Western Grain Transportation Act of 1983 changed that, so CN is now compensated by the federal government for providing this public service.[89]

🏛 MIXED ENTERPRISES

At the beginning of this chapter a mixed enterprise was defined as a corporation whose shares are partially owned by Canada with the balance owned by *private sector parties.*

Presumably one reason governments enter into mixed enterprises, particularly commercial ventures, is that they want the best of both worlds. They want an organization that will be influenced by the business partners to operate in an efficient, businesslike manner, but one that the government will still be able to influence in order to implement public policy. Stephen Brooks has studied the activities of many mixed enterprises and his conclusion is that this simply does not work.

> [T]he MOC [mixed ownership corporation] involves an ambiguous form of organization that limits the ability of the government shareholder to impose its policy goals on that organization when these seriously conflict with those of management and/or private sector shareholders.[90]

When governments attempt to exercise *effective* control over mixed enterprises, they run into two arguments from company management. The first stems from the general pro-business, anti-government bias in society. Management will argue that business people know what is best for businesses and that the inefficiency caused by the imposition of political values is bad for business. The second, more pragmatic, argument is that if the business does not act to maximize its income, the value of its shares will go down in the open market, which will cause shareholders to blame government for their losses. The result of this is that it will be more difficult to sell shares in future mixed enterprises, because potential shareholders will fear a repeat of previous government interference.

If this line of argument is accepted, management can have almost complete autonomy because of divisions of power on the board of directors and the inability of the minister to provide directives or other controls.[91] Stephen Brooks's analysis of a formerly prominent mixed enterprise leads him to the conclusion that a Crown corporation can function as *either* an engine for profit *or* an instrument of public policy, *but not both.*[92]

Because of the problems identified above and because of the government's general desire to exit the corporate sphere, mixed enterprises are considerably less common than they were formerly. It is not likely that this trend will turn around until there is a significant change in the way the role of government is viewed.

🏛 CONCLUSION

This chapter has focused on the Crown corporation as an organizational form. Its main value is in carrying on commercial and financial operations at arm's length from the government of the day. The next chapter considers another organizational form that is also at arm's length—the regulatory agency.

NOTES

1. One of the most thoughtful considerations of the definition problem is found in: M.J. Trebilcock and J.R.S. Prichard, "Crown Corporations: The Calculus of Instrument Choice," in J. Robert S. Prichard, ed., *Crown Corporations in Canada: The Calculus of Instrument Choice* (Toronto: Butterworths, 1983), 8–15. John W. Langfgord also does an admirable job of grappling with this same difficult question in "The Identification and Classification of Federal Public Corporations: A Preface to Regime Building," *Canadian Public Administration* 23 (spring 1980): 76–104. For a different but equally plausible definition, see Royal Commission on Financial Management and Accountability, *Final Report* (Hull: Minister of Supply and Services Canada, 1979), ch. 16.

2. Patrice Garant, "Crown Corporations: Instruments of Economic Intervention—Legal Aspects," in Ivan Bernier and Andrée Lajoie, eds., *Regulations, Crown Corporations and Administrative Tribunals*, Research study for the Royal Commission on the Economic Union and Development Prospects for Canada (Toronto: University of Toronto Press, 1985), 4. (Emphasis added.) Reprinted by permission of the University of Toronto Press in cooperation with the Royal Commission on the Economic Union and Development Prospects for Canada and the Canadian Publishing Centre, Supply and Services Canada.

3. These categories are explained further and full information on the holdings are provided in: President of the Treasury Board, *Crown Corporations and Other Corporate Interests of Canada: 1992–93 Annual Report to Parliament* (1994), III-5 and passim.

4. Ibid., III-5.

5. Ibid.

6. A good history of the development of the public enterprise instrument in Canada is Economic Council of Canada, *Minding the Public's Business* (Ottawa: Minister of Supply and Services Canada, 1986), ch. 2.

7. The growth in number and complexity of Crown corporations is well documented in: John W. Langford and Kenneth J. Huffman, "The Uncharted Universe of Federal Crown Corporations," in J. Robert S. Prichard, ed., *Crown Corporations in Canada*, 219–301.

8. This embarrassing situation was described in more detail in previous editions of this book.

9. Sandford F. Borins, "World War Two Crown Corporations: Their Wartime Role and Peacetime Privatization," *Canadian Public Administration* 25 (fall 1982): 380–404.

10. John W. Langford and Kenneth J. Huffman, "The Uncharted Universe of Federal Public Corporations," in Prichard, ed., *Crown Corporations in Canada*, 276.

11. Marsha Gordon, *Government in Business* (Montreal: C.D. Howe Institute, 1981), 11–12.

12. In most provinces, power generation was one of the earliest Crown corporations, but this will remain in government hands in only one province—Quebec.

13. Aidan R. Vining and Robert Botterell, "An Overview of the Origins, Growth, Size and Functions of Provincial Crown Corporations," in Prichard, ed., *Crown Corporations in Canada*, 340.

14. For a discussion of the early history of the hydro-electric companies and their uneven development in different provinces, see: Aidan Vining, "Provincial Hydro Utilities," in Allan Tupper and G. Bruce Doern, eds., *Public Corporations and Public Policy in Canada* (Montreal: The Institute for Research on Public Policy, 1981), 152–75.

15. Gordon, *Government in Business*, 14–15.

16. Marsha A. Chandler, "State Enterprise and Partisanship in Provincial Politics," *Canadian Journal of Political Science* 15 (December 1982): 735.

17. One of the best treatments of these factors is contained in Trebilcock and Prichard, "Crown Corporations: The Calculus of Instrument Choice," in Prichard, ed., *Crown*

Corporations in Canada, 39–75. Two other articles in this book are also useful in considering this area: Thomas A. Borcherding, "Toward a Positive Theory of Public Sector Supply Arrangements," 99–184; and Marsha A. Chandler, "The Politics of Public Enterprise," 185–218.

18. The circumstances surrounding this acquisition are described in Allan Tupper, "The Nation's Businesses: Canadian Concepts of Public Enterprise," Ph.D. diss., Queen's University, 1977, 99–113.

19. There have been a few exceptions to this happy picture, in which government takeover attempts have been the subject of much consternation. Some are mentioned in Garant, "Crown Corporations," 6.

20. J.E. Hodgetts, "The Public Corporation in Canada," in W. Friedmann and J.F. Garner, eds., *Government Enterprise: A Comparative Study* (London: Stevens & Sons, 1970), 202. (Footnote omitted.)

21. V. Seymour Wilson, *Canadian Public Policy and Administration: Theory and Environment* (Toronto: McGraw-Hill Ryerson, 1981), 365–70; C.A. Ashley and R.G.H. Smails, *Canadian Crown Corporations: Some Aspects of their Administration and Control* (Toronto: Macmillan, 1965), 3–10; Tupper, "The Nation's Businesses," ii–iv and passim; Chandler, "State Enterprise and Partisanship in Provincial Politics," 727–35.

22. "Crown Corporations: The Calculus of Instrument Choice," 53.

23. Jeanne Kirk Laux and Maureen Appel Molot, *State Capitalism: Public Enterprise in Canada* (Ithaca, N.Y.: Cornell University Press, 1988), 43.

24. Seven Crown corporations are not covered by the legislation. The Bank of Canada, the Canadian Wheat Board, the International Development Research Centre, and the Canada Council are each governed by their own legislation. The Canadian Broadcasting Corporation, the National Arts Centre, and the Canadian Film Development Corporation were not covered by the legislation because they were to be governed by a new "cultural agencies act" that was being prepared. This separate legislation was intended to recognize the importance of maintaining the independence of these cultural organizations from direct government control. The legislation was never passed and its current status is unclear.

25. R.S.C. 1985, c. F-11, s. 3(1) (a).

26. S.C. 1991, c. 24, s. 1.

27. Hodgetts, "The Public Corporation in Canada," 226.

28. For a good overview of the legal and practical aspects of the use of these different methods, see Garant, "Crown Corporations," 14–22.

29. R.S.C. 1985, c. B-9, s. 24(1).

30. R.S.C. 1985, c. C-10.

31. R.S.C. 1985, c. F-11, s. 90.

32. Pierre Fournier, "The National Asbestos Corporation of Quebec," in Tupper and Doern, eds., *Public Corporations and Public Policy*, 353–64.

33. Jeanne Kirk Laux and Maureen Appel Molot, "The Potash Corporation of Saskatchewan," in ibid., 189–219.

34. This dilemma is not new; it was discussed extensively in Parliament in the 1920s. Ashley and Smails, *Canadian Crown Corporations*, ch. 5.

35. This can be a relatively common occurrence. For example, see the question by Mr. Cossitt in Canada, House of Commons, *Debates*, 1 June 1981, 10, 119–20. The most tumultuous example of this kind of controversy surrounded the show, "This Hour Has Seven Days." The controversy is described in K. Kernaghan, *Canadian Cases in Public Administration* (Toronto: Methuen, 1977), 48–54.

36. Canada, House of Commons, *Debates*, 9 March 1973, 2067.

37. Canada, House of Commons, *Debates*, 13 October 1983, 27986.

38. R.S.C. 1985, c. F-11, s. 122(3).

39. R.S.C. 1985, c. F-11, s. 150(3).

40. R.S.C. 1985, c. F-11, s. 89.

41. Royal Commission on Financial Management and Accountability, *Final Report*, 337–38.

42. The Crown Corporations Directorate of the Department of Finance and Treasury Board Secretariat, *Directors of Crown Corporations: An Introductory Guide to Their Roles and Responsibilities* (Minister of Supply and Services Canada, 1993), 11.

43. See Garant, "Crown Corporations," 18.

44. R.S.C. 1985, c. F-11, s. 105(1).

45. Sandford F. Borins and Lee Brown, *Investments in Failure: Five Government Corporations that Cost the Canadian Taxpayer Billions* (Toronto: Methuen, 1986), 63 and passim.

46. John Langford, "Crown Corporations as Instruments of Policy," in G. Bruce Doern and Peter Aucoin, eds., *Public Policy in Canada* (Toronto: Macmillan, 1979), 257.

47. Borins and Brown, *Investments in Failure*, 151–53.

48. Michael J. Hatton, *Corporations & Directors: Comparing the Profit and Not-for-Profit Sectors* (Toronto: Thompson Educational Publishing, 1990), chs. 3 and 4.

49. *Report of the Auditor General of Canada to the House of Commons*, Chapter 10: Crown Corporations: Fulfilling Responsibilities for Governance (October 1995), 10–18 and 10–19.

50. This problem is discussed very well in: The Crown Corporations Directorate, *Directors of Crown Corporations*, 3 and passim.

51. Crown Investments Corporation of Saskatchewan, *Annual Report 1996*.

52. Douglas F. Stevens, *Corporate Autonomy and Institutional Control: The Crown Corporation as a Problem in Organizational Design* (Montreal: McGill-Queen's University Press, 1993), ch. 1 and 2.

53. D.P. Gracey, "The Real Issues on the Crown Corporations Debate," in Kenneth Kernaghan, ed., *Public Administration in Canada: Selected Readings*, 5th ed. (Toronto: Methuen, 1985), 132.

54. A good overview of this literature is contained in: Anthony E. Boardman and Aidan R. Vining, "Ownership and Performance in Competitive Environments: A Comparison of the Performance of Private, Mixed and State-Owned Enterprises," Faculty of Commerce Working Paper #1206, University of British Columbia, 1988.

55. Sandford F. Borins and Barry E.C. Boothman, "Crown Corporations and Economic Efficiency," in D.G. McFetridge, ed., *Canadian Industrial Policy in Action* (Toronto: University of Toronto Press, 1985), 121. Reprinted by permission of the University of Toronto Press in cooperation with the Royal Commission on the Economic Union and Development Prospects for Canada and the Canadian Publishing Centre, Supply and Services Canada.

56. Tom McKee, "CTV Says CBC's Olympic Bid Out of Touch with Market," *The Globe and Mail*, 24 May 1994.

57. This controversy is described in Allan Tupper, *Bill S-31 and the Federalism of State Capitalism* (Kingston, Ont.: Queen's University, Institute of Intergovernmental Relations, 1983). For a general discussion of the Caisse, see: Claude Forget, ed., *La Caisse de dépôt et placement du Québec: Sa mission, son impact et sa performance* (Montreal: Institut C.D. Howe, 1984).

58. Barrie McKenna and Ann Gibbon, "Caisse under Fire for Putting Hex on Univa Buyout," *The Globe and Mail*, 20 March 1993; David Olive, "A Glass House," *Report on Business Magazine*, November 1993, 23–24.

59. Allan Swift, "Caisse Posts 19.7% Return," *The Globe and Mail*, 1 April 1994.

60. Stephen Brooks and A. Brian Tanguay, "Quebec's Caisse de dépôt et placement: Tool of Nationalism?" *Canadian Public Administration* 28 (spring 1985): 99–119.

61. Ann Gibbon, "Profit First, Caisse Insists," *The Globe and Mail*, 25 September 1995.

62. John Langford, "Crown Corporations as Instruments of Policy," 240.

63. "A Stake in Steaks," *Maclean's*, 16 August 1993, 11.

64. J. Robert S. Prichard, "Challenges Facing the Boards of Crown Corporations: Diagnosis and Prescription," in Thomas H. Mitchell, Executive Bulletin #30, *Canadian Directorship Practices: The Role of the Board of Directors in Crown Corporation Accountability* (Ottawa: The Conference Board of Canada, 1985), 4.

65. Langford, "Crown Corporations as Instruments of Policy," 256.

66. Auditor General of Canada, *Report of the Auditor General of Canada to the House of Commons 1993* (Ottawa: Minister of Supply and Services, 1993), 109. Another review two years later resulted in similar conclusions. See: *Report of the Auditor General of Canada to the House of Commons*, Chapter 10: Crown Corporations: Fulfilling Responsibilities for Governance (October 1995).

67. *Report of the Auditor General of Canada to the House of Commons*, Chapter 10: Crown Corporations: Fulfilling Responsibilities for Governance October 1995 (Ottawa: Minister of Supply and Services, 1995).

68. Patrice Garant, "Crown Corporations," 39–40. (Footnote omitted.)

69. Allan Tupper and G. Bruce Doern, "Canadian Public Enterprise and Privatization," in Allan Tupper and G. Bruce Doern, eds., *Privatization, Public Policy and Public Corporations in Canada* (Halifax: The Institute for Research on Public Policy, 1988), 1.

70. Paul W. MacAvoy, W.T. Stanbury, George Yarrow, and Richard J. Zeckhauser, eds., *Privatization and State-Owned Enterprises: Lessons from the United States, Great Britain and Canada* (Boston: Kluwer Academic Publishers, 1989); Lionel Ouellet, "La privatisation: un instrument de management public?" *Canadian Public Administration* 30, no. 4 (winter 1987): 567–69.

71. W.T. Stanbury, "Privatization in Canada: Ideology, Symbolism, or Substance?" in MacAvoy, Stanbury, Yarrow, and Zeckhauser, eds., *Privatization and State-Owned Enterprises*, 291–300, 307–10. Maureen Appel Molot, "The Provinces and Privatization: Are the Provinces Really Getting Out of Business?" in Tupper and Doern, eds., *Privatization, Public Policy and Public Corporations in Canada*, 399–425.

72. Gail Lem and Kevin Cox, "Chinese Company to Buy Sysco," *The Globe and Mail*, 30 November 1993.

73. The pro and con views are argued in: Douglas S. West, "Alberta's Liquor Store Privatization: Economic and Social Impacts," *Policy Options* 18, no. 3 (April 1997), 24–27; Dean Neu, Duncan Green and Alison Taylor, "Privatizing the ALCB: Ideology and Symbolism or Efficiency and Equity?" *Policy Options* 18, no. 3 (April 1997), 28–31; See also: Miro Cernetig, "Alberta Gets into Free-Market Spirits," *The Globe and Mail*, 3 September 1993; George Oake, "Warning Flags Fly over Alberta's Liquor Proposal," *The Toronto Star*, 18 September 1993.

74. Ann Gibson, "Plan to Sell Quebec Liquor Stores Draws Fire," *The Globe and Mail*, 5 July 1994.

75. Stevens, *Corporate Autonomy and Institutional Control*, 147.

76. Lawrence Surtees, "Edmonton Eyes Sale of Phone Company," *The Globe and Mail*, 13 April 1994.

77. A good statement of the main arguments presented by the federal government can be found in: "Privatization in Canada," News Release of the Office of Privatization and Regulatory Affairs, August 1989.

78. W.T. Stanbury, "Privatization in Canada: Ideology, Symbolism or Substance?" in MacAvoy, Stanbury, Yarrow, and Zeckhauser, *Privatization and State-Owned Enterprises*, 315–16.

79. Borins and Boothman, "Crown Corporations and Economic Efficiency," in McFetridge, ed., *Canadian Industrial Policy in Action*, 75–129.

80. N.J. Baxter-Moore, "Ideology or Pragmatism? The Politics and Management of the Mulroney Government's Privatization Program," *British Journal of Canadian Studies* 7, no. 2 (1992), 310–13.

81. Cathryn Motherwell, "Tory-Style Privatization Process Test Bidders' Stamina, Corporate Coffers," and "Privatization Trend Faces Test Over Big 3," *The Globe and Mail*, 28 February 1987; Christopher Waddell, "Ottawa's Handling of Crown-Sale Talks Criticized by Study," *The Globe and Mail*, 8 June 1987.

82. "How Privatization Works," News Release of the Office of Privatization and Regulatory Affairs, n.d.

83. Tupper and Doern "Canadian Public Enterprise and Privatization," in Tupper and Doern, eds., *Privatization, Public Policy and Public Corporations in Canada*, 32.

84. Ron Graham, *One-Eyed Kings* (Toronto: Collins, 1986), 371.

85. Jeanne Kirk Laux, "How Private Is Privatization?" *Canadian Public Policy* 19, no. 4 (1993), 398–411.

86. Borins and Boothman, "Crown Corporations and Economic Efficiency," 121.

87. David W. Gillen, Tae H. Oum, and Michael Tretheway, "Privatization of Air Canada: Why It Is Necessary in a Deregulated Environment," *Canadian Public Policy* 15, no. 3 (September 1989): 297.

88. Gary Munro, "Ontario's Urban Transportation Development Corporation: A Case Study in Privatization," *Canadian Public Administration* 32, no. 1 (spring 1989), 25–40.

89. Garth Stevenson, "Canadian National Railways and VIA Rail," in Tupper and Doern, eds., *Privatization, Public Policy and Public Corporations in Canada*, 54–55.

90. Stephen Brooks, *Who's in Charge?* (Halifax: The Institute for Research on Public Policy, 1987), 3.

91. For a catalogue of cases in which management has not followed the obvious desires of government, see: Stephen Brooks, "The Mixed Ownership Corporation as an Instrument of Public Policy," *Comparative Politics* (January 1987): 173–91.

92. Stephen Brooks, "The State as Entrepreneur: From CDC to CDIC," *Canadian Public Administration* 26 (winter 1983): 541–43.

BIBLIOGRAPHY

Ashley, C.A., and R.G.H. Smails. *Canadian Crown Corporations: Some Aspects of Their Administration and Control.* Toronto: Macmillan, 1965.

Auditor General of Canada. *Report of the Auditor General of Canada to the House of Commons.* (Various years.)

Baxter-Moore, N.J. "Ideology or Pragmatism? The Politics and Management of the Mulroney Government's Privatization Program." *British Journal of Canadian Studies* 1992, 7, no. 2, 290–325.

Boardman, Anthony E., and Aidan R. Vining. "Ownership and Performance in Competitive Environments: A Comparison of the Performance of Private, Mixed and State-Owned Enterprises." Faculty of Commerce Working Paper #1206, University of British Columbia, 1988.

Borins, Sandford F. "World War Two Crown Corporations: Their Wartime Role and Peacetime Privatization." *Canadian Public Administration* 25 (fall 1982): 380–404.

Borins, Sandford F., and Barry E.C. Boothman. "Crown Corporations and Economic Efficiency." In D.G. McFetridge, ed., *Canadian Industrial Policy in Action.* Toronto: University of Toronto Press, 1985, 751–29.

Borins, Sandford F., and Lee Brown. *Investments in Failure: Five Government Corporations that Cost the Canadian Taxpayer Billions.* Toronto: Methuen, 1986.

Brazeau, Jean, and Cathy Schutz. "Crown Corporations and Competition Policy." In *Government Enterprise: Roles and Rationale.* Papers presented at a symposium sponsored by the Economic Council of Canada in Ottawa. (September 1984): 424–46.

Brooks, Stephen. "The State as Entrepreneur: From CDC to CDIC." *Canadian Public Administration* 26 (winter 1983): 525–43.

_____. "The Mixed Ownership Corporation as an Instrument of Public Policy." *Comparative Politics* 19:2 (January 1987): 173–191.

_____. *Who's in Charge?* Halifax: The Institute for Research on Public Policy, 1987.

Brooks, Stephen, and A. Brian Tanguay. "Quebec's Caisse de dépôt et placement: Tool of Nationalism?" *Canadian Public Administration* 28 (spring 1985): 99–119.

Canada. Royal Commission on Financial Management and Accountability. *Final Report.* Hull: Minister of Supply and Services Canada, 1979.

Carter, Richard. "Les enterprises publiques: pourquoi et pour qui?" *Canadian Public Administration* 26 (summer 1983): 239–54.

Chandler, Marsha A. "State Enterprise and Partisanship in Provincial Politics." *Canadian Journal of Political Science* 15 (December 1982): 711–40.

The Crown Corporations Directorate of the Department of Finance and Treasury Board Secretariat. *Directors of Crown Corporations: An Introductory Guide to Their Roles and Responsibilities.* Ottawa: Minister of Supply and Services Canada, 1993.

Crown Investments Corporation of Saskatchewan. *Annual Report 1996.*

Economic Council of Canada. *Minding the Public's Business.* Ottawa: Minister of Supply and Services Canada, 1986.

Eichmanis, John, and Graham White. "Government by Other Means: Agencies, Boards and Commissions." In Donald C. MacDonald, ed., *The Government and Politics of Ontario.* 3rd ed. Scarborough, Ont.: Nelson Canada, 1985, 82–99.

Elford, E. Craig, and W. T. Stanbury. "Mixed Enterprises in Canada." In D.G. McFetridge, ed., *Canadian Industry in Transition.* Research study for the Royal Commission on the Economic Union and Development Prospects for Canada. Toronto: University of Toronto Press, 1986, 261–303.

Forget, Claude, ed. *La Caisse de dépôt et placement du Québec: Sa mission, son impact et sa performance.* Montreal: Institut C.D. Howe, 1984.

Garant, Patrice. "Crown Corporations: Instruments of Economic Intervention—Legal Aspects." In Ivan Bernier and Andrée Lajoie, eds., *Regulations, Crown Corporations and Administrative Tribunals,* 1–79. Research Study for the Royal Commission on the Economic Union and Development Prospects for Canada, vol. 48. Toronto: University of Toronto Press, 1985.

Gélinas, André, ed. *Public Enterprise and the Public Interest.* Toronto: The Institute of Public Administration of Canada, 1978.

Gillen, David W., Tae H. Oum, and Michael W. Tretheway. "Privatization of Air Canada: Why It Is Necessary in a Deregulated Environment." *Canadian Public Policy* 15, no. 3 (September 1989): 285–99.

Gordon, Marsha. *Government in Business.* Montreal: C.D. Howe Institute, 1981.

Hatton, Michael J. *Corporations & Directors: Comparing the Profit and Not-for-Profit Sectors.* Toronto: Thompson Educational Publishing, 1990.

Hodgetts, J.E. "The Public Corporation in Canada." In W. Friedmann and J.F. Garner, eds., *Government Enterprise: A Comparative Study.* London: Stevens & Sons, 1970, 201–26.

Hogg, Peter W. *Constitutional Law of Canada.* Toronto: Carswell, 1985.

Langford, John. "Crown Corporations as Instruments of Policy." In G. Bruce Doern and Peter Aucoin, eds., *Public Policy in Canada.* Toronto: Macmillan, 1979, 239–74.

_____. "The Identification and Classification of Federal Public Corporations: A Preface to Regime Building." *Canadian Public Administration* 23 (spring 1980): 76–104.

_____. "Privatization: A Political Analysis." In Thomas E. Kierans and W. T. Stanbury, eds., *Papers on Privatization.* Montreal: Institute for Research on Public Policy, 1985.

Langford, John W., and Neil A. Swainson. "Public and Quasi-Public Corporations in British Columbia." In O.P. Dwivedi, ed., *The Administrative State in Canada.* Toronto: University of Toronto Press, 1982, 63–87.

Laux, Jeanne Kirk. "How Private Is Privatization?" *Canadian Public Policy* 19, no. 4 (1993), 398–411.

Laux, Jeanne Kirk, and Maureen Appel Molot. *State Capitalism: Public Enterprise in Canada.* Ithaca, N.Y.: Cornell University Press, 1988.

MacAvoy, Paul W., W.T. Stanbury, George Yarrow, and Richard J. Zeckhauser, eds. *Privatization and State-Owned Enterprises: Lessons from the United States, Great Britain and Canada.* Boston: Kluwer Academic Publishers, 1989.

Nelles, H.V. *The Politics of Development: Forests, Mines & Hydroelectric Power in Ontario, 1849–1941.* Toronto: Macmillan of Canada, 1974.

Neu, Dean, Duncan Green, and Alison Taylor, "Privatizing the ALCB: Ideology and Symbolism or Efficiency and Equity?," *Policy Options* 18, no. 3 (April 1997): 28–31.

Ohasi, Theodore M., T.P. Roth, Z.A. Spindler, M.L. McMillan, and K.H. Norrie. *Privatization: Theory & Practice.* Vancouver: The Fraser Institute, 1980.

Ontario. Agencies, Boards and Commissions Project. *First Report.* 1985.

_____. *Second Report: Privatization of Ontario Crown Corporations.* Report prepared for the Ministry of Treasury and Economics and the Management Board of Cabinet, n.d.

Ouellet, Lionel. "La privatisation: un instrument de management public?" *Canadian Public Administration* 30, no. 4 (winter 1987): 566–84.

Perl, Anthony. "Public Enterprise as an Expression of Sovereignty: Reconsidering the Origin of Canadian National Railways," *Canadian Journal of Political Science* 27, no. 1 (March 1994), 23–52.

Prichard, J. Robert S., ed. *Crown Corporations in Canada: The Calculus of Instrument Choice.* Toronto: Butterworths, 1983.

Report of the Auditor General of Canada to the House of Commons, Chapter 10: Crown Corporations: Fulfilling Responsibilities for Governance, October 1995. Ottawa: Minister of Supply and Services, 1995.

Stanbury, W.T. "Privatization and the Mulroney Government." In Andrew W. Gollner and Daniel Salée, eds., *Canada Under Mulroney: An End-of-Term Report.* Montreal: Véhicule Press, 1988, 119–57.

Stevens, Douglas F. *Corporate Autonomy and Institutional Control: The Crown Corporation as a Problem in Organizational Design.* Montreal: McGill-Queen's University Press, 1993.

Treasury Board of Canada Secretariat. *Crown Corporations and Other Corporate Interests of the Government of Canada.* Annual publication.

Tupper, Allan. "The Nation's Businesses: Canadian Concepts of Public Enterprise." Ph.D. diss., Queen's University, 1977.

_____. *Bill S-31 and the Federalism of State Capitalism.* Kingston, Ont.: Queen's University, Institute of Intergovernmental Relations, 1983.

Tupper, Allan, and G. Bruce Doern, eds. *Public Corporations and Public Policy in Canada.* Montreal: The Institute for Research on Public Policy, 1981.

_____. *Privatization, Public Policy and Public Corporations in Canada.* Halifax: The Institute for Research on Public Policy, 1988.

West, Douglas S. "Alberta's Liquor Store Privatization: Economic and Social Impacts." *Policy Options* 18, no. 3 (April 1997), 24–27.

Wilson, V. Seymour. *Canadian Public Policy and Administration: Theory and Environment.* Toronto: McGraw-Hill Ryerson Limited, 1981.

10

Regulatory Agencies and Deregulation

Most of us agree that there's too much government regulation in this country. At least, we agree on that most of the time. But when a former glamour company—Bre-X—suddenly went bankrupt and left many investors penniless, people were asking the same question as the headline in *The Globe and Mail*: "Where Were the Regulators?"[1]

People have an ambivalent attitude toward government regulation. There are many examples of government regulations which seem foolish and wasteful. Everyone has a favourite story about an attempt to obtain a simple document in a government office that turned into an odyssey of several days through numerous government offices. Then, there are the opposite cases where government seems to be too weak and timid in exercising its regulatory role. The case of Bre-X was already mentioned; there is also a great public outcry whenever a child is injured by an unsafe toy. In these cases, the cry always is, "Why isn't the government more aggressive in regulating?"

Why do people complain so much in the abstract about too many regulations, but then expect government regulators to be there when they need them?

This chapter will discuss the large and diverse group of governmental units commonly referred to as regulatory agencies. These units are probably the most misunderstood agencies of government because few ordinary citizens come into direct contact with them on a regular basis. Compared to the Crown corporations discussed earlier, which deliver the mail, provide transportation, generate electrical power, and employ large numbers of people in fields such as fishing and mining, regulatory agencies have a much lower profile.

However, this lack of *direct* contact between citizens and regulatory agencies masks the very great influence that these agencies have over our everyday lives. They determine which channels will operate on cable TV; they influence the content of programs broadcast on radio and television through Canadian content and other regulations; they control the rates charged for transportation and telephone services, the rents charged for apartments in some provinces, and even the importation of hog-bristle paint brushes. The ongoing discussion about the proper form and scope of regulation is a reflection of the very significant, if indirect, impact that the actions of these agencies have on all of us, and the very direct impact that they have on most businesses.

This chapter begins by establishing the definition of a regulatory agency. In keeping with the theme of this section of the book—the choice of service-delivery method—there will then be a discussion of some of the reasons politicians choose regulatory agencies to accomplish particular objectives. This discussion relates to the following section, which describes the powers of regulatory agencies. Next, the important aspects of political and judicial control of regulatory agencies will be discussed. Then, the operating procedures and organizational structure of a typical regulatory agency will be described. Finally, the current problems associated with regulatory agencies and some proposed solutions to these problems will be addressed.

While this chapter deals with the general phenomenon of government regulation, it focuses specifically on regulation by regulatory agency rather than by government department. A significant amount of regulation does emanate from government departments, and a lesser amount from other government organizations such as Crown corporations. Some obvious examples are the consumer protection regulations administered by the various federal and provincial departments responsible for consumer affairs, and the regulation of technical aspects of aviation by the federal Ministry of Transport. This chapter focuses solely on regulatory agencies, not only because they perform extremely important regulatory functions, but also because they differ in structure and operation from operating departments.

🏛 DEFINITION OF A REGULATORY AGENCY

Defining the phrase "regulatory agency" is a bit like trying to describe the shape of an amoeba. Regulatory agencies come in so many sizes and shapes and with such a variety of duties that it is difficult to generalize about them. The name of the agency is also of little help in identifying a regulatory agency. A study done for the Ontario government found that Ontario used sixteen different words to identify its regulatory agencies, but the word "agency" was not one of them.[2] In spite of this difficulty, one expert defined a regulatory agency as:

> A statutory body charged with responsibility to administer, to fix, to establish, to control, or to regulate an economic activity or market by regularized and established means in the public interest and in accordance with government policy.[3]

Two phrases in this definition—"regularized and established means" and "the public interest"—deserve special attention. First, regulatory agencies must set out *specific rules of procedure* and must follow those rules in working toward a decision. Although regulatory agencies are different from the ordinary law courts in ways that will be discussed later, these agencies do have certain judicial-like trappings, and the emphasis on "regularized and established means" of acting is one of them. This is one of the main characteristics that separates regulatory agencies from operating departments and Crown corporations. Of course, these latter two types of organization also have restrictions on their actions, but, in general, they are able to make decisions in a manner that is considerably more flexible, and sometimes more secretive, than that of regulatory agencies.

Second, regulatory agencies are frequently directed to act in "*the public interest*," but it can be very difficult to define exactly what that means. When an agency is making a decision on rate setting, it must decide between the interests of consumers, who are members of the public, and shareholders of the company, who are also members of the public. In this situation, the strongest and most principled adherence to the public interest is not a very helpful guide to action. Still, a commitment to the public interest, however defined, is an important influence on the work of regulatory agencies.

Two improvements might be made in the definition given above. First, the emphasis on "economic activity or market" has more to do with traditional forms of regulation than with some of the newer forms of regulation in cultural, environmental, and social areas. A distinction is sometimes made between economic or direct regulation and social regulation:

> *Economic [or direct] regulation* is a term that has been used to describe the early type of government regulation, which of course continues to be applied, where regulations were concerned with industry practices involving pricing, marketing and competition. The regulations had a direct impact on industry structure and practices and were frequently aimed at specific industries or markets. From the characteristics of this type of regulation, it also became known as direct regulation and "old style" regulation.

> *Social regulation* is the term which has been applied to describe that category of regulations which has become prominent in the last few decades and relates to the welfare of society. Regulations in this category tend to focus on the conditions under which goods and services are produced and distributed and on the attributes or physical properties of the products. They are primarily in the form of standards described above and relate to issues of safety, health, employment, the environment and a variety of social or welfare-related issues. The regulations for the most part are not directed at any one specific industry or market but tend to cut across industries. Pressure for these regulations generally originated from social groups including consumer interest groups, environmentalists, labour unions and others, and stem from social considerations related to improving the quality of life. This category of regulations has sometimes been referred to as the "new style" regulation or "new wave" regulation.[4]

One of the major changes in the regulatory environment in recent years has been the movement toward more social regulation, e.g., regulation in areas of culture, such as more stringent rules on Canadian content in broadcasting, and environmental and social concerns such as pollution control, occupational health and safety, and consumer protection.

The second problem with the definition is that it does not mention that a regulatory agency is insulated from direct political intervention when it is making decisions in specific cases, although there is some political control over its general policy direction.

The question of the appropriate role of the minister raises a conundrum. He or she is responsible for the policy outcomes of the activities of the agency, but cannot interfere in the making of individual decisions. The purpose of this apparent contradiction is to balance accountability to the minister in policy matters and autonomy in the making of specific decisions. As will be seen later, this need for balance poses one of the more awkward dilemmas in regulatory reform.

These considerations bring about some changes in the definition presented. The main advantage of this revised definition is its emphasis on the lack of direct ministerial control over individual decisions made by the regulatory agency. The legislature and the minister set the overall policy of the regulatory agency, but the concept of ministerial responsibility does not have the same meaning with regard to regulatory agencies as it does in the case of operating departments. In fact, it would be inappropriate for a minister to intervene when the agency is making a decision on a specific case.

Thus, a *regulatory agency* may be defined as a statutory body charged with responsibility to administer, fix, establish, control, or regulate an economic, cultural, environmental, or social activity by regularized and established means in the public interest and in accordance with general policy guidelines specified by the government. This body is under the general direction of the legislature and a responsible minister with regard to policy matters but possesses relative autonomy of action in making individual decisions within those policy guidelines.

🏛 FUNCTIONS OF REGULATORY AGENCIES

It is difficult to generalize about the functions of regulatory agencies because the powers and duties assigned to them by their enabling statutes vary widely. Richard Schultz has identified the five most common functions, each of which is examined below.

Adjudicative

This is really the defining function of a regulatory agency, so it is performed by all regulatory agencies. It involves "the determination of outcomes in individual cases which typically deal with control over entry, the setting of prices or rates of return, and the setting of standards or rules of conduct by regulated enterprises."[5]

To understand the adjudication function, it is necessary to distinguish a regulatory agency from an ordinary court of law.[6] The law courts are called upon to make a finding of fact and to relate that finding to a relatively precise piece of legislation. If the legislation is not precise in some area, there is usually some precedent set out in a decision on a similar case that can be used to assist in the application of the law.

In the case of a regulatory agency, the terms of the law that must be applied are considerably more vague. Statutes containing phrases such as "the public interest" or "public convenience and necessity" are very imprecise guides to action. Therefore, the regulatory agency must act much more on its own initiative in shaping policy than an ordinary court does.

> Granting that the [regulatory agency] which applies these legislative standards should maintain a judicial attitude, it cannot give a decision which is judicial in the narrow sense because there is no law for it to apply. If a decision is to be made at

all, it must be made on grounds of policy and therefore the function in question is primarily legislative rather than judicial.[7]

There is a paradox here in that regulatory agencies are required to behave in a judicial-like manner in considering a case, but they actually make the decision based on policy considerations. This latter point explains why agencies are not bound by precedent. In the many cases in which agencies are allocating scarce resources, they simply could not follow precedent anyway. If all of the available slots on the radio dial have already been assigned, then the quality of the next application received is not relevant. The scarcity of slots on the dial precludes approval on the basis of precedent.

The adjudicative function tends to be the core activity of most regulatory agencies, but there are several other activities that are also a part of the responsibilities of many agencies.

Legislative

This function comprises "the ability to make general rules or regulations, in the form of delegated legislation, that have the force of law."[8] Most legislation that establishes regulatory agencies gives them some power to prescribe more specific regulations within the guidelines set out in the legislation. These regulations are referred to as *delegated legislation* because they are made pursuant to powers delegated to the agency in the legislation. They could relate to either policy matters, i.e., specify the agency's approach to particular issues, or procedural matters, i.e., specify how applications are to be filed and hearings conducted.

Research

Most agencies employ some staff to conduct general research in the policy area that they regulate. The purpose of this research is to allow members to remain conversant with recent trends in the field. For example, it could provide them with an early warning when there is a need for a policy shift. The research staff is also sometimes used to evaluate applications and to provide advice to agency members in making specific decisions.

Advisory

In many ways, the advisory function follows from the research function. As a result of the research conducted and the findings flowing from hearings, the agency members and staff are frequently able to advise the minister and/or the operating department about the need for a fresh consideration of certain policy issues. The regulatory agencies are close to the regulated industry and its clientele. Therefore, they have a good knowledge of emerging problems.

Administrative

Some agencies also have direct administrative responsibility for operating programs. For example, the National Transportation Agency formerly provided subsidies to railways under the Western Grain Transportation Act and to railways, marine, and truck lines under the Atlantic Region Freight Assistance Act. These kinds of functions are being eliminated because they could create conflict when an agency must both operate a program affecting an industry and regulate that industry.

This listing of some of the duties of regulatory agencies provides an idea of the rather broad scope and diversity of this organizational form. Therefore, it should not be surprising that there are many varied reasons given for employing the regulatory agency form of organization.

🏛 THE RATIONALE FOR REGULATORY AGENCIES

The administrator, the economist, and the politician see regulation in somewhat different lights.[9] The practising administrator frequently sees regulation as the easiest and cheapest method of attaining a particular objective. The economist is usually opposed to regulation, except in those relatively rare cases where it corrects some market imperfections.[10] The politician must respond to the frequently conflicting demands of electors, and so sometimes views regulation as an easy method of farming out complex problems to independent agencies to be dealt with over the long term. Therefore, there are many different reasons for the creation of regulatory agencies. The reasons discussed below constitute only a partial list.

Remove an Issue from "Politics"

The word politics is used here in the negative sense of relying too much on partisanship, compromise, and expediency, and not enough on fairness and hard economic facts.

Many of the decisions made by regulatory agencies are in rather delicate areas. In cases such as the regulation of broadcasting, there may be a fear that one political party would attempt to use the media for partisan advantage. There are also cases in which regulatory agencies are rationing scarce resources. These resources could be slots on a radio or television dial or the right to develop a particular piece of land. Not only is there usually a large amount of money at stake in these cases, but they also frequently involve highly technical questions that require the attention of experts. For example, the question of whether an applicant has the engineering expertise and financial support to operate a radio station is a technical question best addressed by engineers and accountants. In this sense, it is sometimes reassuring to have decisions removed from the partisan political process so that they can be viewed more objectively.

However, this argument must be put in perspective. Most delicate issues of this kind consist not only of technical questions, but also of contentious political ones. In the broadcasting case, the questions of engineering competence and financial viability are predominantly technical ones, but questions of Canadian content, sex-role stereotyping, pornography, or appropriate programming mix are inherently political ones.

For this reason, the idea of using the vehicle of the regulatory agency to remove an issue from politics must be approached carefully. If it means providing experts with some scope to review technical problems outside the vagaries of the political process, then it is probably highly beneficial. If it implies that mixed technical and political questions can be resolved by technical experts, then it is not only naive, but dangerous, because it would suggest that politicians should not be held accountable for certain decisions simply because those decisions contain some technical element.

Provide an Impartial, Judicial-Like Hearing

This reason is related to the previous one. It is the nature of parliamentary governments that cabinet decisions are made in closed sessions and rely on information that is not necessarily available to the public. In this context, it is difficult for someone submitting an issue to cabinet to know whether all important arguments have been considered before a cabinet decision is made.

Thus, it is sometimes considered important to have a public forum such as a regulatory agency where all the facts in a case can be presented. The forum usually involves a relatively formal hearing in which petitioners can present their arguments and cross-examine one another. This process ensures that all parties have a fair opportunity to state their case as well as they can. Since the members of the agency presiding over the hearing and making the decision must be free from bias, it also ensures that a decision that takes account of the arguments of all sides will be rendered.

If the decisions were made in an overtly political arena, it might be difficult for politicians to escape at least the appearance of bias. For example, some people who own companies that hold broadcast licences are prominently identified with a particular political party. There could be an appearance of bias in either the renewal or the refusal to renew a licence depending on the political stripe of the government.

Apply Specialized Expertise

Many kinds of concerns assigned to regulatory agencies could be handled in ordinary courts. After all, judges become very proficient at sorting through conflicting arguments, separating the important from the trivial, and rendering an impartial decision. These are all activities performed by members of regulatory agencies.

However, while judges are learned in the law, they are not expected to have detailed knowledge of the activities of a particular industry. Also, one cannot expect different judges to apply an integrated, coherent policy in making decisions about an industry; judges decide individual cases based on the law.

By way of contrast, the members of a regulatory agency develop specialized knowledge over the years and so are capable of making decisions reflecting consciously conceived policies. Also, these specialized decision makers can arrive at decisions more quickly than someone who must become familiar with a new issue from the ground up, as judges would have to do.

Deal with Future Conditions that the Legislature Could Not Foresee

Frequently, technical and economic conditions are changing so rapidly that it is dysfunctional for the legislature to prescribe hard-and-fast rules in legislation that can only be changed by new legislation. It is preferable for the legislature to specify general principles and to allow the regulatory agency flexibility within those principles to respond to changing conditions.

Regulate a Natural Monopoly

A natural monopoly exists when the lowest cost for a good or service is obtained when there is only one producer of that good or service.[11] In other words, certain technical aspects of production mean that competition would increase its cost. For example, the delivery of electricity in a particular geographic area is a natural monopoly. The capital cost of installing two or more electrical service lines into every area of a city could not possibly be lower than with one monopoly supplier.

The problem with a natural monopoly is that the discipline of the market is not available to force the supplier to deal fairly with consumers. In the absence of that discipline, most economists argue that the natural monopoly situation is one of the few cases in which government regulation is justified to ensure appropriate prices and adequate service.

Smooth Market Instability

In recent years, there has been a trend toward the use of regulatory agencies for "supply management." The best examples are the marketing boards for such farm products as eggs, milk, and chicken. These agencies work by setting quotas on the overall quantity of the product that can be produced and allocating this quota among specific producers. The effect is to ensure that an excess of supply does not reduce prices paid to producers.

Marketing boards have been criticized on the grounds that they increase the price that consumers pay. However, they also assure reasonable security of supply by preventing injurious competition that would force some suppliers from the market. In other words, consumers must pay a premium for eggs every time they buy them to ensure that there will always be some eggs available at a reasonable price. Whether the cost is worth the benefit is something that each voter must decide.

Prevent Discrimination Where a Situation of Inequality Exists

This rationale bears some similarity to the natural monopoly argument in that there is some perceived inequality of bargaining power that government feels should be corrected. Most of the new kinds of social regulatory agencies in fields such as human rights, occupational health and safety, and rent control were created for this reason. The role of the regulatory agency in this case is to protect the weaker party by preventing the stronger party from taking unfair advantage of its position.

The agencies created as a result of this rationale have been the most controversial because the existence of an inequality that requires government intervention is frequently in the eye of the beholder. Rent control, around which there is considerable controversy, is one obvious example of an area in which not everyone agrees on the need for protection.

Control Externalities or "Spill-Overs"

A nontechnical definition of an externality is a cost imposed by one person on another person, or on society as a whole, when the person imposing the cost has no market incentive to minimize or control the cost. The most common example is pollution. The obvious market incentive is for polluters to minimize their expenditure on pollution-control equipment so that the entire cost of pollution will be borne by society as a whole. Of course, people damaged by the pollution could seek remedy through the court system, but this avenue is more difficult than it might seem.[12] Therefore, a regulatory agency with the power to enforce particular standards is the obvious solution.

Provide a Low-Cost Option from the Standpoint of Government

As discussed in Chapter 6, when a government wants to have an impact on a particular kind of behaviour, it has a number of options, ranging from exhortation, through tax incentives and grants, to coercive legislation. One of the lowest cost options from the standpoint of the government is simply to say: "Thou shalt not." There is a cost to the government of establishing and operating a regulatory agency, but the impact per dollar spent is usually greater than that of an operating department or Crown corporation because of the regulatory agency's coercive powers.

A classic example of the use of this rationale is the treatment of the Niagara escarpment in southern Ontario. The escarpment is a unique geological formation and prime recreation area. In fact, it is so attractive that private interests would love to develop it for resorts, housing, golf courses, and so forth. In the 1960s, there was considerable pressure on the Ontario government to control development in this area. A number of options were considered, including buying the entire escarpment or strategic portions of it. Not surprisingly, the Ontario government decided to establish a regulatory agency, the Niagara Escarpment Commission, and give it the power to say: "Thou shalt not develop here without prior permission." This was clearly the low-cost option from the standpoint of the government.

Regulation is the low-cost option *only* from the standpoint of the government. As will be discussed in more detail later, regulation can impose significant costs on others. In the Niagara escarpment example, many people saw the value of their land plummet when it became unlikely that it could be used for subdivisions or resorts. It has been suggested that the low cost of regulation makes it particularly attractive to governments facing simultaneous demands for decisive action and for financial restraint.[13]

The reasons noted above constitute only a partial listing of the reasons for establishing and preserving regulatory agencies. This diversity of reasons demonstrates why these agencies have such a wide variety of roles. However, the main characteristics that cut across all agencies are their relative autonomy from direct political control, and their judicial-like methods of operation. These characteristics will be examined in the next two sections.

🏛 POLITICAL CONTROL OF REGULATORY AGENCIES

The Conundrum of Accountability and Autonomy

A central feature of parliamentary control of regulatory agencies is that the legislature, the cabinet, and individual ministers set general policies and guidelines for their activities but are kept at arm's length from their day-to-day operations. This creates a conundrum in that the agency must be accountable to the minister and the legislature, but at the same time it must have autonomy in making individual decisions.[14] This problem was well illustrated when the Opposition demanded that the federal solicitor general take some action against members of the National Parole Board who had been responsible for the release of prisoners who had gone on to commit violent crimes.[15] The minister cannot maintain an arm's length relationship with an agency and at the same time be held responsible for its actions.

Some of the problems that this setup raises were identified by a report of the Economic Council of Canada:

> This form of compromise between regulatory independence and political control has led in recent years to a great deal of tension, confusion and compromise. The record of both the federal and provincial governments' relationships with their regulatory agencies raises a number of challenging questions. Who should make regulatory policy? How should such policy be made—through open, participatory hearings in advance of specific cases or as a result of appeals to the cabinet following a specific case? Should [regulatory agencies] perform *both* adjudicative functions, for which they appear to be well suited, as well as policy advisory, research, and administrative functions, for which they may be less well suited. In particular, if a policy advisory role is retained, should the agency's advice to the government be confidential or made only in public documents? Finally, is it realistic to expect a government to be able to clearly articulate its policy positions, except in rather general terms, in advance of specific choices that embody the means of implementing them?[16]

Weak political control of the agency might allow it to act at cross-purposes with other government agencies, or to make decisions that are not in the overall public interest. However, excessive political control deflates the morale of the agency and could lead to dominance by powerful interest groups. The conundrum of accountability and autonomy is one of the most difficult problems to handle in discussing regulatory reform.[17] This section will discuss the method of accomplishing this balancing act.

Enabling Statutes and Other Legislation

Regulatory agencies are similar to operating departments and most Crown corporations in that they are formed as a result of enabling legislation, which specifies the structure of the agency, the procedures it must follow in considering cases, the limits of its authority, and the general policies it must apply in making decisions. In some instances, all of these components are specified in one statute; in others, they are divided among a number of pieces of legislation. For example, the Canadian Transportation Agency was created by the Canada Transportation Act,[18] but it draws many of its powers from the Atlantic Region Freight Assistance Act,[19] Pilotage Act,[20] and Railway Safety Act,[21] among others.

Legislative committees also check the work of regulatory agencies. They scrutinize the operation of regulatory agencies in the same manner as that of operating departments and Crown corporations. Thus, the committee members can question the minister responsible for an agency and/or the members of the agency about its implementation of policies or its operating procedures.

Standing Joint Committee on Scrutiny of Regulations

In addition to the policy-oriented legislative committees that oversee the activities of regulatory agencies, there can be specialized committees that review all regulations and delegated legislation. This was first employed in Saskatchewan in the early 1960s and came to the federal government in 1971 in the form of the Senate and House of Commons Standing Joint Committee on Regulations and Other Statutory Instruments,[22] which has now been retitled the Standing Joint Committee on Scrutiny of Regulations.[23]

All regulations made under delegated legislation by either operating departments or regulatory agencies are referred to this committee.[24] Its mandate includes reviewing whether the regulation is in line with the authorizing legislation, whether it violates the Charter of Rights and Freedoms, and whether it intrudes into an area that is the prerogative of Parliament. Beyond these specific areas, it does not generally delve into the merits of the regulation. Therefore, the committee has a somewhat legalistic and limited mandate.

In a recent report this committee criticized the government's decision to exempt the Kemano II dam project in British Columbia from environmental assessment.[25] The committee argued that the government exceeded its legislative powers in providing such an exemption. The legal terminology of this situation is *ultra vires*, literally "beyond the powers."

Appointment of Members

The decisions of regulatory agencies are made by a panel of members who are appointed by the governor in council, usually after consultation with the minister responsible for the agency. The minister will normally recommend the appointment of persons who share her or his views on the policy area.

David Johnson has argued that the power of appointment is the most important of all these powers because it allows the government to establish the "culture" of the agency. In the absence of any direct control over agency decisions, the ability to establish this overall cultural tone is a very important element of accountability.

> Recent empirical research probing the relationship between governments, ministries, and agencies in [Ontario] suggests that the strongest link between these centres of authority is "cultural." Shared values, ideas, beliefs concerning the proper approaches which agencies should adopt respecting the development and administration of regulatory policy, and not formal legal controls, are the key elements binding agencies to their responsible ministries and governments. Former premiers David Peterson and William Davis, and various senior officials within ministries, have all commented that governments will only appoint persons whom they trust to positions of power within agencies. The point is simple yet important. Governments will usually have a basic conception of the strategic policy approaches which they wish their agencies to follow. In making appointments to these bodies they will then select persons who share the same general policy perspectives. Having appointed such officials, ministers will then trust these delegates to undertake their responsibilities without the need for ministers having to directly intervene in the routine activities of the agencies.[26]

This "cultural" approach is particularly important since appointees immediately attain a high level of independence after they are appointed. Most appointments are for lengthy fixed terms of office and members can be removed only "for cause." Therefore, the ability of anyone, including the minister, to interfere in a specific decision is limited.

The allegation has often been made that this power of appointment has been used for patronage purposes.[27] Clearly, there have been instances of ministers appointing people of their own political stripe, but allegations of patronage must be considered carefully. Evidence provided later in this chapter indicates that political appointments are not as common as popular opinion suggests. Ontario has taken steps to open up the appointment process by advertising vacancies in the *Ontario Gazette* and there is some emphasis on appointing people who represent a broad cross-section of Ontario society. Appointments are also subject to review by a legislative committee, although there is some question about how effective this is in a majority government situation.[28]

Policy Statements and Directives

As noted above, it is inappropriate for a minister to intervene in specific cases before an agency. However, a minister, or the cabinet collectively, can issue policy statements or directives to inform the regulatory agency of the government's desires in a particular area. For some agencies it is not clear whether these are binding,[29] but for others the legislation makes it clear that they are binding. These must be general policy statements and not directions concerning specific cases. Thus, it would be inappropriate for a minister to tell an agency: "You must grant this broadcast licence to person A instead of person B." However, it would be quite appropriate for the minister to direct the agency that: "The only applicants who should be considered for this broadcast licence are those who will agree to provide X percent of Canadian content."

These policy statements or directives can be made secretly to the agency, but it is usually considered important that they be made publicly so that all parties appearing before the agency will know what policy statements and directives have been made. It also acts as a constraint on any potential abuse of power by the minister.

Prior Approval of Decisions

In some instances, the decision of a regulatory agency does not become binding until it is approved either by the responsible minister or by the cabinet collectively.[30] The role of the agency in this situation is to provide an impartial hearing to all concerned and to apply its specialized expertise in arriving at a recommendation for a decision. These recommendations are usually given publicly so that the cabinet must consider very carefully both the recommendations and the supporting documentation. If this advice is ignored, allegations of inappropriate political influence can be made.[31]

Appeal

Some legislation dealing with regulation provides the right of appeal to the minister or to the governor in council, i.e., the cabinet. Where this provision exists, the appellant usually has no right to appear personally before the minister or cabinet but must state in writing the reasons why the decision should be overturned. The minister or cabinet considers these appeals carefully but is usually somewhat reluctant to overturn a decision, partly to preserve the morale and integrity of the agency and partly to prevent a flood of similar appeals. This reluctance to overturn decisions probably explains the small number of appeals made to cabinet.

However, this appeal mechanism is still a valuable safety valve. At the extreme, it prevents the members of the agency from behaving in some entirely inappropriate manner because they know that their decision could be appealed to a higher level. In a less extreme vein, the minister or cabinet can use the selective acceptance of certain appeals to signal changes in policy at the political level.[32] Regulatory agency members are usually sensitive to this sort of signal.

Political control of regulatory agencies is geared to ensuring that they follow the policy guidelines set out by the government. Judicial control of regulatory agencies, which is discussed in the next section, is geared to ensuring fairness in the handling of individual cases.

🏛 JUDICIAL CONTROL OF REGULATORY AGENCIES

Chapter 18 contains a full treatment of judicial control of administrative actions in general and of regulatory decision making in particular. It is useful to note here that there is usually much discussion about which type of redress is more effective—political or judicial.[33] The answer depends on a number of factors. First, a court rarely *changes* the decision of a regulatory agency. This has been described as *judicial deference*, i.e., the courts will defer to the decision of the agency as long as the appropriate process was followed.[34] Thus, the court considers only the *process* followed by the agency, not the *merits* of its decision. A court can find that an agency followed an improper procedure, and so overturn the decision. At this point, the agency is free to reconsider the matter, follow the proper procedure, and arrive at exactly the same decision. The court would then be satisfied. Of course, there is also the possibility that a different procedure will produce a different result.

If it is clear that the agency has followed the proper procedure but there is still dissatisfaction with the decision reached, then the most likely source of redress lies at the political level. It is usually only the minister or cabinet who can consider the *merits* of the decision and substitute another final and binding decision.

🏛 ORGANIZATIONAL STRUCTURE OF REGULATORY AGENCIES

It is very difficult to generalize about the structure of regulatory agencies because each agency is somewhat different. However, this section will describe some of the usual structures.

Regulatory agencies are virtually always headed by a panel of members. The panel usually consists of five to ten members, but the number can vary quite widely. For example, the National Parole Board has had as many as fifty-nine members.[35] Panel members are collectively responsible for the agency's operation.

The method of appointment and removal of panel members obviously has an impact on the independence of the agency from political control.[36] To maximize independence, members should be appointed for relatively lengthy terms and should be removable only for cause. This is the case for most federal agencies, but Brown-John found that many members of regulatory agencies do not have the security of tenure needed for independence.[37]

One member of the panel is designated as the chairperson or president of the agency.[38] This individual is considered the administrative head of the agency and usually has the responsibility of assigning fellow panel members to cases, as well as of supervising the public servants who work for the agency.

The fact that the agency is headed by a panel means that there is scope for the representation of diverse interests on the panel, e.g., geographic regions, special interest groups. Members of the Canadian Radio-television and Telecommunications Commission are traditionally appointed from different regions of the country, and labour relations boards contain a roughly equal balance between members with backgrounds in labour and management.

The background of panel members obviously has some impact on agency decisions. The specialized knowledge possessed by former employees of the regulated industry makes them choice candidates for appointment to the agency. It has sometimes been suggested that a preponderance of these people as panel members will make the agency "soft" on the industry.

However, a (now somewhat dated) Canadian survey indicates that members of regulatory agencies are more likely to be former public servants than former employees of the regulated industry.[39] This same survey found that there were not large numbers of former politicians serving as members of regulatory agencies, thus negating somewhat the image of these agencies as repositories of patronage appointees. However, a report of the Law Reform Commission of Canada suggests that the highly political nature of the appointments to these agencies can have a detrimental effect on their operations.[40] The commission recommends that the process be opened up considerably by advertising the open positions and by consulting with interested groups about potential members.

The members preside over hearings and make decisions, but it is unusual for all members to be present at any one hearing.[41] The agency's legislation will specify the minimum number of members necessary to conduct a hearing. This can be as few as one. Thus, several hearings can be held at the same time, and the work of the agency can be accelerated. Members can be assigned to cases by the chairperson on a random basis, or there can be a committee system that allows members to specialize.

All regulatory agencies have a fairly extensive staff of experts in law, economics, accounting, engineering, or whatever other specialties are required. The main functions of this staff are supporting the work of the members in arranging hearings, conducting both general research and specific investigations concerning individual applications, and advising members on legal and/or technical aspects of their work.

🏛 CREATING OR CHANGING A REGULATION

The enabling legislation usually gives the agency or department[42] some discretion in establishing specific regulations within the framework set out in its act or acts. This section describes that regulation-making process. It will become clear that this process has a predisposition that has led past governments to use the regulatory tool too quickly, too frequently, and in too cumbersome a manner. This process puts a fairly heavy onus on the agency proposing the regulation to prove that regulation is the best tool in the circumstances.

Step 1: Agency Initiation of a Change[43]

The process begins when the agency decides that it might need to establish a new regulation or modify an existing one. It will then identify and assess its available alternatives. The federal government's current regulatory policy stresses that:[44]

a) regulation should be employed only when absolutely necessary (i.e., less coercive measures should be tried first); and

b) when it is determined that regulation is absolutely necessary, the regulations established should be as unintrusive as possible.

This sort of thinking is embodied in the federal government's new Citizens' Code of Regulatory Fairness, excerpts of which are in the following box.

CITIZENS' CODE OF REGULATORY FAIRNESS

1. Canadians are entitled to expect that the Government's regulation will be characterized by minimum interference with individual freedom consistent with the protection of community interests.

2. The Government will encourage and facilitate a full opportunity for consultation and participation by Canadians in the federal regulatory process.

. . .

10. The Government will not use regulation unless it has clear evidence that: a problem exists; government intervention is justified; and regulation is the best alternative open to the Government.

11. The Government will ensure that the benefits of regulation exceed the costs and will give particularly careful consideration to all new regulation that could impede economic growth or job creation.

Source: Treasury Board of Canada Secretariat, The Federal Regulatory Process: An Interim Procedures Manual for Departments and Agencies 1991, 11–12. Reproduced with the permission of the Minister of Public Works and Government Services Canada, 1998.

At the same time that the agency is undertaking its internal review, it will notify all interested parties that it is considering changing regulations. It can do this in a variety of ways. The preferred method is to include some mention of the proposal in the annual *Federal Regulatory Plan*. This is published by the Treasury Board and provides all interested parties with information about changes that are being considered in the federal regulatory regime. The sample in the box on the next page illustrates a representative entry. Note that it provides a brief outline of the proposed action in reasonably nontechnical language, although it is a bit difficult to understand its effect unless one is familiar with the Student Debt Management Strategy and some of the other documents mentioned. It gives the name of a contact person who can provide additional information or accept comments from interested parties.

While the *Federal Regulatory Plan* is the preferred method of disseminating this information, agencies can use other methods, such as the *Canada Gazette*, formal legal letters, advertisements in newspapers or trade publications, and news announcements in the media. In some cases, this notice is an open-ended request for any comments that interested parties want to tender. In other cases, the staff of the agency prepares some tentative working documents on which comments are invited.

Interested parties are usually requested to submit written comments first. On the basis of these comments, some people will be invited to attend a hearing to present their views and be questioned by the members of the agency. In some cases, these hearings are held at the home base of the agency, but in others, the members travel to major cities across the country or province to obtain a wide cross-section of views.

If the agency decides to go forward with its new or amended regulation, the next step is the preparation of a *Regulatory Impact Analysis Statement (RIAS)*. The RIAS is the agency's formal justification of the regulation that it is

---

SAMPLE ENTRY FROM FEDERAL REGULATORY PLAN 1997

HRDC/97-6-1

CANADA STUDENT LOANS PROGRAM (CHANGES)

It is proposed to introduce new regulations under paragraph 15(1) of the Canada Student Financial Assistance Act to implement elements of the Student Debt Management Strategy, which was announced on August 1, 1995. Other regulations to enhance assistance to students, to place greater emphasis on education results and to ensure harmony in program delivery are being considered. Further amendments may also be required to ensure consistency between the Canada Student Loans Regulations and the Canada Student Financial Assistance Regulations.

　　Legal authority: Canada Student Financial Assistance Act; Canada Student Loans Act.

　　Contact: Jo Anne Denis, Senior Policy Analyst, Youth, Learning Programs Policy, Human Resources Development Canada, 15 Eddy Street, Hull, Quebec, K1A 0M7. Tel. (819) 994-5018; Fax (819) 953-8147.

---

proposing. It provides a description of what the government is going to deliver, how Canadians have been consulted, and what they have said. It then offers a final chance for Canadians to have input to the regulation-making process.

Within government, the RIAS is intended to provide better information for decision makers both inside and outside the initiating department. Outside the government, the RIAS is intended to give the public better information with which to evaluate proposed regulations, and on which to base any questions and final comments they may have about specific regulations.[45]

The RIAS has six sections:

1. *Description* outlines the regulations, defines the problem, and shows why action is necessary.

2. *Alternatives* examines the options besides regulation, as well as lighter forms of regulation.

3. *Benefits and Costs* quantifies the impact.

4. *Consultation* shows who was consulted and the results.

5. *Compliance and Enforcement* explains the procedures and resources that will be used to ensure the regulation is respected.

6. *Contact Person* is the individual best able to answer questions from RIAS readers.[46]

The most important part of the RIAS is the review of costs and benefits because there is now a strong emphasis that an agency should be able to justify any new regulation by demonstrating that its benefits exceed its costs.

In addition to the RIAS, the agency must use the Business Impact Test (BIT) to assess the proposed regulation's impact on the industry. Developed by the federal government and the Canadian Manufacturers Association, BIT is a piece of computer software that allows an agency to determine "the direct costs of proposed regulations, as well as the effect the proposals may have on the way firms operate, organize and innovate."[47]

Step 2: Review by Other Agencies

The *Department of Justice* reviews the proposed regulation to ensure that it has a proper legal basis and that it conforms with the Charter of Rights and Freedoms.

The *Treasury Board Secretariat* examines the proposed regulation to ensure that it complies with the various regulatory policies discussed in this chapter, particularly to see if alternatives to regulation were considered, costs and benefits assessed, and adequate consultation sought.

The *Privy Council Office* ensures that the proposed regulation meshes with overall government policy and that a proper communications strategy is in place.

Step 3: Ministerial Approval and Submission to Cabinet

If the proposed regulation withstands these various tests, the minister then approves its submission to the Special Committee of Council, which is a cabinet committee. This committee reviews the regulation from a political perspective to ensure that it conforms to broad government policy initiatives, particularly in terms of its impact on jobs and economic growth.

Step 4: Prepublication in the *Canada Gazette*

The draft regulation is then published in the *Canada Gazette*, which commences a thirty-day period for final comment from interested parties.

Step 5: Registration and Publication

The regulation is then officially registered with the Privy Council Office and given approval by the governor in council. The regulation takes effect when it is published in Part II of the *Canada Gazette*.

Step 6: Review by the Standing Joint Committee on Scrutiny of Regulations

After the regulation has been approved, it goes to the Standing Joint Committee on Scrutiny of Regulations for review. As discussed earlier, the committee has a fairly narrow mandate to review the regulation to ensure that it is within the purview of the enabling legislation and that it does not intrude on a prerogative of the legislature. If the committee is dissatisfied with some aspect of the regulation, it can only draw this to the attention of the House of Commons. The committee has no authority to delay or overturn the regulation.

🏛 DECIDING A CASE

The adjudication process—the consideration of individual cases—can begin in a number of ways. Usually, an individual case begins when an application is submitted to the agency requesting, for example, a rate increase or a change in service level. The process can also be initiated by the agency or a third party where, for example, there is concern that a regulated company is not meeting some obligation.

In accordance with the standards of natural justice,[48] there is usually a requirement that *notice* be provided to all interested parties that an application is under review. Any party who comes forward at this time is called an *intervener*. An intervener can prepare a submission supporting or opposing the application or proposing some middle ground. Typically, the interveners will be individual consumers, consumers' groups, or companies in the industry affected by the application. However, even government departments or other governments can intervene before a regulatory agency.

As interventions are received, the public servants who work for the regulatory agency will begin to analyze both the original application and the comments provided by interveners. They will then prepare a summary of the relevant issues for the panel and possibly even a recommendation concerning the final disposition of the application.

Whether a full hearing will then be held depends on the requirements in the legislation and regulations, and the importance of the case. When there is a full formal hearing, the process begins with a presentation explaining the applicant's position. Then the agency will usually invite some of the interveners to explain their positions.

The hearings of some agencies are very formal, almost judicial, procedures held in settings that resemble a courtroom and involve the presence of lawyers, formal presentation of evidence, and cross-examination of witnesses. Other agencies strive to keep their proceedings as simple and informal as possible. In this situation, the members might only leave the room for a few minutes and return to present their decision verbally. In more complex cases, several months could be required for members to deliver a lengthy, written decision with the underlying reasons.

These procedures are carefully worked out to ensure fairness to all sides and a thorough consideration of the issue. A survey has indicated that most of those involved in the regulatory process are quite satisfied with the process,[49] but some commentators have identified flaws in the system.

🏛 PROBLEMS IDENTIFIED WITH REGULATION

The role of regulation and regulatory agencies in society is currently the subject of much debate. Agencies are attacked on one side for being too assertive and intrusive, and on the other for being too docile and "captive" of the interests that they were established to regulate. In this section, some of the main criticisms of regulatory agencies will be considered and in the next section some of the possible reforms will be discussed.[50]

Cost of Regulation

Although regulation is usually seen as the low-cost option from the standpoint of government, it can impose sizable costs on other parties. The most obvious examples are the direct costs incurred by the regulated industry and by other affected parties. The firms in the regulated industry must maintain extensive records in a format specified by the regulatory agency. All parties affected by regulatory agencies incur substantial information costs to keep themselves abreast of initiatives by the agency and by other groups affected by the agency. Then there are legal and other costs involved in preparing a case and actually appearing before the regulatory agency.

However, these direct costs might be only the tip of the iceberg.[51] The major costs of regulation could come from the delay it causes in implementation. Hearings on environmental issues such as approval of landfill sites can take years. In the meantime, municipalities must make other arrangements, which can be very costly. The pharmaceutical industry has long claimed that the lengthy tests required for approval of new drugs slow down the delivery to the market of those much-needed drugs.

It is important to emphasize that benefits as well as costs arise from regulation. The record keeping required of regulated industries allows the regulatory agency to consider intelligently requests for rate increases. The slowness in the introduction of new innovations sometimes keeps dangerous products off the market. This is not to suggest that all forms of regulation are justified. Clearly, there are cases in which legislators or regulators have been overzealous.

There are also *hidden* costs of regulation. Economists argue that the optimum competitive situation occurs when barriers to entering an industry are low. Easy entry for new firms forces existing firms to be competitive in both price and quality of product. Regulatory agencies virtually always raise barriers to entry in the regulated industry and so could limit competitiveness in the industry.[52] Barriers can be direct, such as the need for prior approval from the regulatory agency, or indirect, but equally effective, such as residence or minimum capitalization requirements. Still other barriers can be psychological in that entrepreneurs will simply choose not to enter an industry in which the regulations are seen as intrusive, particularly if the barriers are felt to be unfair or unreasonable.

Regulations and Competitiveness

Regulation can limit the competitiveness of Canadian companies in several ways. First, the cost that regulation imposes on Canadian companies increases their costs of doing business. Second, the regulatory system can introduce impediments to innovation. Third, some regulations stifle competition and actually drive up prices to consumers. An analysis of Air Canada suggested that when price competition was effectively prohibited in the airline industry, the companies competed by increasing the frequency and quality of their service. This meant that all airlines were operating inefficiently because of excess capacity, but government regulation made it impossible for any of them to change their method of operation.[53]

Of course, these increased costs are passed along to consumers. But probably the worst part of the cost of regulation is that it weakens the competitive position of Canadian companies in the international market. These problems will become more urgent as the globalization of the economy proceeds.

The federal government has taken two initiatives to deal with this problem. It has established a subcommittee of the House of Commons, which has produced a report that reviewed the competitiveness issue thoroughly and offered some recommendations to improve the situation.[54] Second, agencies are now required to use the Business Impact Test (BIT) to assess the impact that a new regulation will have on an industry.[55]

Compliance

Traditionally, it has been assumed that regulatees will automatically comply with the rulings of regulatory agencies. Agencies have a number of mechanisms, such as the imposition of fines or the lifting of licences, that tend to ensure compliance. For this reason, the question of compliance has received little study. However, there is a growing understanding that ensuring compliance can be a real problem because regulatees can circumvent rulings in both subtle and overt ways.

Some of the best examples of subtle evasion are in the area of broadcasting regulation. The CRTC usually issues a licence to a broadcasting company with the condition that it provide a certain level of Canadian content. After a period of operation, the licencee sometimes argues that it has not quite fulfilled its obligation for economic or practical reasons. The CRTC is then confronted with a difficult dilemma. It can either lift the company's licence and leave an area with reduced or, in some cases, no service, or it can slap the company on the wrist and ask it to do better in the future. So far, the CRTC has usually pursued the latter course and has been subjected to some criticism for being too weak.

> Time and again, ... the CRTC has gone through the charade of extracting promises of performance only to forgive or cancel these once the licence was issued. It has paid lip service to broadcasting licences as public property while allowing them to be trafficked as private goods. No major broadcaster has ever lost a licence or come close to doing so even though the principles and goals of the broadcasting act have been torn in shreds.[56]

Of course, the CRTC would likely be subject to criticism from other quarters if it pursued the firmer course.

Similar enforcement problems can develop when a government agency tries to take action to control pollution caused by companies that are major employers.[57] When the company threatens to close, the regulator is in a very difficult position. Thus, in the real world, compliance is not as automatic as some assume.

There are also examples of more overt refusal to comply with agency directives. Some of the most awkward examples have occurred as a result of federal-provincial disputes,[58] but the most colourful incidents occurred in the mid-1970s when the dish-type satellite-receiving antennas were illegal. On numerous occasions when RCMP officers attempted to seize these devices at remote mining or lumber camps, they were simply chased away by the irate residents, thus prompting one commentator to suggest that while the Mounties may always get their man, they don't always get their dish.[59]

The Empty Consumers' Chair

It is sometimes said that the purpose of a regulatory agency is to protect the consumer. While some legislators might intend this, it is not, strictly speaking, legally correct. The members of a regulatory agency listen to the arguments presented by the various parties and attempt to arrive at an optimum decision based on those arguments. They are clearly restrained from favouring one side or the other; they must decide on the basis of the arguments presented. If one side is able to present its arguments more persuasively or more forcefully, then, other things being equal, it is likely to win.

This premium on the ability to make one's case well is significant, because it has been suggested that producers have an advantage over consumers in the regulatory process.[60] There is usually a relatively small number of producers (sometimes only one); therefore, in actions such as rate increase applications, each producer has a significant sum of money at stake. This pressure causes producers to work together and spend large sums of money to defend their claims.

However, there are a large number of consumers, each of whom has a fairly small amount of money at stake in any given rate increase. Therefore, it is difficult for consumers to band together to fight rate increases. To put it directly: How much would you be willing to spend to prevent your telephone bill from increasing by fifty cents per month? Probably considerably less than a telephone company would be willing to spend to gain the several million dollars that it has at stake in the same application.

The Captive Agency Theory

The *captive agency theory* is in many ways complementary to the above arguments about the lack of consumer power in the regulatory process. This theory suggests that, over time, the agency is captured by the industry that it was set up to regulate, and so becomes supportive of that industry.[61] This is a gradual process in which the agency develops a concern for the orderly development of the industry; this concern gradually comes to mean the protection of the companies currently in the industry from any disruptive forces, such as excessive competition from new entrants.

Marver H. Bernstein has developed a life cycle theory of regulatory agencies that explains this capture.[62] An agency is usually born as the result of political activism by groups concerned about some perceived problem. These groups work long and hard against difficult odds to encourage legislators to introduce some regulatory legislation.

However, when the necessary legislation is passed, these groups run out of steam, partly because it is innately difficult to hold such large and diverse groups together, and partly because people drift away when they feel that the battle is won. Paradoxically, it is at precisely this time, when the fledgling agency is just beginning its operations and drafting its regulations, that it needs public input and support the most.

The people staffing the new agency are unlikely to be knowledgeable about the industry since it has never been regulated before. Where should they turn for assistance and advice? The groups that agitated for the legislation in the first place are no longer strong and active. The only other source of knowledge about the industry is the industry itself. Therefore, the new regulators seek the advice of the regulated industry about how it wants to be regulated. This close contact allows the regulated industry to have a subtle but effective impact on the regulatory agency at its crucial formative stage. Once the pattern of close consultation between regulator and regulatee—with limited public involvement—is established, then it simply continues and becomes closer over the years.

At the same time, politicians tend to lose interest in the agency. They feel that the problem has been solved by the mere creation of the agency and would rather not become involved in the sometimes very antagonistic atmosphere that exists when specific decisions are made. This is more likely to happen in the United States, where agencies are truly independent of executive control, than in Canada, where there is some element of ministerial responsibility. However, there is some evidence that this occurs in Canada as well.[63]

According to Bernstein's theory, over time the agency becomes highly judicialized and totally unwilling to take any policy initiatives. When people making budgeting decisions see the organization in this state, they are likely to decrease the agency's budgetary allocation, thus driving away good employees and worsening the downward spiral. The organization can continue in this spiral almost indefinitely unless some crisis snaps it out of its lethargy. It simply no longer possesses the drive and initiative to regulate the industry effectively.

Following this theory, the outcome ultimately is that the regulatory agency in actuality protects the existing shape of the industry, meaning that it protects the existing company or companies in the industry from any rude shocks such as excessive competition. Further support for this thesis comes from the fact in 1991 regulated prices increased by 9.6 percent while nonregulated prices increased by 4.5 percent.[64] Ted Rogers, the president of the largest cable TV company in Canada and several related enterprises, said, "We are comfortable with regulation." He went on to say that without the CRTC, "I would feel naked." His regulated companies usually generate a return on investment of about 20 percent.[65]

This is a very complex issue that has been the subject of more anecdotal comment than serious testing. One serious review of environmental regulation suggests that agencies can go through stages in which they are somewhat captured by the industry. However, this can then provoke reaction on the part of other interests, which causes the agency to become more sympathetic to those other interests.[66]

Regulatory Agencies and Federalism

In recent years, regulatory agencies have made decisions that have had a substantial impact on federal-provincial relations. In some cases, decisions by federal regulatory agencies have allowed the federal government to intervene in provincial areas in a manner that ignored the concerns of provincial governments about both the content of decisions and the process by which the decisions were made.

Aside from their predictable opposition in principle to federal-led economic decision-making, there are three specific reasons for provincial concerns. The first is the now commonplace and widespread provincial criticism that federal economic policy making is unfairly discriminatory in favour of some regions and industries, at the expense of others. This argument has long been routinely invoked, not without some justification, in battles, for example, over transportation and energy policies.

Secondly, in the past three decades especially, provincial opposition to federal economic dominance has been based on doubts about the capacity of the federal government to perform effectively as an economic decision maker. Provinces are simply not prepared to accept that the federal government possesses greater competence than they as justification for it having more power or influence over economic decision making.[67]

The third reason relates to the use of the regulatory agency form and the fact that the "distinguishing feature of these agencies is their exceptionally high degree of independence within the federal parliamentary system."[68]

Schultz has described this sort of situation as being characterized by *regulatory agency independence* and *federal-provincial interdependence*.[69] Federal and provincial governments frequently enter into agreements to share authority in particular policy areas. However, regulatory agencies, asserting their independence of executive control, can take the position that they are not bound by such agreements. This is exactly what the CRTC did with regard to an agreement between the federal and Manitoba governments in the field of cable television.[70]

The federal government and the three prairie provinces have been feuding over telecommunications regulation in recent years. In the past, the federal government has regulated telecommunications in most of Canada, but each of the three prairie provinces has had its own telephone company that was not subject to federal regulation. This has been very important to these provinces partly because telecommunications have been a good source of revenue, but mostly because the companies have taken advantage of cross-subsidies to provide a high standard of relatively inexpensive service to rural areas. Politically, this is very important to these three provincial governments.

The federal government has now moved to create one regulatory regime for all Canada. This will also effectively create one market across the entire country for long-distance and other specialized services. The Minister of Communications has explained that there are very good economic and technological reasons for this regulatory regime.[71] The fact that it happens to benefit private companies located in central Canada is simply a coincidence.

The prairie provinces fear these moves for two reasons.[72] If the federal regulatory agency demands an end to the cross-subsidies, then rural rates could rise. However, the more serious problem would occur if the regulatory agency allowed the large (central Canada-dominated) companies such as Bell Canada and CN/CP Telecommunications to compete for long-distance and other services in the prairie provinces. For practical reasons, the smaller prairie companies would have no way of reciprocating by moving into Ontario and Quebec to compete against Bell Canada.

Sometimes the conflict is less direct, but it is no less significant. Both energy-producing and energy-consuming provinces have a real stake in certain decisions of the National Energy Board. Provincial governments feel that they should have some sort of special status in board hearings because they are the legitimate representatives of the people of their provinces. However, most regulatory agencies adopt the position that provincial governments have the same status as any other intervener.

It would be inappropriate to leave the impression that regulation always results in federal-provincial clashes. There are reported cases in which the presence of the federal and provincial governments in the same regulatory arena resulted in a complementary and mutually supportive arrangement,[73] but these cases seem to be fewer in number than the more contentious ones.

🏛 PROPOSALS FOR REFORM

These perceived problems with regulation have generated many proposals for changes in the regulatory process. The most important of these are discussed below.

Deregulation

Obviously, deregulation is the ultimate in regulatory reform. Canadian governments have tended not to use the word because it has become somewhat ideologically loaded by associations with Margaret Thatcher and Ronald Reagan. However, it is quite clear that successive federal governments and all provincial governments have become concerned with reducing the excesses of regulation. The current government's regulatory policy is an example of balancing a desire for reducing regulation with the need to maintain vigilance in some areas. When regulating, regulatory authorities must demonstrate the following points:

1. A problem of risk exists, federal government intervention is justified, and regulation is the best alternative.

2. Canadians are being consulted, and have an opportunity to participate in developing or modifying regulations and regulatory programs.

3. The benefits outweigh the costs to Canadians, their governments and businesses.

4. Adverse impacts on the capacity of the economy to generate wealth and employment are minimized and no unnecessary regulatory burden is imposed ...

5. Inter-governmental agreements are respected and full advantage is taken of opportunities to coordinate with other governments and agencies.

6. Systems are in place to manage regulatory programs effectively ...[74]

This sort of thinking is found in governments at all levels.[75] Thus, we seem to be moving in the direction of lessened regulation while steering clear of using the word deregulation. The general idea seems to be to introduce just enough procedural impediments to the establishment of new regulations that ministers will think twice about whether they really need a particular regulation.

However, the public's view of deregulation is decidedly ambivalent. In the abstract, everyone opposes regulation, associating it with excessive red tape, government intrusiveness, and so forth. However, in concrete cases, such as increases in telephone or cable-TV rates, the general public usually asks what a *Globe and Mail* headline asked in the wake of the spectacular failure of Bre-X: "Where Were the Regulators?"[76] Deregulation is attractive because it seems clear that there is too much regulation is some areas, but not everyone agrees on which fields should be deregulated.

Sunset Legislation

Sunset legislation has some of the same characteristics as deregulation. The basic idea is that regulatory agencies would be established for a certain period of time, and if they were unable to prove their worth over that period, they would be allowed to die.[77] This is a remedy for the frequently discussed phenomenon that a government agency seldom dies, even when its *raison d'être* seems to have passed. Under sunset legislation, the onus would be on the agency to prove its continued value.

Use Economic Incentives Instead of Command and Control

Regulations are usually concerned with attaining a particular objective, e.g., a safe workplace. However, in practice, many regulations involve command and control procedures that specify certain rules, e.g., detailed regulations about certain physical aspects of the workplace. This focus on rules rather than a specification of desired objectives can discourage the development of innovative ways of accomplishing the same objectives. It might be better to specify the objectives desired, impose severe penalties if they are not attained, and allow those most directly involved to decide on the best way to achieve the objective.

For example, instead of a government agency specifying detailed workplace safety rules and spending a great deal of time and money ensuring that the rules are followed, the government could impose severe penalties for organizations with a poor workplace safety record. This would reduce the cost to the government of policing the rules and allow employers and employees to work together to determine the best ways to improve safety in their particular environment.

There are cases of pollution being handled in a similar way. Some manufacturers have found it more economical to redesign their entire production process to limit the creation of pollution throughout the process. If these companies had been forced to install expensive equipment to treat the pollution at the end of their process, they might never have considered the alternative that turned out to be a more efficient way of dealing with the problem.[78]

Tabling Estimate of Costs and Benefits of Federal Regulations

The House Subcommittee on Regulations and Competitiveness recommended that the president of the Treasury Board produce a document annually that would list the costs and benefits of all federal regulations. This document would be tabled each year at the same time as the government's expenditure estimates, which would serve as a reminder that government regulation also imposes a cost on society.

The government did not respond to this recommendation when it responded to the committee's other recommendations.[79] Preparing a document of this kind would be very difficult. Many government regulations are geared to protecting the environment or saving lives. It would be very difficult to quantify these kinds of benefits.

More Consumer Involvement

The significance of greater consumer involvement in the regulatory process is clear, but there are so many specific proposals to accomplish this that it is impossible to cover more than a few of them here.[80] They are all designed to put the consumer on a more even footing with the producer.

Consumers' Associations. Among the associations representing Canadian consumers are the broad-based Consumers' Association of Canada and specific associations representing such groups as automobile owners and airline travellers. For reasons discussed earlier, these associations are usually weaker than the producers and producers' associations with which they must do battle. Therefore, it is sometimes suggested that the strength of these consumers' groups ought to be bolstered. The usual suggestions include an infusion of government funding, tax incentives, or some payments from the regulated industry.

Intervener Funding. Another proposal is that the government, the regulated industry, and/or its association should provide funding to all legitimate interveners in regulatory proceedings. Regulated industries point to the difficulties of controlling costs and of distinguishing legitimate from nuisance interveners.

The Agency as Advocate. The current legal situation of the agency makes it an impartial referee between the various interests before it. It has been proposed that the agency should instead be charged with defending the interests of the consumer. This proposal would weight the regulatory process in favour of the consumer, and so place the onus on the industry to prove the efficacy of its claim for higher rates or different service levels.

Better Accountability to Parliament

There is also a perceived need for better accountability to Parliament, which is the ultimate source of the authority of all regulatory agencies. The House of Commons Special Committee on Regulatory Reform has pointed out that

[t]he Standing Joint Committee on Regulations and other Statutory Instruments reviews regulations and other published statutory instruments using criteria that relate to the legality and propriety of the measures examined. There is, however, no analogous arrangement facilitating parliamentary examination of subordinate legislation from the point of view of policy or merit.[81]

The committee went on to recommend a considerably enhanced parliamentary committee system in which each of the standing committees would review the activities of regulatory agencies in its substantive area. Specifically, the committees would monitor the regulatory process in general, review the merits of specific regulations, and review the activities of the agency itself using the program evaluations prepared under the auspices of the Treasury Board Secretariat. These and other recommendations of the committee were all geared to improving the accountability of regulatory agencies to Parliament.

Resolving the Accountability-Autonomy Conundrum

Of course, there are broader questions about balancing accountability to the legislature and autonomy in making decisions. A number of different proposals have been made to resolve the apparent conflict between the need for accountability to political forces and the need for some autonomy from the vagaries of partisan politics.

Douglas G. Hartle has recommended that all agencies be designated as either *advisory agencies* or *decision-making agencies*.[82] The *advisory agencies* would emphasize accountability in that they would conduct research in their policy field and *advise* the government concerning new policy initiatives. These agencies would differ from operating departments in that they would have an element of independence in how they gathered evidence and prepared recommendations. They could hold public hearings and present their advice to the minister publicly. However, accountability would be emphasized with these kinds of agencies because the minister would be able to accept or reject the advice offered.

Decision-making agencies would emphasize autonomy. These agencies would be guided by government policy directives in making decisions on individual cases, but their decisions could not be overturned by politicians, except in unusual circumstances.

These classification schemes possess the virtues of simplicity and clarity. However, they might be too abstracted from the real world to be very useful. The accountability-autonomy conundrum simply reflects the love-hate relationship that many Canadians have with politicians. On the one hand, we mistrust politicians and fear that they will act for improper, self-serving motives; on the other hand, we sometimes see appeals to politicians as a way of escaping the tyranny of the bureaucracy. It might well be that there is no simple way out of this accountability-autonomy dilemma. The ideal arrangement might involve a continued balancing of the two to ensure both are present in appropriate levels in the decision-making process.

Policy Directives

One recommendation that would modify the current accountability regime suggests that cabinet should be able to issue policy directives to regulatory agencies.[83] Through this means, the government could convey its desires regarding particular policy areas to the regulatory agency before the agency made any specific decisions. This would allow the regulated industry, consumers, and other interested parties to know the rules of the game before they started to play. It would also improve accountability, because it would make it clear when the agency was acting at the request of the government and when it was making its own policy.

The fear about this proposal is that it would "enhance the power of those with greater access to cabinet, namely the large regulated firms and departmental officials."[84]

A More Flexible Decision Process

Traditionally, the economic kinds of regulatory agencies have borrowed some trappings from the courts in that they hear arguments concerning an issue, go away to discuss it, and return with a decision that is binding on all parties. There is no room for negotiation or compromise between the parties after the process has started.

There are many other more flexible and less formal and costly ways of arriving at decisions.[85] Agencies can provide *mediation and conciliation services* to the parties to help them arrive at their own decision. Since the matter at hand is rarely a private one between two parties but usually involves some broader public policy issue, the agency must retain the right to accept or reject an agreement made by these parties.

There are a number of other innovations that can improve the agency decision-making process. However, many agencies cannot take advantage of these because their enabling legislation or their own rules set out some very specific and sometimes cumbersome procedures. One way that agencies could deal with criticisms about the cumbersome nature of regulation is by streamlining their decision-making process.

An Increased Provincial Role in the Federal Regulatory Process

As mentioned earlier, one of the sore points with provincial governments is that their interests are sometimes very directly affected by the actions of federal regulatory agencies, yet they have no special status with those agencies. The federal government also experiences embarrassment in this area because it is sometimes unable to issue directives to its regulatory agencies, even in areas in which it has entered into an agreement with a province.[86]

One of the most radical remedies suggested is that there should be "joint regulatory mechanisms" involving the federal and provincial governments, or several provincial governments, as the case may be. This could be accomplished in a number of ways. One way would have existing regulatory agencies, federal or provincial, meet together to conduct a joint hearing and possibly even issue one joint decision.[87] Another alternative would be to have the two spheres of government work together to jointly regulate areas where they both have an interest. This would also benefit the regulated industry, which would be facing a single, coherent regulatory regime. The federal and Ontario governments have discussed the joint regulation of financial institutions.[88]

This system would pose some obvious practical problems, such as agreeing on common rules of procedures, not to mention the tension involved in working out a joint decision. This arrangement might be difficult at first, but over time the agencies would learn how to work with one another. Ontario already has a provision for several agencies within its jurisdiction to hold one consolidated hearing on a proposal.

"A second major variant would entail the power of appointment by one level of government of members of a regulatory agency established by another level."[89] This would produce some of the same tensions as the previous proposal, and it raises the difficult issue of which governments appoint how many members.

Another proposal is what has been called "political regulation." This "option involves a fully politicized model of regulation without recourse to independent authorities."[90] This would require cabinet or the minister to make decisions that are currently delegated to a regulatory agency. This is clearly not a panacea. Recent events make it clear that federal and provincial politicians have a great deal of difficulty arriving at agreements. However, it might be an improvement on the status quo because it would convert an odd trilateral relationship involving two (or more) politicians and a somewhat independent agency into a bilateral relationship. This simplified structure ought to make it easier to resolve problems.

Some of these proposals are radical and/or highly problematic, but the tensions caused by the existing system are so serious that some better arrangement must be found. The impact of regulatory agencies on federalism (and vice versa) is an area that bears watching over the next few years because federal-provincial relations could become extremely tense if federal regulatory agencies do not deal with provincial concerns in a sensitive manner.

🏛 CONCLUSION

The most common service delivery mechanisms used by governments are the operating department, the Crown corporation, and the regulatory agency. In this and the previous two chapters, these forms have been discussed and the reasons for choosing one to accomplish a particular objective have been considered. However, the story is not quite complete. There are a number of other methods of delivering government services, which fall under the very broad heading of alternative service delivery. These will be discussed in the next chapter.

NOTES

1. Karen Howlett and Janet McFarland, "Where Were the Regulators?" *The Globe and Mail*, 10 May 1997.
2. *Directions: Review of Ontario's Regulatory Agencies* (Toronto: Queen's Printer for Ontario, 1989), 2–4.
3. C. Lloyd Brown-John, *Canadian Regulatory Agencies* (Toronto: Butterworths, 1981), 35.
4. John C. Strick, *The Economics of Government Regulation*, 2nd ed. (Toronto: Thompson Educational Publishing, Inc., 1994), 8. (Emphasis added.) A further elaboration of this distinction is explained in: Stephen Brooks and Andrew Stritch, *Business and Government in Canada* (Scarborough, Ont.: Prentice-Hall Canada Inc., 1991), 334–37. See also: Economic Council of Canada, *Reforming Regulation* (Ottawa: Minister of Supply and Services Canada, 1981), 7.
5. "Regulatory Agencies and Accountability," a study prepared for the Royal Commission on Financial Management and Accountability, May 1978, unpublished manuscript, as referred to in Economic Council of Canada, *Responsible Regulation: An Interim Report* (Hull: Minister of Supply and Services Canada, 1979), 56. For a similar but slightly different list of functions, see Canada, Privy Council Office, *Submissions to the Royal Commission on Financial Management and Accountability* (Hull: Minister of Supply and Services Canada, 1978), 2–77 to 2–93.
6. An extensive discussion of the differences in these organizations is found in: *Directions*, ch. 3.
7. J.A. Corry, "Introduction: The Genesis and Nature of Boards," in John Willis, ed., *Canadian Boards at Work* (Toronto: Macmillan, 1941), xxxvi.
8. Economic Council of Canada, *Responsible Regulation: An Interim Report*, 56.
9. Roderick A. Macdonald, "Understanding Regulation by Regulations," in Ivan Bernier and Andrée Lajoie, eds., *Regulations, Crown Corporations and Administrative Tribunals* (Toronto: University of Toronto Press, 1985), 84–89.
10. A good discussion of the economic rationales for regulation is contained in Strick, *The Economics of Government Regulation*, ch. 2.
11. Economic Council of Canada, *Responsible Regulation: An Interim Report*, 46.
12. Donald N. Dewees, "The Role of Tort Law in Controlling Environmental Pollution," *Canadian Public Policy* 18, no. 4 (December 1992), 425–42.
13. G. Bruce Doern, "Introduction," in G. Bruce Doern, ed., *The Regulatory Process in Canada* (Toronto: Macmillan, 1978), 17–18.
14. This seeming contradiction has been the subject of two very insightful reviews: *Directions*, and Canadian Bar Association Task Force on the Independence of Federal Administrative Tribunals and Agencies in Canada, *The Independence of Federal Administrative Tribunals and Agencies in Canada* (Ottawa: The Canadian Bar Association, 1990).
15. Ross Howard, "Minister to Review Fatal Parole Rulings," *The Globe and Mail*, 5 May 1994.
16. Industry Canada, *Responsible Regulation: An Interim Report*, 57. (Emphasis in original; footnote omitted.) Reproduced with the permission of the Minister of Public Works and Government Services Canada, 1998.
17. Richard Schultz, "Regulatory Agencies and the Canadian Political System," in Kenneth Kernaghan, ed., *Public Administration in Canada: Selected Readings*, 4th ed. (Toronto: Methuen, 1982), 70–80.
18. S.C. 1996, c. 10.
19. R.S.C. 1985, c. A-15.
20. R.S.C. 1985, c. P-14.
21. R.S.C. 1985, c. 32 (4th supplement).
22. Macdonald, "Understanding Regulation by Regulations," 96.
23. The role of this committee will be discussed further in Chapter 15.
24. R.S.C. 1985, c. S–22, s. 19.

25. "Dam Exemption Illegal, MPs Say," *The Globe and Mail*, 24 May 1993.

26. David Johnson, "Regulatory Agencies and Accountability: An Ontario Perspective," *Canadian Public Administration* 34, no. 3 (autumn 1991), 428. Footnotes in original omitted.

27. D.J. Mullan, "Administrative Tribunals: Their Evolution in Canada from 1945 to 1984," in Bernier and Lajoie, eds., *Regulations, Crown Corporations and Administrative Tribunals*, 184; Canadian Bar Association Task Force ..., *The Independence of Federal Administrative Tribunals and Agencies in Canada*, 53.

28. These recent changes are described in: Donald C. MacDonald, "Ontario's Agencies, Boards, and Commissions Come of Age," *Canadian Public Administration* 36, no. 3 (fall 1993), 349–63.

29. Lucinda Vandervort, *Political Control of Independent Administrative Agencies* (Ottawa: Law Reform Commission of Canada, 1979), 12–13; a good discussion of this issue is found in: *Directions*, 9–74 ff.

30. This is the case with certain decisions of the National Energy Board. R.S.C. 1985, c. N–7, s. 52.

31. Harvey Enchin, "PC Backers Win Review of TV–Station Licences," *The Globe and Mail*, 13 November 1985.

32. Vandervort, *Political Control of Independent Administrative Agencies*, 35, 59–60.

33. For a good comparison of the two remedies see: *Directions*, 4–27, 8–104 ff., 9–67 ff.

34. Ibid., 4–9 ff.

35. Ross Howard, "Minister to Review Fatal Parole Rulings," *The Globe and Mail*, 5 May 1994.

36. Canadian Bar Association Task Force ..., *The Independence of Federal Administrative Tribunals ...*, ch. 3.

37. Brown-John, *Canadian Regulatory Agencies*, 118.

38. The role of the chairperson is discussed in: *Directions*, 8–69 ff.

39. Caroline Andrew and Rejean Pelletier, "The Regulators," in Doern, ed., *The Regulatory Process in Canada*, 150–52; Brown–John, *Canadian Regulatory Agencies*, 114–16.

40. Law Reform Commission of Canada, *Report on Independent Administrative Agencies: A Framework for Decision Making*, Report 26 (Ottawa: Law Reform Commission of Canada, 1985), 77.

41. For a discussion of this issue, see: *Directions*, 9–10 ff.

42. While this chapter deals with regulatory agencies, the regulation-making process is the same for both agencies and departments.

43. This process is described in more detail in: Treasury Board of Canada Secretariat, *Managing Regulation in Canada* (Ottawa: Minister of Supply and Services Canada, 1996), 9–12.

44. "Citizen's Code of Regulatory Fairness," reproduced in: House of Commons, Standing Committee on Finance, *Regulations and Competitiveness*, 107–8.

45. Treasury Board Secretariat, *RIAS Writer's Guide* (Ottawa: Minister of Supply and Services Canada, 1992), 3–4.

46. Ibid., 4.

47. Government of Canada—Canadian Manufacturers' Association, "News Release," 4 February 1994.

48. Natural justice is described in more detail in Chapter 18.

49. Brown-John, *Canadian Regulatory Agencies*, 143.

50. An excellent recent review of problems and reforms is contained in: David J. Mullan, "Administrative Tribunals: Their Evolution in Canada from 1945 to 1984," in Bernier and Lajoie, eds., *Regulations, Crown Corporations and Administrative Tribunals*, 155–201.

51. A good discussion of the nature of some of these costs is contained in Economic Council of Canada, *Responsible Regulation: An Interim Report*, 34–38.

52. D.W. Gillen, T.H. Oum, and M.W. Tretheway, "Privatization of Air Canada: Why It Is Necessary in a Deregulated Environment," *Canadian Public Policy* 15, no. 3 (September 1989), 285–99; Edwin H. Neave, "Canada's Approach to Financial Regulation," *Canadian Public Policy* 15, no. 1 (March 1989), 1–11.

53. Gillen, Oum, and Tretheway, "Privatization of Air Canada," 285–99.

54. House of Commons Standing Committee of Finance, *Regulations and Competitiveness*.

55. Treasury Board of Canada Secretariat, *Managing Regulation in Canada* (Ottawa: Minister of Supply and Services Canada, 1996), 10.

56 Ralph Heintzman, "Paper Tiger," *Saturday Night*, November 1988, 33. See also: Robert Fulford, "Promises, Promises," *Saturday Night*, July 1987, 5–7; "CBC Program Cuts 'Dismaying' Says Author of Task Force Report," *The Globe and Mail*, 5 March 1987.

57. William F. Sinclair, "Controlling Effluent Discharges from Canadian Pulp and Paper Manufacturers," *Canadian Public Policy* 17, no. 1 (March 1991), 86–105.

58. Richard Schultz, "Regulation and Public Administration," in Kenneth Kernaghan, ed., *Canadian Public Administration: Discipline and Profession* (Toronto: Butterworths, 1983), 209.

59. Ibid.

60. Anthony Downs, *An Economic Theory of Democracy* (New York: Harper & Row, 1957), ch. 13, esp. 254 ff; Michael J. Trebilcock et al., *The Choice of Governing Instrument* (Ottawa: Minister of Supply and Services Canada, 1982), 7–10.

61. There is an alternative interpretation of how this close relationship between regulator and regulatee develops. See: Brooks and Stritch, *Business and Government in Canada* (Scarborough, Ont,: Prentice-Hall Canada, Inc.), 343–46.

62. Marver H. Bernstein, *Regulating Business by Independent Commission* (Princeton, N.J.: Princeton University Press, 1955), ch. 3.

63. W.H.N. Hull, "Captive or Victim: The Board of Broadcast Governors and Bernstein's Law, 1958–68," *Canadian Public Administration* 26 (winter 1983): 560.

64. Alan Freeman, "Regulated Prices Soared in 1991," *The Globe and Mail*, 17 April 1992.

65. Brenda Daglish, "The King of Cable," *Maclean's*, 22 March 1993, 34.

66. Mark Winfield, "The Ultimate Horizontal Issue: The Environmental Issue: The Environmental Policy Experiences of Alberta and Ontario, 1971–1993," *Canadian Journal of Political Science* 27, no. 1 (March 1994), 129–152.

67. Richard Schultz and Alan Alexandroff, *Economic Regulation and the Federal System* (Toronto: University of Toronto Press, 1985), 29. Reprinted by permission of the University of Toronto Press in cooperation with the Royal Commission on the Economic Union and Development Prospects for Canada and the Canadian Publishing Centre, Supply and Services Canada.

68. Ibid., 30.

69. Richard Schultz, "The Regulatory Process and Federal-Provincial Relations," in Doern, ed., *The Regulatory Process in Canada*, 128–31 and passim.

70. Vandervort, *Political Control of Independent Administrative Agencies*, 40–42.

71. "Debalkanizing Telecom," *The Globe and Mail*, 11 November 1989.

72. "Federal Phone Takeover Infuriates 3 Provinces," *Toronto Star*, 20 October 1989.

73. Peter N. Nemetz, "The Fisheries Act and Federal-Provincial Environmental Regulation: Duplication or Complementarity?" *Canadian Public Administration* 29, no. 3 (fall 1986): 401–24.

74. Government of Canada, *Federal Regulatory Plan 1997* (Minister of Public Works and Government Services, 1996), vii.

75. James Rusk, "Ontario Fights Red Tape with Control on Regulations," *The Globe and Mail*, 18 July 1996.

76. Karen Howlett and Janet McFarland, "Where Were the Regulators?"

77. Economic Council of Canada, *Responsible Regulation: An Interim Report*, 78–81.

78. Standing Committee on Finance, *Regulations and Competitiveness*, 25–6, 32–3.
79. Treasury Board of Canada Secretariat, *Responsive Regulation in Canada* (Highlights) (Ottawa: Minister of Supply and Services Canada, 1993).
80. This issue is treated very well in: Liora Salter, "Capture or Co-management: Democracy and Accountability in Regulatory Agencies," in Gregory Albo, David Langille, and Leo Panitch, eds., *A Different Kind of State? Popular Power and Democratic Administration* (Toronto: Oxford University Press, 1993), 87–100.
81. Canada, House of Commons, Special Committee on Regulatory Reform, *Report* (Ottawa: Minister of Supply and Services, 1981), 24.
82. Douglas G. Hartle, *Public Policy Decision Making and Regulation* (Toronto: Institute for Research on Public Policy, 1979), 131–33.
83. Canada, House of Commons, Special Committee on Regulatory Reform, *Report*, 15–17.
84. Richard Schultz, "Regulatory Agencies," in Michael S. Whittington and Glen Williams, eds., *Canadian Politics in the 1990s*, 3rd ed. (Scarborough, Ont.: Nelson Canada, 1990), 475.
85. These are considered in more detail in: *Directions*, 9–13 ff.
86. Vandervort, *Political Control of Independent Administrative Agencies*, 91–92.
87. Schultz and Alexandroff, *Economic Regulation and the Federal System*, 149.
88. John Partridge, "Ontario, Ottawa Eye Regulatory Union," *The Globe and Mail*, 16 February 1993.
89. Schultz and Alexandroff, *Economic Regulation and the Federal System*, 149. (Footnote omitted.)
90. Ibid., 152.

BIBLIOGRAPHY

Bernier, Ivan, and Andrée Lajoie, eds. *Regulations, Crown Corporations and Administrative Tribunals*. Research study for the Royal Commission on the Economic Union and Development Prospects for Canada. Vol. 48. Toronto: University of Toronto Press, 1985.

Bernstein, Marver H. *Regulating Business by Independent Commission*. Princeton, N.J.: Princeton University Press, 1955.

Brooks, Stephen, and Andrew Stritch. *Business and Government in Canada*. Scarborough, Ont.: Prentice-Hall Canada Inc., 1991.

Brown-John, C. Lloyd. *Canadian Regulatory Agencies*. Toronto: Butterworths, 1981.

Canada. House of Commons. Special Committee on Regulatory Reform. *Report*. Ottawa: Minister of Supply and Services Canada, 1981.

Canada. Office of Privatization and Regulatory Affairs. *Regulatory Reform: Making It Work*. Ottawa: The Office of Privatization and Regulatory Affairs, 1988.

_____. *Regulatory Reform Strategy*. n.d.

Canada. Office of Regulatory Reform. *Report on Regulatory Reform*. Various issues.

Canada. Privy Council Office. *Submissions to the Royal Commission on Financial Management and Accountability*. Ottawa: Minister of Supply and Services Canada, 1978.

Canada. Senate and House of Commons. Standing Joint Committee on Regulations and Other Statutory Instruments. *Minutes and Proceedings*, no. 1, 16 February 1984.

Canadian Bar Association Task Force on the Independence of Federal Administrative Tribunals and Agencies in Canada. *The Independence of Federal Administrative Tribunals and Agencies in Canada*. Ottawa: The Canadian Bar Association, 1990.

Dewees, Donald N. "The Role of Tort Law in Controlling Environmental Pollution." *Canadian Public Policy* 18, no. 4 (December 1992), 425–42.

Directions: Review of Ontario's Regulatory Agencies. Toronto: Queen's Printer for Ontario, 1989.

Doern, G. Bruce, ed. *The Regulatory Process in Canada*. Toronto: Macmillan, 1978.

Economic Council of Canada. *Responsible Regulation: An Interim Report.* Hull: Minister of Supply and Services Canada, 1979.

———. *Reforming Regulation.* Ottawa: Minister of Supply and Services Canada, 1981.

Gillen, David W., Tae H. Oum, and Michael W. Tretheway. "Privatization of Air Canada: Why It Is Necessary in a Deregulated Environment." *Canadian Public Policy* 15, no. 3 (September 1989), 285–99.

Hartle, Douglas G. *Public Policy Decision Making and Regulation.* Toronto: Institute for Research on Public Policy, 1979.

Hull, W.H.N. "Captive or Victim: The Board of Broadcast Governors and Bernstein's Law, 1958–68." *Canadian Public Administration* 26 (winter 1983): 544–62.

Johnson, David. "Regulatory Agencies and Accountability: An Ontario Perspective." *Canadian Public Administration* 34, no. 3 (autumn 1991), 417–34.

Law Reform Commission of Canada. *Report on Independent Administrative Agencies: A Framework for Decision Making,* Report 26. Ottawa: Law Reform Commission of Canada, 1985.

MacDonald, Donald C. "Ontario's Agencies, Boards, and Commissions Come of Age." *Canadian Public Administration* 36, no. 3 (fall 1993), 349–63.

Neave, Edwin H. "Canada's Approach to Financial Regulation." *Canadian Public Policy* 15, no. 1 (March 1989), 1–11.

Nemetz, Peter N. "The Fisheries Act and Federal-Provincial Environmental Regulation: Duplication or Complementarity?" *Canadian Public Administration* 29, no. 3 (fall 1986): 401–24.

Ontario. Committee on Government Productivity. *Report Number Nine* (1973).

Reschenthaler, Gil, Bill Stanbury, and Fred Thompson. "Whatever Happened to Deregulation?" *Policy Options* (May–June 1982): 36–42.

Salter, Liora. "Capture or Co-management: Democracy and Accountability in Regulatory Agencies." In Gregory Albo, David Langille, and Leo Panitch, eds., *A Different Kind of State? Popular Power and Democratic Administration* Toronto: Oxford University Press, 1993, 87–100.

Schultz, Richard J. *Federalism and the Regulatory Process.* Montreal: Institute for Research on Public Policy, 1979.

———. *Federalism, Bureaucracy, and Public Policy: The Politics of Highway Transportation Regulation.* Montreal: McGill-Queen's University Press, 1980.

———. "Regulation and Public Administration." In Kenneth Kernaghan, ed., *Canadian Public Administration: Discipline and Profession,* 196–210. Toronto: Butterworths, 1983.

———. "Regulatory Agencies." In Michael S. Whittington and Glen Williams, eds., *Canadian Politics in the 1990s,* 3rd ed. Scarborough, Ont.: Nelson Canada, 1990, 468–80.

Schultz, Richard, and Alan Alexandroff. *Economic Regulation and the Federal System.* Toronto: University of Toronto Press, 1985.

Sinclair, William F. "Controlling Effluent Discharges from Canadian Pulp and Paper Manufacturers." *Canadian Public Policy* 17, no. 1 (March 1991), 86–105.

Strick, John C. *The Economics of Government Regulation.* 2nd ed. Toronto: Thompson Educational Publishing, Inc., 1994.

Treasury Board of Canada Secretariat. *The Federal Regulatory Process: An Interim Procedures Manual for Departments and Agencies 1991.*

———. *How Regulators Regulate.* Ottawa: Minister of Supply and Services Canada, 1992.

———. *RIAS Writer's Guide.* Ottawa: Minister of Supply and Services Canada, 1992.

———. *Responsive Regulation in Canada* (Highlights). Ottawa: Minister of Supply and Services Canada, 1993.

Treasury Board Secretariat. *Federal Regulatory Plan 1994.* Ottawa: Minister of Supply and Services, 1993.

———. *Managing Regulation in Canada.* Ottawa: Minister of Supply and Services Canada, 1996.

Trebilcock, Michael J., Douglas G. Hartle, J. Robert Pritchard, and Donald N. Dewees. *The Choice of Governing Instrument.* Ottawa: Minister of Supply and Services Canada, 1982.

Tupper, Allan, and G. Bruce Doern, eds. *Public Corporations and Public Policy in Canada.* Montreal: The Institute for Research on Public Policy, 1981.

Vandervort, Lucinda. *Political Control of Independent Administrative Agencies.* Ottawa: Law Reform Commission of Canada, 1979.

Willis, John, ed. *Canadian Boards at Work.* Toronto: Macmillan, 1941.

11

Alternative Service Delivery

After a long meeting, Jean walks by Michelle's desk, and the following conversation takes place.

Michelle: "How are things, this morning?"

Jean: Not so great. It looks like we're going to have to cancel that new program that I was involved in starting last year.

Michelle: That's too bad. You were very keen on that program and it served such a needy group. What's the problem?

Jean: Well, first it's the budget crunch. We've been hit with more reductions, and it's clear that some programs are going to have to go.

Michelle: Yeah, sure. That's happening everywhere, but why this program?

Jean: The deputy says that she isn't certain that the people most affected by it are really interested in it. I know that's not true. Every time I talk to the head of their group, he tells me how much they need this program, but I don't know how to convey that to the deputy.

Michelle: Have you considered entering into a partnership with the group?

Jean: What do you mean by a partnership? How would that solve my problem?

Michelle: You enter into a legal agreement with the group which requires them to provide some funding and handle the administration of the program while you provide the rest of the funding. It reduces your cost of the program, and it will show the deputy that these people are really committed to the program.

Jean: Well, I don't know. You mean we would let some outside organization run a government program and spend government money. Sounds kind of scary to me. What if they do something wrong and it embarrasses the government?

Michelle: You're right to be concerned. That certainly can happen. You'll have to draw up a proper legal agreement stating what commitments they're making, then you will have to monitor the administration of the program on a regular basis. It will require some effort on your part, but it solves a number of problems.

Partnerships are one of the innovations which governments are using to deliver services. The previous three chapters discussed three traditional types of organizations which are used by governments for service delivery. Until a few years ago, this was the end of the story about service delivery—virtually all services fit into one of these three moulds and were delivered by one of these three entities. However, in recent years, governments have adopted more flexible mechanisms in the delivery of services. Figure 11.1 identifies a very broad range of program delivery alternatives. It is likely that even this list is not complete.

Figure 11.1 explores different mechanisms along three dimensions. One is the distinction between the public sector and the private sector. The significance of this dimension is that it shows that private sector organizations have a role in the delivery of government services through mechanisms like contracting out and partnering, which will be discussed in this chapter.

The second dimension measures the extent of federal government control of the delivery mechanism. The newer approaches to service delivery do not require the government to control delivery completely. There is a recognition that partnerships with provincial and municipal governments and community enterprises, for example, will require that the federal government relax some of its direct control over a service and give the partner some influence in how the service is provided.

Figure 11.1
OPPORTUNITIES FOR PROGRAM DELIVERY ALTERNATIVES

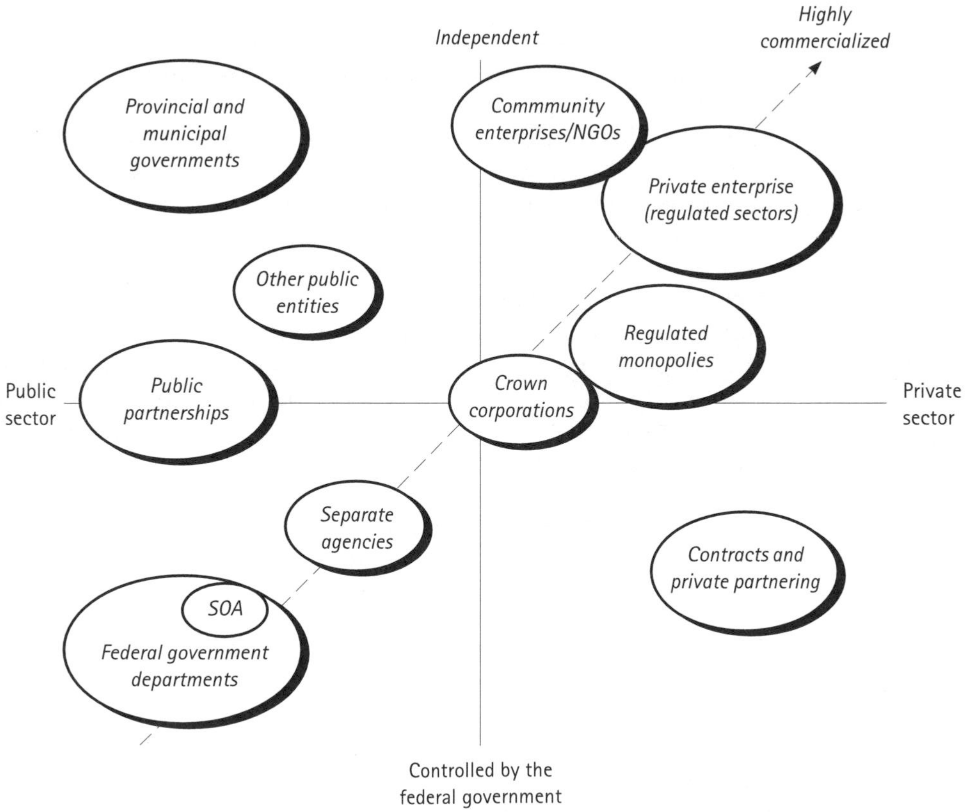

Source: Treasury Board of Canada Secretariat, Framework for Alternative Program Delivery. Reproduced with the permission of the Minister of Public Works and Government Services Canada, 1998.

The third dimension illustrated on the chart is the level of commercialization. This refers to the extent to which the organization makes a profit by selling its goods or services. One of the changes we have seen in recent years is that more services that the government formerly provided for free are now paid for by the user. Of course, no service is really free; we pay for all government services through our taxes. The increasing level of commercialization means that the user is being asked to pay for the service rather than charging the general taxpayer.

The lower-left quadrant consists of the traditional kinds of government organizations, although there are some innovations in this area. For example, this chapter will discuss SOAs (special operating agencies) and separate agencies. Crown corporations are placed to span the public and private sectors and also to be somewhat, but not totally, removed from government control.

The other three quadrants identify methods of service delivery that were not previously viewed as significant. For example, in the upper-left quadrant are provincial and municipal governments and other public bodies that do not fit neatly into one level of government. Some of these entities have been around longer than the federal government, but the federal government now recognizes that the three spheres of government and the other public bodies could cooperate in the delivery of services.

The upper-right quadrant contains a number of nongovernmental organizations that are separate from, but somehow controlled by, government. Good examples would be cable TV (regulated monopolies), airlines (regulated sector), and community development corporations (community enterprises). These are autonomous entities, but they all have a particular relationship with government, which means that they are involved in delivering a public service.

The lower-right quadrant identifies cases in which governments and private sector organizations have partnership or contractual relationships, which allow a sharing of responsibilities between government and nongovernmental entities.

This chapter will focus on those items in Figure 11.1 that can be grouped under the very broad heading of alternative service delivery (ASD)—a phrase with a number of different meanings. The assertion that governments are slow to espouse new ideas might be correct, but when governments seized upon the idea of ASD, they did so with a vengeance. This chapter is not meant to be comprehensive. There are so many examples of ASD being developed everyday that there can be no comprehensive catalogue. The purpose of this chapter is to provide a flavour of the concept of ASD and address some of the political issues it raises.

The first section will provide a definition of the term ASD, followed by a discussion of some of the reasons why governments have chosen to employ ASD mechanisms. The next section will provide a selective discussion of some ASD approaches. The final section of the chapter will raise some of the potential problems in the use of ASD mechanisms.

🏛 DEFINITION

The origin of the consideration of ASD as a separate entity or topic of discussion is frequently dated from the landmark book with the portentious title

Reinventing Government, by David Osborne and Ted Gaebler,[1] although some of these mechanisms have fairly lengthy histories. What has happened recently is that we have developed a name for something that many governments, particularly local governments, have been doing for many years.

Osborne and Gaebler make the distinction between "steering" and "rowing," and argue that the role of government should be to steer society. However, governments do not have to row in order to steer. In fact, the authors feel that government's excessive allocation of resources to rowing has inhibited its ability to steer. They suggest that governments would be able to steer better if they concentrated on steering and allowed others to row. So a simple definition of ASD might be the choice of who should row and how they should row.

The steering and rowing analogy is another way of suggesting the separation of the policy/advice functions from the operations function. Many of the ASD initiatives are based on the separation of policy making from policy execution. As will be discussed later, this is both the strength and the weakness of ASD. Too much concern about policy making complicates service delivery. For example, a policy prescription that every service must be provided equally in all regions of the country will increase the cost of delivering the service. However, a focus on delivery without due regard to political issues is also a recipe for disaster. Governments must make sure that both steering and rowing are done properly, and ASD is one way of balancing those two functions.

Osborne and Gaebler do not suggest that governments should never row; there might be situations in which governments are uniquely situated to row. However, in the past, governments have been too quick to assume that steering and rowing are always coupled. Osborne and Gaebler suggest that governments reconsider that mode of thinking.

There are many definitions of ASD because it is a new term that covers a broad variety of activities, but a good working definition is.

> a creative and dynamic process of public sector restructuring that improves the delivery of services to clients by sharing governance functions with individuals, community groups and other government entities.[2]

The same authors go on to say:

> ASD approaches provide a toolbox from which governments can tailor various options to meet their own prevailing needs and demands. ASD is a dynamic spectrum of delivery options that challenge hierarchical public service structures and allow public servants the flexibility to adapt to their future environment.[3]

The definition emphasizes that ASD is "a creative and dynamic process." The traditional approach was that government chose the "one best way" to deliver a service (through an operating department, Crown corporation, or regulatory agency) when a policy was created and stayed with that mechanism for the indefinite future. ASD suggests that there is no "one best way" of delivering a service. The best approach is to consider service delivery as a "toolbox from which governments can tailor various options" to meet the needs of a particular set of circumstances.[4] As those circumstances (e.g., technology of service delivery, characteristics of service users) change, different ASD mechanisms might be employed.

The next part of the definition refers to "public sector restructuring." It is important to understand that ASD is not a minor adjustment in approach, such as a restructuring of field offices. ASD constitutes a form of "sharing governance functions with individuals, community groups and other government entities." Thus, it gives other groups some involvement in the governing process, at least at the level of rowing.

One of the common features found in most ASD arrangements is some combination of contractual arrangements, business plans, and performance measures. Basically, this arrangement allows the agency to operate free from onerous day-to-day controls as long as it complies with the terms of its contract, operates according to the business plan prepared in advance, and meets the performance measures agreed to. All of the ASD mechanisms discussed below involve one or all of these features. It is a way of ensuring that the minister can still maintain an appropriate level of accountability.[5]

🏛 CITIZEN OR CUSTOMER?

One of the issues that ASD has aroused is how to refer to people who use these services. Some of the initiatives emphasizing service quality come from the private sector, so the word "customer" is naturally a part of their vocabulary. The term customer also emphasizes the direct relationship between the service provider and the service user, and the similarity in method of service provision between private and public sector organizations.

However, many people have objected strongly to the use of the word customer to refer to citizens.

> I am not a mere customer of my government, thank you. I expect something more than arm's length trading and something less than the encouragement to consume ... But, most important, I am a *citizen*, with rights that go far beyond those of customers or even clients.[6]

One basic difference between the two terms is that citizenship confers certain rights with regard to receipt of a service. This means that governments have certain obligations to their citizens that private sector organizations do not have with regard to their customers. As a customer, you can choose not to use a service, but you have no right to tell the service provider how the service should be provided, and the provider has no obligation to be accountable to customers.

The clerk of the Privy Council put the issue very succinctly in her annual report to the prime minister. She pointed out

> the importance of the role of citizens well beyond their role as customers and clients. Citizens have a rich and profound relationship to their governments as equal bearers of rights and duties in a democratic setting. The relationship bears no resemblance to that which exists between consumers and enterprises in the private sector.[7]

The strength of people's reaction to the word customer stems from the fact that its use is seen as putting citizens at arm's length from government and denying that government must be accountable to its citizens. In this book we will generally use the word citizen or the more general and neutral "service user." The word customer will be used when it is the most appropriate word to describe a certain situation.

🏛 ORIGINS OF ASD

Proponents of ASD arrive at their positions from a number of different directions. From the right-wing anti-government perspective, ASD is a way of reducing the size and scope of government to make society a better place. For the left-wing critic of how government deals with some of its more disadvantaged citizens, ASD is a way of wresting control of service delivery from an unfeeling bureaucracy. For those with a more middle-of-the-road, pragmatic bent, ASD is a way of going beyond the knee-jerk attitude that government action is the best solution to every problem to considering a whole range of tools for solving a problem. Therefore, it should not be surprising that a number of seemingly mutually contradictory arguments have been made in favour of ASD.

Improving Service Quality by Making Government More Citizen-Centred

By now it is a cliché that people are losing confidence in society's major institutions. For some people, this means large corporations generally, and banks specifically; for others, it means organized religions; for almost everyone, it means governments. Governments have long been the organizations that people love to hate, but the recent disaffection with large institutions has had a major impact on governments.

Governments have responded by attempting to restore public confidence in their ability to deliver services. In the past, service-delivery issues have frequently revolved around "turf wars," i.e., disputes between different governments or even within governments over who will deliver a service. The needs of citizens have too often been the last consideration in service delivery.

ASD should begin by asking: "What is the best way to serve the interests of citizens?" All those other inter- and intragovernmental and labour-management issues should become subsidiary to that most important question.

Reduction in Size and Scope of Government

One of the most frequent arguments heard in favour of ASD is that it will reduce government spending, reduce the deficit, and improve the quality of service delivery. Some examples of ASD involve restructuring within government to provide the service better at lower cost. This will occur if governments restructure to rise above the turf wars and focus on the quality of service delivery.

ASD also involves giving private sector and nonprofit sector organizations a greater role in service delivery. This will automatically reduce the size of government by hiving off certain responsibilities. Whether this action will result in greater efficiency depends on how efficient the service-delivery organization is.

Some of these arguments for ASD are based on a blind faith that private sector, or at least nongovernmental, delivery mechanisms will always be superior to governmental ones. A later section of this chapter will address this somewhat complex issue, but it is clear that many people see the reduction in the size of government as a positive goal in and of itself.

Flexibility in Service Delivery

Related to the idea of reducing the cost of service delivery is a desire to increase the flexibility in how services are delivered. One of the problems hampering government in service delivery is an excessive emphasis on process control rather than on achievement of results. Because of the large size of most government organizations and the need to maintain ministerial responsibility, there can be excessive amounts of red tape to ensure that rules are honoured. These rules are important to ensure prudence and probity and to prevent mistakes and embarrassment, but they can also sometimes get in the way of good service delivery.[8]

Ideally, governments should be able to adjust their operation and shed the unnecessary red tape, but there are some valid reasons why government organizations will always put more emphasis on process control than will smaller, more flexible organizations. To get around this emphasis, it might be useful to use other agents for the delivery of certain services. For example, governments have been notoriously slow to respond to new issues because inflexibilities in budgeting systems and staffing rules prevent existing organizations from moving into new areas. In these kinds of situations, it might be better for governments to provide grants to organizations that are already working in the field than to try to establish a new government organization.

Motivating Employees

One of the major inflexibilities in government administration is the human resource management system. It can be very difficult for governments to move employees around to meet changing demands or to reward or penalize employees based on their performance. These are valuable safeguards for protecting the rights of employees, but they can also introduce rigidities that make it difficult to respond to the needs of citizens.

Private sector and other nongovernmental organizations usually have the flexibility to redeploy employees more quickly and to reward employees more directly for a job well done. For this reason, many people would prefer to work for these types of organizations. They feel a greater sense of accomplishment from being able to get beyond the red tape and meet the needs of citizens directly.

Involvement of Users in Service Delivery

The presence of nongovernmental organizations provides a way of involving users and others who are directly affected by a service in its provision. The traditional governmental approach is based on a concept of ministerial responsibility that emphasizes top-down, hierarchical decision making, with users on the receiving end of decisions made in capital cities.

ASD mechanisms can bring users directly into the decision-making process to ensure that services are provided in ways that are more directly responsive to their needs. There are many examples of sport and recreation clubs taking over activities previously run by governments, and providing them in a more responsive manner at a lower cost.

The involvement of users and others can be particularly helpful in dealing with what have been called "wicked" problems—"problems flowing from issues in which goals either are not known or are ambiguous, *and* in which the means-ends relationships are uncertain and poorly understood."[9] Thus, users will have an idea of what is wrong with the existing situation, but they cannot foresee exactly what needs to be done to change it. Nongovernmental organizations have more flexibility to experiment with different approaches. They can start and stop initiatives fairly quickly without going through a long chain of command.

🏛 EXAMPLES OF ALTERNATIVE SERVICE-DELIVERY MECHANISMS

This section will discuss some of the many ASD mechanisms that governments are beginning to employ.

Restructuring within Governments

There is sometimes a sense that ASDs must involve a radical change in delivery method, usually involving several other organizations. In fact, some very important and positive changes in service delivery have been made by simply restructuring the operation of government departments.

Better Cooperation Between Departments: Breaking Down Silos. Members of the public are frequently angered when they hear about several departments being engaged in very similar activities, seemingly duplicating work or working at cross-purposes. Citizens are also frustrated when they must wander through myriad government channels with little assistance to obtain multiple approvals to engage in what seems like a fairly simple activity.

This is viewed as the silo approach to management and service delivery. Departments operate in their own vertical silos with no horizontal interaction. The idea is that individual government departments are each acting in their own interest, and it is up to the individual citizen to figure out how to coordinate the requirements of different departments.

One of the goals of ASD is to break down those silos and increase horizontal interaction among departments. *Horizontality* is one of the key words of

ASD. It refers to the concept of encouraging interaction among departments, across levels of government, and even between government and nongovernment organizations. In the words of the secretary of the Treasury Board:

> From our clients' perspective, problems don't organize neatly by department or jurisdiction. Our clients are forcing us to work across disciplines, across functions and across jurisdictions and are therefore forcing us to think in terms of larger portfolios. We are learning to align our actions in a way that makes sense to those we serve.[10]

One of the most widely discussed initiatives in this area is the Canadian Food Inspection Agency (CFIA). This agency combines the food inspection and quarantine services previously provided by three federal departments (agriculture and agri-food, health, and fisheries and oceans) into one agency. It is estimated that it will save the federal government $44 million annually by 1999.[11] It will also improve relations with industry because regulatees will no longer have to deal with a succession of several federal inspectors each looking at a different aspect of their operations. Because this is a separate agency rather than a department of the federal government, it allows for provincial and even municipal governments to become involved in its operations as well, which will streamline the entire food inspection system even more.

A second example is a memorandum of understanding entered into by the four federal government departments involved in natural resources (agriculture and agri-food, environment, fisheries and oceans, and natural resources). This is an agreement "to address issues of common concern that are either current or beginning to emerge."[12] This has resulted in the establishment of program-based working groups (cutting across departmental lines) to address such issues as climate change and variability, metals in the environment, ecosystem effects of UV-B radiation, and coastal zone management.

Creation of Agencies. One innovation in ASD is the creation of agencies that are not under the same direct ministerial control as operating departments. Figure 11.2 shows a continuum of different types of government organizations based on the level of ministerial control exercised over the organization. Agencies still have a high level of ministerial control, but they are removed from operating departments.

The Canadian Food Inspection Agency discussed above is one example of an agency; another is the new Canada Customs and Revenue Agency. It will be responsible for the collection of most federal taxes such as customs duties, income taxes, and the goods and services tax. This agency will still be responsible to the minister with regard to policy matters. However, it will be managed by a board of directors with provincial representation, which will allow it to better coordinate its involvement with provincial governments. Agency status also allows it to establish its own administrative policies in such areas as human resource and financial management.

Figure 11.2
MINISTERIAL ACCOUNTABILITY AND INVOLVEMENT

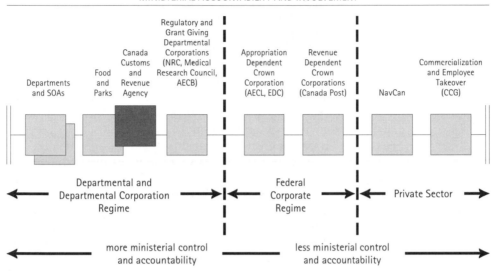

Source: "Canada Customs and Revenue Agency," Presentation to the Canadian Centre for Management Development University Seminar (7 May 1998).

Use of New Technology. There are many examples of departments using computer and communications technology to deliver services more efficiently. This will eventually allow people to access many government services from their own homes, but it currently provides for relatively cheap service delivery points in many shopping centres and other public places that are much more accessible than government offices.

Human Resources Development Canada has about 5000 computer kiosks similar to the ATMs used for banking to provide information on job opportunities.[13] Similar computer access points are also used in some provinces to deliver information about government services or even renewal of drivers' licences.

In 1997, approximately 4.8 million individuals chose to "e-file" their income tax return. Electronic filing means that the return is processed in eleven days instead of twenty-one.[14] It also reduces the labour cost to the department. Revenue Canada has an overflow call centre so that calls to local offices, which would have formerly received a busy signal, are automatically diverted to the central number and answered promptly.[15]

User Charges. Many organizations that used to provide free services are charging user fees to ensure that service users pay at least a portion of the cost. The introduction of user charges has several goals.

One goal is simply to raise some revenue for government to offset the increasing cost of providing these services. As citizens have become more concerned about increasing taxes, governments have sought ways of broadening their revenue base, one of which is the imposition of user charges.

However, user charges are also imposed to try to change users' behaviour or at least make them reconsider their behaviour. Many municipalities are now imposing charges for garbage collection. Usually, residents are entitled to put out a certain number of bags for free, but must pay a per-bag charge for additional bags. This raises revenue to offset the rapidly increasing cost of operating landfill sites, but the main purpose of these charges is to discourage residents from creating excess garbage and encourage them to reduce, reuse, and recycle.

User charges are also a way of ensuring that those who benefit from a service pay for its full cost and do not transfer this cost to other taxpayers. If someone can afford to go on an international vacation, why shouldn't he or she pay the full cost of the passport? Why should 100 percent of Canadian taxpayers subsidize the cost of airports when only 20 percent of the population will travel by air in any year? If a homeowner can afford to build an addition onto his or her home, why shouldn't he or she have to pay the full cost associated with issuing the building permit and inspecting the work?

The ability to pay is one of the major questions that makes user charges a very hot political issue. The cases of the airline traveller or wealthy homeowner are fairly straightforward, but user charges for health services or for children to use recreational facilities are much more contentious.

Colocation.   One of the least radical changes is colocation, but it can be very effective. This involves the location of a number of related departments in the same building or even the same suite of offices. It allows service users to move easily from one service to another without the time and expense of travelling between departments in different parts of town to handle a variety of related transactions.

Ideally, the colocation of offices would cross governmental boundaries and even extend to nongovernmental groups, so that a person could go to one grouping of offices and obtain services related to federal employment insurance, provincial retraining programs, municipal employment opportunities, and a community-based job search assistance program. While cost saving is not the main purpose of colocation, it could well occur if departments are able to share some common services such as office equipment. Prince Edward Island has had several Regional Service Centres for many years, which provide colocation of provincial and some federal services.[16] Service New Brunswick is a similar initiative that provides a broad range of services and is open Thursday and Friday evenings and Saturday morning.

Single Window.   In colocation the different organizations are located close together but still maintain their separate identities in distinct offices. The single window approach provides seamless service to users across several departments or even levels of government. Ideally, people would not even be aware that they were dealing with different organizations. The organizations would coordinate the services among themselves rather than expecting the service users to figure it out.

An example is the federal-provincial business centres operating in most provinces. Traditionally, people wanting to start new businesses have had to trek to several government offices to meet their obligations with regard to federal income tax, federal employment insurance, provincial sales tax, provincial workers' compensation, and various kinds of municipal business licences. The federal government and most provinces have now established federal-provincial business centres[17] to streamline this process by providing a single window where people can obtain all the information they need about the requirements of various governments. In Vancouver, this centre "provides a seamless one-stop service for business information from 27 federal and 18 provincial agencies."[18]

At the provincial level, the British Columbia Agents have a very long history as a single-window service in rural areas and small towns. Table 11.1 provides a sample of some of the services that they provide. In addition, there is a tradition that the B.C. Agent will find the answer to any question regarding government, whether it is directly within the agent's area of responsibility or not.[19]

Table 11.1
SERVICES PROVIDED BY B.C. AGENTS

Air Brake Manuals	Gold Commissioner	Provincial Voters Lists
Birth Certificates	Hunting Licences	Senior Citizen Assistance
Dog Licences	Mining Claim Tags	Strike Vote Observer
Drivers Licences	Mobile Home Registry	Tourist Information
Fur Royalties	Ombudsman Complaints	Will Registration

Crown Corporations.   These are a fairly traditional method of hiving off certain government activities to an organization that will be flexible in responding to the needs of users. As discussed in Chapter 9, Crown corporations have come to be seen as more a part of the problem than a part of the solution, so they are now used less than in the past. The structure is still used but not in the conventional manner.

The newest federal Crown corporation, created in 1996, is the Canadian Race Relations Foundation. "Its purpose is to facilitate the exchange of information that would assist government in developing effective race relations policies and practices."[20]

Special Operating Agencies.   SOAs are a half-way house. They have more flexibility than operating departments but less autonomy than Crown corporations. They have a separate identity, but since they report to the deputy minister, they are accountable in the same way as other units of the department. They produce a clearly defined product, which is separable from the other services of the department, and they generate revenue. In many cases, they are self-funding, such as the Passport Office, which was one of the first SOAs. In most cases, they are expected to be more entrepreneurial than a standard department.

EXAMPLES OF SPECIAL OPERATING AGENCIES

Passport Office

Training and Development Canada

Canadian Grains Commission

Consulting and Audit Canada

Race Track Supervision

Indian Oil and Gas Canada

Transport Canada Training Institute

The rationale for SOA status is to improve the service delivery and cost-effectiveness of certain government services through increased management flexibility, in return for agreed-upon levels of performance and results.

The SOA model separates the policy role of the Minister and supporting bureaucrats from the managerial role of the SOA, usually under a Chief Executive Officer (CEO). An SOA differs from past reform movements and other innovative models in that it introduces *extensive structural and operational changes in the rules* aimed at moving the agency toward management practices more consistent with those of the private sector.[21]

The Audit Services Bureau of the Department of Supply and Services was once a fairly reactive common service agency, which performed financial audits and consulting work for federal government departments. Since it has became an SOA called Consulting and Audit Canada, it bids on all sorts of work both inside and outside government. It has even undertaken work for international agencies, which it likely would not have done under its previous manifestation. Its mandate is simply to make money.

These are the main examples of restructuring within governments. The next sections discuss some of the ways in which governments have begun to work with nongovernmental organizations.

Partnerships

The use of *partnerships* is one of the most widely heralded innovations in ASD. Partnerships can involve the cooperation of:

- several departments of the same government,
- several levels of government, or
- government organizations and private sector or not-for-profit organizations.

The variations are almost endless.[22]

Legally speaking, most of these are not true partnerships. For purposes of ASD, a partnership can be defined as "a relationship involving *the sharing of power, work, support and/or information* with others for the achievement of joint goals and/or mutual benefits."[23]

Partnerships frequently come about when a government that had previously been the exclusive provider of a service begins to face severe financial restraint that requires it to close some of its service offices. At the same time, a local not-for-profit community service group could have a number of volunteers searching for a mandate but only limited funds. The government department could provide enough funds to keep the community group operating even though the funds would not be enough to operate a full-fledged branch office. Coincidentally, the fact that the service is now provided closer to the users means that the providing agency will likely be more responsive to users' needs than would a government department in a far-away capital city.

Almost everyone benefits from this kind of arrangement. Government gets its service delivered at lower cost; the community agency receives more funding than it was receiving before and establishes a renewed mandate in the community; and users receive a service that is more responsive to their needs.[24] The plight of the previous government employees will be discussed later.

There can be quite an alphabet soup associated with partnerships, as the next sections indicate.

BOOT (Build-Own-Operate-Transfer). A good example of this is the Confederation Bridge between New Brunswick and Prince Edward Island. A private sector company built the bridge and was responsible for the full construction cost including any overruns. It was required to complete construction by June 1, 1997, or pay a substantial penalty. The company then operates the bridge for thirty-five years, collecting the tolls (at a regulated rate) and paying all operating expenses. At the end of the thirty-five years, ownership is transferred to the federal government.

In this arrangement, the government transfers both the cost of the construction and the risk of cost overruns to the private sector. In return, the private sector organization can make a substantial profit if it operates the structure efficiently. Then the government can profit from the operation of the bridge after thirty-five years. Since the bridge is built to last one hundred years, operating it could yield a substantial amount of money.

COGO (Company-Owned-Government-Operated). In this case, a private company builds something for the government, which the government would then operate. For example, Nova Scotia has adopted the P-3 (public-private partnerships) program. Under this program, a private company built a large number of school buildings. The company retains ownership of the buildings and the government pays an annual rent to use them.

This arrangement saves the government the large initial construction cost, although it ends up paying the same amount eventually in annual rents. However, this defers the cost over several years, instead of requiring the government to pay a lump sum up front. The government has some flexibility in that it can discontinue use of the buildings if they are no longer needed. Of course, this is limited by the fact that the owner will demand a lease of a certain length of time before it will agree to build the buildings.

GOCO (Government-Owned-Company-Operated). This is the inverse of the previous case. In this case, the government owns a facility and allows a private company to operate it.

A good example of this is the situation with regard to several large airports. The government has retained ownership of the building but is allowing local airport authorities to operate them in exchange for a fee. This allows government to withdraw from a commercial-type operation for which it is not suited and transfer its operation to a private sector company, which has greater expertise in this area. It also provides for decentralized, local decision making, rather than having all decisions referred to Ottawa.

Contracting Out

Contracting out or outsourcing is another method of ASD. Traditionally any service that was *funded* by government was also *provided* by government—the equation of steering and rowing. However, contemporary thinking is that separating funding from provision will increase citizens' choice in the use and acquisition of services, and ultimately improve the quality of the service.

One of the earliest and still most radical suggestions along this line was the provision of vouchers that parents could use for the education of their children. Government would provide funding for education in the form of vouchers, ensuring that all children had access to education, but service would be provided by a variety of organizations, including possibly for-profit businesses. Parents would have the freedom to choose which organization they wanted to patronize. Schools would be required to prove their worth in order to get parents to spend their vouchers with them. Thus, only high-quality schools could remain in business.

While few jurisdictions have gone to this extreme, there are many examples of contracting out.[25] In fact, contracting out might be one of the oldest innovations discussed in this section. Provincial and municipal governments have been contracting out road construction and maintenance from the days of the first roads. It has also been very common for governments to contract out such services as cafeteria operations and office cleaning in government buildings. What sets off more recent initiatives is that they are more extensive, sometimes extending to such core government services as social services.

It is expected that when governments contract out services instead of providing them internally, the services will be provided more cheaply. There are a number of reasons for this expectation. Some governments are not large enough to benefit from the economies of scale and specialization that larger, more specialized organizations can generate. Many municipalities contract with a computer service bureau to carry out some of their accounting functions, particularly the preparation of tax bills. It is more efficient for one large service bureau to develop specialized software to sell to all municipalities in an area than for each municipality to write its own.

Another reason for contracting out is the expectation that the competition generated by the process will force organizations providing the service to be efficient, which will, in turn, increase quality and/or reduce costs. In many cases, the tendering process is open to both private sector organizations and the government organization that formerly delivered the service on a monopoly basis. Some people might be surprised to find that government organizations frequently submit the successful tender, but this is usually only after these organizations have assessed their structures very critically and made a number of changes.[26]

Much of contracting out is done between different public sector organizations or between governments and parapublic sector organizations. For example, eight provinces have contracted to have the Royal Canadian Mounted Police provide some police services within their province. The Regional Municipality of Hamilton-Wentworth provides certain land-use planning and engineering services to the City of Hamilton. A similar arrangement is employed in the regional districts in British Columbia. There are also many cases in which governments contract with not-for-profit social agencies for the delivery of social services.

In addition to economic efficiency, contracting out provides governments with a significant amount of flexibility.[27] Governments are frequently their own worst enemies in service delivery because they establish a plethora of rules and regulations that then make it difficult for them to respond quickly and flexibly to changing situations. This means that private sector organizations appear to be more efficient in meeting certain needs. Of course, the ideal solution to this situation is to determine whether all the restrictive rules are necessary, but, in the shorter term, it will probably be more efficient to use the services of the flexible private sector organizations.

Governments also benefit from contracting out in that they do not have to purchase expensive, specialized equipment and hire and train permanent staff, which would make it difficult to abandon the service when public tastes change.

However, some caveats must be registered about contracting out. It works better for some services than for others. It has generally worked well where it is relatively easy to monitor the amount and quality of work done. Solid waste collection has been a popular candidate for contracting out,[28] but the contracting out of social services is more complicated.[29]

Apparent savings in the actual provision of the service can disappear if the costs of monitoring the quality of service delivered are high. Governments can be particularly vulnerable if they are dealing with a private sector firm that has an effective monopoly.[30]

Commercialization

The most radical form of ASD comes about when government decides that it simply no longer needs to be involved in both the funding and the provision of a service. Therefore, it decides to stop providing the service so that it can be delivered by a private sector or other organization, which might be more interested in it.

An example of this is NavCanada, which is the new organization responsible for providing air navigation services in Canadian air space.[31] This nonprofit corporation was established when the federal government did not want to continue to provide this service, and the airlines were not happy with the way the government was providing it anyway. However, the airlines were also concerned about turning this service over to a profit-making private monopoly over which they would have only limited influence. The compromise reached was a nonprofit corporation with a board of directors consisting of five members selected by the users of the system (the airlines); two by the employee unions, and three by the federal government. These ten would then select four additional members. NavCanada sets its own rates so that it will break even.

This constitutes a partial list of ASD approaches. There are many more and more ideas are being added every day. The concept of ASD has been beneficial in letting a breath of fresh air into government's previous traditional ways of doing things. There are many success stories arising from ASD.

🏛 PROBLEMS WITH ASD

There is no question that opening up the issue of service delivery rather than always assuming that there is a "one best way" is quite beneficial. However, certain caveats must be raised because there have been some problems with the implementation of ASD.

Real Savings?

In some cases, the apparent cost savings are not all they claim to be. Sometimes the expected cost savings identified early in the planning stage disappear when the actual tenders are opened. It often turns out that the actual costs are higher than expected.

Sometimes the *full* cost of the contracted service ends up being higher than expected. There are always costs of monitoring the contract, which are frequently underestimated or even totally overlooked at the planning stage. These are the costs of negotiating the contract, ensuring that the contractor complies with its conditions, dealing with citizens' complaints about the contractor, and so forth. Then there is the occasional situation of what is euphemistically called "contract failure," e.g., the contractor goes out of business or its performance becomes so bad that the contract must be terminated. These kinds of situations are expensive, disruptive, and embarrassing to the government.

In some cases, the cost savings come along with reductions in the level of service provided by the contractor. Contractors provide exactly the level of service stipulated in the contract; sometimes, citizens became accustomed to a higher service level provided by government employees.

Governments can be in a particularly difficult situation when the contractor has an effective monopoly over the provision of the service. When the government disbands its organization that formerly provided the service, it now becomes dependent on the one other provider in the area. This could put users in a situation where they are paying the same amount for a lower quality of service, but they are deprived of both the ability to find another provider and "their ultimate revenge—getting even at the next election."[32]

Labour Relations

Many forms of ASD involve moving government employees into a different regime within government or even into a private sector organization. On the positive side, this will frequently loosen the constraints of government human resource management systems and allow employees greater flexibility in working conditions, including the opportunity to earn merit pay. However, many employees fear that they will lose the protection that comes with the government human resources management regime. The right to provide merit pay for a job well done is also the right to withhold merit pay for possibly venal reasons. Some employees do not like moving out of the protective situation of the government system. Some make even stronger claims that ASD initiatives are aimed at breaking strong unions or preventing the establishment of a union. These issues all must be considered by the government spinning off the service and the organization taking over the service.

ASD is also changing the nature of the workforce. Long-serving, full-time employees are being replaced by limited-term contract employees. This is beneficial to governments to the extent that it increases their flexibility and reduces labour costs. However, this temporary workforce will have very little loyalty to their present employer. It is also very difficult to develop an organizational culture or an organizational memory with so many employees passing through the revolving door.[33]

Loss of Accountability or the Difficulties of Steering without Rowing

The whole idea of ASD is that services will be delivered at arm's length from government so that they can be delivered in a more flexible manner with greater responsiveness to users. The danger is that accountability linkages will be weakened at the same time. In some cases, the traditional governmental accountability linkages will be supplanted by other types of accountability mechanisms. In the case of NavCan, the users now have direct representation on the board of directors. However, there are other cases where the weakening of accountability poses serious problems.

> In the case of partnerships, accountability and management can be problematic. Regardless of who delivers a "public" service, government will ultimately be held accountable by the electorate for service shortfalls or outcomes. For example, who is accountable when a prisoner escapes from a provincially regulated facility which is operated by a private sector company? In Ontario, when some young offenders found their way out of a newly opened "boot camp," it was the government through the Ministry of the Solicitor General and Correctional Services who was called to account—not the company that was contracted and responsible to operate the facility.[34]

The moral of this story is that governments need to choose very carefully the types of services that are given this arm's-length treatment. In some cases, other mechanisms work very well in ensuring accountability, but not always.

Where Is the Public Interest?

Increasing responsiveness to users and more emphasis on the bottom line sound like two very positive values, but is it possible to be too responsive to users or too profit-driven so that the broader public interest is ignored? David Zussman raises the question of what a national parks agency that has the opportunity to make huge sums of money from tour operators should do?[35] If there is excessive emphasis on the profit motive, then the agency will be forced to behave in a way that many Canadians would not see as beneficial in the long run.

It is probably inappropriate to judge certain types of agencies based on consumer satisfaction. A tax collection agency must be fair and courteous with taxpayers, but it is in the public interest that the agency collect a fair amount from all taxpayers. In doing that, it is likely to incur the wrath of some people who would rather not pay taxes. That can be seen as a sign that it is doing its job well.

The emphasis on the bottom line and being user-friendly is important, but governments are elected to further the public interest.

🏛 REBALANCING THE SYSTEM

There is no doubt that the advent of alternative service delivery has had a very beneficial impact on service delivery. It has prompted governments to review virtually every service that they deliver. Even when this review has not resulted in contracting out, it has frequently caused governments to revise and improve their own way of delivering services. However, as frequently happens with innovations, ASD has been somewhat oversold. It is beneficial; it is not a cure-all.

NOTES

1. David Osborne and Ted Gaebler, *Reinventing Government* (Reading, Mass.: Addison-Wesley Publishing Company, Inc., 1992).
2. Robin Ford and David Zussman, "Alternative Service Delivery: Transcending Boundaries," in Robin Ford and David Zussman, eds., *Alternative Service Delivery: Sharing Governance in Canada* (Toronto: KPMG Centre for Government Foundation and Institute of Public Administration of Canada, 1997), 6.
3. Ibid., 7.
4. There is no such thing as a complete listing of possible ASD arrangements, but the federal government has prepared a document that sets out some categories and a checklist of considerations in deciding on how to select the proper tool from the toolbox. Treasury Board of Canada Secretariat, *Framework for Alternative Program Delivery* (n.d.).
5. F. Leslie Seidle, *Rethinking the Delivery of Public Services to Citizens* (Montreal: Institute for Research on Public Policy, 1995), 18–19 and ch. 1 *passim*.
6. Henry Mintzberg, "Managing Government, Governing Management," *Harvard Business Review*, (May–June, 1996), 77.

7. Jocelyne Bourgon, *Fifth Annual Report to The Prime Minister on The Public Service of Canada* (Her Majesty the Queen in Right of Canada, 1998), 12.

8. Barbara Wake Carroll and David Siegel, *Service in the Field* (Montreal & Kingston: McGill-Queen's University Press, 1998).

9. Gilles Paquet, "Alternative Service Delivery: Transforming the Practices of Governance," in Ford and Zussman, eds., *Alternative Service Delivery*, 33.

10. V. Peter Harder, "Public Administration in Canada: New Ideas," presentation at Rendez-vous 97 (14 July 1997), 3.

11. Ronald L. Doering, "Alternative Service Delivery: The Case of the Canadian Food Inspection Agency (CFIA)," paper presented to Alternative Service Delivery workshop sponsored by the Department of Justice (25 November 1996). See also: Robert Howse, "Reforming the Canadian Food Inspection System: An Opportunity to Build a New National System," in Ford and Zussman, eds., *Alternative Service Delivery*, 138–53.

12. Government of Canada, *1996–97 Annual Report on the Memorandum of Understanding among the Four Natural Resources Departments on Science and Technology for Sustainable Development* (Ottawa: Minister of Public Works and Government Services Canada, 1997), 1.

13. Jocelyne Bourgon, "Notes for an Address to the APEX Forum," 27 May 1997, 8.

14. Revenue Canada, *Ensuring Fair Customs and Revenue Administration in Canada* (March 1998), 12.

15. Treasury Board of Canada Secretariat, *Treasury Board Secretariat Initiatives in Support of Good Governance* (March 26, 1998), 6.

16. Carroll and Siegel, *Service in the Field*, ch. 4.

17. Ibid.

18. Bourgon, "Notes for an Address ...," 7.

19. Carroll and Siegel, *Service in the Field*, ch. 4.

20. President of the Treasury Board, *Crown Corporations and Other Corporate Interests of Canada 1997* (Ottawa: Minister of Public Works and Government Services Canada, 1997), 88.

21. Consulting and Audit Canada, *The Historical and International Background of Special Operating Agencies* (Ottawa: October 1992), 6. (Emphasis in original.)

22. A good overview of some of the possibilities is found in: Pierre A. Letarte, "Partenariats locaux et sociétés d'economie mixte," *Policy Options* 18, 4 (May 1997), 39–43; F.X. Alan Gratias and Melanie Boyd, "Beyond Government: Can the Public Sector Meet the Challenges of Public-Private Partnering," *Optimum* 26, no. 1 (summer 1995), 3–14.

23. Kenneth Kernaghan, "Partnership and Public Administration: Conceptual and Practical Considerations," *Canadian Public Administration* 36, no. 1 (spring 1993), 61. (Emphasis in original.)

24. A somewhat less sanguine view is expressed in: Michael H. Hall and Paul B. Reed, "Shifting the Burden: How Much Can Government Download to the Non-Profit Sector?" *Canadian Public Administration* 41, no. 1 (spring 1998), 1–20.

25. James C. McDavid and Eric G. Clemens, "Contracting Out Local Government Services: The B.C. Experience," *Canadian Public Administration* 38, no. 2 (summer 1995), 177–93.

26. David Osborne and Ted Gaebler, *Reinventing Government* (Reading, Mass.: Addison-Wesley Publishing Company, Inc., 1992), 76–78; David Siegel, "'Market Testing' in the UK," *Public Sector Management* 4, no. 2 (1993), 4–5; James C. McDavid and Gregory K. Schick, "Privatization Versus Union-Management Cooperation: The Effects of Competition on Service Efficiency in Municipalities," *Canadian Public Administration* 30, no. 3 (fall 1987): 472–88.

27. John Johnston, "Public Servants and Private Contractors: Managing the Mixed Service Delivery System," *Canadian Public Administration* 29, no. 4 (winter 1986): 549.

28. E.E. Savas, "Policy Analysis for Local Government: Public vs. Private Refuse Collection," in Charles H. Levine, ed., *Managing Fiscal Stress*, 281–302.

29.   Philip de L. Panet and Michael J. Trebilcock, "Contracting-out Social Services," *Canadian Public Administration* 41, no. 1(spring 1998), 21–50; Lorna F. Hurl, "Privatized Social Service Systems: Lessons from Ontario's Children's Services," *Canadian Public Policy* 10, no. 4 (December 1984): 395–405.

30.   Lydia Manchester, "Alternative Service Delivery Approaches and City Service Planning," in Lawrence K. Finley, ed., *Public Sector Privatization: Alternative Approaches to Service Delivery* (New York: Quorum Books, 1989), 15.

31.   Chandran Mylvaganam, "Flying the User-Managed Skies: The Story of NavCanada," in Ford and Zussman, eds., *Alternative Service Delivery*, 223–34.

32.   Madelaine Drohan, "Perils of Privatization," *Report on Business Magazine* (May 1996), 39.

33.   Ruth Hubbard, "The Professional Public Service," *The Alternative Network* 1.6 (n.d.), 3.

34.   David Zussman, "Ensuring Successful Partnerships through Performance-Based Management," *The Alternative Network* 2.3 (n.d.), 1.

35.   "Government's New Style," *Management* 8, no. 2 (n.d.), 22.

BIBLIOGRAPHY

Bish, Robert L. "Improving Productivity in the Government Sector: The Role of Contracting Out." In David Laidler, research coordinator, *Responses to Economic Change*. Toronto: University of Toronto Press, 1986, 203–37.

Bourgon, Jocelyne. "Notes for an Address to the APEX Forum." 27 May 1997.

———. *Fifth Annual Report to the Prime Minister on the Public Service of Canada*. Her Majesty the Queen in Right of Canada, 1998.

Carroll, Barbara Wake, and David Siegel. *Service in the Field*. Montreal & Kingston: McGill-Queen's University Press, 1998.

Consulting and Audit Canada. *The Historical and International Background of Special Operating Agencies*. Ottawa: October 1992.

Doering, Ronald L. "Alternative Service Delivery: The Case of the Canadian Food Inspection Agency (CFIA)" Paper presented to Alternative Service Delivery workshop sponsored by the Department of Justice, 25 November 1996.

Finley, Lawrence K., ed. *Public Sector Privatization: Alternative Approaches to Service Delivery*. New York: Quorum Books, 1989.

Ford, Robin, and David Zussman, eds. *Alternative Service Delivery: Sharing Governance in Canada*. Toronto: KPMG Centre for Government Foundation and Institute of Public Administration of Canada, 1997.

Government of Canada. *1996–97 Annual Report on the Memorandum of Understanding among the Four Natural Resources Departments on Science and Technology for Sustainable Development*. Ottawa: Minister of Public Works and Government Services Canada, 1997.

Gratias, F.X. Alan, and Melanie Boyd. "Beyond Government: Can the Public Sector Meet the Challenges of Public-Private Partnering." *Optimum* 26, no. 1 (summer 1995), 3–14.

Hall, Michael H., and Paul B. Reed. "Shifting the Burden: How Much Can Government Download to the Non-Profit Sector?" *Canadian Public Administration* 41, no. 1 (spring 1998), 1–20.

Harder, V. Peter. "Public Administration in Canada: New Ideas." Presentation at Rendez-vous 97 (14 July 1997).

Hubbard, Ruth. "The Professional Public Service." *The Alternative Network* 1.6 (n.d.), 2–3.

Hurl, Lorna F. "Privatized Social Service Systems: Lessons from Ontario's Children's Services." *Canadian Public Policy* 10, no. 4 (December 1984): 395–405.

Johnston, John. "Public Servants and Private Contractors: Managing the Mixed Service Delivery System." *Canadian Public Administration* 29, no. 4 (winter 1986), 549–53.

Jones, L.R., and Jerry L. McCaffery. *Government Response to Financial Constraints: Budgetary Control in Canada.* New York: Greenwood Press, 1989.

Kernaghan, Kenneth. "Partnership and Public Administration: Conceptual and Practical Considerations." *Canadian Public Administration* 36, no. 1 (spring 1993).

Letarte, Pierre A. "Partenariats locaux et sociétés d'economie mixte." *Policy Options* 18, 4 (May 1997), 39–43.

Manchester, Lydia. "Alternative Service Delivery Approaches and City Service Planning." In Lawrence K. Finley, ed., *Public Sector Privatization: Alternative Approaches to Service Delivery.* New York: Quorum Books, 1989.

McDavid, James C., and Eric G. Clemens. "Contracting Out Local Government Services: The B.C. Experience." *Canadian Public Administration* 38, no. 2 (summer 1995), 177–93.

McDavid, James C., and Gregory K. Schick. "Privatization Versus Union-Management Cooperation: The Effects of Competition on Service Efficiency in Municipalities." *Canadian Public Administration* 30, no. 3 (fall 1987): 472–88.

Mintzberg, Henry. "Managing Government, Governing Management." *Harvard Business Review* 74, 3 (May–June, 1996), 75–83.

Osborne, David, and Ted Gaebler. *Reinventing Government.* Reading, Mass.: Addison-Wesley Publishing Company, Inc., 1992.

Panet, Philip de L., and Michael J. Trebilcock. "Contracting-out Social Services." *Canadian Public Administration* 41, no. 1 (spring 1998), 21–50.

Revenue Canada. *Ensuring Fair Customs and Revenue Administration in Canada* (March 1998), 12.

Savas, E.E. "Policy Analysis for Local Government: Public vs. Private Refuse Collection." In Charles H. Levine, ed., *Managing Fiscal Stress: The Crisis in the Public Sector.* Chatham, N.J.: Chatham House, 1980, 281–302.

Seidle, F. Leslie. *Rethinking the Delivery of Public Services to Citizens.* Montreal: Institute for Research on Public Policy, 1995.

Siegel, David. "'Market Testing' in the UK." *Public Sector Management* 4, no. 2 (1993), 4–5.

Treasury Board of Canada Secretariat. *Framework for Alternative Program Delivery* (n.d.).

_____. *Treasury Board Secretariat Initiatives in Support of Good Governance* (26 March 1998).

Zussman, David. "Ensuring Successful Partnerships through Performance-Based Management." *The Alternative Network* 2.3 (n.d.), 1–2.

_____. "Government's New Style." *Management* 8, no. 2 (n.d.), 21–23.

IV

Politics, Values, and Public Administration

12

Institutional and Value Frameworks

Somalia. This word evokes a variety of images for Canadians, including images of scandal, lies, and cover-up. The torture and killing of a Somalian civilian by Canadian soldiers during a 1992–93 U.N. peace-keeping mission put the minister and the employees of the Department of National Defence at the centre of a huge public controversy. Surrounding these departmental officials were many other interested parties, including the prime minister, a former prime minister, a former deputy minister of defence, the cabinet, Members of Parliament, members of a commission of inquiry into the killing, the Freedom of Information Commissioner, pressure groups representatives, journalists, and, behind the scenes, public servants working in central agencies and other government departments.

The Somalia affair illustrates the broad range of actors with whom public servants interact in the policy process. This chapter sets out an *institutional* framework for organizing and understanding this complicated web of interaction. The Somalia affair also draws attention to the importance of the values that guide—or should guide—the behaviour of government employees. Among the public service values that came into play during the affair were integrity, accountability, openness, leadership, loyalty, and professionalism. A second framework in this chapter—a *value* framework—identifies the values that are central to the decisions and operations of the public service.

Before moving to a discussion of these frameworks, it is important to explain the relationship of this new part of the book, Part IV, to Parts III and V. Part III described the program delivery mechanisms in the executive-bureaucratic sphere of government. However, reading a description of the central components of the machinery of government is similar to visiting a factory in the dead of night. You can see the machinery and be told how it is supposed to operate, but you cannot understand how it really works until you see it humming, whirring, clanking, and, occasionally, breaking down. Moreover, you need to see how the operators use the machinery and how they relate to one another. Thus, the primary purpose of Parts IV and V is to explain the ways in which the machinery of government operates in practice. Part IV provides frameworks for understanding this operation and explains the central concepts of bureaucratic values, power, and responsibility that underlie the operation.

Part V focuses on the role of the public organizations (departments, agencies, boards, and commissions) discussed in Part III and on the public servants who manage them. It examines interaction in the executive-bureaucratic sphere among public servants and between public servants and cabinet ministers; it also examines interaction between public servants and actors outside this sphere, namely legislators, the courts, provincial governments, pressure groups, journalists, and the general public. This is the complex web of relationships illustrated by reference to the Somalia case.

🏛 THE INSTITUTIONAL FRAMEWORK

Given the large number of actors involved in the public policy process, it is essential to provide a means of identifying and classifying them. Moreover, since this book is concerned with the role of *the public service* in the policy process, it is necessary to devise a framework that permits a focus on public organizations.[1] Thus, we have set out below an institutional framework that facilitates an examination of interactions:

1. within public organizations;

2. between and among public organizations; and

3. between public organizations and actors outside the public service.

The term public organization is used here to refer to either a department or a nondepartmental body (e.g., Crown corporation, regulatory agency, advisory council).

The Concept of Power

The key concept underlying the institutional framework, as well as the value framework (discussed later), is one that is central to scholarly writings in political science, organization theory, and public administration—namely, power. Social science literature contains various definitions and usages of power and the closely related concepts of influence, control, and authority.[2] It is generally agreed that power is a relational concept. It is, therefore, extremely useful for describing and explaining relations between and among organizations, groups, and individuals—and indeed, as we shall see, between and among governments. *Power* is defined here as "the capacity to secure the dominance of one's values or goals."[3] A similar definition explains power as "the capacity of an individual, or group of individuals, to modify the conduct of other individuals or groups in the manner in which he desires, and to prevent his own being modified in a manner which he does not."[4]

Control and Influence

There are two forms of power: control and influence. *Control* refers to that form of power in which A has authority to direct or command B. For example, a deputy minister wields control over a subordinate when he or she exercises statutory or other authority to order the subordinate to act in a certain way.

Influence is a more general and pervasive form of power than control. When B conforms to A's desires, values, or goals by suggestion, persuasion, emulation, or anticipation, then A exercises influence over B. For example, a deputy minister may influence another deputy minister by persuading him or her to take a particular action. Influence can sometimes cause power to flow upwards when administrative subordinates who possess special expertise in some field exercise influence over hierarchical superiors in the form of "authority of expertise" or "expert power." Bachrach and Lawler assert that influence "is the mode of power that both gives subordinates the capability of manipulating superiors and gives superiors the capability of getting more from their subordinates than is specified in the formal role obligations."[5] They also state that "influence is two-directional in hierarchical relations, but it also applies to horizontal relations not lodged in an authority structure."[6] Thus, for example, influence is at work in interdepartmental and intergovernmental relations.

To exercise control, A must have authority in the sense of having access to the inducements, rewards, and sanctions necessary to back up commands. This is "authority of position" or "position power." A may also exercise influence over B through "authority of leadership" or "personal power," which involves the use of such means as persuasion, suggestion, and intimation rather than direction, supervision, and command. Moreover, authority of position allows A to exercise influence as a result of "the rule of anticipated reactions."[7] Application of this rule is evident in the innumerable instances in which administrative officials "anticipate the reactions" of those who have the power to reward or constrain them. Officials tend to act in a fashion that would be applauded—or at least approved—by those whose favour they seek. Thus, those actors ordinarily perceived as exercising control, such as hierarchical superiors, can also exercise influence by affecting another actor's decisions in an informal, unofficial— even unintentional—way.[8] Heclo and Wildavsky's observation about the British government is equally applicable to Canada: "Most of the time on most issues, ministers, sitting alone at the top of their departmental empire, can exercise their political leadership only through civil servants' second-, third-, or fourth-hand anticipation of ministers' likely reactions."[9]

What distinguishes actors with the capacity to exercise both control and influence from those possessing only influence is that the former have at their disposal sanctions and inducements formalized by law and the organization chart. Influence over public organizations and public servants within these organizations can be exercised by those who do not have legally or formally sanctioned power to command or supervise. For example, pressure groups may seek favours from public servants by offering inducements (e.g., gifts) or imposing penalties (e.g., criticism), but they have no legal or formal capacity to compel compliance to their wishes. This does not mean, however, that such influence cannot be as effective as control or, in some instances, even more effective. A public servant may well grant special favours to pressure groups despite formal directions to the contrary from an administrative superior. Thus, influence can be exercised by those without either authority of position or authority of leadership through a variety of means, including persuasion, friendship, knowledge, and experience.

Internal and External Interactions

The preceding analysis provides the basis for the development of a framework showing the patterns of interaction both within public organizations and between these organizations and other participants in the public policy process. These interactions involve in large part the reciprocal exercise of power in the form of control and/or influence. From the perspective of any one organization, these interactions can be classified as internal, external-within government, and external-outside government. This classification is depicted in Figure 12.1 and Table 12.1.

Figure 12.1
INTERNAL AND EXTERNAL INTERACTIONS OF
PUBLIC ORGANIZATIONS

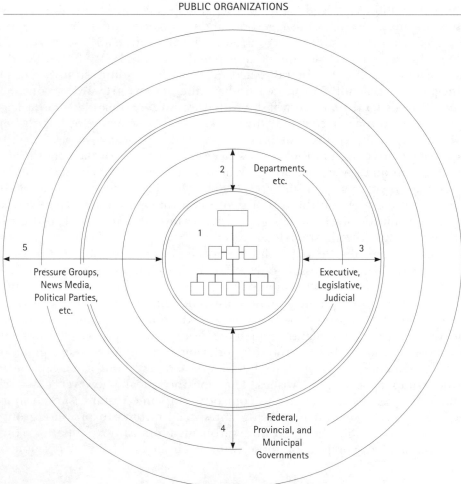

Table 12.1
INTERNAL AND EXTERNAL INTERACTIONS OF PUBLIC ORGANIZATIONS

1 Broad Patterns of Interaction	2 Major Categories of Interaction	3 Actors	4 Power Resources
internal	intradepartmental	line units staff units field units	
external (within government)	intradepartmental	public organization other public organizations	
	executive-bureaucratic	public organization prime minister cabinet central agencies	expertise experience discretionary power clientele support appointment/removal powers information and advice from central agencies chairmanship of cabinet
	legislative-bureaucratic	public organization parliament auditor general	
	judicial-bureaucratic	public organization federal courts provincial courts	
external (outside government)	intergovernmental	public organization institutions and organizations of other levels of government intergovernmental bodies	
	governmental-nongovernmental	public organization nongovernmental organizations	

Figure 12.1 consists of five concentric circles with the major actor—a public organization—at the centre. The order in which these circles are labelled from the centre outward represents the proximity of the other actors to the organization. Proximity to the centre does not, however, indicate the extent of power exercised over the organization or over officials within the organization. For example, in some situations, a pressure group can exert more power over a department than can a central agency.

The innermost circle (circle 1) depicts the internal pattern of interaction, i.e., the public organization and its subunits. For the sake of simplicity, the organization's administrative pyramid has been greatly compressed to indicate merely the major lines of interaction within the organization. Circles 2 and 3 portray the external-within government pattern of interactions; this pattern includes those actors outside the organization but within the particular government under consideration (e.g., other public organizations, political executives, legislators, the courts).

The outer limit of circle 3 is the boundary between actors within and outside government—the external-outside government pattern of interaction. Circle 4 includes actors in other governments, either in the same sphere or in different spheres of government. Finally, circle 5 contains the broad range of nongovernmental actors (e.g., pressure groups, political parties, journalists). Each of these categories of interaction is covered in later chapters of Part IV.

This framework for classifying interactions involving public servants and other policy actors is explained in greater detail in Table 12.1. Here the framework is specifically applied to the parliamentary-cabinet form of government as it operates in Canada's federal and provincial governments. The framework can be modified slightly to apply to the municipal sphere of government as well. In addition, it can be used to examine systematically the vertical and horizontal relations of public organizations with other relevant actors and to identify the participants and their interactions in a particular policy field.[10]

In Table 12.1, the three broad patterns of interaction in the first column are subdivided to show, in the second column, the major categories of interaction in which a public organization may be involved, namely:

1. intraorganizational (e.g., intradepartmental);

2. interdepartmental;

3. executive-bureaucratic;

4. legislative-bureaucratic;

5. judicial-bureaucratic;

6. intergovernmental; and

7. governmental-nongovernmental.

These various categories of interaction are discussed in Chapters 15 to 21. Thus, the institutional framework provides the basis for organizing much of this part of the book.

Column 3 in Table 12.1 contains a further refinement of these categories into the potential actors in each category. Column 4 lists the most significant means by which these actors can exercise control and influence, i.e., power, over one another. The interaction of these actors can be explained largely in terms of power relations, i.e., relations between actors for the purpose of, or with the result of, affecting behaviour in a specific direction.

There is insufficient space in Table 12.1 to provide a detailed list of the actors involved in the policy process and of their power resources (i.e., the means of control and influence available to them). It is evident, however, that column 3 could be subdivided to show the subunits of the various actors, such as departmental divisions and sections, cabinet committees, and legislative committees. An even finer subdivision could be achieved by identifying individual roles associated with each of the organizations or groups listed in column three, such as those of public servants, ministers, and legislators. The effective application of the framework to a particular public organization in a specific policy field (e.g., Health and Welfare in aging policy) would require these more detailed subdivisions. In column 4, some elaboration is provided, by way of example, of the interaction between the public organization and the prime minister or a provincial premier.

Power relations between public organizations and other actors flow in two directions. Public servants are not defenceless against pressures put on them by actors outside the public service. An examination of the real or potential impact of controls and influences over the public service must account for the potent resources that public servants can use to resist pressure and to exert power over others. Among the resources public servants possess to control and/or influence other actors are expertise, experience, budgetary allocations, confidential information, and discretionary powers to develop and implement policies and programs. These resources may be utilized in various ways. For example, public servants may prevail over political superiors by virtue of special knowledge of a policy area (authority of expertise); they may feed selected bits of information to journalists to enhance support for a certain program; or they may disarm external critics by organizing them into advisory bodies.

In summary, the institutional framework provides a means of examining interactions among participants in the public policy process, and it places public organizations at the centre of these interactions. It can be applied at any level of government and can focus attention on a specific public organization or policy field. Finally, it provides a linkage between intraorganizational and interorganizational relations.

🏛 THE VALUE FRAMEWORK

Values are enduring beliefs that influence the choices made by individuals, groups, or organizations from among available means or ends. Values are organized into value systems, in which values are ranked in terms of their relative importance. Thus, each public servant has a value system or framework in which various social, political, administrative, and personal values are ranked, admittedly very roughly, even subconsciously, in order of importance. The focus here is on *administrative* or *public service* values.

A review of Canadian administrative history shows that among the most important public service values are neutrality, accountability, efficiency, effectiveness, responsiveness, representativeness, and integrity. Moreover, in the past few decades, equity (or fairness) has become an increasingly central public service value. These are often described as "traditional" values. Since each of these values is discussed in one or more of the subsequent chapters, only a brief explanation is provided here.

Neutrality

As explained in the next chapter, it is essential to distinguish between political neutrality, in the sense of nonpartisanship, and value neutrality. Most public servants preserve their neutrality in terms of partisan politics; they cannot, however, reasonably be expected to be value neutral because they are actively involved in politics in the broad sense of the authoritative allocation of values for society. The value system of individual public servants is central to an analysis of bureaucratic behaviour and bureaucratic power because they *cannot* be completely value neutral in making and recommending decisions. Indeed, public servants have never been value neutral and they have become less so as their discretionary powers have increased. Many of the decisions they make oblige them, or give them the opportunity, to inject their own views as to which values should take priority. The difficulty of ensuring the responsible exercise of power under these circumstances helps to explain the importance of accountability.

Accountability

The quest for *administrative accountability* arises largely from the reality that public servants are not value neutral. Accountability involves concern for the legal, institutional, and procedural means by which public servants can be obliged to answer for their actions. It is a pervasive theme in this book both because it has been one of the major values in the evolution of Canadian public administration and because of its current importance. Since the early 1990s, there has been a major shift in emphasis from accountability for *process*—for the way things are done—to accountability for *results*—for what is achieved.

Efficiency and Effectiveness

Despite the current concern with accountability, the dominant value in Canadian public administration over the broad sweep of the 20th century has been efficiency. Moreover, much of the emphasis on accountability has really been directed to holding public servants accountable for the economic, efficient, and effective use of public funds. The values of economy, efficiency, and effectiveness are interdependent but distinct in meaning. *Economy* refers to the

Figure 12.2
THE THREE Es OF AN EMPLOYMENT TRAINING PROGRAM

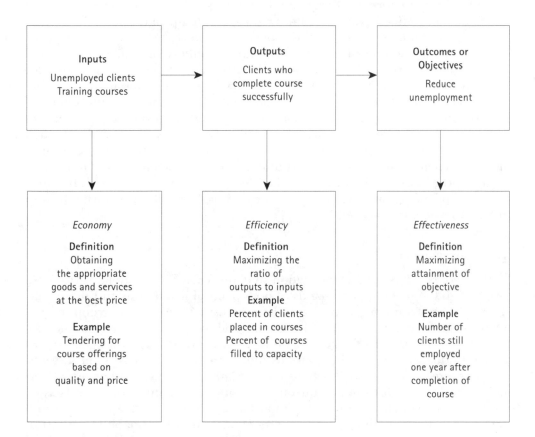

acquisition of the appropriate goods and services at the best possible price. *Efficiency* is a measure of performance that may be expressed as a ratio between input and output. *Effectiveness* is a measure of the extent to which an activity achieves the organization's objectives. Figure 12.2 demonstrates the meaning of these values with respect to an employment training program.

We shall see in subsequent chapters that there has been increasing emphasis, especially since the late 1960s, on these so-called three Es of economy, efficiency, and effectiveness. During this period, effectiveness has gradually superseded economy as the major companion value of efficiency. Efficiency and effectiveness may complement one another, but they may also conflict. For example, the construction of a thousand houses for aboriginal peoples at appropriate cost and quality, and on schedule, is efficient and effective. The completion of these houses at appropriate cost and quality but long after they are needed is efficient but ineffective. The timely construction of adequate homes at very high cost is effective but inefficient.

The Treasury Board has been the prime mover in promoting efficiency and effectiveness throughout the public service. The board has supported the introduction of more sophisticated techniques of achieving and assessing efficiency and effectiveness, including the planning-programming-budgeting system, cost-benefit analysis, the operational performance measurement system, management by objectives (MBO), program evaluation, and Increased Ministerial Authority and Accountability (IMAA). The Office of the Comptroller General, which became part of the Treasury Board Secretariat in 1993, has responsibility for developing systems to stimulate the efficiency and effectiveness of government operations, in part by designing and promoting procedures for program evaluation. Moreover, the Auditor General Act of 1977 broadened the auditor general's powers to include reporting on instances where money has been spent without "due regard to economy or efficiency" or where "satisfactory procedures have not been established to measure and report the effectiveness of programs, where such procedures could appropriately and reasonably be implemented."

Responsiveness

Responsiveness refers to the inclination and the capacity of public servants to respond to the needs and demands of both political institutions and the public. Thus, public servants are expected to be responsive to two major groups of participants in the political system. The first includes political executives and legislators; the second includes the general public as well as various "publics," i.e., groups and individuals affected by the decisions and recommendations of public servants.

Responsiveness is usually discussed in relation to the second group of participants. The Royal Commission on Government Organization (the Glassco Commission) concluded that "the importance to the public of efficiency and integrity in the machinery of government … is unquestionably great.... But even greater is the importance of a service responsive to public wants and expectations."[11] As will be noted in Chapter 21, a major purpose of the movement for increased public participation is greater government responsiveness to the public's wants and needs. The current emphasis in public sector management on improving service to the public is part of a continuing effort to achieve the value of responsiveness. Public servants are of course required to reconcile responsiveness with such other values as accountability and efficiency. For example, the emphasis on these latter two values during times of financial restraint in government is usually to the detriment of administrative responsiveness to the public.

Representativeness

A representative public service is one in which employees are drawn proportionately from the major ethnic, religious, and socioeconomic groups in society. Representativeness in the public service is closely tied to several other public service values. For example, the argument is frequently made that a more representative public service is a more responsive public service. In the belief that the attitudes of representatives of a group will be similar to the attitudes of the whole group, a representative public service is deemed to be more responsive to the needs of the public and more effective in giving policy advice. However, it is also argued that if efforts to achieve a representative public service mean that the most qualified persons are not hired, the efficiency and effectiveness of the service will be adversely affected. Thus, as we shall see in Chapter 24, the representativeness of the public service is tightly tied to the issues of equal opportunity, employment equity, and managing diversity.

Fairness and Equity

For most practical purposes, the terms fairness and equity can be used inter-changeably. We shall see in Chapter 23 that equity is one of the major values to be balanced in determining the merit of persons seeking appointment to the public service and in Chapter 18 that the courts and governments are now putting greater emphasis on procedural fairness. Considerations of procedural fairness have gradually expanded beyond the boundaries of administrative law to the administrative processes of the public service. Public servants are increasingly expected—or required—to consider whether their decisions and recommendations are fair both in substance and in procedure. This heightened emphasis on fairness and equity is based largely on the recognition of the significant power that public servants exercise over the rights and livelihood of individual citizens.

There is a complementary relationship between the values of fairness and responsiveness in that procedural fairness could be said to require that public servants be responsive to the public through various mechanisms for public participation. It is also obvious that fairness can clash with such values as efficiency and effectiveness.

Integrity

Integrity refers here to ethics in public administration. The integrity of public servants is extremely important to the preservation of public trust and confidence in government. Recent experience in Canada and elsewhere indicates that increased vigilance is required to ensure that public servants adhere to high ethical standards. Chapter 14 provides evidence that the ethical dimension in public administration is a pervasive one, and that governments are paying increased attention to the various means by which ethical conduct can be maintained and nurtured.

New Values

As a result of the extensive public service reforms that have taken place since the mid-1980s, a number of so-called *new* public service values have emerged.[12] Several of these new values are closely associated with the new public management approach to public administraion, which was discussed in Chapter 4.

Among the most prominent of these new values are service, innovation, team-work, and quality. Other values of increasing importance are openness, com-munication, trust, and leadership. Some of these new values (e.g., service) complement certain traditional values (e.g., responsiveness), but other new values (e.g., innovation) clash with some of the traditional values (e.g., account-ability). We shall refer in subsequent chapters to both traditional and new values and will return to a discussion of values in the concluding chapter, which examines the future of public administration.

Facts and Values

If an administrative issue is significant enough to require the conscious prepa-ration of alternative solutions and the evaluation of their possible conse-quences, each alternative will be an amalgam of what Herbert Simon refers to as the value and factual elements in any decision.[13] The mix of fact and value will, of course, vary greatly from one decision-making circumstance to another. Many decisions of a routine and repetitive nature (programmed decisions) require little, if any, conscious value selection. Decisions of a unique or novel nature (nonprogrammed decisions) may contain a substantial mix of value and factual elements.

Sources of the Bureaucrat's Values

A focus on the bureaucrat's values is especially important in that bureaucratic behaviour may be explained or interpreted in terms of the interplay among the individual bureaucrat's values, and between the bureaucrat's values and the values of those with whom he or she interacts. Before an individual joins the public service, his or her general value system, as well as particular attitudes and orientations toward the public service, are molded by powerful and enduring forces. This is accomplished through the process of *socialization*, i.e., "an indi-vidual's learning from others in his environment the social patterns and values of his culture."[14] The socializing "agencies" involved in this process include family, peer groups, schools, prior employment, and adult organizations. Thus, an individual enters government service with values that will significantly affect his or her decisions. Moreover, in varying degrees, the socializing agencies con-tinue to affect the bureaucrat's values during his or her public service career.

However, the organization that employs the individual is itself a powerful socializing agent. The individual's personal values and perceptions of the public service are altered by a process of *organizational socialization* that begins the very day he or she is recruited for a public service position. Organizational socialization refers to the process through which the individual learns the expectations attached to the position he or she occupies in the organization, and selectively internalizes as values some of the expectations of those with whom he or she interacts.

🏛 THE CRUCIAL LINK

It is at this point that the theoretical link between the value framework and the institutional framework can be demonstrated. The public servant is expected to be responsive to the values of the various policy participants as these values are expressed through the exercise of specific controls and influences. The policy participants shown in Table 12.1 are then the primary sources of the official's public service values.

Since various policy participants pursue different, and sometimes mutually exclusive, objectives in their relations with public servants, the public servant will be the object of conflicting expectations and pressures as to his or her behaviour. The purpose of each participant's interaction with the public servant will usually be the dominance of the participant's particular values and goals over those of both the public servant and other participants. The problem for the public servant is clearly posed: How can he or she be responsive to the multiplicity of values expressed?

The linkages between the institutional and the value frameworks help explain the means by which the number and assortment of variables impinging on the public servant may be reduced to more manageable proportions. Over a considerable period of time, and in a variety of bureaucratic positions, an official might conceivably interact with virtually the whole range of policy participants and be subjected to a wide variety of controls and influences. As the occupant of a specific position over a shorter period, an official will, however, only interact with a limited number of actors. The range of these actors will be confined to those with a stake in either the activities of the official or the issue at hand. For example, a deputy minister of consumer relations is the object of much greater pressure from outside the public service (e.g., interest groups and journalists) than a deputy minister of government services. More importantly, during the process of organizational socialization, the public servant learns what kinds of behaviour will bring reward or punishment from various policy actors and what values they are seeking to realize. The bureaucrat's value system is usually most directly molded by the values of those hierarchical associates on whom he or she relies most heavily for approval and reward, i.e., political and administrative superiors, peers, and subordinates. Of course, the public servant is also expected to be responsive to the values of such other policy actors as legislators, interest group representatives, and the general public. Faced with complementary, conflicting, and contradictory expectations issuing from various sources, the public servant can inculcate only some of the values held by those with whom he or she interacts.

This socialization experience provides practical and psychological benefits for the public servant. Over time, the public servant internalizes a commitment to certain public service values. He or she develops a value framework that facilitates decision making because there is a point beyond which he or she will not go in contemplating, much less yielding to, pressures in his or her decision-making environment. The public servant will refuse to examine his or her value system *a priori* in each decision situation and will be predisposed to accept or reject the exercise of power (i.e., control and influence) from certain directions.

The existence of this value framework for individual decision making relates also to the earlier discussion of the resources available to public servants to withstand the exercise of power by other policy participants. The situation in which the official chooses to wield countervailing power and the resources he or she selects to control or influence others are, in very large measure, determined by this value system.

Value Conflict

Despite efforts to minimize the number of variables involved in any given decision-making situation, value conflict is frequent, especially for senior public servants. Herbert Simon contends that at the lower levels of the organization, the framework for decision making is usually well established in that "the factors to be evaluated have already been enumerated, and all that remains is to determine their values under the given circumstances."[15] At the senior levels of the organization, however, "the task is an inventive one. New values must be sought out and weighed; the possibilities of new administrative structures evaluated. The very framework of reference within which each decision is to take place must be constructed."[16]

The major categories of value conflicts that public servants encounter are those

- between personal values and public service values;

- between and among public service values; and

- between public service values and the values of other policy participants.

The resolution of value conflicts involving personal and public service values (e.g., ambition versus accountability, or avarice versus integrity) depends on the personality and character of the particular public servant. Anthony Downs contends that "most officials are significantly motivated by self-interest when their social function is to serve the public interest."[17] He provides a typology of public servants ranging from "purely self-interested officials" (i.e., climbers and conservers) through to "mixed-motive officials" (i.e., zealots, advocates, and statesmen). Statesmen are the least self-seeking and most public-oriented of public servants. They are "motivated by loyalty to society as a whole and a desire to obtain the power necessary to have a significant influence upon national policies and actions. They are altruistic to a high degree because their loyalty is to the 'general welfare' as they see it."[18] The "statesman" type of public servant will have comparatively little difficulty reconciling personal and public service values but will occasionally be obliged to choose between and among public service values he or she holds equally dear (e.g., accountability versus integrity or accountability versus responsiveness). Similarly, bureaucrats' values come into conflict with the values held by those with whom they interact (e.g., accountability versus responsiveness to an interest group's request, or account-ability versus efficiency expected by a professional colleague).

The relative importance of each public service value varies according to the particular circumstances of time, place, and policy within which value choices are made. For example, the values of representativeness and respon-siveness may become predominant during a period when the general public or the government feels that the interests of certain disadvantaged minority groups must be better represented and their needs and demands better under-stood and satisfied. During such a period, considerations of efficiency and neu-trality may be relegated to a secondary order of importance.

Public servants may conceivably pass through one, two, or all three stages of value conflict. In practice, of course, these stages are not chronological; rather, they overlap and interact with one another. Thus, a choice between the public service values of accountability and responsiveness is likely to be made in conjunction with, and to be affected by, controls and influences reflecting the values of other policy actors. We shall see in Chapter 14 that there is an inti-mate connection between the resolution of value conflicts and the concept of the public interest.

In summary, the role of the public service in the public policy process can be illuminated by using the institutional and value frameworks outlined above. The institutional framework may be used separately to examine relationships among bureaucratic actors and between these actors and other participants in the policy process. The value framework complements the institutional frame-work by showing that the values of individual public servants are significantly affected by the values of those actors who exercise power over them.

🏛 COORDINATION

The foregoing analysis provides a useful basis for examining the concept of *coordination*, which is critically important in the making and implementation of public policy in Canada. The prime minister, at the centre of the machinery of government, looks out on a vast constellation of public organizations, including operating departments, central agencies, Crown corporations, regulatory agen-cies, advisory councils, and royal commissions. Moreover, beyond the bounds of the federal government is an even larger number of public organizations in the provincial and municipal spheres of government with which the federal gov-ernment must deal. Provincial premiers face a similar but somewhat smaller array of organizations.

Coordination is the process of two or more parties taking one another into account for the purpose of bringing their activities into harmonious or recip-rocal relation. This process can be formal or informal, and it can be pursued both within public organizations and between these organizations and other policy actors. Coordination of both the formulation and implementation of public policy is widely viewed as essential to efficient, effective, and responsive government, and is considered especially desirable during periods of financial restraint. Consequently, in recent years greater attention has been paid to the coordination of the activities of public organizations and to coordination between governments and policy actors outside government. In addition, the challenge of managing intergovernmental relations, especially in federal states, requires increasingly vigorous efforts to coordinate the activities of organizations and officials in two or more orders of government. Since the mid-1990s, much greater emphasis has been placed on improving policy coordination between government departments, between governments within Canada, and between Canadian and foreign governments.[19] We will return to this subject in Chapter 16 under the heading of "horizontal relations."

Both the general public and public officials frequently bewail the absence or inadequacy of coordination in government. Coordination is often viewed as a means of ensuring that appropriate policy and program decisions are made, duplication and overlap are avoided, and effective and responsive services are provided. It is important, therefore, to dash false hopes and unrealistic expectations about the nature and utility of coordination. It is not a panacea for such government ills as inefficiency, ineffectiveness, and unresponsiveness. Nor is it a substitute for shared values and goals among participants in the policy process. It is evident that coordination can be used to achieve different and sometimes conflicting values and goals (e.g., efficiency and responsiveness).

Virtues and Limitations of Coordination

The curative effects of coordination can be impressive, but they are limited. Requirements that coordination be sought through time-consuming consultative techniques, such as extensive citizen participation, can lead to delay and indecision that may aggravate, rather than remedy, a problem. Also, the process of coordination can lead to overcoordination. A convincing case can be made that redundancy in the form of duplication and overlap often serves a valuable purpose.[21] Landau

> The quest for coordination is in many respects the twentieth-century equivalent of the philosopher's stone. If we can find the right formula for coordination, we can reconcile the irreconcilable, harmonize competing and wholly divergent interests, overcome irrationalities in our government structures, and make hard policy choices to which no one will dissent.
>
> Source: Harold Seidman and Robert Gilmour, Politics, Position and Power.[20]

contends that "'streamlining an agency,' 'consolidating similar functions,' 'eliminating duplication,' and 'commonality' are powerful slogans … But it is just possible that their achievement would deprive an agency of the properties it needs most—those which allow rules to be broken and units to operate defectively without doing critical injury to the agency as a whole."[22]

Coordination is sought and attained not simply through formal structures and processes, but also through informal relations between and among policy actors. Moreover, it is often difficult to know when coordination is actually taking place. Charles Lindblom argues persuasively that through a process of *partisan mutual adjustment* a very large measure of coordination in government occurs without any deliberate, conscious attempt to coordinate. He contends that there are no coordinators in this process; rather, coordination comes about as "a by-product of ordinary decisions, that is, of decisions not specifically intended to coordinate."[23] He distinguishes this process from that of central coordination whereby, for the most part, "decision makers adapt to one another on instruction from a central decision maker."[24] He acknowledges also the existence of situations characterized by a mixture of central coordination and partisan mutual adjustment, "where somebody can be both a central supervisor to a degree and a mutual adjuster."[25]

While central coordination is sought primarily through the exercise of control, partisan mutual adjustment is pursued through a broad range of techniques, most of which (e.g., negotiation, bargaining) require the exercise of influence. Lindblom's mixture of central coordination and mutual adjustment, which is commonly found within public organizations and frequently within government as a whole, involves the use of both control and influence. In a later work, Lindblom states that some political systems, such as the British, "rely more heavily on central coordination," whereas other systems, such as the American, depend "more heavily on mutual adjustment."[26] Canada's political system, like that of Britain, relies more on central coordination than mutual adjustment. His analysis, which has been greatly simplified here, indicates the large extent to which coordination is achieved as a result of the exercise of power for other purposes.

Lindblom acknowledges the utility of central coordination and recognizes that governments cannot rely solely on partisan mutual adjustment. We shall see in subsequent chapters that formal coordinating activities by governments are often needed to supplement coordination sought or attained by other means.

NOTES

1. Although it is analytically convenient to speak of decisions being made by institutions and organizations, decisions are in reality made by individuals and groups within these institutions and organizations.
2. For example, some writers use the terms power and influence interchangeably; other writers distinguish power from influence by interpreting power as a force backed by coercive authority. Note that Max Weber "used power to refer to the ability to induce acceptance of orders; legitimation to refer to the acceptance of the exercise of power because it is in line with values held by the subjects; and authority to refer to the combination of the two., i.e., to power that is viewed as legitimate." Amitai Etzioni, *Modern Organizations* (Englewood Cliffs, N.J.: Prentice-Hall, 1964), 51.
3. John F. Pfiffner and Frank P. Sherwood, *Administrative Organization* (Englewood Cliffs, N.J.: Prentice-Hall, 1960), 77.
4. R.H. Tawney, *Equality* (London: G. Allen and Unwin, 1931), 229.
5. Samuel B. Bachrach and Edward J. Lawler, *Power and Politics in Organizations* (San Francisco: Jossey-Bass Publishers, 1980), 41.
6. Ibid.
7. A good treatment of this concept may be found in Carl J. Friedrich, *Man and His Government* (New York: McGraw-Hill, 1963), ch. 11.

8. Some organizational theorists distinguish between "formal" and "informal" controls. In the context of our definition of control and influence and throughout this book, all controls are of a formal nature; informal controls are subsumed under the broad definition of influences.

9. Heclo and Wildavsky, *The Private Government of Public Money: Community and Policy Inside British Politics* (Berkeley: University of California Press, 1974), 376.

10. For an application of the framework to the policy field of aging, see Kenneth Kernaghan and Olivia Kuper, *Coordination in Canadian Governments: A Case Study of Aging Policy* (Toronto: Institute of Public Administration of Canada, 1983).

11. Canada, Royal Commission on Government Organization, *Report*, vol. 1, 63 (Ottawa: Queen's Printer, 1962).

12. Kenneth Kernaghan, "The Emerging Public Service Culture: Values, Ethics and Reforms," *Canadian Public Administration* 37 (winter 1994): 614–40.

13. Herbert A. Simon, *Administrative Behaviour*, 2nd ed. (New York: The Free Press, 1957), 45–60.

14. Kenneth P. Langton, *Political Socialization* (New York: Oxford University Press, 1969), 3.

15. Simon, *Administrative Behaviour*, 217.

16. Ibid.

17. Anthony Downs, *Inside Bureaucracy* (Boston: Little, Brown, 1967), 87.

18. Ibid., 88.

19. Canada, Deputy Ministers' Task Force, *Managing Horizontal Policy* (Ottawa: Privy Council Office, December 1996).

20. Harold Seidman and Robert Gilmour, *Politics, Position and Power,* 4th ed. (New York: Oxford University Press, 1986), 219.

21. See Martin Landau, "Redundancy, Rationality and the Problem of Duplication and Overlap," *Public Administration Review* 29 (July–August 1969): 346–58.

22. Ibid., 356.

23. Charles Lindblom, *The Intelligence of Democracy* (New York: The Free Press, 1965), 9.

24. Ibid., 25.

25. Ibid., 27.

26. *The Policy-Making Process* (Englewood Cliffs, N.J.: Prentice-Hall, 1968), 82.

BIBLIOGRAPHY

Aucoin, Peter. "A Profession of Public Administration?" *Canadian Public Administration* 40 (spring 1997): 23–9.

Aucoin, Peter. "Portfolio Structures and Policy Coordination." In G. Bruce Doern and Peter Aucoin, eds., *Public Policy in Canada*. Toronto: Macmillan, 1979.

Bachrach, Samuel B., and Edward J. Lawler. *Power and Politics in Organizations*. San Francisco: Jossey-Bass Publishers, 1980.

Downs, Anthony. *Inside Bureaucracy*. Boston: Little, Brown, 1967.

Dunsire, Andrew. *Control in a Bureaucracy*. Oxford: Martin Robertson, 1978.

Canada, Deputy Minister's Task Force, *Discussion Paper on Values and Ethics in the Public Service* (Ottawa: Privy Council Office, December 1996).

Kernaghan, Kenneth. "Towards a Public Service Code of Conduct—and Beyond." *Canadian Public Administration* 40 (spring 1997): 40–54.

———. "The Emerging Public Service Culture: Values, Ethics and Reforms." *Canadian Public Administration* 37 (winter 1994): 614–30.

———. "Values, Ethics and Public Service." In Jacques Bourgault et al., eds., *Public Administration and Public Management: Canadian Experiences* (Quebec: Les Publications du Quebec, 1997): 101–11.

————. "Shaking the Foundation: Traditional Versus New Public Service Values." In Charih, Mohamed and Arthur Daniels, eds. *New Public Management and Public Administration in Canada.* Toronto: Institute of Public Administration of Canada, 1997, 47–65.

Kernaghan, Kenneth, and Olivia Kuper. *Coordination in Canadian Governments: A Case Study of Aging Policy.* Toronto: Institute of Public Administration of Canada, 1983.

Landau, Martin. "Redundancy, Rationality and the Problem of Duplication and Overlap." *Public Administration Review* 29 (July–August 1969): 346–58.

Lindblom, Charles E. *The Intelligence of Democracy.* New York: The Free Press, 1965.

————. *The Policy-Making Process.* Englewood Cliffs, N.J.: Prentice-Hall, 1968.

Simon, Herbert A. *Administrative Behaviour.* 2nd ed. New York: The Free Press, 1957.

Tait, J. "A Strong Foundation: Report of the Task Force on Public Service Values and Ethics (the summary)." *Canadian Public Administration* 40 (spring 1997): 1–22.

Wamsley, Gary L., and Mayer N. Zald. *The Political Economy of Public Organizations.* Bloomington, Ind.: Indiana University Press, 1976.

13

Power, Politics, and Bureaucracy

At first it was a fairly innocuous event. Three scientists from outside government published a paper in the *Canadian Journal of Fisheries and Aquatic Sciences* titled "Is Scientific Inquiry Compatible with Government Information Control?"[1] The paper may not have received much public attention if senior public servants in the federal Department of Fisheries and Oceans had not responded to it so strongly. However, they had reason to be unhappy. The paper suggested, among other things, that the department had tried to repress research showing that overfishing rather than seal predation or environmental change was the main cause of the collapse of the Atlantic fishery; that the minister of the department may have been behind this effort; and that the department's scientists were routinely reprimanded for speaking out in public on contentious issues. Then, a university professor alleged to the *Ottawa Citizen* that the department had made politically motivated efforts to suppress some of his research on the role of seals in the fishery's collapse. Senior departmental officials sued him, but a large number of scientists publicly supported him; moreover, pressure groups wanting to protect the seals took on his legal defence.

When the department's head of science subsequently appeared before the House of Commons Committee on Fisheries and Oceans, he was subjected to scathing personal attack by several Members of Parliament. One member asked why government scientists didn't have the backbone to stand up to damaging political decisions. The committee discussed the department minister's decision to raise the quota for turbot despite specific warnings from the science branch. A court decision on this matter had quoted the assistant deputy minister as saying in a letter that raising the quota "would be completely irresponsible." The committee went so far as to recommend that "senior DFO personnel who are viewed by the fishing community as being responsible for the crisis in the fishery be removed from the Department."[2] However, some committee members argued that this recommendation "would appear to advocate punishing individuals merely for being accused ... of some undefined failing" and that it "created a conflict with the constitutional principles of parliamentary supremacy and ministerial responsibility."[3]

This case illustrates how individual citizens, journalists, and legislators can turn what seems initially to be a relatively harmless administrative matter into an important political matter. It also raises the issues of how much power public servants have in relation to ministers and legislators and how fully they can enjoy the political rights accorded to citizens in general. These are some of the major issues discussed in this chapter.

🏛 BUREAUCRATIC POWER

Power was defined in the previous chapter as the capacity to secure the dominance of one's values or goals. In this sense, public servants wield substantial power by virtue of their role in policy development and execution. If the machinery of government could be arranged so that public servants simply implemented laws spelled out in very specific terms by the legislature, enforced judicial decisions interpreting these laws, and administered policies and programs under the close supervision of political executives, few value problems would exist for most public servants. The realm of politics and policy would belong to elected representatives and would be sharply delineated from the administrative sphere. The value issues in any situation would be worked out by others so that the public servant's primary concern would be to adhere to those values emerging from the executive, legislative, and judicial spheres of government.

The historical record shows that an era of such bureaucratic innocence has never existed in modern democratic states. There is, in reality, much room for the injection of the public servant's values into decisions and recommendations. It is generally acknowledged that public servants exercise significant power in both the development and the execution of policy. In a lecture on the threat to parliamentary responsible government, Robert Stanfield, a former leader of the Progressive Conservative party, stated that "while the House of Commons has been losing control, so also has the Government. The ministers just do not have the time to run such a vast show and make such a vast range of decisions. Consequently, more and more is for all practical purposes being decided by and implemented by the bureaucracy."[4] In a reminiscence on thirty years as a senior public servant and a minister, Mitchell Sharp observed that

> top public servants are powerful persons in the machinery of government at the federal level. They wield great influence. They do so because they are, in the main, professionals who have been selected for their proven administrative ability and who devote their full time to government. In many cases, they have a greater influence upon the course of events than have Ministers, particularly the weaker and less competent.[5]

The extent of this bureaucratic power clearly varies in accordance with such factors as the government's view of the proper role of public servants in the political process, the policy or program under consideration, the department or agency involved, and the style and competence of ministers and their officials.

The Concept and Practice of Political Neutrality

Political neutrality is a constitutional doctrine or convention according to which public servants should avoid activities that are likely to impair—or seem to impair—their political impartiality or the impartiality of the public service. The several interrelated ideas traditionally associated with the concept of political neutrality provide a useful model for examining the nature of interaction between public servants and other actors in the political system.[6] The model also permits a consideration of the changing nature of bureaucratic power and of the role of public servants in the policy process. The major elements of the traditional doctrine may be summarized as follows:

1. politics and policy are separated from administration; thus, politicians make policy decisions and public servants execute these decisions;

2. public servants are appointed and promoted on the basis of merit rather than of party affiliation or contributions;

3. public servants do not engage in partisan political activities;

4. public servants do not express publicly their personal views on government policies or administration;

5. public servants provide forthright and objective advice to their political masters in private and in confidence; political executives protect the anonymity of public servants by publicly accepting responsibility for departmental decisions; and

6. public servants execute policy decisions loyally, irrespective of the philosophy and programs of the party in power and regardless of their personal opinions; as a result, public servants enjoy security of tenure during good behaviour and satisfactory performance.

In order to explain the nature and extent of bureaucratic power in the Canadian political system, each of these six elements will be examined separately. Special attention is centred on the degree to which actual practice has departed from the requirements of the model. Note that this is an ideal-type model in that its description of the relations between politicians and public servants in a government is characterized by absolute political neutrality.

> A vital challenge ... is preserving the essence of a professional and politically neutral Public Service. The hallmark of that professionalism is the ability to give the government of the day the best possible advice without fear or favour, based on the long-term public good, to loyally carry out the orders of the democratically elected government, to obey the law and to act with probity in the public interest.
>
> Source: Federal Public Service Commission, Annual Report 1995–96[7]

1. The Politics-Administration Dichotomy

The political neutrality of public servants has traditionally rested on the possibility of the separation of politics and administration, and on a related distinction between policy and administration. Frequently, the two dichotomies are treated as synonyms—as if the terms politics and policy are interchangeable. However, the scope of activity covered by the term politics is much broader than that embraced by the term policy. "*Politics* is concerned, throughout the sphere of government, with the whole business of deciding what to do and getting it done. *Policy* is the decision as to what to do; *administration* is getting it done."[8] According to the *politics-administration dichotomy*, political executives and legislators are concerned with the formation of policy, and public servants are concerned with its implementation. Policy decisions are political; administrative decisions are nonpolitical. However, abundant evidence points to the important political and policy advisory roles of public servants.

The distinction between politics and policy on the one hand and administration on the other has been central to the evolution of both the study and the practice of public administration. V. Seymour Wilson, who uses interchangeably the terms politics-administration dichotomy and policy-administration dichotomy, states that the dichotomy

> remains a powerful philosophy.... It has guided, and will continue to guide, many aspects of the actions and perceptions of politicians, public servants and the public.... The policy/administration dichotomy has a profound influence on just about every aspect of theory and practice in public policy and administration.[9]

From 1887 to the end of World War II, most prominent writers on public administration wrote within a framework of a dichotomy between politics and administration. Woodrow Wilson's celebrated essay of 1887, "The Study of Administration," is usually taken as the point of departure for academic and theoretical writing on public administration in North America. Wilson asserted that

> the field of administration is a field of business. It is removed from the hurry and strife of politics ... [A]dministrative questions are not political questions ... "Policy does nothing without the aid of administration," but administration is not therefore politics.[10]

Wilson's distinction between politics and administration was accepted and perpetuated by such other pioneers as Frank Goodnow (1914), L.D. White (1926), and W.F. Willoughby (1927). In their writings, "the politics-administration dichotomy was assumed both as a self-evident truth and a desirable goal; administration was perceived as a self-contained world of its own, with its own separate values, rules and methods."[11] Set in proper historical perspective, these questionable views are more comprehensible.

During the late 19th and early 20th centuries, administrative reform efforts in both the United States and Canada were devoted to eradicating patronage from the public service, with a view to promoting efficient administration. A separate but overlapping development that had its origins in industrial organization in the United States was the scientific management movement described in Chapter 3. This movement, which pursued efficiency in large-scale organizations by seeking the most rational means—the "one best way"—of performing any organizational task had an enormous impact on the public service reform movement in the United States. The tenets of the scientific management movement spread also to Canada and several European countries.

In both the United States and Canada, the two elements of the reform movement—efficiency through the elimination of patronage and efficiency through scientific management—reinforced one another and became integral components of the merit system. In Canada, the 1917–18 Report of the Civil Service Commission noted that the merit system in the Canadian civil service "consisted of two distinct parts: the first is concerned with the selection and appointment of individuals 'without regard to their politics, religion or influence'; the second is concerned with 'applying the methods of scientific employment to maintain the efficiency of these selected employees after they enter the service.'"[12] While the Civil Service Act of 1918 was a landmark event in establishing a merit system for the Canadian public service, political interference with the application of the system hindered efforts to eliminate patronage appointments.

Although there were no Canadian counterparts to American writers on public administration who articulated the notion of a separation between politics and administration, Canadian reformers operated within a similar framework. Implicit in their efforts to remove partisan political considerations from appointments to the public service was acceptance of the possibility and desirability of separating politics from administration—at least insofar as staffing the service was concerned. For example, the 1917–18 Report of the Civil Service Commission stated that the purpose of the 1918 Civil Service Act was to promote "efficiency and economy in the *non-political* Civil Service."[13]

Concurrent with this pursuit of impartial and efficient administration was a steady growth in the discretionary powers of public servants. While efficient staffing of the service required the separation of politics and administration, the need for effective development and execution of public policy drew administrative officials into the political maelstrom—not in the sense of partisan activity but in the sense of involvement in the authoritative allocation of values for society. Public servants formulated rules and regulations to put flesh on the skeletons of vaguely worded statutes, enforced these rules and regulations, and adjudicated disputes arising from this enforcement. Moreover, the complicated and technical nature of public policy issues meant that political executives had to rely increasingly on public servants for policy advice and for the management of large-scale public organizations.

During the 1930s, writers on public administration who recognized the significant and growing political role of the bureaucracy lived uncomfortably with the textbook dichotomy between politics and administration.[14] The dichotomy came under increasing attack during the war years as many scholars gained practical administrative experience in government. Shortly after the war, a number of political scientists launched a devastating assault on the notion that politics and administration were, or could be, separated. Among this group of postwar authors, Paul Appleby stands out for his defence of the proposition that "public administration is policy making ... Public administration is one of a number of basic political processes."[15] In less celebrated and more broadly focused works than those written by Americans, British and Canadian writers during this period demonstrated a growing recognition of the blurring of the traditional constitutional line between politicians and public servants in the parliamentary-cabinet system of government.

By 1960, the interdependence of politics and administration had been enshrined in the theoretical literature on public administration and accepted by the major actors in the political system. By this time, however, recognition of the reality of bureaucratic power in the political process led to suggestions that public servants should become "agents of social change." Public servants were encouraged to promote new and creative ideas and solutions in social policy by aggregating and articulating the needs of unorganized and disadvantaged groups (e.g., consumers, the poor), and by stimulating groups and individuals to make demands on government for remedies to their social and economic ills. It was clear that public servants who undertook such activities were likely to clash on occasion with political and administrative superiors who did not perceive the proper role of public servants to be active initiators of social change. The basic question was the extent to which appointed public officials could, or should, share with elected representatives the responsibility for stimulating and responding to social change. Discussion of public servants as social change agents was intermingled with the movement for increased citizen participation in governmental decision making. This movement brought both politicians and public servants into more direct contact and confrontation with the general citizenry.

In the United States, these and other developments culminated in the late 1960s in a loose confederation of scholars and practitioners seeking a so-called *new public administration*.[16] Among the major concerns of the advocates of this movement were social equity, sensitivity to and representation of disadvantaged minority groups, increased citizen participation in governmental decision making, and new forms of public organization.

The relevance of the new public administration movement for the relation between politics and administration was that some of its supporters called for a reformulation of the traditional roles of politicians and public servants.[17] It was argued that public servants, because of their expertise and experience and their close contacts with members of the public, are better qualified than political executives or legislators to determine the public interest. Public servants must, however, establish a value system with a focus on human dignity or administrative humanism; they should not simply reflect the values of their political masters. Implicit also was a resistance to political control over public administration. The new public administration movement drew attention to the actual and potential power of public servants and to the importance of their value system for decision making in government; however, it did not resolve—indeed, it complicated—the issue of finding an appropriate balance between the power of public servants and that of elected representatives.

Thus, the scholarly literature on public administration records an evolution since 1945 from a situation in which only a few writers recognized the necessary involvement of public servants in politics to one in which some writers suggested that leadership in policy development rightly belongs to public servants rather than to politicians. The new public administration movement had little spillover effect on the study and practice of public administration in Canada. Nevertheless, scholars and practitioners in Canada are acutely aware that the line between politics and administration has become increasingly indistinct as both politicians and public servants participate actively in policy development. Moreover, the line fluctuates according to the expansion of bureaucratic power and the gradual politicization of the public service.

Policy Development and Policy Implementation.   Since the political role of public servants is attributed primarily to their contribution to policy development, much attention in the literature has focused on the intermingling of policy and administration. The conventional view that a clear division may be made between policy and administration has always been a fiction; whatever distinction could be made has become increasingly untenable with the continuing growth of government activities and bureaucratic power. The terms policy and administration are of limited use in distinguishing between the roles of political executives (i.e., cabinet ministers) and those of public servants because political executives and public servants are jointly involved in both the development and the administration of policy. Gordon Robertson, former clerk of the Privy Council, observed:

> I can hardly claim to be capable of complete objectivity. It would be easier to achieve such detachment if I could shelter behind the dictum so solemnly delivered from editorial pages and professorial podia that politicians, and not civil servants, make policy and civil servants, and not politicians, apply it. It is unfortunate that so clear and helpful a distinction should have so little truth about it.[18]

In the late 1970s, public administration scholars began to study more vigorously "the missing link" in the policy-making process, namely *policy implementation*.[19] It is now widely recognized that the power of public servants is greatly enhanced by their dominant role in program implementation and service delivery. Subsequent discussion will, therefore, examine the exercise of bureaucratic power in both policy formation and policy implementation.

Writers on bureaucratic power have long recognized the enormous influence of public servants on *policy formation*. Senior public servants in particular make significant discretionary decisions as to the policy options to be set before their political masters. In the development and presentation of these policy options, public servants are expected to be attuned to the political, as well as the administrative, financial, and technical implications of their recommendations. Some public servants are especially influential in policy formation because of their central positions in the policy process (e.g., the Deputy Minister of Finance, the clerk of the Privy Council). Thus, despite the variety of available sources of policy advice outside government, the very technical, complex, and time-consuming nature of certain policy issues obliges ministers to continue to rely heavily on the advice of their officials. Moreover, since the late 1960s, the power of the so-called public service mandarins (a small group of influential senior public servants) has been diffused among a broader range of political actors and a greater number of senior public servants.[20]

In the sphere of *policy implementation*, public servants also exercise substantial power. The extent of bureaucratic power in policy implementation depends largely on the specificity of the statute enacted by the legislature. In an early, but very perceptive, discussion of *administrative discretion*, the philosopher Wayne A.R. Leys developed a threefold classification of discretion depending on the willingness and capacity of elected representatives to set down in statutes the criteria on which administrative decisions are to be based. Ley's classification of discretionary powers distinguishes among:

1. merely technical discretion, where the legislature has stated or assumed that the administrator knew the results which it desired;

2. discretion in social planning, where the legislature does not know exactly what it will ultimately want in the way of results; and

3. discretion in the work of reconciliation, where the legislature has, in effect, asked the administrator to break a political deadlock.[21]

The first category, where discretionary judgment is limited, illustrates that care must be taken not to exaggerate the number of value-laden issues confronting officials. A large percentage of the thousands of administrative decisions made each day present value problems of such minor significance that officials are scarcely aware of any value content in the decisions made. The second and third categories demonstrate the discretionary powers exercised by officials, either because of the complexity of the issue or because of the inability of the executive or legislature to resolve the political conflicts involved. Both situations shift the burden of decision making from political executives, legislators, and judges to public servants. The making of decisions and recommendations on complex and technical matters of "social planning" requires the exercise of discretionary powers of a legislative and judicial nature. Further, the participation of officials in negotiation, bargaining, compromise, and reconciliation in order "to break a political deadlock" is undeniably a *political* activity.

In the course of interpreting, clarifying, and applying policy, public servants can significantly influence the success of policy decisions made by ministers and legislators. The care and enthusiasm with which public servants administer policy determine to a large extent the success of that policy. A series of individual, relatively minor decisions in a particular policy area can have a significant cumulative impact on the extent to which the original intent of cabinet and Parliament is realized. Moreover, such decisions can help to determine the content of subsequent changes in existing policy. In wielding such discretionary powers, public servants are, of course, expected to ensure that their decisions are attuned to the general policy of their minister and their department.

The discretionary powers of public servants in policy implementation are especially evident in the making and enforcement of regulations under authority delegated to them by Parliament, or subdelegated to them by a minister or by cabinet.[22] The statutory provisions authorizing the making of regulations are often phrased in general or imprecise language that permits public servants to exercise significant discretion both in the wording of the regulations and in the application of their provisions to particular cases. Eric Hehner repeatedly warned of the danger of "dispersed discretions." He argued:

> If regulations extend only to details of mechanical procedures, no real discretionary powers are delegated. However, where the statutory provisions are only a skeleton and it is left to regulations to say "what, where, when, why, how and who,"

then we have created meaningful discretionary powers.... When regulations are issued by the governor-in-council, or even by a minister of the Crown, there is at least a degree of accountability for this first step. Where the power is conferred upon a board or commission, review of its exercise becomes more difficult and remote.... If persons or bodies possessed of delegated powers redelegate them, we come to a state that may be described as "dispersed discretions."[23]

The exercise of discretionary powers is pervasive in that they are dispersed to various levels of the hierarchy. However, both the scope and importance of discretionary powers increase as one moves up the administrative pyramid into the upper echelons of the bureaucracy. It is, therefore, among senior public servants that value problems and priorities are most crucial for the determination of public policy and the state of administrative responsibility. It is important, however, not to overestimate the value problems of the most senior public servants and thereby to minimize the substantial, sometimes critical, significance of value choices made by professional, technical, and administrative personnel at lower levels of the hierarchy. The failure of such officials to act responsibly, particularly by failing to make decisions that are efficient, effective, and responsive, may seriously jeopardize policies and programs determined at the executive levels of the organization. Decisions judged to be irresponsible may be taken with the best of personal intentions; other irresponsible decisions may constitute deliberate efforts to obstruct or sabotage the implementation of government policies. Instances of this latter type of irresponsible administrative conduct are difficult to document, but there are numerous opportunities for such conduct. In a large organization—whether in the public or the private sector—the decision-making process may involve inputs and judgments by so many individuals that the person or persons guilty of irresponsible behaviour are extremely difficult to pinpoint. This is the condition Robert Presthus described as "organized irresponsibility."[24]

Despite the fact that politics and policy cannot be easily separated from administration, the distinctions commonly made between politics and administration, policy and administration, and policy formation and implementation serve an extremely useful analytical and practical purpose. They enable political theorists to distinguish—not in an absolute sense but as a matter of degree and emphasis—between the constitutional and legal functions of political executives and public servants. While the policy role of public servants has led some writers to refer to them as "permanent politicians" and "ruling servants," they remain, in fact and in democratic theory, subject to the overriding authority of elected representatives and the courts. It is useful, then, to refer to the *predominance* of ministers in policy formation and the *predominance* of public servants in policy implementation, while acknowledging that both ministers and public servants are involved in both policy formation and implementation.

These dichotomies also serve a practical end in that they enable politicians to preserve the appearance before the public that they, not public servants, are the policy makers. Elected representatives have a stake in preserving the notion that public servants are neutral instruments of political masters. This notion in turn supports the doctrine that ministers must accept responsibility for the decisions of their administrative subordinates. Public servants also have an interest in preserving these convenient fictions so that they may retain their anonymity and be sheltered from public attack.

2. Political Appointments

Merit and Patronage. A second component of the ideal model of political neutrality is the practice whereby "public servants are appointed and promoted on the basis of merit rather than of party affiliation or contributions." Political *patronage* involves the appointment of people to government service on the grounds of contributions, financial or otherwise, to the governing party; it is a blatant violation of the doctrine of political neutrality.[25] Indeed, the appointment is made on the basis that the appointee is *not* politically neutral but is politically partisan. Such appointments clash with the *merit principle*, according to which:

1. Canadian citizens should have a reasonable opportunity to be considered for employment in the public service;

2. Selections must be based exclusively on merit, or fitness to do the job.[26]

The *merit system* "is the mechanism in use at any time by which these goals are achieved." It is "an administrative device which can and should be adapted to changing circumstances."[27]

The merit system established by the Civil Service Act in 1918 greatly diminished, but by no means eliminated, patronage appointments. As late as 1944, H.M. Clokie claimed that Canada had not "fully emancipated herself from the laxness of appointment by favour which tends to paralyze all efforts to attain a sound merit system."[28] By 1945, however, the number of patronage appointments had been greatly reduced, and by 1962 the Glassco Commission was able to conclude that "for all practical purposes ... the Civil Service Commission [now the Public Service Commission] has managed to eliminate political patronage appointments to those positions falling within its jurisdiction."[29]

Recipients and Effects of Patronage. Patronage appointments have certainly not disappeared. A review of debates in the House of Commons in recent decades reveals numerous allegations and denials regarding the use of patronage in staffing the public service. Many of the alleged patronage appointments have been to lower-level or part-time positions where the appointees are so far removed from policy development that their appointment has negligible effect on the status of political neutrality. Opposition parties, the news media, and the general public have shown greater interest in senior positions that are filled by patronage appointees rather than on a competitive basis by persons from within or outside the public service. The prime minister and the cabinet have the authority to appoint deputy ministers; heads and members of agencies, boards, and commissions; ambassadors; high commissioners; consuls general and certain other diplomatic representatives; and federal judges. Moreover, officials in the Prime Minister's Office are selected by the prime minister, and cabinet ministers' assistants are also chosen in an overtly partisan manner. All these appointments are exempt from the appointing power of the Public Service Commission.

Among the persons who may be, and frequently are, appointed to exempt positions are retired legislators, defeated candidates of the governing party, and party supporters who have made significant financial or other contributions to the party's fortunes. Defeated or retired cabinet ministers have also enjoyed particular success in finding a comfortable niche in government service.[30] Finally, the expansion of the personal staff of cabinet ministers has increased the importance of this group as a source of patronage appointments.[31]

Such appointments are often denounced on the grounds that they are made more on the basis of partisanship than merit. Nevertheless, the government has the authority to make these appointments on whatever basis it deems appropriate. A measure of merit is achieved with respect to the most senior posts because the government is usually unwilling to bear the embarrassment that the appointment of an incompetent partisan may bring. Moreover, party supporters are more likely to find their reward in appointments to Crown agencies, boards, and commissions than to the regular departments of government. There have been few partisan appointments to deputy ministerial posts, at least in the federal sphere.

The number of patronage appointments in each of the categories examined above is relatively small, but, taking all the categories together, the number of *senior* positions filled by patronage appointees is substantial. The impact of these appointments on bureaucratic power is difficult to measure with any precision. However, such appointments limit the influence of career public servants by blocking access to some of the highest positions in government. Moreover, long-serving officials are obliged to share their influence in the policy process with newcomers who may have fresh ideas and unorthodox approaches and who may not share the administrative values to which most public servants have become socialized.

Patronage in the Provinces. The evolution of political patronage in Canada's provinces has been very similar to that in the federal government. Civil service acts were passed and public service commissions or their equivalent were created to promote public service neutrality and efficiency through a merit system of personnel management.[32] The timing of these reforms varied greatly from province to province, but in all cases effective reforms occurred more slowly than on the federal scene. Hodgetts and Dwivedi note that "until the early '60s, most provinces continued to present only the facade of a merit system, while combatting charges of patronage and personal favouritism in their public services." However, "by the mid-'60s nearly all provinces had made their central personnel agencies powerful enough to implement the merit principle."[33] Patronage appointments to agencies, boards, and commissions and to lower-level positions in certain operating departments remain a common practice in several provincial governments.[34] Some provinces (e.g., Saskatchewan)[35] have recently been more inclined than others to make political appointments to senior posts in *departments* as well as in semi-independent bodies.

3. Political Partisanship

Political Sterilization.   The ideal model of political neutrality requires that public servants not "engage in partisan political activities."[36] Indeed, the federal government recently stated that

> there is nothing more important to the effectiveness of the Public Service than that Ministers of successive Governments have confidence in the loyalty of Public Servants. Those who advise them ... must be without partisan associations.... These conditions form the basis of careers in the Public Service, enabling Public Servants to carry out their essential duty of serving successive Governments of different political parties without any legitimate questioning of their loyalty and commitment.[37]

We shall see, however, that in practice these conditions apply more to senior public servants than to those at lower levels of the hierarchy.

During the first fifty years of Canada's political history, the issues of political partisanship and political patronage were intimately linked. Patronage appointments were rewards for service to the governing party. Many of the appointees sought to enhance their progress within the public service by continuing their partisan support of the governing party after their appointment. Thus, when a new party came to power, it replaced these persons with its own supporters.

In an effort to eliminate this practice, legislators provided in the 1918 Civil Service Act that no public servant could "engage in partisan work in connection with any ... election, or contribute, receive or in any way deal with any money for any party funds."[38] Violations were punishable by dismissal. The penalty was so severe and so clearly stated that, with the exception of the right to vote, the impact of the act was the political sterilization of Canada's federal public servants. Despite this effective weakening of the link between patronage and political activity, the rigid restraints imposed in 1918 remained virtually unchanged until 1967. The primary explanation was the desire to ensure the political impartiality of public servants in the performance of their advisory and discretionary powers.

The Public Service Employment Act of 1967 liberalized the longstanding restrictions on political activity. Section 33 of the act provided that public servants, unless they were deputy heads, could stand for election to public office if the Public Service Commission believed that their usefulness would not be impaired by their candidacy. Employees were not permitted to work for or against a candidate for election to a federal or provincial office, or for or against a political party; they were permitted, however, to attend political meetings and to make contributions to the funds of a political candidate or party. In 1991, the Supreme Court of Canada struck down Section 33 with the result that, except for deputy ministers, there are virtually no statutory restrictions on the political rights of federal public servants.

Political Activity in the Provinces. In provincial governments, a common pattern has emerged with respect to public servants who wish to become candidates for public office. Although the number of senior and other officials who are prohibited from such activity varies from province to province, most public servants seeking candidacy and election may receive a leave of absence for a period preceding the date of the election. Employees who are elected must resign their public service position. In several provinces, however, an employee who is elected but who ceases to be a representative within five years will be reinstated to government service.

In regard to other forms of political activity (e.g., membership in political parties; attendance at political meetings, rallies, and conventions; making and soliciting financial contributions; canvassing for a political candidate), the rules vary considerably among provinces. In virtually every province, the right of public servants to support the party of their choice or no party at all is specifically protected by statute. For example, the Saskatchewan Public Service Act provides that no public servant:

- shall be obliged to contribute to a political party or to participate in political activities;

- use his or her authority or influence to "control or modify" political action of another person;

- engage in political activities at the workplace; or

- participate in political activities likely to impair his or her usefulness in the public service.

The fact that most public servants may now stand for election and engage in a broader spectrum of political activities has heightened the general level of partisan activity and consciousness in Canada's public services, especially among younger employees. However, officials in senior and sensitive posts are usually required to refrain from partisan activity; thus, those officials most actively involved in policy formation and in the discretionary application of

---

In cases where individuals are identified, or even suspected, of having party connections of the wrong kind, there is only so much deputy ministers can do to protect them.... [T]here will of course still be consenting adults in the public service who are prepared to accept the consequences of ending up on the wrong side after an election. For the others, however, I would suggest they approach the question of political activity in the same manner that the Anglican prayer book prescribes for marriage: it is "not by any to be entered upon ... lightly or wantonly; but ... discreetly, advisedly, soberly, and in the fear of God."

Source: Arthur Kroeger, former federal deputy minister, "On Being a Deputy Minister"[39]

policy retain their impartiality. Also, officials with many years of government experience have difficulty overcoming their ingrained avoidance of political activity. Some public servants may justifiably perceive overt partisanship as an obstacle to promotion to the senior ranks of what is, substantially, a politically neutral public service.

Restrictions on the political partisanship of public servants, in both the federal and provincial spheres of government, have been challenged in the courts under the Canadian Charter of Rights and Freedoms. The issue is, for the most part, framed in terms of the need to strike the most appropriate balance between the political rights of public servants and the political neutrality of the public service. Section 2 of the Charter guarantees the fundamental freedoms of expression, peaceful assembly, and association, and Section 1 provides that the guarantees to rights and freedoms under the Charter are subject to "such reasonable limits prescribed by law as can be demonstrably justified in a free and democratic society." The issue before the courts, then, is whether the limits on the political partisanship of public servants can be demonstrably justified to be reasonable in contemporary Canadian society. Recent court decisions indicate that there is a clear trend in the direction of extending the political rights of public servants. As noted, the Supreme Court struck down Section 33 of the federal Public Service Employment Act, largely on the grounds that the wording of the section was so vague as to be unduly restrictive and, therefore, unreasonable.[40]

4. Public Comment

Restrictions.   The admonition that public servants "not express publicly their personal views on government policies or administration" is an integral component of the ideal model of political neutrality. The prime reason given by contemporary governments for restrictions on public comment is the need to preserve the confidence of the public and of political superiors in the impartiality of public servants.

Strict interpretation of this rule of official reticence requires that public servants not express personal opinions on government policies, whether they are attacking or supporting those policies. As explained below, this convention has been supplemented by statutory prohibitions relating to political partisanship and to the use of confidential information, by decisions of administrative tribunals, and by written guidelines.

Public servants on leave of absence to seek election are of course obliged to express personal and partisan views on campaign issues. Those who wish to return to government service if they are defeated may find it prudent to show discretion in their public statements, especially with respect to the policies and programs of the department to which they may wish to return. Public servants, whether seeking election or not, are normally prohibited by an oath of office and secrecy, and by the Official Secrets Act, from disclosing or using for personal gain confidential information acquired by virtue of their government position. It is a serious offence to criticize government policy or administration;

the use of confidential information for this purpose would greatly compound the offence.

Formal written guidelines on public comment are so sparse that considerable uncertainty exists as to the rights of public servants in this area. It is well established in the public service legislation of modern democratic states that the role of public servants in policy development and implementation requires that they enjoy fewer political rights than other citizens. In the area of public comment, the difficulty is to strike an appropriate balance between freedom of expression and political neutrality. The dilemma for a public servant who engages in public criticism of government is illustrated well by the celebrated Fraser case.

Neil Fraser, an employee of the Department of National Revenue, began his public protest with attacks on the government's compulsory imposition of the metric system; he then extended his criticism to the proposed Charter of Rights. When Fraser's appeal against his subsequent dismissal was being heard by an adjudicator of the Public Service Staff Relations Board, Fraser said that if he discontinued his protests, he would be breaking "the common law that the citizen has a duty to speak out against a Government that lies to the people."[41] The adjudicator's decision that Fraser's dismissal was appropriate was upheld by the Supreme Court of Canada. The Court stated that:

> [P]ublic servants have some freedom to criticize the government. But it is not an absolute freedom.... In some circumstances a public servant may actively and publicly express opposition to the policies of a government. This would be appropriate if, for example, the government were engaged in illegal acts, or if its policies jeopardized the life, health or safety of the public servant or others, or if the public servant's criticism had no impact on his or her ability to perform effectively the duties of a public servant or on the public perception of that ability.[42]

Beyond Public Criticism. The decisions of the adjudicator and of the Supreme Court are of limited value in dealing with forms of public comment other than criticism of government. The issue of public comment is much more complex than the conventional rule suggests. This rule does not take adequate account of the extent to which public servants are inescapably involved in public comment in the regular performance of their duties. In speaking or writing for public consumption, public servants may serve such purposes as:[43]

1. providing information and analysis of a scientific or technical nature for consideration primarily by their professional colleagues within and outside government;

2. describing the administrative process and departmental organization and procedures;

3. explaining the content, implications, and administration of specific government policies and programs;

4. discussing, within the framework of governmental or departmental policy, the solution of problems through changes in existing programs or the development of new programs;

5. discussing issues on which governmental or departmental policy has not yet been determined;

6. explaining the nature of the political and policy process in government;

7. advocating reforms in the existing organization or procedures of government;

8. commenting in a constructively critical way on government policy or administration;

9. denouncing existing or potential government policies, programs, and operations; and

10. commenting in an overtly partisan way on public policy issues or on government policy or administration.

This list moves from types of public comment that are generally expected, required, or permissible, to those that are questionable, risky, or prohibited. Few public servants have ventured beyond the first four categories. The fourth category often involves public servants in bargaining, accommodation, and compromise on behalf of their political superiors. It is on these occasions that members of the public may see most clearly the nature and extent of bureaucratic power in the policy process. These meetings usually take place in private, but public servants are sometimes required to make presentations and answer questions in public forums where a larger measure of risk exists. Public servants have to be especially careful not to move beyond the fourth category by speculating about future government or departmental policy on which ministers have not yet made a decision.

As a result of the intimate links among politics, policy, and administration described earlier, public servants often enhance understanding of the political and policy process through their speeches and writings on the machinery of government and the administrative process. However, the major burden of explaining the political system to the public is likely to remain with politicians and scholars.

Public advocacy of administrative reform and constructive criticism of government activities may complement the public servants' information and conciliation functions. However, the participation of public servants in these forms of public comment is restricted by their political superiors, who bear public responsibility for the operations of government.

Denunciations and overtly partisan assessments of government policy or administration tend to be clearer than other forms of public comment in their manifestation, and in the certainty of their punishment. Both the traditional admonition against public comment and recent decisions by administrative tribunals prohibit such activity unless public servants are on leave of absence to seek election.

The unwritten rule against public comment is subject to varying interpretations and applications in contemporary society. Public servants are now involved in forms of public comment not explicitly covered by the conventional rule, and the nature of this involvement constitutes a significant departure from a position of political neutrality. It appears that public servants will increasingly be required to attend public meetings to provide information about the substance and implementation of government policies and programs. As a result, the public will become more aware of the influence that public servants bring to deliberations on public policy matters. It is often difficult for public servants to discuss government policy without indicating, inadvertently or otherwise, some measure of the influence they have—or could have—over the content of policy.

5. Anonymity and Ministerial Responsibility

As noted early in this chapter, the ideal model of political neutrality requires that public servants provide forthright and objective advice to their political masters in private and in confidence; political executives protect the anonymity of public servants by publicly accepting responsibility for departmental decisions. The anonymity of public servants depends, in large measure, on the vitality of the doctrine of individual ministerial responsibility, according to which ministers are personally responsible to the legislature both for their own actions and for those of their administrative subordinates. Thus, public servants are not directly answerable to the legislature and their minister protects their anonymity. Recent events have shown, however, that ministers will not invariably protect the anonymity of their officials by refusing to name or blame them publicly. This issue and the relationship of ministerial responsibility to political neutrality and anonymity are discussed in Chapter 17.

The Decline of Official Anonymity.   Public service anonymity depends significantly on factors other than the operation of ministerial responsibility. Departures from political neutrality in the areas of patronage and political activity also diminish official anonymity, but the greatest threat is probably the expansion of public comment described earlier. The increased interaction of public servants with both individual citizens and specific "publics," or clientele groups, reveals the nature of official involvement in policy development. The cumulative impact of the growing information and conciliation functions performed by public servants is a gradual, but significant, decline in official anonymity.

The anonymity of public servants has also been diminished by their more frequent appearances before legislative committees. Their diplomatic skills are often severely taxed as they strive to describe and explain their department's programs fully and frankly, while preserving their loyalty to their minister and their reputation for impartiality. On occasion, however, legislators, pressure groups, journalists, and others concerned with the committees' deliberations can discern the actual or potential power of public servants in the policy process. Elaboration on the interaction between public servants and legislators is contained in Chapter 17.

The pervasive role of the news media in contemporary society has been reflected in increased media coverage of the activities and identities of public servants. As explained in Chapter 21, the media and public servants share a mutual desire to inform the public about government programs. Public servants utilize the media for public relations and publicity—to tell their department's story and to sell their department's programs. The media serve as excellent channels of communication to the public for officials engaged in public comment that requires the description and explanation of government programs. The media, in turn, analyze the purposes and, whenever possible, identify the personalities involved in the development and administration of programs. This media coverage helps to limit bureaucratic power by exposing the activities of public servants to public questioning and criticism.

The extent to which public servants are exposed to the public's gaze through the news media depends largely on the position they occupy, on current interest in their department's activities, and on their personal views and those of their minister on anonymity. Certain public servants (e.g., a deputy minister of finance) are better known because of the enduring importance of their position; others receive publicity during periods of public controversy in their sphere of responsibilities.

Since the early 1990s, there has been greatly increased emphasis on improving government service to the public by pushing decision-making power down the administrative hierarchy and out to field offices. This means public servants will be in more direct and more frequent contact with their clients and other stakeholders, thereby becoming more visible to the public generally.

Although the tradition of anonymity remains strong among public servants, their visibility has been heightened by changes in political institutions and practices, and by the media's response to demands for more public information. This gradual decline in official anonymity is likely to continue, revealing the significant role of public servants in the political process. A federal deputy minister has noted that "[a]nonymity and invisibility are disappearing. The public is demanding communication with a senior public service with names, faces and telephone numbers they can call."[45]

> [P]ublic service anonymity is not an absolute. It has been significantly qualified both here and abroad, and could be qualified still further, as the practice of parliamentary government continues to evolve. If and as it does so, an important question will become not so much whether public servants are anonymous, but how they behave when they are in the public eye, [and] whether this behaviour is consistent with other public service values, including the principles of responsible government itself.
>
> *Source: Federal Deputy Ministers, Task Force on Public Service Values and Ethics*[44]

6. Permanence in Office

The Case for Security of Tenure.   As previously noted, the preservation of political neutrality requires that "public servants execute policy decisions loyally, irrespective of the philosophy and programs of the party in power and regardless of their personal opinions. As a result, public servants enjoy security of tenure during good behaviour and satisfactory performance." Thus, in the event of a change of government, official neutrality helps to ensure continuity of administration by competent and experienced public servants, as well as the provision of impartial advice on policy options and the loyal implementation of policy decisions. Security of tenure enables a career public servant not only to establish and wield influence in the policy process but also to continue to exercise such influence even if there is a change in the governing party. Long tenure enables public servants to acquire knowledge and experience, both in specific policy fields and in the political-administrative system within which policy decisions are made. Permanence in office for public servants increases their power vis-à-vis politicians. Ministers cannot match the expertise of their senior officials, and the frequent rotation of ministers among departments prevents them from accumulating much experience in particular policy areas.

As public servants, especially at the senior levels, become more overtly or apparently political, the argument for political appointments to senior posts is strengthened. Thus, permanence in office depends largely on adherence to the elements of political neutrality already described. The merit system is designed to bring about a more permanent public service[46] by minimizing the number of patronage appointments and avoiding a turnover of personnel following a change of government. Senior public servants are not permitted to engage in partisan political activity or public criticism of government. Finally, the preservation of ministerial responsibility and public service anonymity helps to protect officials from public identification as supporters or opponents of particular policies.

Despite these efforts to achieve the fact and the appearance of administrative impartiality, Opposition party leaders have frequently promised, if elected, to turf out senior officials because of their assumed contribution to government policies to which these leaders are opposed. Therefore, public servants must be able to demonstrate the capacity to adapt quickly and effectively to the requirements of a new governing party.

When permanence in office for public servants has been combined with longevity in office by a particular political party, a change of government presents an especially difficult challenge to the capacity of public servants to serve different political masters impartially. It is understandable that senior officials who have worked closely with ministers in the development of existing policies should be apprehensive about the arrival of a new governing party. During the Diefenbaker government, unhealthy tension often existed between senior public servants and the government. There were, however, "few resignations and few drastic changes in policy. The new ministers soon discovered that a good civil servant conceives it his duty to serve his political master to the best of his ability, and that the higher civil service was as effective at advising the new government as it had been the old."[47] In general, subsequent new governments have come to the same conclusion.[48]

During the brief Clark period, few senior officials were invited or decided to resign, but ministers in the Clark government disagree as to whether they were well and faithfully served by senior public servants. Flora MacDonald, the Secretary of State for External Affairs, stated that her efforts to seek advice from persons outside government were resisted almost entirely by "those who really have their hands on the levers of power—the senior mandarins." She also complained about the use by senior public servants of such "entrapment devices" as the many "crisis corridor decisions" with which she was faced, unduly lengthy and numerous memos, the late delivery of her submissions to cabinet, and "the one-dimensional opinions put forward in memos." She noted that she "was expected to accept the unanimous recommendation of the Department" and that she was "seldom, if ever ... given the luxury of multiple-choice options on matters of major import."[49]

The experience of other ministers was different.[50] One minister stated that his experience with officials in his own department and "indeed, generally, was not similar to Miss MacDonald's. I am not suggesting there might not have been some incidents where public servants with deep political or policy convictions which differ from mine might have endeavoured to frustrate or mislead me. However, generally I found them to be hard-working, dedicated and professional."[51]

These differing views support the argument presented earlier in this chapter that the extent of bureaucratic power varies according to such factors as the policy or program under consideration, the department or agency involved, and the style and competence of ministers and their officials. Former prime minister Clark stated that he and his government had no complaint regarding the treatment they received from the senior public service. He did ask, however, whether "a large and diverse country like ours can be as well served as Britain is by the exclusive reliance upon a professional Public Service, or whether we should be leaning more towards elements of the American system which allow a new government to bring in people who agree with its point of view."[52]

The Case for Politicization.   There is some support in Canada for a system of political appointments similar to that in the United States. Supporters of a politicized public service usually cite the following benefits from political appointments to senior public service posts:

- a strong commitment to implementing the policies of the new government;

- an injection of new ideas and approaches toward government policies and processes;

- the restoration and preservation of political (ministerial) control over permanent officials and the decision-making processes of government;

- advice on policy issues that is more sensitive to their partisan political implications;

- greater trust by ministers in their policy advisors.

Under this system, the incumbents of the most senior public service positions would be replaced whenever a change in government occurred. Some senior appointments would thus be held on a temporary rather than a permanent basis. The power of career public servants would be reduced because they would not normally be appointed to the highest administrative posts. However, assuming regular changes in the governing party, the tenure of senior political appointees would be too brief to enable them to exercise as much power based on experience and expertise as do career public servants.

At present, a shift to a system of political appointments either in the federal government or in most provincial governments is unlikely. Career public servants in Canada can normally expect security of tenure during good conduct, adequate performance, and political neutrality. Note must be taken, however, of a gradual politicization of the senior bureaucracy in certain provinces. For example, the Conservative government that came to power in Saskatchewan in 1982 dismissed about two hundred senior public servants. The rationale for the sweeping nature of the dismissals is unclear; many of those dismissed were career public servants with no partisan affiliation. In Ontario, the New Democratic Party government that took office in 1990 made a considerable number of partisan political appointments to the deputy minister ranks. This created the risk that these appointees would be dismissed with a change of government and that a new round of partisan hirings would occur. However, the Progressive Conservative government that succeeded the New Democrats committed itself to the traditional model of a professional, nonpartisan public service.

Political Neutrality and Bureaucratic Power

The several components of the concept of political neutrality are interrelated; changes in one component tend to affect one or more of the others. For example, a substantial increase in patronage appointments to senior public service posts is likely to have a significant impact on the anonymity and the security of tenure of public servants—and indeed on ministerial responsibility. Similarly, a substantial increase in high-profile partisan political activity by public servants can lead to a greater measure of political patronage.

The present operations of Canada's public services are not in accord with a strict interpretation of the traditional doctrine of political neutrality. Some of the requirements of the traditional doctrine remain substantially unchanged; but some have never been met, and others have been altered to keep pace with changing political, social, and technological circumstances. A summary of the extent to which governments have, in general, departed from the requirements of political neutrality outlined earlier in this chapter is shown below.

1. Politics, policy, and administration are closely intertwined. Politicians and public servants are involved in both the making and the implementation of policy decisions. Elected officials, notably cabinet ministers, make final decisions on major policy matters, but public servants influence these decisions and make decisions of their own under authority delegated by cabinet and the legislature.

2. The vast majority of public servants are appointed on the basis of merit. A substantial number are appointed on the grounds of contributions to the governing political party, but, at a senior level, most of these political appointments are made to agencies, boards, or commissions rather than to regular government departments. Patronage appointments continue to be made at relatively low levels of the public service in several Canadian jurisdictions.

3. Public servants are permitted to engage in certain partisan political activities. The extent of permissible participation varies among governments but it is gradually increasing. Public servants who wish to stand for public office are required in most governments to seek permission for a leave of absence. They are also forbidden to engage in partisan political activity while at work and their political and administrative superiors are forbidden to coerce them into performing partisan work.

4. Public servants in most governments are prohibited from expressing publicly their personal views on government policies or administration, especially if these views are critical of the government or partisan in nature. Moreover, they are forbidden by law and tradition to engage in any forms of public comment in which they make use of confidential information to which they are privy by virtue of their official position. However, many public servants are required to engage in public comment during the performance of their official duties. The difficulty of drawing a clear line between permissible and unacceptable forms of public comment prompts public servants to be cautious when speaking or writing for public consumption.

5. Public servants provide forthright and objective advice to their political masters in private and in confidence; political executives normally protect the anonymity of public servants by publicly accepting responsibility for departmental decisions. Public service anonymity has been diminished to some extent by the role that public servants are required to play in explaining policies and programs to the public and to legislators. In playing this role, public servants must be careful not to infringe on their minister's sphere of responsibility by justifying or speculating on government policy.

6. Public servants usually execute policy decisions loyally, irrespective of the philosophy and programs of the party in power and regardless of their

personal opinions; as a result, public servants usually enjoy security of tenure, except in the event of staff cutbacks, unsatisfactory performance, or bad behaviour. With a change of government, however, public servants who are political appointees are likely to lose their positions.

Thus, public servants are actively involved in the political system both by necessity in the areas of policy development and execution, and by choice in the sphere of political partisanship. This involvement accounts, in large part, for the nature and extent of bureaucratic power in contemporary Canadian governments. The next chapter assesses the implications of this bureaucratic power for the concept and practice of administrative responsibility.

NOTES

1. Jeffery A. Hutchings, Carl Walters, and Richard L. Haedrich, "Is Scientific Inquiry Cimpatible with Government Information Control?" *Canadian Journal of Fisheries and Aquatic Sciences,* 54, May 1997, 1198–1210.
2. Standing Committe on Fisheries and Oceans, *The East Coast Report,* Interim Report tabled March 1998, para. 153, rec. 20.
3. Ibid., supplementary opinion to recommendation 20.
4. The George C. Nowlan Lecture, Acadia University, 7 February 1977. Reprinted in *The Globe and Mail* (8 February 1977).
5. Mitchell Sharp, "Reflections of a Former Minister of the Crown." Address to the Toronto Regional Group of the Institute of Public Administration of Canada, 29 November 1976, 6–7.
6. This model was first set out in Kenneth Kernaghan, "Politics, Policy and Public Servants: Political Neutrality Revisited," *Canadian Public Administration* 21 (fall 1976): 432–56. For the application of the model to municipal government, see: David Siegel, "Politics, Politicians, and Public Servants in Non-Partisan Local Governments," *Canadian Public Administration* 37 (spring 1994): 7–30. See also the chapter on the "Politically Neutral Public Servant," in Kenneth Kernaghan and John Langford, *The Responsible Public Servant* (Toronto: Institute of Public Administration of Canada, and Halifax: Institute for Research on Public Policy, 1990).
7. Canada, Public Service Commission, *Annual Report 1995–96* (Ottawa: Minister of Supply and Services, 1996).
8. R.J.S. Baker, *Administrative Theory and Public Administration* (London: Hutchison, 1972), 13.
9. *Canadian Public Policy and Administration* (Toronto: McGraw-Hill Ryerson, 1981), 99.
10. Woodrow Wilson, "The Study of Administration," reprinted in Peter Woll, ed., *Public Administration and Policy* (New York: Harper & Row, 1966), 28–29.
11. Wallace S. Sayre, "Premises of Public Administration: Past and Emerging," *Public Administration Review* 18, no. 1 (1958): 103.
12. Quoted in J.E. Hodgetts et al., *The Biography of an Institution: The Civil Service Commission of Canada, 1908–1967* (Montreal: McGill-Queen's University Press, 1972), 56.
13. Ibid. (Emphasis added.)
14. See, for example, Luther Gulick's "Politics, Administration and the New Deal," in *Annals of the American Academy of Political and Social Science* (New York: Russell, 1967, originally published in 1933); and Pendleton Herring, *Public Administration and the Public Interest* (New York: Russell, 1967; originally published in 1936).

15. Paul Appleby, *Policy and Administration* (University, Ala.: University of Alabama Press, 1949), 170. See also Dwight Waldo, *The Administrative State* (New York: Ronald Press, 1948); and Harold Stein, *Public Administration and Policy Development: A Casebook* (New York: Harcourt, Brace and Co., 1952).

16. See Frank Marini, ed., *Toward a New Public Administration: The Minnowbrook Perspective* (Scranton, Pa.: Chandler, 1971).

17. See especially Eugene P. Dvorin and Robert H. Simmons, *From Amoral to Humane Bureaucracy* (San Francisco: Canfield Press, 1972); and Louis C. Gawthrop, *Administrative Politics and Social Change* (New York: St. Martin's Press, 1971).

18. Gordon Robertson, "The Coming Crisis in the North," *Journal of Canadian Studies* 2 (February 1967): 3.

19. See Chapter 7.

20. See Kenneth Kernaghan and T.H. McLeod, "Mandarins and Ministers in the Canadian Administrative State," in O.P. Dwivedi, ed., *The Canadian Administrative State* (Toronto: University of Toronto Press, 1982), 17–30.

21. Wayne A.R. Leys, "Ethics and Administrative Discretion," *Public Administration Review* 3 (winter 1943): 23.

22. See Denys C. Holland and John P. McGowan, *Delegated Legislation in Canada* (Toronto: Carswell, 1989), chs. 1–6.

23. Eric Hehner, "Growth of Discretions—Decline of Accountability," in Kenneth Kernaghan, ed., *Public Administration in Canada: Selected Readings*, 5th ed., (Toronto: Methuen, 1985), 342.

24. Robert Presthus, *The Organizational Society* (New York: Vintage Books, 1962), p. 53.

25. For an account of the evolution of patronage in the federal and provincial spheres, see Jeffrey Simpson, *Spoils of Power: The Politics of Patronage* (Toronto: Collins, 1988).

26. R.H. Dowdell, "Public Personnel Administration," in Kenneth Kernaghan, ed., *Public Administration in Canada*, 4th ed. (Toronto: Methuen, 1982), 196. Not everyone agrees that the "reasonable opportunity" component should be included in the definition and there is disagreement on what constitutes a reasonable opportunity. The courts have consistently defined merit as best qualified.

27. Ibid.

28. H. McDonald Clokie, *Canadian Government and Politics* (Toronto: Longmans, Green, 1944), 190.

29. Canada, Royal Commission on Government Organization, *Report*, vol. 1 (Ottawa: Queen's Printer, 1962), 371.

30. Between 1948 and 1972, 12.1 percent of retiring or defeated ministers were appointed to patronage positions. See W.A. Matheson, *The Prime Minister and the Cabinet* (Toronto: Methuen, 1976), 121.

31. See Chapter 16 for elaboration on the role of ministerial staff.

32. See J.E. Hodgetts and O.P. Dwivedi, *Provincial Governments as Employers* (McGill-Queen's University Press, 1974), ch. 2.

33. J.E. Hodgetts and O.P. Dwivedi, "Administration and Personnel," in David J. Bellamy, Jon H. Pammett, and Donald C. Rowat, eds., *The Provincial Political Systems: Comparative Essays* (Toronto: Methuen, 1976), 347.

34. See Doug Love, "The Merit Principle in the Provincial Governments of Atlantic Canada," *Canadian Public Administration* 31 (fall 1988): 335–81.

35. See S.M. Lipset, *Agrarian Socialism: The Cooperative Commonwealth Federation in Saskatchewan* (Berkeley: University of California Press, 1959); Evelyn Eager, *Saskatchewan Government* (Saskatoon: Western Producer Prairie Books, 1980), 164–67; and Hans J. Michelmann and Jeffrey S. Steeves, "The 1982 Transition in Power in

Saskatchewan: The Progressive Conservatives and the Public Service," *Canadian Public Administration* 28 (spring 1985): 1–23.

36. For a definition of political activity and an account of the arguments usually raised for and against the political activity of government employees, see Kenneth Kernaghan, "Political Rights and Political Neutrality: Finding the Balance Point," *Canadian Public Administration* 29 (winter 1986): 639–52; and "The Political Rights of Canada's Federal Public Servants," in Michael Cassidy, ed., *Democratic Rights and Electoral Reform in Canada* (Toronto: Dundurn Press, for the Royal Commission on Electoral Reform and Party Financing, 1991), 213–67.

37. *Public Service 2000. The Renewal of the Public Service of Canada* (Ottawa: Supply and Services, 1990) 63, 64. (Emphasis added.)

38. *Canada Statutes*, 8–9 Geo. v, c. 12.

39. Arthur Kroeger, "On Being a Deputy Minister," *Policy Options* 13 (May 1992): 6.

40. *Osborne* v. *Canada (Treasury Board)* (1991), 82 D.L.R. (4th) 321 (S.C.C.)

41. *Neil A. Fraser, Grievor,* v. *Treasury Board (Department of National Revenue, Taxation) Employer,* Public Service Staff Relations Board Decision, 31 May 1982, 16.

42. Supreme Court of Canada, *Neil Fraser and Public Service Staff Relations Board* (1985) 2 S.C.R., 468, 470.

43. This classification is an expansion of that set out in Kenneth Kernaghan, *Ethical Conduct: Guidelines for Government Employees* (Toronto: Institute of Public Administration of Canada, 1975), 36.

44. Task Force on Public Service Values and Ethics. Discussion Paper on Values and Ethics in the Public Service (Ottawa: Privy Council Office, 1996), 13.

45. Bruce Rawson, "Public Service 2000 Service to the Public Task Force: Findings and Implications," *Canadian Public Administration* 34 (fall 1991): 495.

46. See the discussion of career public service in Chapter 23.

47. J.R. Mallory, *The Structure of Canadian Government* (Toronto: Macmillan, 1971), 116.

48. Jacques Bourgault and Stéphane Dion conclude that the Mulroney government did not politicize the role of deputy ministers. See Brian Mulroney: "A-t-il politisé les sous-ministres?" *Canadian Public Administration* 32 (spring 1989): 63–83.

49. See "The Ministers and the Mandarins," *Policy Options* 1 (September–October 1980): 29–31.

50. Reported in confidential communications with Professor Kernaghan in October 1980.

51. Ibid.

52. Transcript of an Address (including Question and Answer Period) to the 11th Annual Leadership Conference sponsored by the Centre for the Study of the Presidency, Ottawa, 19 October 1980, 14.

BIBLIOGRAPHY

Atkinson, Michael M., and William D. Coleman. "Bureaucrats and Politicians in Canada: An Examination of the Political Administration Model." *Comparative Political Studies* 18 (April 1985): 58–80.

Baker, Walter. "Power and the Public Service." *Canadian Public Administration* 30 (spring 1987): 14–33.

Blakeney, Allan, and Sandford Borins. *Political Management in Canada.* Toronto: McGraw-Hill Ryerson, 1992.

Bourgault, Jacques, and Barbara Carroll. "The Canadian Senior Public Service: The Last Vestiges of the Whitehold Model?" In Jacques Bourgault et al., eds. *Public Administration and Public Management: Experiences in Canada.* Quebec: Les Publications du Quebec, 1997, 91–100.

Bourgault, Jacques, and Stéphane Dion. "Brian Mulroney a-t-il politisé les sous ministres." *Canadian Public Administration* 32 (spring 1989): 63–83.

———"Governments Come and Go, But What of Senior Civil Servants? Canadian Deputy Ministers and Transitions in Power (1867–1987)." *Governance* 2, no. 2 (1989): 124–51.

Campbell, Colin. *Governments Under Stress: Political Executives and Key Bureaucrats in Washington, London and Ottawa.* Toronto: University of Toronto Press, 1983.

Cassidy, Michael. "Political Rights for Public Servants: A Federal Perspective I." *Canadian Public Administration* 29 (winter 1986): 653–64.

D'Aquino, Thomas. "The Public Service of Canada: The Case for Political Neutrality." *Canadian Public Administration* 27 (spring 1984): 14–23.

Dawson, R.M. "The Civil Service of Canada." *Canadian Journal of Economics and Political Science* 2 (August 1936): 291.

Dvorin, Eugene P., and Robert H. Simmons. *From Amoral to Humane Bureaucracy.* San Francisco: Canfield, 1972.

Hodgetts, J.E. "The Civil Service and Policy Formation." *Canadian Journal of Economics and Political Science* 23 (November 1957): 467–79.

Hodgetts, J.E., William McCloskey, Reginald Whitaker, and V. Seymour Wilson. *The Biography of an Institution: The Civil Service Commission of Canada, 1908–1967.* Montreal: McGill-Queen's University Press, 1972.

Hutchings, Jeffrey A., Carl Walters, and Richard L. Haedrich. "Is Scientific Inquiry Compatible with Government Information Control?" *Canadian Journal of Fisheries and Aquatic Sciences.*

Kernaghan, Kenneth. "Politics, Policy and Public Servants: Political Neutrality Revisited." *Canadian Public Administration* 19 (fall 1976): 432–56.

———. "Changing Concepts of Power and Responsibility in the Canadian Public Service." *Canadian Public Administration* 21 (fall 1978): 389–406.

———. "Power, Parliament and Public Servants: Ministerial Responsibility Reexamined." *Canadian Public Policy* 5 (autumn 1979): 383–96.

———. "Political Rights and Political Neutrality: Finding the Balance Point." *Canadian Public Administration* 29 (winter 1986): 639–52.

———. "The Political Rights of Canada's Federal Public Servants." In Michael Cassidy, ed., *Democratic Rights and Electoral Reform.* Royal Commission on Electoral Reform and Party Financing. Vol. 10. Toronto: Dundurn Press, 1993, 213–67.

Kernaghan, Kenneth, and John Langford. *The Responsible Public Servant.* Toronto: Institute of Public Administration of Canada, and Halifax: Institute for Research on Public Policy, 1990, ch. 3.

Kernaghan, Kenneth, and T.H. McLeod. "Mandarins and Ministers in the Canadian Administrative State." In O.P. Dwivedi, ed., *The Administrative State in Canada.* Toronto: University of Toronto Press, 1982.

Love, Doug. "The Merit Principle in the Provincial Governments of Atlantic Canada." *Canadian Public Administration* 31 (fall 1988): 335–51.

MacDonald, Flora. "The Ministers and the Mandarins." *Policy Options* 1 (September–October 1980): 29–31.

Nakamura, Robert T., and Frank Smallwood. *The Politics of Policy Implementation.* New York: St. Martin's Press, 1980.

Peters, B. Guy. *The Politics of Bureaucracy.* 2nd ed. New York: Longman, 1984.

Pressman, Jeffrey L., and Aaron Wildavsky. *Implementation.* Berkeley: University of California Press, 1965.

Siegel, David. "Politics, Politicians, and Public Servants in Non-Partisan Local Governments." *Canadian Public Administration* 37 (spring 1994): 7–30.

Simpson, Jeffrey. *Spoils of Power: The Politics of Patronage.* Toronto: Collins, 1988.

Wilson, V. Seymour. *Canadian Public Policy and Administration.* Toronto: McGraw-Hill Ryerson, 1981, ch. 4.

Zussman, David. "Walking the Tightrope: The Mulroney Government and the Public Service." In Michael J. Prince, ed., *How Ottawa Spends, 1986–87: Tracking the Tories.* Toronto: Methuen, 1986, 25–82.

———. "Managing the Federal Public Service as the Knot Tightens." In Katherine A. Graham, ed., *How Ottawa Spends, 1990–1991: Tracking the Second Agenda.* Ottawa: Carleton University Press, 1990, 247–75.

14

Responsibility, Accountability, and Ethics

Public organizations that try to be more efficient and effective by being more innovative can run into problems of accountability and ethics. Consider the partnership created by a provincial government department to provide improved service to the public at lower cost.[1] The department and a business firm named Data Corp each invested $40 million to computerize a new client registration system. Another firm, Info Tech, which lost the partnership bid to Data Corp, complained that the government had not lived up to its promise to make the whole deal, including the names of the Data Corp owners, public. The opposition parties in the legislature demanded full accountability in the form of detailed information on the firm's ownership and on the terms of the partnership agreement—and the news media began to report the story. Then, Info Tech charged that confidential information had been leaked during the bidding process, an accusation that was investigated by the provincial police. The government said that it wanted to release the requested information but Data Corp used the province's Privacy Act to prevent this disclosure.

This case raises several issues that are examined in this chapter. Are public servants held sufficiently accountable for the power they exercise? What ethical standards do they bring to their recommendations and decisions? What constitutes ethical behaviour? How much transparency in government operations is feasible? Where does the public interest lie when public servants are balancing such values as efficiency, accountability, and integrity?

It is notable that the public service values outlined in Chapter 12 are central not only to the evolution of Canadian public administration but also to the theoretical literature on administrative responsibility. The responsible public servant is commonly perceived as one who pursues such values as accountability, integrity, neutrality, efficiency, and effectiveness. This chapter focuses on accountability and integrity.

🏛 THE IMPORTANCE OF ADMINISTRATIVE RESPONSIBILITY

During the past thirty years in particular, public concern about responsibility in government has been stimulated in Western democratic states, including Canada, by events involving illegal, unethical, or questionable activities by both politicians and public servants. Discussion of incidents of political espionage, conflicts of interest, disclosures of confidential information, and alleged wasteful spending have revealed that both the general public and students of government disagree among themselves as to what constitutes irresponsible conduct, who should assume blame in particular cases, and what penalty should be paid.

The scope and complexity of government activities have become so great that it is often difficult to determine the actual—as opposed to the legal or constitutional—locus of responsibility for specific decisions. As explained in Chapter 17, political executives (i.e., cabinet ministers) are held responsible for personal wrongdoing. They are not, however, expected to assume responsibility by way of resignation or demotion for acts of administrative subordinates about which they could not reasonably be expected to have knowledge. Yet it is frequently impossible to assign individual responsibility to public servants for administrative transgressions because so many public servants have contributed to the decision-making process. The allocation of responsibility in government has been complicated even further by the interposition of political appointees or temporary officials between political executives and permanent public servants.

While the involvement of political executives in unlawful or questionable activities has drawn much public attention to the issue of *political* responsibility, the status of *administrative* responsibility has also become a matter of increasing anxiety. As noted in the previous chapter, elected officials make the final decisions on major public policy issues, but public servants have significant influence on these decisions and have authority to make decisions on their own that affect the individual and collective rights of the citizenry.

Concern about the preservation of administrative responsibility is shared in varying degrees by all major actors in the political system—whether they be political executives, legislators, judges, interest group and mass media representatives, members of the general public, or public servants. As a result of efforts by these various actors to promote responsible administrative conduct, the decisions of public servants are subject to an almost bewildering assortment of controls and influences, many of which are examined in Chapters 15 to 21.

🏛 THEORIES OF ADMINISTRATIVE RESPONSIBILITY

The Conventional Theories

The traditional concepts of administrative responsibility may be explained by reference to the celebrated debate between Carl Friedrich and Herman Finer during the period 1935–41.[2]

Both Friedrich and Finer correctly identified the source of burgeoning bureaucratic power as the rapid expansion of government's service and regulatory functions. However, they disagreed vehemently on the most effective means of guarding against abuse of administrative discretion so as to maintain and promote responsible administrative conduct. Their disagreement was, in large part, an outgrowth of their differing conceptions of the capacity of political systems to adapt to change and of the proper role of public servants. To achieve administrative responsibility, Finer placed primary faith in controls and sanctions exercised over public servants by the legislature, the judiciary, and the administrative hierarchy. In his insistence on the predominant importance of political responsibility (i.e., responsibility to elected officials), he claimed that "the political and administrative history of all ages" had shown that "sooner or later there is an abuse of power when external punitive controls are lacking."[3]

Friedrich relied more heavily on the propensity of public servants to be self-directing and self-regulating, the measure of which was their responsiveness to the dual standard of technical knowledge and popular sentiment. While he admitted the continuing need for political responsibility, he argued that a policy was irresponsible if it was adopted

> without proper regard to the existing sum of human knowledge concerning the technical issues involved ... [or] without proper regard for existing preferences in the community, and more particularly its prevailing majority. Consequently, the responsible administrator is one who is responsive to these two dominant factors: technical knowledge and popular sentiment.[4]

Friedrich asserted also that "parliamentary responsibility is largely inoperative and certainly ineffectual"[5] and that "the task of clear and consistent policy formation has passed ... into the hands of administrators and is bound to continue to do so."[6]

Finer admitted this problem but stressed the necessity of remedying the several deficiencies of political control over administrative officials. He believed that the means of legislative control should be improved.[7] He argued further that public servants should not determine their own course of action. Rather, the elected representatives of the people should "determine the course of action of public servants to the most minute degree that is technically feasible."[8] Finer presented an excellent summary of both his position and his critique of Friedrich's stand in his explanation of "the two definitions" of administrative responsibility:

> First, responsibility may mean that X is accountable for Y to Z. Second, responsibility may mean an inward personal sense of moral obligation. In the first definition the essence is the externality of the agency or persons to whom an account is to be rendered, and it can mean very little without that agency having authority over X, determining the lines of X's obligation and the terms of its continuance or revocation. The second definition puts the emphasis on the conscience of the agent, and ... if he commits an error it is an error only when recognized by his own conscience, and ... the punishment of the agent will be merely the twinges thereof. The one implies public execution; the other hara-kari.[9]

Finer described the sum of Friedrich's arguments as *moral* responsibility, as opposed to his own emphasis on *political* responsibility.

Friedrich's contention that administrative responsibility can be more effectively elicited than enforced raises a critical issue for contemporary discussion of the subject. He believed that responsible conduct depended to a large extent on "sound work rules and effective morale."[10] To this end, he suggested that the environment of government employment be changed. Public servants were to be granted the right to organize into staff associations and to bargain collectively with the government. Furthermore, responsibility to technical knowledge could not be assured unless public servants were permitted to discuss policy issues publicly. He noted that "in matters of vital importance the general public is entitled to the views of its permanent servants."[11] Finer argued for the preservation of the official's anonymity so that the official may avoid "bringing himself and his colleagues into partisan contempt"[12] and making himself "the instrument of conflict between 'the general public' … and the legislature."[13]

An understanding of the Friedrich-Finer debate is an essential foundation on which to construct subsequent discussion. It raises several of the major issues of administrative responsibility still being debated by contemporary scholars, albeit in a vastly different social and political environment. The strength of Finer's approach lay in his recognition of the continuing need for political controls over the bureaucracy. Its primary weakness lay in his failure to anticipate the inadequacy of these controls to ensure administrative responsibility in a period of ever-accelerating political and social change. The strength of Friedrich's argument rested on his awareness of the deficiency of solely applying political controls. Its major weakness lay in the difficulty of reconciling conflicts between the two criteria of technical knowledge and popular sentiment.

Although the Friedrich-Finer controversy preceded the postwar assault on traditional principles and tenets of public administration, the seeds of change had already borne enough fruit for Friedrich to see the emerging trends. Among the developments he foresaw were the rejection of the politics-administration dichotomy, with the acceptance of the role of public servants in policy development; the increased need to delegate to public servants powers of a legislative and judicial nature; the strikingly rapid growth and significance of professionalism in the public service; recognition of the effect of employee morale on work performance; agitation for the extension to public employees of the rights to bargain collectively and to speak publicly on issues of public policy; and, finally, demands for direct citizen participation in the administrative process. It is instructive to note the similarities between some of Friedrich's main arguments and the current emphasis on empowering public servants discussed in Chapter 5.

Criticisms of the Conventional Theories

The Friedrich and Finer approaches have been subject to a number of critiques, and alternative interpretations have been formulated.[14] However, their approaches have remained the major contending ones; and most writers on administrative responsibility have referred to the Friedrich-Finer debate with a view to supporting, attacking, or updating one or both sides of the argument.

Michael Harmon, for example, argues that, despite their differences, both Finer and Friedrich take a negative view of human nature and of administrators in particular because they agree that "without the checks provided by either the law or the processes of professional socialization, the resultant behaviour of administrators would be both selfish and capricious."[15] Harmon looks to the existentialist's notion of self-development and self-actualization as a basis for a new theory of administrative responsibility. Officials are expected to become much more actively engaged in the initiation and promotion of policy. Harmon fails, however, to reconcile this increased participation with the conventional idea that administrators' decisions should be guided by the values and goals of elected politicians within the constraints of the law and the administrative hierarchy.

Theodore Lowi, writing in the context of the United States, recommends that the Supreme Court declare "invalid and unconstitutional any delegation of powers to an administrative agency that is not accompanied by clear standards of implementation."[16] This call to the legislature to specify in more precise terms the course of action for public servants is complemented by a plea for "early and frequent *administrative rule-making*."[17] Rather than relying primarily on case-by-case adjudication under a statute delegating broad powers in vague language, public servants should formulate rules that provide standards for the adjudication of cases under that statute. Harmon and Lowi offer a different but related version of the Finer-Friedrich debate.

Objective and Subjective Responsibility

Frederick Mosher provides a broader, more inclusive classification than the Friedrich-Finer categories by making a distinction between objective responsibility (or accountability) and psychological or subjective responsibility. According to his widely accepted definition, *objective responsibility* "connotes the responsibility of a person or an organization to someone else, outside of self, for some thing or some kind of performance. It is closely akin to *accountability* or *answerability*. If one fails to carry out legitimate directives, he is judged irresponsible, and may be subjected to penalties."[18] Psychological or *subjective responsibility*, by way of contrast, focuses

> not upon to whom and for what one is responsible (according to law and the organization chart) but to whom and for what one *feels* responsible and *behaves* responsibly. This meaning, which is sometimes described as *personal* responsibility, is more nearly synonymous with identification, loyalty and conscience than it is with accountability and answerability.[19]

Thus, Mosher views administrative responsibility as a broad concept that includes administrative accountability as one of its two major components.

The presence of subjective or psychological responsibility is more difficult to discern than that of objective responsibility, but there is some evidence of its existence and its influence. The deputy ministers surveyed by the Royal Commission on Financial Management and Accountability (the Lambert Commission) were in complete agreement that they felt "personally responsible" for ensuring that they had good financial controls.[20] Moreover, when asked to what persons and organizations they considered themselves *most* responsible for specific subjects, a large number of deputies answered "myself" in regard to performing the role of leader for the department's employees, managing their executive team, and building their department's management capability.[21] Despite the importance of this notion of subjective responsibility, it is accountability (objective responsibility) that has received by far the most public and scholarly attention.

🏛 ADMINISTRATIVE ACCOUNTABILITY

The questions commonly asked about the accountability of public servants are: *Who* is accountable? *To whom* is accountability owed? *For what* is accountability owed? *By what means* can accountability be achieved?[22] These questions are dealt with in Chapters 15 to 21 as an integral part of an examination of interactions between public servants and other actors in the political system.

The current emphasis on accountability is a result of both the need to strengthen accountability in government generally and the very broad interpretations that the word accountability has gradually acquired. For example, the Lambert Commission viewed accountability as "the activating, but fragile, element permeating a complex network connecting the government upward to Parliament and downward and outward to a geographically dispersed bureaucracy grouped in a bewildering array of departments, corporations, boards and commissions."[23] This definition portrays well the breadth of meaning currently given to the notion of accountability in government. It is, however, too sweeping a definition to be very useful in operational terms; moreover, it covers the accountability of both politicians and public servants, whereas our primary concern is with public service accountability. A narrower and, for our purposes, a more useful definition of *administrative accountability* is:

> the obligation of public servants to be answerable for fulfilling responsibilities that flow from the authority given them.… Internal accountability holds public servants answerable to their line superiors for their own actions and the actions of their subordinates.… External accountability holds public servants answerable to the public as well. The normal channel through which this requirement is satisfied is the minister.[24]

This definition draws attention to the fact that public servants are only *directly* accountable to a limited number of political actors, and that to hold public servants accountable, one must be able to exercise authority over them. Indeed, a more useful distinction than that between internal and external accountability is that between direct and indirect accountability. Public servants are directly accountable only to political and administrative superiors, to the courts, and to any internal governmental authorities (e.g., central agencies) to which accountability is required by law or the administrative hierarchy. They are not *directly* accountable to the legislature, to pressure groups, to the news media, or to the general public. However, they are generally required to explain their decisions and actions to these entities, and they may feel a sense of psychological or personal responsibility toward them.

Enforcing accountability for the exercise of bureaucratic power has become more difficult as our public services have grown in size and their responsibilities have grown in complexity. The decision-making process in government is often so lengthy and complicated that it is difficult to single out those public servants who should be held responsible for specific recommendations and decisions. Moreover, as will be explained in Chapter 17, the present application of the doctrine of ministerial responsibility does not ensure that ministers will be held responsible for maladministration in their departments.

Another obstacle on the road to accountability is the wide range of authorities to which public servants are deemed to be accountable. While, in general, it is agreed that public servants are accountable first of all to their minister, in practice public servants receive directions, rewards, and penalties from a variety of sources. This is one of the major differences between public and private sector administration. Subsequent chapters will show that governments have an impressive array of mechanisms to promote administrative accountability.

🏛 ADMINISTRATIVE ETHICS[25]

As noted in Chapter 12, *integrity* is a central public service value. It can be interpreted to cover a broad range of bureaucratic behaviour, but it is used here in a limited sense to refer to *administrative* or *public service ethics*, i.e., to principles and standards of right conduct for public servants. Certain principles and standards of ethical behaviour (e.g., honesty, promise keeping) are of such enduring importance in all walks of life that they can be described as *ethical values*. These ethical values can be used to resolve conflicts between such public service values as responsiveness and efficiency; they can also be applied to clashes between public service values on the one hand, and social values like liberty and equality, or personal values like success and wealth, on the other. Consider, for example, public servants whose political superiors direct them to conceal information about a threat to the public's health. The conflict between accountability to their superiors and their sense of responsiveness to the public could be resolved according to the ethical value of honesty. Integrity in the sense of ethical behaviour can in some instances override all other values.

Opportunities for public servants to become involved in unethical conduct arise from the power they exercise in the development and administration of public policy. Senior public servants with discretionary authority and confidential information have the greatest opportunities to benefit from unethical conduct. But temptations to engage in unethical behaviour exist at all levels of the administrative hierarchy and at all levels of government (e.g., a senior official with contracting authority in a federal department or a secretary in a municipal government with access to confidential development plans).

Historically, the public's interest in the ethical conduct of government officials, whether politicians or public servants, has waxed and waned as instances of wrongdoing have been exposed, publicized, debated, punished, and then forgotten. But since the early 1970s, there has been continuing anxiety among the public and within governments about the ethical standards of public officials. There is increasing recognition that the ethical dimension of public administration has been unduly neglected in the past.

Much of the recent public and media concern about public service ethics has centred on conflicts of interest and, to a lesser extent, on issues of political partisanship, public comment, and confidentiality. Among the many questions of current concern in these problem areas are the following: What kinds of gifts or entertainment should public servants accept from someone with whom they do business? Under what circumstances is moonlighting acceptable? Is an apparent conflict of interest as serious as an actual conflict? To what extent should public servants participate in partisan political activity? To what extent should public servants criticize government policies and programs in public? Under what circumstances, if any, are public servants justified in leaking government information?

The effective management of these issues is generally considered to be essential to public trust and confidence in government. Over the past two decades, governments have responded to heightened public concern about these issues by drafting statutes, regulations, guidelines, and codes dealing with ethical conduct. However, these high-profile issues constitute only a small proportion of the total field of ethical problems. Many other ethical issues of considerable importance receive comparatively little public attention. These are issues that relate less to the use of public office for private, personal, or partisan gain and more to ethical and value conflicts and dilemmas that arise in the performance of administrative duties. Among these issues are the following: Under what circumstances, if any, should public servants lie to the public? Should public servants zealously implement a policy that they think is misguided? Do public servants owe their ultimate loyalty to their political superiors? To the public? To their perception of the public interest? To their conscience? Is it appropriate to bend the rules to assist a member of the public who is especially needy or especially deserving? Is the public interest the same thing as the interest of the government in power? What level of risk should a public servant take with the public? Where should the balance be struck between a representative public service and an efficient and effective public service? An important, emerging ethical issue is the extent to which practices within the public service should be altered to accommodate the beliefs of persons of various cultural backgrounds. The management of a culturally diverse work force requires sensitivity to different views and values and the capacity to resolve ethical problems arising from these differences. This issue is discussed at greater length in Chapter 24 under the heading of "Managing Diversity."

Compared to issues like conflict of interest and confidentiality, the several questions raised above have not only received less public attention but are also less amenable to management by written ethics rules. Thus, the effective management of these issues requires

> Recruiting members of ethnic minorities can really muddle our morals. How, for example, do you conduct a fair job interview when, in certain cultures, making direct eye contact is considered bad form? In other cultures it is unheard of to talk positively about yourself. Our notions of "right" and "wrong" go right out the window when confronted with other ways of doing things.
>
> *Source: Elaine Todres, an Ontario deputy minister,*
> *"The Ethical Dimension in Public Service"[26]*

that ethics rules in general and ethics codes in particular be supplemented by other means of promoting ethical behaviour. Indeed, an ethics framework for a government department could include the following components:[27]

1. the evaluation of ethical performance as a basis for appointing and promoting all members of the public service, but especially its leadership;

2. a statement of values, including ethical values, either as part of a strategic plan or as a separate document;

3. a code of ethics (or conduct), linked to a value statement (if one exists), which sets out general principles of ethical conduct;

4. elaboration on the code, usually as commentary under each principle, which explains more fully the meaning of the principle and/or provides illustrations of violations of the principle;

5. reference to the existence of ethics rules (statutes, regulations, etc.) related to the problem areas covered in the code and/or to problem areas covered elsewhere;

6. elaboration on the code, either following each principle or in a separate part, which adapts the code's principles to the particular needs of individual organizations;

7. provisions for administering the code, including publicity, penalties for violations, and provisions for grievance;

8. an ethics counsellor to perform advisory and administrative functions for senior public servants across the government;

9. an ethics counsellor, ombudsman, or committee to provide advice on ethics rules and ethics issues within a single department or agency; and

10. ethics education/training for public servants, beginning with the most senior echelons and new employees.

These approaches could be supplemented by other measures that are less common or more controversial, namely,

11. an ethics audit to evaluate the organization's policies and procedures for preserving and nurturing ethical behaviour;

12. the raising of ethical considerations in a deliberate and regular way at meetings and through such other means of communication as newsletters;

13. the provision of a confidential hotline that public servants can use to discuss concerns about their personal ethical behaviour or that of others; and

14. the inclusion of exit interviews (i.e., interviews with employees leaving the organization) to ask questions about the employee's view of the ethical culture of the organization.

Despite the several components of this framework, the most common approach to promoting ethical conduct is the use of a code of ethics, especially for dealing with conflict of interest problems. Thus, the remainder of this section examines, in turn, the costs and benefits of codes of ethics; the form, content, and administration of these codes; and their implications for administrative responsibility.

Costs and Benefits of Codes of Ethics

Disclosures of unethical conduct by government officials during the early 1970s prompted several governments to assess the desirability of providing or improving ethics rules. By the end of the decade, the federal government and most provincial governments had adopted written rules, often in the form of codes of ethics, to regulate the ethical behaviour of public servants. Developments in the municipal sphere of government were slower.

A code of public service ethics is a statement of principles and standards about the right conduct of public servants. It usually contains only a portion of a government's rules on public service ethics and is, therefore, a more narrow term than ethics rules, which refer to statutes, regulations, and guidelines. The form, content, and administration of ethics codes differ significantly from one government to another. Indeed, much of the dispute over the usefulness of codes of ethics arises from the fact that such a wide variety of instruments are described as codes. The situation is further complicated in that public servants may be subject not only to their government's code of ethics but also to codes developed for their own profession (e.g., law, engineering).

Even the most vigorous advocates of codes of ethics for public servants acknowledge that they are not a panacea for preventing unethical behaviour. There is, however, much disagreement over how useful codes actually are. Perhaps the most common criticism of codes is that the broad ethical principles contained in many codes are often difficult to apply to specific situations. For example, what precisely does it mean in practice to "put loyalty to the highest moral principles and to country above loyalty to persons, party, or Government department"?[28] A second and related concern is that codes of ethics, even if they contain detailed provisions, are difficult to enforce; indeed, many codes contain no provision for their enforcement. Third, the large scale and complexity of government make it difficult to draft a code that can be applied fairly and consistently across a large number of departments. Fourth, codes can adversely affect the individual rights and private lives of public servants whose ethical behaviour is beyond reproach. Consider the effect on individual privacy of the requirement in some governments that public servants disclose not only their own financial interests but also those of their spouses and dependent children. Finally, certain ethical and value issues, such as determining what measure of risk to the public is acceptable, are not easily amenable to management by ethics rules in general or ethics codes in particular.

However, codes can reduce uncertainty among public servants as to what constitutes ethical and unethical behaviour. First, unwritten rules in the form of understandings and practices leave much room for argument as to the content of rules and what penalties must be paid for violating them. Second, codes can promote public trust and confidence in the ethical behaviour of public servants. Taxpayers can be better assured, for example, that they will be treated fairly and impartially, and that public servants are less likely to use their positions for personal gain. Third, codes can reduce unethical practices by discouraging and punishing them. They provide one of several means by which political leaders and senior managers can hold public servants accountable for their activities. Fourth, codes can sensitize public servants to the reality that the ethical and value dimensions of their decisions and recommendations are as important as, and often more important than, the technical, legal, and political dimensions. Finally, the development of a code of ethics may prompt governments to reassess their existing written or unwritten rules so that the rights and participation of public servants in regard to certain activities (e.g., political partisanship, outside employment) may be enhanced.

The Style and Substance of Ethics Rules

Although Canadian governments have taken varying approaches to the *form*, *content*, and *administration* of their ethics rules, it is widely acknowledged that the best approach is a code of ethics that contains comprehensive coverage of the major ethical problem areas and effective means for the code's administration. It is useful to codify existing rules by bringing them together in a single document, or at least incorporating in that document reference to service-wide rules already existing in statutes and regulations.

British Columbia's *Standards of Conduct for Public Service Employees*[29] begins by stating that the government "believes that the highest standards of conduct among public service employees are essential to maintain and enhance the public's trust and confidence in the public service." It provides also that the requirement to "comply with these standards is a condition of employment. Employees who fail to comply with these standards may be subject to disciplinary action up to and including dismissal." On the subject of loyalty, the Standards assert that

> [P]ublic servants have a duty of loyalty to the government as their employer. The duty of loyalty ... requires public service employees, irrespective of political preferences or affiliations, to serve the government of the day to the best of their ability.

> The honesty and integrity of the public service demands that the impartiality of employees, in the conduct of their duties, be above suspicion. Employees' conduct should instill confidence and trust and must not bring the public service into disrepute.

This is followed by provisions on the ethical problem areas of confidentiality, public comments, political activity, service to the public, workplace behaviour (e.g., harassment), conflicts of interest, allegations of wrongdoing, legal proceedings, working relationships (e.g., the hiring of relatives), personnel decisions, and outside remunerative and volunteer work.

Form.   Safeguards against unethical conduct can take the form of statutes providing for prosecution and punishment by the regular courts (e.g., Criminal Code provisions on bribery and corruption) or of regulations or guidelines administered within the government itself. Prosecution by the courts (e.g., under the Criminal Code) is too blunt an instrument to apply to most unethical practices. Many instances of unethical conduct fall into a "grey zone" in that they are unacceptable but cannot be effectively handled by the courts. In other cases, it is debatable whether an offence has actually been committed, since many ethical issues are complex and the offence may be more apparent than real. In such circumstances, governments are required to exercise judgment as to what penalty, if any, is appropriate. Penalties can range from a reprimand to dismissal.

Content.   The content of codes of ethics has focused so heavily on conflicts of interest that it is useful to elaborate on this problem area. A *conflict of interest* may be defined as a situation in which a public employee has a private or personal interest sufficient to influence, or to appear to influence, the objective exercise of his or her official duties. Conflicts of interest receive a great deal of public attention because of the prospect of financial gain from such activities and because of the many varieties of the offence.[30] Among the varieties of conflict of interest are accepting benefits, outside employment, and post-employment.

Accepting benefits of significant value from individuals, groups, or firms with whom the employee has official dealings sometimes borders on bribery and corruption, which is punishable under the Criminal Code. However, the propriety of accepting gifts or hospitality is usually judged on the basis of whether the benefit to the employee is of sufficient value to be likely to influence—or *appear* to influence—the objective discharge of that person's responsibilities. Twenty-five employees of the Ontario Housing Corporation (OHC) were charged under the Criminal Code with having accepted gifts from developers. The gifts included colour television sets, trips to the Caribbean, and amounts ranging from \$200 to over \$12 000.[31] However, employees of the Central Mortgage and Housing Corporation (CMHC) who accepted developers' gifts in the form of liquor, cheese, chocolates, and lunches were simply reprimanded.[32] And the RCMP decided not to lay charges against 11 out of an original 260 federal diplomats allegedly involved in making false travel claims; the RCMP felt that, despite reasonable grounds to lay charges, convictions would be unlikely and, if there were convictions, the penalties likely would be insufficient to act as deterrents.[33] A less obvious example involves public servants who accept free lunches or dinners from persons who could benefit from the public servants' official decisions.

Outside employment, or "moonlighting," constitutes a conflict of interest when that employment reduces significantly the time and effort that public servants devote to their official duties, or when that employment is incompatible with their duties. Thus, a public servant who slept all day on the job after driving a taxi all night would be in a conflict of interest situation; so would a public servant responsible for regulating marine safety who also worked for, or owned, a company selling marine safety equipment. A similar example would be a government plumbing inspector with a part-time plumbing business who offers to come back after hours to fix, for a price, some plumbing he or she had just inspected.

The *post-employment* problem arises when a public servant resigns or retires from government to join a firm with which he or she has had official dealings, or that could benefit unduly from information that the public servant acquired while in government. There is often concern that this person may have conferred benefits on the firm in the hope of future employment, or that the firm might gain a competitive advantage by gaining access to confidential information, including trade secrets.

Administration.   The effective administration of ethics rules in these several problem areas is critical to success in promoting high ethical standards. Provisions for administration of the rules ideally should include publicity, enforcement, and grievance procedures. In governments with a large number of employees and administrative units, it is usually necessary to delegate to individual departments and agencies responsibility for elaborating on service-wide rules and for administering the rules for their own employees.

Most varieties of conflict of interest are covered in the federal government's *Conflict of Interest and Post-Employment Code for the Public Service.*[34] Both new and current employees are required to certify that they have read and understood the code, and that they will observe it as a condition of appointment and employment.

Are the tasks of drafting and administering a code of ethics worth the effort? Governments provide little or no data on the number and nature of ethical offences committed, but it appears that the percentage of public servants involved in unethical conduct

> [E]thical standards in [Canadian] government compare very favourably with those in the private sector and with those of governments in other countries. However, Canadians are concerned about integrity in government. If Canadians do not trust their governments to act ethically, governments will find that their actions have less and less legitimacy and effectiveness. Thus ... it is important to discuss ethics in government and to take action to maintain and promote ethics in government.
>
> *Source: The Auditor General of Canada, "Ethics and Fraud Awareness in Government"[35]*

is very low. Ethics rules are, however, not designed simply to catch offenders but to provide guidance to public servants who are uncertain as to which activities are permissible and which are prohibited. Moreover, a comparatively large cost in time and effort may be justified by the benefit of increased public confidence in government and in the responsibility of public servants.

Ethics Rules, Education, and Leadership

Written rules can be useful in promoting the high ethical standards required of public servants. However, as noted earlier, not all ethical problems can be handled by ethics rules. Such rules are of limited use in helping public servants to develop skills in the analysis of ethical and value issues and in the resolution of these issues. It is desirable to complement formal rules with formal education, training programs, and exemplary role models.

An increasingly important means of promoting ethical behaviour is to sensitize public servants to the ethical and value dimensions of public service during their pre-employment education and in-service training. Recognition of the importance of this approach can be seen in the growing number of courses on public service ethics in universities and government departments.

The influence of administrative superiors is also an extremely important means of promoting ethical behaviour. However, some contemporary governments, and many individual departments, are so large that even senior officials have personal contact with a relatively small percentage of their employees. Therefore, there is now less assurance than there used to be that the influence of public service leaders on ethical matters will flow down the administrative pyramid. This explains in part why many senior public servants support the codification of ethical standards as a means of nurturing responsible administrative behaviour.

🏛 THE PUBLIC INTEREST

The Meaning of the Public Interest

The concept of the public interest is very closely related to the issues of administrative responsibility and administrative ethics. Indeed, responsible administrative behaviour is frequently assessed in terms of the public servant's ability to resolve conflicts among administrative and other values according to the criterion of the public interest. Moreover, the public interest has been proposed as the dominant ethical principle or standard for bureaucratic behaviour. One author describes the public interest as "the highest ethical standard applicable to political affairs."[36]

> The notion of the public interest is a touchstone of motivation for public servants. It is for the public service what liberty and justice are for the legal profession, or what healing and mercy are to the medical profession.... [T]he desire to serve the public interest is one of the normative foundations for public employment, and any approach to public service that treats it ... as if it were the same as private enterprise risks undermining not only the structure of motivation for public service but, more important, its capacity to serve democratic government in an ethical and accountable manner.
>
> *Source: Federal Deputy Ministers' Task Force. Discussion Paper on Values and Ethics in the Public Service .[37]*

The concept of the public interest, like that of administrative responsibility, has been interpreted in various ways.[38] It has been defined as "the general will," "the wisest and most foresighted interest," a moral imperative "resting on natural law foundations," and "compromise ... as the optimum reconciliation of the competing claims of special and private interests."[39] Each of these definitions is, to some extent, partial or deficient. In the context of administrative decision making, for example, the first three definitions are too nebulous to provide sufficient guidance to the public servant. However, the interpretation of the public interest as the best possible accommodation of conflicting interests provides an essential element of specificity.

The accommodation of the claims of various interests connotes a power struggle among competing groups, each possessing approximately equal access to the decision maker and devoting roughly equivalent resources to the struggle. In reality, as will be explained in Chapters 20 and 21, both access and resources of money, organization, supporters, and research capacity vary among different groups. Moreover, the interests of some segments of the population may not be represented because these segments are underprivileged, uneducated, uninformed, inarticulate, unorganized, underfunded, or simply uninterested. Even if the whole range of relevant interests is taken into account, the definition is still incomplete. Public interest theorists commonly assert that the public interest is not the mere sum of particular interests, no matter how evenly and equitably these interests are represented. Frequently, these interests are too shortsighted or are unable, on their own, to reach an accommodation of their various claims. In these cases, the critical contribution to the determination of the public interest comes from the decision maker—who is often a public servant.

However, as explained in Chapter 12, the avenue to some decisions runs through myriad conflicting and complementary values. Among the obstacles along the road is the temptation to succumb to personal or narrow interests when a decision in the broader interest of the general public or of substantial segments of the general public is required. The extent to which public servants are likely to suppress self-interest in a quest for the public interest is a matter for debate. Should the ultimate aim be the development of officials who, like Downs' *statesmen*, have a broad, altruistic, and idealistic devotion to government policies and programs? Or is the inculcation of loyalty to specific programs or administrative units, as in the case of Downs' *zealots* and *advocates*,[40] a sufficient and more realistic goal? Do those who envisage the eventual predominance of self-directing public servants actively pursuing human dignity in every decision[41] have an unduly optimistic view of human nature? Downs contends that, with rare exceptions, "bureaucracies have few places for officials who are loyal to society as a whole" (e.g., for statesmen), and that "this is true even though all administrative textbooks and nearly all administrators at least verbally exhort all officials to exhibit such loyalty."[42]

Determining the Public Interest[43]

The resolution of value conflicts in the light of the public interest is sometimes a difficult challenge for public servants. This is demonstrated well by the following letter to the editor of the *Journal* of the Professional Institute of the Public Service:

> I have been concerned that too rigid an application of ... "the Oath of Secrecy" conflicts with professional integrity. Now that environmental concerns, which are

frequently matters of opinion, not fact, are being accorded increasing attention, the question becomes more urgent. Many … of Canada's professional biologists who are well-qualified to speak on environmental matters are muzzled because they are Civil Servants and so any environmental debate is frequently left to extremist and partisan voices.

If one considers a hypothetical case where pressure is being applied, perhaps from ministerial level, to have a contract awarded to a firm which, for professional reasons, is deemed unsatisfactory, how far dare a Civil Servant go in opposing such seemingly unethical practices? What of an employee who is sufficiently troubled by such an incident to discuss it with a priest under "Seal of the Confessional?" …

[S]urely, our responsibility to Canada is greater than any duty we owe to our political masters of the day. We have standards of professional integrity to maintain and a moral position to uphold. The glib, cynical retort, "Well, you can always resign," is hopelessly inadequate…. (Name withheld by request.)[44]

Except in situations where public servants have been given complete discretionary authority, they may be able to shift the burden of choice among contending values to their hierarchical superior. Hierarchy in administration is a prime safeguard of administrative responsibility in that it forces "important decisions to higher levels of determination or at least higher levels of review where perspectives are necessarily broader, less technical and expert, more political."[45] At the highest policy-making levels of government, it may be argued that, in the final analysis, the determination of the public interest is the task of the elected representatives. Public servants cannot, however, escape the responsibility of providing their political masters with the best possible advice. Moreover, if only in the cause of personal survival, public servants cannot evade the responsibility of pointing out the political, economic, and social costs and benefits of selecting one course of action over another.

Scholarly writings on the public interest demonstrate the difficulty of establishing specific and immutable criteria for how the public interest is determined in any given situation. The public interest may fruitfully be viewed as a dynamic concept. Its content changes from one situation to another and depends, in large part, on the values of both the decision maker and the interests whose claims are considered. Nevertheless, public servants can be provided with some guidelines for acting in the public interest. They need to recognize their biases to ensure that they do not ignore important considerations and interests, and to ask the right questions of themselves and others before making a decision. Among the questions to be asked are: Am I certain that my personal values—and my self-interest—are not overwhelming all other values? Have I identified and consulted "all stakeholders likely to be affected" by my decision? Have I ensured that "the procedures followed in obtaining information and consulting those affected are fair and open"? Have I done "the most comprehensive analysis of the costs and benefits that is possible in the circumstances"?[46]

An important distinction may be made between a *passive* and an *active* pursuit of the public interest. The public servant who considers the claims only of *organized* special interests, and whose range of values is narrow and inflexible, is passive in the search for the public interest. By way of contrast, the public servant who seeks the views of *all relevant interests*, and whose value framework is comparatively broad and flexible, is in active pursuit of the public interest. Both orientations have their virtues and drawbacks, depending on the issue at hand and the level of the organizational pyramid at which the decision is being made.

🏛 ADMINISTRATIVE RESPONSIBILITY AND THE PUBLIC INTEREST

The passive and active orientations toward the public interest may be linked with our earlier distinction between objective and subjective (psychological) responsibility. In a brief and admittedly oversimplified fashion, the main characteristics of two hypothetically extreme types of public servant—the objectively responsible and the subjectively responsible official—are suggested here.

Objectively responsible public servants feel responsible primarily to the legal or formal locus of authority and take a passive approach to the determination of the public interest. Their most prominent characteristic and value is accountability to those who have the power to promote, displace, or replace them. The controls and influences that they internalize in the form of public service values are those expressed by their hierarchical superiors. In making and recommending decisions, they anticipate and reflect the desires of their superiors, who have legitimate authority and who may easily threaten or impose penalties to ensure compliance. Public servants of this type do not actively seek the views of policy actors other than their superiors unless they are required to do so. For example, they consult parties with an interest in impending regulations only if such consultation is required by law or is expected by their superiors. Their foremost public service values include accountability and efficiency. They do not take initiatives or risks that may get them or their superiors into trouble. They are, for example, likely to err on the side of caution in their communications with the media. They also prefer, if possible, that their political and administrative superiors resolve any value dilemmas and determine the content of the public interest for them.

Objectively responsible public servants perceive themselves as ultimately responsible to the general public through the administrative hierarchy, the political executive, and the legislature. Their behaviour is based on the possibility and the desirability of separating policy and administration—even at the senior levels of the public service. In Finer's terminology, they are, therefore, "politically" responsible.

Subjectively responsible public servants are a striking contrast. They feel responsible to a broad range of policy participants and are active in the pursuit of the public interest. Their most outstanding characteristic and value is commitment to what they perceive to be the goals of their department or program. Since they view the expectations of a variety of policy actors as legitimate, the sources of their public service values are numerous and diverse. Subjectively responsible public servants are frequently in conflict with their superiors, but they are not influenced much by the threat of negative sanctions. They seek the views of interests affected by their decisions and recommendations in the absence of, and even in violation of, any legal or formal obligation to do so. Their primary public service values include responsiveness and effectiveness. They are innovative, take risks, and bend the rules to achieve their objectives. They urge their superiors to follow certain courses of action and are prepared to resolve for themselves the value dilemmas they encounter in their search for the public interest. Subjectively responsible public servants are, for example, more likely than others to engage in "whistle-blowing," i.e., exposing actions of political and administrative superiors that are illegal, unethical, or unduly wasteful of public funds.[47]

The subjectively responsible public servant rejects the possibility and desirability of separating policy and administration—especially at the senior echelons of the bureaucracy. To use Finer's language again, officials of this type are "morally" responsible in that they look to their own consciences rather than to "external punitive controls" for guidance.

Neither the purely objective nor the purely subjective type is appropriate as a model of the responsible public servant. Some characteristics of both types produce conduct that scholars and public officials generally view as undesirable. Undue emphasis on certain elements of objective responsibility may lead to behaviour that is unresponsive or ineffective. At the other extreme, too great an emphasis on particular aspects of subjective responsibility may bring equally undesirable results in the form of behaviour that is unaccountable or inefficient.

If the public service was composed predominantly of either objectively or subjectively responsible public servants, it would tend to manifest the same objectionable features. The "ideal" situation, then, is a public service in which each public servant strikes that balance between the objective and subjective elements of responsibility that is appropriate to his or her responsibilities and level in the hierarchy.

There is a close link between the concept of administrative responsibility and the concept of empowerment discussed in Chapter 5. It is argued that holding public servants accountable (objectively responsible) through an arsenal of formal controls is an important, but inadequate, means of promoting responsible behaviour. Empowerment involves emphasis on subjective (or personal) responsibility in the sense of loyalty to, and identification with, the organization's objectives.

A recurring theme in many of the remaining chapters of this book is the extent to which controls and influences over the exercise of bureaucratic power promote administrative responsibility. Keep in mind that in popular discussion, the terms administrative responsibility and administrative accountability are frequently used interchangeably.

NOTES

1. Based on "The Too Silent Partner," Case #21 in La Releve, *Discussion Guide for a Strong Foundation, The Report of the Task Force on Public Service Values and Ethics* (Ottawa: Canadian Centre for Management Development, 1997), 60–61.

2. Carl J. Friedrich, "Responsible Government Service Under the American Constitution," in Friedrich et al., *Problems of the American Public Service* (New York: McGraw-Hill, 1935), 3–74, and "Public Policy and the Nature of Administrative Responsibility," in Carl J. Friedrich and Edward S. Mason, eds., *Public Policy* (Cambridge: Harvard University Press, 1940), 3–24. Herman Finer, "Better Government Personnel," *Political Science Quarterly* 51, (December 1936): 569 ff., and "Administrative Responsibility in Democratic Government," *Public Administration Review* 1, no. 4 (1941): 335–50. The most comprehensive statements of the opposing positions are found in the 1940–41 exchange of articles.

3. Finer, "Administrative Responsibility," 337.

4. Friedrich, "Public Policy," 12.

5. Ibid., 10.

6. Ibid., 5.

7. Finer, "Administrative Responsibility," 339–40.

8. Ibid., 336.

9. Ibid.

10. Friedrich, "Public Policy," 19.

11. Ibid., 23.

12. Finer, "Administrative Responsibility," 349.

13. Ibid.

14. See, for example, the excellent summary and critique of five major interpretations in Arch Dotson, "Approaches to Administrative Responsibility," *Western Political Quarterly* 10 (September 1957): 701–27.

15. Michael M. Harmon, "Normative Theory and Public Administration: Some Suggestions for a Redefinition of Administrative Responsibility," in Frank Marini, ed., *Toward a New Public Administration: The Minnowbrook Perspective* (Scranton, Pa.: Chandler, 1971), 173.

16. *The End of Liberalism* (New York: Norton, 1969), 298.

17. Ibid., 299.

18. Frederick C. Mosher, *Democracy in the Public Service* (New York: Oxford University Press, 1968), 7–10.

19. Ibid., 7. (Emphasis added.)

20. See Kenneth Kernaghan and John Langford, *The Responsible Public Servant* (Toronto: Institute of Public Administration of Canada, and Halifax: Institute for Research on Public Policy, 1990), ch. 7.

21. Royal Commission on Financial Management and Accountability, *Final Report* (Ottawa: Supply and Services, 1979), 458.

22. Ibid., 471.

23. Royal Commission on Financial Management and Accountability, *Final Report*, 9.

24. Government of Ontario, Management Board of Cabinet, Accountability, OPS Management Series (Toronto: Queen's Printer, 1982).

25. For a detailed treatment of administrative ethics in Canada, see Kernaghan and Langford, *The Responsible Public Servant.*

26. Elaine Todres, "The Ethical Dimension in Public Service," in Kenneth Kernaghan, ed., *Do Unto Others: Ethics in Government and Business* (Toronto: Institute of Public Administration of Canada, 1991), 16.

27. This framework is drawn from Kenneth Kernaghan, *The Ethics Era in Canadian Public Administration* (Ottawa: Canadian Centre for Management Development, 1996).

28. United States, *Code of Ethics for Government Service,* House Concurrent Resolution 175, 85th Congress, 2nd session (1985).

29. British Columbia, Public Service Employee Relations Commission, *Standards of Conduct of Public Service Employees* (Revised October 1997). Reprinted with permission of the British Columbia Public Service Employee Relations Commission.

30. For an explanation and illustrations of eight varieties of conflict of interest, see Kernaghan and Langford, *The Responsible Public Servant,* ch. 6.
31. *The Globe and Mail* (2 October 1974).
32. *The Globe and Mail* (4 May 1979).
33. *The Globe and Mail* (27 March 1993).
34. Ottawa: Minister of Supply and Services, 1985.
35. Canada, Office of the Auditor General, "Ethics and Fraud Awareness in Government," *Report May 1995* (Ottawa: Minister of Supply and Services, 1995), 1–24.
36. C.W. Cassinelli, "The Public Interest in Political Ethics," in Carl J. Friedrich, ed., *Nomos V: The Public Interest* (New York: Atherton Press, 1962), 46.
37. Privy Council Office, *Discussion Paper on Values and Ethics in the Public Service* (Ottawa: Privy Council Office, 1996), 46. Reproduced with the permission of the Minister of Public Works and Government Services Canada, 1998.
38. See especially Pendleton Herring, *Public Administration and the Public Interest* (New York: McGraw Hill, 1936); Frank Sorauf, "The Public Interest Reconsidered," *Journal of Politics* 19 (November 1957): 616–39; Glendon Schubert, *The Public Interest: A Critique of a Political Concept* (Glencoe, Ill.: The Free Press, 1960); Friedrich, *Nomos V: The Public Interest;* Herbert J. Storing, "The Crucial Link: Public Administration, Responsibility and the Public Interest," *Public Administration Review* 24 (March 1964): 39–46; and Richard E. Flathman, *The Public Interest* (New York: John Wiley & Sons, 1966). For a list of definitions of the public interest and a bibliography on this subject, see W.T. Stanbury, "Definitions of the Public Interest," in Douglas G. Hartle, *Public Policy Decision Making and Regulation* (Montreal: Institute for Research on Public Policy, 1979), 213–18.
39. Rowland Egger, "Responsibility and Administration: An Exploratory Essay," in Roscoe Martin, ed., *Public Administration and Democracy: Essays in Honor of Paul H. Appleby* (Syracuse: Syracuse University Press, 1965), 311–13.
40. A. Downs, *Inside Bureaucracy* (Boston: Little, Brown, 1967), 88. "Zealots are loyal to relatively narrow policies or concepts, such as the development of nuclear submarines. They seek power both for its own sake and to effect the policies to which they are loyal. Advocates are loyal to a broader set of functions or to a broader organization than zealots. They also seek power because they want to have a significant influence upon policies and actions concerning those functions or organizations."
41. See especially Eugene P. Dvorin and Robert H. Simmons, *From Amoral to Humane Bureaucracy* (San Francisco: Canfield, 1972).
42. Downs, *Inside Bureaucracy,* 111.
43. For an examination of four major approaches to operationalizing the public interest, see Kernaghan and Langford, *The Responsible Public Servant,* ch. 2.
44. *Journal* 52 (November 1973): 9–10.
45. Mosher, *Democracy and the Public Service,* 212.
46. Kernaghan and Langford, *The Responsible Public Servant,* 49–50.
47. See the discussion of whistle blowing in Chapter 21.

BIBLIOGRAPHY

Aucoin, Peter. "A Profession of Public Administration?" *Canadian Public Administration* 40 (spring 1997): 23–9.

Bowman, James S., ed. *Ethical Frontiers in Public Management.* San Francisco: Jossey-Bass, 1991.

Canada, Office of the Auditor General. "Ethics and Fraud Awareness in Government," *Report May 1995* (Ottawa: Supply and Services, 1995).

Canada, Privy Council Office. *Values and Ethics in the Public Service* (Ottawa: Privy Council Office, December 1996).

Canada, Royal Commission on Financial Management and Accountability. *Final Report.* Ottawa: Supply and Services, 1979.

Cooper, Terry L. *The Responsible Administrator,* 3rd ed. Port Washington, New York: Kennikat Press, 1990.

Denhardt, Kathryn G. *The Ethics of Public Service.* Westport, Conn.: Greenwood Press, 1988.

Finer, Herman. "Administrative Responsibility in Democratic Government." *Public Administration Review* 1 (summer 1941): 335–50.

Friedrich, Carl J. "Responsible Government Service Under the American Constitution." In Friedrich et al., *Problems of the American Public Service.* New York: McGraw-Hill, 1935, 3–74.

———. "Public Policy and the Nature of Administrative Responsibility." In Carl J. Friedrich and Edward S. Mason, eds., *Public Policy.* Cambridge, Mass.: Harvard University Press, 1940, 3–24.

———. *Nomos V: The Public Interest.* New York: Atherton Press, 1962.

Hiebert, Janet. *Political Ethics: A Canadian Perspective.* Toronto: Dundurn Press, for the Royal Commission on Electoral Reform and Party Financing, 1993.

Hodgetts, J.E. "Government Responsiveness to the Public Interest: Has Progress Been Made?" *Canadian Public Administration* 24 (summer 1981): 216–31.

———. "Implicit Values in the Administration of Public Affairs." *Canadian Public Administration* 25 (winter 1982): 471–83.

Jabbra, Joseph G., and O.P. Dwivedi, eds. *Public Service Accountability: A Comparative Perspective.* West Hartford, Conn.: Kumarian Press, 1988.

Kernaghan, Kenneth. "Responsible Public Bureaucracy: A Rationale and a Framework for Analysis." *Canadian Public Administration* 16 (winter 1973): 572–603.

———. "Codes of Ethics and Administrative Responsibility." *Canadian Public Administration* 17 (winter 1974): 527–41.

———. *Ethical Conduct Guidelines for Government Employees.* Toronto: Institute of Public Administration of Canada, 1975.

———. "Codes of Ethics and Public Administration: Progress, Problems and Prospects." *Public Administration* 58 (summer 1980): 207–24.

———. "The Conscience of the Bureaucrat: Accomplice or Constraint?" *Canadian Public Administration* 27 (winter 1984): 576–91.

———. "The Emerging Public Service Culture: Values, Ethics and Reforms." *Canadian Public Administration* 37 (winter 1994): 614–30.

———. "Towards a Public Service Code of Conduct—and Beyond." *Canadian Public Administration* 40 (spring 1997): 40–54.

———. "Shaking the Foundation: Traditional Versus New Public Service Values." In Charih, Mohamed and Arthur Daniels, eds., *New Public Management and Public Administration in Canada* (Toronto: Institute of Public Administration of Canada, 1997), 47–65.

———. "Values, Ethics and Public Service." In Bourgault, Jacques et al., eds., *Public Administration and Public Management: Canadian Experiences* (Quebec: Les Publications du Québec, 1997): 101–11.

———. ed. *Do Unto Others: Ethics in Government and Business.* Toronto: Institute of Public Administration of Canada, 1991.

———. "Whistle-blowing in Canadian Governments: Ethical, Political and Managerial Considerations." *Optimum: The Journal of Public Sector Management* 22, no. 1 (1991–92): 34–43.

Kernaghan, Kenneth, and John Langford. *The Responsible Public Servant.* Toronto: Institute of Public Administration of Canada, and Halifax: Institute for Research on Public Policy, 1990.

Laframboise, H.L. "Conscience and Conformity: The Uncomfortable Bedfellows of Accountability." *Canadian Public Administration* 26 (fall 1983): 325–43.

Lewis, Carol W. *The Ethics Challenge in Public Service: A Problem-Solving Guide.* San Francisco: Jossey-Bass, 1991.

Osbaldeston, Gordon. *Keeping Deputy Ministers Accountable.* Toronto: McGraw-Hill Ryerson, 1989.

Rohr, John A. *Ethics for Bureaucrats: An Essay on Law and Values,* 2nd ed. New York: Marcel Dekker, 1989.

Schubert, Glendon. *The Public Interest: A Critique of a Political Concept.* Glencoe, Ill.: The Free Press, 1960.

Tait, J. "A Strong Foundation: Report of the Task Force on Public Service Values and Ethics (the summary)." *Canadian Public Administration* 40 (spring 1997): 1–22.

Thompson, Dennis F. "Moral Responsibility of Public Officials: The Problem of Many Hands." *The American Political Science Review* 74 (1980): 905–16.

———. *Political Ethics and Public Office.* Cambridge, Mass.: Harvard University Press, 1987.

V

The Bureaucracy in the
Political System

15

The Executive and the Bureaucracy

Let's listen in on a confidential discussion between two deputy ministers.[1]

Paul: I've just about had it. Between you and me, Lynn, I'm thinking of throwing in the towel and moving to the private sector. If I do stay in government, it will have to be with a different minister.

Lynn: Don't do anything drastic. The system can handle such personality conflicts.

Paul: It's not really a personality conflict. The problem is that the minister doesn't seem to have any confidence in me—or my recommendations. Every time he presents me with a new idea or proposal, I do my duty by pointing out the pitfalls and potential problems. The minister always listens politely and patiently to my concerns, but he often proceeds with his proposals regardless, and, of course, he asks me to carry them out. I see myself as speaking the truth to the minister, but I think he sees me as an obstacle. I guess I should start telling him what he wants to hear. Perhaps I have the wrong understanding of what loyal service requires.

Lynn: Well, the tell-them-what-they-want-to-hear approach is practiced by a few of our colleagues, but not the most admirable ones. I urge you again not to do anything drastic. I'll nose around and see if I can cast any light on the problem.

(Two weeks later)

Lynn: Paul, you've got it all wrong about your relationship with the minister.

Paul: I don't think so. Nothing has changed in the past few weeks.

Lynn: Will you just listen for a moment? An academic friend of mine interviewed your minister recently on relationships between politicians and public servants. Your minister is reported to have said: "Let me tell you about my excellent deputy. Every time I have a proposal, I can count on him and the department to give me a thorough review and to point out all the problems that could arise if I decide to go ahead. They give me everything I need to think clearly about the way ahead. But when I have made my decision, they carry it out like professionals, as if it were their own decision. I couldn't be more fortunate in the quality of my senior officials."

Paul: What great news! How could I have misunderstood? As you know, I love public service. But I hate it when the minister understands the system better than I do.

Does the minister understand the system correctly? What is the relationship between deputy ministers on the one hand and their minister and the prime minister on the other? How do deputy ministers serve their own minister while at the same time helping to coordinate government activities by serving the cabinet and cabinet committees? What is the cabinet decision-making process? These and other issues are examined in this chapter.

In Canada, the executive sphere of government includes the *nonpolitical* executive (the governor general, provincial lieutenant governors)[2] and the *political* executive (the prime minister or provincial premiers and the cabinet). In addition, the term *executive* is often used to encompass the public service as well. Thus, the executive sphere of government includes three of the major categories of interaction shown in Table 12.1 in Chapter 12, namely executive-bureaucratic, interdepartmental, and intradepartmental. The main actors involved in these categories are the prime minister (or premier), cabinet, cabinet ministers, central agencies, departments, and other administrative units. The functions of these actors were outlined in Chapters 8 to 10. This chapter is primarily concerned with the relations between the political executive and the public service; the next chapter deals with interdepartmental and intradepartmental relations.

🏛 KEY PRINCIPLES OF EXECUTIVE–BUREAUCRATIC INTERACTION

Coordination and ministerial responsibility are centrally important in explaining relations between and among political executives and public servants. Chapter 12 explained the importance and pervasiveness of coordination in Canadian governments. In this chapter, we will see that the cabinet and the public service are the primary instruments for coordinating the development and implementation of public policy. Moreover, coordination is closely related to the principles of collective ministerial responsibility (or cabinet responsibility) and individual ministerial responsibility, which were discussed briefly in Chapter 8.

Ministerial Responsibility

According to the principle of *collective ministerial responsibility*, ministers are responsible as a group (i.e., as members of the cabinet) for the policies and management of the government as a whole. The cabinet must resign if it loses the confidence of the legislature, i.e., if it loses the support of the majority of the members of the House of Commons (or of a provincial legislature). Individual ministers must, in public, support the decisions of the cabinet, acting as a collectivity, so as to maintain at least the appearance of cabinet solidarity. More specifically, ministers are required, in private, to work out a consensus on the content of public policies and on the allocation of resources for developing and implementing these policies. Ministers who cannot support a cabinet decision in public are expected to resign from the cabinet.

The principle of *individual ministerial responsibility*, which will be explained at length in Chapter 17, is subject to varying interpretations. In general, however, it refers to the responsibility of the minister, as the political head of a department, to answer to the legislature and, through the legislature, to the public both for his or her personal acts and for the acts of departmental subordinates. The minister is also legally responsible for the policies, programs, and administration of his or her department.

Coordination and Hierarchy

The principles of collective and individual ministerial responsibility significantly determine the nature of power relations both between politicians and public servants and among public servants themselves. The principles have an especially important effect on the organizational design of the executive sphere of government. Organization charts of the government of Canada typically depict this sphere as a hierarchical arrangement of offices. Aside from the governor general, the prime minister and the cabinet stand at the pinnacle of the hierarchy from which lines of authority flow down to departments headed by cabinet ministers and to Crown agencies reporting to cabinet ministers. Those central agencies that have departmental form and that report to a minister (e.g., Finance, Treasury Board Secretariat) are normally portrayed as equal in status to the regular operating departments strung horizontally across the chart. Other central agencies (e.g., the Prime Minister's Office and the Privy Council Office) are shown in a staff (advisory) relationship to the prime minister and the cabinet.

However, the organization chart discloses little about the complex pattern of power relations in the executive realm, especially insofar as these relations involve the exercise of influence rather than control. The organization chart exposes only the bare bones of political-bureaucratic interaction. This organizational skeleton reveals simply the formal lines of authority through which control moves down the governmental pyramid and accountability moves up; the "informal organization" is hidden from view. Similarly, an organization chart of a single department or agency that purports to describe the reality of administrative life as simply a hierarchy of superior-subordinate relationships or as a chain of command is misleading.

The deficiencies or "pathologies" of bureaucracy in general, and of its hierarchical feature in particular, have been discussed at length elsewhere.[3] Hierarchy does, however, serve several important purposes. One of these is particularly relevant to a discussion of ministerial responsibility in that hierarchy provides for unity of command and of direction both at the top of the government (by the prime minister or premier and the cabinet) and at the top of government departments (by ministers). In other words, hierarchy promotes accountability. Hierarchy also facilitates coordination. Beginning with the cabinet as the central coordinating mechanism of government, various means of pursuing policy and administrative coordination permeate the executive-bureaucratic arena. We shall see that ministers, in fulfilling both their collective responsibility for coordinating government as a whole and their individual responsibility for coordinating their departments, are obliged to rely heavily on senior public servants in central agencies and departments. We explain in the next chapter the increasing emphasis in recent years on horizontal relations between government departments.

Aside from hierarchical control, power in the executive sphere is exercised in the form of influence. This is demonstrated well by the literature on the *bureaucratic politics* approach to policy making.[4] This approach focuses "primarily on the individuals within a government, and the interaction among them, as determinants of the actions of a government."[5] The interaction of these individuals, either within or between administrative units, may involve conflict, bargaining, compromise, and persuasion rather than hierarchical control.

The Key Role of the Deputy Minister

While ministers play the leading roles in the political system as a whole, they share centre stage with their deputies in the executive-bureaucratic theatre of government. "Any defence of ministerial responsibility that did not take into account the real and independent role of the deputy in the administration of government would ultimately prove destructive to the doctrine itself."[6] Easily the most dominant *bureaucratic* actors in executive-bureaucratic relations are the deputy ministers of government departments[7] and their central agency equivalents (e.g., the clerk of the Privy Council, who is also secretary to the cabinet; the secretary of the Treasury Board, who is also comptroller general). Deputy ministers play such a pivotal role in the decision-making process that an effective means of understanding the place of the public service in the Canadian political system is to view the system from their perspective.

Deputies yield the spotlight to ministers on policy decisions, but as supporting actors they perform onerous advisory and administrative roles. In carrying out these responsibilities, deputies must be sensitive not only to administrative, technical, and financial considerations but also to the partisan political implications of their advice and actions. They are, in addition, entangled in the net of bureaucratic politics within their departments, and between their departments and other administrative units. In short, deputies are challenged to perform the difficult feats of keeping their noses to the grindstone, their ears to the ground, and their backs to the wall. Moreover, deputies are required to look in three directions to find the audience for their performance. They must look upward to their political superiors, laterally to their administrative peers, and downward to their departmental subordinates. The pervasive role of deputy ministers will be evident in this chapter's discussion of relations among public servants, the prime minister, and the cabinet. This chapter covers the deputies' role of supporting their ministers' collective responsibility to cabinet; the next chapter examines their central role as the administrative heads of government departments.

🏛 THE PRIME MINISTER AND THE CABINET

The Prime Minister

In the Canadian political system, the prime minister (or a provincial premier) and his or her cabinet colleagues possess the foremost power and responsibility for making and implementing public policy. In very large part, they determine the political and policy parameters within which the many participants in the political system interact. In the executive realm of government, the cabinet, acting in part through cabinet committees, provides the general framework of policies for which public servants must devise programs and for which resources must be allocated to the many departments and agencies. Given the individual and collective responsibility of ministers for the performance of the public service, they must strive to control and influence bureaucratic behaviour. They evaluate and coordinate policy and program proposals emanating from departments and bring partisan political considerations to bear on these proposals. They also initiate policy proposals of their own. In their capacity as cabinet members, federal ministers receive a great deal of political, policy, and administrative support, primarily from the central agencies described in Chapter 8 (the Prime Minister's Office, the Privy Council Office, the Treasury Board Secretariat, the Department of Finance). This central agency support is generally channelled to ministers in their capacity as members of cabinet and cabinet committees. In their capacity as political heads of government departments, ministers receive this assistance primarily from their deputy ministers and, to a lesser extent, from the political staff in their ministerial offices.

The federal cabinet is located at the centre of a complicated network of political-bureaucratic relations, and the prime minister is the central figure in that network. It is generally acknowledged that the prime minister is much more than "first among equals" in relation to cabinet colleagues. In fact, it is sometimes suggested that the prime minister's power has been aggrandized to the point where Canada has "prime ministerial" rather than cabinet government. This argument has *not* been made so strongly about the role of provincial premiers. In any event, it is widely agreed that while claims about the expansion of prime ministerial power have some basis in reality, they have been overstated. The power of the prime minister in the political system generally, and in relation to government departments specifically, is often exaggerated. Certainly the prime minister is a dominant figure by virtue of his or her responsibilities for leading the governing political party, chairing the cabinet, acting as chief spokesperson for the government, and appointing and removing both ministers and deputy ministers. Moreover, the prime minister can control and influence government departments (and individual public servants) both directly, and indirectly through ministers.

There are, however, severe constraints on the ability of the prime minister and, indeed, of provincial premiers to exercise their powers fully. Their time is so precious that they can afford to become actively involved only in those few policy areas or issues in which they have a personal interest or that command attention on the grounds of urgency or partisan politics. Certainly, as chairperson of cabinet, the prime minister is the key actor in the central policy-making and coordinating institution of government, but he or she alone cannot direct or coordinate the activities of the vast number of bureaucratic actors in government. The prime minister must rely on the assistance of cabinet colleagues and central agencies.

Especially since the late 1960s, Canadian prime ministers as well as several provincial premiers have made vigorous efforts to strengthen political control, especially cabinet control, over the making and coordination of public policy. Among the primary means of pursuing this objective have been the reform of the cabinet committee system and changes in the role of central agencies. The development and current status of each of these is discussed below. Table 15.1 provides a chronology of the evolution of cabinet committees and central agencies from the beginning of the Pearson government in 1963 to the present.

Cabinet Committees

Taken together, cabinet committees are responsible for helping to coordinate policies and programs, to allocate human and financial resources, and to control the public service. Except for the Treasury Board, which is a cabinet committee provided for in the Financial Administration Act, the existence and responsibilities of cabinet committees are determined by the prime minister. The number, duties, and importance of cabinet committees vary over time, especially from one government to another.

The significance and sophistication of the cabinet committee system in the federal government have increased greatly since the late 1930s, and especially since the mid-1960s. Before World War II, there were only three cabinet committees. In 1939, ten new committees were created to facilitate and coordinate Canada's war operations; the most important of these was the War Committee chaired by the prime minister. Between 1945 and 1964, cabinet committees were largely ad hoc; they were usually created to consider specific issues referred to them by cabinet, and they were abolished when their job was done.[8]

In 1968, however, then-prime minister Lester Pearson modified the cabinet committee system by replacing the ad hoc committees with nine standing committees so as "to obtain, under the Prime Minister's leadership, thorough consideration of policies, co-ordination of government action, and timely decisions in a manner consistent with ministerial and Cabinet responsibility."[9] In 1968, Pearson created the Priorities and Planning Committee, which he chaired, to set overall government priorities as a framework for expenditure decisions. The practice of requiring that matters be considered by cabinet committees before coming to the full cabinet was initiated, and public servants were permitted to attend cabinet committee meetings on a more regular and frequent basis.

The general configuration of the cabinet system that existed until mid-1993 dates from the election of Pierre Elliott Trudeau as prime minister in 1968. He reorganized the cabinet committee system "to permit a greater centralization of functions and the delegation of certain powers of decision to the committees."[10] The reduction of the number of standing committees to eight

Table 15.1
EVOLUTION OF CABINET STRUCTURES AND CENTRAL AGENCIES

Prime Minister	Ministry Size	Cabinet and Central Agenices
Pearson (1963–68)	25–26	• 9 standing committees (1968: issues generally to committee before cabinet) • cabinet meetings weekly • Priorities and Planning Committee (1968) • TBS split from the Department of Finance (1966) with separate minister
Trudeau (1968–79)	27–33	• fewer committees with more authority • FPRO split from PCO (1975) • OCG split from TBS (1977) • MSED established (1979)
Clark (1979–80)	30	• inner cabinet plus 12 committees • PEMS established • MSSD set up (proclamation 1980)
Trudeau (1980–84)	32–37	• Priorities and Planning with authority to issue decisions • PEMS elaborated • MSERD with FEDCs (1982)
Turner (1984)	29	• Communications, Labour Relations, and Western Affairs committees wound up • MSERD and MSSD wound up; FEDCs to DRIE • "mirror committees" wound up
Mulroney (1984–88)	40	• envelopes consolidated • PEMS rules simplified • cabinet papers further streamlined • Communications Committee set up • Privatization, Regulatory Affairs, and Operations established
Mulroney (1988–93)	40	• PEMS abolished • sectoral committees abolished • Environment, Economic Policy, Human Resources, and National Identity committees set up • ERC created • size of committees reduced • ERC abolished (1993)
Campbell (1993)	25	• Priorities and Planning Committee abolished • cabinet committees reduced from 11 to 5 • size of committees decreased • status of full cabinet restored • FPRO reintegrated into PCO • Office of Comptroller General integrated into TBS
Chrétien (1993–97)	24	• cabinet committees reduced to 4 • 8 secretaries of state appointed (not cabinet members)
(1997–)	27	

Source: Updated since 1985 by the authors, and abridged from Ian D. Clark, "Recent Changes in the Cabinet Decision-Making System in Ottawa," Canadian Public Administration 28 (summer 1985): 188–89.

and the setting of regular times for the weekly meeting(s) of each committee improved the attendance of ministers. An extremely important innovation was expanding the powers of the committees from making recommendations to cabinet to allowing them to take certain "decisions" on their own. These decisions, called "committee recommendations," were annexed to the agenda for cabinet meetings and were routinely ratified unless a minister specifically requested that they be discussed in full cabinet. As a result of these changes, the number of cabinet meetings declined considerably while the number of cabinet committee meetings increased dramatically.

Joe Clark reformed the cabinet committee system in 1979. The Priorities and Planning Committee was replaced by an Inner Cabinet of twelve ministers that had final decision-making authority; the full cabinet, which met less frequently than under Trudeau, confined its deliberations primarily to coordination and to politically sensitive or controversial questions. The most important organizational initiative of the Clark government was the introduction of the Policy and Expenditure Management System (PEMS), also called the "envelope" system.

The overall aim of PEMS was to give cabinet greater control over the management of both policies and expenditures. This objective was pursued by integrating the processes of policy making and fiscal and expenditure planning within the cabinet committee system. More specifically, PEMS was designed to ensure that the government's decisions on priorities and policies were closely integrated with the allocation of resources. Policy decisions and related expenditure decisions were made by the same cabinet committee and at the same time. With the intent of increasing ministerial direction and control, PEMS decentralized decision-making authority for both policies and expenditures from cabinet to cabinet committees. In addition, PEMS provided for the setting of priorities and expenditure limits before developing expenditure plans. This was intended to allow sufficient time in the planning process for ministers to review and change policies and to reallocate resources. A central feature of this system was the establishment of specific expenditure limits, called resource envelopes. Total expenditures covering a five-year period were divided into eight envelopes for eight policy sectors. Responsibility for managing the eight policy sectors within the expenditure limits was assigned to five cabinet policy committees. For example, the Social Development envelope was assigned to the Cabinet Committee on Social Development, which allocated funds to various departments and agencies in that policy sector.

When Trudeau returned to office in 1980 he abolished the Inner Cabinet, restored the Priorities and Planning Committee, and strengthened PEMS. Then, in 1984, John Turner simplified the cabinet system by reducing the number of cabinet committees and dismantling two so-called new central agencies—the Ministries of State for Economic and Regional Development and for Social Development—that had been created under Trudeau and Clark. He also eliminated what were called "mirror committees," i.e., committees composed of deputy ministers that served as public service counterparts to the policy committees of cabinet.

Brian Mulroney made several changes in the cabinet system designed, in large part, to centralize and strengthen control over expenditure decisions. PEMS was abolished, but the already central role of the Priorities and Planning Committee was enhanced. It had authority to review the decisions of the other cabinet committees and became the sole cabinet committee with authority to approve expenditures on new "big ticket" items. Treasury Board had responsibility for approving expenditures on smaller items. Thus, the policy committees of cabinet no longer determined the allocation of funds from the resource envelopes; rather, they were expected to focus their attention on policy. To this end, the committee system was further restructured. The former broad sectoral committees (e.g., Social Development, Economic and Regional Development) were abolished, but the number of committees increased from ten to fourteen because four new policy committees were created. Membership on each committee was reduced from twenty-two to twenty-three ministers to eight to twelve ministers.

The Priorities and Planning Committee was also reformed. During the period from 1968 to 1993, this was the leading cabinet committee. Until early 1989, it was composed of the prime minister as chairperson, the chairpersons of the other cabinet committees, the Minister of Finance, and a few additional ministers chosen either because of the prime minister's respect for their views or to achieve regional representation. The committee was responsible for deciding upon the fiscal framework, for establishing overall government priorities, for detailed consideration of major policy issues, for federal-provincial matters of general import and problems of a cross-cutting nature that involved more than one cabinet committee, and for managing the expenditure of public funds in several policy sectors. In 1989, the size of the committee was expanded and its membership was made more representative of the various regions of the country. This was appropriate because the committee had effectively replaced the cabinet as the executive decision-making body of the government. Cabinet became largely a forum for partisan political discussion.

Since the Priorities and Planning Committee was now about the same size as the full cabinet had been thirty years earlier, the Operations Committee, which had emerged as an informal committee early in 1988, became extremely influential. It had formal authority to review the agendas of the policy committees and to examine any policy proposals that might create expenditure problems before these proposals were considered by the policy committees. In effect, it acted as a gatekeeper to the Priorities and Planning Committee and set the cabinet agenda. The final Mulroney reform was the creation of the Expenditure Review Committee, chaired by the prime minister. It was responsible for ensuring that expenditures were directed to the government's top priorities and that expenditure control contributed to deficit reduction. This committee was abolished in late 1992.

In 1993, Kim Campbell effected a major reorganization of the federal government. She reduced the number of departments from thirty-two to twenty-five and eliminated six cabinet committees, including the Priorities and Planning Committee. The five remaining cabinet committees were the Operations, Treasury Board/Special Committee of Council, Economic and

Environmental Policy, Social Policy, and House Leader's committees. The full cabinet was restored as the central decision-making body for the most important issues facing the government. Prime Minister Jean Chrétien, who succeeded Campbell in 1993, retained most of the changes made by Campbell and made some changes of his own. He appointed twenty-four ministers, who were members of cabinet, and eight secretaries of state, who were part of the ministry but not cabinet members. Upon reelection in 1997, Chrétien increased the number of ministers to twenty-seven. During his two terms, there have been only four cabinet committees (Figure 15.1) and full cabinet has remained as the central decision-making body.

Central Agencies

As noted earlier, there is much debate as to which administrative units should be described as central agencies. In this chapter, the focus is on the Prime Minister's Office (PMO) and the so-called traditional central agencies, i.e., the Department of Finance, the Privy Council Office (PCO), and the Treasury Board Secretariat (TBS). The senior officials of these agencies have been described as "superbureaucrats" because they "are among the most powerful public servants in government" and because "in performing their duties they often cross the line between bureaucrat and policy maker."[11] The detailed description of the functions of these agencies provided in Chapter 8 will not be repeated here. This chapter is concerned with the interaction between these central agencies and other actors in the executive-bureaucratic sphere of government.

The role of central agencies in assisting political executives to control and coordinate government policies and programs began to expand in the late 1960s. In serving both the prime minister and the cabinet, central agency officials control and influence departmental officials by affecting the allocation of human and financial resources, the organization of governmental and departmental machinery, and the coordination of intergovernmental relations. Central agencies thereby help to promote such administrative values as efficiency, effectiveness, and accountability.

Figure 15.1
THE CABINET COMMITTEE SYSTEM

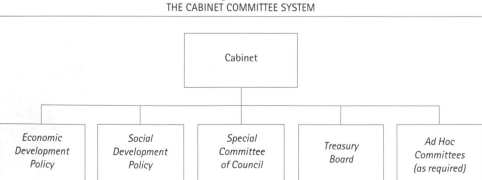

During the early years of the first Trudeau government, elected in 1968, the PMO and the PCO were reorganized and expanded so as to improve their advisory and coordinating functions. The growth in the staff and expenditure of these offices led some commentators to compare them to the White House staff and the Executive Office of the President in the United States, and to suggest that the expansion of these offices was part of the prime minister's objective of "presidentializing" the Canadian political system and enhancing prime-ministerial power. This suggestion is now seen to have been greatly exaggerated. Moreover, there is wide recognition that "political executives require elaborate machinery and large staffs devoted to coordination and control just to get on with the job of governing."[12] The relative importance of the PMO and the traditional central agencies has shifted since 1968, but all have continued to play a prominent role in supporting the prime minister and the cabinet. The interaction and shifts in relative power among the central agencies themselves will be explained in the next chapter on interdepartmental and interagency relations. It is sufficient here to note that the balance of power among the agencies was altered as a result of the creation in 1979 of two new central agencies—the Ministry of State for Social Development (MSSD) and the Ministry of State for Economic Development, which in 1982 became the Ministry of State for Economic and Regional Development (MSERD). As noted, these two agencies were abolished by Turner in 1984 as part of an effort to simplify the cabinet decision-making system.

It is notable that the PMO is a central agency unlike the others in that it is primarily a partisan instrument of the prime minister. The overriding concerns of PMO officials, who are political appointees rather than career public servants, are the political fortunes of the prime minister and the governing party. While they owe their first loyalty to the prime minister, these officials also serve the political interests of the cabinet as a whole. The PMO helps to ensure that the prime minister is knowledgeable about major policy issues, especially their political implications, and that he or she has an alternative source of policy advice to that provided by departmental ministers and officials.

In contrast to the PMO, officials in the PCO are generally career public servants who are nonpartisan; they are, however, highly sensitive to political considerations. The Department of Finance and TBS are also composed of career public servants. The prime minister and cabinet rely heavily on the central agencies to control and influence the behaviour of departmental public servants. This is especially evident in the sphere of financial management. We shall see in Chapters 26 and 27 that the Department of Finance and the TBS are critical forces in influencing and facilitating cabinet decisions on the management of financial resources.

The prime minister and, to a lesser extent, cabinet ministers, with the assistance of central agencies, exercise important functions in the sphere of human resource management, particularly in the staffing area. The prime minister and the cabinet make what are called governor in council appointments to the senior levels of the public service. The choice of deputy ministers is, by convention, the prerogative of the prime minister who receives advice from the secretary to the cabinet and normally discusses possible candidates with the minister of the department in question. With respect to senior positions in agencies, boards, and commissions, the prime minister usually consults with those ministers whose portfolio or region of the country is affected by an appointment. These appointments are made by the governor in council, i.e., by the governor general upon the recommendation of the prime minister and his or her colleagues.

The prime minister wields substantial power both in expenditure and human resource management and in the organization of the machinery of government. He or she is advised in performing this function by the clerk of the Privy Council and secretary to the cabinet, who is supported by the PCO's Machinery of Government Secretariat. This advice can involve the allocation of new policy and program responsibilities to specific departments, as well as major reallocations of existing responsibilities. The prime minister's control in this area is beneficial because it helps to avoid clashes among cabinet ministers over the allocation of governmental responsibilities. The prime minister creates new departments as part of his or her machinery of government responsibilities. Moreover, the prime minister and cabinet have frequently made substantial modifications in existing government organizations under the authority of the Public Service Rearrangement and Transfer of Duties Act, which provides that the governor in council may:

(a) transfer any powers, duties or functions or the control or supervision of any part of the public service of Canada from one minister of the Crown to any other minister of the Crown, or from one department or portion of the public service to any other department or portion of the public service; or

(b) amalgamate and combine any two or more departments under one minister of the Crown and under one deputy minister.[13]

The prime minister is still the dominant decision maker with respect to the machinery of government.

Cabinet Approval and Cabinet Documents

Figure 15.2 shows the process by which departmental proposals for new policies are approved, amended, or rejected by cabinet committees and by cabinet, and how the cabinet's decision, in the form of a record of decision, serves as authority for the allocation of resources for the implementation of those policies. Also, it illustrates the formal and informal interaction among the major players in the executive-bureaucratic arena. Cabinet committees and central agencies clearly play an important role, but policy proposals are formally prepared by government departments and are presented by a minister to the appropriate cabinet committee, usually in the form of a document called a *Memorandum to Cabinet*. A minister's policy proposals can, of course, be influenced by a variety of sources, including political parties, interest groups, and individual citizens.

Figure 15.2
PROCESS OF CABINET APPROVAL

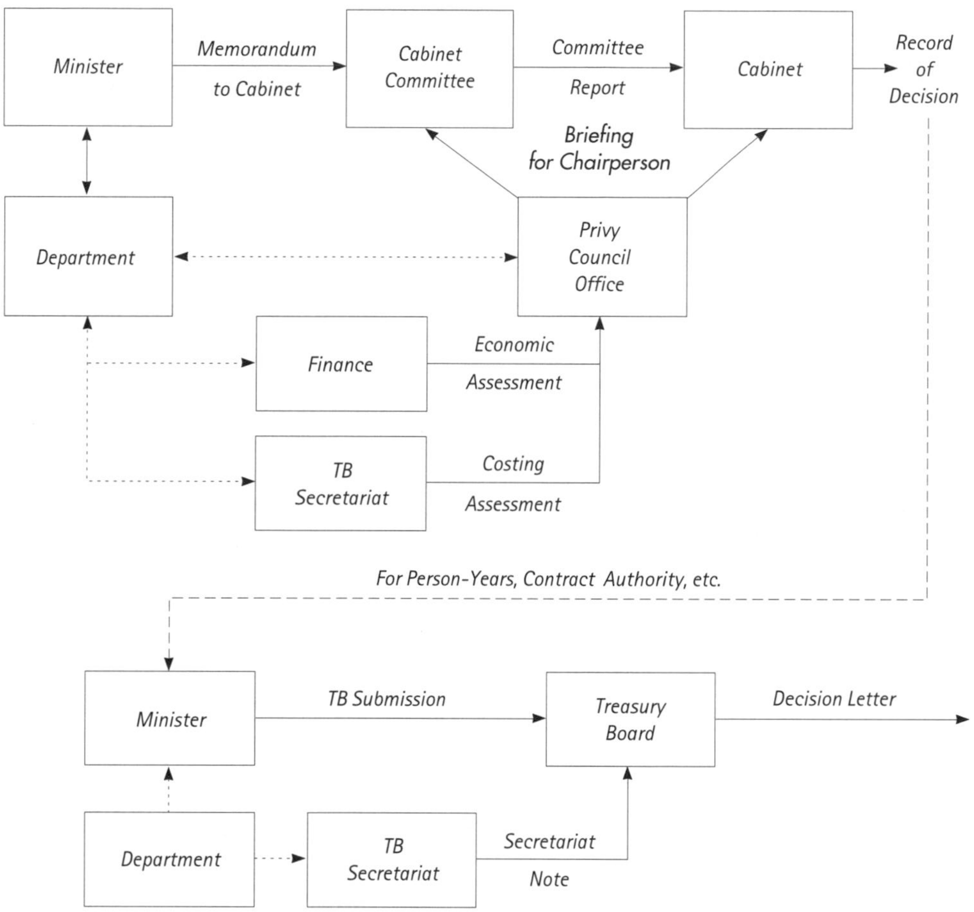

The two principles on which the cabinet approval process is based are that "all ministers have the right to bring to their colleagues proposals for government action in their area of policy responsibility" and that "all ministers should have the opportunity to express an informed view within the cabinet process on a proposal for which they will share collective responsibility."[14] The *Memorandum to Cabinet* is the key mechanism by which policy proposals are brought forward by ministers for consideration and approval by their cabinet colleagues. It is also the formal means by which deputy ministers provide confidential policy advice to their ministers. Cabinet memoranda, which are usually based on extensive research and interdepartmental consultations, set out as concisely as possible the issues associated with a particular problem or proposal;

alternatives for dealing with these issues; the implications of these various alternatives for such concerns as finances, public relations, interdepartmental relations, federal-provincial relations, and the party caucus; and recommendations for action. A cabinet memorandum has two parts—a three-page "Ministerial Recommendations" (MR) section, which contains key information for ministers, and an "Analysis" section, which contains a much lengthier treatment of substantially the same matters covered in the MR, with the exception of the recommendations and politically sensitive matters.

Following its consideration of a cabinet memorandum, a cabinet committee makes a recommendation that is passed on to cabinet in the form of a committee report. Formal approval takes the form of a record of decision that is circulated to all ministers for any necessary follow-up. PCO officials play a sensitive and influential role both in briefing committee chairpersons and in drafting committee reports and records of decision. Note the important role of the Department of Finance and the TBS in providing cabinet committees, through the PCO, with an economic and a costing assessment of policy proposals contained in cabinet memoranda.

The record of decision serves as a basis for ministers, on behalf of their departments, to request approval from Treasury Board and the TBS for the human and financial resources needed to implement approved policies. Ministers seek Treasury Board approval through what is called a Treasury Board submission. The TB Secretariat reviews each submission and recommends to the board whether it should be approved, rejected, or altered. The decision to approve or reject is provided in the form of a "decision letter." Figure 15.2 indicates, by dotted lines, the consultation between departments and central agencies that accompanies the preparation and processing of both cabinet memoranda and Treasury Board submissions.

A primary purpose of the several reforms of the cabinet decision-making system since the mid-1960s has been to enhance the power of political executives over public servants in the making of public policy. Yet, even after these changes, senior officials from departments and central agencies were permitted to attend cabinet committee meetings to provide advice and support to their ministers or the prime minister. This participation provided an opportunity for public servants to use their knowledge and experience to influence a policy at a critical stage of its development. The Mulroney government decided in 1985 to limit strictly the attendance of public servants at cabinet committee meetings to ensure the predominance of ministers in the making of policy decisions. These strict limits have been retained by the Chrétien government.

In general, reforms in the structures and processes of provincial cabinet decision-making systems followed a pattern similar to the federal reforms discussed above and aimed to achieve the same objectives of cabinet coordination and control of policy making.[15] In most provinces, these objectives were pursued through an expanded cabinet committee system dominated by planning and priorities committees, treasury boards or management boards, and standing policy committees. As on the federal scene, cabinet secretariats and other central agencies were established or upgraded to support the premier, the cabinet, and cabinet committees.

The emphasis in this chapter has been on interaction between the prime minister and the cabinet on the one hand, and central agencies and departments on the other. We now turn to an examination of interaction between government departments, between departments and central agencies, and among the central agencies themselves.

NOTES

1. Based on "Speaking Truth to Political Power", Case #5 in La Releve, *Discussion Guide for A Strong Foundation,* The Report of the Task Force on Public Service Values and Ethics (Ottawa: Canadian Centre for Management Development, 1997), 32–33.
2. The governor general and the lieutenant governors are representatives of the Queen.
3. See, for example, J. March and H. Simon, *Organizations* (New York: John Wiley & Sons, 1958); Victor A. Thompson, *Modern Organization* (New York: Knopf, 1961); and Robert K. Merton, "Bureaucratic Structure and Personality," in Robert K. Merton, ed., *Reader in Bureaucracy* (New York: The Free Press, 1952).
4. See the explanation of the bureaucratic politics approach in Chapter 6.
5. Graham T. Allison and Morton H. Halperin, "Bureaucratic Politics: A Paradigm and Some Policy Implications," *World Politics* 24 (Supplement, 1972): 43.
6. Royal Commission on Financial Management and Accountability, *Final Report* (Ottawa: Supply and Services, 1979), 42.
7. See the discussion of deputy ministers in Chapter 16.
8. See W.A. Matheson, *The Prime Minister and the Cabinet* (Toronto: Methuen, 1976), 83–91.
9. Lester B. Pearson, Press Release, Office of the Prime Minister, 20 January 1968.
10. Pierre Elliott Trudeau, Press Release, Office of the Prime Minister, "Statement by the Prime Minister on Cabinet Committee Structure," 30 April 1968.
11. Colin Campbell and George J. Szablowski, *The Superbureaucrats: Structure and Behaviour in Central Agencies* (Toronto: Macmillan, 1979), 1.
12. Colin Campbell, "Central Agencies in Canada," in Kenneth Kernaghan, ed., *Public Administration in Canada: Selected Readings* (Toronto: Methuen, 1985), 13.
13. Canada, *Statutes,* 1918, c. 6 as amended in 1925, c. 23.
14. Ian Clark, "Recent Changes in the Cabinet Decision-Making System in Ottawa," *Canadian Public Administration,* 20 (summer 1985): 198.
15. See Christopher Dunn, "Changing the Design: Cabinet Decision-Making in Three Provincial Governments," *Canadian Public Administration* 34 (winter 1991): 621–40; and Marsha A. Chandler and William M. Chandler, *Public Policy and Provincial Politics* (Toronto: McGraw-Hill Ryerson, 1979), ch. 4, and "Public Administration in Canada's Provinces," in Kenneth Kernaghan, ed., *Canadian Public Administration: Practice and Profession* (Toronto: Butterworths, 1983), 145–50. On the evolution of the cabinet system in Ontario, see Richard A. Loreto and Graham White, "The Premier and the Cabinet," in Graham White, ed., *The Government and Politics of Ontario,* 4th ed. (Scarborough, Ont.: Nelson, 1990), 79–102.

BIBLIOGRAPHY

Aucoin, Peter. "Organizational Change in the Machinery of Canadian Government: From Rational Management to Brokerage Politics." *Canadian Journal of Political Science* 19 (March 1986): 3–27.

Balls, Herbert R. "Decision-Making: The Role of the Deputy Minister." *Canadian Public Administration* 19 (fall 1976): 417–31.

Anderson, G. "The New Focus on the Policy Capacity of the Federal Government." *Canadian Public Administration* 39 (winter 1996): 469–88.

Campbell, Colin. *Governments Under Stress: Political Executives and Key Bureaucrats in Washington, London and Ottawa.* Toronto: University of Toronto Press, 1983.

Campbell, Colin, and George Szablowski. *The Superbureaucrats: Structure and Behaviour in Central Agencies.* Toronto: Macmillan, 1979.

Canada. Royal Commission on Financial Management and Accountability. *Final Report.* Ottawa: Supply and Services, 1979, ch. 4.

Clark, Ian. "Recent Changes in the Cabinet Decision-Making System in Ottawa." *Canadian Public Administration* 28 (summer 1985): 185–201.

———. "Restraint, Renewal and the Treasury Board Secretariat." *Canadian Public Administration* 37 (summer 1994): 209–48.

Doern, G. Bruce, and Richard W. Phidd. *Canadian Public Policy*, 2nd ed. Toronto: Methuen, 1992, ch. 10.

Doerr, Audrey. *The Machinery of Government in Canada.* Toronto: Methuen, 1981, chs. 2–3.

Dunn, Christopher. "Changing the Design: Cabinet Decision-Making in Three Provincial Governments." *Canadian Public Administration* 34 (winter 1991): 621–40.

French, Richard. *How Ottawa Decides: Planning and Industrial Policy Making, 1968–1984*, 2nd ed. Toronto: James Lorimer, 1984.

Jauvin, Nicole. "Government, Ministers, Macro-Organization Chart and Networks." In Bourgault, Jacques et al., eds. *Public Administration and Public Management: Canadian Experiences.* Quebec: Les Publications du Québec, 1997, 45-58.

Johnson, A.W. "The Role of the Deputy Minister." *Canadian Public Administration* 4 (December 1961): 363–69.

Kernaghan, Kenneth, and Olivia Kuper. *Coordination in Canadian Governments: A Case Study of Aging Policy.* Toronto: Institute of Public Administration of Canada, 1983.

Kroeger, Arthur. "A Retrospective on Policy Development in Ottawa." *Canadian Public Administration* 39 (winter 1996): 457–68.

Lalonde, Marc. "The Changing Role of the Prime Minister's Office." *Canadian Public Administration* 14 (winter 1971): 538–55.

Lindquist, Evert and Graham White. "Analyzing Canadian Cabinets: Past, Present and Future." In Charih, Mohamed and Arthur Daniels, eds., *New Public Management and Public Administration in Canada.* Toronto: Institute of Public Administration of Canada, 1997, 113–38.

Loreto, Richard. "Making and Implementing the Decisions: Issues of Public Administration in the Ontario Government." In Graham White, ed., *The Government and Politics of Ontario*, 5th ed. Toronto: University of Toronto Press, 1997, 93–125.

Matheson, W.A. *The Prime Minister and the Cabinet.* Toronto: Methuen, 1976.

———. "The Cabinet and the Canadian Bureaucracy." In Kenneth Kernaghan, ed., *Public Administration in Canada: Selected Readings*, 5th ed. Toronto: Methuen, 1985, 266–80.

Nossal, Kim Richard. "Allison through the (Ottawa) Looking Glass: Bureaucratic Politics and Foreign Policy in a Parliamentary System." *Canadian Public Administration* 22 (winter 1979): 610–26.

Osbaldeston, Gordon F. *Organizing to Govern*, 2 vols. Toronto: McGraw-Hill Ryerson, 1992.

Plumptre, Timothy. "New Perspectives on the Role of the Deputy Minister." *Canadian Public Administration* 30 (fall 1987): 376–98.

Robertson, Gordon. "The Changing Role of the Privy Council Office." *Canadian Public Administration* 14 (spring 1971): 487–508.

Schultz, Richard. *Federalism, Bureaucracy and Public Policy.* Montreal: McGill-Queen's University Press, 1980.

Van Loon, R. "The Policy and Expenditure Management System in the Federal Government: The First Three Years." *Canadian Public Administration* 26 (summer 1983): 255–84.

Zussman, David. "Walking the Tightrope: The Mulroney Government and the Public Service." In Michael J. Prince, ed., *How Ottawa Spends: 1986–87: Tracking the Tories.* Toronto: Methuen, 1986, 250–82.

16

Interdepartmental and Intradepartmental Relations

"Officials Chastised for Major Blunder."[1] This was the headline that accompanied a *Globe and Mail* story about strained relations between two government departments. Each spring, in the Magdalen Islands, the federal Department of Public Works dredges from around harbour docks the sand that has been deposited there by winter storms. To ensure that environmental damage is avoided, Public Works must receive a permit for the dredging from the Department of the Environment. In 1990, Public Works received authorization to dredge near the docks adjacent to Cap-Vert Lagoon, so long as the work was not done during the lobster-spawning season, that is, between May and September. Public works officials misread the authorization, with the result that a large amount of sand was dredged and dumped into the lagoon during those months. The Department of the Environment sued the Department of Public Works for creating what the judge in the case referred to as a disaster because of its adverse impact on the lobster population, which is the foundation of the local economy. The Department of Public Works pleaded guilty to a violation of the Environmental Protection Act and was fined. The judge recognized that the error was not malicious but said that government officials must be held to the strictest of standards because they are entrusted with the responsibility of protecting the environment.

This case highlights the fact that government departments perform substantially different functions from one another and that tension and competition, rather than harmonious collaboration, are often the result. There is a variety of mechanisms to promote coordination among government departments and between departments and central agencies. Similar mechanisms exist to ensure appropriate coordination of policy development and implementation *within* each government department. We shall see in this chapter that deputy ministers play a key role in both *inter*departmental and *intra*departmental relations.

🏛 INTERDEPARTMENTAL RELATIONS

The Importance of Horizontal Relations

In recent years, governments have become increasingly sensitive to the fact that virtually all policy issues cut across *departmental* boundaries and that many of them cut across governmental and even national boundaries. Many policy issues do not fall neatly under the jurisdiction of a single department—or even of a single government or country. For example, it is difficult to develop and implement health policies without giving attention to their implications for such policy areas as taxation and competitiveness. And three departments are significantly involved in administering the income tax system. The Department of Finance formulates tax policy and introduces new tax legislation, Revenue Canada administers tax laws, and the Department of Justice provides legal advisory and litigation services to the other two departments.

Financial constraints have increased the pressure to avoid duplication and overlap within and between departments and governments; and globalization has obliged governments to weigh the international consequences of their domestic policy decisions and the domestic consequences of decisions by other governments, global corporations, and international institutions such as the World Bank. Thus, there is a pressing need within governments for improved horizontal coordination of policy decisions by such means as consultation, cooperation, and collaboration. However, "coordination in government is hard work; there is no 'easy recipe for success.' It depends in part on the processes and machinery of government. It depends in part on the working relationships within Cabinet, between Ministers and their senior advisors and between departments. And it depends in part on the culture regarding collaboration and teamwork within the public service."[2]

While there are many important informal contacts between and among government departments and central agencies, *formal* contacts take the form primarily of interdepartmental committees. This section discusses briefly the evolution of senior-level committees and then explains the functions and effectiveness of interdepartmental committees in general.

> The values that support interdepartmental collaboration and cooperation ... include the democratic values of neutrality and accountability to Parliament, service to the public, and devotion to the public interest; the ethical values such as integrity, as well as respect and concern for others; and the quality values such as professionalism and effectiveness. Together these core values support the development of a collegial policy community, which recognizes its individual and collective responsibilities, and which is committed to working towards policy excellence.
>
> *Source: Federal Deputy Ministers' Task Force, Managing Horizontal Policy*[3]

Senior-Level Interdepartmental Committees

Consultation between and among departments is, of course, essential to the effective development of policy and program proposals. Over the decade before the Turner government of 1984, sectoral deputy minister committees, often called mirror committees, were established to facilitate interdepartmental consultation on matters that were to be considered by the cabinet policy committees composed of ministers. Privy Council Office (PCO) officials promoted interdepartmental coordination by participating in these meetings. As part of an effort to shift some power in the direction of the departments, Turner abolished these committees. However, there was still a need to ensure appropriate interdepartmental consultation. Since that time there has been more burden on the sponsoring department to ensure that items coming to cabinet have been subject to adequate interdepartmental consultation. For example, departments are expected to consult the Department of External Affairs when Canada's international relations might be affected. PCO has the responsibility of ensuring that appropriate interdepartmental work has been done before items are brought forward to cabinet committees.

A valuable coordinating role continues to be played by the Coordinating Committee of Deputy Ministers, chaired by the secretary to the cabinet and whose membership includes the deputy ministers from the TBS and the finance, external affairs, and justice departments. This committee provides an opportunity for an exchange of views between the secretary to the cabinet and the administrative heads of central agencies on matters of general concern to the government. Other meetings, including a monthly deputy ministers' luncheon, a weekly deputy ministers' breakfast, and occasional retreats, are called by the cabinet secretary for the purpose of informal discussion of matters of general interest. Still other interdepartmental committees at the deputy minister level (e.g., the Committee of Senior Officials on Executive Personnel) and at the assistant deputy minister level (e.g., the Interdepartmental Panel on Energy Research and the Committee on International Affairs) serve a variety of purposes. Below these very senior levels, there are many other committees involving public servants from two or more departments.

Functions of Interdepartmental Committees

Audrey Doerr classified interdepartmental committees according to their major function.[4] *Committees to initiate* are created to mobilize departmental interest and support early in the policy process. For example, one of these committees might be created to review a royal commission report and make recommendations on the appropriate governmental response to its proposals. Either a department or a central agency could chair and lead the committee in its work.

Committees to negotiate or arbitrate are concerned with sorting out and reaching compromises on the appropriate allocation of roles and responsibilities for a particular matter. For example, the Interdepartmental Committee on Oceans coordinates the activities of departments and agencies in this area.

Committees to advise are concerned with providing advice to senior departmental officials and ministers with respect to the substance of policy or the coordination of policy development. An example is the Deputy Ministers' Steering Committee on Program Review, which was set up in 1994 to advise ministers on submissions for program reductions prepared by their departments.

Committees to evaluate are often created to assess policies or programs and to make appropriate recommendations for action. An example is the Committee of Senior Officials on Executive Personnel, chaired by the secretary to the cabinet, which, among other things, evaluates the performance of senior officials.

Committees to monitor "maintain a 'watching brief' on departmental activities in a particular policy or program area."[5] For example, an Interdepartmental

Committee on Climate Change was one of several committees established to monitor activities in the environmental area.

Finally, *interdepartmental task forces* are usually temporary bodies composed of public servants loaned by departments and agencies for a particular task. For example, ten task forces, composed of more than ninety deputy ministers, assistant deputy ministers, and regional officials, were set up in 1989 under the Public Service 2000 initiative.

Effectiveness of Interdepartmental Committees

It is important to keep in mind that many of these interdepartmental bodies, whatever their primary function, are composed of representatives of both departments and central agencies. They can, therefore, help to coordinate policy development and implementation among departments, and they can assist central agencies in their support of cabinet and its committees.

Interdepartmental committees have been described as "the principal means of communication and deliberation in the federal bureaucratic establishment."[6] Attention has also been drawn to their value as "important means for central agencies to initiate or coordinate new undertakings. They support departmental policy making by bringing together a number of interested parties and resolving conflicts before recommendations are made to ministers. In each instance, consensus and support are sought through coordination."[7] Other observers have cautioned against expecting much effective coordination through interdepartmental committees. In addition, "some participants have dubbed the interdepartmental committee system 'institutionalized discord'—the coordinate mechanism, in other words, has simply become in several respects one of the battlegrounds where interdepartmental combat occurs."[8] Richard Schultz has noted the enormous growth of what he calls "interdepartmentalism," which has resulted in more and more public servants being required "to negotiate with officials in other departments. This negotiation process, bureaucratic politics, can only reinforce both the political role of members of the public service and correspondingly their influence in the system."[9] Similarly, H.L. Laframboise suggested that "the blurring of departmental boundaries," together with such things as "the spread of collegial decision making" and "the proliferation of watchdog agencies," has resulted in "an emphasis on interdepartmental negotiations, and this emphasis has been translated into a corps of interdepartmental diplomats of considerable dimensions."[10]

The effectiveness of interdepartmental committees varies from one committee to another, but in general they serve a useful purpose in assisting cabinet and central agencies to coordinate government activities. As noted earlier, governments have recently placed great emphasis on overcoming barriers to interdepartmental coordination. According to the federal deputy ministers' task force on managing horizontal relations, "[w]hile the policy debate among departments is an important part of reconciling competing demands and of developing rigorous policies, at the same time, collaboration across government can result in the development of new and innovative policies by drawing on the perspectives and creativity of a range of departments. It can also broaden the debate beyond the narrow, single issue interests to the broader public interest, and can contribute to the development of richer, more integrated policy initiatives."[11]

🏛 RELATIONS BETWEEN DEPARTMENTS AND CENTRAL AGENCIES

It is widely held that the expansion in the size and power of central agencies that occurred in the late 1960s and early 1970s reduced the power of both the ministers and senior officials of operating departments. The control and influence exercised by central agencies in the coordination of policy development, and in the allocation of human and financial resources for departmental programs, led to considerable tension in the relations between the agencies and line departments. The filtering of departmental policy and program proposals through cabinet committees and central agencies helped ensure that ministers and their senior officials understood the implications of their proposals for other departments and for the government as a whole. However, ministers and their officials spent a great deal of time and effort lobbying and bargaining with their counterparts in other departments and in the central agencies. It was an extremely time-consuming process for ministers, and it tended to reduce their individual authority and influence in the cabinet decision-making system.

In the mid-1980s, the Turner and Mulroney governments decided that the number and influence of central agencies, combined with the complexities of the cabinet committee system and the Policy and Expenditure Management System (PEMS), made the decision-making system too complicated. Too much emphasis was being placed on the process of policy formulation as compared to policy content. Several reforms, some of which have already been mentioned in Chapter 15, were introduced to bring about a simpler, more hierarchical model of cabinet government. These reforms included the abolition of two central agencies (the Ministry of State for Economic and Regional Development and the Ministry of State for Social Development), the simplification of the processes of cabinet and its committees, and a reduction in the number of committees. The reforms were designed in large part to restore a greater measure of power in the decision-making process to the ministers of line departments.

In 1986, the Mulroney government initiated a new managerial process called Increased Ministerial Authority and Accountability (IMAA).[12] It involved a general review of Treasury Board policies to bring about a greater measure of delegation and deregulation, to reduce reporting requirements, and to emphasize performance rather than compliance with rules. IMAA also involved the negotiation of Memoranda of Understanding (MOUs) between the Treasury Board and individual departments. Departments were invited to present proposals for altering Treasury Board policies and to request delegated authority and diminished reporting requirements. Each MOU incorporated agreements on these matters and set out an accountability framework within which the department's performance could be assessed. IMAA has been displaced by broader reforms designed to reduce rules and increase accountability for results throughout the public service.

The trend toward greater departmental autonomy accelerated during the 1990s as the argument became widely accepted that departments could be more flexible and responsive if they were subject to fewer central agency controls. However, the traditional tension between departments and central agencies endured because of the continuing need for central agency intervention to promote interdepartmental coordination.

Richard Schultz, among others, has suggested that the role of central agencies in the decision-making process has been somewhat exaggerated. He has argued that the line departments possess powerful resources in any competition with central agencies. He notes that central agencies lack the human resources and the expertise available to operating departments, that policy initiatives and policy implementation are primarily the responsibility of departments, that departments control the timing of their proposals and the information supporting them, and that departments may at times resist the coordinating efforts of central agencies.[13]

Despite various efforts to strengthen the role of departments in relation to central agencies, the traditional central agencies, i.e., the PCO, the Treasury Board Secretariat, and the Department of Finance, continue to exercise considerable power in policy development and implementation. Over time, however, there have been shifts in the relative power of central agencies both in their relations with departments and in their relations with one another. Indeed, competition among the central agencies helps to prevent the dominance of any one agency and, on occasion, helps departments get their way by setting one agency against another. There is an obvious need for cooperation and consultation among the central agencies themselves to ensure an appropriate measure of interdepartmental coordination. "As central agencies try ... to cope with powerful forces pulling in different directions, they will ... have to review the kind of relationships they have with line departments and with one another. They will have somehow to strike a proper balance between the need to decentralize decision making and the need to ensure consistent standards across the government. They will also need to define new ways to monitor the performance of line departments in a systematic fashion."[14]

We turn now to an examination of the relations *within* departments: between ministers and public servants, between public servants and the ministers' political staff, and among public servants.

🏛 INTRADEPARTMENTAL RELATIONS

As explained in detail in Chapter 8, the internal structure of administrative organizations varies from one category of organization to another (e.g., from departments to Crown agencies to central agencies); it also varies from one organization to another within each category. In general, however, departments and those central agencies with departmental form are organized in a broadly uniform manner. They are structured in a pyramidal fashion, with a minister as the political head and a deputy minister as the administrative head of a formal organization, with layers of interlocking superior–subordinate relationships descending to the base of the pyramid.

The Deputy Minister

The Deputy and the Minister

The individual responsibility of ministers as political heads of departments links the cabinet to the bureaucracy, and it establishes the minister as the locus of formal authority in the departmental hierarchy for both policy formulation and policy execution. Ministers not only make the final decisions on policy questions; they also bear constitutional, legal, and political responsibility for the proper administration of their departments. In practice, ministers look for assistance to their senior departmental officials, especially to the deputy minister, who is the administrative head of the department.

> The top officials in the major policy departments are key players in the Canadian system of government. It is essential that they be well informed with well developed views about public policy and, if possible, a wide acquaintanceship with the movers and shakers in the private sector. Politically neutral they should be. Politically ignorant they cannot be. The ministers I served wanted to know the views of their non-partisan advisers on all aspects of the matters under discussion. When I became a minister, I expected my deputy ministers to be frank and open in the expression of their views. Top officials worth their salt should be prepared to tell the minister, politely of course, that his or her pet ideas are for the birds.
>
> *Source: Former minister and deputy minister Mitchell Sharp.*[15]

As noted in the previous chapter, the deputy minister occupies a pivotal position at the border between the political and bureaucratic spheres of government. He or she is expected to provide the minister with technical, managerial, legal, and financial advice, as well as political advice. A federal deputy minister has explained that "the advice provided by deputy ministers and senior officials includes advice that is 'political'—not partisan in the sense of advising the government how to do in the Opposition, but political in the sense of giving ministers assessments of likely reactions, particularly by the department's clientele, to a course of action that is under discussion."[16]

Although the prime minister has the power to appoint, transfer, and remove deputy ministers, their first loyalty is to their minister. This seemingly illogical arrangement reflects the reality that ministers have both individual and collective responsibilities and that deputies are expected to serve their ministers in both capacities. Deputies not only serve their own ministers; through their support of the ministers' collective responsibilities, they also serve the government as a whole. Moreover, deputies perform certain functions according to statute or on the authority of the cabinet rather than of their minister. The prime minister's power to select deputies helps ensure continuity in departmental administration despite a change of ministers, reminds deputies "of their need for a perspective encompassing the whole range of government," and "emphasizes the collective interest of ministers, and the special interest of the prime minister in the effectiveness of management in the public service."[17]

The fact that the prime minister selects both ministers and deputy ministers enables him or her to seek a compatible team in each department—both in terms of policy and management skills and in terms of personal chemistry. The prime minister is in a position to arbitrate the occasional disputes that arise between deputies and their ministers, and he or she can even refuse to transfer deputies who are unacceptable to their ministers. For example, former prime minister Joe Clark is reported to have granted a few ministers their request for a new deputy but to have refused the request of the Minister of External Affairs that her deputy be dismissed or transferred.[18]

The Deputy's Control and Influence

The authority of the deputy minister is based on both statutes and conventions. Many of the deputy's administrative responsibilities are spelled out in departmental acts as well as in the Interpretation Act, the Financial Administration Act, the Public Service Employment Act, and the Official Languages Act. Departmental acts usually provide for the appointment by the governor in council of a deputy minister who is to hold office at pleasure (i.e., he or she may be replaced by the prime minister at any time). Some acts actually delegate authority to the deputy for certain specified matters. The Interpretation Act is especially important, however, because it provides in Section 23(a) that "words ... empowering a Minister ... to do an act or thing, include ... his ... deputy." Thus, the minister can delegate a wide range of authority to the deputy. However, the act states specifically that the deputy cannot substitute for the minister in the making of regulations. Moreover, the deputy cannot answer to Parliament on behalf of the minister or sign cabinet memoranda. The other acts noted above delegate authority directly to the deputy or provide for delegation to the deputy by the Treasury Board or the Public Service Commission. In contrast to the deputy's administrative responsibilities, his or her responsibilities to provide policy advice to the minister and to the government as a whole are based more on tradition and practice than on statutes.

A.W. Johnson contends that, in the realm of policy *development*, the deputy minister's role as policy advisor entails the initiation of policy recommendations and policy studies, without usurping the minister's initiative in these matters. He notes that "the cynics may suggest that this is power without responsibility; I suggest that it is more akin to responsibility without power."[19] The fact is that deputy ministers often do exercise power—in the form of influence—through policy initiatives in which their minister has had little involvement. In this connection, Mitchell Sharp, a former minister and senior public servant, has observed that the typical senior civil servant seems to be thought of as a quite intelligent but passive agent of government, waiting to be set in motion by his Minister and producing in time a memorandum of well-balanced pros and cons. There are occasions, of course, when the senior advisor has to perform exactly that function. But when I think back over my experience, I remember more occasions when civil servants by fruitful initiatives led the Government to adopt lines of policy which would have never occurred to them otherwise.[20]

The challenge, then, is to ensure that the deputy's role in policy formation combines power with responsibility. We shall see that deputies are either accountable, or feel a sense of personal responsibility, to a wide variety of participants in the political system.

In the realm of policy *implementation*, cabinet ministers may become involved in virtually any matter within the ambit of their departmental portfolio, including the organization and management of the department. While ministers are responsible for the administration of their department, their burdensome duties oblige them to leave most of this administration to the deputy and other senior officials. Moreover, deputies tend to guard jealously their managerial responsibilities. They do not wish, or expect, ministers to intervene in administrative matters without their knowledge and consent. Ministers do on occasion become involved in administrative matters, and senior officials are obliged to accommodate them and obey their directions. Indeed, A.W. Johnson has asserted that one of the important jobs of the deputy head is "to try to interpret to his staff the rationale for ministerial forays into the day-to-day work of the civil service."[21]

The extent to which ministers become involved in administration (and public servants in policy formation) depends on individual personalities and capacities, as well as on situational and time factors related to a department's particular activities. Some ministers will, by virtue of past experience and personal predisposition, be very interested in administrative questions; others will prefer to leave departmental administration almost solely in the hands of the public servants. There appears to be no strong correlation between a minister's interest in administrative matters and his or her status as a strong or weak minister. The effective minister appears to be one who will intervene forcefully on important or urgent matters of administration. Senior public servants may head off ministerial excursions into the administrative hierarchy by anticipating and responding quickly to ministerial requests and by providing suggestions to deal with emerging problems that have not yet become matters of ministerial concern.

Policy Advice or Management?

For reasons of partisan politics and personal advancement, both the prime minister and departmental ministers are primarily concerned with the formulation, rather than the implementation, of policy. It is not surprising, therefore, that many deputies have perceived that their own careers will prosper if they focus on policy advice rather than on departmental management. It is notable also that deputies are obliged to compete with other sources of advice for their ministers' attention on policy matters, whereas they have little competition in the sphere of departmental administration. Although deputies reported to the

Lambert Commission that, on average, they spent two-thirds of their time on management, a majority of them ranked the tasks of "supporting my minister" and "ensuring that my department is responsive to the policy thrusts of government" as more important than management responsibilities.[22] Between the mid-1980s and the mid-1990s, the managerial component of the deputies' responsibilities became relatively more important as governments stressed the need for public servants to focus on improved efficiency, effectiveness, and responsiveness in the delivery of government programs. Governments sought policy advice more frequently from political advisors and outside consultants. In more recent years, while the concern for good management has endured, there has been a renewed emphasis on the policy capacity of the public service.

Deputy ministers can, and do, become overloaded by the combined burden of their policy and managerial duties. What has long been said about ministers can now be said about many deputy ministers—they have too much to do and they do too much. A persuasive argument could be made that deputies should be viewed more as experts in the machinery and process of government than as experts in the substance of public policy. The tendency to rotate deputies fairly quickly among departments means that they cannot gain sufficient knowledge about the content and implications of departmental policy. They must, therefore, rely more heavily on the advice of their departmental specialists. The deputies' effective performance of their managerial duties is essential to their policy advisory responsibilities. "Deputy heads must be actively involved in the administration and operation of their departments if they are to be effective in offering policy advice and in developing programs that can be designed and carried out with value for money in mind."[23]

The Accountability of the Deputy Minister[24]

"Effective accountability for the Public Service as a whole ... very largely depends on effective accountability for Deputy Ministers."[25] However, the deputies' job is complicated by the many authorities to whom they are accountable. Deputies are *directly* accountable only to political and administrative superiors, to the courts, and to any internal governmental authorities (e.g., central agencies) to which accountability is required by law or the administrative hierarchy. They are not directly accountable to the legislature, to pressure groups, to the news media, or to the public. While it is agreed that, in general, deputies are accountable first of all to their minister, in practice they receive directions, rewards, and penalties from a variety of sources. As shown in Figure 16.1, the sources of direct accountability include not only their minister but also the prime minister, the Public Service Commission, and Treasury Board. A former public servant, in a hypothetical letter from the secretary of the cabinet to the prime minister, wrote that "we have been remarkably successful in multiplying the number of authorities to which deputy ministers are accountable, and it would be difficult, even for a hostile observer, to find a gap in the web we have spun."[26]

Despite the heavy burden of these existing accountability relationships, the Royal Commission on Financial Management and Accountability recommended that deputy ministers be required to account directly to the Public

Figure 16.1
ACCOUNTABILITY OF THE DEPUTY MINISTER

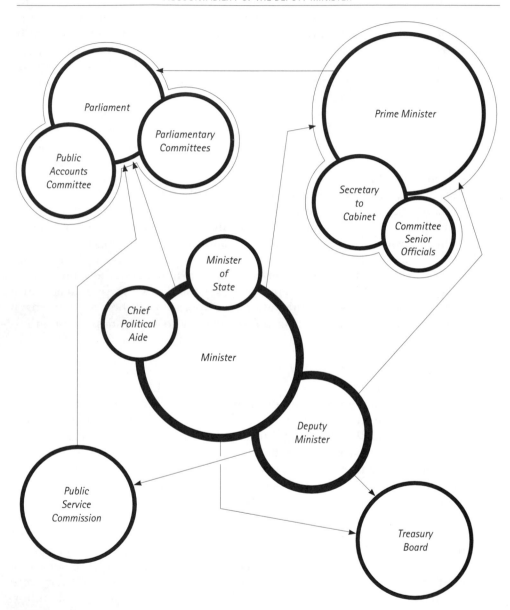

Source: Reproduced with permission from Gordon F. Osbaldeston, Keeping Deputy Ministers Accountable (Toronto: McGraw-Hill Ryerson, 1989), 8.

Accounts Committee of the House of Commons for the performance of specific or assigned duties, including those "relating to the probity and legality of expenditures, the economy and efficiency with which programs are run, and their effectiveness in achieving policy goals."[27] This proposal has been widely discussed in Canada's public administration community.

Critics of the proposal argue that the administrative matters for which deputies would be accountable cannot easily be separated from the policy matters for which ministers would be accountable; that holding deputies accountable for "their effectiveness in achieving policy goals" suggests, incorrectly, that ministers can usually provide clear policy objectives; that a formal, written division of responsibilities between a minister and his or her deputy is not in keeping with the traditional, informal pattern of relations between them; and that if public servants are held accountable to parliamentary committees, their anonymity will suffer.

Supporters of the proposal contend that the direct accountability of deputies would stimulate them to pay greater heed to their management tasks and to seek from their superiors clear statements of their responsibilities. Moreover, while at first glance the proposal seems to threaten the doctrine and practice of ministerial responsibility, it is similar to the "accounting officer" mechanism in Britain whereby a senior departmental official, usually the equivalent of our deputy minister, accounts directly to the Public Accounts Committee for the expenditure of public funds. There has been no suggestion that this British practice encroaches to any significant extent on ministerial responsibility. It is argued further that in Canada deputies already appear before parliamentary committees to explain departmental policy and its administration and that the responsibility for the defence of policy and administrative matters that are not delegated or assigned to deputies would remain with ministers. The anonymity of deputy ministers would decline somewhat, but the anonymity of their advice on policy matters would be preserved.

The outcome of this debate appears to be that no change will soon be made in the existing accountability relationships between deputies and parliamentary committees.

Ministerial Staff

Staff Assistance to Ministers

Relationships between ministers and deputy ministers are complicated further by the role of the minister's office staff. Ministerial assistants, often referred to as political aides or political staff, are appointed by the minister and are usually described as "exempt staff" because they are not subject to the provisions of the Public Service Employment Act. Since the tenure of ministerial assistants is tied directly to that of the minister, they are subject to the vicissitudes of partisan politics. A measure of employment protection is assured, however, by the Public Service Employment Act, which provides that a person who has served at least three years as an executive assistant, a special assistant, or a private secretary to a

minister is entitled to a position in the public service for which he or she is qualified at a level at least equivalent to that of private secretary to a deputy minister.
Ministerial assistants frequently take advantage of this opportunity. It was reported
that during the first six months of 1993, thirty Conservative aides obtained public
service jobs and another thirty were placed on priority waiting lists.[28]

Since the early 1960s, the size of the minister's office staff has gradually
increased; however, the influence of ministerial staff has not only waxed and
waned over that period but has also varied among ministers and departments.
Until the Progressive Conservative government of 1984, ministers were usually
authorized under Treasury Board guidelines to hire an executive assistant, a
policy advisor, as many special assistants as funds permitted, one private secretary, and support staff. Some ministers supplemented this staff by seconding
departmental public servants and/or using departmental funds to hire
employees on a contract basis. Upon its election in 1984, the Progressive
Conservative government upgraded the quality of ministerial staff by authorizing each minister to hire a *chief of staff* at a substantial salary. The chiefs of staff
were intended to function not as senior policy advisors to the minister but as the
minister's chief political advisors and as the managers of the minister's office.[29]
They did, however, play a more significant policy role than their predecessors.
Following its election in 1993, the Chrétien government abolished the chief of
staff role and reduced the resources devoted to ministerial assistants.

The Functions of Ministerial Assistants

The role of the ministerial assistant is meant to complement, rather than compete with, that of the deputy head and other senior public servants. The functions of the minister's staff relate to the management of the minister's office
and the enhancing of his or her political fortunes, rather than to the day-to-day
administration of the department or to the development of substantive policy.

Jeanne Flemming has identified four major roles performed by ministerial
assistants.[30] The role of *political advisor* includes giving advice on the political
implications of policy decisions and on appointments and facilitating effective
relations between the minister and the department, other ministers, the cabinet, the party, Members of Parliament, and the minister's constituency. The
role of *officer manager* requires careful handling of matters of organization,
staffing, budgeting, work flow, and correspondence. The role of *time manager*
involves juggling the minister's extremely onerous schedule to ensure that the
best possible use is made of his or her time. And, finally, the role of *crisis manager* requires ministerial assistants to help keep the minister out of trouble and
to limit the adverse consequences of a politically damaging situation.

Ministerial Staff and Departmental Officials

Harmonious relations between the minister's staff and departmental officials
require a clear understanding of their respective spheres of action. Tension and
conflict have resulted when ministerial assistants have tried to usurp the role of
senior public servants by interfering in departmental administration or by

impeding contacts between the minister and departmental officials. A ministerial assistant should "be careful not to abuse his [or her] authority, which is quite extensive. He or she should refrain from disagreeing with departmental officials on policy or practice merely for the sake of doing so. This unnecessary show of power is not likely to benefit the minister."[31] The ostensible reason for the Liberal government's abolition of the position of chief of staff was that these partisan appointees interposed themselves unduly between the minister and career public servants, especially the deputy minister. Prime Minister Chrétien's view was that "the important role played by ministerial staff should not duplicate the role of the department. Ministers should look to their Deputy Ministers for professional advice and support, on both policy and operations, across the full range of their responsibilities."[32] The government also announced that, compared to the previous government, the number of ministerial assistants would be severely restricted.

Departmental Management[33]

Effective management of government departments is primarily the responsibility of deputy ministers.

> It is the job of the deputy minister to harness the capabilities of the department and manage it on behalf of the minister. By managing, we mean the entire range of activities associated with directing a large and diverse organization within a complex environment. Depending on the department and circumstances, this normally includes some combination of activities such as budgeting, organizing and planning, and activities such as negotiating, motivating, communicating and influencing.... The value they [deputy ministers] should add to the minister's direction is threefold: knowledge of the department; familiarity with the requirements of collective management; and the objectivity of a non-partisan perspective.[34]

The incentive in the past for deputy ministers to pay more attention to the quality of their policy advice than that of their departmental management was explained earlier. The relative importance of policy advisory and management skills does, of course, vary from one department to another. Some departments (e.g., finance) are mainly policy-oriented, whereas others (e.g., health) are mainly program-oriented. In any event, sound departmental management is central to both the policy advisory and policy implementation responsibilities of the deputy minister. The quality of the deputy's performance depends greatly on the quality of the advice and assistance received from departmental subordinates. Thus, the success of the deputy, and indeed of the department and its minister, rests significantly on the extent to which the deputy is able to recruit, develop, and motivate competent departmental officials, especially senior managers.

In the federal public service, senior managers are members of the Executive Group. The Public Service Commission has the authority to appoint public servants to this category, to promote them and move them from one department to another, and to appoint people from outside the public service to the category. However, deputy ministers have the authority to appoint or reassign members of the Executive Group within their department, so long as there is no change in their occupational group or level. This arrangement gives deputy ministers some flexibility to deploy senior staff to meet their operational and career development needs.

In the management of their departments, deputies are constrained by both the regulations and guidelines of the Public Service Commission and by those of such central agencies as the PCO and the Treasury Board Secretariat. This chapter has already covered the diverse accountability mechanisms, including central agencies, to which deputy ministers are subject, and later chapters will examine the constraints on deputies and their departments in their management of human and financial resources. It is important to emphasize here that deputies are required to manage their departments in a political, legal, and bureaucratic environment that considerably restricts their freedom of action. This is one of the points of contrast between public and private sector management. The cabinet, usually acting through central agencies, imposes various service-wide requirements on government departments with a view to achieving such objectives as efficiency and effectiveness, integrity, and representativeness. For example, the Planning Programming Budgeting System (PPBS), the Operational Performance Measurement System (OPMS), and program evaluation were introduced to promote efficiency and effectiveness;[35] conflict of interest guidelines were formulated to stimulate a high level of integrity; and an employment equity program was adopted to bring about a more representative public service. But recent reforms have reduced the number of service-wide constraints on departments. The job of deputy ministers and their senior managers is to fulfil their responsibilities to the best of their abilities within the various constraints imposed by political executives and central agencies.

Deputy ministers play a critical role in pursuing *inter*departmental coordination as well as *intra*departmental coordination. Most government departments are so large that deputies can pursue coordination through regular, personal contacts with only the most senior departmental officials. Deputies are required, therefore, to delegate authority for coordinating departmental activities to their subordinates and to create formal coordinating mechanisms. Many departments have a management committee or an executive committee composed of the deputy and his or her immediate subordinates. This committee determines the overall objectives and priorities of the department and deals with major managerial issues. Deputies, in concert with these senior managers, devise structures and processes to facilitate the coordination of policies and programs at all levels of the department. Formal mechanisms such as committees are supplemented by a broad range of informal means of seeking coordination (personal contacts, telephone calls, etc.).

Provincial governments, like the federal government, seek coordination through cabinet committees and central agencies and through both interdepartmental and departmental committees. They have, as a result, experienced many of the same tensions as those between central agencies and line departments in the federal government.

The story of interaction among the major players in the executive-bureaucratic arena is clearly a complicated one, but in essence it is one of swings in the pendulum of power between political executives and public servants, and between departments and central agencies. Public servants exercise a great deal of control and influence in the policy process, and political executives are not always successful in holding public servants accountable for the exercise of this power. No matter what changes are made in the decision-making system, public servants continue to play a pervasive and significant role. Control over the bureaucracy by the prime minister (or premier) and the cabinet is, however, only one means of holding public servants accountable and responsible for their actions and decisions. The bureaucracy is far from a monolithic entity. We have seen in this chapter that public servants compete with, and are constrained by, other public servants. Subsequent chapters will show that additional actors in the political system—namely, legislators, judges, pressure groups, and the public—also check bureaucratic power.

NOTES

1. *The Globe and Mail* (8 June 1992), A9.
2. Canada, Deputy Ministers' Task Force, *Managing Horizontal Policy* (Ottawa: Privy Council Office, December 1996), 5.
3. Ibid., 26.
4. Audrey Doerr, *The Machinery of Government in Canada* (Toronto: Methuen, 1981), 138–42.
5. Ibid., 141.
6. Colin Campbell and George Szablowski, *The Superbureaucrats: Structure and Behaviour in Central Agencies* (Toronto: Macmillan, 1979), 24.
7. Doerr, *The Machinery of Government in Canada* , 138–39.
8. R.J. Van Loon and M.S. Whittington, *The Canadian Political System*, 4th ed. (Toronto: McGraw-Hill Ryerson, 1987), 563.
9. Richard J. Schultz, *Federalism, Bureaucracy and Public Policy: The Politics of Highway Regulation* (Montreal: McGill-Queen's University Press, 1980), 188.
10. H.L. Laframboise, "The Future of Public Administration in Canada," *Canadian Public Administration* 24 (winter 1982): 513.
11. Canada, Deputy Ministers' Task Force, *Managing Horizontal Policy*, 32.
12. Treasury Board, Draft, *The IMMA Handbook: A Guide to Development and Implementation* (Ottawa: Treasury Board Secretariat, 1 April 1988), 4.
13. Schultz, *Federalism, Bureaucracy and Public Policy*, 182–89.
14. Savoie, Donald J., "Central Agencies: A Government of Canada Perspective," in Jacques Bourgault, Maurice Demers, and Cynthia Williams, eds., *Public Administration and Public Management: Canadian Experiences* (Quebec: Les Publications du Québec, 1997), 68.
15. Mitchell Sharp, *Which Reminds Me ...: A Memoir* (Toronto: University of Toronto Press, 1994), 82.
16. Arthur Kroeger, "On Being a Deputy Minister," *Policy Options* 13 (May 1992): 4.
17. Royal Commission on Government Organization, *Report*, vol. 1 (Ottawa: Queen's Printer, 1965), 60.
18. J. Simpson, *The Discipline of Power* (Toronto: Personal Library, 1980), 132.
19. A.W. Johnson, "The Role of the Deputy Minister," in Kenneth Kernaghan, ed., *Public Administration in Canada: Selected Readings*, 5th ed. (Toronto: Methuen, 1985), 295.

20. Mitchell Sharp, "The Bureaucratic Elite and Policy Formation," in Kenneth Kernaghan, ed., *Bureaucracy in Canadian Government*, 2nd ed. (Toronto: Methuen, 1973), 73.
21. Johnson, "The Role of the Deputy Minister," 292.
22. Royal Commission on Financial Management and Accountability, *Final Report* (Ottawa: Minister of Supply and Services, 1979), 452.
23. Ibid., 179.
24. For an excellent examination of the role of the deputy minister in the Canadian political system, see: Gordon F. Osbaldeston, *Keeping Deputy Ministers Accountable* (Scarborough, Ont.: McGraw-Hill Ryerson, 1989). See also the discussion of the concept of accountability in Chapter 14.
25. Public Service 2000, *The Renewal of the Public Service of Canada* (Ottawa: Minister of Supply and Services, 1990), 91.
26. H.L. Laframboise, "A Note on Accountability," *Optimum* 13–14 (1982): 84.
27. Royal Commission on Financial Management and Accountability, *Final Report*, 374–75.
28. *The Globe and Mail* (14 December 1993), A6.
29. David Zussman, "Walking the Tightrope: The Mulroney Government and the Public Service," in Michael J. Prince, ed., *How Ottawa Spends: 1986–87: Tracking the Tories* (Toronto: Methuen, 1986), 265. For a succinct examination of the nature and evolution of the chief of staff position, see Loretta J. O'Connor, "Chief of Staff," *Policy Options* 12 (April 1991): 23–26. See also Jacques Bourgault and Stephane Dion, "Managing Conflict in a Context of Government Change: Lessons from the Federal Government of Canada," *The International Journal of Conflict Management* 1 (October 1990): 375–95. For an analysis of relations between chiefs of staff and senior public servants in Quebec, see Andrew F. Johnson and Jean Daigneault, "Liberal 'chefs de cabinets ministeriels' in Quebec: Keeping Politics in Policy Making," *Canadian Public Administration* 31 (winter 1988): 501–17.
30. Jeanne M. Flemming, "The Role of Executive Assistant to a Federal Minister," *Optimum* 27 (1997), 64–68.
31. O'Connor, "Chief of Staff," 26.
32. Office of the Prime Minister, *Release*, 4 November 1993, 2.
33. For an examination of the management of government programs, see Chapter 22.
34. Osbaldeston, *Keeping Deputy Ministers Accountable*, 107.
35. See the discussion of these matters in Chapters 26 and 27.

BIBLIOGRAPHY

Most of the items listed in the bibliography for Chapter 15 are also relevant to this chapter. See in addition the following items:

Bourgault, Jacques, and Stéphane Dion. "Managing Conflict in a Context of Government Change: Lessons from the Federal Government of Canada, 1984–1988." *The International Journal of Conflict Management* 1 (October 1990): 373–95.

Canada. Royal Commission on Financial Management and Accountability. *Final Report*. Ottawa: Ministry of Supply and Services, 1979, chs. 9–14.

Doerr, Audrey. *The Machinery of Government in Canada*. Toronto: Methuen, 1981, chs. 4, 6.

Flemming, Jeanne M. "The Role of Executive Assistant to a Federal Minister." *Optimum* 27 (1997): 63–68.

Mallory, J.R. "The Minister's Office Staff: An Unreformed Part of the Public Service." *Canadian Public Administration* 10 (March 1967): 25–34.

O'Connor, Loretta J. "Chief of Staff." *Policy Options* 12 (April 1991): 23–26.

Prince, Michael J., and John Chenier. "The Rise and Fall of Policy Planning and Research Units: An Organizational Perspective." *Canadian Public Administration* 23 (winter 1980): 519–41.

Savoie, Donald J. "The Minister's Staff: The Need for Reform." *Canadian Public Administration* 26 (winter 1983): 509–24.

Sharp, Mitchell. "The Bureaucratic Elite and Policy Formation." In Kenneth Kernaghan, ed., *Bureaucracy in Canadian Government,* 2nd ed. Toronto: Methuen, 1973, 69–73.

Williams, Blair. "The Para-political Bureaucracy in Ottawa." In H.D. Clarke et al., eds., *Parliament, Policy and Representation.* Toronto: Methuen, 1980, 215–30.

17

The Legislature and the Bureaucracy

Mohammed Al-Mashat—you may remember seeing him frequently on television during the Gulf War crisis, when he was Iraq's ambassador to the United States. On March 30, 1991, he was admitted to Canada as a landed immigrant. His entry seemed to have been considerably expedited by Canadian officials. No minister of the Mulroney government accepted responsibility for this politically controversial decision; indeed, the government blamed a senior public servant and a political aide for not informing Joe Clark, then Minister of External Affairs, about Al-Mashat's application for admission to Canada.

During an investigation of the affair by a parliamentary committee, Canadians witnessed a remarkable display of finger pointing and blame avoidance. Ministers laid blame on public servants, opposition members blamed ministers, public servants disagreed among themselves, and when Canada's top public servant asked an opposition member to "shut up for half a minute" the member responded: "Who the hell do you think you are?" However, the performance of one deputy minister was exemplary in its elegant conformity to the requirements of ministerial responsibility. What are these requirements? How is minsterial responsibility related to political neutrality and public service anonymity? What are the appropriate relationships between public servants and politicians? What is the role of the legislature in general, and legislative committees in particular, in holding public servants accountable for their recommendations and decisions? These are the main issues discussed in this chapter.

The conventional wisdom among students of Canadian government and politics is that during this century there has been a decline in the power of the federal Parliament and the provincial legislatures, and a rise in the power of the public service. The growth in the power of the public service, especially since the beginning of World War II, is generally acknowledged. Whether the overall power of the legislatures has actually declined is a debatable and complex issue. Nevertheless, it is widely recognized that, at present, the legislatures do not exercise effective power, in the sense of control and influence, over the executive in general or the public service in particular. The Royal Commission on Financial Management and Accountability (the Lambert Commission) expressed a view that is still widely held:

> Under our system, Parliament must be the beginning and the end of the governmental process. It must scrutinize and approve all legislation and all proposals for the raising of revenues and the expenditure of funds, and must watch over the Government's implementation of the proposals to which it has assented. We think

that Members of Parliament have not been adequately fulfilling their duty of forcing the Government to account for its administration.[1]

The power of the legislature over the public service is wielded primarily in an indirect fashion, through questioning and criticism of ministers responsible to the legislature for the administration of their departments. Since ministers are the formal constitutional intermediaries between legislators and public servants, the legislature's ability to affect the recommendations and decisions of public servants rests heavily on the interpretation and application of the constitutional convention of *ministerial responsibility*. Ministerial responsibility is in turn tightly bound with the conventions of *political neutrality* and *public service anonymity*. The definition and usage of these three constitutional conventions (often referred to as principles or doctrines) shape, to a large extent, the pattern of interaction between public servants on the one hand, and legislators and ministers on the other. For convenience, public service anonymity is included here under the broad heading of political neutrality.

🏛 MINISTERIAL RESPONSIBILITY AND POLITICAL NEUTRALITY

The meaning and relevance of ministerial responsibility have been subjects of continuing controversy in Canada. Some politicians, journalists, and scholars contend that the convention is a myth or that it is dead. But other commentators, who acknowledge the deficiencies of the traditional interpretation of ministerial responsibility, continue to treat it as a central feature of constitutional theory and practice. The Lambert Commission described the doctrine of ministerial responsibility as "a cornerstone" of the Canadian Constitution in that "it identifies who has the final responsibility for decisions taken—the minister, and provides a forum in which he is publicly accountable—Parliament"[2] (or, in the provinces, the legislature).

It is important to clarify the meaning of ministerial responsibility, and its relation to the political neutrality of public servants, as a foundation for informed discussion of its effects on the exercise of legislative and bureaucratic power. The following analysis focuses on the federal Parliament, but the experience in the provincial legislatures is very similar.

As explained in Chapter 15, collective and individual ministerial responsibility are separate but interrelated conventions. *Collective responsibility*, in its application to the government as a whole, prescribes that the prime minister and the cabinet must resign or ask the governor general for a dissolution of Parliament if the House of Commons passes a vote of no confidence in the government. In its application to individual ministers, collective responsibility prescribes that a minister must support government decisions in public, or at least suppress any public criticism of them. If ministers find a particular decision unacceptable, they must either stifle their objections or submit their resignation.

This chapter centres on *individual* rather than collective responsibility. In the academic literature, several meanings and implications are given to *individual ministerial responsibility*, but there is widespread agreement that it has two major components.[3] The first is that the minister is accountable to Parliament for all the administrative errors of his or her departmental subordinates, in the sense that he or she must resign in the event of a serious error by these subordinates. This component of ministerial responsibility is often described as a myth. The second component of the convention is that the minister is answerable to Parliament in that he or she must explain and defend the actions of his or her department before Parliament. The importance of this component is ignored or minimized by some commentators on ministerial responsibility in Canada.

The convention of *political neutrality,* like that of ministerial responsibility, merits analysis in terms of the extent to which it reflects contemporary political and administrative practice.[4] Interpreted broadly and including the convention of public service anonymity, political neutrality entails the separation of administration from politics and policy; the selection and promotion of public servants on the basis of merit rather than partisanship; the avoidance by public servants of partisan political activity and the public expression of personal views on government actions; the provision by public servants of confidential advice to their ministers; ministerial protection of public service anonymity; and the loyal implementation of government decisions by public servants, regardless of their personal views.

The Resignation of Ministers

The first component of ministerial responsibility requires that a minister must resign if a serious administrative error committed by her or his department is exposed. Despite frequent calls by opposition parties for ministerial resignations on the grounds of actual or alleged departmental mismanagement, in practice ministers do not resign as penance for administrative bungling in their department. It is now almost universally accepted that it is unreasonable to hold ministers personally responsible, in the form of resignation, for the administrative failings of their subordinates. Ministers cannot hope to have personal knowledge of more than a small percentage of the administrative actions taken by their officials. Moreover, they must restrict their attention to those administrative matters that are especially important or politically sensitive. Former prime minister Trudeau stated that a minister "can't possibly know everything which is done in the Department by every last Civil Servant and therefore it would be folly to try and pretend that the Minister will be held accountable and must resign when somewhere down the line at the end of a corridor the ten thousandth person committed something illegal or contrary to Government standards or norms."[5]

These factors of size and complexity, together with the burden of the ministers' political obligations, compel them to rely on their senior officials for advice on the administrative, technical, and political implications of policy proposals and decisions. The power of public servants to make discretionary decisions in the implementation of policies further enhances their policy role, in that the implementation process has a substantial impact on the success of policy decisions and on the content of future policies. Thus, public servants are actively involved in politics in the sense of determining or influencing the allocation of public resources among competing forces. It is clear that the first element of the doctrine of political neutrality outlined earlier, namely that administration is separated from politics and policy, is a fiction. In a formal sense, ministers do make decisions and public servants execute those decisions, but public servants exercise enormous influence on both policy development and implementation. It is, therefore, unrealistic to expect ministers to accept personal responsibility for all the acts of their departmental officials. Why should ministers "carry the can" when they have little or no knowledge of its contents?

Thus, the vicarious responsibility of ministers for departmental actions is limited and tied to the particular circumstances of the case at hand. This view was supported by a committee of senior public servants who asserted that

> a Minister is subject to various degrees of responsibility. He must certainly accept full responsibility for matters done properly under his instructions or in accordance with his policy. However, in the case of a problem not affecting an important question of policy, he is generally thought to have met his responsibility if he takes the matter in hand. Where the matter is essentially between a complainant and a particular official, the Minister can hardly be expected to have had prior knowledge of the case or to have had an opportunity to influence it personally. He cannot be acquainted with, or personally criticized for, every detail of administration in his department.[6]

This statement implicitly raises the often ignored issue of distinguishing the minister's personal mistakes from those of his or her officials. It is usually a formidable task for Parliament and the public to discover whether specific administrative acts were "done properly under his [the minister's] instructions or in accordance with his policy." Ministers are understandably reluctant even to admit that an administrative error has been made by their department. And when confronted with proof of error, they will usually deny personal knowledge of, or involvement in, the events in question. On this basis, they then contend that they should not have to accept full responsibility in the form of resignation or, indeed, assume any personal blame. If departmental failures are admitted or apparent, ministers are inclined to blame their officials rather than to accept personal or vicarious responsibility. The usual practice is that ministers inform Parliament that the fault lies with departmental officials and promise that the offenders will be disciplined and their mistakes corrected.

Cases do arise where the personal culpability of a minister is evident or where the magnitude of the error causes the government considerable embarrassment. Even if the minister "accepts full responsibility" in such situations, the practical effects on his or her career depend largely on personal, partisan, and situational factors. If the minister under attack is an unpopular member of cabinet, if the electorate is unusually outraged, or if the government is in a minority position in Parliament, the prime minister might be tempted to seek or accept the minister's resignation. The longstanding practice in Canada, however, is to enfold the offending minister in the cabinet's protective cloak, so that a matter of individual ministerial responsibility becomes one of collective responsibility. Nevertheless, a minister's reputation suffers from the unfavourable publicity that accompanies demands for his or her resignation so that after the next cabinet shuffle or the next election, he or she may be heading a less prestigious department or sitting on a government backbench.

Two other aspects of ministerial resignation deserve brief mention. First, a number of recent cases in Canada show that ministers will almost invariably be compelled to resign if personal misconduct in the form of unethical, immoral, or illegal activities is revealed. For example, a federal minister resigned when it was revealed that he had forged the signature of his friend's husband so that she could obtain an abortion, and a provincial minister resigned when he was charged with having arranged the murder of his wife. Second, incumbent ministers cannot be held responsible, especially by way of resignation, for administrative sins allegedly committed within their departments during their predecessors' tenure.

It is clear that, in practice, ministers do not resign to atone for either serious mismanagement by their officials or personal administrative mistakes. Indeed, if ministerial protestations of innocence are accepted at face value, ministers rarely make mistakes. Thus, the demand for ministerial resignations on the grounds of maladministration may appear to be a feeble weapon in the parliamentary arsenal of opposition parties. Yet this component of ministerial responsibility has important consequences for both ministers and public servants. Parliamentary and public calls for one's resignation, like the probability of being hanged the next morning, effectively concentrate one's attention. A minister's efforts to refute or defuse the allegations are vigorously supported by his or her senior officials, whose duty it is to keep their minister out of trouble. The reputation and career prospects of public servants tend to prosper or suffer along with those of their minister.

In the event of maladministration by departmental officials, the conventions of both ministerial responsibility and political neutrality require that ministers protect the anonymity of the wrongdoers by declining to identify them publicly. Since public servants are expected to serve their minister loyally by supporting departmental policy in public even if they oppose it vigorously within the confines of the department, ministers are expected to shield them from public criticism. However, there have been some notable departures from conventional practice by ministers who have named, and blamed, officials in public. For example, in 1978, Jean-Pierre Goyer, then federal Minister of Supply and Services, was sued for libel by a public servant whom he had criticized both inside and outside the House of Commons. Mr. Justice Lieff of the Ontario High Court, who awarded damages to the official for Goyer's statement outside the House, observed:

> It is a long standing convention of parliamentary democracy and the doctrine of ministerial responsibility which it encompasses that civil servants are to remain faceless to the public. Civil servants are responsible to their ministers. Ministers, as elected officials, are responsible to the public ... Furthermore, ... no matter how advanced the state of erosion of public service anonymity ... a minister should not

be able to blame or castigate personally a civil servant of a department under his control in public and then fall back on the legal defence of qualified privilege. If that were the case and the civil servant were defamed he would be in the peculiar position of being prevented from obtaining vindication for spurious allegations by the minister.[7]

Another celebrated case involving ministerial responsibility was described at the beginning of this chapter. The 1991 "Al-Mashat affair"[8] arose when the former ambassador of Iraq to the United States who was a prominent spokesperson for Iraq during the Gulf War was admitted to Canada as a landed immigrant. Public outrage led federal ministers, supported by certain public service advisors, to blame publicly a senior public servant and a minister's chief of staff. The affair raised serious questions about the government's commitment to the constitutional conventions of ministerial responsibility, political neutrality, and public service anonymity.

Although the instances in which ministers have publicly criticized their officials are exceptional, officials cannot invariably rely on their ministers to protect their anonymity. Moreover, in return for ministerial protection, public servants must not abandon the shelter of ministerial responsibility by engaging in unapproved forms of partisan political activity or in public criticism of government policies. Also, public servants must moderate their public praise of government actions and avoid public identification with specific policies, decisions, or views so that they may retain their office in the event of a change in the governing party. Ministers have a corresponding responsibility not to praise public servants in a manner that identifies them publicly with specific policy initiatives. Yet, at a press conference on December 22, 1969, then prime minister Trudeau announced the move of a deputy minister from one department to another and observed that when the official was deputy minister of Indian Affairs and Northern Development, "he did a first-class job in developing the north ... one of his brain children, I suppose, was the Pan-Arctic which he developed with Mr. Laing, who was minister there and the whole Indian policy, I think, was largely the result of [the deputy] and his team."[9]

All these considerations point to the strong links between political neutrality and ministerial responsibility. It is notable, however, that some advocates of legislative reform believe that a weakening of these conventions is justifiable to achieve the greater good of increased administrative accountability. For example, the 1985 Special Committee on Reform of the House of Commons concluded that "the doctrine of ministerial accountability undermines the potential for genuine accountability on the part of the person that ought to be accountable—the senior officer of the department [the deputy minister]."[10]

The Answerability of Ministers

The second component of ministerial responsibility corresponds closely to its current practice. Ministers do explain and defend their department's policies and administration before Parliament, especially during Question Period. Opposition members and, on occasion, government backbenchers utilize a variety of other opportunities (e.g., motions, Opposition days) to seek information and explanations from ministers. But an inordinate amount of parliamentary, media, and public attention centres on the daily oral Question Period. It is notable that ministers almost always respond to questions in their sphere of responsibility, although they can neither be obliged to answer nor to give reasons for refusing to answer.[11] A strong impetus to answer to Parliament is that a minister may suffer adverse political consequences for declining to do so. The speaker of the House of Commons has observed that he "is not in a position to compel an answer—it is public opinion which compels an answer."[12] Certainly, a minister who refuses to answer questions on an important issue, especially if he or she does not provide a reasonable explanation for his or her position, receives severe criticism from opposition members and the media. There is, therefore, both constitutional and political pressure on ministers to justify their department's actions to Parliament.

The willingness of ministers to answer questions in the legislature does not ensure that all their replies are informative, plausible, or even comprehensible. Experienced ministers tend to be artful dodgers who often bob and weave to avoid direct hits from opposition inquiries and allegations. Brian Chapman admits that ministerial responsibility "may be a useful tag for harrying ministers in Parliament," but he notes that "even then it smacks rather of a verbal game of cowboys and Indians."[13] Nevertheless, on the premise that ministerial evasion and circumlocution on a serious matter may be motivated by a desire to conceal politically embarrassing information, both opposition members and journalists may be prompted to investigate the matter more vigorously.

The fact that a single, identifiable minister is answerable for the activities of a specific department assists backbench members of the legislature in their handling of constituents' inquiries or complaints about government administration. A question in the legislature is sometimes the last recourse of a member who has been unable to obtain a satisfactory answer through private correspondence with a minister.

Although, as noted earlier, ministers are not expected to resign for departmental errors made during their predecessors' term of office, they must answer to Parliament for those errors. This rule ensures a focus of continuing responsibility for government administration, despite changes in the political heads of departments or in the governing party itself. Parliament's capacity to control and influence public servants is enhanced because one minister is required to answer for administrative actions, no matter when these actions took place. Incumbent ministers will usually be obliged to rely heavily on their departmental officials for knowledge of what occurred during the tenure of their predecessors. In such situations, the ability of ministers to answer to Parliament for their department rests largely on the continuity of administration provided by their permanent public servants. Thus, the operation of ministerial responsibility is closely tied to the permanency in office of public servants. Permanency, in turn, depends on the preservation of several of the other elements of political neutrality described earlier.

An important corollary of the answerability of ministers for their departments' administration is that public servants do not answer directly to Parliament for their decisions and recommendations. In the words of S.E. Finer, "the minister alone speaks for his Civil Servants to the House and to his Civil Servants for the House."[14] The application of this principle protects the anonymity of public servants, since it provides that the minister, and only the minister, is answerable to Parliament. The occasional willingness of a few ministers to name and blame their officials has had no significant effect on the status of official anonymity. The impact of allegations made against public servants by members of Parliament has, in general, also been minimal.

Nevertheless, a combination of factors related to the growth of bureaucratic power is bringing about a gradual decline in public service anonymity. These factors are:

- the heightened visibility arising from officials increasingly being required to explain government policies in public forums;

- the expanded media coverage of the activities and identities of specific officials;

- the more frequent appearances of public servants before legislative committees; and

- the increased number of direct contacts between public servants and members of the public.

The traditional interpretation of ministerial responsibility not only precludes public servants from answering directly to Parliament, it also prevents them from responding publicly to parliamentary criticism of their administrative actions. The minister replies to public accusations against his or her officials. However, in the face of allegations of serious administrative error, public servants, with the permission of their minister, have appeared before parliamentary committees to explain and defend their actions. The practice of official reticence and ministerial defence that normally prevails extends to attacks on public servants by persons outside Parliament, notably journalists. As a result, responsibility for departmental administration is focused on the minister, and public servants try to preserve official anonymity by avoiding involvement in public or political controversy.

> [T]he principles of anonymity and ministerial responsibility do not mean an absence of sanctions for public service errors or misconduct. Sanctions can be and regularly are brought to bear, just as they are in the private sector. In both the public and private sectors, however, such actions are normally taken in private. In most cases, no purpose is served, and much damage can be done, by public hangings.
>
> *Source: Federal Deputy Ministers' Task Force, Discussion Paper on Public Service Values and Ethics[15]*

The preceding analysis indicates that the resignation component of the convention of ministerial responsibility may be restated as follows: a minister is not accountable to Parliament for all the administrative errors of his or her department in the sense that he or she must resign in the event of a serious error by the department. The second component of the convention, namely that the minister is answerable to Parliament in that he or she must explain and defend the actions of the department before Parliament, is unchanged.

Reports of the death of individual ministerial responsibility are greatly exaggerated. If the life of the convention depended on ministerial resignations for the misdeeds of departmental subordinates, it would be mortally wounded. But because of the vitality of its answerability component, ministerial responsibility remains a central, operative convention of the Canadian constitution. Indeed, parliamentary debate on ministerial responsibility has centred on its interpretation and application, not on its existence. The concept of ministerial responsibility helps to define and determine how power is, and should be, exercised in the Canadian political system, and who is, or should be, held responsible for the exercise of that power. It provides a major frame of reference for the allocation of power and responsibility among ministers, legislators, and public servants. That the practice of ministerial responsibility does not correspond in full to its theory does not justify denial of the existence or importance of the convention, especially in the absence of a viable alternative. V. Seymour Wilson, in his insightful analysis of ministerial responsibility and bureaucratic accountability, concludes that "Canadian discourse on administrative power continues to be dominated by the doctrine of ministerial responsibility,"[16] and that "ministerial responsibility and all its trappings will continue to be around for a long time."[17]

🏛 LEGISLATIVE CONTROL AND INFLUENCE

An essential condition for a complete and comprehensible system of responsibility in government is that elected and appointed officials bear responsibility for all government actions. In a parliamentary democracy, if officials waste public funds, break the law, or violate citizens' rights, the public expects that someone will be held accountable for these misdeeds. If ministers do not accept responsibility for departmental transgressions, the focus of blame shifts to public servants. But the conventions of ministerial responsibility and political neutrality still protect the anonymity of public servants and restrict their answerability to Parliament. As a result, some commentators claim that these conventions permit public servants to exercise power without publicity or responsibility.[18] On those exceptional occasions when blame is publicly attributed to specific officials, disciplinary action is handled as an internal administrative matter with the result that the public rarely learns what penalties, if any, are imposed. Consequently, it appears to the public that on some occasions neither ministers nor public servants are held accountable for maladministration.

Can the federal and provincial legislatures help to ensure responsibility in government by controlling or influencing bureaucratic action?[19] There are three major means by which this can be done:

1. debates, questions, and other procedures in the legislature;

2. reliance on certain "watchdog" agencies that report directly or indirectly to the legislature; and

3. the use of legislative committees.

The first means, which involves influencing the public service indirectly by influencing ministers, has been discussed at length above.

Watchdog Agencies

The second means of ensuring responsibility in government involves the use of such agencies as ombudsmen and auditors to assist legislators to affect bureaucratic behaviour. The office of the ombudsman, an extremely important watchdog agency in the provincial sphere, does not exist in the federal government. There are, however, a number of important federal agencies that are often described as "specialized ombudsmen" or "mini-ombudsmen." These are the offices of the Correctional Investigator, the Official Languages Commissioner, the Canadian Human Rights Commissioner, the Privacy Commissioner, and the Information Commissioner. The most prominent watchdog agencies in the federal sphere are the Public Service Commission and the Office of the Auditor General.

The Ombudsman

Among the most popular of the various institutional and procedural safeguards designed to check bureaucratic power is the *ombudsman*. The office of the ombudsman originated in Sweden in 1809 and was adopted by Finland in 1919. No other countries appointed an ombudsman until after World War II. Then, a large number of countries around the world adopted the institution to help deal with the problem of ensuring that citizens' rights were protected in the face of rapidly growing bureaucracies in virtually every governmental jurisdiction.[20] An ombudsman has now been appointed in every Canadian province except Prince Edward Island, which has less need for the institution because of its small size. The first office of the ombudsman in Canada—indeed, the first in North America—was established in Alberta in September 1967. The office of the ombudsman has also been widely adapted for use in nongovernmental organizations, notably in universities.

The major function of an ombudsman is to investigate citizens' complaints about improper, unfair, or discriminatory administrative treatment. An ombudsman is usually authorized by statute to obtain access to the government documents and to call the witnesses necessary to investigate these complaints. If he or she believes that certain complaints are justified, the public servants involved will be requested to remedy the mistakes. The ombudsman is responsible to the legislature and presents an annual report to that body, which describes the cases that have been dealt with by his or her office and the progress that has been made in redressing any administrative injustices. It is important to emphasize that

> ombudsmen possess influence rather than control. They cannot alter administrative decisions. But they are well placed to cause those who have this power to review and change decisions which, after careful examination, appear to be unreasonable, oppressive or simply wrong in the circumstances. This influence, like that of auditors general, derives from their authority to investigate matters in depth and, as a last resort, to report their findings publicly to the legislature.[21]

There are, of course, other means of recourse available to citizens who believe they have suffered injustice at the hands of the bureaucracy. These include direct appeals to the public servant responsible for the action at issue and/or to the public servant's superiors, to members of Parliament, to administrative tribunals such as the Tax Review Board, and to the courts. However, the hearing of appeals by officials in the same department or agency responsible for the original decision may not result in the fact or the appearance of impartiality; members of Parliament have neither the time nor the resources equivalent to those of an ombudsman; the jurisdiction of appeal tribunals is limited; and court action can be both costly and time-consuming. Citizens are usually required to exhaust all the legal remedies available to them before complaining to the ombudsman. Thus, ombudsmen deal with complaints about unfair, rather than illegal, administrative action. The simple and inexpensive process of bringing grievances to an ombudsman has great appeal for the average citizen.

A study by a group of federal senior public servants noted that a federal ombudsman "would increase the awareness of ministers and officials of the need to deal promptly and equitably with individuals who perceive that they are victims of an administrative injustice," and concluded that an ombudsman "would be a desirable adjunct to the existing system of complaint handling in the departments and agencies of the federal government."[22] Despite considerable discussion over the years of the desirability of creating a federal ombudsman,[23] including the introduction of a bill for that purpose,[24] there is little current interest in the proposal.

Mini-Ombudsmen

Part of the explanation for the absence of a federal ombudsman is that, as mentioned before, the federal government has several "specialized ombudsmen" who serve a purpose similar to, but considerably narrower than, that of a general purpose ombudsman. These include:

1. the Office of the Correctional Investigator, established in 1973 to investigate complaints made against prison authorities by, or on behalf of, inmates;

2. the Office of the Official Languages Commissioner, created in 1970 to administer the Official Languages Act by protecting the language rights of individuals, monitoring all federal agencies to ensure proper applica-

tion of the act, and making recommendations for improved adherence to the spirit and the letter of the act;

3. the Canadian Human Rights Commission, which was established to implement the Canadian Human Rights Act (1976–77) and is responsible for investigating complaints of discrimination, trying to resolve or settle these complaints, and using research and public education to reduce discriminatory attitudes and behaviour;

4. the Office of the Information Commissioner, set up in 1983 to administer the Access to Information Act by investigating complaints against denial of access to government information; and

5. the Office of the Privacy Commissioner, established in 1983 to implement the Privacy Act and, specifically, to inquire into complaints from persons who believe that their privacy rights have been abridged.[25]

The Office of the Correctional Investigator reports to Parliament through the solicitor general, whereas the Human Rights, Information, and Privacy commissioners report to Parliament through the Department of Justice. The Office of the Official Languages Commissioner is more independent of the executive in that its reports go directly to Parliament, where its work is scrutinized by a joint committee of the House and the Senate.

The Public Service Commission

The federal Public Service Commission is an independent agency that serves Parliament as the guardian of the merit principle in human resource management.[26] The promotion of merit through the elimination of patronage has traditionally been a dominant concern of the commission. In this regard, J.E. Hodgetts has observed that the commission, "from its neutral vantage point, represents the institutionalized conscience of legislators, warding off the demon patronage rather like Alcoholics Anonymous wards off the demon rum on behalf of its membership."[27] The commission's annual report is tabled in Parliament by the Minister of Canadian Heritage.

The Auditor General

Aside from the Official Languages Commissioner, the only federal watchdog agency that reports to Parliament directly rather than through a minister is the Office of the Auditor General, which is discussed at length in Chapter 27.

The auditor general reports annually to Parliament on whether departments have kept proper financial records and whether public funds have been spent as appropriated by Parliament. Moreover, the auditor general is authorized to report cases where "money has been expended without due regard for economy and efficiency; or … satisfactory procedures have not been established to measure and report the effectiveness of programs."[28] The auditor general enjoys considerable autonomy from executive control and can, therefore, significantly influence relations between Parliament and the executive. Ministers and public servants are fearful that the annual report of the auditor general will single out their department or programs for criticism. Traditionally, the annual reports have provided powerful ammunition for the guns of the parliamentary opposition by describing instances of inappropriate, questionable, and illegal government spending that are widely publicized in the media. Provincial auditors play a role similar to, but less publicized than, that of the auditor general.[29]

Parliamentary Committees

Functions and Types of Committees

Parliamentary committees are the third major means by which the legislature can exercise control or influence over the public service. The functions of parliamentary committees may be divided into policy development (primarily involving evaluation of the purpose and content of proposed legislation), review of existing policies, and scrutiny of departmental administration (especially through examination of the estimates). In practice, these functions often overlap and committee members place varying emphasis on each function.

The House of Commons has three types of committees: standing committees, special committees, and legislative committees. Most of the *standing committees* (e.g., Agriculture and Agri-Food, Canadian Heritage, Environment and Sustainable Development) focus on a substantive sphere of government policy. Each committee covers one or more departments and agencies. For example, the Committee on Agriculture and Agri-Food deals with the Department of Agriculture, the Canadian Dairy Commission, the Farm Credit Corporation, and the National Farm Products Council. The other standing committees are called specialist standing committees; they include such committees as the Public Accounts Committee. There are also a few joint standing committees of the Senate and the House of Commons (e.g., the Joint Committee on the Scrutiny of Regulations). In all there are about twenty-two standing committees. They may, within their spheres of responsibility, undertake studies on their own initiative.

In addition to the standing committees, *special committees* are set up as required to examine such specific issues as acid rain and child care; once the committee presents its final report, it ceases to exist. *Legislative committees* are established to examine specific government bills after they have passed second reading in the House of Commons. One advantage of legislative committees has been that the expertise, experience, and interests of the legislators can be matched to the subject matter of the legislation.

The Public Accounts Committee and the Standing Joint Committee (i.e., of the Senate and the House of Commons) on the Scrutiny of Regulations deserve special attention. They enjoy a greater measure of independence from cabinet control because, unlike other committees, they are chaired by a member of the Opposition. In a majority government situation, however, most of the committees' members are from the government party.

The Public Accounts Committee examines both the *public accounts* (i.e., the government's year-end financial statements) and the auditor general's report as a basis for making recommendations to the House of Commons. With the assistance of the auditor general, the committee has uncovered, investigated, and reported on several scandals involving the expenditure of public funds and has recommended corrective action in many other instances where public money has been improperly spent.

The primary function of the Standing Joint Committee on the Scrutiny of Regulations is to scrutinize the use of delegated legislative authority by cabinet, ministers, and public servants.[30] The committee reviews *statutory instruments,* i.e., the rules, regulations, orders, etc. made by the executive under delegated legislative authority. As noted in Chapter 13, the contemporary power of the public service rests, in part, on authority delegated to the executive by Parliament, whose members do not have the time or the expertise to provide for every contingency in legislation. The committee examines statutory instruments in the light of fifteen criteria, including, for example, whether a regulation trespasses unduly on the rights and liberties of the subject or appears for any reason to infringe the rule of law or the rules of natural justice. The committee's frequent warnings that the executive often does not exercise delegated authority in keeping with the intent of Parliament have received surprisingly little media attention.

The Accountability of Public Servants

Among the most common proposals for parliamentary reform are measures that would enhance the effectiveness of committees in evaluating the policies and scrutinizing the administrative actions of the executive. Public servants already answer to parliamentary committees by explaining the administrative and technical implications of existing and proposed policies. An increase in the investigative work, specialization, and expertise of committee members would enable them to engage in better informed and more penetrating questioning of officials. This would encourage public servants to perform their administrative tasks more economically, efficiently, and effectively, especially if committee members focused their attention on the scrutiny of departmental administration. If members devoted a substantial portion of their efforts to policy development and review, officials would continue to refer to their minister those inquiries involving policy matters. But the enhanced competence of committee members, combined with the difficulty of separating policy and administrative considerations, would cause public servants to reveal more frequently and clearly their influence on policy formation. The effect on ministerial responsibility would be negligible because ministers would continue to deal with questions on the substance and direction of government policy.

The reinforcement and extension of the activities and expertise of parliamentary committees would improve Parliament's capacity to hold public servants accountable for the *administration*, but not for the *content*, of government policies. Thus, these reforms would not satisfy those who contend that the responsibility of public servants should be commensurate with their power in the political process. Some observers claim that, in order for Parliament to play a significantly greater role in promoting administrative responsibility, there must be some shift in answerability for *policy* from ministers to public servants. The implementation of this proposal would have important implications for Canada's parliamentary institutions and practices in both the federal and provincial spheres.

Relations between ministers and public servants would be complicated by the difficulty of distinguishing their respective contributions to the development of specific policies. The answerability of public servants to Parliament would compete with their accountability and loyalty to their minister. The remaining healthy component of ministerial responsibility—the answerability of ministers—would be severely weakened. Even the convenient fiction of a separation between policy and administration would be extremely difficult to maintain. There would be a dramatic decline in public service anonymity, and the senior echelons of the service would be politicized. Public servants would be compelled to defend their policy recommendations before parliamentary committees and the public. Officials would become personally associated with particular policies and would, therefore, become involved in political controversy. Security of tenure for senior officials would be replaced by a system of political appointments and a consequent turnover of public servants with a change of government.

This hypothetical pattern of relations between politicians and public servants indicates that public servants cannot be held answerable to Parliament for *policy* matters without major modifications in the present practice of ministerial responsibility and political neutrality. It also demonstrates the small extent to which the conventions have evolved from their traditional interpretation toward this pattern of behaviour. The formal position of the federal government is that

> matters of policy and political controversy have been reserved more or less exclusively for Ministers, principally because political answerability on the part of officials would inevitably draw them into controversy, destroy their permanent utility to the system and, indeed, undermine the authority and responsibility of their Ministers.[31]

Current trends suggest that the conventions will continue to evolve, or will be altered, in the direction of greater administrative answerability to Parliament but that ministers will retain formal responsibility for the defence of government policy. Thus, Parliament has the potential to increase its power over the public service, especially in the sphere of overseeing administration, without breaching those constitutional conventions most directly affecting the conduct of the public service.

The power of Parliament over the public service rests largely on its ability and inclination to control and influence the executive as a whole. But Parliament's success in checking the executive hinges on such factors as the devotion of committee members to their work, the creation of a nonpartisan atmosphere in committee deliberations, the government's willingness to take committee reports seriously, and improved access to much government information now treated as confidential. Reforms in the structures and processes of Parliament would help to augment Parliament's power over both ministers and public servants. In particular, several measures could be adopted to increase the answerability of public servants for departmental administration. The Royal Commission on Financial Management and Accountability (the Lambert Commission)[32] made several useful recommendations for reforms to enhance the accountability of both ministers and senior public servants to Parliament.[33]

These recommendations involved a much more active role for parliamentary committees. The commissioners suggested that the deputy minister be designated the chief administrative officer of the department and be held directly accountable to Parliament through the Public Accounts Committee for specified administrative duties.[34] Ministers would remain accountable for policy objectives and decisions. Several years later, the Special Parliamentary Committee on Reform of the House of Commons (the McGrath Committee) discussed the possibility of an even broader measure of deputy ministerial responsibility:

> We have heard many arguments that a new doctrine of deputy ministerial responsibility relating exclusively to matters of administration should be established … Such a doctrine would set out the obligations of senior public servants and include the obligation to testify before parliamentary committees on matters of administration. Under this system, the testimony of deputy ministers before committees would be an everyday occurrence. Furthermore, regular open contact between the senior public service and Members of Parliament should lead to a more realistic understanding of administrative practices and more precise pinpointing of accountability.[35]

The Lambert commissioners also proposed that the number and size of standing committees in the House of Commons be reduced, and that these committees be allowed to recommend the partial reduction of proposed government expenditures and to submit substantive reports on the Estimates (i.e., the government's annual request for money) to the House. In addition, each committee would have a chairperson elected for the life of a Parliament and a budget to hire staff.

The Lambert commissioners did not believe that their proposed reforms would erode the doctrine of ministerial responsibility. Indeed, they argued that "the concept of direct accountability of officials before Parliament through one of its committees would reinforce the minister's and the Cabinet's ability to be responsible for the conduct of the affairs of government."[36] The commissioners did acknowledge, however, that the success of efforts to increase government's accountability to Parliament on administrative matters depends largely on the determination of ministers and parliamentarians to achieve this end. J.R. Mallory notes that, in trying to improve the operations of the House of Commons, we must remember that "it is a political body made up of political parties whose *raison d'être* is to win the electoral battle and become the government. No activity, no matter how worthy, which does not accord with this primary objective is likely to be embraced by the House."[37]

The report of the McGrath Committee contained many of the same proposed reforms as the Lambert Report. The Mulroney government implemented some of the committee's recommendations, including those that reduced the size of parliamentary committees, ensured continuity in committee membership so as to encourage the development of special expertise among members, and provided committees with their own budgets for research staff and legal counsel. The committee also proposed that

> each standing committee have before it the full departmental policy array to review and to report on, including, but not restricted to the following: the reasons for a department's statutes; the statutes themselves; a department's objectives in relation to its statutory mandate; the activities carried out in pursuit of these objectives; a department's immediate and long-term expenditure plans for these activities; and the achievements of the department measured against its objectives.[38]

This proposal, designed to enable members of Parliament to scrutinize government departments more effectively, was also accepted by the government.

As a result of these changes, there was a modest move in the direction of more effective parliamentary control and influence over the executive in general and the public service in particular. Franks contends that "committees are now stronger and more influential than they ever have been in the past," but he notes also that "they can fill only a secondary place in parliament and the concerns of MPs. The responsibility still remains with the government to devise policies and administer the executive branch."[39] This judgment is confirmed by Sutherland and Baltacioglu, who conclude that "the reforms to the standing committee system have not realized the aim of the McGrath Committee members to force a truly routine diminution of the government's monopoly over planning, spending and making policy."[40]

Since its election in 1993 the Chrétien government has continued the efforts of previous governments to enhance the capacity of parliamentary committees to hold accountable the political executive and the public service. In particular, efforts have been made to provide more timely and comprehensible information to Parliament, including reports on departmental plans and priorities and on departmental performance.[41] Yet, in late 1997, the auditor general lamented the slow progress in this area. After identifying parliamentary review of the government's annual Estimates as one of the best opportunities for committees to influence the management of government, he quoted a parliamentary committee as concluding that "[t]he inadequacy of committee study of the Estimates has become depressingly obvious."[42] He argued further that "one thing hampering parliamentarians from making better use of the Estimates process has been that government has not provided them with appropriate information.... [P]arliamentarians need information, tailored to their needs that clearly and concisely explains what departments plan to do, what it will cost, what results they hope to achieve, and what results they have achieved. The lack of information on results has been a chronic problem ...."[43] On occasion, however, legislative committees assert their influence. In May 1998, for example, the House of Commons Committee on the Environment released an extremely critical report of the government's failure to enforce environmental laws.[44]

In addition to the three major forms of political control over the public service described above, senior public servants, with the consent of the minister concerned, provide occasional briefings to parliamentary caucuses on such matters as departmental structures and functions, and the operation and content of new programs. "The briefings are to provide factual and background material necessary to allow informed discussion of the subject under discussion, consistent with preserving the necessary confidences of government and with maintaining the traditional impartiality of public servants."[45] Finally, there are various informal contacts between legislators and public servants at social events and through oral or written requests for information about such matters as programs, budgets, and constituents' complaints.

Many students of the federal Parliament and provincial legislatures are pessimistic that the changes in government machinery and attitudes needed for a significant increase in legislative power over the public service will be made. Senior public servants do not view Parliament and its committees as a major focus of their accountability, and, for the middle and lower ranks of the public service, "parliament is a distant and unimportant control."[46] Nevertheless, as noted, some important reforms have recently been made and there is continuing pressure for more reform. One expert on the workings of Parliament has recently argued that

> [s]ince public servants are the repository of knowledge about departmental programs and expenditures, parliamentary committees need their cooperation if they are to be effective. The more active participation of officials could be healthy if it makes the process less partisan and more businesslike.[47]

It was explained in Part III that the difficulty legislatures have in exercising control and influence over departments is compounded with respect to Crown corporations and regulatory agencies, which enjoy a greater measure of autonomy than departments from executive, as well as legislative, control. In any event, even a more powerful legislature would be an insufficient instrument to ensure responsible public bureaucracy. The role of the legislature must be supplemented by controls and influences exercised by other actors in the political system, including the judiciary, which is discussed in the next chapter.

NOTES

1. Royal Commission on Financial Management and Accountability, *Final Report* (Ottawa: Minister of Supply and Services, 1979), 52–53.
2. Ibid., 371.
3. See, for example, S.E. Finer, "The Individual Responsibility of Ministers," *Public Administration* 34 (winter 1956): 379; A.H. Birch, *Representative and Responsible Government* (London: George Allen and Unwin, 1964), 139–40; R.M. Punnett, *British Government and Politics* (New York: Norton, 1968), 182; Jeffrey Stanyer and Brian Smith, *Administering Britain* (Glasgow: Fontana/Collins, 1976), 180–81; Geoffrey Marshall and Graeme C. Moodie, *Some Problems of the Constitution,* 4th ed. (London: Hutchinson, 1967), 67–74.
4. For an analysis of the evolution and present status of the convention of political neutrality, see Chapter 13.

5. Office of the Prime Minister, Transcript of Press Conference, 18 November, 1977.
6. Government of Canada, *Report of the Committee on the Concept of the Ombudsman*, Ottawa, July 1977, 16. Reproduced with the permission of the House of Commons, 1998.
7. *Stopforth v. Goyer*, Ontario Reports 20 (2d) 1978: 273. This decision was overturned in the Ontario Court of Appeal on the grounds that the occasion of Goyer's comments outside Parliament "was one of qualified privilege." *Ontario Reports* 23 (2d) 1979: 700.
8. For a comprehensive analysis of this case, see S.L. Sutherland, "The Al-Mashat Affair: Administrative Responsibility in Parliamentary Institutions," *Canadian Public Administration* 34 (winter 1991): 551–72.
9. Office of the Prime Minister, Transcript of Press Conference, 22 December, 1969.
10. House of Commons, *Special Committee on Reform of the House of Commons*, 3rd Report, June 1985.
11. Arthur Beauchesne, *Rules and Forms of the House of Commons of Canada*, 4th ed. (Toronto: Carswell, 1958), sec. 181 (3), 153.
12. House of Commons, *Debates*, 6 February 1978, 567.
13. Brian Chapman, *British Government Observed* (London: George Allen and Unwin, 1963), 38.
14. Finer, "The Individual Responsibility of Ministers," 394.
15. Privy Council Office, Deputy Ministers' Task Force, *Discussion Paper on Values and Ethics in the Public Service* (Ottawa: Privy Council Office, 1996), 11.
16. *Canadian Public Policy and Administration* (Toronto: McGraw-Hill Ryerson, 1981), 197.
17. Ibid., 220.
18. See, for example, J.R. Mallory, "Responsive and Responsible Government," Presidential Address, section II, *Transactions of the Royal Society of Canada*, series IV, 12 (1974): 221.
19. For a general discussion of bureaucratic power and administrative responsibility respectively, see Chapters 13 and 14.
20. For an account of the evolution of the office of the ombudsman, both in Canada and other countries, see Donald C. Rowat, *The Ombudsman Plan: The Worldwide Spread of an Idea*, 2nd ed. (Lanham, Md.: University Press of America, 1986).
21. Committee on the Concept of the Ombudsman, "The Ombudsman," in Kenneth Kernaghan, ed., *Public Administration in Canada: Selected Readings*, 5th ed. (Toronto: Methuen, 1985), 374–75.
22. Ibid., 379.
23. See Henry J. Llambias, "Canada: Introduction," in Gerald E. Caiden, ed., *International Handbook of the Ombudsman: Country Surveys* (Westport, Conn.: Greenwood Press, 1983), 27–28, 34; Stephen Owen, "Why We Need a Federal Ombudsman," *Policy Options* 13 (July/August 1992): 3–6; and Rowat, *The Ombudsman Plan*, ch. 13.
24. In April 1978, the Liberal government introduced Bill C-43, entitled the Ombudsman Act. For a critical analysis of the bill, see K.A. Friedmann and A.G. Milne, "The Federal Ombudsman Legislation: A Critique of Bill C-43," *Canadian Public Policy* 6 (winter 1980): 63–67.
25. For additional information on the Offices of the Information Commissioner and the Privacy Commissioner, see Chapter 21.
26. For elaboration on the commission's functions and its relationship with the Treasury Board Secretariat, see Chapter 22.
27. J.E. Hodgetts, *The Canadian Public Service* (Toronto: University of Toronto Press, 1973), 264.
28. The Auditor General Act, Canada, *Statutes*, 1977, c. 34, s. 7 (2).
29. See Simon McInnes, "Improving Legislative Surveillance of Provincial Public Expenditures: The Performance of the Public Accounts Committees and Auditors General," *Canadian Public Administration* 20 (spring 1977): 36–86.

30. See Denys C. Holland and John P. McGowan, *Delegated Legislation in Canada* (Toronto: Carswell, 1989), ch. 5.
31. Government of Canada, Privy Council Office, *Notes on the Responsibilities of Public Servants In Relation to Parliamentary Committees,* December 1990, 3.
32. *Final Report,* chs. 21 and 22.
33. See also Special Committee on Reform of the House of Commons, *3rd Report,* June 1985; and the recommendations in Thomas D'Aquino, G. Bruce Doern, and Cassandra Blair, *Parliamentary Democracy in Canada: Issues for Reform* (Toronto: Methuen, 1983).
34. See the discussion of this proposal in Chapter 14.
35. Special Committee on Reform of the House of Commons, *3rd Report,* 21. Reproduced with the permission of the House of Commons, 1998.
36. Ibid., 375.
37. J.R. Mallory, "Parliament in the Eighties," in R. Carty and W. Ward, eds., *Entering the Eighties: Canada in Crisis* (Toronto: Oxford University Press, 1980), 132.
38. Special Committee on Reform of the House of Commons, *3rd Report,* 16–17.
39. C.E.S. Franks, *The Parliament of Canada* (Toronto: University of Toronto Press, 1987), 185.
40. S.L. Sutherland and C. Baltacioglu, *Parliamentary Reform and the Federal Public Service.* London, Ont.: National Centre for Management Research and Development, 1988), 47.
41. Treasury Board Secretariat, *Accounting For Results* (Ottawa: Treasury Board Secretariat, 1997), 10–11.
42. Auditor General of Canada, *Report: December 1997* (Ottawa: Minister of Supply and Services, 1997), 15.
43. Ibid., 15–16.
44. *The Globe and Mail,* 23 May 1998, A1.
45. Office of the Prime Minister, *Cabinet Procedures and Ministerial Guidelines,* 18 September 1984; Annex A: Briefings by Officials to Parliamentary Caucuses, dated June 1981.
46. Franks, *The Parliament of Canada,* 233.
47. Peter Dobell, "Give MPs the Tools to Cut Spending," *The Globe and Mail* (18 February 1994) A27.

BIBLIOGRAPHY

Canada. House of Commons. Special Committee on Reform of the House of Commons. *3rd Report.* Ottawa: June 1985.

Canada. Royal Commission on Financial Management and Accountability. *Final Report.* Ottawa: Supply and Services, 1979, chs. 21–22.

Committee on the Concept of the Ombudsman. "The Ombudsman." In Kenneth Kernaghan, ed., *Public Administration in Canada: Selected Readings,* 5th ed. Toronto: Methuen, 1985, 374–79.

Denton, T.M. "Ministerial Responsibility: A Contemporary Perspective." In R. Schultz et al., eds., *The Canadian Political Process.* Toronto: Holt, Rinehart and Winston, 1979, 344–62.

Doerr, Audrey. "Parliamentary Accountability and Legislative Potential." In Harold D. Clarke et al., eds., *Parliament, Policy and Representation.* Toronto: Methuen 1980, 144–59.

Franks, C.E.S. "Not Anonymous: Ministerial Responsibility and the British Accounting Officers." *Canadian Public Administration* 40 (winter 1997): 626–52.

Holland, Denys C., and John P. McGowan. *Delegated Legislation in Canada.* Toronto: Carswell, 1989.

Kersell, J.E. *Parliamentary Supervision of Delegated Legislation: The United Kingdom, Australia, New Zealand and Canada.* London: Stevens, 1960.

————. "Statutory and Judicial Control of Administrative Behavior." *Canadian Public Administration* 19 (summer 1976): 295–307.

Levy, Gary. "Delegated Legislation and the Standing Joint Committee on Regulations and Other Statutory Instruments," *Canadian Public Administration* 22 (fall 1979): 349–65.

Mallory, J.R. "Curtailing 'Divine Right': The Control of Delegated Legislation in Canada." In O.P. Dwivedi, ed., *The Administrative State in Canada.* Toronto: University of Toronto Press, 1982, 131–50.

Molloy, J. "Reconciling Expectations and Reality in House of Commons Committees: The Case of the 1989 GST Inquiry." *Canadian Public Administration* 39 (fall 1996): 314–35.

Rowat, Donald C. *The Ombudsman,* 2nd ed. Toronto: University of Toronto Press, 1968.

————. *The Ombudsman Plan.* Toronto: McClelland & Stewart, 1973.

Slatter, Frans F. *Parliament and Administrative Agencies.* Study paper for the Law Reform Commission of Canada. Ottawa: Supply and Services, 1982.

Sutherland, S.L. "Responsible Government and Ministerial Responsibility." *Canadian Journal of Political Science* 24 (March 1991): 91–120.

————. "The Al-Mashat Affair: Administrative Accountability in Parliamentary Institutions." *Canadian Public Administration* 34 (winter 1991): 573–603.

Vandervort, Lucinda. *Political Control of Independent Administrative Agencies.* Study paper for the Law Reform Commission of Canada. Ottawa: Supply and Services, 1979.

18

The Judiciary and the Bureaucracy

At the time of his death, Médard Dorion had been receiving a war veterans allowance. Margaret Johnson, who claimed to be his common-law widow, applied to the Department of Veterans Affairs for a veteran's widow allowance. A complicated series of events then ensued, including two *denials* of the application; an *approval* of the application; a claim for an allowance by Euphemia Dorion, who was Mr. Dorion's former legal wife; the *denial* of Mrs. Dorion's application, which she then appealed; the *cancellation* of Margaret Johnson's allowance by a letter also saying that she owed a reimbursement of over $14 000; the *approval* of Euphemia Dorion's application; an *appeal* by Margaret Johnson to the War Veterans Allowance Board, which *upheld the cancellation* decision; and the reconsideration of this cancellation by the War Veterans Appeal Board (formerly the Allowance Board), which also *upheld the cancellation*. The official decision makers included a district authority, a departmental review committee, and the two boards. Margaret Johnson appealed the board's decision to the Federal Court of Appeal.

The point of this short account of a long story is not to demonstrate how complex the legal dimension of public administration can be, but how *important* it can be for individual citizens and how administrative power can be abused. The Federal Court of Appeal ordered the department to reconsider the case *de novo* on the grounds that the department "blatantly denied a proper and fair hearing in accordance with the requirements of natural justice and procedural fairness." The court described the case as having the flavour of a textbook example of why the courts must protect citizens from administrative abuse and said that it defies belief that such a decision could be made "so quickly and so easily—without even giving the individual concerned prior notice of the case that appears to be existing against him or her and letting him or her have an opportunity to meet it."[1]

You are probably asking yourself why authorities within government departments are making decisions that sound like they should be made by the courts. You may also be wondering about such things as the meaning of terms like natural justice and procedural fairness; where the Federal Court of Appeal fits into the Canadian judicial system; under what circumstances the courts will review the decisions of public servants; why the court didn't simply reverse the War Veterans Appeal Board's decision; and whether the Canadian Charter of Rights and Freedoms might have been helpful in this case. These are some of the questions considered in this chapter.

🏛 THE CANADIAN JUDICIARY

Unlike the executive and legislative branches of government, which are integrally linked to one another, the judiciary is independent from the others. The independence of judges is considered crucial to the impartial administration of justice and is guaranteed by various measures, including tenure in office for judges during good behaviour.

The structure of the courts in Canada is shown in Figure 18.1. This structure is determined by the Constitution Act of 1867, which provides for separate federal and provincial courts but permits cases to be appealed from provincial to federal courts, including the Supreme Court of Canada, which stands at the apex of the judicial hierarchy. Section 101 of the act authorizes Parliament to establish a court of appeal for Canada and any other courts required for "the better administration" of federal laws. Section 92(14) grants to the provinces exclusive jurisdiction over the administration of justice in the provinces, "including the Constitution, Maintenance, and Organization of Provincial Courts, both of Civil and Criminal Jurisdiction, and including procedure in Civil Matters in those Courts." However, Section 91(27) confers on the federal Parliament exclusive jurisdiction over criminal procedure, and Sections 96, 99, and 100 give the federal government power over the appointment, salaries, and removal of all superior, county, and district judges in the provinces. Since the provinces are authorized to create and operate certain courts for which the federal government is authorized to appoint and pay the judges, federal and provincial governments are required to cooperate in the administration of justice.[2]

The structure and the names of courts in the provinces vary, but there are some broad similarities.[3] At the top of the court system in each province is a superior court that, depending on the province, bears the name of Supreme Court, Superior Court, or High Court. These superior courts have jurisdiction in both criminal and civil cases, and they hear appeals from decisions of the lower courts.

The level below is composed of county or district courts that traditionally have had original jurisdiction over a certain geographical area in criminal cases and in civil cases in which the amount of money at stake is less than a certain amount. However, most provinces have merged their county or district courts with their superior courts. Thus, an intermediate level of courts whose judges are federally appointed has been eliminated. Surrogate courts responsible for such matters as the settlement of estates are also at this level.

Below the county or district courts and the surrogate courts are the provincial courts, which deal with criminal acts, juvenile offences, family problems, and small claims. The judges of these courts are appointed and paid by the provincial government.

The two major federal courts are the Federal Court of Canada, which is the primary court with which we are concerned in this chapter, and the Supreme Court of Canada. The Supreme Court is the highest court in the land and is a general court of appeal for both civil and criminal cases. It hears appeals from the Federal Court of Canada and from the provincial appeal courts. It also deals with questions of law or fact referred to it by the federal cabinet (e.g., on

Figure 18.1
THE HIERARCHY OF CANADIAN COURTS

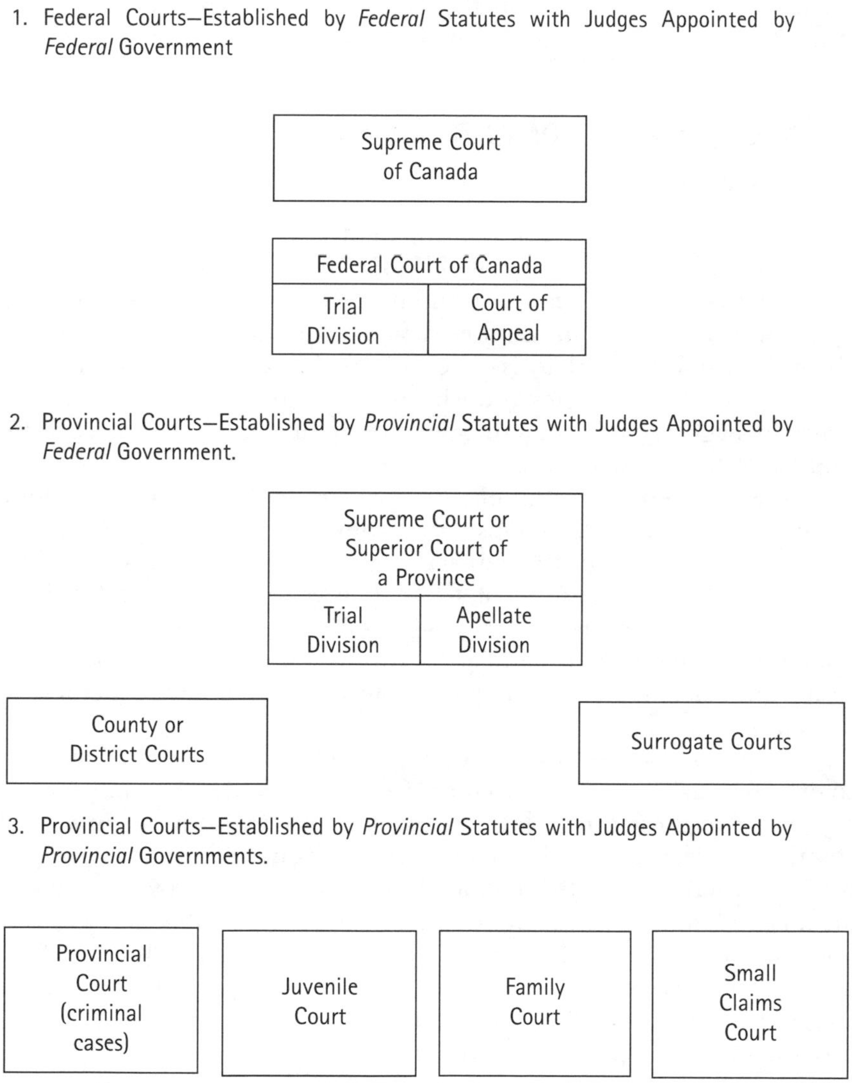

1. Federal Courts—Established by *Federal* Statutes with Judges Appointed by *Federal* Government

Supreme Court of Canada

Federal Court of Canada	
Trial Division	Court of Appeal

2. Provincial Courts—Established by *Provincial* Statutes with Judges Appointed by *Federal* Government.

Supreme Court or Superior Court of a Province	
Trial Division	Apellate Division

County or District Courts

Surrogate Courts

3. Provincial Courts—Established by *Provincial* Statutes with Judges Appointed by *Provincial* Governments.

Provincial Court (criminal cases)	Juvenile Court	Family Court	Small Claims Court

such matters as interpretation of constitutional acts and the validity of federal or provincial legislation).

The Federal Court of Canada is composed of the Trial Division and the Appeal Division (often referred to as the Federal Court of Appeal). Under the Federal Court Act,[4] as amended in 1990, the Trial Division has *original* jurisdiction to hear and grant relief in cases involving claims against the Crown, and *exclusive* jurisdiction to hear and grant relief in cases involving appeals against the decisions of *most* federal boards, commissions, and other tribunals. The Federal Court of Appeal hears appeals from the Trial Division and has *original* jurisdiction to review the decisions of certain federal tribunals.[5] The judicial review jurisdiction conferred on the Federal Court has been interpreted to embrace a broad range of decision makers in the federal government.

🏛 JUDICIAL REVIEW OF ADMINISTRATIVE ACTION

The Focus on Agencies

The public administration community, in its examination of the means by which responsible administrative behaviour may be pursued in Canada, has devoted relatively little attention to the utility of administrative law in general and judicial review of administrative action in particular. *Administrative law* is that branch of public law that "is concerned with the legal limits on the actions of government or its agencies and with the remedies that are available to persons who feel aggrieved by an improper, illegal, or unauthorized act by the government or one of its agencies."[6]

Despite the neglect of administrative law in the field of public administration, since the early 1970s a substantial volume of publications has resulted from increased interest in the subject by the legal community. This development was partly a recognition of the extensive regulatory and adjudicative powers now exercised by administrative officials, especially those in semi-independent agencies. But the major stimulus was the creation in 1970 of the Federal Court of Canada and the court's subsequent review of the decisions of public authorities.

Like Britain, Canada has a large number of conventional government departments organized in hierarchical form and headed by ministers. Unlike Britain, but like the United States, many government activities in Canada are conducted by agencies enjoying a measure of independence from government. John Willis noted that, in the field of administrative law, Canadians "have inherited from England the principle of ministerial responsibility and the common law of judicial review, but have borrowed the institution of the 'independent regulatory commission' and many of the matters regulated from the United States and have modified them to suit our own peculiar conditions."[7] In particular, regulatory agencies in Canada are not as independent of the political executive as the independent regulatory commissions in the United States.

Nevertheless, as explained in Chapter 10, Crown agencies in Canada are less accountable than conventional departments to cabinet, ministers, and Parliament. Thus, in the search for responsible administrative behaviour, judicial control is relatively more important with respect to agencies (boards, commissions, and tribunals) than to regular departments. Included among these agencies are those that perform centrally important and politically sensitive regulatory functions, such as the National Energy Board, and those that play a specialized adjudicative role bearing on individual rights, such as the Immigration Appeal Board.

Discretionary Powers

The importance of judicial review and of other means of control over administrative action arises in large part from the exercise of discretionary powers by public officials. Discretionary powers "are those which involve an element of judgment or choice by the person exercising them and comprise all government functions from fact finding to setting standards."[8] As noted in Chapters 13 and 17, public servants exercise a striking number and variety of discretionary powers under delegated legislative authority. Most of these discretionary powers are delegated to the governor in council (i.e., the cabinet), but they are also conferred on ministers and individual officials and on agencies, boards, commissions, and tribunals. (Throughout the rest of this chapter, the term "tribunal" will be used to encompass all of these individual officials or groups of officials.)

Some statutes delegate discretionary powers to more than one authority. For example, under the Canadian Environmental Protection Act, much is left to be prescribed by the cabinet; authority to determine standards and who should be required to conform to them is delegated to the minister; and inspectors are given powers of enforcement such as the authority to "do such reasonable things as may be necessary in the circumstances." Rules made under delegated legislative authority are described by a variety of names, including regulations, statutory instruments, and orders in council. These rules constitute "subordinate" or "delegated" legislation. Although the courts do review the exercise of legislative functions, notably to determine whether the exercise is *ultra vires* (beyond the powers of) the organization exercising them, the major concern of the courts, and thus of this chapter, is the review of judicial and quasi-judicial functions, which are described below.

Neither the cabinet nor individual ministers can be expected to exercise their delegated powers solely on their own. For example, a minister could not find time to decide upon every application for a licence. Thus, statutes often permit the cabinet and ministers, either expressly or by "necessary intendment," to subdelegate authority. There is a rule that ministers "are generally entitled to exercise their statutory powers through responsible persons in their departments and that in such circumstances ministerial decisions cannot be questioned on the basis that they were not made by the Minister personally."[9] Further, "this rule is founded on the doctrine of ministerial responsibility. The Minister is accountable to the Legislature but not to the courts for actions of his subordinates."[10] The subdelegation of discretionary powers has led to a condition of "dispersed discretions" and a consequent decline in the accountability of public authorities to the legislature and, through the legislature, to the public. It is notable also that public servants, on the basis of their experience and expertise, influence ministers by advising them about the appropriate exercise of powers within ministerial discretion.

Appeal and Review

Judicial control over the decisions of tribunals may be founded on:

1. statutory provisions for appeal;

2. statutory provisions for review (known as statutory or direct remedies); or

3. the courts' inherent supervisory jurisdiction over inferior tribunals.

No right of *appeal* against a tribunal's decision exists unless that right is expressly conferred by statute. Statutory provision may be made for appeals to the courts, to the cabinet, to ministers, to deputy ministers, or to an administrative body either within a government department (e.g., the Income Tax Appeals Division within the Appeals Branch of Revenue Canada), or outside a government department (e.g., the Immigration Appeal Board). The legislature often provides for statutory *review* as well as statutory appeal, but when neither is provided the courts may exercise their *inherent supervisory authority to review* the decisions of inferior tribunals.

Classification of Function

A central issue with respect to judicial review of administrative discretion has traditionally been the *classification* of the function (i.e., administrative, judicial, or quasi-judicial) being performed by the tribunal. The nature of the function being exercised is important in deciding whether, and on what grounds, the courts will grant relief. "The main distinction between judicial and quasi-judicial functions is based on the complete absence of discretion in the former as contrasted with the existence of some discretion in the latter."[11] Despite this distinction, the courts normally use the terms judicial and quasi-judicial interchangeably.

Another important distinction is that between an administrative function and a quasi-judicial function. In classifying functions, the courts consider whether the exercise of the power will affect existing rights; "if it has an effect, the classification will be quasi-judicial; if none it will be administrative. If the decision is based on policy, not law, or made in pursuance of an unfettered discretion, the classification will be 'administrative.' On the other hand, if law, or objective standards, limit the exercise of discretion, it will be classified as quasi-judicial."[12]

Until recently, the courts usually reviewed the exercise of a judicial or quasi-judicial function but not that of an administrative function. However, as explained below in the discussion of natural justice, these distinctions have become significantly less important.

Grounds for Review

Unless otherwise instructed by statute, the courts may review the exercise of administrative discretion if a tribunal has:

1. breached the rules of "natural justice";

2. violated the doctrine of *ultra vires*, i.e., acted outside the jurisdiction conferred on it by statute by exceeding its powers, abusing its powers, or committing errors of procedure; or

3. made errors of law.

Each of these grounds for judicial review will be examined briefly.

Natural Justice

The two fundamental principles of natural justice are *audi alteram partem* (hear the other side) and *nemo judex in sua causa debet esse* (no one should be a judge in his or her own cause.) The *audi alteram partem* principle encompasses the notions that a party whose rights might be affected should have:

1. adequate notice of the allegations against him or her and of the tribunal's intention to make a decision;

2. the right to be heard, specifically to present proofs and arguments;

3. the right to cross-examine witnesses and sometimes the right to legal representation; and

4. the right to an adjournment for a reasonable period of time to allow for preparation of his or her case.

For example, in the case of *Blais* v. *Basford*,[13] the minister of Consumer and Corporate Affairs terminated Blais' business licence on the basis of a report by the superintendent of bankruptcy. The Federal Court ordered the reinstatement of the licence on the grounds that "the Minister must act fairly and impartially and in this case should have offered Blais an opportunity to answer material in the report of the Superintendent." However, the application of the *audi alteram partem* principle depends on the circumstances of the case. Mr. Justice Mahoney of the Federal Court observed that

> what is reasonable in a particular case may run the gamut from merely giving the person to be affected written notice of the bold facts upon which it is proposed to act and inviting his written comments to a full dress oral hearing with witnesses and cross-examination all around. Those seeking certainty from precedents in this area will be disappointed.[14]

According to the *nemo judex in sua causa* principle, all forms of bias should be excluded from the proceedings and decisions of tribunals. The courts may intervene in the event of either "actual" bias or "a real likelihood" or "reasonable apprehension" of bias. The latter form includes such factors as kinship, friendship, or business relations with a party to the proceedings, hearing appeals from one's own decisions, or manifesting undue hostility toward one of the parties.

The two principles of natural justice explained above have traditionally applied only to tribunals exercising judicial or quasi-judicial functions, not to those exercising administrative functions. However, in several decisions over the past two decades, the Supreme Court of Canada has asserted that even tribunals exercising purely administrative functions have a duty to act fairly; this duty requires that where the rights of an individual are affected, a procedure should be followed that not only meets the minimum standards imposed by the statute but also ensures that the case will be heard fairly. A strong affirmation of this duty came in the landmark *Nicholson* case in which the Supreme Court overturned the dismissal of a probationary police constable because he was not given reasons for his dismissal or an opportunity to respond to those reasons.[15] The significance of this decision is that the legislation did not require that reasons and an opportunity to respond be given; the court simply felt that "fairness" required it.

> The result of the *Nicholson* case and of several subsequent cases is that a court of superior jurisdiction may now review decisions of inferior tribunals on the ground that they were made in a manner that was procedurally unfair ... The doctrine of fairness is a part of the rules of natural justice. Indeed, it might be regarded as the core or central requirement of natural justice.[16]

This doctrine of fairness applies to administrative tribunals exercising a purely administrative function, as well as to judicial or quasi-judicial tribunals. Indeed,

> [t]he main effect of fairness has been to destroy the outmoded and dangerous theory that the procedural requirement of justice existed only in matters definable as quasi-judicial. Fairness has become a central concept in administrative law. Thus, arbitrary, complicated and unnecessarily subtle distinctions such as the judicial/administrative quandry have been simplified ... [T]he result of this simplification is that citizens are assured of greater procedural fairness because they can better know and understand their rights.[17]

The importance of procedural fairness in the decisions of administrative authorities can be demonstrated in the Margaret Johnson case discussed at the beginning of this chapter.

Ultra Vires

The courts will generally intervene and grant relief where a tribunal has acted outside the scope of authority bestowed on it by its governing statute. Where there has been an excess of powers, the courts have found all types of decisions *ultra vires*, whether judicial, quasi-judicial, or administrative. Indeed, excess of powers is the primary ground for judicial review. To take a hypothetical and extreme example, the action of an immigration tribunal in granting a driver's licence would be declared *ultra vires*. The determination as to whether there has been an excess of powers obliges the courts to examine the enabling statute very carefully to see if Parliament has empowered the tribunal to act in a certain situation. It is the authority of the tribunal to make a decision, not the merits of the decision itself, which is at issue.

Another ground for review, that of *errors of procedure*, also requires that the courts look to the enabling statute. Parliament may specify that a tribunal exercise its powers according to specific procedures. We have already seen that on grounds of natural justice the courts may require tribunals performing judicial or quasi-judicial functions to follow certain rules of procedure. Regardless of natural justice principles, the courts will insist that tribunals follow the procedural rules set out in the statute; otherwise, the decision stemming from errors of procedure will be declared *ultra vires.*

An *abuse of power* occurs when a tribunal uses its power for a purpose not authorized by Parliament under the enabling statute. Thus, in considering whether there has been an abuse of power, and consequently whether a decision is *ultra vires*, the courts tend to look beyond the enabling statute to examine Parliament's intent. Abuse of power is usually expressed in terms of discretion exercised by a tribunal for improper purposes, in bad faith, or on irrelevant grounds.

In the celebrated case of *Roncarelli v. Duplessis,* the Supreme Court of Canada found abuse of power when the attorney general (who was also the premier) of Quebec directed a licensing commission to cancel a tavern owner's liquor permit because he had acted as bondsperson for persons accused of distributing allegedly seditious literature. The commission's decision was declared to be beyond its powers, and Justice Rand stated:

> In public regulation of this sort there is no such thing as untrammelled "discretion," that is, that action can be taken on any ground or for any reason that can be suggested to the mind of the administrator; no legislative act can, without express language, be taken to contemplate an unlimited arbitrary power exercisable for any person, however capricious or irrelevant, regardless of the nature or purpose of the statute ... "Discretion" necessarily implies good faith in discharging public duty; there is always a perspective within which a statute is intended to operate; any clear departure from its line or objects is just as objectionable as fraud or corruption.[18]

Errors of Law

The courts may review the decisions of tribunals for *errors of law on the face of the record.* The "record" for this purpose includes not only the formal decision but also the reasons for the decision, documents initiating the proceedings, documents on which the decision is based, and documents cited in the reasons for the decision. The words "on the face of the record" indicate that the courts will not review a decision unless the error is apparent.[19]

The Federal Court Act's specification of the common-law grounds for review cover all the grounds noted above. The court may review decisions on the grounds that a tribunal:

1. acted without jurisdiction, acted beyond its jurisdiction, or refused to exercise its jurisdiction;

2. failed to observe a principle of natural justice, procedural fairness, or other procedure that it was required by law to observe;

3. erred in law in making a decision or an order, regardless of whether or not the error appears on the face of the record;

4. based its decision or order on an erroneous finding of fact that it made in a perverse or capricious manner or without regard for the material before it;

5. acted, or failed to act, by reason of fraud or perjured evidence; or

6. acted in any other way that was contrary to law.

Forms of Relief

We turn now to a consideration of the common-law or ancillary remedies that the courts may use after the grounds for judicial review have been established. Statutory or direct remedies, namely appeal and review procedures provided by statute, were discussed above. The common-law remedies are employed when no other form of relief is available, convenient, or effective. They include the prerogative remedies, namely *certiorari*, prohibition, *mandamus, habeas corpus*, and *quo warranto*, as well as the remedies of injunction, declaration, and damages.

The most frequently used writs in Canada are *certiorari* and prohibition. *Certiorari* is a writ issued by a superior court to quash a decision already taken by an inferior tribunal, whereas prohibition is a writ to restrain a tribunal from taking a certain action. Both writs are generally used against tribunals exercising judicial or quasi-judicial functions. Moreover, the grounds on which these writs are available are breach of the rules of natural justice; absence, excess, or abuse of jurisdiction; and error of law on the face of the record. The Supreme Court of Canada held in the case of *Martineau v. Matsqui Institution Disciplinary Board*,[20] that a writ of *certiorari* will also be issued against tribunals exercising an administrative function if there is a violation of the doctrine of fairness.

Mandamus is a writ used to compel an inferior tribunal to exercise the authority conferred on it by statute. Unlike *certiorari* and prohibition, this writ is not restricted to tribunals exercising a judicial or quasi-judicial function. To obtain the writ of *mandamus*, an affected party must show that the tribunal is authorized or required to perform a certain duty, that it has been asked to perform that duty, and that it has refused to perform the duty.

Habeas corpus is used to require that a person who has been detained be brought before a court for the purpose of determining whether the detention is legal. This writ is not used much in the sphere of administrative law. It is normally restricted to immigration cases, where it is often used to challenge orders for custody or deportation.

Quo warranto is a writ used to inquire into whether an appointment to a public office established by statute is legal. Its use has in large measure been made unnecessary by statutory provisions relating to appointments to public office.

An injunction is a remedy that requires an inferior tribunal to take a particular action or, more commonly, to refrain from taking some specified action beyond its powers. An injunction is generally available only if an equally effective alternative remedy is not available. It can be used against tribunals exercising administrative, as well as judicial or quasi-judicial, functions.

An action for declaration (or declaratory judgment) asks the court to declare and define whether some act taken or proposed by a tribunal is beyond its powers. Like an injunction, a declaration is available for administrative as well as judicial or quasi-judicial decisions. Actions for declaration are infrequent. Moreover, they are normally combined with requests for other forms of relief, notably injunctions.

Damages is a remedy that requires that a certain amount of money be paid to compensate for an injury or wrong done to an individual. Tribunals, like ordinary citizens, are liable to an action for damages. Obviously, the remedy of damages is most useful in situations where the tribunal has already taken some action or decision. A remedy like *certiorari* that simply quashes the original decision would be of little help once the harm has been done. The remedy of damages is available for administrative as well as judicial and quasi-judicial functions. Damages were awarded against the attorney general (and premier) of Quebec in the case of *Roncarelli* v. *Duplessis* mentioned earlier.

Privative Clauses

With a view to allowing administrative tribunals to operate efficiently and quickly, Parliament and the provincial legislatures frequently use *privative clauses,* i.e., statutory provisions designed to prevent judicial review of administrative action. These clauses differ in the strength of their wording, but the standard privative clauses are typically worded as follows:

> No decision, order, direction, declaration, or ruling of the tribunal shall be questioned or reviewed in any court, and no order shall be made or proceedings taken in any court, whether by way of injunction, declaratory judgment, certiorari, mandamus, prohibition, or quo warranto, or otherwise to question, review, prohibit, or restrain the tribunal or any of its proceedings.

Until the late 1970s, Canadian courts generally gave little effect to privative clauses on the grounds that the courts should exercise their inherent supervisory jurisdiction over inferior tribunals if these made unreasonable decisions. Since that time, however, the courts have paid more heed to privative clauses as part of a growing confidence in the role of tribunals.

> The judicial attitude to tribunals has changed. Restraint has replaced intervention as judicial policy. Courts now recognize the legitimate role of administrative tribunals in the development and execution of economic, social and political policies ordained by the Legislature. Judges also recognize that tribunals bring to bear in their decisions knowledge and expertise in their particular fields beyond the usual experience of the courts.[21]

🏛 THE CANADIAN CHARTER OF RIGHTS AND FREEDOMS

The Charter, which came into force in 1982, has had a significant effect on administrative law in general and judicial review of administrative action in particular. One legal scholar has noted that "the imposition of the Charter as the supreme law of the land [means] that the sources of Canadian administrative law have been substantially increased. The legality of bureaucratic conduct is now decided not only in accordance with fidelity to legislation, but also by the normative concepts contained in the Charter."[22]

The Charter has already had a considerable effect on the working lives of public servants at all levels of government. Many statutes and regulations have been amended to bring them into harmony with the Charter before they are challenged in the courts. Many decisions, especially in the lower courts, have had a major impact on public servants' day-to-day work. Indeed,

> most Charter cases involve decisions initially made by appointed officials in the executive branch of government. That is especially true of the criminal justice system, from which most Charter litigation has sprung, challenging the actions of a host of police officers, prosecutors, lower court judges, probation officers, and parole officers in the administration of our common law. In the labour field, too, a number of cases have arisen involving the practices and doctrines of appointed labour boards.[23]

The courts use the Charter to assert strongly the rights of individuals. Sections 7, 8, and 15 have an especially important effect on administrative law and, therefore, on the conduct of public administration. Section 7, on legal rights, provides in part that "[e]veryone has the right to life, liberty and security of the person and the right not to be deprived thereof except in accordance with the principles of fundamental justice." In the *Singh* case[24] for example, the Supreme Court held that it was a breach of "the principles of fundamental justice" not to provide an oral hearing to refugee claimants. Legal scholars have observed that the wording of Section 7 "constitutionalizes" the procedural aspects of natural justice (or the duty to be fair), and that the reference to principles of natural justice "may ripen into a substantive [as opposed to a procedural] limitation on ... the content of parent legislation which can be enacted [and] ... provide a method to scrutinize the merits of a delegate's decision."[25]

The Charter must be taken seriously by administrators who, to date, may have had little if any experience with the judicial process. It must be regarded as a limitation upon every administrative action and every statutory instrument. It has "constitutionalized" administrative law, procedure and practice.

There is no point being irritated about it because it reduces administrative efficiency: that was precisely what it was intended to do. If the administration thinks that something is "reasonably justified," it must be prepared not merely to assert it, but to prove it. Gone are the days when one can simply say, "Trust us, we are the public service."

Source: Andrew Roman "The Possible Impact of the Canadian Charter of Rights and Freedoms on Administrative Law"[26]

Section 8 provides that "[e]veryone has the right to be secure against unreasonable search and seizure." The enormous potential for the courts to use this section to protect individual rights against government action is demonstrated in the case of *Mario Duarte*.[27] The issue in the case was whether, under the Charter, the police could legally have an informer record, surreptitiously and without a judicial warrant, his conversation with a suspected drug dealer. The Supreme Court had asserted in previous cases that the primary value served by Section 8 of the Charter is privacy, and in the *Duarte* case the court came to the defence of personal privacy in the face of increasingly sophisticated surveillance technology. Justice La Forest stated:

> The very efficacy of electronic surveillance is such that it has the potential, if left unregulated, to annihilate any expectation that our communications will remain private. A society which exposed us, at the whim of the state, to the risk of having a permanent electronic recording made every time we opened our mouths might be superbly equipped to fight crime, but it would be one in which privacy no longer had any meaning.[28]

Section 15 provides that "[e]very individual is equal before the law and has the right to the equal protection of the law without discrimination and, in particular, without discrimination based on race, national or ethnic origin, colour, religion, sex, age, or mental or physical disability." This section, which deals with equality rights, did not come into effect until 1985, but it has already spawned a large number of cases in the lower courts. The federal Department of Justice has predicted that Section 15 will provide much better protection against discrimination than that provided by human rights laws and the Canadian Bill of Rights because "Section 15 is part of the Constitution. It can be used to strike down laws that offend its principles."[29]

As a result of Section 15, governments must ensure that their hiring and promotion requirements do not discriminate against such disadvantaged groups as women and disabled persons. Thus, this section is especially important to government efforts to promote employment equity. In the case of *Action travail des femmes*,[30] the Supreme Court imposed an employment equity program on Canadian National Railways, which was obliged to hire women for a specific percentage of jobs traditionally held by men.

The Charter has been used to advance the individual rights of public servants themselves. As explained in Chapter 13, restrictions on the political rights of public servants have been reduced as a result of judicial decisions under the Charter.

Jones and de Villars note that "[t]he courts are no longer confined to merely interpreting and enforcing the positive law, which was the theoretical foundation for pre-Charter Administrative Law. Through Charter challenges to administrative action, the courts are now called upon to assess the rationale for particular laws as measured against constitutional criteria which are still developing."[31]

🏛 THE UTILITY OF JUDICIAL REVIEW

Even though the importance of judicial review of administrative action has increased substantially as a result of the Charter, judicial review has several deficiencies as a means of preventing and remedying abuses of bureaucratic power. The courts review only a miniscule number of the millions of decisions made annually by administrative authorities; the success rate of litigants is not high; neither the amount of money nor the issue involved is usually significant enough to justify the high cost of the proceedings; and judicial review tends to focus on certain areas of public administration (labour relations, tax assessment, and licensing) so that many other areas are relatively untouched.

Those scholars favouring a narrow scope for judicial review point to the benefits of having decisions made by tribunals possessing expertise and experience in various areas of administrative activity and of providing more expeditious and inexpensive proceedings than the courts. They acknowledge, however, that judicial review is the best form of control when values fundamental to the legal order as a whole (e.g., civil liberties values and constitutional issues) are in question. "Judicial review is rarely needed, but when it is needed nothing else will do." It remains, however, as only one weapon in the arsenal of controls and influences available to preserve and enhance responsible behaviour.

NOTES

1. *Margaret Johnson v. The Minister of Veterans Affairs*, Reasons for Judgment, Federal Court of Appeal, Ottawa, 9 April 1990, 15.
2. Perry S. Millar and Carl Baar, *Judicial Administration in Canada* (Kingston and Montreal: McGill-Queen's University Press, 1984), ch. 4.
3. Note that Ontario has undertaken a major reform of its court system. For a brief explanation of the reforms, see Gerald L. Gall, *The Canadian Legal System*, 4th ed. (Toronto: Carswell, 1995), 192—94.
4. *Revised Statutes of Canada*, 1970, 2nd Supp., ch. 10, as amended by Canada, *Statutes*, 1990, c. 8.
5. Included among these tribunals are the Tax Court of Canada, the Canadian Radio-television and Telecommunications Commission, the Pension Appeals Board, and the Competition Tribunal.
6. Donald J. Bourgeois, *Public Law in Canada* (Scarborough, Ont.: Nelson, 1990), 195.
7. "Administrative Law in Canada," *Canadian Bar Review* 39 (1961): 254.
8. Law Reform Commission of Canada, *A Catalogue of Discretionary Powers in the Revised Statutes of Canada* (Ottawa: Information Canada, 1975), 2.
9. David J. Mullan *Administrative Law*, (Toronto: Carswell, 2nd. ed. 1979), 3–92.
10. Ibid.
11. René Dussault, "Relationship between the Nature of the Acts of the Administration and Judicial Review: Quebec and Canada," *Canadian Public Administration* 10 (September 1967): 316.
12. Robert F. Reid and David Hillel, *Administrative Law and Practice*, 2nd ed., (Toronto: Butterworths, 1978), 153.
13. (1972) F.G. 151 (C.A.).
14. "Hearings and Decisions: A Judge's Perspective," Speakers' Remarks, Law Reform Commission of Canada, Seminar for Members of Federal Administrative Tribunals, April 5–7, 1978, 105.
15. *Nicholson v. Haldimand-Norfolk Police Commrs. Bd.* (1979), 1 S.C.R., 311.
16. Gerald Gall, *The Canadian Legal System*, 4th ed. (Toronto: Carswell, 1995), 444-5. See also David Philip Jones and Anne S. de Villars, *Principles of Administrative Law*, 2nd ed. (Toronto: Carswell, 1994), 193ff.

17. James Shields and Ian C. Vallance, "Procedural Fairness: Section 11 and the Role of Counsel," in Neil R. Finkelstein and Brian MacLeod Rogers, *Administrative Tribunals and the Charter* (Toronto: Carswell, 1990), 127–28.
18. *Roncarelli* v. *Duplessis* (1959) S.C.R. 121 at 140. Reproduced with the permission of the Minister of Public Works and Government Services Canada, 1998.
19. Errors of law that have led to the quashing of the decisions of tribunals include an error in the interpretation of a statute; the censuring of a manger of a pharmacy when only the pharmacy was charged; failure to make the necessary inquiry; and failure to observe a statutory condition. Reid and Hillel, *Administrative Law and Practice*, 382–83.
20. *Martineau v. Matsqui Inst. Disciplinary Bd.* No. 2 (1980), S.C.R., 602.
21. Mr. Justice Blair, in *Re Ontario Public Service Employees Union and Forer* (1985) 23 D.L.R. (4th) 97 (Ont. H.C.): 104.
22. Andrew J. Roman, "The Possible Impact of the Canadian Charter of Rights and Freedoms on Administrative Law," *Les Cahiers de Droit* 26 (June 1985): 341.
23. Paul C. Weiler, "The Charter at Work: Reflections on the Constitutionalizing of Labour and Employment Law," *University of Toronto Law Journal* 40 (1990): 163.
24. *Singh* v. *Minister of Employment and Immigration* (1985), 17 D.L.R., (4th), 422.
25. David Phillip Jones and Anne S. de Villars, *Principles of Administrative Law* (Toronto: Carswell, 1985), 39–40.
26. Andrews J. Roman, *Les Cahiers de Droit*, 358.
27. *Mario Duarte* v. *Her Majesty The Queen* (1980), 1 S.C.R., 30.
28. Ibid., 44.
29. Canada, Department of Justice, *Equality Issues in Federal Law: A Discussion Paper* (Ottawa: Department of Justice, 1985), 6.
30. (1987) 1 S.C.R., 1114.
31. Jones and Villars, *Principles of Administrative Law*, 65.

BIBLIOGRAPHY

Angus, W.H. "Judicial Review: Do We Need It?" *McGill Law Journal* 20 (1974): 177–212. (Also printed in Daniel J. Baum, ed., *The Individual and the Bureaucracy*. Toronto: Carswell, 1975, 101–35.)

Blake, Sara. *Administrative Law in Canada*. Toronto: Butterworths, 1992.

Borgeat, L. and I. Giroux. "Droit et administration publique: entre tradition et postmodernité." *Canadian Public Administration* 40 (summer 1997): 307–27.

Bourgeois, Donald J. *Public Law in Canada*. Scarborough, Ont.: Nelson, 1990.

Canada. Law Reform Commission. *Judicial Review and the Federal Court*. Report no. 14. Ottawa: Supply and Services, 1980.

———. *Toward a Modern Federal Administrative Law*. Ottawa: Law Reform Commission of Canada, 1987.

Cohen, Davis S. and Peter Finkle. "Crown Liability in Canada: Developing Compensation Policies for Regulatory Failure." *Canadian Public Administration* 37 (spring 1994): 79–107.

de Smith, S.A. *Judicial Review of Administrative Action*. London: Stevens and Sons, 1959.

Dussault, René, and Louis Borgeat. *Administrative Law: A Treatise*, 2nd ed. Toronto: Carswell, 3 vols.—1986, 1988, and 1989.

Finkelstein, Neil R. *Recent Developments in Administrative Law*. Toronto: Carswell, 1987.

Finkelstein, Neil R., and Brian MacLeod Rogers, eds. *Administrative Tribunals and the Charter*. Toronto: Carswell, 1990.

Gall, Gerald. *The Canadian Legal System*, 4th ed. Toronto: Carswell, 1995.

Hogg, Peter. "Judicial Review: How Much Do We Need?" *McGill Law Journal* 20 (1974): 157–66.

Jones, David Phillip, and Anne S. de Villars. *Principles of Administrative Law*. 2nd ed. Scarborough, Ont.: Carswell, 1994.

Kersell, J.E. "Statutory and Judicial Control of Administrative Behaviour." *Canadian Public Administration* 19 (summer 1976): 295–307.

Millar, Perry S., and Carl Baar. *Judicial Administration in Canada*. Kingston and Montreal: McGill-Queen's University Press, 1981.

Moffet, John. "Judicial Review and Environmental Policy: Lessons for Canada from the United States." *Canadian Public Administration* 37 (spring 1994): 140–66.

Morton, F.L., and Leslie Pal. "The Impact of the Charter of Rights on Public Administration: A Case Study of Sex Discrimination in the Unemployment Insurance Act." *Canadian Public Administration* 28 (summer 1985): 221–44.

Mullan, David J. *Administrative Law*, 3nd ed. Toronto: Carswell, 1996.

Reid, Robert F., and David Hillel. *Administrative Law and Practice*, 2nd ed. Toronto: Butterworths, 1978.

Roman, Andrew J. "The Possible Impact of the Canadian Charter of Rights and Freedoms on Administrative Law." *Les Cahiers de Droit* 26 (June 1985): 339–59.

Russell, Peter. *The Judiciary in Canada*, 3rd ed. Toronto: McGraw-Hill Ryerson, 1987.

Smith, G.J. *Charter of Rights and Administrative Law*. Toronto: Carswell, 1983.

19

Intergovernmental Administrative Relations

The prime minister was there, and so were the provincial premiers and territorial leaders. They were seated around a large table at the December 1997 meeting of Canada's First Ministers. But who were all those people sitting behind them, and why did they occasionally lean forward to whisper to the First Ministers? Some of them were cabinet ministers (sixteen in total) from the various governments, and they were there to assist their political leader. Most of them, however, were public servants (ninety-five in total, including some political advisors). Why so many public servants? Because the First Ministers and the cabinet ministers needed expert advice on the policy issues discussed at the conference, namely, social policy renewal, youth employment, and health. But not all of these public servants were experts in these policy fields; many had titles having to do with intergovernmental and constitutional affairs. The province of Quebec brought more intergovernmental officials than officials from regular government departments.

Who are these intergovernmental officials? How much influence do they have and how are they held accountable? What is their relationship to one another and to cabinet ministers and legislators? These are some of the key questions discussed in this chapter. The chapter examines:

1. the meaning and evolution of federalism and intergovernmental relations;

2. the extensive machinery for intergovernmental liaison;

3. models of intergovernmental relations that help explain the functions of intergovernmental officials; and

4. the power and responsibility of these officials.

The impact of intergovernmental relations on government regulation was examined in Chapter 10.

We shall see that intergovernmental relations are vitally important in the Canadian political system. Discussion of the processes and outcomes of interaction among federal, provincial, and municipal governments pervades both scholarly and popular writings on Canadian politics. One author has observed that Canada may be "the only country where you can buy a book about federal-provincial relations at an airport."[1] Intergovernmental relations affect virtually every policy field and have significant political, economic, social, and cultural consequences; they affect the day-to-day lives of Canadians by helping to determine such things as the cost of gasoline and oil and the quality of hospital care.

🏛 FEDERALISM AND INTERGOVERNMENTAL RELATIONS

Meaning and Evolution

Federalism may be defined as a political system in which the powers of the state are formally divided between central and regional governments by a written constitution, but in which these governments are linked in an interdependent political relationship.[2] In the Canadian context, this definition captures the enduring legal and constitutional elements of Canadian federalism, the politics that pervade the federal system, and the necessity for intergovernmental interaction. Federalism and *intergovernmental relations* are not the same thing; rather, federalism provides the structural framework within which the process of intergovernmental relations takes place. The federal form of government ensures that there are at least two orders (or levels) of government (e.g., federal and provincial governments in Canada). In modern federal states, these orders of government tend to be highly interdependent and interactive. Broadly interpreted, the term intergovernmental relations embraces not only federal-provincial relations but also interprovincial, federal-municipal, and provincial-municipal relations. The main emphasis in this chapter is on federal-provincial liaison, but specific reference is made also to the activities of officials involved in interprovincial relations.

A dictionary of almost 500 words and phrases that have been used to describe and explain concepts of federalism has been compiled.[3] While several of Canada's many contributions to concepts of federalism were not acknowledged, Canada was mentioned in more than twenty entries. In Canada, as elsewhere, both the meaning and evolution of federalism have frequently been explained by adding adjectives to the word. For example, James R. Mallory[4] has used five different labels to classify and explain concepts of Canadian federalism.

In Mallory's classification, *quasi-federalism* characterized the early decades of the Canadian federation during which the federal government dominated the provincial governments, in part by making frequent use of the federal constitutional powers to disallow and reserve provincial legislation. The next stage was *classical federalism,* which approached K.C. Wheare's celebrated "federal principle." This principle held that the powers of government are divided "so that the general and regional governments are each, within a sphere, co-ordinate and independent."[5] Between the late 1800s and 1930, with the exception of World War I, provincial powers gradually increased as a result of strong political leadership in certain provinces and judicial decisions favouring the provinces in constitutional disputes with the federal government. Both the federal and provincial governments enjoyed exclusive jurisdiction in certain policy fields, and jurisdictional conflicts were resolved by the courts. Increased federal-provincial consultation was formally recognized by the first federal-provincial conference of First Ministers (the prime minister of Canada and the provincial premiers) held in 1906, and federal assistance for the financing of provincial responsibilities began in such areas as transportation and agriculture. The growing importance and expense of the provinces' responsibilities for health, education, and welfare required not only federal subsidies but also a provincial search for new revenues through the use of such forms of taxation as personal and corporate income taxes.

The period of World War I was one of *emergency federalism*. The courts supported the federal government's exercise of broad powers, enshrined in the constitution, over the economy and over matters of property and civil rights, which, in peacetime, were clearly within provincial jurisdiction. After the war, including the Depression years, the courts resisted the exercise of this emergency power. During World War II, and for a short time afterward, the federal government again used the emergency power to control many matters that were normally within provincial jurisdiction. "There can be little quarrel with Professor Wilfred Eggleston's observation that 'in 1914–19 and again in 1939–45 ... the emergency provisions of the constitution turned Canada for the time being into a unitary state.'"[6]

It is difficult to pinpoint the precise date when *cooperative federalism* emerged, but Donald Smiley noted in the early 1960s that the development of Canadian federalism since 1945 had been "a process of continuous and piece-meal adjustment between the two levels of government," and that these adjustments had overwhelmingly been made through "interaction between federal and provincial executives" rather than through formal constitutional amendment or judicial interpretation.[7] Under cooperative federalism, the constitutional division of powers was preserved, but federal and provincial ministers and public servants engaged in consultation and coordination to reach joint decisions on policies and programs of mutual concern.

During the late 1940s and the 1950s, the federal government dominated federal-provincial relations, but in the 1960s provincial governments gradually acquired the expertise and influence to deal with the federal government from a stronger position. Gradually also, the term *executive federalism,* first used by Smiley, began to be applied more often than cooperative federalism to describe the nature of federal-provincial relations. Garth Stevenson has explained that the main features of cooperative federalism were "the fragmentation of authority within each level of government, the absence of linkages between different issues and functional domains, the forging of specific intergovernmental links by different groups of specialized officials, and the lack of publicity or public awareness of what was happening." Executive federalism, by contrast, involved "the concentration and centralization of authority at the top of each participating government, the control and supervision of intergovernmental relations by politicians and officials with a wide range of functional interests, and the highly formalized and well-publicized proceedings of federal-provincial conference diplomacy."[8]

By the latter half of the 1960s, the term cooperative federalism had become a misnomer because intergovernmental relations were characterized by a great deal of conflict and confrontation, as well as consultation and collaboration. It is notable also that both cooperative federalism and executive federalism have existed alongside another centrally important variant of federalism described by Mallory as *double-image federalism*. This form combines interaction between the central government and the provinces with a special relationship between French- and English-speaking Canadians. Certainly, French-English relations have been a critical and persistent factor in intergovernmental relations, especially since the early 1960s.

Regionalism and Federalism

Regionalism refers to the territorial dimension of the Canadian community, according to which particular areas or regions of the country are distinguished from others by political, economic, historical, cultural, and linguistic characteristics. Since the early 1960s, there has been a substantial increase in conflict between the federal government and the several regions of the country. There has also been much friction between and among the regions themselves. The term region is commonly interpreted in two ways: first, it is used interchangeably with the term province, and second, it is used to refer to one of five major areas in the country: the Atlantic provinces, Quebec, Ontario, the Prairie provinces, and British Columbia.

This regional dimension of Canadian federalism continues to have an enormous impact on both the politics and the management of intergovernmental relations. It affects both the content of government policies and programs and the structures and processes of individual governments and of intergovernmental relations. This can be demonstrated easily by reference to federal economic development policy and to the political and administrative mechanisms devised to formulate and administer this policy.[9]

This concern about regional considerations has led to greater emphasis since the late 1970s on the intrastate dimension of Canadian federalism, as opposed to the traditional interstate dimension. *Interstate federalism* refers to "the distribution of powers and financial resources between the federal and provincial governments as well as the relations between those two orders of government," whereas *intrastate federalism* refers to "arrangements whereby the interests of regional units—the interests either of the government or of the residents of these units—are channelled through and protected by the structures and operations of the central government."[10] These arrangements could include reform of the electoral system to make each party in the House of Commons more representative of the various regions; reform of the Supreme Court to make its members more sensitive to regional and provincial concerns; and reform or replacement of the Senate to provide more effective representation in Parliament of regional and provincial interests. Among the proposed arrangements affecting the public service specifically are a public service that is more representative in its composition of the regions of the country, and formal representation of provincial governments in federal agencies, boards, and commissions.

Alan Cairns has distinguished between centralist and provincial intrastate federalism. The centralist version "is an attempt to weaken provincial governments by increasing the attractiveness of Ottawa to that complex regional/provincial network of interests, values, identities, and socio-economic power whose support is a crucial resource in intergovernmental competition." The provincial version is an attempt to provide direct representation of the provincial governments in the institutions and decision-making processes of the federal government.[11]

Much of the discussion of the intrastate perspective has centred on the federal cabinet, the Senate, the Supreme Court, and the electoral system rather than on bureaucratic institutions and processes.[12] However, it has been suggested that the federal public service would be more sensitive to regional needs and aspirations if its composition were more representative of the regions (e.g., more senior public servants in Ottawa who were from the Atlantic provinces), and if it were restructured with more emphasis on regional considerations (e.g., decentralization of power to federal field units in the regions).[13]

🏛 FEDERAL–PROVINCIAL FISCAL RELATIONS

While federal financial assistance to provincial governments dates to Confederation and was especially important during the Depression, federal-provincial fiscal relations have been an especially prominent theme in Canadian federalism since World War II. A brief explanation of the development and characteristics of these relations is essential to understanding contemporary intergovernmental relations.

The federal-provincial financial relationship is based on four elements: tax collection agreements, conditional grants or shared-cost programs, the Canada Health and Social Transfer, and equalization. Each of these is considered in turn below.[14]

The *tax collection agreement* is an agreement between the federal government and nine provinces that allows the federal government to collect both federal and provincial personal taxes (except for Quebec) and corporate taxes (except for Alberta, Ontario, and Quebec), and to remit the provincial portion of the taxes to the provinces. The purpose of this agreement is to provide an administrative convenience to provincial governments, and to limit tax competition between provinces by establishing some uniformity in the method of calculation. The other three elements of the federal-provincial financial relationship involve transfer payments.[15]

Conditional grants or shared-cost programs[16] involve payments by the federal government to provincial governments choosing to undertake programs according to conditions specified by the federal government. Until 1995, the largest such program was the *Canada Assistance Plan* (CAP) established in 1966. Under this plan, the federal government paid one-half of the cost of provincial social assistance programs. In turn, the provincial programs had to meet certain conditions, e.g., no discrimination against applicants from another province.

In 1995, the *Canada Health and Social Transfer* (CHST) succeeded the Established Programs Financing (EPF) arrangement, which was a transfer payment program begun in 1977.[17] In that year, the federal government terminated three very large conditional grants to the provinces—for medicare, hospital care, and post-secondary education—and replaced them with a combination of cash payments and "tax room." This latter term means that the federal government agrees to reduce its income tax rate by a certain number of "tax points" so that provincial governments can increase their tax rates accordingly. Because of the tax collection agreement discussed above, this type of shift is not evident to the taxpayer.

One of the characteristics of EPF was that provincial governments were not obliged to spend the money on medical or hospital care or post-secondary education; they could use the funds generated for purposes of their own choosing. However, there were still some conditions attached to the receipt of the cash payments. For example, under the Canada Health Act, the federal government could reduce the cash payments to any province that allows physicians to "extra-bill."

The 1995 federal budget combined CAP and EPF into a single block fund called the Canada Health and Social Transfer, covering federal transfers for health, post-secondary education, and welfare. The budget also announced a very substantial reduction in the amount of money to be transferred to the provinces for social assistance programs. The cost-sharing element of CAP was ended, but the requirement that there be no provincial residency requirements for receipt of social assistance was maintained. In addition, the principles of the Canada Health Act noted above were preserved.

Equalization is a program through which the federal government makes unconditional grants to provinces that have a weak tax base.[18] An *unconditional grant* is a payment that can be used for any purpose the province desires; the federal government requires no accounting for how the money is spent. The purpose of the equalization program is to allow the so-called have-not provinces to provide adequate public services to their citizens without imposing excessively high taxes.

The federal government has long been concerned that transfer payments could weaken the accountability of the provincial governments for the expenditure of public funds. A strict concept of accountability would suggest that the government that receives credit for spending funds should be the same as the one that takes blame for raising taxes. The ability to spend someone else's money does little to encourage thrift or accountability. However, there are a number of valid reasons for transfer payments, including the need to redistribute wealth among provinces and the desire to have national programs with uniform national standards.[19]

One of the major controversies surrounding intergovernmental fiscal relations in recent years has been the use of conditional versus unconditional grants. The government providing the grant frequently favours conditional grants because they can be directed to specific purposes and accountability can be ensured through the use of specific regulations or audits. On the negative side, recipient governments sometimes feel that the conditions attached to grants are insensitive to local conditions and that the record-keeping and other administrative requirements imposed are excessive. Therefore, recipient governments tend to favour unconditional grants because this type maximizes their freedom. Governments providing grants are concerned about unconditional grants because they can be used in ways they deem inappropriate and because the government ultimately supplying the funds frequently does not receive the credit when the money is spent. This often gives rise to concern by the federal government about the inadequate visibility it receives for services paid for by federal funds but provided by provincial governments.

In the 1950s and 1960s, the federal government introduced a number of shared-cost programs that encouraged provincial governments to embark on new programs. However, as explained above, the federal government, faced with a weak economy and rising deficits, has taken unilateral action during the 1980s and 1990s to reduce its transfer payments to provinces. This has incited the ire of the provinces, which feel that the federal government pushed them into beginning these programs and is now leaving them "holding the bag." It is clear that the social policy challenges facing federal and provincial governments ensure sustained—and vigorous—debate about the nature and reform of federal-provincial fiscal arrangements.

🏛 FEDERAL–PROVINCIAL CONSTITUTIONAL RELATIONS

The impact of federal-provincial relations on the evolution of Canada's constitution is a long and intricate story in which many of the constitutional issues have had an important financial aspect as well. There have, however, been a number of constitutional developments with special relevance for contemporary federal-provincial relations and, consequently, for the officials involved in these relations. As noted, quasi-federalism and classical federalism gave way to cooperative, executive, and double-image federalism. Dissatisfaction with judicial interpretation of the division of powers contained in the British North America Act, the lack of a formula for amending the act without the consent of the British Parliament, and the expansion in the scope and cost of government activities led to increasing use of extra-constitutional arrangements negotiated by the two orders of government.

A series of federal-provincial conferences that began in 1968 sought agreement on constitutional reform. These efforts were given enormous impetus by the election of the separatist Parti Québécois government in Quebec in 1976 and the 1980 referendum campaign on "sovereignty-association," at which time the federal government promised constitutional change. Also, during the 1970s and early 1980s, intergovernmental tensions were severely exacerbated by sharp disagreements over the ownership of natural resources, especially petroleum, and over the allocation of the revenues flowing from the exploitation of these resources. The dispute raged not only between the federal government and the energy-producing provinces (especially Alberta) but also between these provinces and the energy-consuming provinces (especially Ontario).

For the 1980–81 constitutional meetings, the First Ministers agreed upon an agenda containing twelve contentious items—a statement of principles as a preamble to the constitution; a charter of human rights (including language rights); equalization; the nature of the economic union; a formula for amending the constitution in Canada (referred to as patriation of the constitution); reform of the Upper House with regional representation; reform of the Supreme Court; the ownership of natural resources and related issues of trade and taxation; offshore resources; fisheries; communications (including broadcasting); and family law. However, following the failure of the September 1980 meeting of First Ministers, and after lengthy debate in the federal Parliament, the provinces were presented in November 1981 with a federal proposal for constitutional change, which all provinces, except Quebec, finally accepted. Agreements were reached on only a few of the agenda items, and these agreements were enshrined in the Constitution Act of 1982, which was approved formally by the British Parliament. This act provided, among other things, an amending formula ensuring that all changes to the constitution would henceforth be made in Canada; a charter of rights and freedoms; a commitment to the principle of equalization; confirmation of provincial ownership of natural resources; and affirmation of the existing rights of aboriginal peoples.

Federal action during this period supported former prime minister Trudeau's assertion in 1982 that cooperative federalism was dead. Moreover, there was little evidence of executive federalism at work in that federal-provincial conference diplomacy was replaced by unilateral federal decision making. In 1985 then-prime minister Mulroney announced the rebirth of cooperative federalism as a signal of a renewed federal commitment to consultation and collaboration with the provinces, but federal-provincial disagreements became increasingly severe during his term of office. In late 1993, the new prime minister, Jean Chrétien, promised more harmonious federal-provincial relations; experience since then provides little evidence that harmony will soon be achieved.

During the late 1980s and the early 1990s, the major focus of attention in intergovernmental relations was on the Meech Lake Accord, the Charlottetown Agreement, and the Free Trade Agreement with the United States.

The Meech Lake Accord, formally referred to as the Constitution Amendment, 1987, was negotiated by the First Ministers, with the assistance of their public service advisors, and was signed on June 3, 1987. The accord consisted of a number of proposals for constitutional amendment, including recognition of Quebec as a distinct society, provision for provinces to opt out of any new federal spending programs within provincial constitutional jurisdiction, an amending formula, and arrangements for provincial participation in the selection of members of the Supreme Court and the Senate. From the perspective of the federal and Quebec governments, the primary purpose of the accord was "to bring Quebec back into the constitutional family" after Quebec's refusal to accept the Constitution Act of 1982. The accord was to come into effect when it was ratified by the legislatures of all eleven governments. Under the terms of the Constitution Act, that ratification had to occur within three years, i.e., by June 23, 1990. During the three-year period, federal and provincial public servants played a significant advisory role in the protracted negotiations over the ratification of the accord; these negotiations culminated in a highly publicized and acrimonious First Ministers' Conference in mid-June 1990. The conference appeared to have reached agreement on ratification of the accord, but two provinces (Newfoundland and Manitoba) failed to obtain ratification before the June 23 deadline. Among the major objections to the accord were its recognition of Quebec as a distinct society, its decentralization of power from the federal government to the provinces, its requirement of unanimous consent for Senate reform, and its lack of recognition of the rights of aboriginal peoples.

Intergovernmental tensions were greatly exacerbated by the unwillingness of some provinces to ratify the accord, and by the unwillingness of the federal and Quebec governments to agree to major modifications. Following the death of the accord, the province of Quebec announced its unwillingness to participate in any constitutional conferences for the foreseeable future and began formal consideration of its future association with the rest of Canada.

Beginning in 1991, a renewed effort to reach agreement on constitutional reform began. Widespread consultations involving participants from all parts of the country and many meetings of the First Ministers and senior public servants led to the August 28, 1992, *Consensus Report on the Constitution*. This report was known generally as the Charlottetown Agreement and was agreed to by First Ministers (including the premier of Quebec), territorial leaders, and aboriginal leaders. The agreement's comprehensive proposals for constitutional change included among other things, provisions for a social and economic union, the recognition of Quebec as a distinct society, the protection of minority language rights, the reform of the Senate and the Supreme Court, a reduction of overlap and duplication among governments, and the recognition of the inherent right of self-government for aboriginal peoples. These proposals, which had extremely significant implications for intergovernmental relations, were submitted for approval in a national referendum held on October 26, 1992. The agreement was rejected by a majority of almost 55 percent of voters.

Unlike the Meech Lake Accord and the Charlottetown Agreement, the Canada-U.S. Free Trade Agreement (FTA), which came into effect in January 1989, involved no constitutional change. Like the constitutional initiatives, however, the Free Trade Agreement greatly strained intergovernmental relations because of strong differences of opinion among Canada's First Ministers as to its desirability. The North America Free Trade Agreement (NAFTA), which was concluded in 1993, aroused much less intergovernmental controversy. Both the FTA and the NAFTA, which were negotiated primarily by public servants, will have an enormous impact on public policy and intergovernmental relations. Their effective implementation will also require the advice and assistance of public servants in both federal and provincial spheres of government.

Intergovernmental officials were important players in the extensive bargaining leading up to the major agreements noted. If Quebec were to separate from Canada, these officials would obviously be major participants in the extremely complex and highly charged negotiations over the financial and other terms of the separation.

The active participation of public servants in intergovernmental issues has resulted in an impressive array of intergovernmental administrative structures.

🏛 MACHINERY FOR INTERGOVERNMENTAL RELATIONS

Structures, Processes, and Participants

The network of intergovernmental structures includes separate departments or other administrative units within governments,[20] administrative units within individual departments, intergovernmental secretariats, and a large number of intergovernmental committees. The creation of these structures has both resulted from, and stimulated the proliferation of, intergovernmental conferences and meetings. The major reasons for the development of this complicated web of intergovernmental contacts, especially between federal and provincial governments, have been the expansion of the activities of all governments, the increased interdependence of federal and provincial responsibilities, and the consequent need to design and operate machinery to manage these contacts.

As early as 1972, there were 482 federal-provincial liaison bodies, ranging in scope and importance from the First Ministers' Conference (the prime minister, the provincial premiers, and the territorial leaders) to such specialized federal-provincial committees as those on meteorites and pest control. There are now more than 1000 federal-provincial *committees* of varying degrees of importance. Some of these committees meet more than once, while some do not meet at all during a particular year. Among the more than 500 federal-provincial *meetings* held each year are meetings of First Ministers, ministers, deputy ministers, and public servants below the deputy level.

Intergovernmental secretariats have been established to provide support services for the meetings of the many liaison bodies. The major secretariat is the Canadian Intergovernmental Conference Secretariat, which was established in 1973 to serve the conferences of First Ministers and all other intergovernmental bodies requesting its assistance.[21] It is jointly funded by the federal and provincial governments and provides such services as looking after conference arrangements and agendas, preparing conference transcripts and summary statements, and distributing documents. Some federal-provincial bodies (e.g., the Canadian Council of Resource and Environment Ministers) have established their own secretariat.

The number of officials attending intergovernmental meetings varies greatly from one meeting to another, but it is notable that one of the largest gatherings—the First Ministers' Conference—attracts well over 200 First Ministers, cabinet ministers, and public servants. However, the number of intergovernmental officials attending such meetings does not take account of the large number of officials who do not attend the meetings but who are actively engaged in preparation for the participation of ministers and other officials.

It is difficult to distinguish precisely between *intergovernmental officials* and other public servants. The term is normally used to refer only to so-called intergovernmental affairs specialists. These are senior public servants who are engaged solely or primarily in intergovernmental business. They are usually housed in central agencies and are responsible for the coordination of intergovernmental matters both within their own government and with other governments. But, in varying degrees, many other officials are involved in intergovernmental relations. Thus, the term intergovernmental officials also refers to those officials whose formally designated responsibilities require them to spend the majority of their working hours on intergovernmental matters, but who are not normally described as intergovernmental affairs specialists. The most prominent among these are senior public servants in operating departments who look after intergovernmental issues affecting their departments. In addition, there are officials, notably in senior positions, who devote relatively little time to intergovernmental issues but whose occasional involvement has a major influence on the outcome of intergovernmental negotiations.

Intergovernmental affairs specialists play a central role in government both in the organizational sense and in the development and implementation of policy. They must be adept in *intra*governmental as well as *inter*governmental bargaining. Their influence is based to a large extent on their ability to wend their way skillfully through the labyrinth of intergovernmental affairs in search of agreement with officials in their own government and in other governments. An important element of their expertise is in the *process* of intergovernmental relations. They must also be knowledgeable in a general way about the *substance* of a broad range of policy fields. A primary aim of intergovernmental affairs specialists is to ensure that operating departments in their own government will not weaken that government through the intergovernmental interactions in which they engage.[22]

A critical element in the intergovernmental policy process is the multitude of informal contacts, especially by telephone, that supplement formal meetings. The respect and trust among officials developed during formal contacts pave the way for frank and productive discussions outside of, and between, formal meetings. During these discussions, officials exchange a great deal of information about their government's position on matters of continuing concern and negotiation. An essential attribute of intergovernmental officials is their ability to obtain current information about the perceptions and positions of other governments. This information is crucial in determining the officials' advice to their political and administrative superiors. This ability enables officials to exercise more influence in the policy process.

The critical importance of intergovernmental relations can be seen in the financial and human resources devoted to their conduct. Since the 1960s, the expansion in intergovernmental machinery and in the number and quality of the officials operating this machinery has been striking. The development of administrative structures geared specifically to the management of intergovernmental relations was a response to the growing number of meetings and the desire of governments to coordinate and rationalize the efforts of their departments in various policy fields. There is virtually no policy field in which federal and provincial governments are not engaged in consultation and negotiation. In 1961, the province of Quebec established a Department of Federal-Provincial Relations,[23] and gradually the federal government and other provincial governments developed increasingly sophisticated mechanisms for handling intergovernmental business. In the federal government, the Federal-Provincial Relations Secretariat, which was established in the Privy Council Office (PCO) in 1968, had by 1975 become the Federal-Provincial Relations Office (FPRO), responsible for coordinating federal-provincial relations both within the federal government and between the federal and provincial governments. (Since 1993, these functions have been performed by an Intergovernmental Affairs Branch in the PCO.) In addition, many federal departments developed formal federal-provincial units. All ten provincial governments established intergovernmental units either as separate departments or as part of the premier's office or the cabinet secretariat.

The Enduring Importance of Intergovernmental Machinery

As explained earlier, political, constitutional, and financial pressures have resulted in considerable decentralization of powers to the provinces, especially since the mid-1980s. Continuing movement in this direction in the mid-1990s has taken the form of intergovernmental agreements and of fiscal and administrative arrangements rather than of constitutional change. For example, in 1994, the federal and provincial governments signed the Agreement on Internal Trade (AIT) aimed at reducing barriers to interprovincial trade through a set of generally acceptable rules and standards. In 1996, the federal government announced that it would no longer use its spending power to develop new shared-cost programs in areas of exclusive provincial jurisdiction (e.g., forestry and mining) without the consent of a majority of the provinces.

There has also been an effort to rationalize federal and provincial programs. Through bilateral and multilateral agreements under the 1994 Efficiency of the Federation Initiative, federal and provincial governments have sought to improve administrative efficiency and service to the public. Modest progress has been made in reducing program overlap and duplication and in harmonizing regulations and procedures between the two spheres of government. In addition, an increasing number of mutually beneficial intergovernmental partnerships have been developed at the administrative level to reduce costs and improve efficiency in program delivery. A good example is the federal-Quebec partnership to clean up the St. Lawrence River, to which each government commits resources for their mutual benefit.

On the basis of these and several other developments, Richard Simeon has suggested that a new model of federalism may be emerging. "It is one in which the capacity of Ottawa to shape national policy and influence provincial priorities through use of the spending power is declining; provinces are gaining greater powers, though with fewer resources available to them from Ottawa; and national policies, to the extent that they exist, are developed through *intergovernmental* processes."[24] It is notable that the conduct of these processes is in line with the *executive federalism* approach described earlier. This approach was severely criticized after the failure of the Meech Lake Accord and the Charlottetown Agreement because it involved decision making in closed meetings by ministers and senior public servants, accompanied by a low level of public participation. There is considerable concern that this democratic deficit be reduced by ensuring greater public participation in the processes of intergovernmental decision making.

🏛 INTERPROVINCIAL ADMINISTRATIVE RELATIONS

Interprovincial relations are broadly similar to federal-provincial relations in their organization and participants. Interprovincial interactions occur on both a formal and informal basis; they involve both political executives (premiers and ministers) and public servants, and they cover virtually all provincial policy fields. Most of the intergovernmental bodies created during the formalization of federal-provincial relations are also used to coordinate interprovincial relations.

Provincial political leaders and public servants meet to discuss problems of mutual concern and, when appropriate, to work out joint or common solutions. Among the formal interprovincial mechanisms for collaboration is the Conference of Premiers, which is the provincial version of the First Ministers' Conference. The Premiers' Conference is held annually and is usually attended by all ten premiers and their senior advisors.

Below the level of the premiers, ministers of most provincial departments meet regularly with their counterparts in other provinces not only to exchange information and ideas but also to seek interprovincial coordination. For example, the Canadian Council of Resource and Environment Ministers aims to bring about integrated and comprehensive resource-use planning for social and economic development. Probably the most effective interprovincial interactions for seeking coordination are the meetings of public servants from both the senior administrative and the professional/technical levels of various departments. Aside from the interprovincial meetings, the many federal-provincial meetings provide opportunities for provincial officials to get together informally outside the meeting room. Moreover, many of the same political and bureaucratic officials participate in both types of meeting. These personal contacts are subsequently utilized, via telephone, fax, and letter, to seek interprovincial policy coordination.

There are also important interprovincial meetings organized on a regional basis, notably meetings of the Western Premiers' Conference and the Council of Maritime Premiers. The latter body is composed of the premiers of New

Brunswick, Nova Scotia, and Prince Edward Island and is served by a permanent secretariat. The council was established in 1971 "to promote unity of purpose, ensure maximum coordination of activities and establish the framework for joint actions and undertakings among the three governments."[25]

It is clear that the participation of officials in formal federal-provincial and interprovincial meetings is only the tip of a sizeable iceberg. Below the waterline is a complex network of formal and informal interactions that significantly affect the outcome of intergovernmental negotiations. This network includes interaction between officials and other political actors; among officials in a single department or agency; among officials in different departments and agencies; and among officials in different orders of government.

🏛 MODELS OF INTERGOVERNMENTAL ADMINISTRATIVE INTERACTION

Three distinct, but complementary, models can be used to explain the role and the power of officials in the processes and outcomes of intergovernmental relations in Canada. These are the *cooperation, bargaining,* and *bureaucratic politics* models.

The *cooperation* model refers to intergovernmental relations involving, to a great extent, program specialists from each order of government. Harmonious and productive interaction is facilitated because these program specialists share a body of knowledge and skills and possess a common set of professional attitudes and values relating to their particular policy fields (e.g., welfare officials, foresters).[26] In this model, program specialists are permitted to exercise a large measure of autonomy from control by political and administrative superiors, especially those in intergovernmental relations units, treasury boards, and finance departments. The value of this model for explaining policy development and implementation in certain areas of federal-provincial relations was demonstrated well by the development of the Canada Assistance Plan.[27]

This type of interaction was characteristic of the cooperative federalism period and was more prevalent in the postwar years until the early 1960s than it is now. Gradually during the 1960s and increasingly during the 1970s, the influence of program specialists suffered a relative decline as a result of the growing ascendancy in intergovernmental relations of central agency officials who pursued broader public policy goals than officials from program departments.[28] Donald Smiley anticipated that these central agencies would not develop "the kind of allegiance to common procedures and values which so much facilitates intergovernmental relations among program specialists" because "the concerns of the former relate to fundamental political choices about which consensus is more difficult to establish than in respect to more technical matters."[29]

The reduction in the importance of horizontal relations among program specialists, resulting from the increased influence of central agencies, was accompanied by the creation and growth of new structures and arrangements for the coordination of intergovernmental relations within each government. As a consequence of the institutional centralization of intergovernmental relations under what has been called executive federalism, fewer matters were handled at the lower levels of the governmental pyramid; rather, intergovernmental conflicts gravitated toward the political and senior administrative levels. Since ministers and senior administrators tended not to share values, attitudes, and skills to the same extent as did program specialists, the level of intergovernmental conflict increased. In this milieu, the bargaining model explains the processes and outcomes of intergovernmental relations better than the cooperation model.[30]

The *bargaining* model refers to intergovernmental relations involving primarily ministers and senior administrators from each order of government. Interaction takes the form of a bargaining process in which these ministers and officials present and defend their government's position on specific public policy issues. The focus of attention is on the political resources, strategies, and tactics used by participants in the process. Richard Simeon, on the basis of his study of federal-provincial negotiation over three broad policy issues, concluded that the participants in federal-provincial relations "are not scattered throughout the system in the form of federal cabinet members, members of Parliament, public servants and party leaders; rather they are concentrated and limited largely to provincial Premiers, senior cabinet members, and senior officials on the one hand, and their federal counterparts on the other."[31]

A third model, which complements both the cooperation and bargaining models, is the *bureaucratic politics* model. This model, which has been used most often to study foreign policy, has also been applied to the study of intergovernmental relations in Canada.[32] The model refers to the bargaining over intergovernmental matters among ministers and officials in departments and agencies *within* each order of government. It is *intra*governmental rather than *inter*governmental bargaining that is involved. Despite the use of the term bureaucratic *politics*, the model is concerned with interaction among both ministers and officials.

Richard Schultz and Simon McInnes, in their case studies of federal-provincial negotiations, focus on the impact of *intra*governmental bargaining on *inter*governmental bargaining. Schultz contends that

> the bureaucratic politics model … attempts to answer questions such as why the negotiators adopted the objectives, strategies and tactics they did … Interactions between governments may not … explain, by themselves, the outcomes of intergovernmental negotiations. From the bureaucratic politics perspective, the complex intergovernmental process cannot be separated from the direct relations between governments.[33]

The bureaucratic politics approach suggests that it might be more productive to consider *each* government as a loose coalition of organizations and the negotiating positions of the governments as outcomes of an internal negotiating process.

In the field of intergovernmental relations, governments are often treated as single actors because they usually present a united front in negotiations with other governments. This united front may, however, be a mask that conceals conflict among ministers and officials *within* governments. Neither departments and agencies nor whole governments are homogeneous entities. The process of *intra*governmental bargaining, which is intertwined with that of *inter*governmental bargaining, has been ignored or unduly minimized by many students of Canadian federalism. Intragovernmental bargaining over intergovernmental matters involves both elected and appointed officials, but much of this bargaining takes the form of internal administrative politics. Intragovernmental bargaining occurs not only over the substance of intergovernmental policy but also over the distribution of resources between intergovernmental programs and other government activities.

🏛 THE POWER AND RESPONSIBILITY OF INTERGOVERNMENTAL OFFICIALS

The Power of Intergovernmental Officials

It has been suggested that there has been a politicization of intergovernmental affairs specialists. Politicization refers here to the process by which officials become increasingly involved in politics, either in the partisan sense or in the broader sense of the authoritative allocation of values for society. As explained in Chapter 13, public servants in general have become more politicized as a result of departures from some aspects of the traditional doctrine of political neutrality. The question is whether intergovernmental officials have become politicized and, if so, whether this politicization has taken different forms and emphases from that of other officials.

The overriding objective of intergovernmental relations is the determination of policy. Like other public servants, intergovernmental officials use their knowledge, experience, and discretionary authority to exercise power in the formation and administration of public policy; they engage in consultation and bargaining with other political actors; and their ministers rely heavily on them for advice on complex issues. Thus, in the intergovernmental field, as in other areas of government, the line between the policy contributions of ministers and officials is blurred.

However, the role of intergovernmental officials in the policy process can be distinguished from that of other officials in two significant ways. First, intergovernmental officials cannot exercise control, in the sense of authority, over their counterparts in other governments; rather, they must exercise influence through a process of bargaining. Compared with bargaining with pressure groups, for example, where government officials retain ultimate authority to decide or recommend a course of action, bargaining between governments requires give-and-take among negotiators of roughly equal status.

Second, intergovernmental officials, especially those who participate in formal meetings, enjoy more discretionary power in the bargaining process than most other officials. They are, therefore, more involved in politics in the broad sense than many of their colleagues. In the intergovernmental policy process, usually several governments, and often all eleven governments, are involved in a complicated bargaining process. The outcome of negotiations is frequently a tentative agreement representing a delicate balancing and accommodation of numerous and diverse interests. The Meech Lake Accord and the Charlottetown Agreement are excellent examples. The federal and provincial cabinets, individual ministers, and even legislatures are sometimes reluctant to force a renewal of these intricate negotiations unless they have substantial objections to the agreement worked out by their officials.

Both scholars and practitioners of intergovernmental relations have perceived a tendency among intergovernmental officials to become somewhat more politicized than other public servants. A distinguishing feature of the doctrine of political neutrality is that public servants explain policy and ministers defend it. But in the course of intergovernmental negotiations, the line between explanation and defence becomes blurred. As a result, intergovernmental officials tend to be more involved in politics in the broad sense of that term.

Moreover, some intergovernmental officials occasionally develop an especially intense commitment to the objectives of their own government or their own minister that goes beyond the loyalty expected from public servants. This strong sense of loyalty appears primarily among senior intergovernmental specialists whose working environment is often highly political in the partisan sense, and whose duties require the management of conflict with other governments. They may be motivated both by pressure "not to let the minister down" and by personal commitment to government policies. It is natural for such loyalty and commitment to result from the obligation to continually explain and defend those policies. Vigorous defence by intergovernmental officials of the policies of the government of the day is not usually prompted by partisan support for the governing party, but it does on occasion have that appearance.

The Responsibility of Intergovernmental Officials

In the sphere of intergovernmental relations, it is difficult to pinpoint those who are actually, rather than formally, responsible for government decisions because an important locus of decision making is an intergovernmental body of ministers or officials. There is not space here to examine the broad range of controls and influences that may promote responsible behaviour by intergovernmental officials. Therefore, attention will focus on relations between intergovernmental officials in different jurisdictions and between these officials and cabinet members and legislators.

The increased influence of the provinces in federal-provincial relations rests on several factors, including the constitutional distribution of responsibilities, the relative wealth of a province, and the electoral success of its political leaders. However, a major reason for the growth of provincial power has been the heightened expertise of their intergovernmental officials. The expertise of federal officials, which explained to a large extent the federal government's dominant influence in intergovernmental relations during the 1950s and early 1960s, is now more closely matched by the expertise of their provincial counterparts.

In the intergovernmental policy process, officials exercise significant power, in the sense of influence, over cabinet members and legislators. Gordon

Robertson, former secretary to the cabinet for federal-provincial relations, has asserted that "intergovernmental business in Canada ... is conducted by Cabinet members, notably by First Ministers.... Interministerial conferences are thus an adjunct to executive power, a demonstration of where power actually resides, and the centrepiece of what Donald Smiley has called 'executive federalism.'"[34] This assertion does not take adequate account of the reality that executive federalism involves relations between both ministers *and officials* and that officials exercise significant influence over policy development before, during, and after interministerial conferences. Moreover, as noted earlier, officials exert much policy influence in connection with the very large number of intergovernmental meetings below the ministerial level. This influence arises both from their expertise and from the formal and informal bargaining, often on a multilateral basis, in which they engage on behalf of their ministers.

However, the influence of intergovernmental officials in relation to ministers should not be exaggerated. Cabinet members, both individually and collectively, possess ultimate control over the government's stance on all intergovernmental matters. Officials must be highly sensitive to the desires of the cabinet as a whole, and of individual ministers, in regard to both the substance and strategy of negotiations. Moreover, cabinet members are the central actors in making decisions on major and politically sensitive intergovernmental issues and in much of the negotiation leading to those decisions.

Compared to cabinet members, legislators have little control or influence over intergovernmental activities. Indeed, legislators do not exercise much power over the executive in general or officials in particular in any area of government activity.[35] There is general agreement with the observation that intergovernmental business in Canada "is conducted by governments not by legislatures" and that "this works because a Cabinet in our parliamentary system can normally 'deliver' legislative support on virtually any matter, save possibly in minority situations."[36]

According to the principle of collective ministerial responsibility, the cabinet is responsible to the legislature. Yet there is normally much more discussion of intergovernmental matters in conferences than in the federal Parliament or provincial legislatures. There are few opportunities for legislators to examine intergovernmental policy issues before legislation incorporating agreements reached at conferences is presented to the legislature. Since this legislation is often the outcome of complicated and protracted negotiations among governments, ministers are understandably reluctant to make changes at the legislative stage with which other governments may disagree. Robert Stanfield, former leader of the federal Progressive Conservative party, has noted that "the frustrations of Members of Parliament are increased by federal-provincial deals, agreements and resulting legislation which confront Parliament as faits accomplis."[37] In a comment on Stanfield's remarks, Gordon Gibson, former leader of the Liberal party in British Columbia, said that "federal-provincial agreements are so cast in stone from the time of the agreement that even if the opposition were able to convince the government that amendments should be made it would be too late to change things in any significant respect."[38] It is notable also that the federal Parliament and the provincial legislatures have not developed intergovernmental machinery, e.g., standing committees, to parallel the sophisticated mechanisms established by the executive.

Despite the claims of some journalists and politicians to the contrary, informed observers of the Canadian federal system deny that federal-provincial conferences constitute an additional order of government. There are differences of opinion, however, about the effect of intergovernmental meetings on the accountability of governments to Parliament and the provincial legislatures. Gordon Robertson has stated that "federal-provincial conferences do not in fact reduce the accountability as such of governments to Parliament and to legislatures. Parliament is the locus of responsibility and accountability for our national government but, because of the nature of our system, it is not the public and apparent locus of regional argument and compromise."[39] In a formal sense, this statement is accurate, but the weight of opinion supports Smiley's contention that "to the extent that the actual locus of decision making in respect to an increasing number of public matters has shifted from individual governments to intergovernmental groupings, the effective accountability of executives both to their respective legislatures and to those whom they govern is weakened."[40]

The accountability of intergovernmental officials is a serious concern, but accountability is only one of several values associated with the broad concept of administrative responsibility. Responsible intergovernmental officials must also be concerned with such values as responsiveness and effectiveness. It is important to determine not only whether these officials are accountable to ministers and legislators but also whether they are sensitive to the needs and desires of other political actors and whether they are successful in achieving their government's objectives. Thus, in addition to intergovernmental and intragovernmental conflicts, officials face conflicts between administrative values (e.g., accountability versus responsiveness, or responsiveness versus effectiveness).

Intergovernmental management involves, to a very large extent, the management of conflict and complexity. Alan Cairns has observed that "contemporary intergovernmental coordination is not a simple matter of agreement between a handful of political leaders and their staff advisors. It requires ... the containment of ineradicable tendencies to conflict between the federal vision of a society and economy, and ten competing provincial visions."[41] The key role of intergovernmental officials in seeking to harmonize these diverse perspectives ensures that the management of intergovernmental relations will remain a dominant concern of students and practitioners of Canadian public administration.

NOTES

1. Peter C. Newman, *Maclean's*, 1 October 1979, 3.
2. Adapted from M.J.C. Vile, *The Structure of American Federalism* (London: Oxford University Press, 1961), 199.

3. William H. Stewart, *Concepts of Federalism* (Lanham: University Press of America, 1984).
4. James R. Mallory, "The Five Faces of Federalism," in P.-A. Crépeau and C.B. MacPherson, eds., *The Future of Canadian Federalism* (Toronto: University of Toronto Press, 1965), 3–15. For a different fivefold classification, see Edwin R. Black, *Divided Loyalties: Canadian Concepts of Federalism* (Montreal: McGill-Queen's University Press, 1975).
5. K.C. Wheare, *Federal Government,* 4th ed. (London: Oxford University Press, 1963), 10.
6. Quoted in E. R. Black, *Divided Loyalties,* 43.
7. Donald V. Smiley, "The Rowell-Sirois Report, Provincial Autonomy, and Post-War Canadian Federalism," *Canadian Journal of Economics and Political Science* 28 (February 1962): 54.
8. Garth Stevenson, *Unfulfilled Union,* 3rd ed. (Toronto: Gage, 1989), 224.
9. See, for example, Peter Aucoin and Herman Bakvis, "Regional Responsiveness and Government Organization," in Peter Aucoin, ed., *Regional Responsiveness and the National Administrative State,* Research Study for the Royal Commission on the Economic Union and Development Prospects for Canada, vol. 37 (Toronto: University of Toronto Press, 1985).
10. Donald V. Smiley and Ronald L. Watts, *Intrastate Federalism in Canada,* Research Study for the Royal Commission on the Economic Union and Development Prospects for Canada, vol. 39 (Toronto: University of Toronto Press, 1985), 4.
11. Alan C. Cairns, *From Interstate to Intrastate Federalism in Canada* (Kingston: Queen's University, Institute of Intergovernmental Relations, 1979), 11–12.
12. See Smiley and Watts, *Intrastate Federalism.*
13. For an examination of the value of these suggestions, see Kenneth Kernaghan, "Representative and Responsive Bureaucracy: Implications for Canadian Regionalism," in Aucoin, *Regional Responsiveness.*
14. A good overview of the federal-provincial fiscal relationship is provided in Robin Boadway, *The Constitutional Division of Powers: An Economic Perspective* (Ottawa: Minister of Supply and Services, 1992). See also Paul A.R. Hobson and France St. Hilaire, *Reforming Federal-Provincial Fiscal Arrangements: Towards Sustainable Federalism* (Halifax: Institute for Research on Public Policy, 1994); Peter Leslie, Kenneth Norrie and Irene K. Ip, *A Partnership in Trouble: Renegotiating Fiscal Federalism* (Toronto: C.D. Howe Institute, 1993); and David B. Perry, *Financing the Canadian Federation, 1867–1995: Setting the State for Change* (Ottawa: Canadian Tax Foundation, 1997).
15. A good summary of the provisions of most federal-provincial transfer payment programs is found in Canadian Tax Foundation, *The National Finances* (annual publication of the Canadian Tax Foundation, Toronto).
16. Note that conditional grants and shared-cost programs are not precisely the same thing, but most cost-shared programs are conditional.
17. Thomas J. Courchene, *Refinancing the Canadian Federation: A Survey of the 1977 Fiscal Arrangements Act* (Montreal: C.D. Howe Research Institute, 1979).
18. The details of the equalization formula are given in Canadian Tax Foundation, *The National Finances: 1988–1989* (Toronto: Canadian Tax Foundation, 1990), ch. 16. See also Thomas J. Courchene, *Equalization Payments: Past, Present and Future* (Toronto: Economic Council of Canada, 1984), ch. 2.
19. A general discussion of the rationale for intergovernmental transfers is provided in Robin W. Boadway, *Intergovernmental Transfers in Canada* (Toronto: Canadian Tax Foundation, 1980), ch. 3.
20. For an examination of the evolution of these intergovernmental bodies, see Timothy B. Woolstencroft, *Organizing Intergovernmental Relations* (Kingston, Ont.: Queen's University, Institute of Intergovernmental Relations, 1982); Bruce G. Pollard, *Managing*

the Interface: Intergovernmental Affairs Agencies in Canada (Kingston, Ont.: Queen's University, Institute of Intergovernmental Relations, 1986); and John Warhurst, "Canada's Intergovernmental Relations Specialists," *Australian Journal of Public Administration* 42 (winter 1983): 459–85.

21. This organization is the successor to the Constitutional Conference Secretariat established in 1968.

22. Donald V. Smiley, "An Outsider's Observations of Federal-Provincial Relations Among Consenting Adults," in Richard Simeon, ed., *Intergovernmental Relations in Canada Today* (Toronto: Institute of Public Administration of Canada, 1979), 110.

23. In 1967 this department was renamed the Department of Intergovernmental Affairs. It is notable that for a brief period in 1961, at the end of the Frost era, Ontario had a Department of Economics and Intergovernmental Relations.

24. Richard Simeon, "Rethinking Government, Rethinking Federalism," in Mohamed Charih and Arthur Daniels, eds., *New Public Management and Public Administration in Canada* (Toronto: Institute of Public Administration of Canada, 1997), 81.

25. Council of Maritime Premiers, *Annual Report, 1984–85* (Halifax: Council of Maritime Premiers, 1985), 6.

26. This model is elaborated in Donald V. Smiley, "Public Administration and Canadian Federalism," *Canadian Public Administration* 7 (September 1964): 371–88; and *Constitutional Adaptation and Canadian Federalism Since 1945* (Ottawa: Information Canada, 1970), ch. 7.

27. Rand Dyck, "The Canada Assistance Plan: The Ultimate in Cooperative Federalism," *Canadian Public Administration* 19 (winter 1976): 587–602. Professor Dyck acknowledges some limited relevance for the bargaining model but notes that "the policy development involved in the Canada Assistance Plan can best be understood in terms of Smiley's discussion of shared norms among program administrators" (598).

28. See Simon McInnes, *Federal-Provincial Negotiation: Family Allowances, 1970–1976* (Ottawa: Ph.D. diss., Carleton University, April 1978).

29. Smiley, "Public Administration and Canadian Federalism," 387.

30. For an explanation and application of what we call the bargaining model, see Richard Simeon, *Federal-Provincial Diplomacy: The Making of Recent Policy in Canada* (Toronto: University of Toronto Press, 1972), esp. chs. 2 and 13.

31. Ibid., 38.

32. See Richard Schultz, *Federalism, Bureaucracy and Public Policy* (Montreal: McGill-Queen's University Press, 1980); McInnes, *Federal-Provincial Negotiation;* and Kim Richard Nossal, "Bureaucratic Politics in Canadian Government," *Canadian Public Administration* 22 (winter 1979): 298.

33. Schultz, *Federalism, Bureaucracy and Public Policy,* 434–35.

34. Gordon Robertson, "The Role of Interministerial Conferences in the Decision-Making Process," in Simeon, *Confrontation and Collaboration,* 80.

35. See Kenneth Kernaghan, "Power, Parliament and Public Servants: Ministerial Responsibility Reexamined," *Canadian Public Policy* 5 (summer 1979): 383–96.

36. Robertson, "The Role of Interministerial Conferences," 80.

37. "The Present State of the Legislative Process in Canada: Myths and Realities," in W.A.W. Neilson and J.C. MacPherson, eds., *The Legislative Process in Canada: The Need for Reform* (Toronto: Institute for Research on Public Policy; distributed by Butterworths, 1978), 44.

38. Ibid., 52.

39. Robertson, "The Role of Interministerial Conferences," 83.

40. Smiley, "An Outsider's Observations," 107.

41. Alan Cairns, "The Governments and Societies of Canadian Federalism," *Canadian Journal of Political Science* 10 (December 1977): 722.

BIBLIOGRAPHY

Black, E.R. *Divided Loyalties: Canadian Concepts of Federalism.* Montreal: McGill-Queen's University Press, 1975.

Cairns, Alan. "The Governments and Societies of Canadian Federalism." *Canadian Journal of Political Science* 10 (December 1977): 695–725.

―――. "The Other Crisis of Canadian Federalism." *Canadian Public Administration* 22 (summer 1979): 175–95.

Doerr, Audrey. "Public Administration: Federalism and Intergovernmental Relations." *Canadian Public Administration* 25 (winter 1982): 564–79.

―――. "Building New Orders of Government: The Future of Aboriginal Self-Government." *Canadian Public Administration* 40 (summer 1997): 274–89.

Dyck, R. "The Canada Assistance Plan: The Ultimate in Cooperative Federalism." *Canadian Public Administration* 19 (winter 1976): 587–602.

Elton, David, and Peter McCormick. "The Alberta Case: Intergovernmental Relations." In Jacques Bourgault, Maurice Demers, and Cynthia Williams, eds., *Public Administration and Public Management: Canadian Experiences.* Quebec: Les Publications du Québec, 1997, 209–18.

Hobson, Paul A.R., and France St. Hilaire. *Reforming Federal-Provincial Fiscal Arrangements: Towards Sustainable Federalism.* Halifax: Institute for Research on Public Policy, 1994.

Hurley, James Ross. "Executive Federalism." In Jacques Bourgault, Maurice Demers, and Cynthia Williams, eds., *Public Administration and Public Management,* 113–23.

Kernaghan, Kenneth. "Representative and Responsive Bureaucracy: Implications for Canadian Regionalism." In Peter Aucoin, ed., *Regional Responsiveness and the National Administrative State.* Research study for the Royal Commission on the Economic Union and Development Prospects for Canada, vol. 37. Toronto: University of Toronto Press, 1985, 1–50.

Leslie, Peter, et al. *A Partnership in Trouble: Renegotiating Fiscal Federalism.* Toronto: C.D. Howe Institute, 1993.

Lindquist, Evert A. "Recent Administrative Reform in Canada as Decentralization: Who Is Spreading What Around to Whom and Why?" *Canadian Public Administration* 37 (fall 1994): 416-30.

Phillips, Susan D. "The Canada Health and Social Transfer." In Douglas Brown and J. Rose, eds., *Canada: The State of the Federation.* Kingston, Ont.: Queen's University, Institute of Intergovernmental Relations, 1995, 65–95.

Simeon, Richard. "Rethinking Government, Rethinking Federalism." In Mohamed Charih and Arthur Daniels, eds., *New Public Management and Public Administration in Canada.* Toronto: Institute of Public Administration of Canada, 1997, 69–91.

Smiley, Donald V., and Ronald L. Watts. *Intrastate Federalism in Canada.* Research study for the Royal Commission on the Economic Union and Development Prospects for Canada, vol. 39. Toronto: University of Toronto Press, 1985.

Woolstencroft, Timothy B. *Organizing Intergovernmental Relations.* Kingston Ont.: Queen's University, Institute of Intergovernmental Relations, 1982.

20

Pressure Groups, Political Parties, and the Bureaucracy

The subject of the meeting was Hepatitis C, the potentially fatal liver disease. Jeremy Beaty, head of the Hepatitis C Society of Canada, met in January 1997 with the Minister of Health, David Dingwall, to lobby for compensation for people who had contracted the Hepatitis C virus (HCV) from tainted blood provided by the Red Cross. Documents obtained by the *Ottawa Citizen* under the Access to Information Act contained briefing notes that seemed to have been prepared for the minister by his departmental officials. In these notes, the minister was warned that Mr. Beaty might "use the term 'compensation' which Health Canada avoids due to its tendency to be associated with liability/legal obligations."[1] The notes acknowledged that if Canada had used an available surrogate test, "some, but not all, transfusion-related HCV infection" would have been prevented. The notes recommended that the minister stick with the 1995 position worked out with the provinces, which held that giving compensation to HIV-infected victims of the blood system was an "extraordinary situation" and the government was "at this time" not considering similar assistance for those with "Hep C."

In April 1998, Allan Rock, the new federal Health Minister, announced that compensation would be given to those Hep C victims infected between 1986 and 1990. Soon after, a group of Hep C victims demonstrated on Parliament Hill to lobby for compensation for all victims. Then Ontario and Quebec announced that they would, if necessary, find money in their own coffers to compensate those victims falling outside the federal coverage. A furious federal-provincial controversy erupted and pressure mounted throughout the country to compensate all victims. Mr. Beaty lobbied both levels of government, in part through the news media, and was supported by other pressure groups, including the Canadian Hemophilia Association.

How influential are such pressure groups? Are some more influential than others and, if so, why? What targets do they aim at and what tactics do they use? How do they interact with public servants? Why do we need pressure groups when we have political parties? These are some of the questions that are answered in this chapter.

🏛 PRESSURE GROUPS AND GOVERNMENT LOBBYING

Definition and Classification

Pressure groups (or interest groups)[2] are organizations composed of persons who have joined together to further their mutual interest by influencing public policy. These groups do not have hierarchical or legal authority over government officials. They do, however, exercise *influence* over both the development and the implementation of public policy. Their efforts are commonly described as *lobbying*. To many Canadians, this term has unsavoury connotations of illegal, immoral, or inappropriate means of influencing government decision makers.[3] This perception has its origins in 19th-century United States, when "lobbyists" would frequent the lobbies and corridors of legislative buildings to influence legislators, sometimes with offers of bribes. It is important to emphasize, however, that lobbying is now a legitimate means of attempting to influence government decisions through individual or collective action.

Every policy field and every policy issue attracts the attention of one or more pressure groups. These groups are, therefore, numerous and pervasive in the political system. They include business, labour, agricultural, professional, social welfare, and public interest organizations. Examples of each of these types of organization are the Canadian Manufacturers' Association, the Canadian Labour Congress, the Canadian Federation of Agriculture, the Canadian Bar Association, the Canadian Council on Social Development, and the Canadian Arctic Resources Committee.

Lobbying is not confined to formally established pressure groups; such organizations as corporations and churches also lobby government. Moreover, lobbying is conducted not just by pressure group executives but by professional lobbyists, lawyers, legislators (notably senators), and individual citizens. Lobbying by business people, for example, involves the public affairs departments of business firms, permanent staff members located in Ottawa, trade associations, public affairs consulting companies (which publish newsletters and assist clients to approach the appropriate government officials), and one-on-one contacts between senior business executives and public officials.

While lobbying is a legitimate activity, it is regulated by government for reasons of fairness and transparency. The prominence of pressure groups in the public policy process and, in particular, the activities of professional lobbyists, who lobby government on behalf of third parties, has raised public concern about undue pressure group influence. This concern was exacerbated in the mid-1980s by the activities of professional lobbyists, especially former politicians, who utilized their friends and contacts within government to influence decisions to their clients' advantage. Widespread criticism of this practice was a major factor leading to the enactment of the Lobbyists Registration Act, discussed later in this chapter. In 1997, there were about 2500 *registered* lobbyists in Ottawa, but there are thousands of other lobbyists whose activities do not require registration under the act.

Pressure groups have been classified into a variety of types according to such criteria as their objectives, activities, and structure, but a broad distinction can be made between *institutional* groups and *issue-oriented* groups.[4]

Institutional groups are characterized by organizational continuity and cohesion. They are highly knowledgeable about the policy-making process and about how to get access to public officials, in part because they usually employ a professional staff; their membership is stable; they have concrete and immediate operational objectives, but their ultimate aims are sufficiently broad that they can bargain with government over achieving particular concessions; and their long-term credibility with government decision makers is more important than any single issue or objective. Examples of institutional groups are the Canadian Medical Association and the Canadian Chamber of Commerce.

Issue-oriented groups, however, tend to be less organized and to have less knowledge of government and of how to contact public officials; there is a constant turnover in their membership; they usually focus on only one or two issues; and they are not usually concerned about their long-term credibility with public officials. Examples of issue-oriented groups are those concerned about a particular threat to the environment and those opposed to specific projects of developers. Recently, however, the policy influence of certain issue-oriented groups has increased greatly as they have learned to use the fax, the Internet, and access to the media and outside expertise. A good example is the lobby that operated in the late 1990s, largely on the Internet, to oppose the proposed Multi-Lateral Agreement on Investment.

In reality, virtually all pressure groups fall on a continuum between these two extremes and can be discussed in terms of the extent to which they possess the characteristics of one type or the other. Some issue groups (e.g., Greenpeace) have gradually moved along this continuum toward the institutional pole.

Another distinction is often made between *special interest* groups and *public interest* groups. The vast majority of pressure groups fall into the special interest category on the grounds that they are primarily motivated by particular interests that affect their members directly (e.g., the British Columbia Home Owners' Association or the Canadian Council of Furniture Manufacturers). Public interest groups, by way of contrast, are said to be concerned with the broader, more general interests of the public (e.g., the Consumers Association of Canada, the Canadian Arctic Resources Committee). As in the case of institutional and issue-oriented groups, special interest and public interest groups can best be depicted on a continuum because most groups are motivated by a mixture of self-interest and public interest.[5] For tactical reasons, all groups tend to emphasize the extent to which their activities serve the public interest. It is notable that over the past decade, governments have gradually reduced funding for many public interest groups (for example, the National Action Committee on the Status of Women) with the result that the lobbying activities—and the influence—of these groups have been reduced.[6]

Some pressure groups have been established solely for the purpose of lobbying government, whereas for others lobbying is an incidental part of their activities. Relatively few groups have been organized solely to lobby government; most groups perform such other functions as exchanging information among their members and representing their members to the public.

Advisory Councils and Think Tanks

Advisory councils and think tanks are not normally described as pressure groups, but they do play an advocacy role by trying to influence public policy decisions.

Advisory councils are organizations composed of private citizens that are created by the government, outside of the normal bureaucracy. They provide an independent source of advice to a minister, free of any potential laundering by the public service. Representatives of particular pressure groups are sometimes asked to serve as council members. Appointment to such bodies as the National Advisory Council on Aging or the Nova Scotia Advisory Council on the Status of Women gives pressure group members an opportunity to advance their group's interests.

Advisory councils are in a difficult position because they receive most of their funding from government; they must tread a middle course so that they retain credibility with the government while avoiding being captured by it. They must also be skillful in balancing the interests of their constituents so that they are not captured by any one group. There is often disagreement among these constituents as to whether the best way to maximize their influence on government is to use friendly persuasion or to "go public" in order to bring about overt pressure. There has been a trend in recent years for governments to abolish advisory councils, including such high-profile ones as the Economic Council of Canada and the Science Council of Canada. The limited constituency of these councils and the fact that they do not deliver services directly make them easy targets in budget-cutting exercises.

Think tanks (often call policy institutes) are nonprofit organizations outside of government that are primarily involved in producing research and holding conferences and workshops designed to inform or to influence public policy, or both. Unlike advisory councils, they do not receive direct government funding and are, therefore, more independent.

Think tanks vary considerably in their size, activities, and influence.[7] They include, for example, the Canadian Institute for Economic Policy, which focuses almost exclusively on producing research; the Public Policy Forum, which publishes reports based on roundtable discussions as part of its effort to improve policy making by fostering business-government collaboration; the Fraser Institute, which, through such means as publications and symposia, applies market principles to public policy problems; the Canadian Centre for Policy Alternatives, which applies social-democratic principles in research papers directed to unions and other social organizations; and the Conference Board, which is a large, well-financed organization that produces research and holds conferences on a wide range of public policy issues.

Some academic studies of think tanks are critical of the quality of their research[8] and of their claimed influence. Evert Lindquist concludes that "when it actually comes to designing and implementing policy, and accounting for the concomitant technical and political complexities, institute expertise does not rival that of state bureaucracies." Moreover, think tank leaders have a difficult job because they have to show their members and outsiders that they exercise influence "when, in fact, they rarely do."[9] However, Herman Bakvis contends that think tanks can have considerable influence, especially on agenda setting. "By clever packaging and marketing, relatively mundane analysis can have a disproportionate impact" ... and "think tanks have in many respects pre-empted the political parties in setting the political agenda, at least certainly in between elections."[10]

Functions of Pressure Groups[11]

Communication

Given that the overriding objective of pressure groups is to influence the development and execution of public policies, it is not surprising that their main function is two-way communication between their members and public officials. The *content* of this communication ranges from detailed, technical data on existing or proposed policies, programs, and regulations to irate demands for government action on particular issues (e.g, environmental pollution). The *form* of the communication depends to some extent on its content, but it is determined also by the *type* of pressure group. Institutional groups tend to benefit more than issue-oriented groups from the fact that government–pressure group relations involve a two-way flow of communication and influence. Public officials rely, sometimes very heavily, on the expertise and experience of pressure groups for information on the efficacy of existing policies and on the implications of new proposals. Institutional-type groups, in large part because of the information they are able to provide governments, have greater access to government officials, especially to cabinet ministers and senior public servants.

Public servants and, to a lesser extent, cabinet ministers also utilize pressure group contacts to communicate with the groups' members. Many pressure groups regularly pass along to their members, through newsletters and other internal means of communication, information about government policies and programs. This practice is mutually beneficial in that the groups provide a service to their members and the public servants get their message to the groups' membership.

Legitimation

The communication function of pressure groups is closely related to another important function they perform in the political system—legitimation. Through consultation with pressure groups whose members will be affected by proposed policies, government officials can assess the probable effects of adopting these policies and can seek support for them. Such consultation gives these policies a measure of legitimacy in that groups representing those likely to be affected by the policies have had their views heard and ostensibly taken into account by government decision makers. Certainly, government officials are well advised to consult any group whose opposition to policies could weaken the legitimacy of the policies in the eyes of the public.

Thus, public servants routinely consult certain pressure groups in the development and implementation of policies. Indeed, in a major survey of pressure group behaviour, Robert Presthus found that 50 percent of federal public servants and 68 percent of provincial public servants in Canada described their departments' relations with lobbyists as either "almost an integral part of our day-to-day activity" or "usually taken into account during policy making."[12] The importance of the legitimation function is evident in the efforts of public servants to promote the creation and maintenance of particular pressure groups. Presthus reported that 45 percent of federal public servants and 50 percent of provincial public servants answered yes to the question: "Has your own or any other Department ever created an interest group in order to facilitate the implementation of a policy or program?"[13] This activity ensures a complementary source of outside knowledge and experience; it also serves the legitimation function by ensuring outside support for the government's policies, facilitating group input into the policy process that might not otherwise take place, and promoting the representation of disadvantaged groups. For example, a former senior public servant has acknowledged bureaucratic initiatives in "presenting for ministerial approval measures designed to assist members of disadvantaged sectors of society in forming groups and organizations and otherwise gaining some power in matters affecting their social and economic needs."[14]

Regulation and Administration

Pressure groups often assist governments by regulating their members and administering programs. For example, the governing bodies of the legal, medical, and accounting professions regulate their members by such means as restricting entry to the profession and imposing penalties for unethical behaviour. Pressure groups also conduct research and collect information that assists government's regulatory and legislative activities. For example, the Canadian Home Builders' Association does research on energy efficiency and the National Cancer Institute channels government and private funds to medical research.

Targets of Pressure Group Activity

It is critical to the success of pressure groups that, in their interactions with government, they identify and aim at the right targets. They must decide first whether to direct their efforts to the federal, provincial, or local spheres of government—or to all of them.[15] The federal nature of Canada has important effects on the organization and operations of pressure groups. Many Canadian pressure groups are federations, i.e., they are composed of provincial bodies that lobby provincial governments and a national organization that focuses its efforts on Ottawa. Many other groups are not large enough to have provincial components or affiliates of a national organization and are therefore obliged to channel their limited resources to those governments where the resources will do the most good. Another impact of federalism on pressure group activity is that, in order to be effective on issues that involve more than one level of government, groups may be required to lobby federal, provincial, and local governments simultaneously.

Whether pressure groups lobby federal or provincial governments, the usual targets of their activity are cabinet ministers, public servants, and legislators, all of whom play important roles in the public policy process. This process may be divided into pre-legislative, legislative, and post-legislative stages. Public servants are especially powerful in the post-legislative stage through their implementation of policy decisions.

As a result of their policy advisory responsibilities and the sheer volume of decisions they make, public servants are the most frequent targets of pressure group activity. Canadian public servants are a more common focus of attention by pressure group leaders than either cabinet ministers and legislators in Canada or public servants in the United States. Moreover, close observers of the Canadian political scene have attested to the prominent role of public servants in government–pressure group interaction:

> ... the greatest leverage lies not with the politicians but with the bureaucrats.[16]

> ... civil servants are obviously of key importance and they are a target group that most successful interest groups understand has to be dealt with.[17]

> Any lobbyist ... will tell you that the real levers of power lie with the bureaucracy, among the mandarins whose own concerns and perceptions are the main source of policy.[18]

Most policy initiatives originate in the public service. Thus, it is important for pressure groups to influence a policy before it becomes enshrined in a cabinet memorandum, which is very difficult to change. It makes sense for pressure groups to lobby at the level(s) of the public service where a decision or recommendation affecting their interests can be made. Thus, lobbying will often be aimed at professional and technical personnel rather than at senior executives and managers.

> [M]ost new ideas begin deep in the civil service machine. The man in charge of some special office ... writes a memo suggesting a new policy on this or that. It works its way slowly up and up. At that stage civil servants are delighted ... to talk quietly to people like us, people representing this or that corporation or industry directly involved. This is the time to slip in good ideas.
>
> *Source: Quoted in Clive Baxter, "Familiars in the Corridors of Power"[19]*

Lobbyists are frequently advised to "leave no stone unturned" in their efforts to influence those government officials who can help them achieve their objectives. An Ottawa lobbyist has advised that "the effective lobbyist will maintain contact with the project as it goes up through the department, making sure he or she talks to every rung on the ladder. If you forget to talk to someone, he or she may be offended, and may influence the policy to your detriment."[20] Pressure groups must, however, choose their targets carefully so as not to spread their limited resources too thinly, thereby having little influence anywhere.

The power of public servants does not, of course, give them the final say on major public policy issues; that authority belongs to cabinet ministers. Therefore, pressure groups are frequently obliged to lobby ministers to influence both the decisions of individual departments and those of cabinet committees and cabinet as a whole. Moreover, ministers are often the ultimate target of lobbying aimed at public servants and legislators by pressure groups striving to influence those who can influence ministers. Cabinet ministers have enormous power in all three stages of the policy process—if they decide to exercise that power. In practice, they have neither the time nor the inclination to participate actively in the post-legislative stage; rather, they tend to leave policy implementation to the public servants.

Thus, it is tempting for group representatives to aim their *initial* lobbying efforts at cabinet ministers. But, since ministers are busy people, it is usually inadvisable to approach them before other appropriate avenues of influence have been exhausted. It makes little sense to expend a minister's time and goodwill when a public servant or a legislator will serve as well or even better. Admittedly, if a group gets cabinet approval for a proposal, it has won its case. However, if a group loses at cabinet level, there is no higher body with which it can lodge an appeal. Moreover, access to ministers is generally harder to obtain than to public servants and legislators. For reasons outlined earlier, institutional-type pressure groups tend to receive readier access to ministers than do other pressure groups. Ministers, like public servants, need contacts with experienced, knowledgeable, and influential groups not only to assess better the merits and costs of policy proposals but also to increase political support for their own departments or for the government as a whole. They also use pressure groups as an alternative source of information and advice to that provided by the public service. A former cabinet minister has asserted that "deputy ministers and their supporting policy advisors have no particular monopoly on wisdom and they can as easily become victims of myopia or tunnel vision as anyone else."[21]

It has already been noted that, compared with cabinet ministers and public servants, legislators and legislative committees are a secondary target of pressure group activity. Nevertheless, legislative support for pressure groups can be extremely important, especially on issues of widespread public concern, and can complement a group's efforts to influence officials in the executive-bureaucratic arena. Government backbenchers have opportunities to influence government decisions in party caucus meetings and in formal and informal meetings with ministers and public servants. Opposition members are anxious to receive representations from pressure groups so as to understand better the groups' problems and to obtain ammunition to be used against the government. If individual legislators and legislative committees had more influence on the formulation and implementation of public policy, pressure groups could usefully spend more time and effort trying to influence public policy during the legislative stage of the policy process.

After identifying and selecting their targets from among ministers, public servants, and legislators, pressure groups must focus on more specific targets, i.e., on the most appropriate minister(s), department(s), legislator(s), and legislative committee(s). Pressure groups must know whom to lobby and, as we shall see, what tactics will best ensure success. Above all, groups must gain access to government decision makers; otherwise they are obliged to influence public policy indirectly by influencing the news media and public opinion. This latter method of persuasion can be effective, but in general it is less successful, especially over time.

Recognition of Pressure Groups

Pressure group access to public officials, particularly to public servants, depends largely on the extent to which the group has earned official recognition, i.e., on the extent to which officials perceive the group as useful, credible, and legitimate.

> One of the major prizes in the struggle between competing interest groups ... is tangible *recognition* by government of the status and representative capacity claimed by interest group leaders for their respective organizations. Such recognition is conferred when government canvasses interest group leaders for nomination to official bodies and when government calls a group's leader into consultation on legislative or administrative matters.[22]

Recognition facilitates both access and influence for pressure groups. Those groups regularly consulted by government have an early-warning system that alerts them to governmental initiatives affecting their interests. Therefore, they are in a better position than other groups to anticipate or react to these initiatives. Once groups have achieved this level of recognition, they are wise to ensure that they preserve it by cultivating their contacts in government and continuing to do whatever brought them recognition in the first place.

What are the bases of recognition? The first basis is the *expertise* and *experience* that pressure groups can provide government officials. Public servants naturally tend to consult and to grant readier access to those groups on whom they can rely for accurate data required for informed policy making. A former cabinet minister has attributed the success of an especially effective pressure group to the fact that "their information is as good as the government's.... They do not appear before the executive or ... agencies of government with half-baked information."[23]

Certain pressure groups gain and maintain recognition more easily than others because they constitute the *sole clientele*, or a large part of the clientele, of a specific department (e.g., farmers' organizations vis-à-vis a department of agriculture, or labour organizations vis-à-vis a department of labour). This clientele relationship involves reciprocal costs and benefits. A department can rely on a clientele group as a source of information and as a channel of communication to the group's members. It can also use the group to gain support for its policies from other departments and, indeed, from the general public by claiming to speak for the interests of the major group affected by the department's policies. To do this, the department must maintain good relations with the group and take special pains to avoid open conflict with it. Similarly, the group can benefit in the way of access and influence by receiving such departmental recognition. But if a group is tied too closely to a single department, it may have nowhere else to go, with the result that the department may be able to influence its activities unduly. So far as possible, therefore, a group will usually cultivate support in other departments so that all of its lobbying "eggs" are not in a single basket.

Another important basis of pressure group recognition is the group's *political clout*. Ministers, legislators, and public servants are interested in the political impact pressure group activity can have on the next election. While public servants are expected to be nonpartisan, they are at the same time expected to be politically sensitive. They should be able to advise the minister as to the likely effects of proposed policies on various segments of society, including those represented by influential pressure groups. Thus, public servants should strive to be aware of the possible effects of government decisions on the voting behaviour of a pressure group's membership. Moreover, public servants need to know the likely implications of policy proposals on the bureaucratic or organizational politics within the government itself. A former cabinet minister has stated that "most civil servants are professionally disposed to push or recommend policy that is likely to achieve political support both at the cabinet level and within the public service."[24] Thus, public servants are more likely to grant official recognition to groups that have the resources to influence the political fortunes of their minister or of the government as a whole. Moreover, they will be more favourably disposed toward groups that can help them help the minister.

A final notable source of recognition is the use by pressure groups of lobbying tactics that are approved by, or at least acceptable to, government decision makers.

Pressure Group Tactics

Before deciding on the tactics to be employed, effective pressure groups take special pains to identify the appropriate targets of their lobbying activities (e.g., federal, provincial, and local governments; ministers, public servants, and legislators). They then progressively focus on the organizations and individuals within government most likely to be of assistance to them. It is evident that groups require up-to-date and accurate knowledge of the machinery of government to find their way through the labyrinth to the correct targets. Once this has been done, lobbying tactics can be geared to the needs and biases of these targets.

Ideally, an excellent tactic for pressure groups is to lobby all those government officials who can influence or actually make a decision affecting their interests. Realistically, however, most groups are obliged to utilize their limited financial and staff resources to lobby carefully selected officials. It is important, therefore, that groups lobby at the most appropriate level of the governmental hierarchy. Effective lobbying, in both the short and the long run, requires that groups provide officials with well-researched and relevant data. Thus, once access has been granted, pressure groups must ensure that their arguments are based on thorough homework so as to enhance their success in influencing a specific policy, as well as to increase their long-run credibility and legitimacy.

Groups are also well advised to attempt to influence policy at the earliest possible stage of its development and to follow the progress of that policy all the way through the policy-making process, including the post-legislative or implementation stage. "Any organization seeking to influence public policy must be prepared to come back again and again at whatever level of government is dealing with an issue. In other words, the group must have tenacity."[25] Groups can perform this task more successfully if their contacts with government officials are sufficiently cordial and continuous to allow them to anticipate or learn quickly about policy initiatives. Thus, once again, a group's tactics are determined significantly by the extent of its recognition.

In general, pressure groups seek to influence public officials, especially public servants, through quiet, behind-the-scenes consultations rather than through media campaigns and public demonstrations designed to influence decision makers indirectly. Institutional-type pressure groups are more likely to use the former tactic because they are interested in influencing government decisions on a number of issues over a period of time, whereas issue-oriented groups tend to focus on a single problem or to have fewer of the resources that encourage government officials to grant them recognition and access. In the face of limited opportunities to make their case directly to public officials, they hope to influence public policy indirectly by mobilizing public support for their cause through the news media and even public demonstrations. Institutional groups are more likely to absorb defeat on a particular issue without "going public" because they know that there are other battles to be fought and that using public and media campaigns to win their point is unlikely to be to their long-run advantage. They are inclined to minimize publicity and to avoid the adversarial approach. The head of the Grocery Products Manufacturers Association has stated that "we're not prepared to go on Parliament Hill and slaughter a pig to have our representations heard—unless we're absolutely forced to."[26] The president of the Retail Council of Canada has observed that "the marshalling of public support through the media is sometimes the right recipe for tackling a particular issue, but not often. Only the most simplistic of issues is likely to be well understood by the public."[27] Pressure groups need to remember that official recognition is hard to win but relatively easy to lose. This consideration significantly determines the tactics used by many groups.

The discreet approach to lobbying is more acceptable to public servants because they want to keep their minister out of trouble and keep themselves out of the public spotlight. Neither they nor the department as a whole wish to be the object of public attack as this is likely to affect detrimentally their own, and possibly their minister's, career prospects. Moreover, when government officials and group representatives meet in private and in confidence, where they are removed from the immediate pressure of public and media opinion, it is easier for them to work out an accommodation of their differences.

Certainly, some pressure groups, especially those of the issue-oriented variety, have had great impact on specific policy decisions by mobilizing public opinion. It is also possible for groups to influence decisions without enjoying much in the way of access based on official recognition and without going to the media or the public. This usually will require the pushing of several pressure points at the same time (i.e., ministers, public servants, and legislators). On some occasions, even institutional groups resort to media campaigns or join with issue groups to pressure the government. However, these are exceptional situations; the aim of most groups, including those concerned about a single issue of lasting importance, is to use those tactics most likely to achieve their objectives while preserving or enhancing their official recognition. Representatives of well-recognized pressure groups are more likely than others to be invited to become members of the advisory councils mentioned earlier, which advise ministers on policy.

Well-recognized groups tend to adhere to the "rules of the game" for government–pressure group relations. These rules are not spelled out in any document; rather, they are composed of understandings based on experience as to what kind of behaviour is expected on both sides. With respect to bureaucracy-group relations, perhaps the most important of these informal rules is that private exchanges of information and opinion are to be kept confidential. Public servants do not expect the content of private discussions with group representatives to be reported publicly or used as a basis for criticism of themselves or their department in other parts of the government. Similarly, pressure groups do not expect that the substance of their submissions to government will be shared with competing pressure groups or, without their consent, with other interested parties in the policy process.

Both common sense and the present nature of the policy process suggest that pressure group representations to government should, where feasible, be framed in terms of the public interest. The requests of pressure groups are more likely to be met if they are attuned to the priorities and plans of the government than if they amount to blatant, self-interested pleading. For example, in a time of high inflation and high unemployment, officials are likely to look favourably on proposals that may reduce these. Similarly, proposals that require the expenditure of substantial public funds during a time of severe economic restraint are unlikely to receive a sympathetic hearing. In short, pressure groups can advance their own interests by demonstrating that these interests enhance, or at least complement, the broader public interest. One lobbyist has observed that lobbying

> has evolved into a straightforward process of doing your homework. And the more you know, the more professional your approach to government, the more balanced your presentation, the more willing you are to look beyond your own interests and take the good of the country into account …, the more open government becomes to what you have to say and the more often it solicits direct input when formulating new policy or making changes to current legislation.[28]

One effective and frequently used tactic to demonstrate the public interest—or at least a broad interest—in a group's submission is cooperative lobbying. This requires groups to create formal or informal alliances with other groups who share their views on a particular policy issue. Cooperative lobbying enables several groups to present a united front to government as an indication of widespread concern. At the same time, the groups profit from this cooperative arrangement by sharing information and contacts. Even competing pressure groups may benefit from consultation with one another because they can learn the content and strength of their opponents' arguments, even if they cannot work out a common position to present to government. But the lobbyists "will be better received if they have reached an accommodation with the other interested protagonists—be they labour, other industries, consumers, etc."[29]

As explained in Chapter 6, pressure groups can be influential players in *policy communities* (that is, clusters of interested parties such as other governments, journalists, and individual citizens organized around a particular policy) and in *policy networks* (the interconnections among the various parties). The extent to which a pressure group will play a central role in a policy community will depend on the importance it attaches to the issue at hand and its influence in the community relative to the other parties.

Pressure groups must be knowledgeable about the policy process in general and about the organization and operations of the specific departments and agencies they wish to influence. Groups must be especially vigilant in keeping up to date on changes in structures and processes in both the executive-bureaucratic and the legislative spheres of government.[30] Such changes often signal shifts in the distribution of power within government and can therefore significantly affect the appropriate targets and tactics of pressure group activity.

The Lobbyists Registration Act

This act, passed in 1985 and amended in 1995,[31] requires the registration of all persons who are paid to communicate with politicians and public servants in an effort to influence policies, programs, legislation, regulations, grants, or other financial benefits.[32] A major impetus for the act was the undue influence perceived to be exercised by retired politicians and public servants during the mid-1980s. The problem has been aggravated more recently by staff cutbacks leading former public servants to join or form lobby groups.

The purpose of the act is to make the lobbying process better understood and more transparent by identifying the lobbyists and the issues on which they are lobbying. The act divides lobbyists into three categories. *Consultant lobbyists* are paid to lobby on behalf of a client; they include government relations consultants, lawyers, and accountants. *In-house lobbyists (corporate)* are employees of corporations engaged in commercial activities for financial gain and for whom lobbying is a substantial part of their duties. The senior paid officer of an organization is required to register as an *in-house lobbyist (organizations)* if one or more employees is involved in lobbying and the lobbying of all such employees would make up a substantial portion of the duties of one employee. All lobbyists must provide such information as the name of their client, the subject-matter of the lobbying, the names of the departments contacted, the amount and source of any government funding, and the communications techniques adopted (e.g. grassroots lobbying).

In addition, a Lobbyists' Code of Conduct, administered by the Office of the Ethics Counsellor, came into effect on March 1, 1997. Its purpose "is to assure the Canadian public that lobbying is done ethically and with the highest standards with a view to conserving and enhancing public confidence and trust in the integrity, objectivity and impartiality of government decision-making."[33] The Office of the Ethics Counsellor is responsible for providing advice on, and ensuring compliance with, the code's requirements.

🏛 POLITICAL PARTIES AND IDEOLOGIES

Public administration scholars have paid little attention to the interaction between political parties and the public service. The functions of political parties are usually described as interest aggregation and articulation, the recruitment and training of political leaders, and the education and socialization of the public on political matters; control or influence over the public service is rarely mentioned. In brief, political parties are organizations that seek to get their members elected to political office and to gain and maintain control of the government. They pursue this objective both inside and outside government. The internal and external components of a political party are often referred to as the parliamentary and the extraparliamentary party. Earlier chapters discussed relations between the public service and the parliamentary party, i.e., the parties' elected members in the legislature and in party caucus. The brief treatment of political parties provided here is concerned with the impact on the public service of the extraparliamentary parties, i.e., the parties' national and provincial executives and offices and the constituency associations.

Political parties, whether acting through an executive elected by party members or through party meetings and conventions, are generally perceived to be remote from the operations of the public service. The influence of political parties on bureaucratic decisions and recommendations tends to be indirect and often intangible. However, this influence is greater than is popularly perceived.

There are two general types of interaction between political parties and public servants. The first involves the public servant as citizen; the second involves the public servant as government employee.

The most direct contacts between public servants and political parties take the form of public servants' participation in the activities of political parties. As noted in Chapter 13, restrictions have been placed on the partisan political activities of public servants so as to preserve their political neutrality. Within the bounds of these restrictions, public servants do seek nomination and election to public office and provide various forms of support for individual candidates and political parties. The right of public servants to participate in partisan political activities has gradually been extended over the past thirty years, and there are strong pressures for further relaxation of the constraints on such activities. Through the limited opportunities to contribute directly to political parties, public servants can have some direct influence on the policy positions adopted by parties, but their participation is usually circumspect. The most senior public servants and those in sensitive positions are usually excluded, or deliberately exclude themselves, from any kind of partisan political activity. As noted in Chapter 13, however, some senior public servants are political appointees, i.e., they are appointed by the governing party because they have been involved in partisan politics.

The influence of the extraparliamentary wing of political parties on the public servant as government employee is indirect and difficult to assess. This influence is exercised in the form of policies, proposals, and promises that have implications for the public service as a whole or particular parts of it, and that are made during party meetings, leadership conventions, and election campaigns. Political candidates and political parties, especially if they are in Opposition, frequently join in the bureaucrat bashing that generally falls on such fertile ground among the electorate. Charges of inefficient, ineffective, and unresponsive bureaucratic behaviour are usually accompanied by promises of cutbacks in the number of public servants and in the amount of money they spend. It is understandable that political parties that have been in Opposition for a long time should become antagonistic toward the public service and view some public servants as being too close to the governing party. This leads to threats that many senior public servants will be turfed out with a change in government, and to unhappiness among many of the party faithful when these threats are not carried out.

Aside from attacks on the general performance of the public service, political parties and their leaders adopt party platforms that have implications for public servants working in particular policy fields, which can range from broad promises to reduce expenditure on social policy to specific promises to abolish certain programs or agencies. While experience has shown that once in office, political leaders often deviate substantially from their party's platform, policies set by political parties can be very influential, especially through the publicity received in the news media.

There are often significant differences among political parties in the ways they view the public service. In the federal sphere, for example, the Reform party and, to a lesser extent, the Progressive Conservative party are more likely than the Liberal party to lament the size and expenditures of government and to propose such solutions as privatization of Crown corporations and deregulation. The New Democratic Party, which favours policies likely to require a larger governmental apparatus and which is affiliated with the trade-union movement, generally avoids broad attacks on the public service and gives greater support than other parties to collective bargaining in the public sector.

It is difficult for public servants to separate completely their role as citizen or voter from that of government employee and it is, therefore, reasonable to assume that sympathy for a political party will carry over into decisions or recommendations on the job. Equally problematic is assessing the effect of the ideological commitments of public servants. These commitments need not be manifested by a formal or emotional attachment to a particular political party; the public servant who is politically neutral in the partisan sense still has ample opportunity to inject personal ideological preferences into the policy-making process. These preferences will obviously affect the public servant's views on major policy issues involving such social values as the redistribution of income and the protection of human rights.

There are well-documented cases in Canada where the ideological preferences of public servants appear to have had a significant influence on policy development. There was, for example, substantial and successful resistance by senior public servants to the social values and goals of the CCF government that defeated the Liberals in Saskatchewan in 1944.[34] Another example is provided by Richard Splane, who has described the important influence of federal public servants, notably social workers in the Department of National Health and Welfare, on the reform of social policy in Canada.[35] Within the framework of support for such reform by successive ministers, the credo of these public servants "consisted almost wholly of a belief that in the interests of all Canadians, and particularly of those least-advantaged, a high priority should be given to the development of a comprehensive nation-wide social security system."[36]

The growth in the number and apparent influence of pressure groups has raised concern that they rival, and even threaten to supplant, political parties as the primary channel of communication between citizens and their governments. Unlike political parties, however, pressure groups do not seek, through the electoral process, overall control of government and thereby of policy making and implementation; rather, pressure groups attempt to affect particular government decisions. Moreover, political parties aggregate the needs and wishes of a vast number of interests in society, whereas pressure groups aggregate the views of a much narrower range of interests. While such large pressure groups as the Canadian Labour Congress and the Canadian Manufacturers' Association are concerned about a wide range of policy issues, at the other extreme are pressure groups with very small memberships who are concerned about a single issue (e.g., a group of people opposed to a halfway house in their neighbourhood).

Collectively, pressure groups have, in fact, diminished to some extent the role of political parties as intermediaries between the citizen and the state. But the increasing attraction of pressure group activity is, in large part, a response to the decline of political parties in the political system for reasons other than the proliferation and influence of pressure groups. Members of political parties who become backbench members of the legislature exercise little power in the political system compared to cabinet ministers and senior public servants. Furthermore, lobbyists are usually better able than individual legislators to deal with technical matters. "If a plant manufacturing railway box cars is threatened with closure and the loss of two thousand jobs, that would be an appropriate area of concern for the local Member of Parliament. [However], if that same plant had a problem with the Department of Transport on the safety aspects of the design of a journal box, that would be more appropriate for solution by that company's management or the industry's trade association."[37] It is natural for citizens to pursue their self-interest by using the channels of communication that best enable them to influence public policy.

The public service is influenced not only by pressure groups and political parties but also, as explained in the next chapter, by the news media and the public.

NOTES

1. *Ottawa Citizen,*19 March 1998.
2. For our purposes, these two terms can be used interchangeably. Often, however, the term interest group is used when the broad range of functions performed by these groups is under consideration, whereas the term pressure group is used when the focus of discussion is primarily on the exercise of political pressure.
3. Professor William Stanbury has observed that "our attitude toward lobbying can be likened to that toward sex. At one and the same time they are perceived as healthy and natural acts, but they are also seen as embarrassing, slightly taboo, even 'dirty' activities to be removed from polite conversation." "Lobbying and Interest Group Representation in the Legislative Process," in W.A.W. Neilson and James C. MacPherson, eds., *The Legislative Process in Canada* (Montreal: Institute for Research on Public Policy, 1978), 175.
4. See A. Paul Pross, *Group Politics and Public Policy* (Toronto: Oxford University Press, 1986), 114–27.
5. For a vigorous debate on the extent to which public interest groups are self-interested, see W.T. Stanbury, "A Sceptic's Guide to the Claims of So-Called Public Interest Groups." *Canadian Public Administration* 36 (winter 1993): 580–605; and Susan D. Phillips, "Of Public Interest Groups and Sceptics: A Realist's Reply to Professor Stanbury, *Canadian Public Administration* 36 (winter 1993): 606–16.
6. Andrew Cardoza, "Lion Taming: Downsizing the Opponents of Downsizing," in Gene Swimmer, ed., *How Ottawa Spends 1996–1997: Life Under the Knife* (Ottawa: Carleton University Press, 1996), 303–36.
7. See Evert A. Lindquist, "Think Tanks or Clubs? Assessing the Influence and Roles of Canadian Policy Institutes," *Canadian Public Administration* 36 (winter 1993): 547–79.
8. Allan Tupper, "Think Tanks, Public Debt and the Politics of Expertise in Canada," *Canadian Public Administration* 36 (winter 1993): 530–46.
9. Lindquist, "Think Tanks or Policy Clubs," 576.
10. Herman Bakvis, "Pressure Groups and the New Public Management: From 'Pressure Pluralism' to 'Managing the Contract,'" in Mohamed Charih and Arthur Daniels, eds., *New Public Management and Public Administration in Canada* (Toronto: Institute of Public Administration of Canada, 1997), 304, 305.
11. See Pross, *Group Politics and Public Policy*, 88–95.
12. Robert Presthus and William Monopoli, "Bureaucracy in the United States and Canada: Social, Attitudinal and Behavioral Variables," *International Journal of Comparative Sociology* 18 (March/June 1977): 186.
13. Ibid., 187.
14. Richard Splane, "Social Policy-Making in the Government of Canada: Reflections of a Reformist Bureaucrat," in S.A. Yelaja, ed., *Canadian Social Policy* (Waterloo: Wilfrid Laurier University Press, 1978), 215.
15. For a discussion of the impact of federalism on pressure group activity in Canada, see Helen Jones Dawson, "National Pressure Groups and the Federal Government," in A. Paul Pross, ed., *Pressure Group Behaviour in Canadian Politics* (Toronto: McGraw-Hill Ryerson, 1975), 30–35.
16. Jim Bennett of the Canadian Federation of Independent Business, quoted in *The Globe and Mail* (25 October 1980), A11.
17. Hugh Faulkner, "Pressuring the Executive," *Canadian Public Administration* 25 (summer 1982): 244.
18. John Gray, "Insiders Go to Mandarins before Ministers," *The Globe and Mail* (27 October 1980), 1.
19. Clive Baxter, "Familiars in the Corridors of Power," *The Financial Post* (12 July 1975), 6.
20. Andrew Roman, "Comments on Lobbying," in Neilson and MacPherson, *The Legislative Process in Canada*, 214–15.

21. Faulkner, "Pressuring the Executive," 241.
22. David Kwavnick, "Pressure Group Demands and the Struggle for Organizational Status: The Case of Organized Labour in Canada," *Canadian Journal of Political Science* 3 (March 1970): 58. (Emphasis added.)
23. Faulkner, "Pressuring the Executive," 246.
24. Ibid., 242.
25. Ibid., 247.
26. David Morley, quoted in Julianne Labreche, "The Quiet Persuaders of Parliament Hill," *The Financial Post* (29 November 1980), 34.
27. Alasdair J. McKichan, "Comments on Lobbying," in Neilson and MacPherson, The Legislative Process in Canada, 223.
28. Quoted in Mary Ann Smythe, "Once-a-Year Meetings, Limited Access and Cronyism Are No Longer Enough," *The Globe and Mail* (5 June 1989), B28.
29. McKichan, "Comments on Lobbying," 220.
30. See Peter Aucoin, "Pressure Groups and Recent Changes in the Policy-Making Process," in Pross, *Pressure Group Behaviour*, 174–92.
31. Canada, *Revised Statutes 1985*, c. 44 (4th supp.) as amended by Canada, *Statutes*, 1995, c.12.
32. For information on the content and administration of the Lobbyists Registration Act, see the annual reports on the Act published by Industry Canada.
33. Industry Canada, Office of the Ethics Counsellor, Lobbyists' Code of Conduct: Annual Report 1997 (Ottawa: Industry Canada 1997), 2.
34. S.M. Lipset, *Agrarian Socialism: The Cooperative Commonwealth Federation in Saskatchewan* (Berkeley: University of California Press, 1959), ch. 12.
35. "Social Policy-Making in the Government of Canada: Reflections of a Reformist Bureaucrat," in Yelaja, *Canadian Social Policy*, 209–26.
36. Ibid., 211.
37. McKichan, "Comments on Lobbying," 221.

BIBLIOGRAPHY

Abelson, D.E. "Environmental Lobbying and Political Posturing: The Role of Environmental Groups in Ontario's Debate Over NAFTA." *Canadian Public Administration* 38 (fall 1995): 3352–81.

Bakvis, Herman. "From 'Pressure Pluralism' to 'Managing the Contract.'" In Mohamed Charih and Arthur Daniels, eds., *New Public Management and Public Administration in Canada* (Toronto: Institute of Public Administration of Canada, 1997), 293–315.

Coleman, William D. "Analyzing the Associative Action of Business: Policy Advocacy and Policy Participation." *Canadian Public Administration* 28 (fall 1985): 413–33.

Faulkner, J. Hugh. "Pressuring the Executive." *Canadian Public Administration* 25 (summer 1982): 240–53.

Gillies, James, and Jean Piggott. "Participation in the Legislative Process." *Canadian Public Administration* 25 (summer 1982): 254–64.

Howlett, M., and J. Rayner. "Do Ideas Matter? Policy Network Configurations and Resistance to Policy Change in the Canadian Forest Sector." *Canadian Public Administration* 38 (fall 1995): 382–410.

Kwavnik, D. *Organized Labour and Pressure Politics: The Canadian Labour Congress, 1956–1968.* Montreal: McGill-Queen's University Press, 1972.

Lipset, S.M. *Agrarian Socialism: The Cooperative Commonwealth Federation in Saskatchewan.* Berkeley: University of California Press, 1959.

Pal, Leslie A. *Interests of State: The Politics of Language, Multiculturalism, and Feminism in Canada.*

Montreal and Kingston: McGill-Queen's University Press, 1993.

Paltiel, Khayyam Z. "The Changing Environment and Role of Special Interest Groups." *Canadian Public Administration* 25 (summer 1982): 198–210.

Phillips, Susan D. "Of Public Interest Groups and Sceptics: A Realist's Reply to Professor Stanbury," *Canadian Public Administration* 36 (winter 1993): 606–16.

Presthus, R. *Elite Accommodation in Canadian Politics.* Toronto: Macmillan, 1973.

——. *Elites in the Policy Process.* Cambridge: Cambridge University Press, 1974.

Pross, A. Paul. *Pressure Group Behaviour in Canadian Politics.* Toronto: McGraw-Hill Ryerson, 1975.

——. *Group Politics and Public Policy.* Toronto: Oxford University Press, 1986 (2nd ed., 1992).

——, ed. "Pressure Groups: Talking Chameleons." In Michael S. Whittington and Glen Williams, eds., *Canadian Politics in the 1980s*, 2nd ed. Toronto: Methuen, 1984, 287–311.

Raboy, M. "Influencing Public Policy on Canadian Broadcasting." *Canadian Public Administration* 38 (fall 1995): 411–32.

Stanbury, W.T. "A Sceptic's Guide to the Claims of So-Called Public Interest Groups." *Canadian Public Administration* 36 (winter 1993): 580–605.

Stanbury, W.T. *Business Interests and the Reform of Canadian Competition Policy.* Toronto: Methuen, 1977.

Thorburn, Hugh G. *Interest Groups in the Canadian Federal System.* Special Study for the Royal Commission on the Economic Union and Development Prospects for Canada, vol. 69. Toronto: University of Toronto Press, 1985.

Thorburn, Hugh G., ed. *Party Politics in Canada.* 5th ed. Scarborough, Ont.: Prentice-Hall, 1979.

Winn, C., and J. McMenemy. *Political Parties in Canada.* Toronto: McGraw-Hill, 1976.

21

The Public, the Media, and the Bureaucracy

Mr. Jones "blew the whistle" by disclosing to persons outside the public service what he considered to be government wrongdoing.[1] He was a federal immigration official who expressed concern to his superiors about a program inviting foreign citizens living illegally in Canada to apply to remain lawfully as refugees. He was alarmed that some of the "call-in" letters were being sent to convicted criminals and persons wanted for arrest in Canada and elsewhere. Before getting a reply from his superiors, he took his complaint—and several government files—to an opposition Member of Parliament, who in turn took the story to *The Toronto Star*. Mr. Jones also consulted a criminal prosecutor with the Department of Justice to see whether it was possible to charge a cabinet minister with a criminal offence.

Other immigration officers also expressed concern to management about the letters, and instructions were issued that the letters not be sent to inadmissible persons. However, Mr. Jones was informed that his actions had been incompatible with his Oath of Office, which bound him not to disclose information coming to him by virtue of his public office. Four months later, the Federal Court of Canada dismissed an application from Mr. Jones for writs directed against his department, the minister, the deputy minister, and others. Then, after another four months, Mr. Jones was fired because, in his deputy minister's words, he had "contributed to the media attention and political controversy which ensued and which brought into public question the integrity of the minister, and the legality" of the call-in program. The adjudicator of Mr. Jones' appeal against the dismissal substituted a lengthy suspension for the dismissal.

Such instances of whistle blowing are not common, but they highlight the need for public servants to be careful in their many dealings with the public and the media, especially in their use of confidential information. How should public servants respond to the increasing demand that the public be consulted and have influence on government decisions? What is the proper relationship between public servants and the media? How do governments balance the public's right to know with the government's need to keep certain information confidential? These are the primary issues examined in this chapter.

🏛 THE PUBLIC AND PUBLIC OPINION

Politicians and public servants face significant obstacles in eliciting and assessing public input into government decisions. It is difficult even to define the *public* and so to discern the public's *opinion* on political and administrative issues. The term public is variously defined as the total population, the total adult population, the electorate, an aggregation of pressure groups, the most influential organized interest, and so on. A useful distinction is often made between the public as a whole and the multiple *publics* or segments of the public that make up the total population. The public is clearly not a homogeneous entity whose collective view can easily be obtained; rather, it is fragmented into a large variety of organized and unorganized groups and individuals whose opinions on many issues conflict. Public opinion, then, is an aggregate of individual and group opinions.

The public and public servants have strong incentives to interact. Public servants actively seek the public's views as at least a partial basis for making both recommendations and decisions. They want to inform the public about government activities and to seek the public's reaction to existing and proposed policies and programs; they also want to stimulate widespread support among the population for their departments' undertakings. For the public, the extent of the bureaucracy's power provides good reason for efforts to enhance public influence on government decision making. It has been argued that "the clamour for citizen involvement" arises, in part, from the suspicion among citizens "that decisions that impinge solely on them are actually being made, not by their representatives in the legislatures or by ministers directly responsible to their representatives," but rather "on high by persons nameless and faceless to them."[2] Certainly, members of the public, in their capacity as voters, are far removed from the most important official decision makers—cabinet ministers and senior public servants.

The traditional mechanisms for interaction between government and society, namely the electoral system, political parties, legislators, pressure groups, and the mass media, permit the public to exercise little direct influence over politicians and public servants. The electorate obviously constitutes an extremely large and important segment of the public, but election results are an inexact measure of public attitudes on any specific public policy issue. Similarly, political parties in Canada reflect a wide range of opinion on policy issues. Neither the electoral system nor political parties are effective means by which the public can influence bureaucratic decisions. Furthermore, legislators have insufficient capacity to hold ministers responsible for their administration of departments and agencies. Yet public servants, to whom ministers delegate substantial powers, are even further removed from legislative control and influence. Thus, the public, acting through its elected representatives, has relatively little influence over the public service.

Pressure groups are another extremely important segment of the public, but despite their professed concern for the broad public interest, their primary concern is usually their self-interest. Moreover, these groups are often in conflict with one another. Even so-called public interest groups (e.g., the Consumers' Association of Canada) can legitimately claim to speak for only a portion of the public. As noted in the previous chapter, however, governments benefit from active consultation with pressure groups.

The mass media provide other channels of communication between the public and the bureaucracy by reflecting and, to some extent, shaping public opinion. But, like pressure groups, various media organizations disagree on public policy issues and therefore send conflicting signals to government officials as to the content of public opinion.

🏛 PUBLIC PARTICIPATION AND CONSULTATION

During the 1960s, there was an upsurge of public concern that the traditional mechanisms noted above provided inadequate opportunities for public input into the policy process. The institutions and processes of representative democracy were complemented by a vigorous emphasis on what was popularly described in Canada and elsewhere as participatory democracy. During the 1968 federal election campaign, Pierre Elliott Trudeau frequently used this term to sum up his commitment "to make government more accessible to people, to give citizens a sense of full participation in the affairs of government, and full control over their representatives."[3] To achieve these ends, demands were made both for improvements in the representative system (i.e., public input through popularly elected representatives and political parties) and for instruments to permit more *direct* public participation in the policy process (e.g., task forces and advisory bodies). While opportunities for public participation were considerably enhanced over the following two decades, since the late 1980s there has been another resurgence of demand for public participation in government decision making.

Public participation is a broader concept than citizen participation, although the two terms are often used interchangeably. *Public participation* refers to a broad range of direct and indirect forms of participation, *including* citizen participation. *Citizen participation* connotes *direct* participation of individual citizens and citizens' groups in government decision making. The purpose of citizen participation is more to stimulate decision makers to take account of a wider range of considerations at an earlier stage in the policy process than to enable citizens to scrutinize the administration of government programs.

Sherry Arnstein has provided a helpful means of conceptualizing the gradations of citizen participation by identifying eight rungs on "a ladder to citizen participation."[4] The ascending rungs depict a progression of citizen involvement from forms of "nonparticipation" to participation involving the actual exercise of citizen power. The eight rungs make up three major levels. The first and lowest level is labelled *nonparticipation* and includes:

1. manipulation by the power structure; and

2. therapy for the organization.

The second level is described as *token* participation and includes:

3. communication with the groups;

4. consultation with the groups; and

5. placation of the groups.

The third and highest level, that of *real citizen power*, contains the rungs of:

6. partnership;

7. delegated power; and

8. citizen control.

Much of what has passed for citizen participation in Canada is, in Arnstein's terms, a form of tokenism. Nevertheless, the quality of government decision making is often enhanced by such token forms of participation as communication and consultation.

Virtues and Limitations of Public Participation

Advocates of increased public participation in general and citizen participation in particular contend that participation benefits both members of the public and government officials. It is argued that the overriding benefit to the public is greater *responsiveness* of government decisions, programs, and services to the public's needs and desires. Participation facilitates a valuable exchange of information between the government and citizens who are directly—and often acutely—affected by government activities. Politicians and public servants thereby become more knowledgeable about the impact of their decisions, especially on individuals and groups whose views and concerns might otherwise be overlooked. Easier and more equal access to official decision makers stimulates participation by individual citizens and by such groups as the poor and aboriginal peoples; it thereby helps to reduce the influence of well-organized and well-connected interests that usually enjoy good access to government officials.

In addition, individual participants can receive substantial educational and social returns from participation. Exposure to new ideas and to people with different values develops greater tolerance and sensitivity toward the views of others. Moreover, working with others for common objectives promotes a sense of belonging and can enhance one's self-image. These benefits can accrue to participants even when the government's commitment to meaningful participation is not genuine.

For government officials, public participation helps to ensure that their decisions are more responsive to public wants and needs; it also enhances the legitimacy of these decisions in the eyes of those who have made a direct or indirect input into the policy process. Participating individuals and groups are more likely to accept decisions when they see—or perceive—that their views have been heard and taken into account. The argument is frequently made that public participation enhances the *effectiveness* as well as the responsiveness of public decisions by sensitizing government officials to the likely consequences of their decisions.

Critics of increased participation express, with varying degrees of intensity, one or more of the following concerns. Improving opportunities for indirect public input into the policy process through legislatures and political parties is praiseworthy, but Canadians in general are not inclined to participate actively and directly in the policy process. Thus, the creation or reform of institutions and procedures to promote direct citizen interaction with government officials is not worth the effort. Moreover, the benefits that may result from the heightened responsiveness of public officials and especially of public servants, who make the bulk of government decisions, have offsetting disadvantages. Consultation with citizens, citizens' groups, and advisory bodies can be extremely time consuming and, therefore, an inefficient use of the time and energy of public officials. Such consultation can also lead to less efficient and effective government by causing delays in the making of decisions and the delivery of programs. Efficiency and effectiveness can be further reduced if "expert" public servants are obliged to take undue account of the views of "amateur" citizens. Alan Altshuler has asserted that "groups of laymen—and especially groups of poorly educated laymen with little or no administrative experience—have particular handicaps as decision makers. They have little time to devote to consideration of the issues; their concerns are selfish and immediate; they lack technical competence."[5]

Another concern about the development of participative mechanisms is that they may create a mere facade of increased involvement by traditionally underrepresented groups. For example, the poor and the uneducated may participate more actively but, on balance, enjoy no greater influence than they had before. Organized interests that are already influential often use participative mechanisms to obtain even better access to government officials and thereby exercise even greater influence on government decisions—sometimes at the expense of less well-organized but more deserving citizens. Public servants can also use citizen participation to their advantage. They can blur the lines of accountability by delegating decision making powers to citizens' groups or by sharing these powers. They can encourage participation so as to co-opt or pacify citizens who might otherwise publicly criticize government policies and programs. Finally, public servants can build support for—or reduce opposition to—their activities by involving affected interests in the decision-making process.

Mechanisms for Public Participation

Despite these concerns, efforts to facilitate public participation have, since the late 1960s, been undertaken by all levels of government. Since the late 1980s, these efforts have been given new life, especially as a result of major emphasis on improving the quality of government's *service to the public* through more vigorous *consultation* between citizens, politicians, and public servants.

Over the past thirty years, both political parties and pressure groups have been affected by the trend toward greater public participation. The inner workings of Canada's major political parties have been democratized to allow increased participation by their members in shaping the parties' stance on policy issues. New pressure groups have sprung up to exert influence on behalf of previously unrepresented or underrepresented segments of the population. Government officials have encouraged the participation of groups representing such interests as consumers, environmentalists, and the poor by assisting them with public funds. Citizens' groups (e.g., residents' and ratepayers' associations) concerned with such issues as housing, zoning, and transportation have been especially active in the sphere of local government.

The parliamentary system has been reformed to provide more opportunities for testimony on policy issues by members of the public, including individual citizens, and more appearances by public servants before legislative committees to explain government policies and programs. Parliamentary committees have travelled to various parts of the country to consult individuals and groups on policy questions, and effective use has been made of special committees. These are composed of backbench members of all political parties who, acting largely on a nonpartisan basis, consult members of the public and make recommendations to government on such policy matters as regulatory reform and federal-provincial fiscal arrangements. Legislative committees have also enhanced public participation by holding hearings to examine *coloured papers*,[6] especially *white papers* and *green papers,* issued by government. The publication of these papers provides the public with information about existing and proposed policies (e.g., in the areas of tax reform, immigration, public access to information), as well as an invitation to comment on these policies.

Royal commissions and task forces have also responded to the public participation movement by seeking the public's views more frequently and systematically. Both types of organization use public opinion surveys (often called social surveys) to assess the public's views on current and proposed government activities. The extensive use of such surveys by cabinets, political parties, and individual politicians is well known. However, the public is less knowledgeable about the existence and results of the many public opinion surveys, of varying degrees of sophistication and reliability, that are conducted by or for government departments. The results of these surveys are not routinely disclosed to the public, but many are now available under the Access to Information Act. In general, the data from social surveys are a useful input for the government's assessment of public opinion. One advantage of these surveys is that they can provide information on the needs and desires of all segments of the public, including those who are disadvantaged, unorganized, or uneducated.

Another means by which public participation can be pursued is through the use of advisory bodies to government. The creation of advisory boards and councils is in keeping with the desire for more *direct* citizen participation in government decision making. Unlike most of the mechanisms discussed, advisory bodies can be used for direct interaction between citizens and public officials, especially public servants. A large number of advisory bodies have been established at all levels of Canadian government to provide advice to politicians and public servants (e.g., provincial councils on the status of women, the elderly, the handicapped, etc., advise the relevant government departments). Many advisory bodies containing representatives of citizens' groups have been established as nongovernmental organizations supported by public funds.[7] It is difficult to find genuine cases of an actual delegation of authority over decision making, program administration, and/or the expenditure of public funds to groups of citizens at the community level. In recent years, however, there has been some movement in this direction through the use of partnership arrangements between governments and citizen groups.

In addition to these mechanisms, governments have made increasing use of other consultative mechanisms, including town hall meetings, workshops, toll-free telephone numbers, focus groups, and roundtables. The term "consultation" embraces a spectrum of consultative approaches ranging from listening, through dialogue, debate, and joint analysis, to jointly agreed solutions.[8] The federal government has adopted a list of principles for consultation that reflects the concept's increased importance. The statement includes, among others, the following principles:

- Consultation between government and the public is intrinsic to effective public policy development and service to the public. It should be a first thought, not an after-thought.

- Whenever possible, consultation should involve all parties who can contribute to or are affected by the outcome of consultation.

- Some participants may not have the resources or expertise required to participate, and financial assistance or other support may be needed for their representation to be assured.

- A clear, mutual understanding of the purpose and expectations of all parties to the consultation is necessary from the outset.

- To be effective, consultation must be based on values of openness, honesty, trust and transparency of purpose and process.

- Participants in a consultation should have clear mandates. Participants should have influence over the outcome and a stake in implementing.

- All participants must have reasonable access to relevant information and commit themselves to sharing information.[9]

Conclusions

Despite the advances in the level and means of public participation and consultation since the late 1960s, there remains a gap between promise and performance. Katherine Graham and Susan Phillips contend that public participation, in such forms as "public hearings, public meetings and open forums" and "ostensibly before policies and priorities are set," has recently and increasingly been discredited.[10] They argue that the public participation process had been dominated by professionals who were not well connected to the real political and public service decision makers; that provincial and municipal governments engaged in "tell and sell" rather than genuine consultation; and that the cost of consultations raised questions as to "whether it is worth spending substantial sums to hold meetings attended by small numbers of people, who are frequently cranky and critical."[11] The complexity of this issue is demonstrated by the fact that some citizens and groups feel that they are "overconsulted." Moreover, just because decision makers cannot please all of the various interests, we cannot conclude that consultations are purely cynical exercises.

The fundamental mechanism for public participation in the political system is the process of nominating and electing public officials. But the mechanisms discussed above have provided a vital complementary means of involving members of the public in the policy process. In particular, they have stimulated a greater sense of responsiveness to the public among politicians and public servants. Elected officials, notably cabinet ministers, have neither the time nor the expertise to handle all the representations made by members of the public. Certainly, in the municipal sphere, the result of efforts to facilitate citizen participation has largely been to increase citizen interaction with public employees rather than with councillors. Thus, participation has affected public servants not only indirectly through their political superiors but also directly through increased interaction with individual citizens and citizens' groups.

🏛 THE MEDIA

Like pressure groups, the media of mass communication, commonly known as the mass media or the news media, act as intermediaries between the government and the public. The term mass media includes radio, television, newspapers, and magazines. Unlike pressure groups, the mass media transmit much information for the sake of transmitting information rather than for the purpose of influencing public policy. Moreover, compared to pressure groups, which tend to represent well-defined interests to carefully identified officials, the media's audience, both within government and among the public, tends to be broader and more diffuse.

The Media and the Government

A key function of the media is to provide information to the public. Similarly, a major responsibility of government in a democratic society is to inform the public about the institutions and processes of government and about the programs and services offered by departments and agencies. In varying degrees, all government departments generate news and information. The gathering and disseminating of information to the public is a major function of some departments, such as Statistics Canada. Other departments provide information of importance to the general public (e.g., the Department of Natural Resources on energy conservation), or to more specialized groups (e.g., the Department of Health on income security for the elderly, and several other departments on scientific and technological advances). In addition, as a basis for policy development and implementation, government officials require information on the needs and demands of the citizens they serve. In contrast to their relations with many pressure groups, government officials do not usually look to, or depend on, the media for information of a technical nature; rather, they are interested in media coverage of a political or policy nature bearing on the activities of other governments or the attitudes of the general public—or particular sections of the public.

In the sphere of government-media interaction, the major participants on the government side are ministers, Members of Parliament, and public servants, especially senior public servants and information officers in government departments and agencies. On the media side, the primary participants are journalists, editorial executives, and the owners of print and broadcast organizations. The media and the government pursue different objectives through their provision of information. In very general terms, government officials want to get their message to the public without stirring up the political waters. In some cases, this is useful to the media because it provides them with a ready source of up-to-date news at minimal cost; however, the media's objective of attracting a large audience can often best be achieved by rocking the political boat. It is notable that the media are by no means a homogeneous entity; thus, the government can occasionally achieve its objectives in communicating with the public by taking advantage of competition and conflict among various media organizations.

The media play a critical role as two-way channels of communication between the governors and the governed. Newspapers, magazines, television, and radio carry information from the public to politicians and public servants and from these officials to the public. The media serve as "filters" for this information; they aim also to influence the attitudes and behaviour of both government officials and members of the public. Thus, the media both reflect and influence public opinion.

Governments cannot and do not rely solely on the media to communicate with the public. Much information is exchanged through correspondence and telephone calls between officials and citizens and through government publications and direct mailings aimed at the general public or particular groups. But government information appears to be transmitted most effectively through the media. Indeed, a survey for the federal Task Force on Government Information found that Canadians learn about government programs primarily through the mass media. In order of priority, the reported sources of federal information were "television, newspapers and magazines, radio, friends and relatives, government publications, public servants and Members of Parliament, and associations and clubs."[12] It is noteworthy that a substantial portion of government information transmitted through the media takes the form of advertising paid for by public funds.

A broad, and admittedly oversimplified, distinction can be made between two categories of government-media interaction. The first category involves the exchange of information, largely of a factual nature, on the content and administration of government programs. The main actors in this category are public servants at various levels of the administrative hierarchy. The second category involves an exchange of news and views, primarily on political and policy issues. The most important actors in this category are politicians and senior public servants.

The Media and Public Servants

Most government contacts with the media are handled by public servants who strive to use the media to support their political superiors, to publicize their department's activities, to obtain favourable comment on these activities, and to seek public reaction to proposed policies and programs (sometimes in the form of "trial balloons"). Public servants also attempt to keep secret from the media any information that would adversely affect their departments or themselves; and if damaging information is uncovered by the media, public servants usually work to minimize its negative impact. Moreover, the amount and type of information provided by public servants is significantly affected by rules and conventions on the confidentiality of government documents and on the bounds of permissible public comment. Public servants must be especially careful not to stray too far over the nebulous line between politics and administration by performing the minister's role of defending, or speculating on, public policy.

The media do not perceive their primary function vis-à-vis government as publicizing government activities in a manner designed to please public officials. The media do transmit a great deal of factual material from government to the public, but they serve several other functions in their interactions with government. The media see themselves more as watchdogs of the public interest than as purveyors of government information. They help to set the public agenda by selecting from the enormous volume of available information items to which they give special prominence or continuing attention. They contribute to the development of public policy by subjecting events and personalities to critical analysis through such means as newspaper editorials and television documentaries. They stimulate reform in government by exposing mismanagement, corruption, and illegality. They make judgments as to what government-provided information is publicity that merits dissemination and what appears to be propaganda to be disregarded.

Our earlier discussion of relations between politicians and public servants suggested that media coverage of bureaucratic activities and personalities has somewhat diminished the anonymity of public servants. In addition to assessing the regular activities of public servants, the media have a strong incentive to break through the barriers of government secrecy to get a controversial, dramatic, or exciting story that may involve public servants. The media are, however, subject to such legal restraints on their activities as the Official Secrets Act, the laws of libel, and requirements regarding the revealing of sources of information. Moreover, in Canada, there is not much of a tradition or practice of investigative journalism, especially of the type whereby "crusading" journalists expose and publicize government scandals or mismanagement.

Given the intermediary role of the media between the government and the public, government officials are well advised to develop and preserve cordial relations with both print and electronic media. They can accomplish this, in part, by providing material in an appropriate form and at the proper time. Similarly, media representatives can gain the trust and confidence of public officials by "responsible" use of government information. The development of informal relationships based on friendship and long association are also mutually beneficial to the exchange of information. Certain "friendly" journalists may receive preferential treatment in the form of advance notice of upcoming developments, access to public officials, or confidential information. They must be careful, however, that they are not thereby captured and manipulated by public servants. Where political and policy issues are involved, the desire of politicians and public servants to "tell the department's story" may well conflict with the media's desire to "tell the whole story."

Much of the impact of the media on public servants is, of course, indirect. Although, as noted earlier, the news media do on occasion focus on the activities of individual public servants, bureaucratic anonymity is still basically intact. However, public servants can be greatly affected by news stories dealing in a critical or erroneous way with their departments or with policies or programs for which they have some responsibility. Care should be taken not to exaggerate the overall influence of the media on the public service, but the potential influence of the media and its actual influence in particular circumstances help to constrain the exercise of bureaucratic power.

There are few research studies on which to base an assessment of the media's impact on the attitudes and decisions of public servants. The nature and importance of interaction with the media depend on such factors as the public servants' responsibilities, their level in the hierarchy, and their department. Information officers seek to enhance the reputation of their departments through such public relations efforts as providing briefings for journalists and churning out press releases. Senior public servants are anxious to ensure that media coverage of departmental activities does not embarrass their political superiors. Thus, senior public servants who brief ministers for questions in the legislature or from the media monitor news stories so as to anticipate questions that might be asked. For example, news stories in *The Globe and Mail, The Financial Post,* and *Le Devoir* are often the basis for questions to ministers in the House of Commons.

🏛 FREEDOM OF INFORMATION AND INDIVIDUAL PRIVACY[13]

Freedom of Information

It is widely argued that open access to government information enables the public and the media to make a more informed contribution to government decision making. This issue is important for relations between the public service and both the public and the media, and because of its implications for ministerial responsibility and political neutrality.

The government of Canada has traditionally operated on the principle that all government information is secret unless the government decides to release it. Many proponents of freedom of information legislation contend that this principle should be reversed so that all government information will be released unless the government can make a good case for keeping it secret. Under this latter approach, the burden on the public of justifying requests for the disclosure of information is lifted and the burden of justifying nondisclosure of information is imposed on the government, specifically on ministers and public servants. The federal *Access to Information Act* (the ATI Act)[14] permits the government to keep a great deal of information confidential, but, in general, the act follows the second approach. Its stated purpose is

> to provide a right of access to information in records under the control of a government in accordance with the principles that government information should be available to the public, that necessary exceptions to the right of access should be limited and specific and that decisions on the disclosure of government information should be reviewed independently of government.[15]

Ministerial Responsibility and Political Neutrality

Discussion of freedom of information legislation in both the federal and provincial spheres has centred on the issue of whether such legislation would unduly encroach on ministerial responsibility. Somewhat less concern has focused on the possible reduction in the political neutrality and anonymity of public servants.

It is easy to understand why ministers and senior public servants do not share the enthusiasm of people outside government for freedom of information legislation and for access to material on the decision making process in particular. The release of information revealing ministerial and public service contributions to, and debates over, policy has important consequences for both ministerial responsibility and political neutrality. Documents that expose disagreement among ministers or between ministers and public servants could be exploited by the government's opponents to the ministers' political disadvantage. It is natural that ministers should not want to answer to the legislature and the public for the content of documents that are likely to be controversial and that could be kept secret. Ministers do not deliberately seek trouble.

Similarly, senior public servants generally resist the expansion of public access to official documents that disclose their personal views and values on policy issues. If public servants are drawn into public debate over their contributions to policy development, their anonymity will decline. Moreover, to the extent that a public servant's written advice is at odds with his or her minister's decision, both may be publicly embarrassed. Ministers may strive to avoid such situations by surrounding themselves with political appointees or with "yes men." This would threaten both the frankness and the completeness of departmental advice and would also undermine the security of tenure associated with a career in the public service.

The impact of more open government on the doctrines of ministerial responsibility and political neutrality should not be exaggerated. The evolution of these doctrines has been explained in Chapters 13 and 17. The implementation of freedom of information legislation requires further evolution of these doctrines, but it does not require their drastic alteration or abandonment. The importance of the doctrine of ministerial responsibility in particular will be evident in the following sections on exemptions and the review process. Exemptions refer to classes of information that may, or must be, kept secret; the review process refers to mechanisms for reconsidering and/or overruling decisions by ministers or public servants not to disclose information.

Exemptions

The subjects of exemptions and review mechanisms are closely related. Judgments on the number and nature of exemptions considered desirable depend to a large extent on the method adopted to review complaints about nondisclosure. If ministers have the final authority to determine whether a particular document falls into an exempted category, they will be inclined to approve legislation providing for a small number of specific exemptions. But if a person or body independent of ministers makes the final determination on exemptions, ministers will likely favour legislation that contains a large number of specific exemptions or a smaller number of very broad exemptions. Thus, decisions on the exemptions to be included in legislation are usually taken in relation to the review mechanisms that will be adopted.

There is much agreement among governments that certain types of information should be kept secret, such as documents relating to national defence and security, personal information on individual citizens, financial or commercial information collected by government on a confidential basis, and records of criminal investigations. There is, however, considerable variation among governments in the comprehensiveness of the exemptions within the different classes of information.

In Canada, the exemptions (and exclusions) set out in the ATI Act are substantial. The act provides, subject to a number of exemptions, that a Canadian citizen, a permanent resident, or a Canadian corporation "has a right to and shall, on request, be given access to any record under the control of a government institution." However, records containing information obtained in confidence from a foreign government, an international organization, or a provincial, municipal, or regional government in Canada are exempted from disclosure unless the government or the organization in question agrees to release or permits the release of the records.

The confidentiality of records may be retained if they could reasonably be expected to injure the conduct of federal-provincial relations. Thus, information relating to federal-provincial consultations or deliberations, or to strategy or tactics of the Canadian government bearing on the conduct of federal-provincial affairs, may be exempted from disclosure. Very broad exemption is also provided for information that, if disclosed, could reasonably be expected to harm "the conduct of international affairs, the defence of Canada, or any state allied or associated with Canada or the detection, prevention or suppression of subversive or hostile activities."

In addition, records may be exempted from disclosure if they contain information relating to law enforcement and investigation, or if their release might threaten the safety of individuals or affect adversely the financial interests of Canada. Records are also exempted if they contain personal information or if they contain trade secrets, financial, commercial, scientific, or technical information, which, if disclosed, could harm a third party (i.e., firms and corporations).

Some exemptions and some specific exclusions in the act reflect the concern of ministers and public servants about the preservation of ministerial responsibility and public service anonymity. *Exemptions* include advice developed by or for a government institution or cabinet minister; an account of consultations involving public servants and a cabinet minister (or a cabinet minister's staff); plans developed for negotiations conducted by the government; and plans bearing on personnel management or the administration of a government institution that have not yet been put into operation. *Exclusions* from disclosure relate to "confidences of the Queen's Privy Council for Canada" (i.e., the cabinet). The excluded documents include cabinet memoranda; discussion papers prepared for cabinet; cabinet agendas or records of cabinet deliberations or decisions; records relating to consultation among ministers in respect to government decisions and policies; records used to brief ministers on these decisions and policies; and draft legislation. These exclusions do not apply to "confidences" more than twenty years old; discussion papers relating to decisions that have been made public; and all other discussion papers more than four years old.

The length and breadth of the exemptions and exclusions in the act have been severely criticized by many segments of the Canadian public. Thus, the review mechanism established to make the final decision on the exemptions is a critical component of the ATI Act. Before examining the review process, however, it is an enlightening experience to play the party game called "Airplane." This game was used by Canada's first information commissioner to explain to students that, although in the abstract they may strongly favour unlimited access to government information, they may in practice see some virtue in the act's exemptions. The scenario for the game is as follows:

An airplane skidded off the runway; the passengers were unhurt save for one who died, apparently from a heart attack. For some unknown reason the passengers were left incommunicado at the airport under police protection.

Students are assigned to play the following roles: an arms dealer who holds a new patent on a weapon sought by many governments; a diplomat known to be engaged in high-level peace negotiations; an aging actress and her lover, a well-known sex symbol; an RCMP officer who is escorting a prisoner-informer being taken to protective custody in another penitentiary; a student who was supposed to be at class; a Minister of Transport; a Solicitor General; a commissioner of the RCMP; the Information Commissioner; and a representative of the estate of the dead person. Finally, someone plays the journalist who is assigned to the story and must obtain the passenger list under the Access to Information Act.[16]

The information commissioner noted that "it is amazing how quickly [students] become protective of their characters" and that "it soon becomes clear that freedom of information invariably involves disclosure of information, collected by someone else, affecting yet another person's interests."[17] This game demonstrates well the need to balance the public's right to know with the individual's right to privacy. In addition to the provisions in the ATI Act exempting personal information from disclosure, individual privacy is protected by the Privacy Act discussed later in this chapter.

The Review Process

Initially, the task of applying the exemption provisions to requests for access to government documents is performed by public servants. However, instances arise where citizens wish to appeal to a higher authority against a public servant's decision to deny access to all or part of certain documents. Thus, freedom of information legislation must provide a review process that specifies the person(s) with authority to review the decisions of public servants.

Experience in Canada suggests that ministers and public servants tend to favour a review process in which ministers have ultimate authority to decide whether a particular document will be released. However, those outside government tend to prefer a review mechanism that allows ministerial decisions on access to be overruled. The system adopted for the ATI Act is a *two-tier* review mechanism involving an information commissioner *and* judicial review. Under the act, the information commissioner is authorized to receive and investigate complaints when access to a record is refused; when unreasonable fees are imposed for searching for or producing a record; where a public official unreasonably extends the time limit for producing a record; when a record is not provided in the official language requested; and "in respect of any other matter relating to requesting or obtaining access to records" under the act. The commissioner may also initiate a complaint on "reasonable grounds." After investigating a complaint, the commissioner recommends whether a record should be released; he or she cannot require that a record be disclosed. Following the commissioner's investigation, the complainant, or the commissioner with the complainant's consent, may apply to the Federal Court for review of any refusal to disclose a record. The court may then order the head of a government institution to disclose—or not to disclose—all or part of a record.

Implementation of the Access to Information Act

People seeking information under the act must write to the appropriate department and must identify as precisely as possible the information they require. Assistance in this regard is available in the *Access Register,* which contains a description of the records held by each department. Copies of the register and of access request forms can be obtained in public libraries and government information offices in major population centres, as well as in about 2000 postal stations in rural areas. Each department has an access coordinator to assist applicants to identify the records required. The department has thirty days either to produce the information requested or to provide reasons why a request has been denied. If the request is for a large number of records or is complicated, the department can extend the time limit but must inform the applicant of the situation. The role of the information commissioner and the Federal Court of Canada in cases where access to information is denied was described earlier. A nominal fee is charged for each request for information. Applicants must pay an extra amount if excessive time is needed to process a request and for copying and computer-processing time.

During the 1996–97 fiscal year, the Office of the Information Commissioner received 1382 complaints.[18] Forty-three percent of the complaints investigated during the year arose from a refusal to disclose the information requested and 45 percent were complaints about delays in disclosure. Sixty-four percent of these complaints were resolved to the satisfaction of the commissioner as a result of remedial action by the government institution involved; slightly more than 26 percent of the complaints were unsubstantiated.[19]

A widely held view among proponents of freedom of information legislation is that it will gradually change the attitude of ministers and public servants toward public access to official information. It has been suggested also that government officials will become more supportive of open government when they realize that it has more benefits and fewer disadvantages than they anticipated. Yet, in 1998, the Information Commissioner concluded that

> A culture of secrecy still flourishes in too many high places even after 15 years.... Too many public officials cling to the old proprietorial notion that they, and not the Access to Information Act, should determine what and when information should be dispensed to the unwashed public. If bold boasts are to be believed, some have taken to adopting the motto attributed to an old New York Democratic boss: "Never write if you can speak; never speak if you can nod; and never nod if you can wink."[20]

Whistle Blowing

Through the practice of whistle blowing,[21] public servants can make public some of the sensitive information exempted or excluded from disclosure by the ATI Act. Whistle blowing refers to "both the open disclosure and the surreptitious leaking to persons outside the organization of confidential information concerning a harmful act that a colleague or superior has committed, is contemplating, or is allowing to occur."[22] Thus, the whistle can be blown to legislators and to public servants outside one's own department as well as to the media and the general public.

The kinds of wrongdoing that usually provoke whistle blowing are illegal activity, gross waste of public funds, and threats to public health or safety. There is much disagreement in practice, however, as to how serious the wrongdoing must be to justify the "disloyalty" of disclosure. Moreover, some whistle blowers are motivated by considerations other than the public interest (e.g., vindictiveness, partisanship, publicity), or are simply cranks.

A substantial increase since the early 1970s in the leaking of information has been complemented since the early 1980s by frequent instances of public disclosure of alleged government wrongdoing. Compared with public disclosure, leaking information is generally a risk-free means by which public servants can expose government wrongdoing. Public disclosure usually has adverse consequences for a public servant's career. For example, in 1982, a forester in the Ontario Ministry of Natural Resources was fired for alleging to an opposition member of the legislature that the ministry was violating its own policy by granting timber-cutting rights in an area where volumes of suitable timber were insufficient. In 1986, a deputy registrar of the federal Immigration Board was fired for releasing confidential documents and publicly alleging improprieties by the board. In 1987, a federal immigration officer was fired for alleging to members of the House of Commons Standing Committee on Labour, Employment and Immigration that his superiors were breaking the rules by permitting persons with criminal records to stay in Canada.

Canadian public servants who engage in whistle blowing may be subject to disciplinary action for violating their oath of office and secrecy or such statutes as the Official Secrets Act and the Criminal Code. Moreover, they are subject at common law to the broad duties of loyalty, good faith, and confidentiality. However, there is increasing support for providing whistle blowers with statutory protection from reprisal in those instances where they publicly disclose government information that should, in the public interest, be disclosed.

> If, today, government can no longer justify confidentiality for all information ... then we cannot see how the principle of confidentiality can be invoked in order to cover up serious government wrongdoing. The modern movement toward increased access to, and disclosure of, government information is founded, at least in part, on the perceived needs of a democratic state for openness and for the free exchange of ideas and information. Public awareness of government activity is seen as an essential means of monitoring, and holding the government accountable for, such activity. Is it reasonable, then, to frustrate the purpose of a more liberal access and disclosure regime precisely where serious government wrongdoing is alleged?[23]

In the federal government and in many state governments in the United States, whistle blower protection legislation has been passed to reduce the vulnerability of whistle blowers to retaliation by political or administrative superiors. There is growing, but still modest, support for similar legislation in Canada.

Individual Privacy

Concern about individual privacy is the flip side of the access to information issue. The *Privacy Act*[24] and the Access to Information Act came into effect on the same day, July 1, 1983. The Privacy Act replaces, and expands on, the protection to individual privacy previously provided in the Canadian Human Rights Act. Individual privacy is protected by restricting access to personal information held by the federal government on Canadian citizens and permanent residents.

The act contains principles of fair information practices that direct government institutions to limit their collection of information to that which is necessary to do their work; if possible, to gather the information directly from the individuals concerned; to inform the individuals of what use is to be made of the information; and to "take all reasonable steps" to ensure accuracy and completeness of the information. In addition, individuals have the right to see all information the government has on them in its more than 2000 federal personal information banks. Copies of the *Personal Information Index*, which describes the activities of each department, what kind of information it collects, and whom to contact for access, are available in public libraries and post offices across Canada.

A privacy commissioner is appointed under the act to initiate complaints on his or her own initiative and to investigate complaints from individuals who believe their privacy rights have been denied. Grounds for complaint include denial of some or all of the information requested, denial of the right to correct or annotate some of the information on one's file, and use of information that contravenes the act. The first commissioner described himself both as "a specialized ombudsman for privacy, the single voice in the federal government with a mandate to speak on behalf of privacy rights," and as an auditor responsible for determining "whether personal information is collected, held by, and disposed of by federal government institutions" according to the act.[25]

During the 1996–97 fiscal year alone, the Office of the Privacy Commissioner received 2235 complaints. Ten institutions received 88 percent of these complaints, ranging from 602 complaints about Correctional Services Canada to 45 complaints about the Canadian Security Intelligence Service. Of the 2772 complaints investigated during that year, 30 percent were discovered to be well founded.[26]

The commissioner's annual report makes fascinating reading. He noted in 1990 that the most frequently received question relates to when a social insurance number must be given, but other contacts include media requests for comment on matters with potential privacy implications; citizens' concerns about telephone gadgetry showing a caller's telephone number on a screen; an auditor general's proposal for an anonymous fraud hotline; and a municipal council's proposal to circulate detailed profiles of released offenders. The privacy commissioner noted also that "privacy has moved from a peripheral social issue into the mainstream of public consciousness."[27] He asked:

> What chance does privacy have when satellites can conduct surveillance from more than 300 kilometres in the sky? Audio eavesdropping no longer demands physical access to a building in order to plant listening devices. And, of course, most of us carry in our wallets or purses the key to vast amounts of highly sensitive personal information. Our ubiquitous bank and credit cards leave a trail of where we travel, eat, shop and sleep—perhaps by matching records—even with whom! George Orwell could not have imagined the new possibilities of Big Brother.[28]

Figure 21.1 demonstrates the extent to which our privacy is at stake in our everyday activities.

Information and Privacy Legislation in The Provinces

Nearly all provincial governments have enacted freedom of information legislation. The government of Nova Scotia, with the enactment of its Freedom of Information Act in 1977, was the first in the Commonwealth to make access to

Figure 21.1

A DAY IN THE LIFE OF A CANADIAN WITH NOTHING TO HIDE [ABRIDGED VERSION]

Nothing to hide? It's just as well. ... [F]rom the time we get up in the morning until we climb into bed at night we leave a trail of data behind us for others to collect, merge, analyse, massage and even sell—often without our knowledge or consent. And there is no law against it (except in Quebec).

8:30   Exit apartment parking lot (Cameras, and possibly a card, record departure) ...

8:42   Caught in traffic jam, call work to delay meeting (Cellular phone calls can be easily intercepted; new personal telephones will signal your whereabouts to satellites to deliver calls) ...

9:20   Enter main office/plant door ("Swipe" cards record comings and goings; active badges allow others to locate you anywhere in the building) ...

9:29   Send personal E-mail to friend, business message to colleague (Both can be read by the employer; simple deletion does not erase them from the computer's hard drive) ...

12:05   Stop at bank machine (System records details of transactions, cameras overhead or in machine record your behaviour) ...

12:35   Doctor's appointment (Health cards will soon contain small computer chips to record your complete medical history on the card, blood samples contain DNA which could be tested for wide variety of conditions, doctor's diagnosis may need to be disclosed to insurance company if you buy life or disability insurance and details sent to centralized registry in U.S. run by insurance companies)

1:15   Pick up prescription (Some provinces have on-line drug networks which share your drug history with pharmacies across the province and may be disclosed to police tracking drug abuse) ...

2:45   Provide urine sample for employer's new drug testing program (Reveals use of targetted drugs but not impairment; sample may also reveal use of legal drugs such as birth control pills, insulin and anti-depressants) ...

6:45   Pick up video (Computer records viewing preferences, Social Insurance Number; store may sell your viewing preferences—say, Erotica—to other companies)

7:20   Listen to phone messages (Your phone has recorded callers' phone numbers, displays your number when you call others—unless you enter code to block the display) ...

8:35   Survey company calls (Company gathers political views, social attitudes and personal views. Some surveys are actually marketing calls to collect personal data for future sales. Legitimate surveys destroy personal identifiers once data processed) ...

9:10   Log onto Internet (Your choice of chat groups and your messages can be monitored and a profile assembled by anyone, including police; some Web sites monitor your visits).

Source: Office of the Privacy Commissioner, Annual Report 1995–1996.

information a legal right. The New Brunswick Right to Information Act, which was adopted in 1978 and came into force in 1980, is notable for its review mechanism. An individual who has been denied access to information by a minister may appeal the minister's decision, either to the provincial ombudsman or to a Supreme Court judge. The ombudsman can only *recommend* to the minister that the information be released whereas the judge can *order* its release. Moreover, if an individual is not satisfied with the minister's response to the ombudsman's recommendation, he or she can still appeal the minister's decision to a Supreme Court judge.

The Quebec Act on Access to Documents Held by Public Bodies and the Protection of Personal Privacy,[29] which was enacted in 1982 and came into effect in stages between 1982–84, is also notable. An Access to Information Commission, headed by a chairperson and two other commissioners, was created to enforce the act and to serve as a court to settle disputes between the government and citizens on matters of access to information and individual privacy. The act applies to more than several thousand government administrative units, including departments, agencies, Crown corporations, municipalities, and private and public educational institutions.

Most provincial governments have enacted privacy legislation. In Alberta, British Columbia, Nova Scotia, Ontario, and Quebec, the freedom of information and privacy legislation is combined in a single act. In Ontario, for example, the Freedom of Information and Protection of Privacy Act provides a right of access to citizens while at the same time protecting the privacy of individuals with respect to information held by provincial government institutions. The government publishes a *Personal Information Index* to assist the public in locating information, and, if an access request is denied, an appeal can be made to the information and privacy commissioner.

Conclusions

Although participative mechanisms are still at a rudimentary stage in Canada, advocates of public participation have grounds for optimism. The opportunities for participation incorporated into many of the formal mechanisms for government decision making are unlikely to be withdrawn. There is, therefore, reasonable promise that participative mechanisms will be expanded and refined and that public input into the policy process will be further enhanced.

In addition, the gradual movement toward greater openness at all levels of Canadian government through the enactment of freedom of information legislation helps to ensure that *public* participation is *informed* participation. At the same time, legislative measures are being taken to maintain the privacy of information held by the government on individual citizens. In the Canadian context, legislation on these two matters is quite recent; we can, therefore, expect that it will be modified and refined on the basis of experience with its implementation and new advances in information technology.

NOTES

1. Based on a case reported in Kenneth Kernaghan, "Whistle-blowing in Canadian Government: Ethical, Political and Managerial Considerations," *Optimum*, 22–21 (1991–92): 36–38.

2. J.A. Corry, "Sovereign People or Sovereign Governments," in H.V. Kroeker, ed., *Sovereign People or Sovereign Governments* (Montreal: Institute for Research on Public Policy, 1981), 11.

3. Pierre Elliott Trudeau, *Campaign Speech: Ottawa* (Ottawa: The Liberal Party of Canada, 1968).

4. Sherry R. Arnstein, "A Ladder to Citizen Participation," *Journal of the American Institute of Planners* 35 (July 1969): 216–24.

5. Alan Altshuler, *Community Control* (Washington, D.C.: Urban Institute, 1970), 45.

6. For a more detailed discussion of coloured papers, royal commissions, task forces, and advisory councils, see Chapter 6.

7. For an account and an evaluation of efforts to encourage citizen participation in Winnipeg, see Phil H. Wichern, *Evaluating Winnipeg's Unicity: Resident Advisory Groups, 1971–1984*, Research and Working Papers, no. 11 (Winnipeg: Institute of Urban Studies, University of Winnipeg, 1984).

8. Canada, Privy Council Office, *Task Force Report: Service to the Public* (Ottawa: Privy Council Office, 1993, 41.

9. Privy Council Office, Report of the Task Force on Service to the Public, p. 47. Reproduced with the permission of the Minister of Public Works and Government Services Canada, 1998.

10. Katherine Graham and Susan Phillips, "Citizen Engagement: Beyond the Customer Revolution." *Canadian Public Administration* 40 (summer 1997): 259.

11. Ibid., 260.

12.. Canada, *To Know and Be Known*, Report of the Task Force on Government Information, vol. 2 (Ottawa: Queen's Printer, 1969), 50.

13. For an examination of these two matters in the Canadian context, see Kenneth Kernaghan and John Langford, *The Responsible Public Servant* (Toronto: Institute of Public Administration of Canada, and Halifax: Institute for Research on Public Policy, 1990), ch. 4.

14. Canada, *Statutes*, 1980–83, c. 111, Schedule I.

15. Ibid., 10.

16. See Office of the Information Commissioner, *Annual Report, 1983–1984* (Ottawa: Minister of Supply and Services, 1984), 3.

17. Ibid.

18. Office of the Information Commissioner, *Annual Report, 1996–97* (Ottawa: Minister of Supply and Services, 1997), 80, 81.

19. Ibid., 82.

20. Office of the Information Commissioner, *Annual Report, 1997–98* (Ottawa: Minister of Public Works and Government Services, 1998), 2.

21. For elaboration on this issue, see Kenneth Kernaghan, "Whistle-blowing in Canadian Governments: Ethical, Political and Managerial Considerations," *Optimum* 22 (1991–92): 32–43; and Kernaghan and Langford, *The Responsible Public Servant*, 94–100.

22. Kernaghan and Langford, *The Responsible Public Servant*, 4.

23. Ontario, Law Reform Commission, *Report on Political Activity, Public Comment and Disclosure by Crown Employees* (Toronto: Ministry of the Attorney General, 1986), 325.

24. Canada, *Statutes*, 1980–83, c. 111, Schedule II.

25. Office of the Privacy Commissioner, *Annual Report, 1983–1984* (Ottawa: Ministry of Supply and Services) 2, 7.

26.   Office of the Privacy Commissioner, *Annual Report, 1996–97* (Canada Communications Group) 69.
27.   Office of the Privacy Commissioner, *Annual Report, 1989–1990* (Ottawa: Ministry of Supply and Services) 2.
28.   Ibid., 3.
29.   Quebec, *Statutes*, 1982, c. 30.

BIBLIOGRAPHY

Arnstein, Sherry R. "A Ladder to Citizen Participation." *Journal of the American Institute of Planners* 35 (July 1969): 216–24.

Bryden, Kenneth. "Public Input into Policy-Making and Administration." *Canadian Public Administration* 25 (spring 1982): 81–107.

Canada. *To Know and Be Known*. Report of the Task Force on Government Information. Ottawa: Queen's Printer, 1969.

Doerr, Audrey. "The Role of Coloured Papers." *Canadian Public Administration* 25 (fall 1982): 366–79.

Graham, K.A., and S.D. Phillips. "Citizen Engagement: Beyond the Customer Revolution." *Canadian Public Administration* 40 (summer 1997): 255–73.

Kernaghan, Kenneth. "Whistle-blowing in Canadian Governments: Ethical, Political and Managerial Considerations." *Optimum* 22 (1991–92): 34–43.

Knight, K.W. "Administrative Secrecy and Ministerial Responsibility." *Canadian Journal of Economics and Political Science* 32 (February 1966): 77–84.

Mishler, William. *Political Participation in Canada*. Toronto: Macmillan, 1979.

Pal, Leslie A. *Interests of State: The Politics of Language, Multiculturalism, and Feminism in Canada*. Montreal and Kingston: McGill-Queen's University Press, 1993.

Rowat, Donald C. "How Much Administrative Secrecy?" *Canadian Journal of Economics and Political Science* 31 (November 1965): 479–98.

Rowat, Donald C., ed. *Administrative Secrecy in Developed Countries*. New York: Columbia University Press, 1979.

Siegel, Arthur. *Politics and the Mass Media in Canada*. Toronto: McGraw-Hill Ryerson, 1983.

Tapscott, D. "The Digital Media and the Reinvention of Government." *Canadian Public Administration* 40 (summer 1997): 328–45.

VanNijnatten, D.L., and S.W. Gregoire. "Bureaucracy and Consultation: The Correctional Service of Canada and the Requirements of Being Democratic." *Canadian Public Administration* 38 (summer 1995): 204–21.

Zussman, D. "Do Citizens Trust Their Government?" *Canadian Public Administration* 40 (summer 1997): 234–54.

VI

The Management of Organizational Resources

22

The Management of Government Programs

In the last few years, one of the major trends in municipal organization has been the amalgamation of municipalities. The hope is that this will save money and simplify administration. In fact, the merger frequently creates some initial difficulties which politicians must deal with. This is a fictional conversation between two of these politicians meeting for the first time at the first meeting of their combined councils.

Fred: This consolidation is pretty scary. We're two very different organizations with different cultures and different goals. How are we ever going to pull this off?

Martha: That's true, but I'm more concerned about the financial side of things. The province says that this merger should allow us to reduce our expenses by 15%, but looking at these financial statements—I don't see it. I'm worried that we might have to increase some of our costs to deliver all these programs we have in place.

Fred: Well, it seems clear that we can't just continue doing what we've been doing. We'll never meet our financial targets that way.

Martha: You're right. What we need is a way to step back and make some conscious decisions about what we want to do. If we just continue to drift the way we have been, we'll end up doing everything poorly instead of focusing on our main priorities and being certain that they are done properly.

Fred: We're doing something at work called strategic planning. The idea is that we decide where we want our organization to be in ten years, then plan a way to get there. It's been pretty scary because we've decided to scrap some programs and spend a lot more money on others, but we feel like we have a better sense of where we're going. I wonder if we could use something like that in government?

This part of the book discusses the day-to-day management of government programs. It describes the issues that managers face on a regular basis and the tools they use to deal with them. Chapters 23 to 25 concentrate on such human resource management issues as staffing and classification, managing diversity, and collective bargaining. Chapters 26 and 27 discuss budgeting and financial management. This chapter focuses on some of the broad management issues and techniques that transcend the management of human and financial resources.

The first concept presented will be one of the most comprehensive management techniques developed in recent years—strategic planning. This will be followed by an introduction to another recent innovation that is gaining importance—the use of computers and management information systems. The chapter will conclude with a discussion of how governments have dealt with financial restraint, downsizing, and program terminations.

🏛 STRATEGIC PLANNING

In recent years, a number of new management practices with names like corporate management, corporate planning, and strategic planning have developed. In this chapter, the term strategic planning is used to cover all these, but it is important to understand that practitioners and writers may define each of these terms slightly differently.

This section discusses the general concept of strategic planning and describes in detail one method of implementing it. It then assesses the application of strategic planning in Canadian governments. This entire field is complex, and the literature on it has burgeoned in the past few years. Thus, this section is not intended to be comprehensive, but rather to provide a quick overview of the field. For those interested in more depth, a number of books are listed in the bibliography of this chapter.

The Concept of Strategic Planning

The first part of this book described the operation of standard bureaucratic organizations. It emphasized that these kinds of organizations are good at accomplishing repetitive tasks but that they do not manage change very well. All organizations change over time because both their external environment and their internal culture change. The only issue is whether the change will be planned and systematic or rudderless and free-form. The purpose of strategic planning is to allow organizations to engage in planned, systematic change.

Strategic planning is also very important as a priority-setting exercise. Governments are being pressed to do many different things in an environment of restrained resources. The easy course is to continue to do what has always been done. It is considerably more difficult to introduce new ideas. Strategic planning searches for new problems and opportunities and ensures that they receive an appropriate position on the agenda.

John M. Bryson has defined strategic planning as

> a disciplined effort to produce fundamental decisions and actions that shape and guide what an organization (or other entity) is, what it does, and why it does it. At its best, strategic planning requires broad-scale information gathering, an exploration of alternatives, and an emphasis on the future implications of present decisions. It can facilitate communication and participation, accommodate divergent interests and values, and foster orderly decision making and successful implementation.[1]

Strategic planning involves the entire organization and is broader than any other kind of planning. In fact, strategic planning was developed because of a recognition that narrower forms of financial or human resource planning were too restricted to provide the broad picture of where the organization ought to be going.[2]

Bryson is a prolific writer and an experienced practitioner of strategic planning in the public sector. He suggests an eight-step process.[3]

Step 1. Initiating and Agreeing on a Strategic Planning Process.
Everyone involved in the process, especially senior decision makers, must understand the process and agree on it.

Step 2. Clarifying Organizational Mandates.
Before embarking on change, every organization should understand the core activities that it *must* undertake and the outer boundaries of actions that it can and cannot perform.

Step 3. Clarifying Organizational Mission and Values.
This is the key step in the process because it requires that an organization define what its main role will be. It is surprising that so many organizations exhibit confusion in this area, but it is a symptom of the random change that occurs over time in the absence of a planned change process.

The first part of this step is to perform a stakeholder analysis. Bryson defines a stakeholder as

> any person, group, or organization that can place a claim on an organization's attention, resources, or output, or is affected by that output. Examples of government's stakeholders are citizens, taxpayers, service recipients, the governing body, employees, unions, interest groups, political parties, the financial community, and other governments.[4]

A stakeholder analysis first identifies who the stakeholders are (not always an easy task), then determines what stakeholders want from the organization and what the organization needs from stakeholders (e.g., money, political support).

Out of this process, a mission statement can be established. Figures 22.1 and 22.2 illustrate two types of mission statements. The first is a succinct, one sentence statement. The second is a longer, more detailed treatment. However, the purpose of both is the same—to provide a short description of how the

Figure 22.1
BRITISH COLUMBIA
MINISTRY OF TRANSPORTATION AND HIGHWAYS
MISSION STATEMENT

To provide and maintain safe and efficient movement of people and resources on a provincial transportation system in conjunction with the economic development of the province in a socially and environmentally acceptable manner.

Figure 22.2
MANITOBA
DEPARTMENT OF EDUCATION AND TRAINING
MISSION STATEMENT

The mission of Manitoba Education and Training is to ensure high quality education and training programs for Manitobans to enable them to develop their individual potential and contribute to the economic, social and cultural life of Manitoba. In carrying out its mission, the Department is guided by the following principles:

- *Excellence*—providing a climate for education and training that fosters dedication, determination, creativity, initiative and high achievement.
- *Equity*—ensuring fairness and providing the best possible learning opportunities for Manitobans, regardless of background or geographic location.
- *Openness*—being receptive to ways of thinking and acting that result in on-going renewal, and meaningful involvement of people in decision making.
- *Responsiveness*—meeting the education and training needs of individuals by taking into consideration personal background, individual characteristics and geographic location.
- *Choice*—providing alternatives to meet diverse learning needs and interests.
- *Relevance*—providing education and training that is current and meaningful to students.
- *Integration*—connecting components within and between education and training and social and economic systems in order to increase the effectiveness and efficiency of programs and services.
- *Accountability*—ensuring that the expected educational outcomes are realized through effective and efficient use of resources.

organization sees itself and to delineate what its goals are. It is a way of communicating with outside stakeholders, but it is also valuable as a way of focusing the attention of members of the organization.

In these first three steps, the organization has decided where it wants to go; now it is time to determine how to get there.

Step 4. Assessing the External Environment. Organizations must monitor the **p**olitical, **e**conomic, **s**ocial, and **t**echnological forces and trends (PESTs) facing them. It is important to understand that these PESTs contain both opportunities and threats. Organizations must take particular note of how changes in the PESTs are having an impact on their stakeholders.

Step 5. Assessing the Internal Environment. One way to identify internal strengths and weaknesses is to determine the efficiency with which inputs are converted to outputs. Problems in this conversion process will illustrate problems in the internal environment.

Another part of assessing the internal environment is comparing the output of the organization to the output desired by stakeholders—not the outputs desired by management. This process will determine the extent to which the internal environment is sensitive to external concerns.

At this point, the organization will have completed what Bryson refers to as a SWOT analysis (**s**trengths, **w**eaknesses, **o**pportunities, and **t**hreats). This process helps to determine where the organization sits within its environment; the next steps are geared to developing an organizational strategy for coping with the environment.

Step 6. Identifying the Strategic Issues Facing an Organization.   This step identifies the limited number of issues that will have a real impact on the future of the organization—in either a positive or a negative direction. These must be issues over which the organization has some control, e.g., it would be a waste of resources to decide how to prevent a meteorite from striking the organization's headquarters. These must be very important issues, posing either major threats or opportunities.

Step 7. Formulating Strategies to Manage the Issues.   This involves developing alternative strategies for dealing with the issues, assessing the barriers to implementing each of the strategies, and deciding which alternative to pursue.

> An effective strategy must meet several criteria. It must be technically workable, politically acceptable to key stakeholders, and must accord with the organization's philosophy and core values. It should be ethical, moral, and legal. It must also deal with the strategic issue it was supposed to address.[5]

The last sentence ought to be self-evident, but Bryson contends that many planning exercises become so caught up in satisfying political and other needs that their ultimate aim is overlooked.

This step is not completed until both a long-term strategy (two to three years) and a detailed work plan (six to twelve months) have been established. At this point, the strategic plan acts as a macro-plan for the entire organization and, therefore, provides a framework for other operational plans within individual organizational units. For example, Jennifer McQueen has described how strategic planning in one federal department is an important input for human resource planning.[6]

Step 8. Establishing an Effective Organizational Vision for the Future. This is the organization's vision of what it will look like if it implements its strategies successfully. This is usually not essential to a good strategic planning exercise, but it gives everyone involved in the process a sense of mission. It can act as a very powerful motivating force and help the organization and all of its employees focus their attention.

The Application of Strategic Planning in Canadian Governments

Strategic planning has been employed quite widely in Canadian governments at all three levels.[7] One of the most extensive studies of the implementation of strategic planning suggests that government departments have used it successfully to:

- define their mission and establish priorities;

- reallocate scarce resources;

- steer a plan to fruition; and

- establish a set of values and a philosophy of management.[8]

The literature on the application of strategic planning in Canadian governments indicates that there have been success stories. However, there have been problems as well. The basis of some problems rests in the difficulty of engaging in planning in a volatile political situation. Coldly rational planning is very difficult when governments are pressed to satisfy conflicting goals.

> [G]overnment is expected to set a standard in terms of efficiency, of fair treatment of workers and the public, of diligence, and of cost-effectiveness—a set of objectives which are clearly inconsistent, at least some of the time. But if any one of them is not met, there are political consequences.[9]

The difficulty of reconciling divergent goals was demonstrated in the Alberta Department of Energy and Natural Resources when a planning exercise actually heightened tensions between organizational units when it forced previously separate units to engage in an integrated planning exercise.[10] The tension between the units had quietly simmered for a long time, but this exercise forced it into the open.

The differing perspectives of politicians and public servants can also be a problem. Strategic planning is usually done on the basis of *programs* because that is the way public servants operate. However, politicians are more concerned with *issues* that frequently span a number of programs and departments and that change much more rapidly than programs.[11] Thus, it can be very difficult to obtain ministerial support for a planning process that does not satisfy a political need.

In sum, strategic planning can be a very good way of reconciling conflicting directions and focusing the attention of members of the organization. However, in some circumstances, it can be very difficult to implement and can even heighten tensions.

🏛 COMPUTERS AND MANAGEMENT INFORMATION SYSTEMS

The use of computers has had a major impact on government. In 1996 the Auditor General of Canada estimated that the federal government alone spent more than $3 billion annually on information technology.[12] This should not be surprising because most government work is based on exchange of information. In past times, this exchange of information was accomplished by generating and sending huge volumes of paper to many different locations. Thus, the customs clerk at a border crossing prepared a multiple copy entry form and sent the copies to other customs offices, the importer, the trucking company, and so forth. With the advent of the *information highway*, government departments and their clients are all connected by computers. You can now file your income tax return electronically, go to the kiosk maintained by Human Resources Development Canada to find out about job openings across the country, and have your property taxes paid directly from your bank to your municipality's bank. The one development that has changed the work environment of public servants the most in the last twenty years has been the evolution of computers from specialized tools controlled by experts to personal assistants sitting on everyone's desk. The information highway will continue to produce many changes in work environments and in the broader society.

> The terms *information highway* or *electronic highway* denote the advanced information and communications infrastructure that is essential for Canada's emerging information economy. Building on existing and planned communications networks, this infrastructure will become a "network of networks," linking Canadian homes, businesses, governments and institutions to a wide range of interactive services from entertainment, education, cultural products and social services to data banks, computers, electronic commerce, banking and business services....

> The enabling effects of the information highway will be felt in all industry sectors and regions of Canada. It will stimulate research and development (R&D) in leading-edge technologies; it will facilitate the diffusion of innovative technologies and information-based services; it will strengthen the competitiveness of large and small Canadian businesses; and it will provide cost-effective access to high-quality health care, educational and social services. The information highway initiative is essential for Canada's success in a new global economy in which value, jobs and wealth are based on the creation, movement and application of information.[13]

Management Information Systems

In the 1990s, it is common to view computers and management information systems as being very closely related, but the terms are not synonymous. A computer is a piece of hardware, which, when loaded with software, can provide management information, play video games, or diagnose a fault in a car engine. A management information system (MIS) has been defined as

> an organized method of providing past, present and projection information relating to internal operations and external intelligence. It supports the planning, control, and operational functions of an organization by furnishing uniform information in the proper time-frame to assist the decision making process.[14]

So an MIS can be located in a computer, but it can also be a card file or a pocket notebook. While it is important to distinguish between an MIS and the computer that usually supports it, in the 1990s an MIS is virtually always a computer-based system of some kind.

The first MISs were developed for accounting purposes, but now they are in use in all sorts of areas. When the cashier at the grocery store reads the bar code on an item you are buying, he or she is making an entry into an MIS that records changes in inventory as well as the sale price of the item. At some universities, students can telephone an MIS from the comfort of their homes to register in courses. Many provinces now have an MIS that prevents people from renewing their automobile or driver's licences if they have unpaid traffic tickets.

The strength of computer-based management information systems lies in their ability to provide information on a real-time basis so that managers can make immediate decisions. For example, an airline manager wanting to make a decision about how many seats on a particular flight to offer at a discount fare can obtain up-to-the-minute information about the number of seats already sold and the usual load factor on the flight.

The ideal MIS would provide information about external, as well as internal, events. For example, our airline manager might want to know whether there was heavy competition on the route under consideration and whether the load factor on the flight is likely to be influenced by some unusual situation such as a convention or a major sporting event.

An MIS ought to assist in all aspects of managing. In the airline example, the MIS should help in making fare decisions as well as scheduling crew members, scheduling aircraft, ordering meals, and, finally, providing an early indication of the company's profit picture.

The Evolution of Computer Technology

In earlier times, a computer was a huge machine (called a mainframe) kept in a climate-controlled environment and approached only by those with highly specialized training. Over the years, computers have become smaller and more "user-friendly" so that now many public servants have computers or terminals connected to mainframes on their desks. The user-friendly nature of these new machines means that people do not have to know anything technical about computers to use them, in the same way that a driver does not have to know anything about the mechanics of a car to drive one.

At first, these microcomputers were stand-alone devices located on a desk and unable to communicate with any other computers. However, over time the technology was developed to allow these computers to communicate with other nearby computers through the use of *LAN*s (local area networks), and to communicate with a mainframe (now usually called a server) some distance away. A large number of people located great distances apart can now exchange ideas and information with one another and can use common application packages and databases resident in one central computer.

E-mail (electronic mail) is becoming a very common way to communicate. It allows a person to send a message from her or his computer to someone else's computer virtually anywhere in the world, or send a message to everyone in an organization at the same time. This aspect of e-mail could revolutionize organizational communications because

> [i]nformation which previously was not shared because of the time pressures of other business can now be transmitted over new electronic message circuits. Some of these messages may appear trivial to an outsider, but their sharing may serve an important morale function for the group.[15]

Most organizations now maintain *Web sites*, which are accessible by computer. The Web sites contain huge amounts of information about the organization that were previously available only in paper documents located in the organization's offices or a few select libraries. It is now easy to browse through government documents, newspapers, and magazines from anywhere in the world by just sitting in front of a computer, making Web sites a tremendous research tool. This aspect of Web sites is discussed in the appendix on researching and writing papers.

Computers and Service Delivery

Computers can be a tremendous aid in the delivery of government services. In earlier times, all requests for certain government services (e.g., copies of birth certificates, applications for old age security payments) had to go through one central office. There was only one set of records and these had to be checked by hand before a decision could be made or a document issued. These transactions usually had to be handled by mail with the attendant delay.

In the computer age, everyone on the network has access to the same information at the same time. Now a client can go into any government office that is on the network and find out the necessary information immediately. This means that a decision on an application can frequently be made immediately in a remote branch office.

The British Columbia government has established a network of government agents across the province who provide one-stop shopping for a broad spectrum of government services.[16] A client can visit one of the many kiosks maintained by Human Resources Development Canada to find out about job openings both locally and across the country. Government officials contend that there are more of these kiosks than there are ATM banking machines for any one bank.

The federal government has shown that it is serious about using computers to improve the quality of services by appointing a Chief Informatics Officer who has produced a document outlining the ways in which departments can use computers to provide better service delivery in an economical fashion.[17] However, the huge integrated system proposed by the federal government is very expensive and time consuming to develop and comes with some risk of failure.[18]

There is no question that computers can be a tremendous boon to governments and the citizens who must deal with them, but this computer revolution has raised a number of concerns as well.

Privacy and Security

Governments collect huge amounts of information about everyone.[19] Government computers contain information about our health, income, marital status, level of education, and even the number of flush toilets in our homes. With modern telecommunications and database capabilities, it is *technically* very easy to match and cross-check all of this information, but the ethical issues surrounding this are very difficult.[20] For example, should a government agency concerned with financial support for deserted spouses and children have access to income tax records to locate the delinquent spouse? Should public health authorities have access to an individual's health insurance records to locate people who have been treated for AIDS or other communicable diseases?

Governments have generally responded to concerns about privacy and security by passing legislation that requires that information be used only by the agency that collected it and only for the purpose for which it was collected. This effectively prohibits sharing and cross-matching of data. Unfortunately, one occasionally hears of isolated incidents where these laws are violated. Some citizens are uneasy at even the thought that so much sensitive information about them is transmitted on telecommunications lines and stored on mechanical devices.

This concern has been heightened with the proliferation of devices that can access these files. In the early days, the mainframe was a stand-alone device kept in a secured area. Improvements in technology now allow computers to be connected to other computers and input and output devices. "What use then is the sophisticated security over the mainframe and its data bases when some of the same data are held on mere floppy disks?"[21] The large number of decentralized devices increases the possibility that an irresponsible person will use sensitive data for inappropriate purposes.

There is also the possibility of illegal access to records stored in MISs. It is now a practical necessity in most cases that computers be connected to telephone lines to facilitate movement of data. Systems managers are sensitive to the security problems this causes and attempt to protect their data from unlawful tampering. However, when a system is attached to outside communication lines, it is almost impossible to provide absolute security in the face of dedicated "hackers" or others who attempt to steal information from these systems.

All indications are that the public should not panic. Governments are sensitive to public concerns about privacy and security and exercise great care to ensure that unauthorized access to data does not occur, but absolute security in this regard can never be guaranteed.

Computers and Jobs

Another concern about computer systems has been the impact they will have on jobs. Paper-based systems tended to be labour intensive. One person prepared the source documents; several other people then used the information to update a number of records; and, finally, someone had to file the original paper document. In a computer system, all of these steps can be performed instantly by one person making one entry in a microcomputer or terminal.

The experience of B.C. Hydro is quite illuminating:

> Since 1981 employment levels in B.C. Hydro have dropped approximately 37 per cent while sales have continued to increase. Although technology is not the main cause of this decrease, it appeared that the technological innovations introduced throughout the company have enabled operations to continue with fewer employees.[22]

In practice, there have been few examples of large-scale layoffs as a direct result of computerization. Most reductions have been handled through retirements, transfers, and so forth. The standard argument is that mass layoffs ought to be avoided because workers will be more accepting of the new technology if they do not perceive that their jobs are threatened by it.

However, there is another line of thought that suggests that computers will actually increase job opportunities:

> I know some firms that brought computing devices into the accounting department, expecting that this would reduce the need for accountants and bookkeepers. But what happened is that with the computer they were able to get immediate answers to questions they'd never thought of asking before! As a result, they ended up with a larger staff in the accounting department, because with these new tools at their disposal they were able to increase market share and efficiency of production.[23]

The impact of computers on total employment levels seems unclear at this point, but it is clear that computerization will continue to have a definite effect on both the composition of the workforce and the manner in which work is organized.

Computers will likely reduce secretarial and clerical jobs and increase the need for people with the skills to design hardware and software and interpret the output of the sophisticated software packages. Since women are highly over-represented in secretarial and clerical positions, they will be hurt by these changes much more than men. "Canadian women are on a collision course between their continuing concentration in clerical occupations and industry's apparently diminishing requirements in that line of work."[24]

> The current generation of micro-computers makes typing a letter or even a lengthy report so simple that even a man can do it. They also reduce the total volume of work that needs to be done. Preparing successive drafts of a report is no longer a lengthy typing process for each new draft. One simply makes the necessary changes, enters the print command, and goes to the coffee room to join the ever-lasting conversation about the high level of stress in the modern-day workplace.[25]

In the new workplace, the skills gulf between the clerical employee and the computer analyst is such that mobility is difficult, if not impossible.[26] In the old workplace, it was quite possible for a woman to progress from clerk to senior clerk to supervisor to middle manager and so on. In the new workplace, middle-level employees need skills that can only be obtained in a college or university, so there is little hope for the clerical employee who aspires beyond her current position. "Clerical workers generally have the fewest opportunities for educational leave and staff training, and women have particular problems upgrading their qualifications because of family and related considerations."[27]

Mental and Physical Health Concerns

The increasing use of computers has raised concerns about both the mental and physical health of the people using them. The thoroughness and precision of computers allow supervisors to monitor exactly what employees are doing

every minute of every workday. Goofing off when the boss is gone is an old tradition. Some might consider it laziness, but in monotonous or stressful jobs a
certain amount of relaxation is necessary. The constant feeling that "Big
Brother" is watching is very stressful.

> The computer's silent monitoring of every action and its implicit pressure for
> greater output further depersonalize the work-place. Women interviewed for this
> study complained that having a daily record of their number of keystrokes per hour
> (in data-entry work) or sales volumes (in cashier work), plus a detailed breakdown
> of their time away from the machine, acted as a source of anxiety to them.[28]

There have also been concerns about physical problems. There have been
long-standing complaints about eye strain caused by looking at a monitor for eight
hours a day. Manufacturers have made many changes in the colour projected on
the screen to lessen this problem, but some users still experience migraine
headaches, eye strain, and other problems, which they attribute to the monitor.

A more serious concern has been registered about the effect that various
emissions from computers might have on the physical health of users. This is
usually raised when a cluster of women who work together all experience mis-
carriages or have babies with birth defects. Studies in this area are at a very early
stage. Of course, all manufacturers argue that their machines are safe, but not
all unions and workers agree.[29] One analyst who has reviewed the studies suggests that while "these conflicting reports may be more confusing than helpful
to the average office manager or computer user, there is probably enough evidence linking radiation emissions with health hazards to warrant a conservative, safety-conscious attitude."[30] Some manufacturers have responded to this
concern by developing low-emission displays.[31]

The most serious situation seems to be the condition called *repetitive strain
injury (RSI)*, which affects huge numbers of workers. This is caused by constant
repetition of the same forceful movement with no change in body position, for
example, striking the keys on a computer keyboard for several hours day in and
day out. RSI begins as a mild numbness or tingling in the fingers or arms but
can quickly become a very painful and debilitating condition. It seems to stem
from overuse of certain muscles, but very little is currently known about the
physiology of the condition and even less is known about treatment.

RSI has been called a silent epidemic and the Ontario Workplace Health and
Safety Agency "reported that workplace injuries caused by repetitive and forceful
movements or awkward body positions account for about half of the lost-time
claims processed by the Workers Compensation Board of Ontario."[32] The best
treatment seems to be prevention and many organizations are taking steps to protect their employees from this problem. The idea of sustaining a serious injury by
typing too vigorously seems almost humorous, but a week-long series of articles in
The Globe and Mail has highlighted how serious this problem is.[33]

Telework, Telecommuting, and Home Work

Computers could not only change the size and composition of the workforce,
they could also have an impact on how work will be organized.

> For decades we have been moving workers to information, at high personal and dollar costs. We now have what it takes to move information to the worker in a planned, supervised way, which produces benefits to the employer, the employee and the surrounding area.[34]

People will now be able to work in their own homes and use telephone lines to transmit their work to a central computer. For example, Northern Telecom employs about 73 000 people, almost 5 percent of whom work at home.[35] This is a positive development for many people, including parents of young children, who will not have to struggle with daycare, and people with physical disabilities, who find the journey to work difficult. This development fits in well with the changing attitudes of many workers about the need to balance family considerations and work commitments instead of spending inordinate amounts of time at the workplace.[36]

However, working from home can also have negative impacts. Figures 22.3 and 22.4 summarize many of the advantages and disadvantages of this new approach to work referred to as *flexiplace, telework,*[37] or *telecommuting.* This trend could become a very controversial issue in labour relations. Some employees (and their unions) see this as just another form of exploitative piecework, while others see it as a tremendous benefit.

The federal government evaluated a teleworking pilot project involving 800 employees in several departments. These are some of the study's findings:

> Teleworkers reported a marked increase in job satisfaction since they began to telework. While it is difficult to establish a direct cause-and-effect relationship, this could very likely result from having more control over their work environment and schedule. Such control over aspects of their professional life can, in turn, have a positive influence on their personal life, leading to reduced stress and a better ability to balance work and personal responsibilities.[38]

> [Ninety-two percent] of the supervisors reported that they have either recouped these costs or will be able to do so, primarily through increased productivity, reduced absenteeism, or savings on office space.[39]

> Teleworkers consistently indicated that their productivity has increased since they began to telework.[40]

> The workers' supervisors were a little less positive in their assessment, but they did not disagree with this conclusion.[41]

Overall, the evaluation painted a very positive picture of telework, with a few suggestions for both the employee and the supervisor to ensure that the arrangement works smoothly.

The Public Service Alliance of Canada (a major federal government union) has conducted its own, more limited study of employee satisfaction. The union study was somewhat less positive, but it still indicated that workers had a generally positive attitude toward telework.[42]

Home work is already a very common form of employment and is likely to become more so in the future as more work becomes computer-based. Employers, employees, and unions will have to address this important and controversial issue very carefully.

Figure 22.3
ADVANTAGES OF TELEWORK

For employers:
- Improvements in employee productivity; fewer interruptions
- Expanded pool of potential workers
- Reduction in office and parking space
- Aids in recruiting new employees
- Decline in absenteeism due to minor illness and bad weather
- Able to accommodate employees with disabilities or health problems

For employees:
- Reduced commuting time
- Flexible work schedule to accommodate personal and family needs
- Ability to work in more comfortable surroundings
- Reduction in costs for transportation, food, clothing, and child care.
- Reduced stress arising from greater feeling of freedom
- Renewal of motivation because of new environment

For society:
- Reduction in traffic congestion and accidents
- Fewer roadways and reduced use of polluting fossil fuels
- Better harmonization of work and family life
- Improved employment opportunities for people with physical disabilities or other impediments to normal job access
- Fewer burglaries

Source: Canada, Human Resource Development Council, Telework Pilot Program in the Public Service (Ottawa: Minister of Supply and Services Canada, 1992), 13–17.

🏛 DEALING WITH FINANCIAL RESTRAINT

In the mid-1970s, governments ended a thirty-year growth period and shifted abruptly into a much more restrained mode of operation.[43] At first, it was expected that this was just a temporary phase like some of the short-term hiring freezes that occurred during the growth period, but this restraint has now persisted for more than twenty years and shows no sign of abating. It is a reflection of a general slowing of growth in the economy.

These declining growth rates have forced Western governments to confront some politically sensitive tradeoffs that are inherent in mixed economic systems but are largely ignored during periods of rapid growth. These tradeoffs include (1) the choice between inflation or unsatisfied public demands for goods and services; (2) the choice between providing services through tax-supported bureaucracies or through market arrangements; (3) the choice between attempting to provide equal health, housing, and educational opportunities to all citizens or (in effect) rationing opportunities to those who can afford to pay for them; and (4) the

Figure 22.4
DISADVANTAGES OF TELEWORK

For employers:
- Some loss of direct control over employees
- Potential for distractions at home
- Negative public perception
- Some training and counselling costs

For employees:
- Social interaction is reduced, isolation increased
- Negative impact on promotional opportunities
- Increased electricity and other home costs

For society:
- Businesses in office areas may suffer
- Tax revenue from fuel and goods and services may decrease

Source: Canada, Human Resource Development Council, Telework Pilot Program in the Public Service (Ottawa: Minister of Supply and Services Canada, 1992), 13–17.

---

choice between spending for national defense or spending to alleviate the hardship of the poor, the sick, and the underprivileged (i.e., the dilemma of "guns vs. butter").[44]

The challenge facing government in this period is to provide the same or higher levels of public service with less funding and to maintain staff morale. Obviously, this is a very difficult task.

Causes of Financial Restraint

Many of the causes of financial restraint flow from the generally weakened nature of the economy. Not all of the causes discussed below have affected all governments equally, but these problems are fairly widespread.

Flattened tax revenues have affected some governments severely. There are a number of reasons why tax revenues have levelled off in recent years. The recession of the early 1990s has resulted in a number of business failures, a general decline in business activity, and significant reductions in levels of employment. Obviously, these trends have reduced governments' revenue from both income and sales taxes. Provinces such as Alberta and Saskatchewan, whose economies rely extensively on one resource, are very much at the mercy of the world markets for that resource. This creates "boom-and-bust" cycles, which make planning very difficult.

It has also been suggested that governments are the authors of their own misfortune because they have not used the tax system as fully as they should. In general, they have used the corporate tax system less in recent years and are relying more on the personal income tax. Isabella Bakker points to tax expenditures and tax deferrals that benefit businesses as two reasons why taxes have not kept pace with expenditure.[45]

Many jurisdictions have also suffered from *reductions in transfer payments from other governments.* Some provincial and local governments depend on transfer payments from other levels of government for more than half of their total income. As the federal government has felt the pinch, it has reduced transfer payments to provincial governments. Provincial governments, in turn, have felt that they must compensate for their reduced revenues from the federal government by reducing transfer payments to local governments.

In some jurisdictions, *surging expenditures* in the 1950s and 1960s simply could not be sustained over the longer term. During this period of buoyant revenue, governments launched many new programs without understanding the cumulative impact that all of these programs would have on total expenditures. In the 1960s and 1970s, when that cumulative impact began to be felt, governments quickly realized that they could not allow these programs to continue to grow in an unrestrained fashion. In the 1990s, increasing expenditure has been fuelled by the recession, which has forced all governments to spend more on such social support programs as unemployment insurance and social assistance at precisely the time when their revenues were declining.

Political ideology has also had a significant impact on restraint programs. It is likely that Canadians' views of government institutions[46] and, indeed, of all traditional large institutions are undergoing a fundamental change.

> All Canadian governments are now witnessing (1) a loss of faith in government that is not unlike an earlier loss of faith in private institutions, (2) a restructuring of the balance of interests that underlie our socio-economic order, and (3) a challenge to our structures of government that are perceived to be bureaucratic empires unresponsive to public opinion or political direction.[47]

The positive, activist view of government that prevailed in the post-World War II period has given way to an attitude that is much more suspicious of the increasing role of government. In recent years, politicians have found "bureaucrat bashing" to be a very convenient way to win votes. Frequently it seems that most voters

> believe that government programs are wasteful. As inflation and recession cause them to experience increased personal financial stress, citizens are more inclined to demand that their taxes be lowered, that government productivity be improved, and that waste in government be eliminated.[48]

This has created an odd dichotomy in which outraged citizens have loudly proclaimed that government is evil and government programs should be eliminated but have screamed equally loudly when programs affecting them were slated for cuts.

Some agencies lose *political or societal support* for their goals, which makes it very difficult for them to obtain adequate levels of funding. Sometimes this can come about through changes in political views held by societies. For example, if society begins to feel that those who must rely on social services are responsible for their own fate, then it is more difficult for politicians to provide funding to social service agencies. In other cases, organizations are the cause of their own difficulties, as when an agency is the subject of a serious scandal or a public display of mismanagement.

Organizations have responded to financial constraints in a variety of ways. Some have recognized that the tightening of resources is a long-term trend and they would have to develop a long term strategy to deal with it, while others have simply muddled through.

Strategies for Managing Restraint

Two writers in the field of cutback management have defined the basic problem as "how to wind back bureaucratic spending and staff with the least damage to whatever is held dear (including one's hold on power)."[49] Before discussing specific measures that governments have used to effect cutbacks, it is important to understand that the sort of extreme restraint that all governments have been experiencing for a prolonged period has had a significant impact on virtually all aspects of government organization. It is not simply a matter of reducing expenditure; there have been major changes in government operations and shifts of power within organizations.[50]

The first strategy that an organization could use to deal with restraint is to *resist the imposition of restraint.*[51] Management could engage in such a fight by building a coalition of important individuals and groups to make it clear to budget cutters how important the organization is.

This coalition could involve a wide range of what might, under other circumstances, appear to be strange bedfellows. For example, management and union could combine forces in the common cause of protecting their jobs. Management could also employ client groups, outside interest groups, and professional associations to testify to the importance of the agency under fire. Large public meetings help clarify to both the media and political decision makers how important an agency is in the eyes of the community.

However, there are dangers in these tactics. Fighting back will obviously irritate the decision makers who are trying to impose the cuts. This might cause them to take punitive action against ringleaders, who would otherwise have been spared. Alternatively, the budget cutters might retreat temporarily but return in future years with an even more devastating and well-formulated plan. Also, the support groups are a limited resource. They can be activated once or twice to support the cause, but interest usually wanes as the fight drags on. There is nothing more embarrassing than a public meeting with a sparse turnout; it makes it clear to politicians that support for the organization is very weak.

This is a strategy that is best employed to resist short-term cutback initiatives. In the extensive cutbacks of the 1990s virtually all organizations are suffering to some extent. The best a department can hope for is to minimize the level of reductions it must endure relative to other departments. This has led organizations to develop a variety of strategies that will allow them to continue to deliver most of their services at considerably less cost.

Alternative service delivery (ASD) is a method of maintaining the quality of service delivery at reduced cost to the government organization. This was discussed in more detail in Chapter 11, but the general idea is that governments search for improved ways of delivering services, such as forging partnerships with other organizations or contracting out. Many of the ideas below are ASD-type approaches to the problem of doing more with less.

Many organizations are now using *volunteers* to assist in the performance of some duties. There is a long tradition of volunteerism in firefighting and hospitals, but it is now expanding into such areas as recreation and social services. Sometimes a symbiotic relationship can develop between an educational institution wanting to give its students practical experience and a government needing volunteers. The obvious problem in relying on volunteers is obtaining adequate numbers of appropriately trained people.

Many governments have begun to employ *user fees* more extensively.[52] Some governments are now charging for services that were provided free at one point, and in other cases governments are increasing what were nominal fees to a point where the fee covers the actual cost of providing the service. There are two purposes behind the imposition of user fees. The most obvious is to provide revenue to the government, but the second is to reduce demand for the service. For example, one of the relatively new areas for user fees is solid waste collection. Municipalities are imposing these charges both to raise revenue and to encourage recycling, composting, and other methods of disposing waste.

There is always some controversy surrounding the initial imposition or increase of user fees. People are upset at the idea of being subjected to increasing levels of taxation and also having to pay sharply increased user fees. User fees can be seen as regressive forms of taxation. A charge to use a swimming pool that seems nominal to a wealthy family with one child might pose a significant burden to a poorer family with several children.

For these reasons, politicians have ambivalent feelings about the imposition of user fees. On the one hand, fees are a good source of revenue directed at those who use the service. On the other hand, they can be a political minefield if they irritate well-organized groups such as sports leagues.

Many governments are *contracting out* certain services to save money. Like some other responses to fiscal stress, this is not a new idea. Governments have been contracting out the provision of legal services, specialized computer services, and road construction and maintenance for a long time. What has changed recently is the range of services that governments have been contracting out and the innovative nature of some of the arrangements.[53] This potentially complex and politically divisive issue was discussed more fully in Chapter 11.

Some organizations prefer to use *equal, across-the-board cuts* to implement restraint. One argument for this approach is that it is fair because it forces everyone to bear a portion of the pain. It can also be the easiest alternative politically.

Cutting back equally and across the board is much less risky than suggesting that certain social needs can be more urgent than others. Similarly, there is more political wisdom in pretending that all programs are equally efficient and effective than in trying to identify the real impact of some programs.[54]

However, the very fact that the burden is spread equally is sometimes seen as unfair. Some organizational units are more central to the mandate of the overall organization and, therefore, cuts to these organizations will weaken the overall organization more than cuts elsewhere. Other parts of the organization might have already suffered serious shocks (e.g., a rapidly expanding client load) which make it difficult for them to bear their "fair" share.

Hiring freezes demonstrate some of the same problems as across-the-board cuts. There is no guarantee that hiring freezes will affect all units equally. They could lead to the devastation of some units with high turnover and not touch more stable units. Hiring freezes are not sensitive to changes in the demand for services and could result in serious cutbacks in expanding areas while leaving areas of declining demand with excess resources.

Small, short-term financial restraint can probably be handled by across-the-board cuts and hiring freezes, but these are dangerous techniques for handling more serious, long-term restraint. Their continual imposition could slowly, but systematically, destroy the ability of every organizational unit to provide services. Obviously this would weaken the credibility of the entire organization.

Virtually all government organizations have now employed some form of *wage roll backs and other restrictions on the collective bargaining process.*[55] These are usually introduced unilaterally by governments, although sometimes governments agree to discuss the details of implementation with employee associations or unions. The standard selling point for the rollbacks is that other sectors of the economy are experiencing significant job losses, and the idea of all employees accepting a rollback is preferable to some employees losing their jobs.

The first reaction is for unions and employees to fight these restrictions. However, most employees eventually come to accept the principle of rollbacks, even if they have reservations about certain aspects of their implementation. They are usually imposed, and accepted, on the basis that everyone has to do her or his share.

Over time, this attitude of semi-cooperation, or at least acceptance, has eroded. At first, public servants took the position that their security of employment and the fact that their rates of pay were generally quite adequate more than offset the temporary rollbacks. As the security of employment has declined (see the next section) and the temporary rollbacks have continued for many years with no sign of change, employee dissatisfaction has increased.

The morale of staff has also been affected by the fact that employees are attempting to grapple with a dizzying array of major structural and other changes in government at the same time that they are facing these personal reductions in pay.[56]

This is further exacerbated by the increasing popularity of "bureaucrat bashing" among politicians, the media, and the general public. The irony is not lost on public servants that the chorus of bureaucrat bashing has been increasing at a time when they are working harder, earning less, and losing job security.

In many governments, there is currently a great deal of tension in the workplace as employees continue to try to serve their clients while working with fewer resources and experiencing ever-increasing declines in real income.[57] This was one of the causes of a very nasty strike in the federal government in 1991, the effects of which are still being felt.

In addition to rollbacks, most governments have also begun to *downsize*, or to use the more palatable term, *rightsize*. These are both euphemisms for shedding employees in one way or another. Governments usually move on this progressively. The first step is to offer a very attractive pension package to encourage long-serving employees to retire early. The next step is to engage in what is frequently called *workforce adjustment*.[58] This usually involves declaring certain jobs redundant. The incumbents of these positions are then offered early retirement (if applicable) or are placed on a list of persons who have priority for other positions. At the early stages of this process, the worst consequence is that people are forced to take jobs that they do not like in geographic locations that they do not like. As the process continues over time, more and more employees are added to the list as more and more positions are abolished. It is clear that at some point, many of these employees will be adjusted out of the workplace.

The federal and provincial governments have sometimes been accused of *downloading* programs. This involves the shifting of responsibility for programs to other levels of government. The federal government has recently revised a long-standing policy so that more refugees will now be receiving social assistance from provincial government rather than from the federal government.[59] Municipalities are particularly susceptible to this because they are at the bottom of the chain and because they depend heavily on the provincial governments. In Ontario, the provincial government has dealt with the very sensitive and costly issue of security in courthouses by making municipal police forces responsible for it. Numerous other examples can be found in the social service area.

Sometimes, selective *program termination* is the only solution. When it is clear that restraint will be serious and long term, it is necessary for managers to engage in strategic planning to decide how they want the organization to work after downsizing.[60] Radical restraint will produce not just a *quantitatively smaller* organization, but also a *qualitatively different* organization. Thus, a decision might have to be made to eliminate certain programs or deliver some services in a completely different manner.

It can be very difficult to terminate a program because both managers and clients will probably resist.[61] Robert D. Behn has prepared a series of tips to assist in this difficult process. A few of them are:[62]

- "Don't float trial balloons." This gives supporters of the program an opportunity to mobilize others. It is better to announce termination of the program and stand firm.

- "Focus attention on the policy's harm." All policies, regardless of their benefits, have some harmful side effects, even if it is only that they use resources which could be employed elsewhere.

- "Accept short-term cost increases." With severance pay to employees, and payments to contractors to allow for early termination of contracts, the one-time cost of terminating a program might be greater than the annual cost of operating it. Would-be program terminators will simply have to accept the short-term media and other criticism which this will generate and remember that there is a long-term benefit.

- "Buy off the beneficiaries." Offer the more vocal critics something else instead of this policy. Obviously, care must be taken to ensure that the cost of the sweetener (including all future costs) does not exceed the cost of the program terminated.

One of the most radical concepts for dealing with the current financial situation facing governments is *reinventing government*. David Osborne and Ted Gaebler's book *Reinventing Government* is one of the most widely read books in government circles in years. They debunk the idea that the only options available to governments facing financial restraint are to raise taxes or to cut services. Their basic argument is that governments should be steering society, but in recent years they have been doing *too much rowing and not enough steering*. In other words, governments have been viewed too much as direct providers of goods and services, and they have been devoting so much of their resources to providing services that they have not been directing society.

Osborne and Gaebler's book contains many anecdotes that illustrate how governments were able to use innovative and entrepreneurial ideas to work smarter. Many of their ideas are not new, but their forceful method of presentation has caused many public sector managers to rethink their methods of operation. For example, Osborne and Gaebler discuss the idea of government becoming more of a facilitator or partner and less of a doer. They exhort governments to encourage other organizations to do things rather than do them themselves.

Program Review

Program Review is one of the major initiatives that the federal and many provincial governments have used to try to reduce expenditure.[63]

The federal Program Review exercise was initiated in February 1994. It was clear that this was a top-down process, with the strong support of Prime Minister Chrétien. It began with the target of reducing the federal deficit by 3 percent of gross domestic product over a two-year period. The overall target was then allocated among departments, but not on an across-the-board basis. Some departments were allocated larger cuts than others. Each department was then required to prepare an "action plan" that would allow it to meet its two-year target.[64]

This differed from earlier expenditure reduction exercises that attempted to reduce expenditure by ferreting out waste in government programs. These exercises were singularly unsuccessful because they required managers to admit that there was waste in their programs. The Program Review exercise turned this around by imposing a target cut and making it a matter of patriotic duty to find the funds necessary to fight the deficit.

Program Review went beyond just deficit reduction; it examined the role of government generally and the role of the federal government specifically by asking the six questions listed below about each program. The questions allowed managers to address some very important issues about their program, their department, and even the role of the federal government. The exercise resulted in many changes in programs and some terminations.[65]

SIX QUESTIONS FOR PROGRAM REVIEW

Test	Question
Public Interest	Is the program still in the public interest?
Role of Government	Is its delivery a legitimate and necessary role for government?
Federalism	Is the current federal role appropriate or should the program be realigned with the provinces?
Partnership	Should it be delivered in partnership with the private or voluntary sector?
Efficiency	How can it be redesigned for efficiency?
Affordability	Is it affordable, given fiscal constraints?

A serious evaluation of the overall process has argued that it did not accomplish everything it attempted,[66] but it is quite clear that it succeeded in reducing the deficit.

🏛 CONCLUSION

This chapter has covered some of the significant issues that government managers in the 1990s must face and some of the techniques that they are using to deal with them. The impact of computers on the workplace has been highly visible and very significant. The long-term financial restraint facing government is also having a serious impact. Governments have dealt with short-term restraint before, but there has never such a protracted period of restraint before. While there are signs that the worst of the reductions is over, it is likely that governments will operate permanently at a lower level than they experienced twenty years ago. This means that we have not only a quantitatively smaller government, but also a qualitatively different government. There is no question that this long-term restraint has changed the role of government in society. Strategic planning is one way of making decisions about how governments and other organizations will reshape themselves to deal with the new world they are facing.

NOTES

1. John M. Bryson, *Strategic Planning for Public and Nonprofit Organizations* (San Francisco: Jossey-Bass Publishers, 1988), 5.
2. Jack Koteen, *Strategic Management in Public and Nonprofit Organizations* (New York: Praeger, 1989), 18.

3. Bryson, *Strategic Planning*, ch. 3.

4. Ibid., 52.

5. Ibid., 60.

6. Jennifer McQueen, "Integrating Human Resource Planning with Strategic Planning," *Canadian Public Administration* 27, no. 1 (spring 1984): 1–13.

7. Gaetan Lussier, "Planning and Accountability in Employment and Immigration Canada," *Canadian Public Administration* 28, no. 1 (spring 1985): 134–42; Robert Loo, "Strategic Planning for Mental Health Services in Canada's Federal Police Services," *Canadian Public Administration* 29, no. 3 (fall 1986): 469–73.

8. Mohamed Charih and Michel Paquin, "La planification stratégique à Ottawa et à Québec: une comparaison de quelques ministères," *Canadian Public Administration* 36, no. 2 (summer 1993), 185 and passim; see also: Special Issue on "Strategic Management in the Public Sector," *Optimum* 24, no. 1 (summer 1993).

9. Benjamin Levin, "Squaring the Circle: Strategic Planning in Government," *Canadian Public Administration* 28, no. 4 (winter 1985): 601.

10. Ken Langhorn and Bob Hinings, "Integrated Planning and Organizational Conflict," *Canadian Public Administration* 30, no. 4 (winter 1987): 550–65.

11. Levin, "Squaring the Circle," 602–603.

12. Auditor General of Canada, *Report of the Auditor General of Canada to the House of Commons*, Ch. 16: "Treasury Board Secretariat—Renewing Government Services Using Information Technology" (Ottawa: Minister of Public Works and Government Services, 1996), 7.

13. Spectrum, Information Technologies and Telecommunications Sector, Industry Canada, *The Canadian Information Highway: Building Canada's Information and Communications Infrastructure* (Ottawa: Minister of Supply and Services Canada, 1994), 1.

14. Walter J. Kennevan, "MIS Universe," *Data Management* (September 1970), 63.

15. Ted Grusec, "Office Automation Trials in the Federal Government: Lessons for Managers," *Canadian Public Administration* 29, no. 4 (winter 1986): 559.

16. Brian Marson, "Building Customer-Focused Organizations in British Columbia," *Public Administration Quarterly* (spring 1993), 30–47.

17. Art Eggleton, President of the Treasury Board, *Blueprint for Renewing Government Services Using Information Technology* (n.d.)

18. Auditor General of Canada, *Report of the Auditor General of Canada to the House of Commons*, ch. 16, see also: same report, ch. 24: Systems under Development—Getting Results (November 1996).

19. David Lyon, "The End of Privacy," *Policy Options* 18, no. 3 (April 1997), 3–7.

20. Kenneth Kernaghan and John Langford, *The Responsible Public Servant* (Halifax: The Institute for Research on Public Policy, and Toronto: The Institute of Public Administration of Canada, 1990), ch. 4.

21. Bruce A. Macdonald, "Information Management in the Public Service: Summary of Discussions," *Canadian Public Administration* 29, no. 1 (spring 1986): 9.

22. Jill E. Davidson, "Tech Change: Boon or Bane for Professionals, Supervisors and Middle Managers," *Canadian Public Administration* 29, no. 4 (winter 1986): 563.

23. Stuart L. Smith, *Technology and Work in Canada's Future* (Toronto: The Governing Council of the University of Toronto, 1986), 54.

24. Heather Menzies, *Women and the Chip* (Montreal: The Institute for Research on Public Policy, 1981), 75.

25. David Siegel, "The Changing Shape and Nature of Public Service Employment," *Canadian Public Administration* 31, no. 2 (summer 1988): 187.

26. Eli Ginzberg, Thierry J. Novelle, and Thomas M. Stanback, Jr., *Technology and Employment: Concepts and Clarifications* (Boulder, Colo: Westview Press, 1986), chs. 3 and 4.

27. Menzies, *Women and the Chip*, 65.

28. Ibid., 63.

29. Ontario Public Service Employees Union, *The Hazards of VDTs* (Toronto: Ontario Public Service Employees Union, 1981).

30. Susan King, "Bad for Your Health?" *CGA Magazine*, October 1993, 66.

31. Winn L. Rosch, "Monitor Emissions: Should You Worry?" *PC Magazine*, July 1991, 106–7.

32. Virginia Galt, "Silent Epidemic Disabling Work Force," *The Globe and Mail*, 5 November 1993.

33. The articles began on 27 December 1993.

34. Linda Russell, senior partner with Telecommuting Consultants International, as quoted in: Virginia Galt, "Oh, Give Me a Home ...," *The Globe and Mail*, 19 September 1992.

35. Heather Scoffield, "Nortel Leaves Employees at Home," *The Globe and Mail*, 27 May 1998.

36. This issue has become of great concern to employers. The federal government has been involved in a major study reported in: Symposium on "Balancing Work and Family: A Study of the Canadian Work Force," *Optimum* 23, no. 2 (autumn 1992).

37. The federal government prefers the word telework to emphasize that the work need not take place at home.

38. Treasury Board Secretariat of Canada, *Evaluation of Telework Pilot Policy—Highlights* (Ottawa: Minister of Supply and Services Canada 1996), 8.

39. Ibid., 9.

40. Ibid.

41. Ibid., 10.

42. Public Service Alliance of Canada, *Delivering Public Services from Home: Telework in the 90's* (February 1996).

43. These phases are well-chronicled in L.R. Jones and Jerry L. McCaffery, *Government Response to Financial Constraints: Budgetary Control in Canada* (New York: Greenwood Press, 1989).

44. Charles H. Levine, "The New Crisis in the Public Sector," in Charles H. Levine, ed., *Managing Fiscal Stress: The Crisis in the Public Sector* (Chatham, N.J.: Chatham House, 1980), 3.

45. Isabella Bakker, "The Size and Scope of Government: Robin Hood Sent Packing," in Michael S. Whittington and Glen Williams, eds., *Canadian Politics in the 1990s*, 3rd ed. (Scarborough, Ont.: Nelson Canada, 1990), 440–41.

46. Neil Nevitte, *The Decline of Deference: Canadian Value Change in Cross-National Perspective* (Peterborough, Ont.: Broadview Press, 1996), 54–62.

47. Peter Aucoin, "The Politics and Management of Restraint in Government: An Overview," in Peter Aucoin, ed., *The Politics and Management of Restraint in Government* (Montreal: The Institute for Research in Public Policy, 1981), 3.

48. Levine, "The New Crisis in the Public Sector," 5.

49. Andrew Dunsire and Christopher Hood, *Cutback Management in Public Bureaucracies* (Cambridge: Cambridge University Press, 1989), 186.

50. Peter Aucoin, "The Politics and Management of Restraint Budgeting," in André Blais and Stéphane Dion, eds., *The Budget-Maximizing Bureaucrat: Appraisals and Evidence* (Pittsburgh: University of Pittsburgh Press, 1991), 119–41.

51. Some examples of strategies are described in Cynthia Hardy, "Fighting Cutbacks: Some Issues for Public Sector Administrators," *Canadian Public Administration* 28, no. 4 (winter 1985): 531–49; Cynthia Hardy, *Strategies for Retrenchment and Turnaround: The Politics of Survival* (Berlin: Walter de Gruyter, 1990), ch. 13 and passim.

52. Neil B. Ridler, "Fiscal Constraints and the Growth of User Fees Among Canadian Municipalities," *Canadian Public Administration* 27, no. 3 (fall 1984): 429–36.

53. A partial catalogue of both these things is found in Robert L. Bish, "Improving Productivity in the Government Sector: The Role of Contracting Out," in David Laidler

(research coordinator), *Responses to Economic Change* (Toronto: University of Toronto Press, 1986), 209–11.

54. Eli Teram and Pamela G. Hines, "The Case for Government Involvement in the Management of Cutbacks by Public Service Organizations," *Canadian Public Administration* 31, no. 1 (fall 1988): 333.

55. For a discussion of how this was done in Ontario, see: Michael Decter, "Ontario Social Contract: Restructuring for Productivity and Survival," *Public Sector Management* 4, no. 4 (n.d.), 28–30.

56. This panoply of changes is discussed in: Ian C. Clark, "Restraint, Renewal and the Treasury Board Secretariat," *Canadian Public Administration* 37, no. 2 (summer 1994), pp. 209–48.

57. Kevin Cox, "Teachers Threaten Strike Action over Wage Cuts," *The Globe and Mail*, 9 May 1994.

58. A good survey of the range of policies adopted by governments is contained in: Terry H. Wagar and Shelley Arsenault, "Workforce Reduction in the Public Sector: Evidence from the Maritime Provinces," *Canadian Public Administration* 37, no. 1 (spring 1994), 177–84.

59. Craig McInnes, "Coming and Going Get More Costly, as Immigration, Deportation Fees Rise," *The Globe and Mail*, 16 April 1994.

60. Such an exercise is described in Ivan Robinson, "Managing Retrenchment in a Public Service Organization," *Canadian Public Administration* 28, no. 4 (winter 1985): 513–30.

61. Thomas R. Dye, *Understanding Public Policy*, 7th ed. (Englewood Cliffs, N.J.: Prentice-Hall, 1992), 371–73.

62. Robert D. Behn, "How to Terminate a Public Policy: A Dozen Hints for the Would-Be Terminator," in Levine, ed., *Managing Fiscal Stress*, 327–42.

63. A good overview of the exercises at both levels of government is contained in: Amelita Armit and Jacques Bourgault eds., *Hard Choices or No Choices: Assessing Program Review* (Toronto: The Institute of Public Administration of Canada, n.d.).

64. The federal government has presented reviews of this exercise in: President of the Treasury Board, *Strengthening Government Review* (Ottawa: Minister of Supply and Services, 1995); Treasury Board of Canada Secretariat, *Getting Government Right* (Ottawa: Minister of Public Works and Government Services Canada, 1997).

65. Paul G. Thomas, "Vision versus Resources in the Federal Program Review," in Amelita Armit and Jacques Bourgault, eds., *Hard Choices or No Choices: Assessing Program Review* (Toronto: The Institute of Public Administration of Canada, n.d.), 44.

66. Gilles Paquet and Robert Shepherd, "The Program Review Process: A Deconstruction," in Gene Swimmer ed., *How Ottawa Spends 1996–97: Life Under the Knife* (Ottawa: Carleton University Press, Inc., 1996), 39–72.

BIBLIOGRAPHY

Armit, Amelita, and Jacques Bourgault, eds. *Hard Choices or No Choices: Assessing Program Review* (Toronto: The Institute of Public Administration of Canada, n.d.).

Aucoin, Peter. "The Politics and Management of Restraint Budgeting." In André Blais and Stéphane Dion, eds., *The Budget-Maximizing Bureaucrat: Appraisals and Evidence*. Pittsburgh: University of Pittsburgh Press, 1991, 119–41.

Aucoin, Peter, ed. *The Politics and Management of Restraint in Government*. Montreal: The Institute for Research in Public Policy, 1981.

Auditor General of Canada. *Report of the Auditor General of Canada to the House of Commons*. Ch. 16: "Treasury Board Secretariat—Renewing Government Services Using Information Technology." Ottawa: Minister of Public Works and Government Services, 1996.

Bakker, Isabella. "The Size and Scope of Government: Robin Hood Sent Packing." In Michael S. Whittington and Glen Williams, eds., *Canadian Politics in the 1990s*, 3rd ed. Scarborough, Ont.: Nelson Canada, 1990, 423–47.

Bish, Robert L. "Improving Productivity in the Government Sector: The Role of Contracting Out." In David Laidler (research coordinator), *Responses to Economic Change*. Toronto: University of Toronto Press, 1986, 203–37.

Brown-John, C. Lloyd. "If You're So Damned Smart Why Don't You Run Government Like a Business?" In Katherine A. Graham, ed., *How Ottawa Spends: 1990–91: Tracking the Second Agenda*. Ottawa: Carleton University Press, 1990, 219–45.

Bryson, John M. *Strategic Planning for Public and Nonprofit Organizations*. San Francisco: Jossey-Bass Publishers, 1988.

Canada. Human Resource Development Council. *Telework Pilot Program in the Public Service*. Ottawa: Minister of Supply and Services Canada, 1992.

Charih, Mohamed, and Michel Paquin. "La planification stratégique à Ottawa et à Québec: une comparaison de quelques ministères," *Canadian Public Administration* 36, no. 2 (summer 1993), 175–89.

Clark, Ian C. "Restraint, Renewal and the Treasury Board Secretariat." *Canadian Public Administration* 37, no. 2 (summer 1994), 209–48.

Davidson, Jill E. "Tech Change: Boon or Bane for Professionals, Supervisors and Middle Managers." *Canadian Public Administration* 29, no. 4 (winter 1986): 562–66.

Decter, Michael. "Ontario Social Contract: Restructuring for Productivity and Survival," *Public Sector Management* 4, no. 4 (n.d.), 28–30.

Dunsire, Andrew, and Christopher Hood. *Cutback Management in Public Bureaucracies*. Cambridge: Cambridge University Press, 1989.

Eggleton, Art, President of the Treasury Board. *Blueprint for Renewing Government Services Using Information Technology*. n.d.

Finley, Lawrence K., ed. *Public Sector Privatization: Alternative Approaches to Service Delivery*. New York: Quorum Books, 1989.

Ginzberg, Eli, Thierry J. Novelle, and Thomas M. Stanback, Jr. *Technology and Employment: Concepts and Clarifications*. Boulder, Colo.: Westview Press, 1986.

Grusec, Ted. "Office Automation Trials in the Federal Government: Lessons for Managers." *Canadian Public Administration* 29, no. 4 (winter 1986): 556–62.

Hardy, Cynthia. "Fighting Cutbacks: Some Issues for Public Sector Administrators." *Canadian Public Administration* 28, no. 4 (winter 1985): 531–49.

———. *Strategies for Retrenchment and Turnaround: The Politics of Survival*. Berlin: Walter de Gruyter, 1990.

Jones, L.R., and Jerry L. McCaffery. *Government Response to Financial Constraints: Budgetary Control in Canada*. New York: Greenwood Press, 1989.

Kernaghan, Kenneth, and John Langford. *The Responsible Public Servant*. Halifax: The Institute for Research on Public Policy, and Toronto: The Institute of Public Administration of Canada, 1990.

Langhorn, Ken, and Bob Hinings. "Integrated Planning and Organizational Conflict." *Canadian Public Administration* 30, no. 4 (winter 1987): 550–65.

Levin, Benjamin. "Squaring the Circle: Strategic Planning in Government." *Canadian Public Administration* 28, no. 4 (winter 1985): 600–605.

Levine, Charles H., ed. *Managing Fiscal Stress: The Crisis in the Public Sector*. Chatham, N.J.: Chatham House, 1980.

Lyon, David. "The End of Privacy." *Policy Options* 18, no. 3 (April 1997), 3–7.

Loo, Robert. "Strategic Planning for Mental Health Services in Canada's Federal Police Services." *Canadian Public Administration* 29, no. 3 (fall 1986): 469–73.

Lussier, Gaetan. "Planning and Accountability in Employment and Immigration Canada." *Canadian Public Administration* 28, no. 1 (spring 1985): 134–42.

Marson, Brian. "Building Customer–Focused Organizations in British Columbia." *Public Administration Quarterly* (spring 1993), 30–47.

McQueen, Jennifer. "Integrating Human Resource Planning with Strategic Planning." *Canadian Public Administration* 27, no. 1 (spring 1984): 1–13.

Menzies, Heather. *Women and the Chip.* Montreal: The Institute for Research on Public Policy, 1981.

Nevitte, Neil. *The Decline of Deference: Canadian Value Change in Cross-National Perspective.* Peterborough, Ont.: Broadview Press, 1996.

Northcott, Jim, Michael Fogarty, and Malcolm Trevor. *Chips and Jobs: Acceptance of New Technology at Work.* London: Policy Studies Institute, 1985.

Ontario Public Service Employees Union. *The Hazards of VDTs.* Toronto: Ontario Public Service Employees Union, 1981.

Osbaldeston, Gordon F. *Keeping Deputy Ministers Accountable.* Scarborough, Ont.: McGraw-Hill Ryerson, 1989.

Paquet, Gilles, and Robert Shepherd. "The Program Review Process: A Deconstruction." In Gene Swimmer (ed.), *How Ottawa Spends 1996–97: Life Under the Knife* (Ottawa: Carleton University Press, Inc., 1996), 39–72.

President of the Treasury Board. *Strengthening Government Review* Ottawa: Minister of Supply and Services 1995.

Public Service Alliance of Canada, *Delivering Public Services from Home: Telework in the 90's* (February 1996).

Ridler, Neil B. "Fiscal Constraints and the Growth of User Fees Among Canadian Municipalities." *Canadian Public Administration* 27, no. 3 (fall 1984): 429–36.

Robinson, Ivan. "Managing Retrenchment in a Public Service Organization." *Canadian Public Administration* 28, no. 4 (winter 1985): 513–30.

Siegel, David. "The Changing Shape and Nature of Public Service Employment." *Canadian Public Administration* 31, no. 2 (summer 1988): 159–93.

Smith, Stuart L. *Technology and Work in Canada's Future.* Toronto: The Governing Council of the University of Toronto, 1986.

Special Issue on "Strategic Management in the Public Sector," *Optimum* 24, no. 1 (summer 1993).

Spectrum, Information Technologies and Telecommunications Sector, Industry Canada. *The Canadian Information Highway: Building Canada's Information and Communications Infrastructure.* Ottawa: Minister of Supply and Services Canada, 1994.

Symposium on "Balancing Work and Family: A Study of the Canadian Work Force." *Optimum* 23, no. 2 (autumn 1992).

Tellier, Paul M. "Public Service 2000: The Renewal of the Public Service." *Canadian Public Administration* 33, no. 2 (summer 1990): 123–32.

Teram, Eli, and Pamela G. Hines. "The Case for Government Involvement in the Management of Cutbacks by Public Service Organizations." *Canadian Public Administration* 31, no. 1 (fall 1988): 321–34.

Treasury Board Secretariat of Canada. *Evaluation of Telework Pilot Policy—Highlights.* Ottawa: Minister of Supply and Services Canada, 1996.

Treasury Board of Canada Secretariat. *Getting Government Right.* Ottawa: Minister of Public Works and Government Services Canada, 1997.

Wagar, Terry H., and Shelley Arsenault. "Workforce Reduction in the Public Sector: Evidence from the Maritime Provinces." *Canadian Public Administration* 37, no. 1 (spring 1994), 177–84.

23

The Management of Human Resources

A new vision for managing human resources is required. At least, that's the argument of some advocates of change in the terms and conditions of employment for public servants. One vision of a new employment system calls for the preservation of "core principles such as merit, fairness, transparency and equity," while asserting the need "to fundamentally rethink what these principles mean today."[1] In particular, merit "should not confer universal rights of consideration to all employees for all possible positions for which they might be qualified as it does in large measure today."[2] Proponents of this new vision contend that there is a pressing need for more flexible management of human resources. It is argued, for example, that there should be greater *mobility* of employees, both within the public service and between the public service and the private sector.

Those advocating a more conservative approach agree that such mobility can have positive effects, like getting the right mix of skills at the right time. But they note that it can also have an adverse impact on important public service values. For example, given the uncertainty about the length of their government employment, some public servants would constantly be on the lookout for future job opportunities, wherever these might be found. As a result, traditional values such as *loyalty* and, indeed, new values such as *service*, might take a back seat to the driving force of advancing one's career.

Therefore, it is important to ask what values need to be preserved in the management of human resources. What is meant by *merit*? What is the legislative and organizational environment within which human resource management is set? What are the major processes involved? And to what extent do we have a career public service? This chapter examines each of these questions.

The competence and performance of public employees are key determinants of successful policy formation and execution. Yet it is only since the mid-1980s that governments have fully recognized the central importance of effective human resource management. Moreover, their efforts to improve it have been complicated by such factors as financial restraint accompanied by workforce reductions, concerns about employment equity and pay equity, and adversarial employer-employee relations.

🏛 THE CONCEPT OF MERIT

Merit is the most pervasive and enduring theme in human resource management. To understand the concept of merit, one must distinguish between the merit *principle* and the merit *system*. As noted in Chapter 13, the merit principle has often been explained as requiring that public service appointments be based exclusively on merit, in the sense of fitness to do the job, and that citizens have a reasonable opportunity to be considered for public service employment. Yet this definition allows for considerable interpretation as to what is meant by "reasonable"; moreover, fitness for the job does not necessarily require that the most qualified person be chosen. The merit principle is often interpreted solely in terms of appointing the best qualified person, that is, the "reasonable opportunity" component is omitted. Canadian courts have consistently interpreted merit to mean "best qualified."

In practice, the meaning of the merit principle is worked out through the merit system, which is the mechanism, consisting of policies, procedures, and regulations, by which the merit principle is pursued. The merit system is a dynamic concept in that it can be adapted to changing circumstances. The federal Public Service Commission, which is responsible for safeguarding the merit principle through implementation of the merit system, is obliged to reconcile the merit principle with several other important principles. According to the commission,

> [a]ppointments to the Public Service are based on merit, and Public Service employees advance in accordance with merit. This means that the knowledge, experience, abilities and personal suitabilities of candidates are evaluated against the requirements of the position. It also means that the best qualified person (relative merit) or a qualified person based on a standard of competence (individual merit) is selected, and that treatment of Public Service employees and those seeking employment in the Public Service is fair and equitable. The Public Service must be highly competent, totally professional and politically neutral in providing advice to the government and quality services to the Canadian public. It also must be representative of the population it serves. Its staffing system must be easy to manage, economical to operate and sufficiently flexible to meet changing operational needs and driven by ... values (fairness, equity and transparency)....[3]

Despite the advances in organization theory during this century, public sector human resource management continues to be based to a significant extent on the scientific management school of thought that emerged in the early decades of the century. But "current organizational theory, which views organizations more in terms of social systems, suggests that individuals should know the results expected of them [and] have some influence over the work they perform and over the possible application and development of their own abilities to varying tasks in support of those results."[4] In brief, it is argued that a less rigid interpretation of merit should be complemented by enhanced concern about some of the influences on motivation considered in Chapters 4 and 5.

The human resource policies of our public services do not always reflect what we have learned from organization theorists about the behaviour of people in organizations. The objective of human resource management should be to supply a sufficient number of well-qualified and well-motivated persons at the appropriate time to ensure successful development and implementation of government policies and programs. Greater emphasis has traditionally been placed on providing well-qualified, rather than well-motivated, public employees. Given the evolution of human resource management in the unique Canadian environment and the recency of important insights into organizational behaviour, this emphasis is understandable. However, the long-standing concern about the quality of employees' preparation and performance can now be combined with increased attention to the quality of their working lives and its effect on their performance. The current emphasis on empowering public employees, discussed in Chapter 4, is the primary means by which this combination is being pursued.

There have been few significant events, developments, or reforms in the public service that have not affected human resource management in general and merit in particular. Merit has been pursued within the broader context of the traditional public service values discussed in Chapter 12, namely, neutrality, accountability, efficiency and effectiveness, responsiveness, representativeness, integrity, fairness, and equity. The priority that public servants assign to each of these values at any given time is a reflection of the desires and expectations of the various actors in the political system who control or influence public servants. Among the most important of these actors are political superiors. The uniqueness of human resource management in the public, as opposed to the private, sector can be explained in large part by the political environment within which public servants work. Evidence of the importance of the politics of human resource management has been provided in earlier discussion of such matters as political appointments, political partisanship, public comment, anonymity, permanence in office, and ministerial responsibility. Additional evidence is set forth in this chapter. The subject of merit is examined again in the final section of this chapter dealing with the concept of career public service.

🏛 EVOLUTION OF HUMAN RESOURCE MANAGEMENT

The development of human resource management in Canada may fruitfully be viewed in terms of the effect on merit, and to a lesser degree on motivation, of the shifting importance of the dominant administrative values. In the federal sphere of government, this evolution may for analytical purposes be divided chronologically into six periods—pre-1918, 1918–45, 1946–66, 1967–78, 1979–89, and 1990 to the present. In each of these periods, human resource management has been affected by a different mix of administrative values as the priority of the various values has risen and declined.

The Patronage Era (Pre-1918)

This period was dominated by efforts to promote political neutrality by eliminating, or at least minimizing, political patronage in the appointment of public servants.[5] Indeed, between 1867 and 1918, as many as five royal commissions and a judicial inquiry on the federal public service devoted considerable attention to the evils of patronage. In relation to the staffing of the public service, patronage took several forms. The most common form was appointments based on party affiliation, which occurred at the level of the local constituency and which involved both the Member of Parliament and the local party members. Most of these appointments were to lower-level positions in the public service, and many of the positions were of a seasonal nature. A second form was appointments made by the cabinet to senior-level positions, largely on the basis of partisan political considerations. A third form of appointments were those to positions to be filled from *within* the public service; since many deputy ministers were political appointees themselves, it is not surprising that some "bureaucratic" patronage occurred. Finally, there was a greater number of appointments following a change of government when some appointees of the outgoing governing party were dismissed and replaced by supporters of the incoming party.

The first major step toward the abolition of patronage was the Civil Service Amendment Act of 1908, which established the Civil Service Commission. The act also provided for appointment on the basis of merit and for heavy penalties for partisan political activities by public servants. However, the act applied only to the "inside service," i.e., those public servants working in Ottawa.

From Patronage to Merit (1918–45)

This period began with the passage of the Civil Service Act in 1918. The search for political neutrality was supplemented by concern for efficiency. The major objective of the act was the "promotion of economy and efficiency in the non-political public service." Merit was to be achieved through "selection and appointment without regard to politics, religion or influence," and through "the application of methods of scientific employment to maintain the efficiency of these selected employees after they enter the service." The act applied to both the "inside" and "outside" services. Severe restrictions in this act on partisan political activities remained virtually unchanged until 1967.

Continued pursuit of political neutrality and efficiency had important effects on human resource management. The emphasis during the 1920s on eradicating patronage rather than on improving efficiency led to a significant decline in patronage appointments and partisan political activities by 1930. In the 1930s, the Civil Service Commission, with its persistent focus on merit in terms of selection of the best qualified candidates, lost ground to the Treasury Board, which emphasized economy and efficiency, not only in the human resource area but throughout government. This emphasis continued during the war years.

The Roots of Reform (1946–66)

This postwar period provided a strikingly different environment for human resource management. The rapid expansion of government activities in an increasingly complex and technological society required a much larger number of employees and a greater proportion of employees with professional, technical, and managerial skills. By the end of this period, public service unions had won the right to bargain collectively and to strike. Efficiency remained the paramount public service value as the Royal Commission on Government Organization (the Glassco Commission)[6] examined human resource management as part of its task to recommend changes to "promote efficiency, economy and improved service in the dispatch of public business." Political neutrality was a continuing, but secondary, concern. As will be explained in Chapter 24, representativeness emerged as a primary public service value, specifically in regard to remedying the longstanding discrimination in the public service against French-speaking Canadians.

The Fruits of Reform (1967–78)

This period was an especially momentous one in the evolution of human resource management. Public service managers in general and human resource managers in particular felt the full effects of reforms generated in the previous period. Among the most important reforms were collective bargaining, language training, new management techniques, and departmental reorganizations. Each of these reforms is discussed in other sections of this book.

A larger number of public service values contended for precedence during this period. The former emphasis on economy and efficiency was supplemented by vigorous concern for effectiveness. Disclosures of mismanagement and of inefficient and ineffective use of public funds led to widespread anxiety about the accountability of public servants. Revelations of numerous incidents of unethical conduct involving government officials aroused unprecedented concern about their integrity. The representativeness of the public service became a major issue as the claims of women, aboriginal peoples, and the disabled were added to those of French-speaking Canadians. The Trudeau government's promises of participatory democracy gave responsiveness a higher place among the public servants' value priorities. Finally, the importance of political neutrality was renewed with the increased recognition of the changing role of public servants in the political system.

The Failure to Reform (1979–89)

It was evident by the end of the 1970s that the traditional concept of merit would have to be reinterpreted to take account of important public service values. Since that time, the federal government has consistently argued that the principles of the merit system noted earlier in this chapter (e.g., fairness, equity, efficiency) should govern all aspects of human resource management. These principles are very similar to the public service values discussed in earlier chapters. During the 1980s, the values of efficiency and accountability had an especially important impact on human resource management.

In 1979, the Special Committee on Personnel Management and the Merit Principle[7] (the D'Avignon Committee) reported that the basic human resource problems were a lack of leadership, excessive and inflexible regulation, managers who were ill equipped for managing, and an absence of accountability for the proper management of human resources. The report rejected "authoritarian, non-participative, uncommunicative and centralized systems" and proposed "a flexible, entrepreneurial, professional and participative style of management."[8] Other studies documented the deficiencies of human resource management,[9] including low morale caused in part by staff and expenditure reductions. Since the government's efforts to remedy these problems during the 1980s enjoyed little success, in 1989 the government launched Public Service 2000 (PS 2000), an initiative to revitalize the public service, especially in the sphere of human resource management.

The Road to Renewal? (1990–)

By the time PS 2000 reported in late 1990,[10] human resource management was being affected by the emergence of "new" values that had arisen from extensive public service reform. Notable among these new values were innovation, service, quality, and teamwork. There was also continuing emphasis on the traditional values of efficiency and accountability. PS 2000, which viewed *people* as the main asset of the public service, recommended the pursuit of such human resource objectives as the empowerment of employees, enhanced career planning and professional development, and improved union-management relations.

In 1996, to reinforce the actions taken to achieve these objectives, the government launched La Relève, an initiative designed largely "to ensure that Canada enters the 21st century with a modern, world-class public service." This initiative involves "a major investment in ... all employees of the Public Service of Canada."[11] While La Relève encompasses many specific activities, it is in general terms defined as

- a challenge to build a modern and vibrant institution able to use fully the talents of its people;

- a commitment by each and every public servant to do everything in their power to provide for a modern and vibrant organization now and in the future;

- a duty, as the guardian of the institution, to pass on to our successors an organization of qualified and committed staff ready to face the challenges of their time.[12]

La Relève is a response to what the clerk of the Privy Council and secretary to the cabinet has described as a "quiet crisis" arising from "the loss of talent through many years of downsizing; a demographic skew after years of limited recruitment; constant criticism of the public sector which seriously affected morale; many years of pay freezes; and increasing interest by the private sector in acquiring the skills possessed by public servants."[13] Similar challenges exist in provincial and municipal governments.

🏛 THE LEGISLATIVE AND ORGANIZATIONAL FRAMEWORK

The function of human resource management pervades government, but the development and administration of human resource policy in the federal government are determined largely by a few key statutes and organizations. The scope and objectives of human resource activities and their allocation among these organizations are set out in three major statutes. The Financial Administration Act (FAA) of 1951 states that the Treasury Board is charged, among other things, with broad responsibility for "personnel management in the public service, including the determination of terms and conditions of employment of persons therein." The Public Service Employment Act (PSEA) of 1967 grants the Public Service Commission (PSC) exclusive authority to appoint persons to and within the public service according to merit, and to manage such matters as appeals, layoffs and dismissals, and political partisanship. The Public Service Staff Relations Act (PSSRA), also passed in 1967, sets out the responsibilities of the Public Service Staff Relations Board (PSSRB) and provides for the structure and operation of the collective bargaining process and for the resolution of disputes and grievances. A summary of the responsibilities of the Treasury Board, PSC, and PSSRB is contained in Table 23.1.

Other notable statutes affecting human resource management are the Official Languages Act of 1969 (replaced by a new act in 1988), which designates French and English as Canada's official languages, provides for their use in the federal government, and authorizes an Official Languages Commissioner to report on this usage; the Canadian Human Rights Act (1977), which covers such matters as discriminatory employment practices and the privacy of personal information; and the Public Service Superannuation Act (1975), which is concerned with pension and death benefits.

The major authority for the formulation and implementation of human resource policy is vested in the Treasury Board[14] and the Public Service Commission. The Treasury Board is a cabinet committee supported by the Treasury Board Secretariat, which is, in effect, the central management agency of government. Its very broad responsibilities in the human resource field include the development and interpretation of policies, programs, and procedures in regard to the organization of the public service; positions; compensation; training and development; official languages; discipline; working conditions; human resource needs and their utilization; classification of employees and employee benefits; and other terms and conditions of employment necessary for effective human resource management. In addition, the secretariat represents the government as employer in the collective bargaining process.

The mission of the Public Service Commission is "to ensure that the people of Canada are served by a highly competent Public Service that is nonpartisan and representative of Canadian society."[15] To pursue this mission, the commission has authority to recruit, select, promote, transfer, demote, and dismiss public servants; to provide staff development and training, including language training, within the framework of Treasury Board policies; to hear and decide

Table 23.1
RESPONSIBILITIES FOR HUMAN RESOURCE MANAGEMENT

Agency	Treasury Board	Public Service Commission	Public Service Staff Relations Board
Primary Role	To ensure good administrative management, including fair treatment of employees	Guardian of the merit principle	To administer the collective bargaining system
Governing Structure	Committee of cabinet composed of six members, headed by the president of the Treasury Board	Three commissioners appointed for ten-year periods so that they can be independent of the government of the day	Equal representatives of the employer and unions
Relationship to the Government of the Day	Cabinet committee	Independent	Controlled jointly by government and unions
Specific Responsibilities	Organization of the public service Job classification Official languages Training and development policy Represents employer in collective bargaining	Recruitment Establishes rules for hiring and promotion Hears appeals dealing with hiring, promotion, and dismissal Decides on granting leave for political activities	Defines bargaining units Certifies bargaining units Appoints conciliators, arbitrators, and adjudicators
Main Legislation	Financial Administration Act	Public Service Employment Act	Public Service Staff Relations Act

appeals relating to appointments or to demotions and dismissals for incompetence or incapacity; to investigate allegations of discrimination in public service employment practices; and to administer regulations on political activities by public servants, including decisions on requests for leave of absence to seek political office. The commission, unlike the Treasury Board, does not report to a cabinet minister; rather, under the Public Service Employment Act, the commission is a politically independent agency that is accountable to Parliament for the administration of the act. The commission is headed by a president of deputy minister rank and two commissioners. Both the board and the commission delegate much of their operational authority for various human resource activities to departments under the direction of deputy ministers, and they have created mechanisms and procedures to help ensure that deputy ministers and other departmental officials are accountable for their exercise of that delegated authority. These mechanisms include general statements of procedures to be followed and after-the-fact monitoring mechanisms to ensure that they have been followed.

In addition to the board and the commission, other federal organizations with important roles in human resource management include the Human Resources Development Council, the Privy Council Office (PCO), the Committee of Senior Officials on Executive Personnel, the External Advisory Committee on Senior Level Retention and Compensation, and the Public Service Staff Relations Board (discussed under collective bargaining in the next chapter).

The Human Resources Development Council was established in October 1990 to work with deputy ministers to develop policies and programs to promote the effective management and development of human resources. Its duties include identifying problems and emerging issues in human resources management, developing approaches to address them, and examining "exemplary practices" and models for human resource management.

The PCO's human resource functions are limited in scope but critical in impact because the PCO exercises the major influence on human resource policy and appointments for the most senior ranks of the public service. It is the prime minister's prerogative to make a large number of order-in-council appointments, including deputy ministers, heads of Crown agencies, and federal judges. The clerk of the Privy Council, who is also secretary to the cabinet, advises the prime minister on the qualifications of existing and prospective order-in-council appointees. The clerk is assisted by the Management Priorities and Senior Personnel Secretariat in the PCO, which, in turn, provides advice on career planning and senior personnel policy. In addition, this secretariat provides staff support to the Committee of Senior Officials (COSO) which was established in 1968. COSO, chaired by the clerk of the Privy Council/secretary to the cabinet, undertakes an annual evaluation of the performance of order-in-council appointees and makes salary recommendations to the government. The External Advisory Committee on Senior Level Retention and Compensation was created in 1997. It provides advice to the president of the Treasury Board on the management and compensation of senior executives.

🏛 THE MAJOR HUMAN RESOURCE MANAGEMENT PROCESSES

In practice, the distribution of responsibilities for human resource management among the key organizations discussed above and the many other administrative bodies within government is very complex. A comprehensive examination of the entire field of human resource management in Canadian government cannot be provided here, but an explanation of the major human resource processes—classification, human resource planning, staffing, training and development, and performance evaluation—is provided. (The issue of political neutrality, which has important implications for human resource management, was discussed in Chapter 13.)

Job Classification

Job classification is the process by which jobs are assigned to an occupational group within an occupational category and to a level within that group.[16] Both logically and chronologically, classification usually precedes the other main human resource processes. It supplies an essential basis for effective human resource management in general and appropriate wage and salary administration in particular.

An *occupational category* includes a broad range of occupations of the same type, distinguished by the nature of the duties performed and the education required. The six occupational categories in the federal public service and the number of full-time employees in each category in 1997 were: Executive Group (3528), Scientific and Professional (23 284), Administrative and Foreign Service (69 846), Technical (17 962), Administrative Support (49 273), and Operational (22 755).[17] An occupational *group* within a category includes occupations that require similar types of work involving similar skills (e.g., the actuarial science group within the Scientific and Professional Category or the firefighters group within the Operational Category) and that are often related to the labour market outside the public service.

The primary task in classification is *job evaluation,* which consists of:

1. the analysis of a job in terms of its duties and responsibilities, its physical and mental demands, the knowledge and skills it requires, and the conditions under which it is performed;

2. the writing of a job description that explains the duties, working conditions, and other aspects of the job; and

3. the assessment of these job characteristics against the classification standard established for the relevant occupational group.

Each occupational group has a *classification standard,* which contains a definition of the category within which the group falls, the groups within each category, the job evaluation plan, and the descriptions of benchmark positions[18] to be used as guides for assessing jobs and rating them according to their level in the group. Jobs at the same level are assigned the same salary range. Since classification is essentially a matter of judgment, it is common practice to obtain more than one person's judgment by having jobs evaluated and rated by committees who advise the official responsible for the final decision.

Human Resource Planning

Human resource planning is the process through which a government strives to ensure that it has—and will continue to have—the appropriate quantity and quality of employees to carry out its responsibilities. This process aims to eliminate the gap between the existing supply of qualified employees and the current and anticipated demand. There is a close relationship between this planning and virtually all other areas of human resource management.

> The single biggest challenge facing provincial public services is renewal and retention of intel-
> lectual capital. We will never attract and retain talented public servants unless we value them
> highly and recognize the service they are providing to the public. It reminds me of Adam Smith
> and the paradox of value that he posed.... Why is it, Smith asked, that a diamond, which doesn't
> do much for society, is given so much value and water, which is essential for life, is given so
> little? That is one of the questions underlying the need to invest in public servants.
>
> Source: S. Waterfield, former Ontario deputy minister, "The Challenges Forcing Provincial Public Services"[19]

In the areas of staffing and of training and development in particular, human resource planning requires that an appropriate balance be struck between the government's desire for human resources of specific kinds and the career aspirations of individual employees. Human resource planning would be a much simpler task if governments could treat current and future employees as automatons. Individuals could then be inserted in the appropriate slots in the administrative hierarchy as they completed prescribed forms of management experience and training. However, career development does not always conform to organizational needs. Individuals have career goals, job preferences, and personal idiosyncrasies that often run counter to the government's need for employees with particular qualifications. Individuals may not want to accept positions for which they have the required skills and experience, or they may not wish to engage in training—or in particular forms of it.

It is useful to distinguish between human resource planning *by* managers and *for* managers. Planning *by* managers "must include consideration of the number and kinds of people who will be needed to carry out departmental programs; when, where and how they will be obtained; what training or development they will need; how much they will cost; and the implications for program plans of inability to obtain the people required."[20] Thus, human resource planning is an essential part of both financial and program planning.

Human resource planning *for* managers takes place within the context of managing the Executive Group, which includes senior public servants with responsibility for policy development; program formulation and delivery; the design and operation of management machinery; and the management of human resources, finances, and public affairs. A major reason for creating this occupational category was to facilitate planning for human resource needs that would produce highly qualified executives and senior managers. These senior public servants now receive formal management training to enable them to conduct appropriate human resource planning for the rest of the public service.

Staffing

The integral link between attracting capable employees and attaining program objectives suggests that staffing may well be the key element of human resource management. We have already seen that determining staffing needs and the means of meeting these needs is a central feature of human resource planning.

At the beginning of this chapter, we also saw the importance in the staffing system of balancing the merit principle with other principles. The Public Service 2000 Task Force on Staffing set out the following guiding principles to which the entire staffing system should conform:

- It has sufficient flexibility to respond to the human resource needs of departments to support them in fulfilling their responsibilities to the Canadian public and the government of the day.

- It contributes to a highly competent public service.

- It presents no systemic barriers to a representative public service and it can respond to policies regarding the correction of representation imbalances.

- It meets the requirements of fairness and administrative due process.

- It requires that the recruitment and promotion of public servants be free from political, bureaucratic, or personal patronage.

- It is simple and efficient to operate.[21]

Staffing is a complex process, especially in government where account must be taken of policy and procedural considerations that are absent in most private sector organizations (e.g., language requirements). However, the staffing process in Canadian governments is normally characterized, and to some extent simplified, by a number of policy and program components (e.g., delegation of staffing authority, open and closed competitions) and of sequential and interrelated steps (e.g., written tests, interviews). Moreover, these policies, programs, and procedures are usually spelled out in a human resource management manual.

The central activities in staffing are recruitment, promotion, and deployment. *Recruitment* involves identifying candidates for public service positions from outside the public service by such methods as inviting job applications from within and from outside the public service and using a human resource inventory system. *Promotion* involves the appointment of an employee from within the public service to a position for which the maximum rate of pay is greater than that of the employee's current position. *Deployment* involves the appointment of an employee to another position at the same level as his or her existing position, or to a higher or lower level, provided that there is no change in the employee's personnel classification. In turn, all of these activities involve *selection,* i.e., the screening of candidates through such means as application forms, written examinations, interviews, and a review of the candidate's credentials and past performance. The activities of recruitment and selection are followed by appointment to a specific position or level in the public service.

It is difficult to design and operate a staffing system that will fully satisfy all the parties affected. The D'Avignon Committee noted in 1979 that the staffing system in the federal government was "viewed by managers as slow, inflexible and inefficient; by bargaining agents as misguided and inequitable; and by employees as frequently failing to ensure that their qualifications are fairly and objectively assessed."[22] More than a decade later, the Public Service 2000 Task

Force on Staffing concluded that these problems still existed and that the staffing system failed on two counts. First, its users do not understand it and do not use it to attain their objectives and, second, employees do not believe that it is administered with integrity. "Because managers see the system as a maze of red tape to be circumvented, employees, who see the system being circumvented, have become suspicious of its capacity to ensure fairness and suspicious of the good faith of managers."[23] The task force noted that the individual components of the system worked reasonably well. The major source of the problem

> is the management philosophy that underlies the current staffing system—a philosophy that favours the exercise of external control rather than the exercise of individual responsibility, a philosophy that favours error prevention rather than accountability, a philosophy that relies on rules rather than judgment ... There must be a major shift in the administrative culture in which the staffing system is imbedded.[24]

The obstacles to achieving a satisfactory staffing system can be easily illustrated by reference to the problem area of selection.

Many employees do not believe that selection board procedures necessarily result in the choice of the most meritorious candidate. There is dissatisfaction about the relative weight given to the factors of knowledge, abilities, sensitivity, potential for advancement, and seniority. There is also concern about the inadequate training of board members in selection techniques; about the inadequacy of the interview technique for predicting probable success and assessing the relative merits of candidates with roughly the same qualifications; and about bureaucratic patronage resulting from the bias of board members toward certain candidates. A former public service commissioner has stated that despite efforts to adhere to the merit principle

> we know ... managers are understandably inclined to favour their immediate staff, whose work they have already seen, over other candidates; managers tend to select in their own image; interviews, even if structured, are an imperfect predictor of success in a job; written examinations, while undoubtedly more objective, may in fact be no more reliable a predictor; and the criteria for certain jobs tend to be overblown or to be of questionable relevance to successful job performance.[25]

Another problem in the staffing area is reconciling the merit principle with the desire for a *representative* public service. (This matter is discussed at length in the next chapter.)

Training, Development, and Learning

In some governments, the terms *training* and *development* are used interchangeably, whereas in others a distinction is made between training, which prepares people to perform their present jobs, and development, which prepares them for future jobs. Still other governments include development as part of training. For example, the federal government has defined training as "any learning activity that contributes to the acquisition by employees of knowledge, skills and experience that helps them to do their present jobs efficiently or prepares them to assume other responsibilities."[26] This latter definition will be used here. In the federal government, while Treasury Board is responsible for overall policy direction for training and development, the Public Service Commission conducts central training courses and programs and provides advice and assistance to departments; in addition, individual departments provide programs to meet their own needs.

A great variety of objectives and approaches are involved in the training of government employees. Among the objectives are making sure that employees can perform their current responsibilities adequately, retraining employees who have become surplus, orienting employees who have taken on new jobs, and ensuring through developmental training that qualified employees will be available to meet future needs. The three main approaches to the process are:

1. formal classroom training within government;

2. formal classroom training by universities, colleges, or consulting firms; and

3. on-the-job training and experience.

The programs available range from intensive one-day or weekend sessions through residential sessions lasting from several days to two months, to funded educational leave for as long as a year for senior managers.

Governments have begun to recognize the need for a major shift from the conventional approaches described above to "learning organizations" or what is called "a continuous learning culture." Training must go beyond "traditional instructor-led, classroom training" to "encompass development opportunities such as deployment, attending conferences and seminars, and making presentations."[27] The learning organization develops the capacity to carry out three processes that form the core of organizational learning. These processes are:

- strongly encouraging and supporting individual learning, and then embedding the results of that individual learning into the culture and practices of the organization;

- reviewing and modifying the organization's basic assumptions and mental models to ensure a continuing fit with a changing environment; and

- engaging in learning partnerships with customers to produce results that are valued by society.[28]

Despite the large investment of time and money by some governments to train their employees, it is widely acknowledged that virtually every government needs to do more. It is also generally recognized that there are formidable obstacles to increasing substantially the current level of investment.

Elected politicians in general are not very sympathetic to calls for more training. Many politicians are reluctant to allocate resources for this purpose because the benefits are not immediately evident or easily evaluated, and/or the political payoff is not apparent. Even among some senior appointed officials, there is insufficient recognition of the necessity for adequate training. In some governments, especially at the municipal level, there appears to be little concern about the adequacy of personnel to meet the demands of existing positions, much less about planning for those employees required in the 1990s and beyond. The "hope and a prayer" approach to training, according to which governments trust that qualified personnel will somehow emerge when needed, is woefully inadequate.

The scarcity of financial resources is another major obstacle to developing and preserving a body of highly skilled and knowledgeable employees, even among those governments where the importance of training and development is readily acknowledged. Training and development programs are costly, not only in terms of the infrastructure required to make opportunities available but also in terms of the time lost from substantive work while employees take courses. Financial support for training and development is also related to what is sometimes described as "the great training robbery." It is often difficult to show that those who have completed certain programs are better able to perform their present duties or to take on new and more challenging tasks. It is reasonable for politicians to ask whether a good case can be made for investing in this area. Therefore, more attention needs to be paid to evaluating the wide assortment of available programs.

The Public Service 2000 Task Force on Training and Development proposed several guiding principles as a basis for future policies and priorities in training and development, including:

- Training and development are investments in better government and better service to the public.

- Good human resource management and development policies will be necessary to attract and retain good people in the public service in the future.

- Training and development of staff are integral parts of management at all levels, embracing a broad range of activities and priorities of which classroom training is but one.

- Equity in training and development means responding to the needs of the individual, as well as corporate needs; this includes the necessity of redressing previous inequities.[29]

Governments have recently placed greater emphasis on training managers, who are, in turn, encouraged to ensure that their subordinates are adequately trained. This emphasis is reflected in the importance attributed to the training of the federal Executive Group and its counterpart in other governments. In 1988, the federal government established the Canadian Centre for Management Development as an institution dedicated to excellence in teaching and research in public sector management. The centre aims to provide senior managers with the skills, research, and practical solutions needed to make government operations as efficient and effective as possible.

Performance Evaluation

Performance evaluation (often called employee appraisal) is a process involving the systematic collection and analysis of information about the performance of employees over time. It is integrally linked to the other human resource processes discussed above. Employees must not only be recruited, selected, trained, and paid; they must also be evaluated in terms of their overall performance. Effective employee appraisal must be preceded by the process of *performance review*, which is "a continuous process in which a supervisor and an employee consider the duties to be performed by the employee, the achievements expected, the evaluation criteria and the results actually achieved."[30] *Employee appraisal*, which is based on this performance review, "identifies an employee's various qualifications, estimates potential, identifies and proposes responses to training and development needs, and indicates future assignments."[31] This employee appraisal is contained in a formal, written report that often includes a summary of the performance review.

The overriding purpose of performance evaluation is to improve the contribution and motivation of each employee. More specifically, it provides a means of assessing the advisability of pay increases and promotion, the strengths and weaknesses of an employee's present performance, and his or her potential for advancement and need for training and development. In addition, performance evaluation gives supervisors a regular opportunity to communicate with and motivate their employees and to check the effectiveness of such other human resource processes as selection and training.

A formal appraisal report is typically prepared once each year for permanent employees and more frequently, usually quarterly, for probationary employees. To facilitate comparison of employees within a single department and with employees in other departments, a common set of evaluation categories is normally used across the government as a whole. For example, the federal government uses the five categories of outstanding, superior, fully satisfactory, satisfactory, and unsatisfactory. Performance evaluation, like job classification, is a difficult undertaking because it involves a substantial measure of personal judgment. It is widely recognized that the objectivity, validity, and reliability of rating systems are often questionable. That one supervisor's "superior" is another supervisor's "satisfactory" raises questions about the fairness of the process.

Thus, performance evaluation, which is supposed to help employees to enhance their contribution and motivation, can often have the opposite effect. Employees are aware of the impact of performance evaluations on their compensation and career prospects; thus, they frequently view evaluations with trepidation. If the process and the outcome of the evaluation are seen as unfair, they may actually reduce the employees' motivation to perform at his or her current level. The matter of fairness is complicated by the reality that many employees have an inflated perception of their performance and may well resent even a "satisfactory" rating. Supervisors, in turn, are sensitive to these high expectations and to the career impact of evaluation decisions; they are, therefore, reluctant to assign low ratings which they must then explain and defend in face-to-face meetings with employees. Supervisors are especially reluctant to assign ratings that may get them involved in the time-consuming process of grievances and appeals. Consequently, supervisors are understandably tempted to rate each employee as at least satisfactory. The annual employee appraisal tends to be easier when supervisors provide employees with an informal, ongoing assessment of their performance rather than storing up the good and bad points of performance for discussion at a single session.

🏛 CAREER PUBLIC SERVICE

Principles of Career Service[32]

The difficulty of managing human resources in the public service can be demonstrated by reference to the concept and practice of career public service. A career service has traditionally been defined as one that is composed of persons who have spent, or intend to spend, all or most of their working lives in government and who remain in office with a change of government because they are permanent employees, appointed on the basis of merit, rather than political appointees. The belief underlying the reforms proposed in the federal government's White Paper on public service renewal was that "a professional, career Public Service, capable of attracting and retaining Canadians of talent, commitment and imagination, is essential to Canada's national well-being."[33] The list of career service principles provided here is not designed to reflect the current state of career service in Canadian governments; rather it specifies the principles that would have to be followed to achieve a career service in an absolute or ideal sense. The challenge is to decide, in the light of contemporary and emerging circumstances, the extent to which the public service does adhere—and should adhere—to these principles.

1. Appointments to the public service are made with a view to preserving its political neutrality.

2. Appointments to, and within, the public service are based on merit, in the sense that the person appointed is the one who is best qualified.

3. So far as possible, appointments are made from within the public service.

4. Public servants are assured of assistance in selecting their career goals and the path to those goals.

It is widely recognized that there are significant barriers to achieving a career public service. First, there are barriers arising from external forces—changing social, political, economic, and demographic conditions—over which governments have little or no short-run control. For example, economic restraint resulting in staff cutbacks, combined with an aging workforce leading to an aging public service, have contributed substantially to the plateauing phenomenon, i.e., a blocking of career paths to the senior levels of the public service.[34]

A second set of barriers arises from conflict among some of the career service principles themselves. While in practice the principles tend to complement one another, there is potential for conflict. For example, the requirement that appointments be made from *within* the public service "is the single feature of a career service to be found across the whole of our system."[35] Yet if this requirement is strictly met, often the best qualified person for the position may not be chosen because competent persons outside the public service cannot be appointed.

The third set of impediments flows from the clash between the principles of career public service and other principles, policies, and objectives pursued by public servants, public service unions, and politicians. For example, the personal career goals of public servants can be at odds with the human resource plans of their departments. The desire of public service unions to restrict appointments to those already employed in the service and, therefore, to their members, can clash with efforts to appoint the best qualified persons. Policy decisions to grant special treatment to certain groups of public servants can affect adversely the career prospects of others, and the extensive use of contracting out and temporary staff reduces the number of available career positions.

The optimum system of human resource management is unlikely to adhere strictly to all the principles of career service. For example, career service may require the appointment of the "best qualified" person, whereas, all things considered, the most effective management of human resources may simply require a "qualified" person.

Current Status of the Principles

The principle of political neutrality is generally respected, but, as explained in Chapter 13, it is threatened by such factors as support for patronage appointments at the senior levels of the departmental public service; patronage appointments to agencies, boards, and commissions; and increased involvement of public servants in partisan politics.

In general also, as noted above, the government is committed to the principle of making appointments on the basis of merit, in the sense that the person appointed is the one best qualified. In practice, there is considerable disagreement about the meaning of the merit principle and its application through the merit system. Some view employment equity programs as a means of fulfilling the merit principle while enhancing the career opportunities of members of underrepresented groups; others see these measures as preferential treatment that reduces the opportunities of members of overrepresented groups.

The usual practice is that appointments are made from within the public service where possible. But the future public service is likely to be a more open one as the government seeks to achieve employment equity objectives and to attract persons with the requisite knowledge and skills. Finally, at present, most public servants are not assured of assistance in selecting their career goals and in pursuing the path to these goals.

The management of human resources is a centrally important function of government that is closely related to several of the subjects examined in earlier chapters. Many of the issues discussed in this chapter are of an enduring nature; despite continuing efforts, they have not yet been resolved to the satisfaction of the government or its employees. Two additional issues, namely employment equity and collective bargaining, have emerged more recently. These two issues are likely to have a continuing impact on public administration in all spheres of Canadian government. They are, therefore, discussed separately in the next two chapters.

NOTES

1. See the basis for discussion of this system provided by the Strategic Policy Committee of the federal Personnel Renewal Council in *The Way Ahead for Human Resource Management in the Public Service,* 3 February 1995.
2. Ibid., 1, 2, and 4.
3. Treasury Board of Canada, *The Manager's Deskbook,* 4th ed. (Ottawa: Minister of Supply and Services, 1995), p 3.1–1.
4. Canada, *Report of the Special Committee on the Review of Personnel Management and the Merit Principle* (Ottawa: Minister of Supply and Services, 1979), 78.
5. Valuable information and analysis on the nature and extent of patronage from the pre-Confederation period to the mid-1930s are provided by R. McGregor Dawson in *The Principle of Official Independence* (London: P.S. King and Son, 1922), ch. 3; *The Civil Service of Canada* (Oxford: Oxford University Press, 1929); and "The Canadian Civil Service," *Canadian Journal of Economics and Political Science 2* (August 1936): 288–300. For a detailed treatment of the evolution of merit in the Canadian federal public service, see: J.E. Hodgetts, William McCloskey, Reginald Whitaker, and V. Seymour Wilson, *The Biography of an Institution: The Civil Service of Canada, 1908–1967* (Montreal: McGill-Queen's University Press, 1974).
6. *Report,* 5 vols. (Ottawa: Queen's Printer, 1962–63).
7. Canada, *Report of the Special Committee on the Review of Personnel Management and the Merit Principle,* 5.
8. Ibid., 46.
9. See, notably, David Zussman and Jak Jabes, *The Vertical Solitude: Managing in the Public Sector* (Halifax: The Institute for Research on Public Policy, 1989).
10. Canada, *Public Service 2000: The Renewal of the Public Service of Canada* (Ottawa: Minister of Supply and Services, 1990).
11. Peter Harrison, "La Relève: Investing in Canada's Future," *The Focus Report,* 6 (1997): 7. Various reports on the work of La Relève are available at http://lareleve.pwgsc.gc.ca.
12. Jocelyn Bourgon, *Fourth Annual Report to the Prime Minister on the Public Service of Canada* (Ottawa: Privy Council Office, 1997), 3.
13. Ibid., 2.
14. For an account of the functions of Treasury Board and its Secretariat, see Chapter 8.
15. Canada, Public Service Commission, *Annual Report 1995–1996* (Ottawa: Public Works and Government Services, 1996), 2.
16. See also the discussion of occupational categories and groups in the section of Chapter 25 on the structure of bargaining units.
17. Canada, Treasury Board Secretariat, *Employment Equity in the Federal Public Service: 1996–97* (Ottawa: Minister Supply and Services, 1997), 57–59. The Administrative and Foreign Service Category and the Administrative Support Category were subsequently combined into the new General Services (GE) Category .
18. A benchmark description is "the description of illustrative work performed in a job which exemplifies the degrees of the factors and/or the classification levels in an eval-

uation plan." It is usually made up of "the identification of information, a summary of the duties stating the function and purpose of the job, a list of duties, the percentage of time devoted to each duty, and specifications written in terms of factors used in the rating plan." Canada, Treasury Board Secretariat, *Personnel: A Manager's Handbook* (Ottawa: Minister of Supply and Services, 1982), 82.

19. S. Waterfield "The Challenges Facing Provincial Public Services," *Canadian Public Administration* 40 (summer 1997): 212.

20. Canada, Treasury Board Secretariat, *Personnel: A Manager's Handbook*, 24.

21. Privy Council Office, *Report of the Task Force on Staffing* (Ottawa: Privy Council Office, 8 August 1990), 9. Reproduced with the permission of the Minister of Public Works and Government Services Canada, 1998.

22. Canada, *Report of the Special Committee on Personnel Management and the Merit Principle*, 183.

23. Public Serice 2000, *Report of the Task Force on Staffings*, 3.

24. Ibid., 4.

25. John Edwards, "Equal Opportunity in the Public Service," *Dialogue* 6 (February 1982): 4.

26. Canada, Treasury Board Secretariat, *Personnel: A Manager's Handbook*, 51.

27. Paul Tellier, *Public Service 2000: A Report on Progress* (Ottawa: Minister of Supply and Services, 1992), 59.

28. Auditor General of Canada, *Report of the Auditor General 1992* (Ottawa: Minister of Supply and Services, 1992), ch. 5 on "The Learning Organization."

29. Privy Council Office, *Report of the Task Force on Training and Development, Executive Summary*, May 1991, 5. Reproduced with the permission of the Minister of Public Works and Government Services Canada, 1998.

30. Canada, Treasury Board Secretariat, *Personnel: A Manager's Handbook*, 49.

31. Ibid.

32. This section is based in part on Kenneth Kernaghan, "Career Public Service 2000: Road to Renewal or Impractical Vision?" *Canadian Public Administration* 34 (winter 1991): 551–72.

33. Canada, Public Service 2000, *The Renewal of the Public Service*, 63.

34. For elaboration on these matters, see Public Service Commission, *Annual Report 1987* (Ottawa: Minister of Supply and Services, 1988), 15–21.

35. Canada, *Report of the Special Committee on the Review of Personnel Management and the Merit Principle*, 82.

BIBLIOGRAPHY

Bird, Richard M. *The Growth of Public Employment in Canada*. Toronto: Butterworths, 1979.

Borins, Sandford F. *The Language of the Skies: The Bilingual Air Traffic Control Conflict in Canada*. Montreal: McGill-Queen's University Press, 1983.

Campbell, Colin, and George Szablowski. *The Superbureaucrats: Structure and Behaviour in Central Agencies*. Toronto: Macmillan, 1979.

Canada. *Beneath the Veneer: Report of the Task Force on Barriers to Women in the Public Service*, 4 volumes. Ottawa: Minister of Supply and Services, 1990.

Canada. Civil Service Commission. *Personnel Administration in the Public Service*. Ottawa: Queen's Printer, 1958.

Canada. *Public Service 2000: The Renewal of the Public Service of Canada*. Ottawa: Minister of Supply and Services, 1990.

Canada. *Report of the Special Committee on the Review of Personnel Management and the Merit Principle*. Ottawa: Supply and Services, 1979.

Canada. Royal Commission on Administrative Classification in the Public Service. *Report*. Ottawa: King's Printer, 1946.

Canada. Royal Commission on Financial Management and Accountability. *Final Report.* Ottawa: Minister of Supply and Services, 1979.

Canada. Royal Commission on Government Organization. *Report*, 5 vols. Ottawa: Queen's Printer, 1962.

Canada. Treasury Board. *Public Service 2000. PS 2000: Reports and Summaries of the Task Forces.* Ottawa: Privy Council Office, 14 August 1990)

Hodgetts, J.E. *Pioneer Public Service: An Administrative History of the United Canadas.* Toronto: University of Toronto Press, 1955.

Hodgetts, J.E., and O.P. Dwivedi. *Provincial Governments as Employers.* Montreal: McGill-Queen's University Press, 1974.

Hodgetts, J.E., William McCloskey, Reginald Whitaker, and V. Seymour Wilson. *The Biography of an Institution: The Civil Service of Canada, 1908–1967.* Montreal: McGill-Queen's University Press, 1972.

Laframboise, H.L. "Administrative Reform in the Federal Public Service: Signs of a Saturation Psychosis." *Canadian Public Administration* 14 (fall 1971): 303–25.

Love, J.D. "Personnel Organization in the Canadian Public Service: Some Observations on the Past." *Canadian Public Administration* 22 (fall 1979): 402–14.

———. "The Merit Principle in the Provincial Governments of Atlantic Canada." *Canadian Public Administration* 31 (fall 1988): 335–51.

Manion, John. "New Challenges in Public Administration." *Canadian Public Administration* 31 (summer 1988): 234–46.

Siegel, David. "The Changing Shape and Nature of Public Service Employment." *Canadian Public Administration* 31 (summer 1988): 159–93.

24

Representative Bureaucracy, Employment Equity, and Managing Diversity

"Shameful Record." "Health Canada Guilty of Racial Bias." These were the dramatic headlines in *The Toronto Star*[1] regarding a 1997 decision of the Canadian Human Rights Commission on discrimination against visible minorities in the federal Department of Health and Welfare. The commission characterized the discrimination as "systemic." It concluded that there was significant underrepresentation of visible minorities in the department's senior management, that visible minorities were bottlenecked in the feeder group leading to senior posts, that their failure to advance into management could not "be explained by a lack of interest or lack of technical or professional skills ... ," and that visible minorities were "viewed by senior management as culturally different" and not "suitable for managerial positions."[2] The commission prescribed a wide range of corrective measures, including the requirement that where a visible minority candidate competes for a position and is not selected, the manager must explain to senior departmental officials why the minority candidate was not selected before a final decision in the competition can be made.

What is meant by *systemic* discrimination? To what extent should the public service be representative of the composition of the population as a whole? What measures have been taken to promote employment equity, and how successful have they been? What is meant by managing diversity? These are the key questions examined in this chapter.

🏛 REPRESENTATIVE BUREAUCRACY

Representative bureaucracy is a difficult concept that has been interpreted in a variety of ways.[3] A strict interpretation would require that the public service be a microcosm of the total society in terms of a wide range of variables, including race, religion, language, education, social class, and region of origin. However, there is disagreement in scholarly writings as to what purposes representative bureaucracy serves, what degree of representativeness is desirable, and what variables should be included. Proponents of representative bureaucracy recommend its adoption on the following grounds:

1. Public servants exercise significant power in the political system

2. External controls over public servants by the political executive, the legislature, and the courts are inadequate to check bureaucratic power and thereby to ensure bureaucratic responsibility

3. A public service that is representative of the total population will be responsive to the needs and interests of the general public and will therefore be more responsible.

This third point, which is a central proposition of the theory of representative bureaucracy, is based on several subpropositions:

a. If the values of the public service as a whole are similar to those of the total population, then the public service will tend to make the kinds of decisions that the public would make if it were involved in the decision-making process

b. The values of public servants are molded by the pattern of socialization they experience before they enter the public service, i.e., by such socializing forces as education, social class, occupational background, race, family, and group associations

c. The values arising from this socialization will not be modified by prolonged exposure to bureaucratic values;

d. The values arising from socialization will be reflected in the behaviour of public servants and, therefore, in their recommendations and decisions;

e. Thus, the various groups in the general population should be represented in the public service in approximate demographic proportion so that public servants will be responsive to the interests of these groups both in policy development and in program delivery.

Critics of representative bureaucracy acknowledge the substantial power of public servants and the consequent need to provide controls to preserve and promote bureaucratic responsibility. They contend, however, that the assertion that external controls are inadequate to ensure responsible administrative conduct requires more investigation. These critics also point to the logical and empirical failings of the theory of representative bureaucracy.

Critics contend that in a representative public service, the values of the public service as a whole will not be similar to those of the general population; rather, the values of individual public servants *may* be similar to the values of those groups in the population they are supposed to represent. Moreover, the public service as a whole does not make decisions; rather, decisions are made by individual public servants who, by acting on behalf of groups they represent, would serve the interests of particular segments of the public rather than the total population. Also, it is insufficient for the public service as a whole to be broadly representative of the total population; for all interests to be represented in the decision-making process, each major administrative unit must be representative of the total population, especially at its senior levels where the most important recommendations and decisions are made.

Opponents of representative bureaucracy observe further that a public servant with certain social and educational origins will not necessarily share the values of those outside the public service with similar origins. The lifelong process of socialization continues after entry to the public service in the form of resocialization to the values of the service as a whole or of particular administrative units. Moreover, representatives of a specific group in the population, particularly if they achieve high office in the public service, are likely to be upwardly mobile and may well share the socioeconomic and other values of those with whom they work, rather than of the group from which they came. In this regard, Peta Sheriff regrets the lack of research on the strength of pre-occupational and post-occupational experience, and concludes that although "the very cornerstone of the representative bureaucracy thesis has no direct evidence to support it ... the suspicion that pre-occupational socialization must have some influence is sufficient to maintain the thesis."[4] However, even if public servants continue to share the values of certain groups, despite organizational socialization, these values may not be significantly reflected in the public servants' behaviour.

Thus, it is logically possible to have a representative public service that is not responsive and a responsive public service that is not representative. Indeed, Meier and Nigro conclude that those at the most senior levels in the U.S. public service "are an unrepresentative demographic group holding quite representative attitudes."[5]

Canadian Writings

The major points of contention in a debate on representative bureaucracy in Canada[6] involve the extent to which the values of efficiency, effectiveness, neutrality, and responsiveness conflict with, or complement, that of representativeness. In this debate, Donald Rowat objects to John Porter's sacrifice of representativeness for the sake of efficiency and suggests that both values can be achieved. He argues that representativeness "is essential to the efficiency of the bureaucracy, in the sense of the latter's effectiveness in a democratic, pluralistic society."[7] Porter asserts that people of various social origins will be found in the bureaucracy in roughly the same proportion as in the population as a whole *if* government recruitment and promotion policies do not discriminate against particular groups, *if* educational facilities to qualify persons for public service appointments are equal among these groups, and *if* these groups are equally motivated to join the public service. He contends that "in the theoretically ideal bureaucracy, the candidate for office neither gains nor loses as a result of ethnic, religious or regional origins."[8]

Rowat, who is more concerned with what can be realized in practice than with a search for a theoretically ideal bureaucracy, observes that Porter's conditions of equality do not exist and cannot be easily achieved. He contends that representativeness must be actively sought, even at the expense of technical efficiency and neutrality. Intelligent people with the potential to rise to higher levels in the service could be recruited and provided with the required in-service education and training. Moreover, competent members of underrepresented groups could be brought into the public service from outside. Porter opposes the recruitment of outsiders on the grounds that this practice threatens the neutrality of the service and the concept of the bureaucratic career. He states that "since the basis of power associations are frequently ethnic, regional or religious, the idea that these groups should be represented in the bureaucracy contradicts the notion of the official as the servant of the state."[9] Rowat does not agree that the appointment of "bureaucratic outsiders" would endanger political neutrality, and he argues that a public service that complemented career public servants with outsiders would be more responsive, since a career bureaucracy tends to "lose contact with and lack understanding of the changing feelings, needs and desires of the great variety of people and groups found in our dynamic, pluralistic society."[10]

Rowat does not suggest that underrepresented groups should be represented in precise proportion to their presence in the total population, and he rejects the use of quotas for recruitment and promotion as unworkable. He does suggest, however, that recruitment to the public service should be guided by the principle of representation.

Porter objects on several grounds to Rowat's plea for representativeness. He first poses the basic question as to which of the many groups in society should be represented in the public service. He then contends that Rowat's proposals for recruiting members of underrepresented groups and providing them with in-service training serve the principle of equal opportunity rather than representativeness. He states also that "in a society of classes, the upwardly mobile are seldom representative of the social interests from which they originated."[11] Finally, he notes the assumption in the theory of representative bureaucracy that political institutions are inadequate to cope with modern demands and questions the view that "ways can be found for governmental bureaucracy to make up for the deficiencies in our representative political institutions."[12]

Two decades after the Porter-Rowat debate, Wilson and Mullins expressed doubt that "members of a bureaucracy chosen from various relevant groups will be likely to act as agents or spokesmen for their groups and group interests."[13] Moreover, they concluded that support for representative bureaucracy "on the assumption that it would be politically representative in any meaningful sense is not only bogus, but also dangerous."[14] Like Rowat, Wilson and Mullins assert that technical efficiency should not be stressed at the expense of representativeness.

Another perspective on the issue of representative bureaucracy in Canada has been provided by Dennis Olsen, who updated to 1973 the study of the bureaucratic elite conducted by John Porter in 1953. On the basis of an examination of data on the social backgrounds, careers, and education of federal and provincial bureaucrats, Olsen concluded that, compared with the 1953 bureaucratic elite, the 1973 group is "more open, more heterogeneous, and probably more meritocratic."[15] However, these changes have taken place very slowly, and he envisages that the overall future pattern will be characterized by a "marked persistence of both social class and ethnic preferences in recruitment."[16]

The Representativeness of the Canadian Bureaucracy

Data on several aspects of the current composition of the Canadian public service in relation to the total population are unavailable. The data that are available indicate that the service is *not* a microcosm of Canadian society. Moreover, it is not the policy of the federal government to establish in the public service a microcosm of the Canadian mosaic by pursuing exact demographic representation of all groups in society; rather, the government's aim is to achieve a more proportionate representation of a limited number of politically significant, but underrepresented, groups. In this regard, the government has argued that the underrepresentation of such groups as francophones, women, and aboriginal peoples may diminish the sensitivity of the public service to the needs of certain segments of the population. Thus, a prime motivation underlying efforts to represent these groups more adequately is to make the public service more responsive, both in the provision of policy advice and the delivery of services. As explained above, the assumption that representativeness will promote responsiveness is central to the theory of representative bureaucracy. The government also presumes that members of underrepresented groups who join the public service will remain sensitive to the needs and claims of these groups.

In view of the deficiencies of the theory of representative bureaucracy outlined earlier, the benefits of representation in terms of increased responsiveness are likely to be less than anticipated. However, we know little about the extent to which the expanded representation of members of underrepresented groups has had a policy impact by advancing the substantive interests of these groups.

Increased representation has effects that are not covered by the theory of representative bureaucracy. Representation has a symbolic impact that helps to promote quiescence and stability in the Canadian political system and explains, in part, its appeal to government officials. The statutes, regulations, and administrative units designed to increase the representation of underrepresented groups evoke symbols of equality of opportunity and upward mobility for members of these groups. In the name of equal opportunity, the government has instituted programs to recruit and train group members who have not enjoyed equal access to the public service. Also, recruitment to senior posts from outside the service and post-entry training geared to promotion to the higher ranks of the service demonstrate the opportunities for group members to attain senior policy-making posts. Thus, group members who are appointed to, and promoted in, the public service provide role models for other members of their group.

Government actions to increase the representativeness of the public service serve a partisan political purpose in that they help to sustain or increase electoral support for the governing party. Evidence of partisan motivation can be seen in the fact that the groups for whom increased representation has been sought have mobilized for political action and are highly visible and vocal in their demands for greater participation in the political and administrative systems. The government's efforts on behalf of underrepresented groups have brought about a more representative public service. It is not viable, however, to attempt to represent proportionately all the myriad groups that make up the Canadian mosaic. Experience to date suggests that future government measures toward a more representative public service will be directed primarily to underrepresented groups that become politically influential.

🏛 EQUAL OPPORTUNITY AND EMPLOYMENT EQUITY

The issues of representative bureaucracy and equal opportunity are closely linked in that the attainment of a representative public service depends largely on the extent to which various groups in society have equal access to employment in the public service. The federal, provincial, and municipal governments have adopted a wide range of programs to promote equal opportunity in the public service for segments of the population that have historically been underrepresented. As explained above, the federal government is committed to improving the representation of certain "target" or "designated" groups, namely, women, members of visible minority groups, persons with disabilities, and aboriginal peoples. In the federal sphere, francophones are not treated as one of the target groups; rather, they are treated separately as part of the government's efforts to ensure equitable participation in the public service of Canada's two official language communities. Among the provinces, there is some variation as to the particular groups considered to be inadequately represented. The underrepresentation of women is an important concern in all provinces, whereas concern about the participation of such groups as francophones and aboriginal peoples is limited to provinces where these groups constitute a significant proportion of the population.

The term *equal opportunity* was largely displaced in the early 1980s by the term *affirmative action,* which was in turn soon displaced by the term *employment equity.* The terms affirmative action and employment equity are often used interchangeably; both can usefully be viewed as means to the end of equal opportunity. In June 1983, the government announced its continued commitment to a bureaucracy that is representative of and responsive to the people it serves,[17] and introduced an *affirmative action program* to accelerate the participation in the public service of the target groups. Affirmative action was defined as "a comprehensive systems-based approach to the identification and elimination of discrimination in employment. It makes use of detailed analyses to identify and systematically remove employment policies, practices and procedures which may exclude or place at a disadvantage the three target groups"[18] (which at that time included women, aboriginal peoples, and disabled persons).

The government stressed that the merit principle would be preserved and that the numerical goals being set were not quotas but "an estimate of what can be achieved when systemic barriers are eliminated and some temporary special measures are put in place to accelerate training and development experience."[19] The president of the Treasury Board announced that implementation of the affirmative action program would be viewed as a major consideration in the performance of deputy ministers. Thus, while this program did not establish quotas, it moved in that direction by using temporary special measures, numerical goals, and pressure on senior public servants to achieve these goals.

The legal basis for affirmative action programs was laid in 1977 by the Canadian Human Rights Act, which also established the Canadian Human Rights Commission. Section 16(1) of the act provides in effect that measures taken to redress historical imbalances in the participation of certain groups does not amount to reverse discrimination. More recently, the recommendations of the Royal Commission on Equality in Employment[20] (the Abella Commission) and the coming into force of section 15—the equality rights section—of the Canadian Charter of Rights and Freedoms have supported the federal government's affirmative action programs. The report of the commission argued that

> [s]ometimes equality means treating people the same, despite their differences, and sometimes it means treating them as equals by accommodating their differences ... We now know that to treat everyone the same may be to offend the notion of equality ... Equality means nothing if it does not mean that we are of equal worth regardless of differences in gender, race, ethnicity, or disability ... Ignoring differences and refusing to accommodate them is a denial of equal access and opportunity. It is discrimination.[21]

It is important to note that employment equity programs are protected under the Charter. Section 15 guarantees "equal protection and equal benefit of the law without discrimination," and then goes on to say that this guarantee "does not preclude any law, program or activity that has as its object the amelioration of conditions of disadvantaged individuals or groups including those that are disadvantaged because of race, national or ethnic origin, colour, religion, sex, age or mental or physical disability." In other words, preferential treatment for groups that have historically been disadvantaged does not constitute reverse discrimination.

As noted, the term employment equity, which came into frequent use in 1985, is very similar in meaning to affirmative action. The Public Service Employment Act, as amended in 1992,[22] defines an employment equity program as "a policy or program established by the Treasury Board to improve employment and career opportunities in the Public Service for groups of persons that are disadvantaged, including women, aboriginal peoples, persons with disabilities and persons who are, because of their race or colour, in a visible minority in Canada, and to correct the conditions of disadvantage experienced by such groups in their employment."

In March 1986, the House of Commons passed the federal Employment Equity Act (Bill C-62), which required federally regulated employers with 100 or more employees (primarily in the banking, transportation, and communication industries) and Crown corporations to report annually to the government on the extent to which they have achieved results in promoting employment equity programs for designated groups. In the same year, the Treasury Board issued an employment equity policy for the public service that required departments and agencies, among other things, to identify *systemic barriers* to equitable participation by designated groups, adopt special measures to remedy imbalances in the public service workforce, and meet numerical objectives for the representation and distribution of the designated groups.[23]

The term systemic barriers (or systemic discrimination) refers to an employment policy, practice, procedure, or system that excludes, or has a negative effect on, the designated groups, whether or not that effect was intended, and that cannot be justified as being job related. For example, if 15 percent of geologists in Canada are women but only 6 percent of the geologists in a particular department are women, the burden is on the department to show that this is not the result of discrimination. The explanation could be that the department requires all the geologists it hires to have ten years of work experience and that relatively few female geologists have that experience. Consideration would be given to removing this requirement because it penalizes women more than men, even though no discrimination was intended.

In early 1991, the Treasury Board announced a new approach to setting employment equity targets based on rates of recruitment, promotion, and separation, not just on representation. "This reflects the principle that the workplace should be conducive to attracting and retaining designated group members, that they should receive a fair share of recruitment and promotion opportunities, and that their rate of separation from the Public Service should be no higher than that of other employees."[24] In 1995 a new Employment Equity Act replaced the 1986 act. The new act applies to public servants as well as the previously covered Crown corporations and federally regulated industries; it also authorizes the Canadian Human Rights Commission to audit employers to verify their compliance with the act.

In the federal government, the Treasury Board Secretariat and the Public Service Commission have played the leading roles in developing, implementing, and monitoring employment equity programs. The two agencies devised programs for francophones and women in the 1960s that were strengthened and supplemented by programs for aboriginal peoples, visible minorities, and the disabled during the 1970s and 1980s. Table 24.1 shows the distribution of employees by designated group and occupational category as of December 1997.

Employment equity programs can be grouped into three categories: training and development (e.g., special training opportunities for women); new or modified administrative units and practices (e.g., a special office for aboriginal employment); and vigorous recruitment (e.g., various programs to recruit qualified persons from every target group). Departments and agencies are required to run employment equity programs to promote representativeness and fairness in the public service.

Programs to overcome artificial institutional barriers to public service employment are of limited use in overcoming attitudinal barriers, notably prejudice against the target groups, which exists in the public service and in Canadian society as a whole. There is, however, an ongoing effort in government to sensitize public service managers to the importance of removing obstacles to equal access to public service employment. To ensure that managers are

Table 24.1

DISTRIBUTION OF PUBLIC SERVICE EMPLOYEES BY DESIGNATED GROUP, OCCUPATIONAL CATEGORY, AND WORKFORCE AVAILABILITY AS OF MARCH 31, 1997

Occupational Category	Women	Aboriginal Peoples	Persons with Disabilities	Persons in a Visible Minority
	%	%	%	%
Executive Group	23.0	1.7	2.2	2.6
Scientific and Professional	31.2	1.5	2.0	9.0
Administrative and Foreign Service	50.9	2.4	3.7	4.5
Technical	23.3	1.6	2.1	3.3
Administrative Support	84.0	3.0	4.5	4.7
Operational	13.8	3.1	2.3	2.0
Total % in Public Service	49.5	2.4	3.3	4.7
Availability in Workforce	47.3	2.6	4.8	9.0

Source: Compiled from Tables 1 and 3 of Treasury Board, Employment Equity in the Federal Public Service: 1996–97 (Ottawa: Minister Supply and Services, 1997), 55, 57–59.

sensitive to this effort, success in enhancing the participation of these groups is now deemed to be one element of the managers' performance evaluation. The Public Service Commission has observed that "an important positive re-enforcement to managerial sensitization is the evaluation of managers vis-à-vis their

A PERSON WITH A DISABILITY (i) has a long-term or recurring condition or health problem that limits the kind or amount of work he/she can do in the workplace; OR (ii) feels that he/she may be perceived as limited in the kind or amount of work he/she can do because of a physical, mental, sensory, psychiatric or learning impairment.

AN ABORIGINAL PERSON is a North American Indian or a member of a First Nation, or who is Métis or Inuit. North American Indians or members of a First Nation include status, treaty or registered Indians, as well as non-status and non-registered Indians.

A PERSON IN A VISIBLE MINORITY in Canada is someone (other than an Aboriginal person as defined above) who is non-white in colour/race regardless of place of birth.

Source: Treasury Board Employment Equity in the Federal Public Service: 1996–97[25]

utilization of human resources ... specifically with respect to the participation of under-represented groups."[26]

There have been complaints from public servants and from their unions that equal opportunity programs violate the merit principle and discriminate against candidates outside the designated groups for appointment and promotion. The commission has responded by explaining that merit is a dynamic principle; its application must be reconciled with such other values as responsiveness, representativeness, fairness, equity, and economy. Moreover, according to the commission, the equal opportunity programs do not amount to reverse discrimination because individual abilities, rather than group characteristics, are emphasized in appointments and promotions. A senior official of the commission explained that

> equal treatment is not necessarily equitable treatment and ... discrimination means practices or attitudes that have, by design or impact, the effect of limiting an individual's or group's right to the opportunities generally available to others. It also deprives the Public Service and other employers of valuable talent...
>
> We are learning that selection according to merit is not served if well qualified people are either prevented from entering the Public Service or from moving up in accordance with their experience and ability. We are also understanding and recognizing that it is because their competence was not recognized in the past that some groups are underrepresented today.[27]

Nevertheless, the commission has opposed the setting of *quotas* for the employment of underrepresented groups on the grounds that

1. it is very difficult to decide which groups or interests in society should be represented; and

2. quotas clash with the merit principle by creating two classes of public servants—those who received their jobs because they were meritorious and those who received them because they were members of an underrepresented group.

The commission has supported the Treasury Board requirements that departments set realistic *targets* for increasing the representation of the designated groups. The commission asserts that these targets are not quotas; rather, they are described as yardsticks by which the government's success in attracting qualified candidates from underrepresented groups can be measured.

To assess the extent to which the federal government's employment equity programs have been successful, it is useful to examine briefly the experience of five major groups that, historically, have been underrepresented in the public service: francophones, women, aboriginal peoples, members of visible minorities, and disabled persons.

The Representation of Francophones

Barriers to equal opportunity for French-speaking people existed both in the government and in the francophone community itself for much of this century.

During the post-Confederation period before the 1918 Civil Service Act, francophones were numerically well represented in the public service. They were not, however, as well represented as anglophones at the senior levels. Moreover, many of the francophone appointments rested on patronage, whereas the 1918 act emphasized merit and efficiency. Especially after 1918, the public service was pervaded by an anglophone linguistic and cultural bias. Merit and efficiency were linked to formal education and technical qualifications. French-language, or bilingual, competence was not considered a component of merit or likely to enhance efficiency. Furthermore, written examinations and interviews for recruitment and promotion reflected anglophone values and the anglophone educational system, to the disadvantage of francophones. Finally, the view was widely held that the Quebec educational system was a significant barrier to francophone representation because it emphasized education for such occupations as law, medicine, and the priesthood and did not, therefore, provide its graduates with the technical, scientific, and commercial skills required for appointment to the public service.

All these factors combined to reduce the motivation of francophones to seek or retain positions in the federal public service. The result was a decline in the proportion of francophones from 21.58 percent in 1918 to 12.25 percent in 1946, and a decline at the deputy minister level during the same period from 14.28 percent to zero.[28]

During the early 1960s, the so-called Quiet Revolution in Quebec focused national attention on francophone grievances about their inadequate participation in the public service. The Glassco Commission reported in 1963 that francophones were poorly represented in the service. The commissioners noted that public confidence in the public service will depend on "how representative it is of the public it serves," and that to achieve representativeness, "a career at the centre of government should be as attractive and congenial to French-speaking as to English-speaking Canadians."[29]

Then, in 1966, Prime Minister Pearson promised that the "linguistic and cultural values of the English-speaking and French-speaking Canadians will be reflected through civil service recruitment and training."[30] The Royal Commission on Bilingualism and Biculturalism, which reported in 1967, gave enormous impetus to this objective. Prime Minister Trudeau, in his comments on the commission's report, stated that "the atmosphere of the public service should represent the linguistic and cultural duality of Canadian society, and … Canadians whose mother tongue is French should be adequately represented in the public service—both in terms of numbers and in levels of responsibility."[31] Then, in keeping with the aim of the Official Languages Act passed in 1969,[32] the Treasury Board established the Official Languages Program, with three major objectives—providing services to, and communicating with, the public in both official languages; enabling public servants to work in the official language of their choice; and achieving the full participation in the service of members of both the anglophone and francophone communities.

In a concerted effort since the late 1960s to increase francophone representation in the public service, the major strategies adopted by the government have included more active recruitment of francophones, the designation of language requirements for public service positions, and the development of an extensive language training system.[33] Individual public servants and public service unions severely attacked these measures on the grounds that they violated the merit principle and amounted to reverse discrimination against anglophones. The government's response to these charges was that bilingual competence is an element of merit and that, by increasing the number of positions requiring bilingual competence, the opportunities for qualified francophones are also increased. As a result, the merit principle and the goal of a more representative public service are both achievable.

These remedial strategies have helped to reduce institutional barriers in the government to francophone representation. Francophones are now represented in the public service in almost exact proportion to their numbers in the total population—an increase from 12.25 percent of the service in 1946 to 28.6 percent in 1992.[34] However, only 23 percent of the Executive Group is composed of francophones.

The Representation of Women

The underrepresentation of women in Canada's public services, especially at the middle and senior levels, resulted from obstacles to equal opportunity, both in the government and in society generally. By 1885, only 23 of 4280 public servants were women and more than one-third of these were junior clerks in the Post Office Department. The proportion of women in the service rose gradually to 14 percent in 1928 and to 18.7 percent in 1937. It accelerated during the war years, reaching 35 percent in 1943, but declined after the war and remained at about 27 percent during the 1960s.[35] Since, by 1970, women constituted about 30 percent of the total labour force, they were not badly underrepresented in the public service compared to the private sector. However, they were poorly represented at senior levels of the service. In 1971, only 14.1 percent of officer positions were held by women, whereas women made up 29.3 percent of the service as a whole.[36]

Before 1970, the government took little action to promote female representation in the public service. It was not until 1955 that the restriction against hiring married women for government employment was abolished. The Royal Commission on Government Organization (the Glassco Commission) called upon the government in 1963 to show "creative leadership in providing equal opportunities for women."[37] In the 1967 Public Service Employment Act, sex was included with race, national origin, colour, and religion as a basis on which it was forbidden to discriminate. Then the Royal Commission on the Status of Women reported in 1970 that women do not enjoy equal opportunity to "enter and advance in Government Service, and that their skills and abilities are not being fully used there. Attitudes and practices seem to be at fault."[38] The commissioners made numerous recommendations to ensure equality of opportunity for women in the public service, and the government implemented most of these recommendations.

Barriers to equal opportunity for women have been similar in the public and private sectors of society. The underutilization of women has generally been attributed to differences between men and women in formal education and work experience, and to low career expectations, high absenteeism, and high turnover among female employees. Studies on the role of women in the public service conclude that these factors are not sufficient to explain fully the lower salaries and subordinate positions received by women. The Task Force on Barriers to Women in the Public Service reported in 1990 that the public service loses proportionally more women than men because of one or more of the following barriers:

- attitudes, which keep them away from advancement and development;

- a corporate culture, which seems suffocating, if not hostile; and

- extreme difficulty in balancing work and family responsibilities.[39]

As with francophones, the government has used a variety of strategies to remove barriers to female representation, including new administrative structures, active recruitment, and training. Between 1975 and 1997, the percentage of women in the public service rose from 35.6 percent to 49.5 percent. In late 1997, women made up 84 percent of the Administrative Support Category and 23 percent of the Executive Group[40] (an increase from 5.9 percent of the Executive Group in 1983).

The Representation of Aboriginal Peoples

The underrepresentation of aboriginal peoples reflects the lack of effective aboriginal participation in the Canadian labour force as a whole and results from a formidable array of institutional and attitudinal barriers to representation, both in the government and in the aboriginal community. Aboriginal peoples have been isolated culturally and geographically from the mainstream of Canadian society. Inadequate educational facilities and opportunities have made it difficult for them to obtain the academic qualifications required for entry into the public service, especially at the senior levels. As a result of their small numbers in the public service and of their concentration in the lower ranks, they are not sufficiently aware of career opportunities in the more senior echelons. There is no visible cadre of aboriginal public servants whose achievements they are motivated to emulate. Furthermore, the government's recruitment practices tend to emphasize formal academic qualifications rather than practical experience, and to stress competence in the French or English languages rather than in an aboriginal language. Discriminatory attitudes toward aboriginal peoples that are widespread in Canadian society are found also in the public service.[41] In addition, some aboriginals choose not to work for the Canadian government because they do not recognize this government as *their* government.

These various governmental and societal factors have combined to discourage aboriginal peoples from seeking positions in the service and to confine those who do enter primarily to lower-level positions. To overcome these obstacles, the federal government has adopted strategies similar to those used to increase the representation of francophones and women. New administrative units have engaged in active recruitment and training of aboriginal peoples. Aboriginal peoples constitute 2.6 percent of the labour force. By 1997, largely as a result of the government's special efforts, aboriginal peoples made up 2.4 percent of the public service. However, they comprised only 1.7 percent of the Executive Group.

The Representation of Visible Minorities

Visible minorities make up an increasing percentage of the Canadian population and, therefore, of the labour force. However, they are significantly under-represented in both the federal and provincial public services. The federal government formally recognized the need to make the public service more representative of visible minorities in its September 1995 announcement of special measures to promote employment equity for members of these groups.[42] These measures were in part a response to the recommendations of the 1984 House of Commons Special Committee on Participation of Visible Minorities in Canadian Society.[43] A government survey at that time showed that members of visible minority groups made up about 1.7 percent of the service, compared to more than 4 percent of the labour force. The special measures included revising employment application forms to allow members of visible minority groups to so identify themselves, providing estimates of the availability of qualified members of these groups in the labour market to help public service managers establish targets for hiring such members, and incorporating a special section on visible minorities in training courses for public service managers.

In 1992, a Visible Minority Consultation Group appointed by the Treasury Board found that "employment practices are believed by most visible minority employees ... to be unfair, to lack integrity, and to be racially biased."[44] In 1997, a human rights tribunal ruled that in the federal Department of Health and Welfare the underrepresentation of visible minorities resulted from systemic discrimination.[45] The tribunal's long list of corrective measures included "numerical goals," sensitivity training for managers, and more training opportunities for minority employees. Also in 1997, the Canadian Human Rights Commissioner[46] and a report sponsored by the commission[47] lamented the slow progress made by the government as a whole in increasing the representation of visible minorities. The report concluded that "bias and subtle barriers against visible minorities persist in the public service"[48] and recommended that, among other things, greater efforts be made to promote the career advancement of members of these minorities.

Visible minorities constituted 9 percent of the workforce by the time of the 1991 census and were estimated to make up 12 percent in 1996.[49] Table 24.1 shows their representation compared to their availability in the workforce and the extent to which they are represented in each occupational category; clearly, they are significantly underrepresented in the Executive Group. The federal government has adopted a variety of measures to improve the representation of members of visible minorities, but it has been less successful in its efforts than the federally regulated private sector. Aside from the problem of systemic discrimination, the government's efforts have been hampered by substantial cutbacks in public service employment, which makes it difficult to hire new employees of any kind.

The Representation of Disabled Persons

The federal government has been somewhat more successful in increasing the representation of disabled persons as compared to members of visible minorities, but disabled persons are still significantly underrepresented in relation to their workforce availability. Table 24.1 shows that disabled persons are underrepresented in every occupational category, except the Administrative Support Category, and, like visible minority persons, they are poorly represented in the Executive Group.

Integrating persons with disabilities into the workplace can be costly and complicated, but, in the words of the Canadian Human Rights Commission, "any of us might some day become disabled. It is therefore necessary for managers to familiarize themselves not only with the issues related to hiring or enabling a person in a handicap situation to re-enter the workplace, but also with technical aids and accommodations that may enable people with disabilities to be as productive ... as their co-workers."[50] As with the other target groups already discussed, the government has utilized a number of mechanisms to enhance the representation of disabled persons. These include a Special Measures Initiatives Fund, which, among other things, provides training and career development for disabled employees, *technical aids* such as talking computers and magnifiers, and *accommodations* such as reader services for blind employees and furnishings appropriate to the nature of the disability.

MANAGING DIVERSITY

Employment equity programs have helped make the public service more representative of certain historically disadvantaged groups and, therefore, more diverse in its composition. However, it is widely acknowledged that employment equity initiatives must be complemented by cultural awareness programs generally described as *valuing differences* programs. Hiring members of underrepresented groups and expecting them to fit into the organization's value system is unacceptable because this puts them at a disadvantage and sets them up to fail. Managers must become more sensitive to the different values, backgrounds, and styles of various employees and to the need to resolve in an ethical way conflicts arising from these differences. Among the government initiatives to make diversity work is the federal government's Diversity in Leadership Program, which "provides executive development opportunities to 'high potential' members of visible minority groups, persons with disabilities, Aboriginal peoples, and women from non-traditional occupations."[51] Saskatchewan Telecommunications, a Crown corporation, made diversity an accepted part of its normal business operations by incorporating diversity into its strategic business plan and establishing it as a core value of the organization.[52]

Some basic demographic facts speak eloquently to the practical benefits of valuing differences. It is anticipated that by the year 2000 as many as 85 percent of persons entering the labour force will be members of the designated groups discussed earlier. Women will make up 64 percent of the workforce; among Aboriginal peoples, high birth rates and larger numbers of post-secondary graduates will increase substantially their representation in the workforce; employment possibilities for disabled persons will improve because of new technologies and better educational opportunities; and the number of visible minority persons in the labour force will continue to increase.[53] Proponents of the emphasis on valuing differences argue that for public organizations to compete effectively for skilled employees, the working milieu in government must be conducive to the success of these designated groups.

The concept of valuing differences is often used interchangeably with that of *managing diversity*. Increasingly, however, managing diversity is viewed as a much broader concept. It is defined as a comprehensive managerial *process* (not a program) for developing an organizational environment in which all employees can realize their potential while pursuing the organization's objectives. A leading scholar on this subject argues that while managing diversity is related to the concepts of employment equity and valuing differences, it is a *new* approach.[54] "[A]cceptance, tolerance, and understanding of diversity are not by themselves enough to create an empowered workforce. To empower a diverse group of employees to reach their full potential, managing diversity is needed."[55] Moreover, diversity is not viewed simply in terms of gender, ethnicity, or abilities but also in terms of such factors as age, religion, sexual preference, geographic origin, and lifestyle. "Managing diversity defines diversity broadly; it addresses the many ways employees are different *and* the many ways they are alike.... It is not about white males managing women and minorities; it is about all managers empowering whoever is in their workforce."[56] Managing diversity in this sense is a complicated and time-consuming process that involves examining an organization's culture and changing it to the extent necessary to empower *all* employees. For example, a "cultural audit" may reveal that the organizational understanding of fairness is treating people the same rather than treating them "appropriately." Clearly, managing diversity is closely related to the contemporary emphasis in public organizations on empowerment explained in Chapter 5.

🏛 PAY EQUITY

Over the past decade, *pay equity*—or equal pay for work of equal value—has been an issue of considerable importance in the management of human resources in both the public and private sectors of the economy. It is one component of the broader concept of employment equity already discussed.

Pay equity is a shorthand term for *equal pay for work of equal value*. This concept must be distinguished from that of *equal pay for equal work*, which requires that men and women be paid the same for doing the same job, or for a job that is very similar. The concept of equal pay for work of equal value permits comparisons of different jobs performed for the same employer. For example, if one job classification, such as public health nurse, is of equal value to another, such as public health inspector, employees in these two categories should receive the same base pay.

A primary purpose of pay equity programs is to ensure that women receive equal pay for doing work that has the same value as that done by men. Historically, women have been segregated into certain low-paying jobs (e.g., clerical, sales, and service jobs); these jobs have received lower rates of pay than those of equivalent value traditionally performed by men. Pay equity programs strive to devise a job evaluation method that removes sex bias from job classifications. If the requirements of a female-dominated job category, such as secretary, were found to be equivalent in terms of skill, effort, responsibility, and working conditions to those of a higher-paid job category in which males predominated, then a pay adjustment would be made for the female-dominated category.

The implementation of pay equity usually involves four steps.[57] The first step is the identification of jobs that are predominantly female; gender dominance can be defined, for example, as 70 percent or more of either sex. The second step is evaluation of jobs by a job evaluation procedure that is gender neutral. Third is the comparison of jobs; this may take the form, for example, of formulating rules for comparing male jobs to female jobs. The final step is adjustment of the pay of undervalued female jobs to that of the male-dominated group with which they have been compared.

Among the concerns about pay equity programs is the argument that the value of dissimilar jobs cannot be easily compared. In particular, it is argued that, in addition to the usual components of job evaluation described in the previous chapter, account must be taken of such factors as market considerations, i.e., the supply and demand of people able to perform certain jobs, and the collective bargaining process. Despite these and other concerns about pay equity,[58] most governments in Canada are convinced that the benefits outweigh the disadvantages. Several provinces have enacted pay equity legislation for their employees based on a "proactive" systemwide approach that requires employers to implement pay equity regardless of whether a complaint has been made or whether there is solid evidence of wage discrimination. In March 1990, for example, the Ontario government announced that it would pay out $96 million over a three-year period to remedy wage discrimination against provincial employees. The federal government and the Quebec government have adopted a "complaints-based," rather than a proactive, approach to pay equity. In Newfoundland, pay equity is a formal part of the collective bargaining process.

In the federal government, and in most provincial governments, the battle for pay equity *legislation* has been won, but the issue is still very much alive, in large part because pay equity settlements are so costly. By late 1997, the federal government had paid out more than $1 billion and was in a protracted dispute with the Public Service Alliance of Canada (the major public service union) which was demanding $42 billion in a settlement for 65 000 clerks, secretaries, and data processors.[59] According to the Canadian Human Rights Commissioner, "the fact that in 1995 women working full-time in the federal domain earned about seventy-five cents for every dollar earned by men amply demonstrates that the disparities of compensation today are hardly less blatant then they were a decade ago."[60] The challenges now lie in implementing and enforcing the legislation effectively, and in evaluating the extent to which the goals of pay equity are achieved in practice and the extent to which pay equity contributes to the broader objective of employment equity.

NOTES

1. *The Toronto Star,* 23 March and 20 March 1997, respectively.
2. Canadian Human Rights Commission, National Capital Alliance on Race Relations (NCARR) and Health and Welfare Canada, decision rendered 19 March 1997, 42–45.
3. For an examination of the theory of representative bureaucracy and its inadequacies, see: V. Subramaniam, "Representative Bureaucracy: A Reassessment," *American Political Science Review 61* (December, 1967): 1010–19; Arthur D. Larson, "Representative Bureaucracy and Administrative Responsibility: A Reassessment," *Midwest Review of Public Administration 7* (April 1973): 78–89; Kenneth John Meier, "Representative Bureaucracy: An Empirical Analysis," *American Political Science Review 69* (June 1965): 526–42; and V. Seymour Wilson and Willard A. Mullins, "Representative Bureaucracy: Linguistic/Ethnic Aspects in Canadian Public Policy," *Canadian Public Administration 21* (winter 1978): 513–38.
4. Peta E. Sheriff, "Unrepresentative Bureaucracy," *Sociology* 8, no. 3 (1974): 449.
5. Kenneth John Meier and Lloyd C. Nigro, "Representative Bureaucracy and Policy Preferences: A Study in the Attitudes of Federal Executives," *Public Administration Review* 36 (July–August, 1976): 467.
6. John Porter, "Higher Public Servants and the Bureaucratic Elite in Canada," *Canadian Journal of Economics and Political Science 24* (November 1958): 483–501; Donald C. Rowat, "On John Porter's Bureaucratic Elite in Canada," *Canadian Journal of Economics and Political Science 25* (May 1959): 204–7; and John Porter, "The Bureaucratic Elite: A Reply to Professor Rowat," *Canadian Journal of Economics and Political Science 25* (May 1959): 207–9.
7. Rowat, "On John Porter's Bureaucratic Elite," 204.
8. Porter, "Higher Public Servants," 490–91.
9. Ibid., 490.
10. Rowat, "On John Porter's Bureaucratic Elite," 207.
11. Porter, "The Bureaucratic Elite," 208.
12. Ibid., 209.
13. Wilson and Mullins, "Representative Bureaucracy," 533.
14. Ibid., 534.
15. Dennis Olsen, *The State Elite* (Toronto: McClelland & Stewart, 1980).
16. Ibid., 82.
17. Treasury Board, *Affirmative Action in the Public Service*, News Release, 27 June 1983.
18. Ibid.
19. Ibid.
20. Royal Commission on Equality in Employment, *Report* (Ottawa: Minister of Supply and Services, 1984).
21. Ibid., 3.

22. "Public Service Reform Act," Canada, *Statutes* (1992), ch. 54, sec. 5.1(5).

23. Treasury Board, *Employment Equity in the Public Service: Annual Report 1992–93* (Ottawa: Minister of Supply and Services, March 1994), 6.

24. Paul Tellier, Clerk of the Privy Council and Secretary to the Cabinet, *Public Service 2000: A Report on Progress* (Ottawa: Minister of Supply and Services, 1992), 59–60.

25. Treasury Board of Canada Secretariat, *Employment Equity in the Federal Public Service: 1996–97* (Ottawa: Treasury Board Secretariat, 1997), 7. Reproduced with the permission of the Minister of Public Works and Government Services Canada, 1998.

26. Public Service Commission, *Equality of Access: Equal Opportunity Programs and the Merit Principle* (Ottawa: Public Service Commission, 1982), 3.

27. Lise Pigeon, "Towards a Representative Public Service: The Experience of the Canadian Federal Government." Address to the Conference of the Institute of Public Administration of Canada (New Brunswick Region), Fredericton, N.B., 13 March 1989.

28. Wilson and Mullins, "Representative Bureaucracy," 520.

29. Royal Commission on Government Organization, *Report*, vol. 1 (Queen's Printer, 1963), 27–29.

30. House of Commons, *Debates*, April 6, 1966, 3915.

31. Ibid., 23 June 1970, 8487. (Emphasis added.)

32. A new Official Languages Act was proclaimed in September 1988. Among other things, the new act recognizes that the participation rates of anglophones and francophones may vary from one department to another, depending on such considerations as the department's mandate, clientele, and location.

33. For information on the implementation and effectiveness of these strategies, see the annual reports of the Commissioner of Official Languages. See also the first annual report of the Treasury Board to Parliament entitled *Official Languages in Federal Institutions: Annual Report, 1988–1989* (Ottawa: Minister of Supply and Services, 1989). On the history of language training programs and the Office of the Commissioner of Official Languages, see the 12-volume work by Gilles Bibeau, *Report of the Independent Study on the Language Training Programmes of the Public Service of Canada* (Ottawa: 1975).

34. Public Service Commission, *Annual Report Statistics 1992* (Ottawa: Minister of Supply and Services, 1993), 10.

35. Stanislaw Judek, *Women in the Public Service* (Ottawa: Queen's Printer, 1968), 7–9; and Kathleen Archibald, *Sex and the Public Service* (Ottawa: Queen's Printer, 1970), 106.

36. Calculations based on Public Service Commission, *Annual Report 1971* (Ottawa: Information Canada, 1972), 44–45.

37. Royal Commission on Government Organization, *Report*, vol. 1, 275.

38. Royal Commission on the Status of Women, *Report* (Ottawa: Information Canada, 1970), 138.

39. *Beneath the Veneer: Report of the Task Force on Barriers to Women in the Public Service*, vol. 1 (Ottawa: Minister of Supply and Services, 1990), 116.

40. President of the Treasury Board, *Employment Equity in the Public Service: Annual Report 1996–97* (Ottawa: Minister of Supply and Services, 1997), 35.

41. See *Native People and Employment in the Public Service of Canada*, a report prepared by Impact Research for the Public Service Commission, October 1976, 40–44.

42. Treasury Board, News Release, "Special Employment Measures for Members of Visible Minority Groups," 9 September 1985.

43. Canada, House of Commons, *Equality Now: Report of the Special Committee on Participation of Visible Minorities in Canadian Society*, Issue no. 4, 8 March 1984.

44. Cited in Canadian Human Rights Commission, *Visible Minorities and the Public Service of Canada, section 2.3* (Ottawa: Canadian Human Rights Commission, 1997), 1. Available at http://www.chrc.ca.

45. Between: National Capital Alliance on Race Relations (Complainant) and Health and Welfare Canada, the Public Service Commission and the Treasury Board, 19 March 1997.

46. Canadian Human Rights Commission, *Annual Report 1996–97* (Ottawa: Canadian Human Rights Commission, 1997).

47. Canadian Human Rights Commission, *Visible Minorities*.

48. Ibid, section 7.1.

49. Canadian Human Rights Commission, *Visible Minorities*.

50. *Barrier-Free Employers* (Ottawa: Canadian Human Rights Commission), 1997, 2. Available at http://www.chrc.ca.

51. *Public Sector Management* 6, no. 2 (1995): 15.

52. Ibid., 4.

53. Canada, Department of Natural Resources, Human Resources Services, *A Manager's Guide to Managing a Diverse Workforce and Employment Equity* (Ottawa: Natural Resources Canada, c. 1995), 10.

54. R. Roosevelt Thomas, Jr., *Beyond Race and Gender: Unleashing the Power of Your Total Workforce by Managing Diversity* (New York: American Management Associations, 1991), 26.

55. Ibid., 25.

56. Ibid., 12.

57. Morley Gunderson and Roberta Edgecombe Robb, "Legal and Institutional Issues Pertaining to Women's Wages in Canada." Paper prepared for the Conference on Women's Wages, *Stability and Change in Six Industrialized Countries*, Chicago, March 1990, 4.

58. For an examination of the costs and benefits of pay equity, see: Roberta Edgecombe Robb, "Equal Pay for Work of Equal Value: Issues and Policies," *Canadian Public Policy* 13, no. 4 (1987): 445–61.

59. Margaret Wente, "Who Pays for Pay Equity," *The Globe and Mail*, 27 September 1997, D7.

60. Canadian Human Rights Commission, *Annual Report 1996–97*.

BIBLIOGRAPHY

Agocs, Carol. "Affirmative Action, Canadian Style: A Reconnaissance." *Canadian Public Policy* 12 (March 1986): 148–62.

Archibald, Kathleen. *Sex and the Public Service*. Ottawa: Queen's Printer, 1970.

Beattie, Christopher. *Minority Men in a Majority Setting*. Toronto: McClelland & Stewart, 1975.

Canada. Royal Commission on Bilingualism and Biculturalism. *Report*, Vol. 3. Ottawa: Queen's Printer, 1965.

Chartrand, P.J., and K.L. Pond. *A Study of Executive Career Paths in the Public Service of Canada*. Chicago: Public Personnel Association, 1970.

Cox, T., Jr. *Cultural Diversity in Organizations: Theory, Research and Practice*. San Francisco: Berrett-Koehler, 1993.

Judek, Stanislaw. *Women in the Public Service*. Ottawa: Queen's Printer, 1968.

Kernaghan, Kenneth. "Representative Bureaucracy: The Canadian Experience." *Canadian Public Administration* 21 (winter 1978): 489–512.

Kingsley, J. Donald. *Representative Bureaucracy: An Interpretation of the British Civil Service*. Yellow Springs, Ohio: Antioch Press, 1944.

Krantz, Harry. *The Participatory Bureaucracy*. Lexington: Lexington Books, 1976.

Krislov, Samuel. *Representative Bureaucracy*. Englewood Cliffs, N.J.: Prentice-Hall, 1974.

Larson, Arthur D. "Representative Bureaucracy and Administrative Responsibility: A Reassessment." *Midwest Review of Public Administration* 7 (April 1973): 79–89.

Lum, Janet M. "The Federal Employment Equity Act: Goals vs. Implementation." *Canadian Public Administration* 38 (spring 1995): 45–76.

Olsen, Dennis. *The State Elite.* Toronto: McClelland & Stewart, 1980.

Ospina, Sonia M. "Realizing the Promise of Diversity." In James L. Perry, ed., *Handbook of Public Administration*, 2nd ed. San Francisco: Jossey-Bass, 1996, 441–59.

Porter, John. "Higher Public Servants and the Bureaucratic Elite in Canada." *Canadian Journal of Economics and Political Science* 24 (November 1958): 483–501.

_____. "The Bureaucratic Elite: A Reply to Professor Rowat." *Canadian Journal of Economics and Political Science* 25 (May 1959): 207–9.

Rowat, Donald C. "On John Porter's Bureaucratic Elite in Canada." *Canadian Journal of Economics and Political Science* 25 (May 1959): 204–7.

Wilson, V. Seymour, and Willard A. Mullins. "Representative Bureaucracy: Linguistic/Ethnic Aspects in Canadian Public Policy." *Canadian Public Administration* 21 (winter 1978): 513–38.

Winn, Conrad. "Affirmative Action for Women: More than a Case of Simple Justice." *Canadian Public Administration* 28 (spring 1985): 24–46.

_____. "Affirmative Action and Visible Minorities: Eight Premises in Search of Evidence." *Canadian Public Policy* 11 (December 1985): 684–700.

25

Collective Bargaining

On September 28, 1991, *The Globe and Mail* reported that "thousands of public servants stormed the main entrance of the Parliament Buildings in Ottawa ... as the Public Service Alliance of Canada resumed a nationwide strike."[1] Members of the RCMP riot squad went to the Parliament Buildings; the House of Commons was adjourned early; and the prime minister was taken down a freight elevator and out a side door to his limousine.

This was the largest strike ever in the federal public service. The finance minister, in his February 26 budget speech, had announced that while the collective bargaining process would continue, wage increases would be severely limited for the next three years and if public servants went on strike, they would be legislated back to work. On September 9, about 70 000 of the 109 000 non-designated members of the Public Service Alliance of Canada (PSAC) began a legal strike, causing considerable disruption at border crossings and airports and in grain-handling operations. The union suspended the strike for eleven days while it waited for a new offer from the government. Then, after characterizing the offer as "a slap in the face," the union resumed strike action. On October 2, the government ended the strike by legislation.

To what extent can public servants engage in collective bargaining and take strike action? What is the Public Service Alliance of Canada and what is a "nondesignated" member? What is the legal and administrative system within which collective bargaining is conducted? How does the system work in practice? What does the future hold for collective bargaining in Canada? These are some of the main issues discussed in this chapter.

Public sector collective bargaining is a continuing source of concern and controversy in Canadian society. The processes and outcomes of collective bargaining have significant effects beyond our governments as well as within them. For example, public sector strikes can disrupt the provision of such important government services as mail delivery, air traffic control, and police protection. Moreover, collective bargaining agreements in the public sector on wages, fringe benefits, and working conditions can influence settlements in the private sector.

Compared with the private sector, the emergence of collective bargaining in the public sector is quite recent. It was during the period from the early 1960s to the mid-1970s that the federal government and most provincial governments granted their employees the statutory right to bargain collectively. While the growth of public service unionism was extremely rapid in the 1960s and 1970s, it then levelled off because most eligible employees had been unionized.[2] Public sector employees constitute about one-quarter of the total labour force, but they make up almost one-half of all union members. Moreover, the three largest unions in Canada are public service unions—the Canadian Union of Public Employees (mostly municipal government employees), the National Union of Public and General Employees (provincial employees), and the Public Service Alliance of Canada (federal employees).

🏛 THE EVOLUTION OF PUBLIC SECTOR COLLECTIVE BARGAINING

Municipal government employees received the right to bargain collectively earlier than their federal and provincial counterparts. Aside from police and firefighters, most of whom are prohibited from taking strike action and for whom special legislation is usually provided, municipal employees have long had the same rights under provincial labour legislation as private sector employees, including the right to strike. Most unionized municipal employees belong to the Canadian Union of Public Employees (CUPE), which is affiliated with the Canadian Labour Congress (CLC). (The congress is a central union body with ninety national and international member unions, which, in turn, have more than two million individual members.)

Many other public sector employees, in both the federal and provincial spheres, have long enjoyed the right to bargain collectively under general labour legislation. Included in this group are employees of various government boards and agencies, e.g., the CBC in the federal sphere, and hydroelectric commissions and liquor control boards in the provinces. In addition, in the health and education sectors many employees have, under general labour legislation, the right to bargain collectively, including the right to strike; for other employees in this sector, the right to strike is denied or restricted in some way.

For federal and provincial employees in regular government departments, the right to bargain collectively was slow in coming—except in the province of Saskatchewan. As early as 1944, the Co-operative Commonwealth Federation (CCF) government in that province included its employees under the general provincial labour legislation (the Trade Union Act). Other provincial governments gradually gave their employees the right to bargain collectively, but it was not until 1965 that a second provincial government—the government of Quebec—granted its employees the right to strike. The federal government granted collective bargaining with the right to strike in 1967, and several provincial governments did the same shortly thereafter. Other provinces have adopted collective bargaining for government employees but have substituted third-party arbitration (to be explained later) for the right to strike.

The Evolution of the Federal System

The development of the federal regime for collective bargaining in the public service merits special attention because it is generally perceived to be a unique and imaginative approach to labour relations in the public sector, and because its operation has been the focus of so much controversy. Although public service staff associations did not receive legal recognition until the Civil Service Act of 1961, one of the first associations—the Civil Service Rifle Association—was created exactly one century earlier. Postal workers organized into staff associations as early as 1889 when the Railway Mail Clerks Association was established. This was followed by the Federated Association of Letter Carriers in 1891 and the Canadian Postal Employees Association in 1911. Other categories of employees organized into such associations as the Civil Service Association of Ottawa (1907), the Civil Service Federation (1909), the Professional Institute of the Public Service of Canada (1920), and the Amalgamated Civil Servants of Canada (1920).[3]

The efforts of the staff associations to persuade the government to adopt some mechanism for consulting with them finally led, in 1944, to the creation of the National Joint Council of the Public Service of Canada, which was closely modelled on the National Whitley Council in the United Kingdom.[4] The National Joint Council was constituted as an *advisory* body with an employer side composed of senior public servants and an employee side composed of people chosen from the staff associations, according to the size of their membership. The government explained that the purpose of the council was

> to provide machinery for regular and systematic consultation and discussion between the employer and employee sides of the public service in regard to grievances and conditions of employment, and thereby to promote increased efficiency and better morale in the public service.[5]

The duties of the council were to make recommendations to the cabinet, the Treasury Board, and/or the Civil Service Commission on such matters as recruitment, training, hours of work, promotion, discipline, health, welfare, and seniority.

The council was successful in improving communication and general relations between the government and its employees, and in enhancing employee morale. However, by the early 1950s, the staff associations were sufficiently disillusioned with their ability to influence government policy through the consultative mechanism of the council that they began to agitate for the right to bargain collectively. The Civil Service Act of 1961 granted legal recognition to the staff associations for the first time and gave them the right to be consulted on remuneration as well as on terms and conditions of employment. However, the consultative procedures proved unsatisfactory to the staff associations, who renewed their agitation for collective bargaining. Then, during the 1963 federal election campaign, the Liberal party promised, if elected, to introduce collective bargaining. Following their return to office as a minority government, the Liberals, with the strong support of the New Democratic Party, appointed the Preparatory Committee on Collective Bargaining, which was composed entirely of senior public servants and chaired by A.D.P. Heeney. The committee's terms of reference were "to make preparations for the introduction into the Public Service of an appropriate form of collective bargaining and arbitration, and to examine the need for reforms in the systems of classification and pay applying to civil servants and prevailing rate employees."[6]

In addition to proposing the system of collective bargaining discussed below, the committee recommended that the National Joint Council be preserved "as a forum for the systematic study and discussion of problems that transcend those of particular bargaining units."[7] The government accepted this recommendation, and the council continues to exist as an effective mechanism for promoting the efficiency of the public service and the well-being of public servants by providing for consultation between the government and employee organizations.[8] The council deals with such matters as relocation policy, travel policy, and disability insurance. These are matters for which it is appropriate to have the same policy across the entire public service.

The resistance of the federal and provincial governments to public sector collective bargaining had been founded in part on the principle of *the sovereignty of the state*. The application of this principle to public sector labour relations meant that the government could not adopt a system, such as collective bargaining or compulsory arbitration, which required it to give up its final decision-making authority in order that terms and conditions of employment could be determined jointly. As late as 1964, Jean Lesage, the premier of Quebec, proclaimed that "the Queen does not negotiate."[9] Now, however, the principal reason that the system of collective bargaining in federal and provincial governments is more restrictive than that in the private sector is the need to protect essential public services.

🏛 THE LEGAL AND ADMINISTRATIVE FRAMEWORK OF THE FEDERAL SYSTEM

The Preparatory Committee's recommendations led to the enactment of a statutory framework for collective bargaining[10] made up of two new statutes—the Public Service Staff Relations Act[11] (PSSRA) and the Public Service Employment Act[12] (PSEA)—and an amended statute, the Financial Administration Act[13] (FAA). The PSSRA, which is discussed below, sets out the structures and processes of the collective bargaining system. The PSEA replaced the Civil Service Act and, among other things, abolished the Civil Service Commission's function of making recommendations to the Treasury Board on managerial matters such as pay determination. Amendments to the FAA specified the Treasury Board as employer for most of the public service and gave it the responsibility for negotiating collective agreements and determining other aspects of personnel policy. Major changes to the collective bargaining regime resulted from the amendment of all three statutes by the Public Service Reform Act (PSRA) of 1992.[14]

The Public Service Staff Relations Act

This act is administered by the Public Service Staff Relations Board,[15] which is appointed by the federal cabinet. The board plays an extremely important role in the collective bargaining system. It has responsibility for a broad range of matters, including the determination of appropriate bargaining units, the certification of bargaining agents, the settlement of interest disputes (i.e., disputes arising from the renegotiation of a collective agreement), and the settlement of rights disputes (i.e., disputes arising during the term of a collective agreement). In the collective bargaining process, the interests of the government as employer are represented by the Treasury Board, which is usually assisted by the relevant departmental representatives.

The Structure of Bargaining Units

All employees belong to one of the many occupational groups in the public service, and these groups are classified into the six occupational categories explained in Chapter 23 (e.g., Executive Group, Scientific and Professional, Administrative Support). Employee organizations (i.e., unions such as the Public Service Alliance of Canada and the Professional Institute of the Public Service of Canada) wishing to bargain with the government must be certified as *bargaining agents*. These employee organizations act as bargaining agents for *bargaining units*. A bargaining unit is a group of two or more employees determined under the PSSRA to constitute a unit of employees appropriate for collective bargaining. It is composed of employees with reasonably similar duties and cannot include supervisors and subordinates in the same unit.

Exclusions from Collective Bargaining

The PSSRA provides for the exclusion from collective bargaining of certain managerial and confidential positions. Among the positions excluded are those occupied by persons in the Executive Group, legal officers in the Department of Justice, Treasury Board employees, and advisors on staff relations, staffing, or classification. The rationale for excluding such positions is that the membership of their occupants in a bargaining unit would conflict with their responsibilities for negotiating or administering collective agreements.

The Scope of Bargaining

Under the PSSRA, certain subjects are excluded from collective bargaining. No term or condition of employment may be included in a collective agreement if it requires legislative implementation (except for the appropriation of moneys) or if it is established under certain specified statutes (e.g., the Public Service Employment Act). This means that there can be no bargaining on matters falling within the jurisdiction of the Public Service Commission, including recruitment, promotion, and transfers. The PSSRA also confirms the authority of the employer to determine the organization of the public service, to assign duties to positions, and to classify positions. There can be no bargaining over such matters as job evaluation, the distribution of work, and the determination of duties.

The PSSRA specifically confirms some of these limitations by providing that "standards, procedures or processes governing the appointment, appraisal, promotion, demotion, lay-off or termination of employment, other than by way of disciplinary action, of employees" may not be included in a conciliation board report or an arbitral award (i.e., a decision by an arbitration board). The resolution of interest disputes, whether through binding arbitration or conciliation, *can* deal with rates of pay, hours of work, leave entitlements, standards of discipline, other directly related terms and conditions of employment, grievance procedures, check-off of union dues, occupational health and safety, and career development.

Master Agreement Bargaining

The 1992 PSRA made legislative provision for the practice of *master agreement bargaining*, according to which "the employer and a bargaining agent may jointly elect to engage in collective bargaining with a view to the conclusion of a single collective agreement binding on two or more bargaining units." Thus, a union certified as a bargaining agent (e.g., the Professional Institute of the Public Service of Canada) can negotiate a master agreement for several bargaining units on a number of issues (e.g., benefit plans, grievance procedures) and each bargaining unit can then negotiate separate agreements on other issues (e.g., wages, vacations). In 1991, twenty of the Professional Institute's twenty-six bargaining units adopted the master agreement approach, three units chose conventional arbitration and three units followed the conciliation-strike route.[16]

The Resolution of Interest Disputes

Interest disputes usually arise from a renegotiation of an existing collective agreement. The PSSRA provides an innovative approach to resolving such disputes. While the process may seem complicated at first glance, it is actually quite straightforward; the rights and responsibilities of the parties involved are clearly set out in the PSSRA.

Prior to the beginning of each round of talks for a new agreement, the bargaining agent must specify which of two possible methods of impasse resolution it wishes to have applied during the bargaining process:

1. the referral of a dispute to *binding arbitration*; or

2. the referral of a dispute to *conciliation*[17] followed, if necessary, by *strike* action.

Thus, if the bargaining unit chooses the arbitration route, it has no right to strike and the choice cannot be altered until the next round of negotiations. However, as explained later, if the conciliation-strike route is chosen, the parties may use the option of alternate dispute resolution to refer outstanding issues to arbitration.

Table 25.1
POSSIBLE STEPS IN THE PROCESS OF INTEREST DISPUTE RESOLUTION,
GOVERNMENT OF CANADA

Arbitration Route	Conciliation/Strike Route
negotiation	negotiation
conciliator	conciliator
fact finding	fact finding
arbitration board	alternate dispute resolution*
arbitral award	conciliation
	strike

*This can occur at any point in negotiations prior to the referral of all the remaining issues in dispute to conciliation.

Regardless of the option chosen, if negotiations reach an impasse, either the bargaining agent or the employer may request that the chairperson of the PSSRB appoint a conciliator (often called a mediator) to help reach a settlement. The conciliator must report to the chairperson, within fourteen days or a longer period specified by the chairperson, on the probability of success or failure in reaching a settlement. The role of conciliator should be distinguished from that of a conciliation board, which is explained later.

Another form of third-party assistance the parties may use for dispute resolution is called *fact finding*; this is not a compulsory step in the dispute-resolution process, but, if it is used, it *must* take place before either party requests arbitration or conciliation. The fact finder, who is appointed by the PSSRB after consultation with the two parties in dispute, prepares a report, including any recommendations for settling the dispute that he or she considers appropriate. Within thirty days of appointment, the fact finder must submit his or her report to the board, which will make the report public if the parties in dispute do not conclude a collective agreement within fifteen days after the board has given them its report. The purpose of a public report is to alert the public at an early stage in the collective bargaining process that a potentially disruptive labour dispute has developed and to bring the influence of public opinion to bear in the hope that the parties will come to an agreement.

If no agreement is reached as a result of conciliation or fact finding, the next stage depends on whether the arbitration or conciliation-strike route has been chosen.

If the *arbitration route* of dispute resolution has been selected, the parties are expected to reach agreement on as many issues as possible before either party requests arbitration. If arbitration is requested with respect to the matters still in dispute, an arbitration board is set up.[18] Each party chooses one person for the board, and these two persons choose a third person to act as chairperson.

The PSSRA sets out the following criteria upon which arbitral awards are to be made:

(a) the needs of the Public Service for qualified employees;

(b) the conditions of employment in similar occupations outside the Public Service, including such geographic, industrial or other variations as the Board may consider relevant;

(c) the need to maintain appropriate relationships in the conditions of employment as between different grade levels within an occupation and as between occupations in the Public Service;

(d) the need to establish terms and conditions of employment that are fair and reasonable in relation to the qualifications required, the work performed, the responsibility assumed and the nature of the services rendered; and

(e) any other factor that appears to be relevant to the matter in dispute.

The arbitration board, or a single arbitrator, will listen to the arguments presented on both sides and then produce a decision. The document containing the decision looks like, and has the same status as, a collective agreement, but it is technically referred to as an arbitral award. The award is final and binding on both parties.

If the *conciliation-strike* route of dispute resolution has been selected and if the parties are unable to reach agreement on all or some of the matters on the bargaining table, either party may request that a conciliation board be established.[19] The board is constituted in the same way as the arbitration board described above. The conciliation board, or a conciliation commissioner, is responsible for consulting the parties and reporting its findings and recommendations to the chairperson of the PSSRB within fourteen days or a longer period agreed upon by the parties or specified by the chairperson.

An important precondition to the establishment of a conciliation board is a determination of *designated positions* whose occupants are forbidden to participate in a lawful strike. These are positions "having duties consisting in whole or in part of duties the performance of which at any particular time or after any specified period is or will be necessary in the interest of the safety or security of the public." The purpose of this provision is to ensure that the performance of certain essential services (e.g., by hospital workers, corrections officers) will not be disrupted by a public service strike. Six months before a collective agreement expires (before the arbitration or conciliation-strike route is chosen), the employer and the bargaining agent meet to review the position of each employee in the bargaining unit to determine if the position has safety or security duties. Where the employer and bargaining agent disagree on which positions should be designated, the employer refers the positions in dispute to a designation review panel, which makes a nonbinding recommendation. If the parties continue to disagree over designations, the employer refers the positions in dispute to the PSSRB, which makes a final determination. Once positions have been designated, they are *permanently* designated; they are not determined anew for each round of bargaining.

If a conciliation board is established and its recommendations are unacceptable either to the employer or to the union, the union has *the right to strike* seven days after the report is received by the chairperson of the PSSRB. Employees in a bargaining unit for which the conciliation-strike route has been chosen may not strike during the time that a collective agreement applicable to their bargaining unit is in force. Employee organizations are forbidden to declare or authorize a strike that would involve employees in an unlawful strike.

There is one other mechanism that can be used to avoid strike action by facilitating agreement for bargaining units that have chosen the conciliation-strike process; it is called the *alternate dispute resolution process*. By mutual agreement, the parties can refer any or all issues in dispute (that may be included in a collective agreement) to a form of binding arbitration. The parties can, therefore, refer some issues to arbitration while they continue to seek agreement on others.

Alternative Approaches to Dispute Resolution

The federal government's approach to the resolution of interest disputes has been described as the *choice of procedures* approach. There are several possible alternatives to this approach.[20] First, there is the straightforward *right to strike*, which is prevalent in private sector collective bargaining. Second, there is *conventional interest arbitration*, which is the most common alternative to strike action. If the employer and the union cannot reach a settlement, they submit their differences to an arbitrator who assesses the merits of the arguments made by each side and then makes a decision, which is binding. The choice of procedures approach is a combination of these two approaches. A third approach is the *controlled strike*, which enables unions to take strike action but requires that a number of designated employees from the bargaining unit stay on the job to provide essential services. The federal scheme also incorporates this approach.

A fourth approach is called *final offer selection*. This approach differs from conventional interest arbitration in that the arbitrator is required to select, without proposing or making any change, either the position put forward by the employer or that put forward by the union. It is hoped that both sides will make reasonable concessions during the negotiations out of fear that an arbitrator might choose the other side's total position.

The Resolution of Rights Disputes

Federal public servants have a broad right under the PSSRA to present grievances, not only in relation to the interpretation or application of the provisions of a collective agreement or an arbitral award but also in relation to "a provision of a statute, or of a regulation, by-law, direction or other instrument made or issued by the employer, dealing with terms and conditions of employment."

Moreover, the right to present a grievance extends to employees in managerial or confidential positions who are not permitted to belong to a bargaining unit and even, on some matters, to former employees.

Employees with a grievance are normally required to begin by using the three or four levels of the grievance procedure in their department. However, grievances in the areas of classification and discharge are heard first at the final level of the department's grievance procedure. Grievances relating to the interpretation or application of a collective agreement or arbitral award,[21] and to disciplinary action leading to discharge, suspension, or a financial penalty, or discharge for incompetence or incapacity, may be referred to third-party *adjudication* when the grievor is not satisfied with the results of the departmental grievance procedure. In such cases, the PSSRB selects an adjudicator from among its members, unless the parties have selected their own. Employees may request that their grievance be heard by a board of adjudication. If the employer has no objection to this request, the board will consist of a member of the PSSRB as chairperson and one person selected by each of the parties.

Aside from the right to present grievances under the PSSRA, employees have the right under the PSEA to present appeals to the Public Service Commission in relation to layoffs, rejection on probation, termination of employment for political partisanship, and termination of appointment for engaging in fraudulent practices.

🏛 THE OPERATION OF THE FEDERAL SYSTEM

This section examines areas of disagreement between the federal government and the public service unions. Several bodies of inquiry have examined these problem areas and have recommended changes in the PSSRA to remedy them. Of particular importance are the reports by Jacob Finkelman,[22] the first chairperson of the PSSRB; by the parliamentary committee on employer-employee relations in the public service;[23] by the D'Avignon Committee;[24] and by Public Service 2000.[25]

In general, the unions would prefer to have a collective bargaining system for the public sector that is based on the Canada Labour Code. Under this code, which regulates collective bargaining in the *private* sector, more matters are left to negotiation than under the PSSRA. The Treasury Board in 1987 and the Public Service 2000 Task Force on Staff Relations in 1990[26] proposed a number of changes to the PSSRA; several of these proposed changes are mentioned at the top of page 606.

The Structure of Bargaining Units

A large number of bargaining units have resulted from the requirement that the units must correspond to the occupational groups into which the public service is divided. There are, at present, seventy-two occupational groups and eighty-two bargaining units (ten of the groups are divided into supervisory and nonsupervisory units). This means that bargaining is virtually a constant

> Governments as employers must negotiate with their own citizens. ... Under these conditions, adversarialism and the tactics and goals of private sector industrial relations do not serve the parties or the public well. Governments which seek to provide services at the expense of the living conditions of their employees threaten the contract between public sector workers and their community. Unions which extract the greatest possible advantage for their members risk alienation from the community, which depends on their members for many of the benefits of a civilized society.
>
> *Source: Mark Thompson and Gene Swimmer, "The Future of Public Sector Industrial Relations."[27]*

process for the larger public service unions, which represent several bargaining units, and for the Treasury Board.

It has been argued that a reduction in the number of bargaining units would benefit the unions, the employer, and the public in that it would do away with the need to negotiate similar or identical provisions for inclusion in separate agreements, and it would reduce the number of interruptions of service to the public if negotiations break down. The Public Service 2000 Task Force on Classification and Occupational Group Structures recommended that the occupational categories be abolished and that the number of groups be reduced to twenty-three.[28] As noted in Chapter 23, the federal government is considering a simplification of the classification system by reducing drastically the number of occupational groups.

Exclusions from Collective Bargaining

There has been a great deal of controversy between the government and public service unions over the exclusion from collective bargaining of positions occupied by persons employed in a managerial or confidential capacity.[29] In 1990–91, about 7 percent of employees (14 600) were excluded, 7800 in a managerial capacity and 6800 in a confidential capacity. The unions have complained that some positions have been excluded not because of the duties required, but because the government wants to keep a certain number of people on the job to run the operation in the event of a strike.

One provision of the 1992 PSRA reduced the number of exclusions, but another provision increased it. Exclusions based on confidentiality are restricted to those positions relating to staff relations matters. But departments are now able to exclude a larger number of managers from bargaining units. The Treasury Board expects that, on balance, the number of exclusions will remain about the same, but some unions believe that the changes will result in a significant loss of members.

The Scope of Bargaining

Federal public service unions have been successful in achieving many of the terms and conditions of employment that are standard in private sector collective agreements. However, as noted earlier in this chapter, they are prohibited under the PSSRA from bargaining on such centrally important matters as classification, job security,[30] staffing procedures, and superannuation. The unions continue to press strongly for a broadening of the scope of bargaining, especially in these areas. Gene Swimmer argues that the logic of restricting bargaining on such matters as promotion, transfer, and demotion because the merit principle is at stake does not apply to classification.[31]

The Resolution of Interest Disputes

Arbitration versus Conciliation–Strike

Initially most unions selected the arbitration route rather than the conciliation-strike route to the resolution of interest disputes. However, during subsequent negotiations there has been a gradual move in the other direction so that a majority of the bargaining units now choose the conciliation-strike option. Among the many reasons offered for this shift are that average wage settlements have been higher under the conciliation-strike route, constraints have been placed on arbitrators under the PSSRA to the disadvantage of the unions, and the arbitration route obliges unions to focus on preparing persuasive arbitration briefs rather than mobilizing their members. The 1985 National Convention of PSAC approved a motion requiring all of its bargaining units to follow the conciliation-strike option as part of an effort to negotiate the same expiry date for all contracts so that all bargaining units would be in a position to strike at the same time.

The unions object to being required to select either the arbitration or conciliation-strike option before bargaining begins; they would prefer that bargaining units be permitted to choose the dispute resolution mechanism when an impasse arises in the bargaining process. Another approach would be to permit bargaining agents to change their choice from conciliation-strike to arbitration at any time during the bargaining process. In 1987, the Treasury Board proposed that the PSSRA be amended so that if an impasse occurred under the conciliation-strike route, the PSSRB could appoint a conciliator or the parties could mutually agree to refer all outstanding issues to arbitration. A variation of this proposal has been implemented in the form of the alternate dispute resolution process explained earlier.

The Designation Issue

Despite considerable disagreement over the number of employees to be designated as performing essential services, the government and the bargaining agents had, by 1980, reached a generally acceptable working arrangement on this issue. Then, in 1980, the Minister of Transport proposed to the PSSRB that, in the event of a strike in the air traffic control unit, all operational traffic controllers should be designated. The PSSRB decided that it should designate only the number of employees necessary to maintain a level of service that would ensure the safety and security of the public. However, the Federal Court of

Appeal,[32] in a decision upheld by the Supreme Court of Canada in 1982,[33] ruled, among other things, that the PSSRB could not discriminate between employees performing similar duties by designating only a few of them. As a result, designation became largely a management right. Between 1982 and 1987, the percentage of bargaining units whose members were designated as essential rose from roughly 15 percent to 40 percent and, for some units, as high as 100 percent.[34]

The Public Service 2000 Task Force on Staff Relations recognized that during the 1980s the designation of employees to provide essential services "exceeded a reasonable definition of those required to provide the minimum level of services for the protection of the Public."[35] As already noted, the government responded by amending the PSSRA to provide for designations to be negotiated by the parties and in the event of disagreement to be finally determined by the PSSRB. The amendment also provided that positions, rather than employees, should be designated.

Government Restraints on Public Service Unions

Relations between the government and the unions were greatly aggravated by the enactment of the Public Sector Compensation Restraint Act (PSCRA), which was the cornerstone of the federal government's "6 and 5" program introduced in June 1982. This act suspended federal employees' right to bargain collectively on monetary matters and the right to strike for a period of two years. Compensation increases were limited to specified percentages. Most provincial governments followed the federal lead by introducing similar restraints on employee compensation. Following the expiry of the PSCRA, normal collective bargaining was restored, but public service unions were concerned that Parliament and provincial legislatures would be more inclined in the future to take legislative action to reduce "excessive" wage settlements or to end "disruptive" strikes.

Ever since the enactment of the PSSRA, there has been considerable public pressure to reduce the rights of public servants to engage in collective bargaining and especially to take strike action. Yet "by any measure, strikes in the public sector have not been numerous. The federal public service ... has, with the exception of the Post Office, been especially peaceful ... public sector strikes have occurred most frequently in Quebec."[36] However, there have been major public sector strikes in British Columbia, Saskatchewan, and Newfoundland.

During the first half of the 1990s, both the Conservative and the Liberal governments in the federal sphere and several provincial governments imposed severe restrictions on the collective bargaining process and public service salaries. As noted at the beginning of this chapter, there was in 1991 a nationwide strike of federal employees that was ended by government legislation. Gene Swimmer concluded that this strike should not be viewed as a defeat for the union. PSAC not only showed that it could conduct a nationwide strike, it also received post-strike benefits in the form of a better workforce adjustment policy and better pension legislation than it otherwise would have received. Swimmer noted that once PSAC got the attention of the news media, it "successfully demonstrated that its members were not 'fat cats,' but people struggling to get by on modest salaries. Breaking down the public stereotype of 'over-paid and under-worked federal bureaucrats' may be the greatest legacy of the strike."[37]

The Resolution of Rights Disputes[38]

Until recently, there was some overlap between the PSSRA and the PSEA on the reasons for termination of employees. This led to confusion among managers as to whether action for termination should be taken under the PSSRA provisions for discipline or under the PSEA provisions for incompetence or incapacity. To resolve this uncertainty, the PS 2000 Task Force on Staff Relations proposed that demotions and terminations, whether for discipline or for incompetence or incapacity, be handled under the PSSRA.[39] This solution was adopted by the 1992 Public Service Reform Act (PSRA).

The unions vigorously opposed the PSRA's provisions for deployment, which were explained in Chapter 23. The concern is that managers can use deployment (moving an employee to another position without competition) to reward their favourite employees and to punish others; that the use of deployments will reduce the number of opportunities for promotion; and that the rights of appeal against deployment decisions are inadequate.

🏛 COLLECTIVE BARGAINING IN THE PROVINCES

The structure and operation of collective bargaining differ considerably from one province to another.[40] In the provinces, as in the federal sphere, it is the resolution of interest disputes that has attracted the most public and academic attention. This issue is used here to illustrate the variety of approaches to the conduct of collective bargaining in the provinces.[41] The approaches to interest-dispute resolution vary not only from province to province but also from one group of public employees to another, depending on whether the group is made up of departmental public servants, police, firefighters, hospital workers, teachers, or employees of government enterprises. The focus here is on departmental public servants.

A helpful means of explaining briefly the different approaches to interest-dispute resolution in provincial governments is to locate each province within one of four models of public sector collective bargaining.[42] These are the private sector model, the quasi-private sector model, the limited strike model, and the arbitration model.

The *private sector model* applies to Saskatchewan, where public servants are covered by the same legislation as private sector employees and have the right to strike. However, one group of public sector employees, namely firefighters, is restricted to the use of arbitration.

The *quasi-private sector model* applies to British Columbia and Quebec, where public servants have the statutory right to strike but where legislation stipulates that a number of designated employees *may* have to stay on the job to provide essential services.

The *limited strike model* applies to New Brunswick, Newfoundland, and Ontario, where public service collective bargaining is covered by separate legislation. For New Brunswick and Ontario, the legislation stipulates that a number of designated employees *must* stay on the job to provide essential services. In Newfoundland, the union can insist on arbitration if more than half of the bargaining unit is prohibited from striking by being designated as essential.

The *arbitration model* applies to Alberta, Nova Scotia, Manitoba, and Prince Edward Island. Among the important features of the legislation under this model are that the public service is treated separately from the private sector, strikes are prohibited, and disputes are resolved through an arbitration system.

It is no easy task to fit each province neatly into one of these four categories because there is such variation from one province to another. For example, in Nova Scotia, teachers, police, hospital workers, and firefighters are permitted to strike but departmental public servants are not. In Quebec, departmental public servants are allowed to strike but police and firefighters are not. Attempts at classification are further complicated by the fact that in all provinces municipal employees have the right to strike, subject in a few provinces to possible restrictions on those employees providing essential services.

🏛 THE FUTURE OF COLLECTIVE BARGAINING

In all spheres of Canadian government, collective bargaining for public employees is the most controversial issue in human resource management. In the federal sphere, for example, the PSSRA does not provide a framework for employer-employee relations that is satisfactory to the government, the general public, or the public service unions. The government's hesitation in accepting changes requested by the unions is due, in part, to differences of opinion among members of the public regarding the desirability of permitting government employees to bargain collectively and to take strike action. Collective bargaining in the public sector is not just an economic issue; it is also a highly *political* issue that requires both governments and unions to present their case to the public. The most significant challenge for public service unions is "to convince the public at large and union members in the private and public sectors that their cause is just. Are public employees really overpaid, underworked and blessed with lifetime job security? Given the available evidence, it is possible to confront the stereotype head on and demonstrate it is mythology."[43]

It seems unlikely that the right to strike will be withdrawn in those jurisdictions where it has been granted. However, in several provincial governments, public service unions and their supporters are still waging a campaign for the right to strike. In virtually all jurisdictions, including the federal government, there are continuing pressures for reform of the existing collective bargaining regime. Moreover, employer-employee relations have been severely aggravated in recent years by legislation involving restraints on compensation, restraints on collective agreements, changes to the "rules of the game," and direct legislative intervention, as well as layoffs, cutbacks, and the contracting out of services.

The future of public sector labour relations can be assessed in the light of two contrasting hypotheses.[44] According to the *doomsday* hypothesis, the public sector restraint programs described above were simply part of a series of temporary government measures designed to advance business interests behind a facade of protecting the public. These measures included the frequent use of back-to-work legislation, the jailing of union leaders, and reducing the right to strike by designating an increasing number of public sector workers as essential. Given such measures, combined with the fact that the right to strike was not included as a fundamental freedom in the Charter of Rights and Freedoms, "one can see the emergence of an era of relatively permanent restrictions on the rights of labour."[45] This scenario envisages that many of the rights that public sector employees won during the postwar period will be lost.

The *optimistic* hypothesis holds that the restraint programs since the early 1980s have been imposed because of the severe economic problems of high inflation, high unemployment, and the large budgetary deficit. Thus, when the economy improved, it was argued, normal collective bargaining would resume. By 1988, Swimmer had concluded that recent experience supported the doomsday hypothesis.[46] This view was reinforced by subsequent events, including the 1991 budget, the PSAC strike, and the Liberal government's restraint policies. When the Liberals returned to power in 1993, they maintained the suspension of collective bargaining and the freeze on public service salaries as part of their effort to reduce the budgetary deficit. Moreover, despite the Liberals' election promise of improved relations with public sector unions, they were obliged to legislate changes to the job security program so that layoffs could be made in various departments. Swimmer concluded in 1995 that it was "hard to be optimistic about the future of collective bargaining in the federal public service."[47] In 1996, the Liberal government promised a return to collective bargaining. It is clear that the continuing tensions between governments and public service unions will ensure that collective bargaining remains a dominant dimension of the study and practice of public administration.

NOTES

1. Virginia Galt and Geoffrey York, *The Globe and Mail*, "Civil Servants Storm Parliament," 28 September 1991, A1.
2. For a succinct account of the growth of public sector unionism in the federal, provincial, and municipal spheres, see: Joseph B. Rose, "Growth Patterns of Public Sector Unions," in Mark Thompson and Gene Swimmer, eds., *Conflict or Compromise: The Future of Public Sector Industrial Relations* (Montreal: The Institute for Research on Public Policy, 1984), 97–108.
3. See J.E. Hodgetts, *The Canadian Public Service* (Toronto: University of Toronto Press, 1973), 323–25; and J.E. Hodgetts, William McCloskey, Reginald Whitaker, and V.

Seymour Wilson, *Biography of an Institution: The Civil Service Commission of Canada, 1908–1967* (Montreal: McGill-Queen's University Press for the Institute of Public Administration of Canada, 1972).

4. For an account of the evolution of the council, see L.W.C.S. Barnes, *Consult and Advise: A History of the National Joint Council of the Public Service of Canada, 1944–1974* (Kingston, Ont.: Queen's University, Industrial Relations Centre, 1975).

5. J.L. Ilsley, finance minister, as quoted by P.K. Kuruvilla in "Collective Bargaining in the Canadian Federal Public Service," in Kenneth Kernaghan, ed., *Public Administration in Canada: Selected Readings*, 5th ed. (Toronto: Methuen, 1985), 224.

6. The Preparatory Committee on Collective Bargaining in the Public Service, *Report* (Ottawa: Queen's Printer, 1965), 1.

7. Ibid., 40.

8. See Jacob Finkelman and Shirley B. Goldenberg, *Collective Bargaining in the Public Service: The Federal Experience in Canada* (Montreal: Institute for Research on Public Policy, 1983), vol. 1, ch. 5.

9. Shirley B. Goldenberg, "Collective Bargaining in the Provincial Public Services," in Institute of Public Administration of Canada, *Collective Bargaining in the Public Service*, 11.

10. See Robert A. Vaison, "Collective Bargaining in the Federal Public Service: The Achievement of a Milestone in Personnel Relations," *Canadian Public Administration* 12 (spring 1969): 108–22.

11. Canada, *Statutes*, 1966–67, c. 72.

12. Canada, *Statutes*, 1966–67, c. 71.

13. Canada, *Statutes*, 1966–67, c. 74.

14. Canada, *Statutes*, 1992, c. 54.

15. The board is composed of a chairperson, a vice-chairperson, no fewer than three deputy chairpersons, and such other full-time and part-time members as the cabinet deems necessary to fulfill the board's responsibilities.

16. Gene Swimmer, "Collective Bargaining in the Federal Public Service of Canada: The Last Twenty Years," in Gene Swimmer and Mark Thompson, eds., *Public Sector Collective Bargaining in Canada* (Kingston: Queen's University, IRC Press, 1995): 391.

17. The referral of a dispute to conciliation can lead to the establishment of a conciliation board or, if the parties agree, to the appointment of a conciliation commissioner.

18. If both parties agree, a single arbitrator can be appointed instead.

19. Alternatively, if both parties agree, a conciliation commissioner can be appointed instead.

20. See Allen Ponak and Mark Thompson, "Public Sector Collective Bargaining," in John Anderson, Morley Gunderson, and Allen Ponak, *Union-Management Relations in Canada*, 2nd ed. (Don Mills, Ont.: Addison-Wesley, 1989), 394–98.

21. These grievances may be referred to adjudication only if the bargaining agent agrees.

22. J. Finkelman, *Employer-Employee Relations in the Public Service of Canada: Proposals for Legislative Change*, (Ottawa: Information Canada, 1974), Part I, 301 and Part II, 82

23. See Special Joint Committee of the House of Commons and the Senate on Employer-Employee Relations in the Public Service, *Report to Parliament*, Issue no. 47, 26 February 1976.

24. Special Committee on the Review of Personnel Management and the Merit Principle, *Report* (Ottawa: Minister of Supply and Services, 1979).

25. Canada, Privy Council Office, PS 2000, *Report of the Task Force on Staff Relations* (Ottawa: Privy Council Office, 6 August 1990).

26. See the detailed discussion of the Treasury Board proposals in Gene Swimmer, "Changes to Public Service Labour Relations Legislation: Revitalizing or Destroying Collective Bargaining?" in Michael J. Prince, ed., *How Ottawa Spends, 1987–88* (Toronto: Methuen, 1987), 300–16.

27. Mark Thompson and Gene Swimmer, "The Future of Public Sector Industrial Relations," in Swimmer and Thompson, *Public Sector Collective Bargaining*, 445.

28. Canada, Privy Council Office, PS 2000, *Report* (Ottawa: Privy Council Office, 20 July 1990), 22 ff.

29. See Finkelman and Goldenberg, *Collective Bargaining*, vol. 1, 31–45.

30. It is notable, however, that Daryl Bean, National President of PSAC, has publicly described the provisions of the Workforce Adjustment Directive, negotiated between the employer and the public service unions in the National Joint Council, as providing for "virtually iron clad job security."

31. See Gene Swimmer, with Kjerstine Kinaschuk, "Staff Relations Under the Conservative Government: The Singers Change, but the Song Remains the Same," in Frances Abele, ed., *How Ottawa Spends 1992–93: The Politics of Competitiveness* (Ottawa: Carleton University Press, 1992), 280.

32. *Re the Queen in Right of Canada and Canadian Air Traffic Control Association No. 2* (1982) 128 D.L.R. (3d) 685.

33. (1982) 1 S.C.R. 696.

34. Gene Swimmer, "Changes to Public Service Labour Relations Legislation," in Prince, *How Ottawa Spends: 1987–88*, 296, 313–14.

35. Canada, Privy Council Office, PS 2000, *Report*, 4.

36. Thompson and Swimmer, "The Future of Public Sector Industrial Relations," in Thompson and Swimmer, *Conflict or Compromise*, 458.

37. Swimmer, "Collective Bargaining," in Swimmer and Thompson, *Public Sector Collective Bargaining in Canada*, 400.

38. See Katherine Swinton, "Grievance Arbitration in the Public Sector," in Thompson and Swimmer, *Conflict or Compromise*, 343–71.

39. Canada, Privy Council Office, PS 2000, *Report*, 7.

40. For an account of the evolution of collective bargaining in the provinces, see J.E. Hodgetts and O.P. Dwivedi, *Provincial Governments as Employers* (Montreal: McGill-Queen's University Press, 1974), ch. 10.

41. For two very helpful summaries of dispute resolution processes in the federal, provincial, and municipal spheres of Canadian government, see Ponak and Thompson, "Public Sector Collective Bargaining," Table 15.2, 388–89; and Gene Swimmer, "Critical Issues in Public Sector Industrial Relations," in Amarjit S. Sethi, ed., *Collective Bargaining in Canada* (Scarborough, Ont.: Nelson Canada, 1989), Table 14.3, 408–9.

42. Data for the development of these models is drawn from Gene Swimmer and Mark Thompson, "Collective Bargaining in the Public Sector: An Introduction," in Swimmer and Thompson, *Public Sector Collective Bargaining*, 6–11.

43. Swimmer, "Critical Issues," in Sethi, *Collective Bargaining in Canada*, 419.

44. Thompson and Swimmer, "The Future of Public Sector Industrial Relations," in Thompson and Swimmer, *Conflict or Compromise*, 442–45, 465–66.

45. L.V. Panitch and D. Swartz, "From Free Collective Bargaining to Permanent Exceptionalism: The Economic Crisis and the Transformation of Industrial Relations in Canada," in Thompson and Swimmer, *Conflict or Compromise*, 407–35.

46. Swimmer, "Critical Issues," in Sethi, *Collective Bargaining in Canada*, 419.

47. Swimmer, "Collective Bargaining," in Thompson and Swimmer, *Conflict or Compromise*, 404.

BIBLIOGRAPHY

Arthurs, H.W. *Collective Bargaining by Public Employees in Canada: Five Models.* Ann Arbor, Mich.: Institute of Labor and Industrial Relations, University of Michigan, 1971.

Barnes, L.W.C.S. *Consult and Advise: A History of the National Joint Council of the Public Service of Canada, 1944–1974.* Kingston, Ont.: Queen's University, Industrial Relations Centre, 1975.

Barnes, L.W.C S., and L.A. Kelly. *Interest Arbitration in the Federal Public Service of Canada.* Kingston, Ont.: Queen's University, Industrial Relations Centre, 1975.

Canada. Preparatory Committee on Collective Bargaining in the Public Service. *Report.* Ottawa: Queen's Printer, 1965.

Canada. Privy Council Office. Public Service 2000. *PS 2000, Report of the Task Force on Staff Relations.* Ottawa: Privy Council Office, 6 August 1990.

Canada. Public Service 2000. *The Renewal of the Public Service of Canada.* Ottawa: Minister of Supply and Services, 1990.

Canada. Special Committee on the Review of Personnel Management and the Merit Principle. *Report.* Ottawa: Minister of Supply and Services, 1979.

Christensen, Sandra. *Unions and the Public Interest.* Vancouver: The Fraser Institute, 1980.

Conklin, David W., Thomas C. Courchene, and William A. Jones, eds. *Public Sector Compensation.* Toronto: Ontario Economic Council, 1985.

Daniel, Mark J., and William E.A. Robinson. *Compensation in Canada: A Study of the Public and Private Sectors.* Ottawa: The Conference Board of Canada, 1980.

Finkelman, J. *Employer-Employee Relations in the Public Service of Canada: Proposals for Legislative Change.* Ottawa: Information Canada, 1974.

Finkelman, Jacob, and Shirley Goldenberg. *Collective Bargaining in the Public Service: The Federal Experience in Canada.* 2 vols. Montreal: Institute for Research on Public Policy, 1983.

Hodgetts, J.E., and O.P. Dwivedi. *Provincial Governments as Employers.* Montreal: McGill-Queen's University Press, 1974.

Kuruvilla, P.K. "Collective Bargaining in the Canadian Federal Public Service." In Kenneth Kernaghan, ed., *Public Administration in Canada: Selected Readings,* 5th ed. Toronto: Methuen, 1985, 224–35.

Maslove, Allan, and Gene Swimmer. *Wage Controls in Canada, 1975–1978.* Montreal: Institute for Research on Public Policy, 1980.

Swettenham, John, and David Kealy. *Serving the State: A History of the Professional Institute of the Public Service of Canada, 1920–1970.* Ottawa: The Professional Institute of the Public Service of Canada, 1970.

Swimmer, Gene. "Changes to Public Service Labour Relations Legislation: Revitalizing or Destroying Collective Bargaining?" In Michael J. Prince, ed., *How Ottawa Spends, 1987–1988.* Toronto: Methuen, 1987, 300–16.

Swimmer, Gene, with Kjerstine Kinaschuk. "Staff Relations Under the Conservative Government: The Singers Change, but the Song Remains the Same." In Frances Abele, ed. *How Ottawa Spends, 1992–1993: The Politics of Competitiveness.* Ottawa: Carleton University Press, 1992, 267–312.

Swimmer, Gene, and Mark Thompson, "Collective Bargaining in the Public Sector: An Introduction." In Gene Swimmer and Mark Thompson, eds., *Public Sector Collective Bargaining in Canada.* Kingston, Ont.: Queen's University, IRC Press, 1995.

Thompson, Mark, and Gene Swimmer, eds. *Conflict or Compromise: The Future of Public Sector Industrial Relations.* Montreal: Institute for Research on Public Policy, 1984.

26

The Budgetary Process

One of the surest ways to provoke a reaction from the "person on the street" is to mention government expenditure. Everyone has an opinion. Some will say that it is lavish and out of control; others will say that it is too miserly and more money should be spent on government programs. The establishment of budgets is one of the most important—and most difficult—decisions governments must make. Budgetary decisions determine the kinds of taxes that are imposed and their level. This has an impact on everyone in society. Expenditure decisions determine which programs will be funded, and which will be terminated.

How do governments go about making decisions on how much money to raise through taxes and how much money to spend? This chapter answers that question.

The previous three chapters considered the management of human resources. This chapter will discuss the establishment of revenue and expenditure budgets. The next chapter will focus on financial operations during a fiscal year after the initial budget has been established. The budgetary process has three phases—preparation, adoption, and execution. This chapter will treat preparation; the next will deal with adoption and execution.

This chapter begins with a brief discussion of the preparation of the revenue budget, then proceeds to a discussion of various theories of the expenditure budget and a description of the preparation of the federal expenditure budget.

Establishing a budget is certainly one of the single most important acts that any government performs.

> Government and governing are about the use of power and resources to deliver public sector goods and services and to modify private sector behaviour in pursuit of societal objectives. Along the way, an imposing variety of conflicts and trade-offs must be resolved or, at least, addressed. How are the social objectives determined? Who plays a role in their articulation? What resources (and whose resources) are to be mobilized to fund the operations of government? How are these resources to be conscripted? What quantities of resources on the one hand, and public goods and services on the other, are optimal or appropriate? How does government operate to maintain its capacity to govern over extended periods of time? Budgeting, because it must address all these questions, is the quintessential act of governing.[1]

One of the great difficulties in preparing a government budget is that the budget typically has many objectives, not all of which are consistent with one another. In preparing a personal budget, one usually thinks in terms of the fairly one-dimensional problem of adjusting expenditures to fit a relatively fixed income. The complicating factor in the preparation of government budgets is that they must address at least three objectives.

First is the setting of *macroeconomic policy* or at least that part of it that is influenced by fiscal instruments, i.e., levels of aggregate revenue, expenditure, and surplus or deficit. Governments set total revenue and expenditure targets so as to stimulate the economy or slow it down.

The second objective involves *influencing behaviour at a more micro level.* Governments frequently use tax provisions, not just to raise revenue but also to encourage people to do, or refrain from doing, certain things. For example, customs duties raise a sizable portion of government revenue, but their main objective is to protect domestic industry.

Another example of this use of the budget that has received increasing attention in recent years is tax expenditures. *Tax expenditures* are benefits enjoyed in the form of reduced taxes for individuals or corporations who do (or refrain from doing) certain things. For example, there have been programs that encouraged people to invest in scientific research or Canadian-made movies in exchange for a tax benefit. These tax expenditures were used in place of outright cash grants. Their attraction stemmed from the obviously mistaken notion that tax reductions did not really "cost" anything because they did not show up as expenses.[2] Thus, departments could adopt particular policies through a tax expenditure with no idea of, or concern for, its cost to the treasury.

The third objective of a budget is simply to *raise the resources needed to fund expenditures.* This involves estimating the amounts to be received from various tax and nontax sources of revenue, and adjusting those under the control of the government so that adequate funds are raised. Thus, the mark of a good tax system is that it produces reasonably stable amounts of money from year to year, but, even more important, the amount ought to be predictable well in advance, so that the government knows where it will stand as the year progresses.[3]

The most difficult aspect of these three objectives is that not all point toward the same action at the same time. For example, in difficult economic times, government will need more revenue to fund employment insurance and social assistance plans. However, macroeconomic principles suggest that it is desirable to reduce taxes to stimulate spending in hard economic times. The continuing adjustment of these seemingly irreconcilable factors makes government budgeting a most difficult task.

🏛 THE REVENUE BUDGET

It is an important principle of responsible government that no tax can be imposed without the approval of the legislature. At least once each year, the federal Minister of Finance and all provincial treasurers prepare their revenue budgets that contain, among many other things, a request to their respective legislatures to impose new taxes or modify existing ones. Actually, governments generally use the revenue budget to:

1. describe and interpret the major economic events of the recent past and the government's view of the economic outlook (frequently with the intent of altering private expectations);

2. congratulate itself for any past improvement in the state of the economy and shift the blame for any past deterioration;

3. announce changes (including no change) in fiscal policy (tax/expenditure/borrowing/lending) designed to stabilize the economy;

4. propose changes in the tax/tariff structure designed to (a) implement social (income/wealth redistribution) policy, (b) implement economic (resource allocation) policy, and (c) eliminate "technical" flaws or difficulties with existing tax/tariff structures; and

5. deal with special measures such as incomes policy, federal-provincial fiscal relations, pensions, and special studies.[4]

The fiscal year of the federal and provincial governments begins on April 1 and ends the following March 31. There is a tradition that the Minister of Finance presents the federal revenue budget shortly before the beginning of the fiscal year, usually around February, although there is no set rule for this timing; budgets are sometimes presented at other times of the year and more than one budget can be presented in the same year. These deviations stem from either political considerations (e.g., the desire to present an attractive budget on which to fight an election), or from volatile economic conditions such as changing international trade situations or energy prices.

The revenue budget is presented as a part of the minister's budget speech. There is no set format for this speech, but it usually contains most of the following elements:

1. a review of economic conditions and problems based on information from a White Paper tabled a few days earlier (or at the same time as the budget);

2. a statement of government revenues and expenditures over the past year and a comparison with the previous budget's estimation;

3. an estimation of government expenditures and revenues for the upcoming year and the surplus or deficit; and

4. notice of any ways and means motions—that is, motions to introduce bills to amend various tax acts.[5]

The third and fourth items are usually given the greatest attention. In recent years, when government deficits have been the rule, the level of the deficit and the attendant government borrowing requirements provide important signals to money markets. The notice of ways and means motions holds the greatest interest for most taxpayers because this is the announcement of changes in tax structure or rates, which means that new taxes will be introduced, new items taxed, or tax loopholes opened or closed.

The minister's budget speech is given much more attention than other speeches in the legislature. Because it says so much about the government's financial situation, it can be regarded as a sort of "mini-Throne Speech." The date and time are set several weeks in advance at an hour when stock markets are closed so that the contents of the speech will not affect stock prices precipitously. The media pay great attention to the event and it is usually broadcast live on radio and/or television, followed by analysis by learned economists, representatives of interest groups, and the inevitable homey interviews with the "average family." Several days of the legislature's time are set aside for what is euphemistically called debate on the budget speech. Actually it is a time for the opposition parties to criticize the minister for past mistakes and anticipated future mistakes.

After this debate, there is a vote of confidence concerning the overall budget. Since it is a vote of confidence, if it does not carry, then the government must, by convention, resign. This is what happened to the Trudeau government in 1974 and to the short-lived Clark government in 1979.

Assuming that the government does survive the initial vote of confidence, the Minister of Finance will then introduce, over the next few months, a series of motions implementing the specific taxation measures presented in the budget. Votes on these motions can be matters of confidence if the specific measure is central to the total budget package, but they are not ordinarily considered to be matters of confidence. However, defeat of a major tax measure can pose a serious problem for a government, because alternative sources of revenue will have to be found.

Budget Preparation

A later section of this chapter contains a lengthy discussion of the process involved in the preparation of the expenditure budget. It is difficult to discuss the preparation of the revenue budget in the same manner, because it is very much the personal work of the Minister of Finance or provincial treasurer and her or his senior public servants.[6] The secrecy of the revenue budget has traditionally been considered important because if some taxpayers had advance information about certain tax and other provisions of the budget, they could either profit unfairly or evade the intended effects of the provisions.

The parliamentary tradition is that a minister of finance must resign if there is any leak of information about the budget. Resignations for this reason have occurred in Britain,[7] but there has never been a resignation in Canada. There have been several cases where ministers of finance or provincial treasurers have suffered significant political embarrassment because of alleged violations of secrecy. In 1963, Walter Gordon was pressured to resign as federal Minister of Finance when it was discovered that he had employed certain non–civil servants, who had been sworn to an oath of secrecy, to assist him in the preparation of the budget.[8] In more recent times, a federal employee gave a summary of a federal budget to a journalist who broadcast its contents on television; a journalist found portions of an Ontario budget in the trash of a printing firm; and a Nova Scotia newspaper printed advance reports of the provincial budget, which proved to be remarkably accurate.[9] In none of these cases did the minister resign.

One of the persistent proposals for reform of the revenue budget process is that the convention of secrecy should be relaxed somewhat. Evert Lindquist describes four problems that arise from this secrecy:

> First, many businesses and individual citizens find it difficult to plan their affairs because they perceive a high likelihood of having their plans dislocated by surprise budget announcements. Second, many initial budget proposals must be redrafted and rethought because they are prepared in the absence of information available only from those affected by the measures. The cost of consulting with those who have the information would be to reveal government thinking. Third, long delays frequently occur between the date on which a proposed measure has effect and the [later] date when its provisions are fully specified. As with many problems occasioned by public-sector processes, the underlying issue in all these problems is the generation of additional uncertainties. Outside observers have also identified a fourth problem: a concentration on process rather than policy deflects scarce analytical resources away from important substantive issues.[10]

There have been a number of specific proposals for reform.[11] Bruce Doern has argued convincingly that the convention of budget secrecy as it applies to all aspects of the budget has outlived its usefulness and is really an embarrassment because ministers do not resign. He paints a scenario for a relaxation of budget secrecy that both opens up the budgetary process and preserves the aspects of secrecy that are important.[12]

Over the last ten or fifteen years, successive ministers of finance and provincial treasurers have taken limited steps to open up the process. The basic problem is that they are caught between the long tradition of secrecy and the shorter, but strong, tradition of consultation before important decisions are made. Ministers of finance would like to have the opportunity to float trial balloons with interested groups, which is absent under the current system. What has happened is that the very real need for secrecy in one relatively small area of the revenue budget has spilled over to enshroud all aspects of the entire process in secrecy. This is heightened by a media frenzy that seems to focus more on the secrecy of the budget than its substance.

The actual preparation of the budget speech must be done in secrecy, but this does not preclude consultations with interested groups about the possible contents of the budget. Successive ministers of finance have attempted to open up this early consultative part of the process, but Paul Martin seems to have gone further than his predecessors in the preparation of his first budget in February 1994.[13] Prior to the preparation of this budget, he arranged for a series of open, televised meetings with economists, interest groups, and selected citizens. These meetings encouraged those present to comment on the main areas of decision facing the minister. Mr. Martin made a point of attending all these meetings to show his level of interest. This process has been continued and refined since then; it has now become an institutionalized part of the lead-up to the revenue budget. Ontario has also been experimenting with meetings with interest groups as a part of the budget process, although its approach is less formal than the federal government's.[14]

There are some disadvantages to opening up the budgetary process. One obvious disadvantage is that increased consultation usually leads to increased delay in implementation. A more serious problem could stem from the fact that consultation is always uneven; some groups are able to participate better than others.

> If governments invite public debate of tentative tax changes, it is probable that relatively concentrated, well-organized, and well-financed interests with much at stake will be the most intense and best prepared participants. Their views and assumptions will dominate in the policy arena ... Changes unfavorable to business or other well-organized interests will be strongly resisted, while passive citizens, each losing a little, will be "'nickelled' and 'dimed' into economic oblivion."[15]

The continuing closed nature of the revenue budget process has had the effect of inhibiting comment about the process of budget preparation. However, a great deal of discussion has taken place about the preparation of the expenditure budget.

🏛 THE EXPENDITURE BUDGET

The preparation of the expenditure budget is a much more open process. It usually involves almost everybody in the organization. The remainder of this chapter will discuss some of the different styles of preparation of the expenditure budget, provide a step-by-step illustration of how a budget is prepared, and finish with a discussion of some of the strategies employed by organizations to maximize their budgetary allocation.

Styles of the Expenditure Budget

There are many different styles of budgeting in use in different jurisdictions. There is no general consensus about the ideal approach to the expenditure budget; each organization seems to adopt a slightly different style. Regardless of the approach employed, the ideal budgeting system should serve three purposes: control, management, and planning and policy choice.[16]

"*Control* refers to the process of binding operating officials to the policies and plans set by their superiors."[17] A satisfactory budgeting system must have some method of ensuring that managers do not overspend their budgets or spend money on programs that have not been properly authorized.

A sound system of *management* goes beyond simply ensuring that subordinates are following orders; it also ensures that work is organized so as to achieve efficiency and effectiveness. The ideal budget would provide some method of evaluating the quality of the management of an organization. Of course, control would ensure that managers do not overspend their budgets, but more than that is expected of a competent manager. The budget should allow for comparisons between the operating costs of similar organizations and/or the comparison of costs from previous years. These comparisons would provide an insight into the quality of the organization's management.

"*Planning* involves the determination of objectives, the evaluation of alternative courses of action and the authorization of select programs."[18] If planning is a part of the budgetary system, the system can be used to provide information about the future, which can be used in making tradeoffs among policies. The perfect budgeting system will combine all three factors, but attaining that ideal has been somewhat elusive.

In searching for this ideal style, a number of innovations have been introduced over the years. It is sometimes difficult to find precise dividing lines between approaches, but it is possible to identify three major styles of budgeting that have been employed in recent years: line-item, performance, and program. Some of the characteristics of these styles are illustrated in Table 26.1, and each style will be discussed in more detail below. However, it is important to understand that these different styles are not mutually exclusive. There are many examples of organizations creating hybrid systems by borrowing from different styles.

Line-Item Budgeting

Line-item budgeting was the first style of budgeting employed in modern public administration, and is usually considered to be the most rudimentary.[19] Table 26.2 illustrates a page from a line-item budget. This page covers the entire budget of one department and shows how the requested funds will be spent by object of expenditure, e.g., salaries, rent, supplies. This illustrates the fact that the line-item budget focuses on inputs used rather than outputs achieved.

The key person in the preparation of this type of budget is the accountant, because the process basically involves reviewing last year's budget and making revisions based on inflation and changes in the size of the population served. This process is usually carried out on an annual basis; there is ordinarily no attempt at long-range planning.

The key agency is the operating department because the budget is prepared on a "bottom-up" basis. This means that the process begins with the operating department preparing a request for funds that it then passes upward to decision makers who, frankly, have a great deal of difficulty making any revisions in the original request because of the very detailed manner in which it is prepared. This leads to a decentralized style of decision making because decisions are made in operating departments with little opportunity for meaningful review by politicians.

The use of line-item budgeting makes it somewhat awkward to evaluate a manager's performance. The main sign of a good manager in this system is that he or she does not overspend the assigned budget; clearly, this is a minimal

Table 26.1
COMPARISON OF DIFFERENT STYLES OF BUDGETING

	Line-Item	Performance	Program
Building Block	object of expenditure	unit cost and units of service	program
Key Expert	accountant	cost accountant	economist
Time Horizon	annual	annual	multi-year
Direction of Construction	bottom-up	bottom-up	top-down
Key Agency	operating department	operating department	central agencies
Method of Evaluation of Manager	does not overspend	minimizes unit cost	maximizes program performance
Type of Decision Making	decentralized	decentralized	centralized
Dominant Philosophy of Decision Making	incremental	incremental	rational
Strong Points	emphasizes control; discourages conflict	more information for decision makers; emphasizes: —productivity improvement —cost minimization	emphasizes: —rational process —program and planning
Weak Points	emphasizes status quo; little information for decision makers	no cross-program comparisons	high cost; dubious techniques

requirement for good management, but there is simply too little information available to make any other kind of judgment.

All of this adds up to a style of decision making on budgetary allocations that can only be incremental, i.e., this year's budgetary allocation is determined by making incremental changes in last year's allocation. This usually means uniform, across-the-board increases (or decreases) in the allocations to all departments. Everyone involved in the process recognizes that this is inferior to a thoughtful process that seriously considers the needs of each department separately and provides more funding to agencies with greater needs. However,

Table 26.2
EXAMPLE OF LINE-ITEM BUDGET

City of Strathmoor
Ambulance Service
Fiscal Year Ended December 31, 2000

Account	Budget Request 2000	% Change	Forecast Expense 1999	% Change	Actual Expense 1998
Salaries	2 000 000	5.3	1 900 000	5.6	1 800 000
Overtime	250 000	25.0	200 000	33.3	150 000
Accommodation	350 000	0.0	350 000	0.0	350 000
Rental	195 000	5.4	185 000	2.8	180 000
Fuel	45 000	12.5	40 000	5.3	38 000
Vehicle Repairs	64 000	3.2	62 000	3.3	60 000
Supplies	24 000	-7.7	26 000	-3.7	27 000
Training	18 000	-5.3	19 000	-5.0	20 000
Travel	35 000	0.0	35 000	-5.4	37 000
Miscellaneous					
Total	2 981 000	5.8	2 817 000	5.8	2 662 000

because of the dearth of meaningful information generated in a line-item budgeting system, there is no alternative to the incremental approach.

Line-item budgeting emphasizes the control aspect of the budget. It makes it very easy to prevent overspending or to determine who is responsible if it does occur. It also limits some of the conflict found in other styles of budgeting because it tends to compartmentalize spending rather than emphasize tradeoffs. This characteristic is also a political defect in line-item budgeting. The limited information about output that it generates makes it very difficult for decision makers (politicians or senior managers) to make tradeoffs about the quality of programs. Therefore, line-item budgeting does not lend itself to the management and planning and policy choice orientations that were discussed earlier.

Line-item budgeting is useful in the case of relatively small, simple organizations where all decision makers can grasp the roles of the different organizational units quickly and intuitively. The dearth of output information generated by it, and its lack of a management or planning and policy choice orientation, make it considerably less useful in large, dynamic organizations. Nonetheless, it is still used in some organizations largely because of its simplicity of operation and because the accountants who frequently control the budgetary process feel comfortable with it.

The basic problem in line-item budgeting is its lack of an output orientation, i.e., the absence of any measuring technique to determine what is being accomplished by the expenditures. Therefore, it is not surprising that the next improvement in the budgetary process addressed this concern for output measurement.

Performance Budgeting

The basic difference between line-item and performance budgeting was the output orientation of performance budgeting.[20] Line-item budgeting measured only inputs used; performance budgeting established a relationship between inputs employed and outputs attained. The basic building block of performance budgeting was the unit cost of providing a service (inputs) and the number of units of service provided (outputs). Thus, a budgetary allocation was established by multiplying units of service (clients served, miles of road paved) by the unit cost of providing each service.

The key budgetary expert now became the cost accountant because he or she possessed the esoteric skills needed to collect and calculate information about unit costs. The unit cost information created an additional method of evaluating a good manager besides not overspending her or his budget. Managers performing similar duties could be evaluated by comparing the unit costs of their operations.

In making budgetary allocations, it was possible to escape from incrementalism in a limited way. Reasonable estimates could usually be made about changes in the demand for the service, although, even here, incrementalism frequently had to be used as an aid in calculation. The unit cost could be influenced somewhat by experience in other jurisdictions, but, in the final analysis, incrementalism was a frequent guide here as well.

The strong point of performance budgeting was that it added a management improvement focus to the control focus of line-item budgeting. It provided decision makers with enough information to consider management improvement and cost minimization techniques. However, performance budgeting did not provide any techniques for future planning; nor did it provide enough information to make tradeoffs among programs. These techniques would come later.

Program Budgeting

In proceeding chronologically through the various budgetary styles, one can see a steady ascendancy in the basic building block from the object of expenditure, to the unit of service, to the entire program. But there were many changes that came with program budgeting that involved more than just the emphasis on program.

In general, program budgeting was an attempt to adapt the rational decision-making techniques discussed in Chapter 6 to the budgetary process.

Program budgeting concepts were described in a 1969 federal government publication as:

(a)   the setting of specific objectives;

(b)   the systematic analysis to clarify objectives and to assess alternative ways of meeting them;

(c)   the framing of budgetary proposals in terms of programs directed toward the achievement of the objectives;

(d)   the projection of the costs of these programs a number of years in the future;

(e)   the formulation of plans of achievement year by year for each program;

(f)   an information system for each program to supply data for the monitoring of achievement of program goals and to supply data for the reassessment of the program objectives and the appropriateness of the program itself.[21]

Note the similarity between these steps and those mentioned in Chapter 6 under the general heading of rational techniques, such as determining objectives, examining alternative methods of attaining objectives, implementing the optimum method, and installing feedback mechanisms to measure attainment of objectives.

In practice, the implementation of program budgeting involved the division of the activities of each department into discrete units called programs and the preparation of multiyear budgetary forecasts for each program. The purpose of the multiyear estimates was to alert decision makers to the full future costs of programs, particularly in cases in which programs started with a limited use of resources and expanded in future years.

Table 26.3 provides an example of the budget documentation used under program budgeting for the same ambulance service discussed in Table 26.2. This document deals with only one program in the ambulance department—the operations program, which is the largest program. One of the major differences between this and line-item budgeting is that program budgeting focuses on outputs rather than inputs. This is illustrated by the "Description" and "Objective" sections at the beginning of the document.

A typical feature of a program budget is the separation of basic and growth components of the budget. In federal government terminology these are the A and B budgets. The A budget represents the continuation of existing programs with adjustments made for inflation and changes in the population served. The B budget is the request for either the establishment of new programs or the enrichment and enhancement of existing programs. The idea was that A budget items would not be evaluated in depth because these programs were approved previously, but that there would be a thorough review of the costs and benefits of new programs—the B budget items—before they were implemented. In this example, the request for the B budget contains an explanation about how the service would be improved if the additional funds are provided.

Another major improvement of the program budget was the emphasis on output measures. The bottom part of this budget document contains informa-

Table 26.3
EXAMPLE OF PROGRAM BUDGET

City of Strathmoor
Ambulance Service Operations Program
Calendar Year Ended December 31, 2000

. . . .

Description: To provide and maintain ambulance and paramedical assistance to the public.

Objective: To provide immediate patient care in an effort to minimize fatalities by placing emergency paramedical resources at the scene within a minmum time.

. . . .

Basic Component – "A" Budget

	Budget Request 2000	% Change	Forecast 1999	% Change	Actual 1998
Expenditure	1 600 000	5.3	1 520 000	2.7	1 480 000

Enhancement Component – "B" Budget

Expenditure	50 000

Eplanation: The additional funds are being requested to upgrade the department's training program. these funds will be used to offer additional courses to ensure that staff members are knowledgeable about all the latest techniques. This will allow staff to render better service to victims more quickly, which will reduce the number of fatalities and the seriousness of injuries.

Quantitative Measure

Year	Number of Calls	Index of Change
2000 (estimated)	142 000	118.3
1999 (forecast)	136 000	113.3
1998	130 000	108.3
1997	127 000	105.8
1996	124 000	103.3
1995	120 000	100.0

Qualitative Measure

Community	Average Response Time
Downtown	2.30
Beechmont	2.55
Kenwood	2.45
St. Matthews	4.05
Hurstbourne	4.60
Auburndale	6.20

Trend of Service Levels and Expenditure

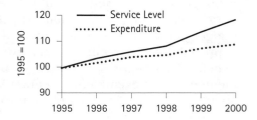

tion on both quantitative and qualitative measures of services provided. The quantitative measures can be used to compare changes in amount of service provided and level of budget requested. In most cases, there should be some correspondence between these two numbers. The last table provides a measure of how well the service is being provided. For emergency services one significant measure of quality is response time. This table indicates a rather marked difference in response times in different parts of the city.

Program budgeting is frequently described as a "top-down" system because it encourages a centralization of decision making by allowing decision makers to escape the excessive detail contained in line-item and performance budgets. In this example, decision makers are provided only with information about total levels of expenditure, not the details of the objects of expenditure. This should encourage them to focus on making choices among programs rather than becoming mired in details. They could communicate messages such as "we need to hold the line on social services," or "this is the year to provide a bit more to defence," by simply allowing smaller increases in social programs and greater increases in defence ones. This sort of movement of macrolevers is possible only because of the emphasis on broad programs instead of details of expenditure.

Program budgeting brought with it a large set of rational economic tools such as cost-benefit analysis, cost-effectiveness analysis, and systems analysis. These tools could maximize government performance by providing a rational, economic comparison of different methods of attaining goals and even comparing the worth of trying to attain different goals. The most extreme proponents of this kind of thinking argued that the ultimate purpose of government was to maximize human well-being—economic, physical, social, psychological—and that this well-being could be measured and rational techniques employed to determine which government programs would best attain its maximization. Others stopped somewhat short of these beliefs, but all practitioners of program budgeting argued that there were rational, economic tools that could be used to make tradeoffs between programs.

Since the economist was the primary person who employed these kinds of techniques, program budgeting caused the mantle of key expert to pass from the accountant to the economist. The other structural change that occurred at the same time was the ascendancy of central agencies, in particular Treasury Board Secretariat. If decision making is more centralized and tradeoffs between departments are more important, then there is an obvious need for a central agency to deal with these various elements.

The strength of program budgeting is that it includes all three of the factors that are important for an ideal budgeting style—control, management, and planning and policy choice. In evaluating the worth of a manager, program budgeting emphasizes not just avoiding overspending or minimizing cost but rather maximizing program performance. In the ambulance service example, one could track the change in expenditure and the change in demand for the service over time. If these seem to be out of line, then the manager should be asked for an explanation. One could also compare the unit cost of providing ambulance service in this city with similar costs in other cities.

The qualitative measures allow for future planning. It is clear that some areas of this city are not served as well as others. This identifies where remedial action needs to be taken. Since response times are determined largely by the location of stations, this helps to determine where the next ambulance stations should be built.

Program budgeting was clearly the major budgeting innovation of the 1960s and the early 1970s. Virtually every government of any size in North America experimented with some form of program budgeting. The success of those experiments has been mixed. It was significant in that it forced people to think in terms of programs and outputs. It was probably unrealistic to think that it could ever live up to its promise to turn budget making into a totally rational process.

There are many reasons for the problems experienced with program budgeting.[22] As noted above, it is an attempt to apply rational modes of decision making to the budget process. Therefore, many of the general criticisms of rational decision-making techniques are also applicable to program budgeting. The high cost, in both dollars and time, of implementing the system and the sheer complexity of some attempts were clearly problems. In some cases, the amount of time spent "getting ready to get ready" seriously weakened the credibility of those seeking to implement program budgeting. Also, the attempt to impose one system of evaluation on diverse programs led to some difficulties. Schick argues that the success of program budgeting in the United States Department of Defense stemmed, in part, from the fact that it was home-grown there; its failure in other departments stemmed from its status as a foreign intruder unable to adapt to the local customs.[23]

There is one outstanding reason for the problems of program budgeting that is too often overlooked. Changes in budgeting systems are not minor technical adjustments in procedures significant only to accountants. Certain changes in budgeting systems amount to vast shifts of power within organizations.[24] This was the case with program budgeting because it required a shift from a decentralized form of budgeting, such as line-item or performance budgeting, to a highly centralized one. In the decentralized systems, individual departments present budget requests, but little information, to politicians. The politicians, in turn, do not have a group of qualified experts from whom they can seek advice. The head of the department, then, has fairly broad latitude to manage the department with minimum scope for intrusion either from any other department or from politicians.

Program budgeting introduces a new actor to the scene—the strong central budget agency. If detailed documentation is to be prepared, cost-benefit analysis performed, and tradeoffs made between various programs, there must be an organization to do these things. If the system is to function properly, this organization must have the right to request significant amounts of information from departments and evaluate that information in order to make recommendations to politicians. This would allow the budget agency to have a clear "window" into the operation of departments and so provide the agency with the ability to exercise some degree of control over operating departments. Thus, operating departments tend to oppose the introduction of program budgeting because they fear the increased exposure that this window provides.

Additional difficulties with a rational system of budgeting surround the related problems of specifying goals, measuring benefits achieved, and predicting future conditions.[25] Government programs usually serve multiple goals and people will disagree on the relative priority of those goals. Is the purpose of a youth employment program to have certain work activities carried out? To assist young people in developing good work habits? To provide funds to young people to continue their schooling? To buy votes? The likely answer is all of these, but which one is seen as paramount will have an effect on how the program is designed and evaluated.

A related problem is the inability to measure in a rigorous, quantified fashion the benefits derived from government services. Everyone agrees that it is beneficial that the garbage is picked up, but how is this value determined objectively in dollars and cents so that costs and benefits can be compared? Some of the public health benefits could be measured, but what about the aesthetic, practical, and other benefits?

A final problem involves the difficulty of predicting the future. Many programs have a large initial cost and a stream of benefits that flow far into the future. The value assigned to those benefits can depend on the number of people who will enjoy them. For example, the total benefit derived from the construction of a second airport in Toronto is highly sensitive to whether one assumes that the level of usage remains steady, increases slightly, or increases significantly.[26] Yet no one is able to predict with sufficient precision which situation will occur.

At this point, most governments have developed systems that contain elements of both line-item and program budgeting. There is a movement toward making budgets more output oriented, but the process seems rather slow.

🏛 THE FEDERAL EXPENDITURE MANAGEMENT SYSTEM

The federal government introduced the Expenditure Management System (EMS) in 1995.[27] This is the latest in a long line of innovations in the budgetary process.[28] EMS is a form of program budgeting but with many variations introduced by the federal government as a result of experience with previous budget processes.

The basis of this system is:

- "steady debt and deficit reduction."[29] This is based on the establishment of two-year targets that will steadily reduce the level of the deficit as a percent of gross domestic product. For individual departments, the principle is that there will be no additional money for new programs; new programs can be initiated only if the department can find funds within its existing operating budget.

- "commitment to a more open, consultative and regular budget process." This is reflected in the more open nature of the revenue budget discussed earlier in this chapter.

- "improved reporting and accountability to Parliament and Canadians." This is reflected in the departmental business plans and a revision in the presentation of the year-end financial reporting to Parliament discussed below.

Figure 26.1 illustrates the budget cycle. One of the main attributes of this system is that it is considerably simpler in execution, less time consuming, and less paper intensive than many of its predecessors. There was a concern that budgeting was becoming too complex and therefore too much under the control of public servants rather than of politicians, who simply did not have the time to take real ownership of a complex budgeting system. The architects of this system wanted to make it simpler and more understandable.

The cycle begins about a year before the budget will be tabled in the House of Commons, so the cycle for the budget year beginning on April 1, 2000, begins in March—June of 1999. In Figure 26.1 the cycle begins in the upper right corner of the diagram, with the preparation and review of departmental business plans. The concept of the business plan is one of the innovations in this system. Business plans were introduced as a part of the federal government's program review exercise, which was discussed in Chapter 22. They require departments to focus on the question: "What business are we in?" This came about because there was some concern that, in times when funds were relatively easily available, departments tended to expand their activities into areas that were not a central part of their mandate. Focusing on the question: "What business are we in?" was meant to bring departments back to their original mandate and encourage them to move away from more peripheral areas. Departments now think of their operations in terms of "business lines." For example, the business lines of Correctional Services Canada consist of

- care—"maintaining a physically and psychologically healthy environment;"

- custody—"safe and secure institutions;"

- reintegration—"safe, timely and effective reintegration of offenders;" and

- corporate services—such as human resources management.[30]

Each spring departments prepare business plans that set out their:

- major challenges, directions and objectives for the planning period [three years] within the context of government priorities and the department's current and prospective position;

- strategies, actions, associated costs and the flexibilities required to deal with major changes;

- associated goals, targets and performance measures to assess program results and management strategies during the planning period; and

- performance information focused on service lines affected by significant change.[31]

Figure 26.1
THE EXPENDITURE MANAGEMENT SYSTEM

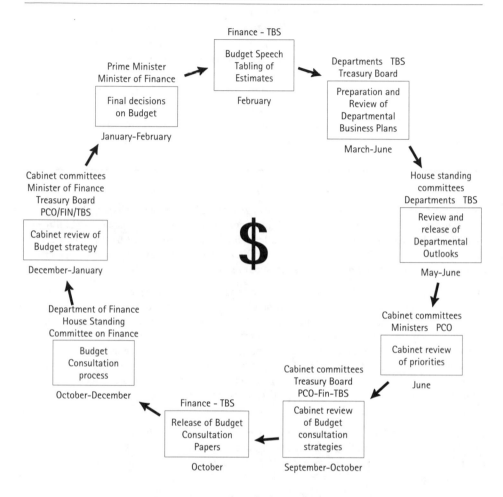

Source: Government of Canada. The Expenditure Management System of the Government of Canada.

These Business Plans are then inputs into the cabinet priority-setting exercise, which occurs in the fall. This results in the preparation and release of a set of consultation papers that are used as part of the prebudget consultation mentioned earlier. Cabinet then assesses the results of these consultations and makes decisions on the level of expenditures.

The process depicted here is considerably more static and one-dimensional than it is in practice. For example, the Department of Finance could and likely will revise its economic forecasts several times throughout the process as the external environment changes. Each new iteration will force cabinet and all the other actors in the process to reconsider their positions. It is unfortunate that the real world cannot be as neat as this diagram, but everyone in the process must be alert to changes in the environment and must change his or her input based on these external changes. A realistic diagram of the process would likely involve several additional loops and other complications.

The final step in the process (located at the top of the diagram) is the tabling of Estimates. The *Estimates,* commonly referred to as the *"Blue Book,"* is the government's formal request to the House of Commons for funds to operate for the coming fiscal year. This document is the result of considerable bargaining between the Treasury Board and the operating departments, which will be discussed in more detail below. The *Estimates* actually consists of several volumes containing a huge amount of information, but the most important part is a listing by department and program of funds requested.[32] The *Estimates*

ESTIMATES

The Estimates or "Blue Book" is actually a multivolume series of documents prepared before the beginning of the fiscal year as an output of the budgetary process. These volumes contain the expenditure budget and represent the formal legislation that, when passed by the legislature, provides authority for spending by the executive. These documents focus entirely on the expenditure budget and so contain no information about revenue.

The Estimates consist of three parts. Part I of the Estimates is called the *Government Expenditure Plan.* In 1998–99, this consists of a two-page overview that contains very little information. In previous years, it contained a multiyear listing of expenditure by department and major program within department. It also contained brief descriptions about the activities of each department and explanations of major increases or decreases in expenditures from previous years. This document was a good starting point to obtain a general understanding of how much of the total budget was consumed by a particular department or program and what the trend was. However, it did not usually provide enough detail about these activities to be satisfactory for most researchers. The 1998–99 version is even less useful than earlier ones.

Part II is called *The Main Estimates.* It provides considerable detail about exactly how much funding is being requested for each department and program. This part also contains a short description of the objectives and activities of each program, as well as some additional budgetary information.

Part II of the Estimates is very useful for research purposes. It provides both financial and narrative background information on the activities of each department. It allows the researcher to locate the organizational unit responsible for a particular activity, and a review of previous years' Estimates allows some consideration of expenditure trends.

Part III of the Estimates is now prepared in two parts. The *Report on Plans and Priorities (RPP)* is tabled at about the same time as the other parts of the Estimates and consists of one volume for each major department and agency. The RPP provides information about the department's objectives and planned results. The *Departmental Performance Reports* are tabled in about November. They compare each department's actual performance to the plans set out in the RPP. If these documents complement one another as planned, they will be very helpful to both parliamentarians and researchers seeking information about departmental activities. The data provided facilitates the identification of trends and the relating of expenditure information to output data.

document is tabled in the House of Commons ordinarily in February, shortly before the beginning of the fiscal year on April 1.

The House then debates the *Estimates* package presented by the government. When it is approved, it becomes law and is called the *Appropriation Act* for that year. Considerably more detail on these latter stages of the process is provided in the next chapter.

One of the main attributes of EMS compared to previous budget processes is the dominance of cabinet as a body. Previous systems were so complex and generated so much paper that there was a sense that the system "belonged" to public servants because only they had the time and detailed knowledge to prepare and understand the documentation. Politicians signed off on the covering letters but did not have time to understand all aspects of the budget submission. The intent of EMS was that it should "belong" to the politicians. This is why the documentation was simplified, the time frames were shortened, and cabinet was given a much more central role as compared to previous processes.

There have not been any systematic evaluations of EMS. Public servants generally speak positively about how business plans have forced them to focus their thinking on determining priorities and defining outputs, and it seems clear that, for whatever reason, the federal government has significantly reduced its level of expenditure and its accompanying deficit. Of course, it is difficult to know how much of this should be attributed to EMS. It is probably too early to offer any strong statements about its long-term value.

🏛 UNDERSTANDING STANDARD BUDGETARY STRATEGIES

Regardless of the style of budgeting used or the specific processes established, there seem to be certain enduring strategies and tactics that participants in any budget-making exercise employ. It is important to understand that the skill with which the various actors employ these tactics will likely have a much greater impact on the eventual shape of the budget than any rational economic techniques.

One of the most common frameworks employed in parliamentary systems to analyze these strategies is "spenders and guardians."[33] Ministers in operating departments with large constituencies score points when they operate attractive, well-funded programs. These ministers are "spenders" not just because they want to aggrandize their own positions (although that could be one motivation), but because they come to understand that their clientele has very real needs that can be met only by adequately funded programs. Ministers also understand that one of their most important jobs is to keep their client groups contented—and therefore quiet. One way to accomplish this is by ensuring that programs affecting these groups are adequately funded. Ministers believe that they receive more political credit for launching new programs than for administering ongoing ones.[34] These factors together can turn the most fiscally conservative, tightfisted minister into an avowed spender.

The "guardians" are the Minister of Finance and the President of the Treasury Board, who score points for reducing deficits and holding the line on taxes. The overall size of the budget and its allocation among programs is an outcome of the "game" played by the "spenders" and "guardians."

This framework is directly related to the bureaucratic or governmental politics style of policy making discussed in Chapter 6. The bureaucratic politics approach sees the expenditure budget as the outcome of a bargaining process involving various governmental and some nongovernmental organizations. Governments are not monolithic entities; rather, they consist of, on the one hand, many departments and agencies that are in competition with one another for limited resources and, on the other hand, agencies that are responsible for deciding how to divide up these funds. The budget, as ultimately determined, is the product of the to-ing and fro-ing that takes place between and among these entities. In spite of its name, this approach is not limited to bureaucrats; politicians and even representatives of nongovernmental organizations become involved.

Just like any game, each side has strategies and tactics that it employs to enhance its position. However, it is important to understand that overarching the seemingly deceptive strategies is a concern for maintaining mutual trust among all the relevant actors. "The sheer mass of budgetary matters means that some people have got to trust others because only rarely can they check up on things."[35] Like all games, there are budgetary tactics that employ trickery and deception, but there are clear limits on how far these prevarications can go. For example, in squash, it is an accepted part of the game to feint one kind of shot and actually hit another. However, lying about the score is not an accepted tactic.

One limit on the deception stems from the fact that most Treasury Board program analysts have worked in departments at some point and have seen these strategies from the other side. Budgeting is like squash in that there are few totally new strategies. The good players are those with the ability to determine quickly which strategy is being employed.

Departments have vast programs that are overseen by a very small group of program analysts from the Treasury Board. It would be relatively easy for a department to deceive its Treasury Board analyst. However, if caught, the consequences for the department would be severe because the Treasury Board can impose very tight controls on departmental operations. The possible benefits are not worth the risk.

The following discussion of tactics must be read in this perspective. There is trickery and deception, but it is confined within understood limits. The most important tactic is maintaining mutual trust, without which the system could never work.

The spenders have the greatest array of potential tactics.[36]

- *Padding the budget.* This is the most basic strategy, but it is not used as crudely as most outsiders probably believe. The budget presented must be close enough to the target to be credible. An obviously heavily padded budget will simply be thrown out by the guardians. However, all budgets must contain some provision for contingencies to give managers some manoeuvring room during the year.

There is a certain irony here in that spenders *must* pad their budget to some extent because guardians always assume that there is some padding. A spender who presents a budget so lean that it cannot sustain any type of cut is in a very dangerous position.

However, padding alone is never enough, unless it is supplemented by other strategies.

- *Mobilize constituency interest groups.* A spending minister will encourage interest groups to make great demands on his or her department, significantly increasing the minister's bargaining power in cabinet. Business groups have been very good at this.

- *The crisis.* Managers can use real or apprehended crises to help them establish the importance of their program. Everyone knows of a particularly bad stretch of road that was only repaired after a serious accident. At a broader level, police departments are very good at using a crisis in levels of criminal activity to support their budget requests. It is unfortunate that important activities can only obtain funding after some serious crisis has developed, but the tremendous pressure on government resources makes it difficult to respond to requests for large increases in resources in the absence of a clear crisis.

- *The thin edge of the wedge.* Start a program with a very small commitment of funds; when people become dependent on the program, the guardians cannot eliminate it and in fact will probably be pressed to increase funding.

- *Kill the Friendly Giant.* When pressed to make budget cuts, always cut the program that is most popular with the public, not least popular. This will bring public pressure to bear on the guardians who demanded the cuts in the first place. A few years ago, when CBC television faced severe budget restraint, it threatened to eliminate the popular program "Friendly Giant," which sparked great concern over the cuts.

- *End run.* In the ordinary budget cycle, when many requests for funding are arrayed against one another, the competition for funds is keen. A resourceful minister will propose a new program part-way through the year and attempt to obtain a snap commitment from cabinet, thus making an end run around the vicissitudes of the ordinary budget process.

- *This program saves money.* It is surprisingly easy to argue that a program that costs a significant amount of money in the short run will actually result in a long-run saving. More money on fitness will reduce future health-care costs. Business development grants will generate future taxes. Of course, these relationships cannot be proven, but they sound good.

- *Fire truck first.* There is an apocryphal story about one of the most audacious strategies. A fire chief wanted a new fire truck and a new fire station

---

POOR FREDDIE THE GIRAFFE

Sometimes the best strategy is the high-profile use of several tactics. When it appeared that the Alberta Wildlife Park would have to close because of lack of funding, Helen Ridgeway, "an 88-year-old dynamo of a woman" who prefers to be called Aunt Helen, became a familiar sight around the Alberta legislature as she lobbied for her favourite cause.

"I'm not just fighting for Freddie," explains Mrs. Ridgway, who says that she likes Billy the Skunk just as much. "But Freddie is a wonderful giraffe."

Source: Miro Cernetig, "Cutbacks Put Freddie the Giraffe's Neck on Line"[37]

---

in the same year. When the city council told him that this was excessive in one year and that he could have either, but not both, he chose to buy the new fire truck. However, when the truck was delivered, it turned out that (you've probably already guessed) the existing fire hall was too small to accommodate the new truck.

Guardians also have tactics of their own, although it is possible that the rapid spending increases of the 1960s and 1970s were a result of an imbalance of power between spenders and guardians. Some of the responses to the above tactics are fairly obvious. For example, most recent budgetary systems have procedures to prevent "end runs," and the claims of program managers that "this program saves money" are usually met with requests to provide hard evidence. The one continuing tactic that guardians have is simply to underestimate revenue and so underestimate the amount available for expenditure. This allows them to paint the picture as being more bleak than it really is and so increases their bargaining power.

Some people object to this "game" theory because they feel that it trivializes an important part of the governing process.[38] However, the theory strikes a responsive note for anyone who has been involved in the process. Game theory should not be equated with deception or a lack of concern for the public interest, but, rather, it can be seen as a committed group of people being certain that all options are considered in arriving at an optimum decision.

This bargaining process usually ensures that budgeting decisions are incremental in the sense discussed in Chapter 6. This means that there are few major changes in budgets from one year to the next.

> The largest determining factor of this year's budget is last year's. Most of each budget is a product of previous decisions. The budget may be conceived of as an iceberg; by far the largest part lies below the surface, outside the control of anyone. Many items are standard, simply reenacted every year unless there is a special reason to challenge to them. Long-range commitments have been made and this year's share is scooped out of the total and included as part of the annual budget.[39]

Budgetary allocations are determined by the relative power and tactics employed by organizations. These seldom change radically from one year to the next, so budgetary allocations are equally slow to change. However, this should not obscure the fact that some changes that seem incremental in fact have longer-term consequences. For example, if a particular program consistently receives a funding increase slightly above the average, this will have major consequences over a ten- or twenty-year period.

Budgeting as an outcome of bureaucratic politics has been fully described in the United States, where it is easy to analyze because the budget-making process is very open.[40] The work in Canada has been somewhat fragmentary,[41] but Donald J. Savoie's recent book, *The Politics of Public Spending in Canada*,[42] provides an excellent insight into the existing system.

The picture that Savoie paints is fairly negative. He uses the analogy of a number of people meeting for lunch and sharing the cost equally, regardless of how much each actually eats. Clearly, the incentive is for each person to eat and drink as much as possible, knowing that the cost will be shared by others. Even people who, at first, show restraint will soon loosen up when they see others gorging themselves. After all, if I am paying for someone else's extravagance anyway, why should I show moderation?[43]

There are simply no incentives for spending ministers to restrain themselves. On the contrary, ministers are frequently judged by their clients on the basis of how much money they spend and how many new programs they can deliver. Regionalism is so important in Canada that ministers must also be seen to be delivering the goods to their regions. Savoie illustrates this with a rather depressing quotation from a minister.

> No doubt, I went for the Cadillac model instead of the Volkswagen model in the case of the golf course, the marina, the highways, the bridges, and so on. Yes, I had some second thoughts about the cost of it all. But that second thought lasted for all of five seconds. All you have to do is sit at the cabinet table and watch ministers from Toronto, Ottawa, and Montreal grab everything that goes by. If I went for the Cadillac model, they went for the Rolls Royce model ... I saw that whenever support for the party in Toronto dropped two points it sent Toronto ministers running around everywhere for new projects. I made sure that my region would get its share of federal spending ... *If Toronto ministers couldn't show restraint surely you don't expect me to do so.*[44]

A person quoted by Savoie expressed his concern about the unfairness of the closing of the CN yards in Moncton in this manner: "In government, especially in the federal government, there is a great deal of waste and inefficiency. Moncton is not getting its share of the waste. In losing the CN shops, we are now getting even less of our share."[45]

It is clear that the overall process is stacked in favour of the spenders. Not only are they more numerous than the guardians, but there are more good political arguments for spending money than for guarding it.

This imbalance has been identified as a major problem and changes have been made in the budgetary process in recent years to redress this imbalance. The Expenditure Management System discussed earlier in this chapter and the Program Review exercise discussed in detail in Chapter 22 were both attempts to bring government expenditure under control and to go beyond the short-sighted and selfish view of government expenditure discussed above. The reduction in government deficits would indicate that these changes have been at least somewhat successful in allowing the guardians to regain control of the budget system.

🏛 CONCLUSION

This chapter has focused on the preparation phase of the budget. This is a very important part of the total budget cycle because it is so important in the determination of overall government priorities. However, budget preparation is still only one-third of the total budget cycle. Adoption and execution are also important; these will be covered in the next chapter.

NOTES

1. Allan M. Maslove, "Introduction: Budgeting in Provincial Governments," in Allan M. Maslove, ed., *Budgeting in the Provinces: Leadership and the Premiers* (Toronto: Institute of Public Administration of Canada, 1989), 1.
2. The illusions involved in tax expenditures are described in Kenneth Woodside, "The Political Economy of Policy Instruments: Tax Expenditures and Subsidies in Canada," in Michael M. Atkinson and Marsha A. Chandler, eds., *The Politics of Canadian Public Policy* (Toronto: University of Toronto Press, 1983), 175–76 and passim.
3. G. Bruce Doern, Allan M. Maslove, and Michael J. Prince, *Public Budgeting in Canada* (Ottawa: Carleton University Press, 1988), 55ff.
4. Douglas G. Hartle, *The Revenue Budget Process of the Government of Canada: Description, Appraisal, and Proposals* (Toronto: Canadian Tax Foundation, 1982), 6. (Footnotes omitted.)
5. Ibid., 31. (Footnotes omitted.)
6. There seem to be only two major discussions of the revenue budget process in addition to Hartle's: David A. Good, *The Politics of Anticipation: Making Canadian Federal Tax Policy* (Ottawa: Carleton University, School of Public Administration, n.d.), ch. 6; and Evert Lindquist, *Consultation and Budget Secrecy* (Ottawa: The Conference Board of Canada, 1985), ch. 2.
7. Robert J. Bertrand, Alice Desjardins, and René Hurtubise, *Legislation, Administration and Interpretation Process in Federal Taxation*, Study for the Royal Commission on Taxation, no. 22 (Ottawa: Queen's Printer and Controller of Stationery, 1967), 44–45.
8. Walter L. Gordon, *A Political Man* (Toronto: McClelland and Stewart, 1977), ch. 8.
9. Robert Martin, "Kerr Won't Quit Over Budget Leak," *The Globe and Mail*, 19 April 1986, A4.
10. Lindquist, *Consultation and Budget Secrecy*, 3–4.
11. The major proposals are recounted in Hartle, *The Revenue Budget Process*, ch. 4.
12. Bruce Doern "Fairness, Budget Secrecy and Pre-Budget Consultation in Ontario: 1985–1992," (Ottawa: Carleton University School of Public Administration, Working Paper Series, 1993).
13. A very good discussion of the development of the process and some speculation on what the future holds is found in: Evert A. Lindquist, "Citizens, Experts and Budgets: Evaluating Ottawa's Emerging Budget Process," in Susan D. Phillips, ed., *How Ottawa Spends 1994–95: Making Change* (Ottawa: Carleton University Press, 1994), 91–128.
14. Jean Daigneault, "Putting Aside Budget Secrecy," *Policy Options* (June 1993), 21–24; Doern, "Fairness, Budget Secrecy and Pre-Budget Consultation in Ontario: 1985–1992."
15. Robert A. Young, "Business and Budgeting: Recent Proposals for Reforming the Revenue Budgetary Process," *Canadian Public Policy* 9 (September 1983): 354. (Footnote omitted.)
16. Donald Gow, *The Process of Budgetary Reform in the Government of Canada* (Ottawa: Information Canada, 1973), 1.

17. Allen Schick, "The Road to PPB: The Stages of Budget Reform," *Public Administration Review* 26 (December 1966): 244. (Emphasis in original.)

18. Ibid. (Emphasis in original.)

19. A good general discussion of the chronological development of the different styles of budgeting is contained in James Cutt and Richard Ritter, *Public Non-Profit Budgeting: The Evolution and Application of Zero-Base Budgeting* (Toronto: The Institute of Public Administration of Canada, 1984), chs. 4–7. A specific description of how the evolution occurred in the Canadian federal government is given in Gow, *The Process of Budgetary Reform in the Government of Canada.*

20. A good description of the strengths and weaknesses of performance budgeting is contained in V. N. Macdonald and P. J. Lawton, *Improving Management Performance: The Contribution of Productivity and Performance Measurement* (Toronto: Ministry of Treasury, Economics and Intergovernmental Affairs, 1977), 32–33.

21. Honourable C.M. Drury, *Planning-Programming-Budgeting Guide* (Ottawa: Queen's Printer, 1969), 8.

22. The strongest critic of the system in Canada is one of its veterans, D.G. Hartle, "Techniques and Processes of Administration," *Canadian Public Administration* 19 (spring 1976): 24–29. One of the most prolific and perceptive critics of PPB in general has been Aaron Wildavsky, "The Political Economy of Efficiency: Cost-Benefit Analysis, Systems Analysis, and Program Budgeting," *Public Administration Review* 26 (December 1966): 292–310, and "Rescuing Policy Analysis from PPB," *Public Administration Review* 29 (March-April 1969): 189–202.

23. Allen Schick, "A Death in the Bureaucracy: The Demise of Federal PPB," *Public Administration Review* 33 (March-April 1973): 147.

24. This shift in power is described very well in A. Clayton, "Brother Could You Spare A Dime?" *Optimum* 12, no. 1 (1981): 7–19.

25. Peter Self, *Econocrats and the Policy Process: The Politics and Philosophy of Cost-Benefit Analysis* (London: Macmillan, 1975).

26. Sandford F. Borins, *The Toronto Airport(s)*, Case Program in Canadian Public Administration (Toronto: Institute of Public Administration of Canada, 1977).

27. Government of Canada, *The Expenditure Management System of the Government of Canada* (Ottawa: Minister of Supply and Services Canada, 1995).

28. There is quite an extensive history of different kinds of budgetary processes. This can be traced through previous editions of this book or in C. Lloyd Brown-John, André LeBlond, and D. Brian Marson, *Public Financial Management: A Canadian Text* (Scarborough, Ont.: Nelson Canada, 1988), ch. 8.

29. This section is based on one of the few commentaries on the new budget system. Peter Harder and Evert Lindquist, "Expenditure Management and Reporting in the Government of Canada: Recent Developments and Backgrounds," in Jacques Bougault, Maurice Demers, and Cynthia Williams, eds., *Public Administration and Public Management Experiences in Canada* (Quebec: Les Publications du Québec, 1997), 82–88.

30. *Estimates 1998–99*, Part III, Correctional Service Canada, 10.

31. Government of Canada, *The Expenditure Management System,* 5–6.

32. Previous editions of this book contained some samples of pages from the Estimates and some advice on how to read them.

33. These terms were popularized by Hugh Heclo and Aaron Wildavsky, *The Private Government of Public Money,* 2nd ed. (London: The Macmillan Press Ltd., 1981), ch. 4.

34. Douglas G. Hartle, "Perceptions of the Expenditure Budget: Survey of Federal and Provincial Legislators and Public Servants," *Canadian Public Administration* 32, no. 3 (fall 1989): 437.

35. Aaron Wildavsky, *The New Politics of the Budgetary Process,* 2nd ed. (New York: HarperCollins Publishers, 1992), 111.

36. One of the most perceptive students of these tactics is Aaron Wildavsky, Ibid., ch. 3. Wildavsky's list has been revised somewhat to reflect structural differences in parliamentary systems of government.

37. Miro Cernetig, "Cutbacks Put Freddie the Giraffes's Neck on the Line," *The Globe and Mail*, 28 February 1991.

38. Hartle, "Perceptions of the Expenditure Budget," 434.

39. Wildavsky, *The New Politics of the Budgetary Process*, 82.

40. There are so many of these studies that it is impossible to mention even the main ones, but some of the classics are ibid., and the same author's earlier classic: *The Politics of the Budgetary Process* (Boston: Little, Brown, 1964); Irene S. Rubin, *The Politics of Public Budgeting* (Chatham, N.J.: Chatham House Publishers, Inc., 1990); Richard F. Fenno, Jr., *The Power of the Purse: Appropriation Politics in Congress* (Boston: Little, Brown, 1966); John P. Crecine, *Governmental Problem-Solving: A Computer Simulation Model of Municipal Budgeting* (Chicago: Rand McNally, 1969).

41. Douglas G. Hartle, *The Expenditure Budget Process in the Government of Canada* (Toronto: Canadian Tax Foundation, 1978); Richard French, *How Ottawa Decides* (Toronto: James Lorimer, 1980); Richard Van Loon, "The Policy and Expenditure Management System in the Federal Government: The First Three Years," *Canadian Public Administration* 26 (summer 1983): 255–85.

42. Donald J. Savoie, *The Politics of Public Spending in Canada*, (Toronto: University of Toronto Press, 1990).

43. Ibid., 19–20.

44. Ibid., 200–201. (Emphasis added.)

45. Ibid., 257.

BIBLIOGRAPHY

Aucoin, Peter. "Organizational Change in the Machinery of Canadian Government: From Rational Management to Brokerage Politics." *Canadian Journal of Political Science* 19 (March 1986): 3–27.

Bertrand, Robert J., Alice Desjardins, and René Hurtubise. *Legislation, Administration and Interpretation Process in Federal Taxation*. Study for the Royal Commission on Taxation, no. 22. Ottawa: Queen's Printer and Controller of Stationery, 1967.

Bird, Richard M. *The Growth of Government Spending in Canada*. Toronto: Canadian Tax Foundation, 1970.

Borins, Sandford. *The Toronto Airport(s)*. Case Program in Canadian Public Administration. Toronto: Institute of Public Administration of Canada, 1977.

Brown-John, C. Lloyd, André LeBlond, and D. Brian Marson. *Public Financial Management: A Canadian Text*. Scarborough, Ont.: Nelson Canada, 1988.

Canada. Treasury Board. *Operational Performance Measurement. Vol. I: A Managerial Overview* and *Vol. II: Technical Manual*. Ottawa: Information Canada, 1974.

_____. *Report on the Study of the Accounts of Canada*. Ottawa: Minister of Supply and Services Canada, 1976.

Clark, Ian D. "Recent Changes in the Cabinet Decision-Making System in Ottawa." *Canadian Public Administration* 28 (summer 1985): 185–201.

Clayton, A. "Brother Could You Spare a Dime?" *Optimum* 12, no. 1 (1981): 7–19.

Crecine, John P. *Governmental Problem-Solving: A Computer Simulation Model of Municipal Budgeting*. Chicago: Rand McNally, 1969.

Cutt, James, and Richard Ritter. *Public Non-Profit Budgeting: The Evolution and Application of Zero-Base Budgeting*. Toronto: The Institute of Public Administration of Canada, 1984.

Daigneault, Jean. "Putting Aside Budget Secrecy." *Policy Options* (June 1993): 21–24.

Danziger, James N. *Making Budgets: Public Resource Allocation.* Beverly Hills, Calif.: Sage Publications, 1978.

Doern, G. Bruce. "Fairness, Budget Secrecy and Pre-Budget Consultation in Ontario: 1985–1992." Ottawa: Carleton University School of Public Administration, Working Paper Series, 1993.

Doern, G. Bruce, Allan M. Maslove, and Michael J. Prince. *Public Budgeting in Canada.* Ottawa: Carleton University Press, 1988.

Downs, Anthony. *An Economic Theory of Democracy.* New York: Harper & Row, 1957.

Drury, C.M. *Planning-Programming-Budgeting Guide.* Rev. ed. Ottawa: Queen's Printer, 1969.

Dye, Thomas. *Understanding Public Policy.* Englewood Cliffs, N.J.: Prentice-Hall, 1972.

Falcone, David J., and Michael S. Whittington. "Output Change in Canada: A Preliminary Attempt to Open the 'Black Box.'" Paper presented to the Annual Meeting of the Canadian Political Science Association, Montreal, Quebec, 4 June 1972.

Fenno, Richard F., Jr. *The Power of the Purse: Appropriation Politics in Congress.* Boston: Little, Brown, 1966.

French, Richard. *How Ottawa Decides.* Toronto: James Lorimer, 1980.

Golembiewski, Robert T., and Jack Rabin, eds. *Public Budgeting and Finance: Behavioral, Theoretical, and Technical Perspectives.* New York: Marcel Dekker, 1983.

Good, David A. *The Politics of Anticipation: Making Canadian Federal Tax Policy.* Ottawa: Carleton University, School of Public Administration, n.d.

Gordon, Walter L. *A Political Man.* Toronto: McClelland and Stewart, 1977.

Government of Canada. *The Expenditure Management System of the Government of Canada.* Ottawa: Minister of Supply and Services Canada, 1995.

Gow, Donald. *The Process of Budgetary Reform in the Government of Canada.* Ottawa: Information Canada, 1973.

Harder, Peter, and Evert Lindquist. "Expenditure Management and Reporting in the Government of Canada: Recent Developments and Backgrounds." In Jacques Bougault, Maurice Demers, and Cynthia Williams, eds., *Public Administration and Public Management Experiences in Canada.* Quebec: Les Publications du Québec, 1997, 71–89.

Hartle, Douglas G. "Techniques and Processes of Administration." *Canadian Public Administration* 19 (spring 1976): 21–33.

―――. *A Theory of the Expenditure Budget Process.* Toronto: Ontario Economic Council, 1976.

―――. *The Expenditure Budget Process in the Government of Canada.* Toronto: Canadian Tax Foundation, 1978.

―――. *The Revenue Budget Process of the Government of Canada: Description, Appraisal, and Proposals.* Toronto: Canadian Tax Foundation, 1982.

―――. "Perceptions of the Expenditure Budget: Survey of Federal and Provincial Legislators and Public Servants." *Canadian Public Administration* 32, no. 3 (fall 1989): 427–48.

Heclo, Hugh, and Aaron Wildavsky. *The Private Government of Public Money.* 2nd ed. London: Macmillan, 1981.

Laframboise, H.L. "Administrative Reform in the Federal Public Service: Signs of a Saturation Psychosis." *Canadian Public Administration* 14 (fall 1971): 303–25.

Linquist, Evert A. *Consultation and Budget Secrecy.* Ottawa: The Conference Board of Canada, 1985.

―――. "Citizens, Experts and Budgets: Evaluating Ottawa's Emerging Budget Process." In Susan D. Phillips, ed., *How Ottawa Spends 1994-95: Making Change.* Ottawa: Carleton University Press, 1994, 91–128.

MacEachen, Allan J. *The Budget Process: A Paper on Budget Secrecy and Proposals for Broader Consultation.* Ottawa: Department of Finance, 1982.

Macnaughton, Bruce D., and Conrad J. Winn. "Economic Policy and Electoral Self-Interest: The Allocations of the Department of Regional Economic Expansion." *Canadian Public Policy* 7 (spring 1981): 318–27.

Maslove, Allan M., ed. *Budgeting in the Provinces: Leadership and the Premiers.* Toronto: Institute of Public Administration of Canada, 1989.

Niskanen, William A., Jr. *Bureaucracy and Representative Government.* Chicago: Aldine-Atherton, 1971.

Pryor, Frederick. *Public Expenditures in Communist and Capitalist Nations.* London: George Allen & Unwin, 1968.

Pyhrr, Peter A. *Zero-Base Budgeting.* Toronto: John Wiley, 1973.

Rubin, Irene S. *The Politics of Public Budgeting.* Chatham, N.J.: Chatham House Publishers, Inc., 1990.

Savoie, Donald J. *The Politics of Public Spending in Canada.* Toronto: University of Toronto Press, 1990.

————. *Thatcher, Reagan, Mulroney: In Search of a New Bureaucracy.* Toronto: University of Toronto Press, 1994.

Schick, Allen. "The Road to PPB: The Stages of Budget Reform." *Public Administration Review* 26 (December 1966): 243–58.

————. "A Death in the Bureaucracy: The Demise of Federal PPB." *Public Administration Review* 33 (March–April 1973): 146–156.

Sherbaniuk, D.J. "Budget Secrecy." *Canadian Tax Journal* 24 (May–June 1976): 223–30.

Treasury Board of Canada. *Guide on Financial Administration for Departments and Agencies of the Government of Canada.* 2nd ed. Hull: Minister of Supply and Services Canada, 1979.

Van Loon, Richard. "Ottawa's Expenditure Process: Four Systems In Search of Co-ordination." In G. Bruce Doern, ed., *How Ottawa Spends: The Liberals, the Opposition & Federal Priorities—1983.* Toronto: James Lorimer, 1983, 93–120.

Van Loon, Richard J., and Michael S. Whittington. "Kaleidoscope in Grey: The Policy Process in Ottawa." In Michael S. Whittington and Glen Williams, eds., *Canadian Politics in the 1990s.* Scarborough, Ont.: Nelson Canada, 1990, 448–67.

Wildavsky, Aaron. *The New Politics of the Budgetary Process.* 2nd ed. New York: HarperCollins Publishers, 1992.

————. *The Politics of the Budgetary Process.* Boston: Little, Brown, 1964.

————. "The Political Economy of Efficiency: Cost-Benefit Analysis, Systems Analysis, and Program Budgeting." *Public Administration Review* 26 (December 1966): 292–310.

————. "Rescuing Policy Analysis from PPB." *Public Administration Review* 29 (March–April 1969): 189–202.

Wilson, Michael H. *The Canadian Budgetary Process: Proposals for Improvement.* Ottawa: Department of Finance, 1985.

Woodside, Kenneth. "The Political Economy of Policy Instruments: Tax Expenditures and Subsidies in Canada." In Michael M. Atkinson and Marsha A. Chandler, eds., *The Politics of Canadian Public Policy.* Toronto: University of Toronto Press, 1983, 173–97.

Young, Robert A. "Business and Budgeting: Recent Proposals for Reforming the Revenue Budgetary Process." *Canadian Public Policy* 9 (September 1983): 347–61.

27

The Management of Financial Resources

Waste and corruption in government are hot topics. There always seem to be news stories about fraud and misuse of government funds. The stories range from the individual public servant who gets caught cheating on an expense claim, to entire programs gone awry where millions of dollars are spent in a wasteful manner. How can these things happen?

Given the huge amount of money that governments spend on so many varied programs, it should not be surprising that some funds go astray from time to time. Governments by their nature are large, decentralized organizations. It is impossible for a few legislators and senior managers to control all the activities of the government taking place across a wide area.

What sorts of controls do governments have in place to prevent these embarrassments from occurring? How do we know that government funds are used wisely? And how do we know that the published government financial statements really tell the true story?

The previous chapter discussed the budgetary process, i.e., the process of allocating funds to be spent on specific programs. This chapter will consider what happens to those funds after they have been appropriated. Of course, operating departments have the main role because they operate programs and therefore spend the bulk of the funds. However, there are a number of other agencies involved in the process of ensuring that funds are spent wisely and with appropriate controls. This chapter will examine in detail each of the agencies involved in the process.

🏛 THE FINANCIAL ADMINISTRATION ACT

The *Financial Administration Act*[1] defines the responsibilities of the Treasury Board and the Department of Finance in the area of financial management. It establishes the general rules for the handling and safeguarding of public funds and other assets. It specifies rules for the management of the public debt and sets out procedures for maintaining the government accounting system. It also establishes the accountability regime for Crown corporations and other agencies. In sum, the Financial Administration Act provides the general framework of financial and administrative management within which the departments and agencies of the federal government must function.

🏛 PARLIAMENT

The best way to view the system is as an annual cycle as illustrated in Figure 27.1. The process begins when Parliament appropriates funds for a new fiscal year. The fiscal year of the federal and provincial governments runs from April 1 to March 31.

Most aspects of the appropriation process were covered in the previous chapter, but it is important to remember that it is a basic tenet of responsible, parliamentary government that Parliament must approve the expenditure of any funds before the expenditure occurs. This is the first step in the financial administration cycle.

As discussed in the previous chapter, quite a bit of work goes into the preparation of the budget before it is tabled in the House of Commons. In this chapter, the role of Parliament in the approval of the expenditure budget will be considered.

The President of the Treasury Board begins the process, usually in February of each year, by tabling a series of documents collectively referred to as the *Estimates*.[2] These documents list the budget allocations requested by each department, as well as some supporting detail about the operation of the programs for which funding is requested. In recent years, this supporting information has expanded so that the *Estimates* consist of several volumes, with a separate volume for each department providing supplementary information about the priorities of the department and its strategies in pursuing those priorities. The *Estimates* can be a valuable research tool.

The *Estimates* and all other "money bills," as they are called, are always tabled and approved in the House of Commons before going to the Senate. This is a long tradition stemming from the fact that the House of Commons is the elected body of Parliament and is, therefore, the only body that is directly responsible to the electorate.

Figure 27.1
CYCLE OF FINANCIAL ADMINISTRATION

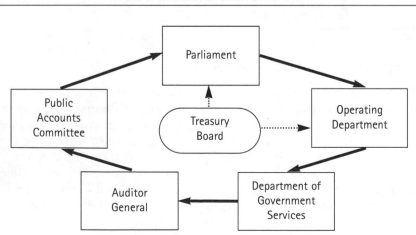

After the *Estimates* documents have been tabled in the House of Commons, they are then sent to the various committees of the House for further consideration. Each committee specializes in a department or a related group of departments so that the *Estimates* are divided up and sent to the appropriate committees for more in-depth consideration. Since this usually takes some time and since the *Estimates* are not tabled until a rather short time before the beginning of the fiscal year on April 1, it is unlikely that Parliament will approve the *Estimates* before the beginning of the fiscal year. Obviously, this creates a serious problem because departments cannot begin to spend money until Parliament has appropriated it. To circumvent this problem, Parliament provides Interim Supply before the beginning of the fiscal year.

Interim Supply is a piece of legislation that provides for the operation of the government for the period from April 1 to June 30 by appropriating approximately one-fourth of the total budget requested. This allows departments to continue operating even though the full budget has not yet been considered. It is customary that interim supply should include funds only for the continuation of existing programs. Funding for new programs must usually await the approval of the *Estimates*.

Shortly after the *Estimates* are tabled, the various parliamentary committees begin to hold hearings on the part of the *Estimates* that most closely concerns them. Usually, ministers and senior officials will appear before these committees to explain and defend their budget requests. The committees also like to hear from clientele groups and interested experts. The committees then recommend to Parliament what the appropriate budgetary allocation ought to be. Since these committees usually operate along highly partisan lines, it is unusual for the committee recommendation to deviate from the government's request, but that should not be taken as a sign of the committees' impotence. These budget hearings are an excellent place for opposition members to learn about the activities of departments and can also provide an important forum for holding ministers and public servants accountable.

After the committee reports have been received by the House of Commons, there is a vote on the full budget as contained in the *Estimates*. This vote is very important because the expenditure budget is always a matter of "confidence," meaning that if the budget were defeated it would be an indication that the government no longer had the "confidence" of the House and, therefore, as a matter of convention, ought to resign.

The rules of the House provide that if a budget has not been acted upon by the House before June 30, then it is voted upon on that date. This means that the opposition is free to defeat a budget, but it cannot hamstring the government by merely delaying the passage of the budget. In fact, the *Estimates* legislation is almost always passed in exactly the form proposed by the government. When it becomes law, it is known as the *Appropriation Act* for that year.

The government always attempts to estimate its needs as accurately as possible when it prepares its *Estimates* at the beginning of the year, but it is not surprising that sometimes these beginning-of-the-year estimates do not prove completely accurate. Since all expenditures require parliamentary approval, the government cannot unilaterally shift funds from one program to another or spend more than was allotted by Parliament in the original Appropriation Act. In order to meet unforeseen circumstances, the government presents *Supplementary Estimates* to the House at various times during the fiscal year. The Supplementary Estimates are pieces of legislation that request either additional funds beyond those originally approved or a shift in funds between programs. In recent years, governments typically have presented Supplementary Estimates from three to five times each year.

There is one other way of dealing with these unforeseen circumstances. *Governor General's Warrants* can be issued to meet an unforeseen need at a time when Parliament is not in session. In this case, the president of the Treasury Board notifies the governor general that funds must be spent even though there has been no parliamentary appropriation. The governor general then issues a warrant authorizing the expenditure of these funds.

To ensure that the use of these warrants is not abused the government is required to provide official notice whenever they are used. First, they are always announced in the *Canada Gazette*, which is the publication of the Government of Canada in which all official government announcements are publicized. Then, the issuance of these warrants must be approved by Parliament when it resumes sitting before it considers any new expenditure legislation.

While there is nothing that Parliament can do at this point to recapture the funds that have already been spent, it is an opportunity for the opposition parties to question the government about the expenditure of these funds. The warrants are a limited violation of the principle that all expenditure requires prior parliamentary approval, but they are an important safety valve. For example, Governor General's Warrants were used extensively during the 1979–80 period when, because of transitions in government, Parliament was not sitting for an extended period. Without some mechanism such as these warrants, absolutely no money could have been spent in that rather lengthy period.

The role of Parliament in financial administration is crucial. Legally, it is Parliament—and only Parliament—that can start the process by appropriating funds. Still, there have been criticisms of Parliament's role. Some Members of Parliament have complained that they have very limited time to consider the lengthy and complex *Estimates* before they are passed. The Royal Commission on Financial Management and Accountability echoed this concern when it suggested that individual MPs were overworked in terms of their committee activities,[3] and when it further pointed out that there was no single committee that was charged with an overview of the budget and the economy.[4] However, while it seems that most people recognize the existence of the problem, no action has been taken to resolve it.

🏛 THE TREASURY BOARD

The *Treasury Board* is a cabinet committee consisting of six cabinet ministers including the President of the Treasury Board and the Minister of Finance. The board has been called the cabinet committee on the expenditure budget and the cabinet committee on management.[5] In fulfilling its first role, it assembles the budget requests of departments and recommends the budget to Parliament. This aspect of its work was covered in detail in the previous chapter. In this chapter, the main focus will be on the latter role.

There are two things that distinguish the Treasury Board from other cabinet committees. First, there is a rather large group of civil servants working directly under the supervision of the president. In 1999, there were 780 employees in the *Treasury Board Secretariat*,[6] as the bureaucratic organization reporting to the president is called. The effect of this bureaucratic contingent is that the Treasury Board has a considerably higher profile as a committee touching on the day-to-day activities of public servants than other cabinet committees.

The Treasury Board is also distinguished from other cabinet committees in that its existence has been established by an act of Parliament (the Financial Administration Act), unlike the other cabinet committees, which are created by, and can be abolished by, a decision of the prime minister. The Financial Administration Act defines the general framework for financial and administrative management in the federal government, and as a part of that framework it establishes the Treasury Board's status as a central control agency, meaning that the board has supervisory powers over certain activities of operating departments.[7] Specifically, the Treasury Board has the power to make regulations in most areas of general administrative and financial management. Some examples of the Treasury Board's authority are set out below.

- establishing allotments, i.e., subdivisions of parliamentary appropriations, that cannot be varied without the Treasury Board approval;

- prescribing rules for the disbursement of public funds, i.e, procedures to be followed before a cheque can be issued;

- prescribing rules for the receipt and control of funds paid to the government;

- prescribing rules for the safeguarding of public property;

- ensuring coordination of administrative functions and services within departments and within government as a whole, i.e., ensuring effective interdepartmental coordination;

- prescribing the form and manner in which government accounting records will be maintained; and

- establishing regulations for entering into contracts and for purchasing.

The Treasury Board has promulgated these rules and regulations and communicated them to departments in two thick loose-leaf binders entitled *Comptrollership*, which are sections of the multivolume *Treasury Board Manual*. The *Comptrollership* volumes set out in detail the procedures that must be followed with regard to receipt and payment of public funds, handling inventories and other assets, and so forth. The box below provides a few examples of other Treasury Board publications that establish guidelines for activities in departments. The Treasury Board also shares with the Department of Public Works and Government Services the responsibility for developing government accounting policy and the system of accounts used in the preparation of the Public Accounts.

The Treasury Board is also responsible for the evaluation of government programs—a process that has been of great concern in the federal government recently. Evaluation, which was discussed in detail in Chapter 7, involves the systematic, in-depth review of a program to determine its contribution to public policy.

> SAMPLE OF TREASURY BOARD PUBLICATIONS
>
> *The Manager's Deskbook* (a quick reference guide found on the desk of most managers)
> *Security*
> *Contracting*
> *Privacy and Data Protection*
> *Insurance and Related Benefits*
> *Information Technology Standards*
> *Material, Service and Risk Management*

The Treasury Board does not actually evaluate the programs itself; that is better left to the operating departments, which understand their programs better than would outsiders. However, the Treasury Board has developed expertise in the evaluation area so that it can advise departments on undertaking evaluations and, to some extent, evaluate the evaluations. In general, it provides leadership in this area by using both moral persuasion and producing publications such as *Principles for the Evaluation of Programs by Federal Departments and Agencies.*[8]

An overview of these activities indicates that the main role of the Treasury Board is to ensure prudence and probity in government, and to ensure uniformity in administration between operating departments. In a small organization, this kind of function would not be necessary, but this role is frequently found in large organizations. It is necessary to have some central agency to ensure that all the diverse and decentralized units of the total organization are conducting their administrative activities in an appropriate and reasonably uniform manner.

In order to carry out this function, the Treasury Board has prepared a number of manuals containing guidelines and regulations that are binding on all departments and agencies of the government. The regulations sometimes specify in great detail rules for everything from the steps that must be followed before a government cheque can be issued to the size of offices for officials of various ranks. In some cases, a department can obtain an exemption from following certain regulations if it is able to make a satisfactory argument to the Treasury Board that special circumstances require this exemption. The staff of the Office of the Auditor General are familiar with the Treasury Board regulations and uses them in the performance of audits.

The status of the Treasury Board as a central control agency gives it a key role in the system of financial administration. However, it is precisely this status that frequently leads it into conflict with operating departments and raises questions about accountability.

Operating departments usually feel a great deal of pressure to organize programs so that significant results are produced quickly. Officials in these departments sometimes see uniform, cross-departmental regulations as obstacles to smooth and efficient service delivery.

The Treasury Board is not unsympathetic to this problem, but officials in the Treasury Board Secretariat are mindful that regulations are established to serve particular purposes and should not be circumvented lightly. The operating department might see that there are ways of saving time and money by cutting corners, for example, by shortcutting certain purchasing procedures or by skimping on some financial control mechanisms. This raises the classic staff-line conflict, but it is exacerbated in this case because the Treasury Board, unlike the classic staff agency, has control over some aspects of the department's work.

This raises the question of accountability. Is it really appropriate to hold the line department accountable for results if it does not have full authority to take whatever action is necessary to obtain those results? This is an old question, which really cannot be answered in the abstract. Every situation is slightly different. The important point to be made is that some controls over the activities of line departments are important, but sensitivity must be employed in exercising this control so as not to cripple the activities of operating departments.

🏛 OPERATING DEPARTMENTS

The line departments are involved in actually operating most large government programs, so this is where the bulk of government expenditure takes place. These departments are clearly in the front line, in terms of making expenditure decisions, but the above discussions about the role of the Treasury Board should make it clear that the authority of a department to act unilaterally is somewhat limited.

Departments are required to establish *pre-audit procedures*—procedures to confirm that appropriate conditions have been met before payment is approved. These procedures must ensure that the expenditure has been authorized by Parliament, that adequate funds still remain in the appropriation, that appropriate goods or services have been received, and that these were in line with the contract. If the payment is a grant or transfer payment, obviously the specific procedure is different, but the general idea is the same. The department must establish procedures to ensure that the person receiving the payment is entitled to it. These procedures are called a pre-audit because they are required, by Treasury Board guidelines, to occur before any public funds are paid out. These same guidelines specify similar rules for the protection of revenue received and the safeguarding of noncash assets such as inventories.

Departments are also responsible for establishing an internal audit group with free access to the deputy minister. The purpose of this is to provide the deputy with objective information about the adequacy and effectiveness of the management framework that each department has established for:

- the achievement of its operational and program objectives;
- the reliability and integrity of the information;

- the economical and efficient use and safeguarding of resources; and

- compliance with policies and regulations.

Departments receive a budgetary allocation and approve the payment of funds to be charged to that allocation, but they do not actually issue cheques. This is done by the Department of Public Works and Government Services.

🏛 DEPARTMENT OF PUBLIC WORKS AND GOVERNMENT SERVICES

The Department of Public Works and Government Services is responsible for many common services provided to all departments and agencies, such as accommodation, purchasing, and central accounting.[9] It is this latter function that will be discussed in this chapter.

The department is the central accounting agency of the Government of Canada. This means that the Receiver General for Canada, which is another title that the Minister of Public Works and Government Services always holds, is responsible for the receipt and disbursement of all public funds and for accounting for those funds in the Consolidated Revenue Fund. The *Consolidated Revenue Fund* is the one large cash account that the government maintains for all federal funds that are not earmarked for some specific purpose. The name comes from the fact that at one time there was a large number of cash funds held by a variety of different agencies and used largely for their own purposes. This created some confusion and raised the possibility of inappropriate use of, or accounting for, government funds. For this reason, it was felt desirable to consolidate all government funds in one account under the control of one minister—the Receiver General—and his or her department—the Department of Public Works and Government Services.

The department receives cheque requisitions from operating departments and agencies and then issues cheques as requested. Before the cheque is issued, the Department of Public Works and Government Services ensures that the department will not be overspending its appropriation, but it undertakes no other reviews beyond that because it assumes that the department has conducted a proper pre-audit.

The Department of Public Works and Government Services handles all receipts and deposits of public funds and acts as a central accounting agency; it shares with the Treasury Board the responsibility for the establishment of the government accounting system.

The department is also responsible for the preparation of the government's year-end financial statements referred to as the *Public Accounts*. These statements contain the government's balance sheet, which lists assets owned and liabilities owed, the Statement of Revenue and Expenditure, and certain other financial statements. The Public Accounts also contains a great deal of detailed information about sources of revenue and objects of expenditure by program and activity. This makes it a valuable source of information for researchers.

The Department of Public Works and Government Services is responsible for preparing the government's financial statements, but these statements must bear the scrutiny of an audit by an independent agency.

🏛 AUDITOR GENERAL

The Office of the Auditor General (OAG) is one of the most visible and well-known actors in the financial management system. The auditor general can be seen as having two roles—one narrow and one much broader. The narrow role is the least contentious and requires the auditor general to act in the same manner as an auditor would act in the private sector. The auditor general's more contentious, broader role requires her or him to be something of a watchdog of government spending.

In the auditor general's narrow role, he or she performs an attest audit. An *attest audit* is an audit performed to ensure that the financial statements accurately reflect the financial position and activities of the government. The outcome of the attest audit is the auditor's opinion, which becomes a part of the *Public Accounts.* This opinion should be read by anyone working with the *Public Accounts* to provide an insight into the level of accuracy of the statements presented. In recent years, the federal government's financial statements have been given a "clean" or unqualified opinion meaning that the auditor general concurs that the *Public Accounts* truly reflects the government's financial position. However, British Columbia's provincial auditor has contemplated issuing a qualified opinion, i.e., an opinion stating certain reservations about the quality of the province's financial statements.[10]

In order to fulfil this attest function, the staff of the OAG must undertake a post-audit of a random selection of financial transactions that occurred during the year. This *post-audit* means that these selected transactions are traced through the accounting process to evaluate the adequacy of the pre-audit performed within departments and to determine the accuracy of the accounting records. This is how the auditor general forms an opinion as to whether the financial statements contained in the Public Accounts, and prepared by the Department of Public Works and Government Services, accurately reflect the financial position of the government.

In addition to the attest audit, the auditor general is also responsible for the performance of a compliance audit. A *compliance audit* is an audit performed to ensure that all legislative enactments and government regulations have been complied with in the operation of programs. It goes beyond the attest audit in ensuring not just that transactions have been recorded correctly, but also that there was appropriate statutory authority for all expenditure and, further, that the regulations specified by the Treasury Board have been followed. This role of the auditor general has never been very contentious because it can usually be objectively established if rules have been violated.

However, the auditor general's broader role has always been somewhat more contentious. The auditor general is an officer of Parliament, rather than simply an ordinary public servant. This means that he or she has the right to report directly to Parliament and has protection from arbitrary dismissal from office by the government, which will be discussed in more detail later. In this role, the auditor general is frequently seen as Parliament's watchdog on government spending. To carry out this role, the auditor general is required to report to Parliament at least once each year.[11] Different auditor generals have produced different types of reports.

Under the terms of legislation in existence prior to 1977, the auditor general was charged with reporting on any "nonproductive expenditure." Previous auditor generals who have taken this responsibility to heart have produced annual reports that contained lists of "horror stories." These were lists of specific incidents that, in the opinion of the auditor general, indicated some inappropriate expenditure by the government. This kind of report was much loved by the media, because it provided a succession of juicy headlines. One of the most widely heralded examples was the story of the refitting of the aircraft carrier Bonaventure.[12] The auditor general found numerous examples of cost overruns and excessive prices paid during the refit. Then, to add insult to injury, the ship was sold for a very low price almost immediately after the refit was complete.

These kinds of findings are important in reminding ministers and public servants that there is a check on their activities and that they must carry out their responsibilities with due care. However, not all of the auditor general's horror stories were as clear-cut as the Bonaventure.

In 1969, the government of the day became incensed over the auditor general's criticism of its expenditure on a study of a causeway to Prince Edward Island.[13] The federal government had commissioned a feasibility study of the construction of the causeway. After considering the findings of the study, it was decided not to build the causeway at that time. At this point, the auditor general suggested in his annual report that the cost of the study was a nonproductive expenditure. The government of the day argued that this finding was unfair because it made more sense to study the feasibility of a major project first, rather than build it and then discover that it was unnecessary. This incident provides some insight into the problems that the auditor general encounters when he or she goes beyond the narrow confines of the attest audit.

In 1977, provisions governing the auditor general were removed from the Financial Administration Act, and the Auditor General's Office was for the first time governed by its own legislation. In this new legislation, the phrase "nonproductive expenditure" was replaced by a requirement to report on any case in which "money has been expended without due regard to economy or efficiency."[14]

At about this time, the style of the Auditor General changed from an emphasis on individual horror stories to a more systematic approach to general problems in financial management. This change came about partly because of misunderstandings such as the causeway, and partly because the accounting profession was taking a more systematic approach to auditing. However, the change mostly came about as a result of the coming to office of James J.

Macdonell—an individual who had spent his entire career in accounting and management consulting in the private sector. Macdonell moved away from the horror stories approach and toward the more systematic approaches of what was first called "value-for-money" auditing and then comprehensive auditing.

Comprehensive auditing is defined as

> an examination that provides an objective and constructive assessment of the extent to which:
>
> - financial, human and physical resources are managed with due regard to economy, efficiency and effectiveness; and
>
> - accountability relationships are served.
>
> The comprehensive audit examines both financial and management controls, including information systems and reporting practices, and recommends improvements where appropriate.[15]

Comprehensive auditing is more extensive than the traditional forms of auditing because it goes beyond a concentration on financial activities to consider the way in which the organization uses all its resources and the general manner in which the organization is managed. This comes through a concentration on the three Es—economy, efficiency, and effectiveness.[16] These three Es can be complementary, but it is

---

THE THREE Es DEFINED

Economy—obtaining the appropriate goods and services at the best possible price.
Efficiency—maximizing ratio of outputs produced to inputs employed.
Effectiveness—maximizing the attainment of the objective.

---

also possible to maximize some of them, but not others. For example, one could maximize economy in obtaining resources but then employ those resources in an inefficient manner. Probably the more usual situation is that economy and efficiency are present, but they are misdirected in some way so that effectiveness is not served, i.e., steps toward the desired objective are not maximized. The concept of effectiveness is the most problematic because its application in specific cases can be highly political. Politicians are frequently reluctant to state the true goals they see for a policy. If the goals of a policy or program are unclear, then it can be a very subjective exercise to evaluate effectiveness.

The introduction of comprehensive auditing caused a change in the style of auditing. In the former style, staff of the audit office reviewed the activities of each department and agency in as much depth as time allowed, performing mostly a post-audit, but always with an eye to uncovering horror stories.

In comprehensive auditing, there is still a concern for the ordinary attest function and post-audit. However, the random search for horror stories was replaced by a systematic and detailed review of a limited number of programs each year. An extensive, but shallow, approach was replaced by a selective, intensive approach.

The style and content of the annual report also changed. The listing of horror stories was replaced by three main types of chapters. One type reported on the comprehensive audits of specific programs. These reports go far beyond the narrow financial reviews that characterized early audits. For example, a review of Parks Canada concluded that some parks could suffer environmental degradation because of an excessive number of visitors.[17]

A second kind of audit dealt with government-wide reviews of a general nature, commenting on the value of program evaluation[18] or the use of computers. These provided an overview of how well these resources were used and offered some advice for improvement.

The third type, and in many ways the most interesting and useful, is more broadly philosophical. The 1983 report contained a chapter titled "Constraints to Productive Management in the Public Service,"[19] which has had a significant influence on recent management reforms in the federal government. Two more recent reports have dealt with the effect of public service reforms on accountability,[20] and values, service, and performance in federal government organizations.[21]

This expanding role of the auditor general has provoked a great deal of controversy. In the first place, comprehensive auditing is, by its nature, a more subjective exercise than attest or compliance auditing. Efficiency and effectiveness, like beauty, are frequently in the eye of the beholder. For example, some people are quick to denounce subsidy programs to others as wasteful, while benefitting from other kinds of subsidy programs themselves.

The second element of controversy in the auditor general's expanded role stems from the heavily political content sometimes involved in assessing effectiveness. It is within the appropriate sphere of the auditor general to comment on economy and efficiency, but a consideration of effectiveness frequently requires some comment on government objectives that clearly goes beyond the mandate of the auditor general and may venture into political territory. The auditor general must exercise care lest at some point he or she usurp the role of the leader of the Opposition.

> The auditor general in the last ten years has moved light-years beyond the role of auditor, toward a broad assessment of government management and decision-making. Ironically, as there is less waste and fewer horror stories to report, the AG's annual report goes further and further toward a general second-guessing of government.[22]

Comprehensive auditing attempts to avoid this dilemma by limiting its role to commenting on economy and efficiency. These are not such contentious areas. In principle, there is no attempt to comment on effectiveness as such, but Macdonell took the position that all programs should have indicators to measure their effectiveness and that his office ought to have responsibility to comment on the existence (or nonexistence) and adequacy of those indicators. This attempt to define the auditor general's role more carefully has probably limited the conflict somewhat, but Mr. Macdonell and his successors have frequently been accused of overstepping their appropriate role.[23]

One of the most significant conflicts occurred around the cabinet decision to allow Petro-Canada to use $1.7 billion in public funds to purchase

Petrofina.[24] The auditor general felt that he needed supporting information to determine whether these funds were spent with appropriate regard to economy and efficiency. Initially, both Petro-Canada and the relevant government departments refused to allow him access to the information on the grounds that these documents were secret cabinet documents. This principle of the secrecy of cabinet documents is important for the maintenance of a neutral public service, which was discussed in Chapter 13 of this book.

In the face of the government's continuing refusal to release the information, the auditor general eventually took the matter to the Supreme Court of Canada. The court ruled that the auditor general did not have right of access to confidential cabinet documents. The ruling held that, where access is denied, the auditor general can report that to Parliament, but it is then up to Parliament to decide what should be done.

The auditor general must be careful about becoming involved in political controversies. The audit function derives its credibility from its objectivity. While it is very tempting to move into controversial areas, this constitutes a movement away from pure objectivity to greater subjectivity, which could weaken the credibility of the office.

Many people, especially the opposition parties, would like to use the auditor general for their own political ends. In this environment, the auditor general must move very carefully to avoid weakening the office by bringing it into political controversy.

In order to carry out the audit function appropriately, the auditor general must have what private sector auditors refer to as "independence," i.e., the auditor must not be under the direct control of the organization being audited—in this case, the executive branch of government.

One aspect of this independence is ensured by the fact that the auditor general is an officer of Parliament. In practice, this means that he or she can deliver all reports directly to Parliament without intervention by the government; he or she can appeal directly to Parliament if he or she feels that the office is not being funded appropriately; and he or she can be dismissed only for cause after an address of both Houses of Parliament. This last point means that an auditor general can be dismissed only for some inappropriate behaviour, and even then only after a majority vote of the House of Commons and Senate and the concurrence of the governor general. This is the same procedure that is followed for the dismissal of a judge.

The method of appointment also helps ensure the independence of the auditor general. The appointment is made by Parliament on the nomination of the prime minister. However, to help ensure the highest quality appointment, there is a tradition that, in making this nomination, the prime minister will rely on the advice of a committee of professional accountants. Further, the Auditor General's Act's requirement that the appointee be a "qualified auditor"[25] would make it difficult for a government to appoint an inappropriate person.

Once appointed, the auditor general serves a fixed term of ten years or until he or she reaches sixty-five years of age, whichever comes first. The independence of the auditor general is very important, and there is a general consensus that this independence is adequately served by the safeguards that are in place.

🏛 PUBLIC ACCOUNTS COMMITTEE

The Public Accounts Committee (PAC) is a committee of the House of Commons charged with the responsibility for reviewing the auditor general's annual report. In most ways, it functions just as any other parliamentary committee with the exception that, by tradition, the chair of the committee is a member of the Opposition. It is quite possible that the committee will be composed of a majority of members from the government party, but this does not make the chair powerless. The chair establishes agendas and provides leadership to the committee. The presence of an opposition member as chair ensures that important topics will be on the agenda and will be discussed in the presence of interested Members of Parliament and the media. This high visibility does much to ensure accountability even if the contents of the committee's reports are dominated by government input.

The committee reviews the auditor general's annual report on a section-by-section basis. Usually, it considers the comprehensive audits of each program separately. Relevant ministers and/or senior public servants are invited to appear before the committee to comment on the findings of the auditor general and possibly explain what steps have been taken to solve the problems. Throughout the process, the members of the PAC are advised by staff of the auditor general's office.

> The auditor general and the public accounts committee must work hand in hand to ensure effective accountability. Without the auditor and his report the committee is unable to dig into government's finances, or to choose from among the millions of transactions and thousands of issues those which are important and deserve study. Without the committee the auditor general can only report and express an opinion; he has no backing or guidance by parliament, and his findings have less publicity and attention without the media interest in proceedings of the public accounts committee.[26]

During the course of the hearings, the committee sends a series of short reports to Parliament, providing its recommendations for what ought to be done as a result of each of the auditor general's observations.

This series of reports closes the loop that was set out in Figure 27.1. Parliament will have the comments of the Public Accounts Committee before it when deciding what to do about the continued funding of a particular program in the next budget.

It is difficult to assess the significance of the role of Parliament in this process, since it does not typically alter the Estimates as presented by the government. However, it is likely that the government would want to move to correct problems identified by the auditor general and the Public Accounts Committee before having to take strong criticism in the House and the media. In this sense, the benefits of these organizations are sometimes more real than apparent.

🏛 ASSESSMENT OF THE EXISTING SYSTEM

In recent years, there has been a great deal of concern about financial account-ability and the quality of financial management in the federal government. The government has responded to this concern in a number of ways: the Treasury Board Secretariat has prepared comprehensive manuals dealing with financial and general administrative practices; program evaluation has been imple-mented across the government; the internal audit function has been empha-sized; and the staff of the Office of the Auditor General has been increased significantly. These steps have made managers much more conscious of the need for good financial management.

However, some people are now questioning whether all of these changes have gone too far and become dysfunctional. Timothy W. Plumptre has written of "an overdose of accountability in Ottawa."[27] In particular, he takes issue with the spe-cific forms of accountability employed, which he describes as "finan-centric"—a view of accountability "which places accounting and financial administration at its heart, subordinating all other dimensions of management."[28] He argues that this form of accountability focuses too much on whether managers are dotting their i's and crossing their t's and not enough on whether overall goals are being attained. It is entirely possible that inappropriate forms of accountability can both prevent good managers from being innovative and provide a hiding place for incompetent managers, who can say "I followed all the rules."

Governments also need to be realistic about the impact of better financial management and accountability on controlling expenditure and public debt. Good management and proper accountability are important, but hopes that better financial management will significantly reduce public expenditure are mis-placed. The major reason that Canada has improved its financial position in the last few years is that difficult decisions have been made to downsize programs.

NOTES

1. R.S.C. 1985, c. F–11.
2. The contents of the *Estimates* are described more fully in Chapter 26. Previous editions of this book contained a lengthy appendix that explained how to read both the *Estimates* and *Public Accounts*.
3. Canada, Royal Commission on Financial Management and Accountability *Final Report* (Hull: Minister of Supply and Services Canada, 1979), ch. 22.
4. Ibid., 381–83.
5. A.W. Johnson, "The Treasury Board of Canada and the Machinery of Government of the 1970s," *The Canadian Journal of Political Science* 4 (September 1971): 346–66.
6. *1998–99 Estimates: Part III-Report on Plans and Priorities: Treasury Board of Canada, Secretariat*, 51.
7. In the past, the Treasury Board shared much of this responsibility with the Office of the Comptroller General (OCG). In 1993, these two organizations were combined.
8. Canada, Treasury Board, *Principles for the Evaluation of Programs by Federal Departments and Agencies*, (Ottawa: Minister of Supply and Services Canada, 1981).

9. For a complete review of the responsibilities of this department and its recent history, see: Alasdair Roberts, "Public Works and Government Services: Beautiful Theory Meets Ugly Reality," in Gene Swimmer, ed., *How Ottawa Spends 1996–97: Life Under the Knife* (Ottawa: Carleton University Press, 1996), 171–203.

10. Anne Giardini, "Morfitt Threatens Reservation on B.C. Accounts," *The Bottom Line* (May 1994), 3.

11. S.C. 1994, c. 32.

12. Sonja Sinclair, *Cordial but Not Cosy* (Toronto: McClelland & Stewart, 1979), 69.

13. Auditor General of Canada, *Report of the Auditor General to the House of Commons for the Fiscal Year Ended March 31, 1967* (Ottawa: Queen's Printer and Controller of Stationery, 1968), 54–56.

14. R.S.C. 1985, ch. A–17, s. 7(2) (d).

15. Canadian Comprehensive Auditing Foundation, *Comprehensive Auditing in Canada: The Provincial Legislative Audit Perspective* (Ottawa: Canadian Comprehensive Auditing Foundation, 1985), 8.

16. The most complete reference on comprehensive auditing is Ibid.; see also *Report of the Auditor General of Canada to the House of Commons—Fiscal Year Ended 31 March 1983* (Ottawa: Minister of Supply and Services Canada, 1983), 200 ff.

17. Auditor General of Canada, *Report of the Auditor General of Canada to the House of Commons*, ch. 31, Canadian Heritage-Parks Canada (Ottawa: Minister of Public Works and Government Services Canada, 1996), 31–11.

18. Auditor General of Canada, *Report of the Auditor General of Canada to the House of Commons*, ch. 3, Evaluation in the Federal Government (Ottawa: Minister of Public Works and Government Services Canada, 1996).

19. Auditor General of Canada, *Report of the Auditor General of Canada to the House of Commons—Fiscal Year Ended March 31, 1983* (Ottawa: Minister of Supply and Services Canada, 1983), 53–87.

20. Auditor General of Canada, *Report of the Auditor General of Canada to the House of Commons 1992* (Ottawa: Minister of Supply and Services Canada, 1992), ch. 4.

21. Auditor General of Canada, *Report of the Auditor General of Canada to the House of Commons—Fiscal Year Ended 31 March 1990* (Ottawa: Minister of Supply and Services Canada, 1990), ch. 7.

22. John L. Manion, "New Challenges in Public Administration," *Canadian Public Administration* 31, no. 2 (summer 1988): 240.

23. Sharon Sutherland, "On the Audit Trail of the Auditor General: Parliament's Servant, 1973–80," *Canadian Public Administration* 23 (winter 1980): 616–44; and by the same author, "The Politics of Audit: The Federal Office of the Auditor General in Comparative Perspective," *Canadian Public Administration* 29 (spring 1986): 118–48.

24. This story is told from the Auditor General's perspective, but quite accurately, in Auditor General of Canada, *Report of the Auditor General of Canada to the House of Commons, Fiscal Year Ended 31 March 1989* (Ottawa: Minister of Supply and Services Canada), 23–27.

25. R.S.C. 1985, c. A–17, s. 3 (1).

26. C.E.S. Franks, *The Parliament of Canada* (Toronto: University of Toronto Press, 1987), 239.

27. Timothy W. Plumptre *Beyond the Bottom Line: Management in Government* (Halifax: The Institute for Research on Public Policy, 1988), 185.

28. Ibid., 187.

BIBLIOGRAPHY

Auditor General of Canada. *Report of the Auditor General to the House of Commons.* (Various years.)

Brown-John, C. Lloyd, André LeBlond, and D. Brian Marson. *Public Financial Management: A Canadian Text.* Scarborough, Ont.: Nelson Canada, 1988.

Canada. Office of the Comptroller General. *Guide on Financial Administration for Departments and Agencies of the Government of Canada.* Ottawa: Minister of Supply and Services Canada, 1979.

Canada. Receiver General for Canada. *Public Accounts of Canada.* (Various years.)

Canada. Royal Commission on Financial Management and Accountability. *Final Report.* Hull: Minister of Supply and Services Canada, 1979.

Canadian Comprehensive Auditing Foundation. *Comprehensive Auditing in Canada: The Provincial Legislative Audit Perspective.* Ottawa: Canadian Comprehensive Auditing Foundation, 1985.

Johnson, A.W. "The Treasury Board of Canada and the Machinery of Government of the 1970s." *Canadian Journal of Political Science* 4 (September 1971): 346–66.

Manion, John L. "New Challenges in Public Administration." *Canadian Public Administration* 31, no. 2 (summer 1988): 234–46.

Roberts, Alasdair. "Public Works and Government Services: Beautiful Theory Meets Ugly Reality." In Gene Swimmer, ed., *How Ottawa Spends 1996–97: Life Under the Knife* (Ottawa: Carleton University Press, 1996), 171–203.

Savoie, Donald J. *The Politics of Public Spending in Canada.* Toronto: University of Toronto Press, 1990.

Sinclair, Sonja. *Cordial but Not Cosy.* Toronto: McClelland & Stewart, 1979.

Sutherland, Sharon. "On the Audit Trail of the Auditor General: Parliament's Servant, 1973–80." *Canadian Public Administration* 23 (winter 1980): 616–44.

———. "The Politics of Audit: The Federal Office of the Auditor General in Comparative Perspective." *Canadian Public Administration* 29 (spring 1986): 118–48.

VII

The Future of Public Administration

28

The Future of Public Administration in Canada

The challenges facing the public service in the early years of the 21st century will include intense global economic competition; increased public demand for programs and services; the increasingly open and participative nature of the public policy process; the effects on government operations of the Charter of Rights and Freedoms; rapid and widespread social change (e.g., the changing composition and the aging of the workforce, more frequent career changes); the impact of information technology; the cumulative effect of government austerity; and a negative public image of public officials.[1] To meet these challenges successfully, the public service at all levels of government must undergo significant changes. This chapter explores changes that are in progress or are likely to occur over the next decade. We begin with an examination of three major scenarios concerning the future of the public service. This is followed by an explanation of emerging issues in the field of public administration. The final section examines the implications of ongoing and anticipated changes for both traditional and new public service values.

🏛 SCENARIOS OF THE FUTURE

It is difficult to predict the direction that public administration will take in a future that is bound to contain sudden and unexpected changes. A federal task force on the future of the public service responded to this problem by developing governance scenarios, which set out three ways in which Canada may evolve over the next decade in response to current and anticipated challenges.[2] These scenarios are not options; rather, they are analytical tools for strategic thinking, planning, and dialogue. The future public service is likely to have elements of all three scenarios. The scenarios can be usefully applied to provincial and municipal governments as well as the federal government.

In the *evolution* scenario, success lies in reaching pragmatic compromises. Change is incremental; the focus is on the short to medium term; various groups, institutions, and regions vigorously seek their self-interest; there are continuing cutbacks in social programs, government employment, and levels of service; and there are continuing transfers of federal power to the provinces. Among the challenges to the federal government are preserving social cohesion despite severe financial constraints; working out compromises with increasingly demanding provincial governments and other political actors; and preserving basic programs and services in the face of continually declining resources. Challenges to the public service include developing new management reforms, including new delivery mechanisms and new accountability regimes; dealing with low morale; and fostering creativity in a risk-averse milieu.

In the *market* scenario, success is measured by wealth creation in a world of global economic competition; economic and social issues are defined and managed through market mechanisms; and governments play only a supporting and facilitating role. Among the challenges for the federal government are providing an environment that fosters private sector innovation and competitiveness, and preserving Canada's identity and sovereignty in a borderless world. Challenges for the public service include reducing its role to a number of core functions; operating in a more businesslike fashion; encouraging mobility between the public and private sectors; and dealing with the value and ethical issues arising from such changes. This scenario is in keeping with what many advocates of the New Public Management approach (discussed in Chapter 4) would like to see as the future of public administration.

In the *renaissance* scenario, success consists of working and learning together. The public and private sectors and a broad range of stakeholders from civil society collaborate in the belief that neither the evolutionary nor the market approach is sustainable. Government focuses on the longer term and on those functions that cannot be handled better outside government. Technology is exploited to bring about a learning society and to promote successful competition in the global information economy. The challenges for the federal government include fostering the trust necessary for effective collaboration with other governments and a wide range of political actors; preserving a federal presence in a more decentralized political system; and balancing the demands of "adversarial politics, a hierarchical structure and ministerial responsibility with the requirements for developing new partnerships, alliances and cooperative ways of working."[3] Among the challenges for the public service are strengthening its strategic capacity; making an attitudinal change in the direction of redistributing and sharing power; encouraging employee mobility across the public, private, and other sectors; and recruiting high-quality employees motivated to serve the public good.

In the late 1990s, several governments have entered a *post-deficit* period in which difficult choices must be made as to how much of their revenue surplus should be devoted to reducing the national debt as opposed to, for example, expanding social programs or reducing taxes. This richer public purse, combined with efforts to revitalize the public service and with new approaches to managing and organizing, will enhance the relative importance of the renaissance scenario.

🏛 EMERGING ISSUES IN PUBLIC ADMINISTRATION

This section examines selected major issues[4] arising in large part from the economic, social, and political factors noted above.

A fundamental issue is *the appropriate role of the state* and the consequent role of the public service. No government in Canada has provided a detailed statement as to which functions *must* be performed by the state and which functions should be performed outside government by the private or voluntary sectors. Nevertheless, such measures as program and staff reductions, privatization, and deregulation provide an *implicit* statement of governments' views on the proper scope of the state's activity. The current thrust of government policies is in the direction of the market scenario, with an emphasis on market mechanisms and on a strategic and facilitative role for governments, resulting in a reduced role and a businesslike style for the public service. However, the emergence of a post-deficit period may slow the use of market approaches and foster a modest expansion in the role of the state. In addition, there is considerable concern that continuing program and staff reductions may lead to a "hollowing out of the state," that is, to a situation where governments cannot adequately perform their essential functions.

Concern has also been expressed about the prospect of a *democratic deficit* in the form of an erosion of basic democratic principles resulting from public sector reform. For example, it is argued that public servants need more discretionary authority so that they can be innovative and entrepreneurial in the pursuit of better service to the public. Consideration will have to be given to the implications of such proposals for traditional relations between politicians and public servants and for democratic accountability. A related issue is the impact of reform on the central constitutional conventions of *ministerial responsibility, political neutrality,* and *public service anonymity.* The inroads that have gradually been made on the practice of all three conventions call for a rigorous examination of their meaning and application.

Another significant issue is *the adequacy of data on the probable consequences of public sector reforms.* To help ensure that reforms actually improve governance, it is useful to answer the W5 question about reforms in general and service delivery mechanisms in particular, namely: What Works Well Where and Why?[5] *What* mechanisms can be used? Which ones *work well,* and which ones work better than others (e.g., privatization versus deregulation versus contracting out)? According to what values or standards do various mechanisms work well (e.g., accountability, efficiency, effectiveness, responsiveness)? *Where* do these mechanisms work well? Do they work better in some policy fields than others (e.g., in health versus agriculture versus defence)? And finally, the most difficult question to answer, *why* do certain mechanisms work well?

A closely related issue is *the performance of traditional government functions by business and "third sector" organizations* (e.g., voluntary, nonprofit, and community organizations) rather than by government. Certainly, the line between the public and private sectors has become increasingly blurred and, as explained in Chapter 11, new ways of delivering government services have emerged. The market scenario envisages that government functions will continue to be transferred to, performed by, or shared with business organizations. The renaissance scenario, however, envisages that third sector organizations will be more actively involved in the delivery of government services. The actual and potential role of the third sector has been little examined in Canada. However, it is clear that, as with government-business relations, increased resort to third sector organizations will involve greater use of partnership arrangements and contracting out. This in turn will require public servants with sophisticated skills in managing contracts and ensuring that there is adequate public accountability for the expenditure of public funds by nongovernmental entities.

Among the many issues in the sphere of human resource management, the issue of *career public service* discussed in Chapter 23 deserves re-emphasis. Both the market and renaissance scenarios foresee much greater mobility of employees between the governmental and nongovernmental sectors. The anticipated benefit of improved flexibility in human resource management could be offset by a decline in values like loyalty, neutrality, and security of tenure, which have traditionally been associated with the notion of career public service. However, a federal government task force has argued that it is possible to have a professional public service without having a career public service in the sense of one that provides employment for the duration of an employee's working life. According to the task force, the significant feature of security of tenure is the assurance of nonpartisanship, not permanent employment.[6] Another important human resource issue—that of *managing diversity*—is discussed below in connection with representativeness.

Two interrelated issues that are likely to receive more attention in the future are the need to *improve the policy capacity of governments* and the need to *promote horizontal relationships* among departments and among governments. The capacity of departments to provide adequate policy advice declined during the decade from the mid-1980s to the mid-1990s. Yet, effective policy capacity is essential if governments are to meet successfully the challenges noted at the beginning of this chapter. Moreover, since most policy issues (e.g., environmental protection) have implications beyond a single department, there is a pressing need, which was identified in the renaissance scenario, to promote coordination and collaboration across departmental, governmental, and state boundaries.

Advances in computing and communication technologies have made it easier to foster horizontal relationships, but *the advent of "electronic government"* is a multifaceted issue with both positive and negative implications for governance. "The electronic government is an inter-networked government" that links "government information structures externally to everything digital, and with everybody—the taxpayer, suppliers, business customers, voters; and with every other institution in the society—schools, laboratories, mass media, hospitals, other levels of government; and with other nations around the world."[7] These electronic links can be of enormous benefit to governments by helping them, for example, to improve service delivery. At the same time, however, these links pose a threat to the individual privacy of citizens and the confidentiality of government data banks.

David Brown has identified several other issues arising from new electronic information technologies.[8] Among these issues is the impact of the technologies on government's dealings with the public, including its ability to satisfy the needs of the technologically sophisticated segment of the population, while ensuring that citizens who are technologically disadvantaged are not left behind. Another issue is the effects of electronic government for the democratic and constitutional milieu within which public servants work and especially for interaction between government and the governed. A related issue is the impact of new technologies on intergovernmental relations and the legal system, which must adapt to the huge and rapid flow of information across governmental and national boundaries. It is important to also examine the implications for the internal operations of the public service where developments include "computing and telecommunications technologies as normal working tools; major technologically driven changes in service delivery, including widespread collaboration with other jurisdictions and non-governmental actors; and shared information environments and direct accessibility of public servants through Internet and electronic mail."[9]

The foregoing discussion has illustrated the nature and magnitude of the challenges facing the public service in the future. It is evident that these issues will have important ramifications for public service values like neutrality, accountability, and service. Since the relative importance of these values changes over time and new values appear, it is useful to examine the future of the public service in relation to both traditional and new public service values.

🏛 CHANGING VALUES

The federal government has set out the "simple and unchanging" values that have characterized the public service since the early years of this century and that provide the basis for dealing with current and emerging challenges. These values are service to Canada and Canadians; loyalty to the duly elected government; honesty, integrity, and nonpartisanship; prudence in the use of taxpayers' money; faithfulness to the principles of fairness and impartiality; professionalism in carrying out duties; and respect for ministers, other parliamentarians, members of the public, and other members of the public service.[10] This list of values overlaps considerably with the traditional public service values highlighted in this book, especially in Chapter 12, namely, neutrality, accountability, efficiency, effectiveness, responsiveness, representativeness, integrity, fairness, and equity. Most of the traditional values continue to be among those emphasized by public organizations, but, as explained below, several new values have emerged.[11]

Traditional Values

Neutrality. As noted in Chapter 12, public servants have never been *value* neutral, and this fact has become more important as their discretionary powers have expanded. This trend is likely to continue as decision-making authority is increasingly delegated down the hierarchy and out to front-line public servants in government field offices as part of the movement towards empowering public servants and providing improved service to the public.

Political neutrality, in the sense of nonpartisanship, is on the decline. We noted in Chapter 13 that the political rights of public servants have been considerably expanded; the number of partisan political appointments to senior posts has increased; the convention of ministerial responsibility has been weakened; and the anonymity of public servants has diminished. Taken together, these several developments are bringing about a more politicized public service. The extent of this politicization varies from one government to another, but all governments need to ensure that the political neutrality of the public service does not become unduly eroded.

Accountability.   This value remains among the most important and most contentious of the traditional public service values. Thus, considerable concern is aroused by developments that threaten to weaken it.

As noted earlier in this book, there is a strong movement in the direction of holding public servants accountable for results achieved rather than for adherence to rules and procedures, especially those prescribed by central agencies. At the same time, some public servants are being empowered to exercise more discretion and to be innovative so that they can use the resources allocated to them in the most efficient, effective, and responsive manner. However, innovation often involves risk taking that can lead to mistakes, which might upset the public and the media and thereby embarrass the political authorities. The public service's traditional pursuit of accountability through rules and procedures "has as much to do with the increasingly critical attitude of the public, the media and politicians towards mistakes as it has do with the fundamental requirements of probity and safeguarding against political and bureaucratic patronage."[12] A careful balance will have to be struck between the creativity and innovation of public servants on the one hand and their accountability to ministers and legislators on the other hand.

Other changes raising concern about accountability include the creation of semi-autonomous units, like the Special Operating Agencies discussed in Chapter 11, and the expansion of managerial spans of control resulting from the flattening of organizational hierarchies. In addition, the recent reduction in some governments of the number of departments and the consequent increase in their size and responsibilities have raised concerns about the ability of ministers to hold public servants sufficiently accountable to political direction.

Efficiency and Effectiveness.   Many of the current efforts to reform the public service are designed to improve its efficiency and effectiveness in response to public demands for more services despite severe budgetary constraints. Managerial and technological innovations are encouraged as a means of promoting more efficient and effective performance. The purpose of such innovations as partnerships and service kiosks is to enable government to do more—or better—with less.

Improving public service competence and morale through better human resource management is critical to improving efficiency and effectiveness. Among the most important future-oriented developments in this area are the movement toward employee empowerment (discussed in Chapter 5) and toward a more flexible human resource system characterized by greater mobility between government and the private sector. While there are frequent calls for improving human resource management through more harmonious labour relations, it seems unlikely that there will be significant improvement in the adversarial relations described in Chapter 25.

Responsiveness. This value has traditionally included the notion of *service*, both to the public and to political authorities. Use of the term service has become so central to public service reform that it has largely displaced references to responsiveness. However, the emphasis on service is in reality a reflection of the increasing importance of responsiveness in relation to other traditional public service values. Greater responsiveness through improved service to ministers, the general public, and individual citizens is a central theme of government efforts to revitalize the public service and to enhance public confidence in government.

In keeping with the private sector model on which it is based, service to the public is often expressed as service to *clients*—and even to *customers*. The gradual movement toward a client-oriented public service will constitute a significant change because it has not been customary for public servants to regard Canadians as clients. This emphasis on developing a client-oriented public service will remind public servants of the need to provide good service. However, they must also keep in mind that Canadians cannot be treated as clients or customers in the business sense because they are citizens with rights as well as obligations. Moreover, it is much tougher in government than in business to decide who exactly is the client to be served.

Representativeness. The importance of this value will not diminish until the target groups discussed in Chapter 24 are represented in the public service in proportion to their numbers in the population as a whole. Efforts to promote representativeness by appointing members of these groups will continue to be complicated by government austerity measures that reduce the overall number of appointments. It is widely argued that governments have not done enough to improve the representation of the target groups and that many business organizations are more representative of the target groups than public organizations. This is cause for concern because the majority of new entrants to the labour force over the next decade will be women and members of visible minority groups, and the representation of aboriginal peoples and disabled persons in the labour force will also expand. Given the anticipated competition for skilled workers between the public and private sectors, governments must create a public service milieu that will attract and retain members of the target groups. Thus, the pressure is on governments to devote more resources to employment equity and to the effective management of diversity.

Equity and Fairness.   In the sphere of human resource management, these two values are closely related to that of representativeness. A constant theme in discussions of employment equity programs is whether these programs are fair. Some persons view employment equity initiatives as a means of fulfilling the merit principle while enhancing the career opportunities of members of under-represented groups; others see these measures as preferential treatment that reduces the opportunities of members of overrepresented groups. There is no doubt, however, that employment equity will continue to be a government priority. The equality provisions of the Charter of Rights and Freedoms alone will go a long way towards ensuring this.

Moreover, judicial decisions made under the Charter will continue to increase the significance and pervasiveness of fairness and equity considerations, not just in human resource management but also in the day-to-day decision making of public servants on a wide range of policy and managerial issues.

Integrity.   In a recent study of the relative importance of organizational values, integrity and ethics, taken together, topped the list.[13] While integrity and ethics are not synomyms, they are often used interchangeably to refer to the disposition to distinguish right from wrong and to do the right thing.

Over the next decade, concerns about the ethical behaviour of government officials, both politicians and public servants, are more likely to increase than to diminish. Problems relating to conflict of interest, employment equity, and workplace harassment will continue to arise; issues of confidentiality and privacy will become more problematic; and ethical dilemmas in such policy areas as the regulation of hazardous products and the use of reproductive technologies are likely to become more common. To sensitize existing and potential public servants to the ethical implications of their decisions, governments and universities will have to put more emphasis on ethics education.

New Values

While the importance of the traditional values will persist, they will have to compete with such popular new values as service, quality, teamwork, innovation, and openness. These new values are closely related to the current emphases in management and organizational reform discussed at various points in this book. The staying power of these new values will depend on whether such reforms as empowerment and various forms of alternative service delivery are simply passing fads or are here to stay. However, their staying power will depend also on such political considerations as the ability of public servants to be innovative within the constraints of ministerial responsibility and parliamentary sovereignty.

There will be clashes between traditional values such as accountability and new values such as innovation. There will also be tensions among the traditional values themselves (e.g., efficiency versus accountability) and among the new values (e.g., innovation versus openness). It is crucial for public servants to find the optimum balance among the central public service values, for it is upon these values that the decisions and actions of Canada's public servants are based.

NOTES

1. Canada, Privy Council Office, *Public Service 2000, The Renewal of the Public Service of Canada* (Ottawa: Minister of Supply and Services, 1990), 15–21.
2. Canada, *Deputy Ministers' Task Force on The Future Public Service* (Ottawa: Privy Council Office, 1997), available at http://www.ccmd-ccg.gc.ca/documents/dmtf/intromtf.htm, p. 4. Emphasis in the original. Note that a fourth, but less likely, scenario is included. This crisis wild card scenario covers a situation where an unexpected event (e.g., finan cial crisis) alters the agenda and the challenges in the short run.
3. Ibid., p. 9.
4. These issues have been drawn from an agenda for future research in public adminis-tration developed at a national conference. See Keneneth Kernaghan and Mohamed Charih, eds., *Research in Public Administration: An Agenda for the Year 2000* (Ottawa: École nationale d'administration publique, 1996). For elaboration on most of the issues dis-cussed in this chapter, see Kernaghan and Charih, "The Challenges of Change: Emerging Issues in Contemporary Public Administration," *Canadian Public Administration* 40 (summer 1997), 218–33.
5. Kernaghan and Charih, *Research in Public Administration,* 16.
6. Canada, Privy Council Office, *Discussion Paper on Values and Ethics in the Public Service* (Ottawa: Privy Council Office, 1996), 25–26.
7. Don Tapscott, "The Digital Media and the Reinvention of Government," *Canadian Public Administration* 40 (summer 1997), 331.
8. David Brown, "New Information Technologies and Canadian Public Administration," in M. Charih and Arthur Daniels, eds., *New Public Management and Public Administration in Canada* (Toronto: Institute of Public Administration of Canada, 1997), 93–112.
9. Ibid., 109.
10. Canada, *Public Service 2000,* 13.
11. See Kenneth Kernaghan, "The Emerging Public Service Culture: Values, Ethics and Reforms," *Canadian Public Administration* 37 (winter 1994), 614–30.
12. Canada, *Public Service 2000,* 16.
13. Kernaghan, "The Emerging Public Service Culture," 620.

BIBLIOGRAPHY

Aucoin, Peter. "The Design of Public Organizations for the Twenty-First Century: Why Bureaucracy Will Survive in Public Management." *Canadian Public Administration* 40 (summer 1997): 290–306.

Canada. Privy Council Office. *Public Service 2000, The Renewal of the Public Service of Canada.* Ottawa: Minister of Supply and Services, 1990.

Canada. *Deputy Ministers' Task Force on the Future of Public Service.* Ottawa: Privy Council Office, 1997.

Charih, Mohamed, and Arthur Daniels, eds. *New Public Management and Public Administration in Canada.* Toronto: Institute of Public Administration of Canada, 1997.

Kernaghan, Kenneth. "The Emerging Public Service Culture: Values, Ethics and Reforms." *Canadian Public Administration* 37 (winter 1994): 614–30.

Kernaghan, Kenneth, and Mohamed Charih, eds. *Research in Public Administration: An Agenda for the Year 2000.* Ottawa: École nationale d'administration publique, 1996.

_____. "The Challenges of Change: Emerging Issues in Contemporary Public Administration." *Canadian Public Administration* 40 (summer 1997): 218–33.

Parenteau, R.E. "L'administration publique du Québec: a l'orée du 21e siecle." *Canadian Public Administration* 40 (summer 1997): 186–203.

Waterfield, S. "The Challenges Facing Provincial Public Services." *Canadian Public Administration* 40 (summer 1997): 204–17.

Appendix

How to Write a Research Paper in Public Administration

One of the assignments frequently required of students in public administration courses is the writing of a major essay. This kind of assignment not only increases and reinforces a student's knowledge in the field but also develops research and writing skills. However, it can be a very difficult task when a student is just becoming familiar with a new field of study. This appendix provides some guidance on choosing a good topic and on doing the research.

The starting point of a good essay is selecting a good topic, if a specific topic or list of topics is not provided by your instructor. The topic should interest you, and there should be an adequate amount of background material available. One obvious source of ideas is either this book or a similar overview text such as Richard J. Van Loon and Michael S. Whittington, *The Canadian Political System: Environment, Structure and Process*, 3rd ed. (Toronto: McGraw-Hill Ryerson, 1981); Michael Whittington and Glen Williams, eds., *Canadian Politics in the 1990s*, 3rd ed. (Scarborough, Ont.: Nelson Canada, 1990); Robert F. Adie and Paul G. Thomas, *Canadian Public Administration*, 2nd ed. (Scarborough, Ont.: Prentice-Hall, 1987); G. Bruce Doern and Richard W. Phidd, *Canadian Public Policy* (Toronto: Methuen, 1983); or V. Seymour Wilson's *Canadian Public Policy and Administration* (Toronto: McGraw-Hill Ryerson, 1981).

Check the table of contents and decide which chapter interests you most. Read that chapter to see the areas covered. There will always be some ideas mentioned that could be extended or reviewed in a research paper. For example, Chapter 9 of this book discusses the accountability regime of federal Crown corporations. You could compare this regime to that of your province. Which is better? By what criteria? Chapter 12 discusses certain administrative values held by public servants. To what extent are these same values important in your province?

Another potential source of ideas for topics is articles contained in scholarly and professional journals. Spend some time in the library flipping through the main journals in the field (discussed later) to get an idea of which topics have been covered by others. Do you see an article with which you strongly disagree? Your paper could be a detailed critique of that article. Do you see an idea applied in one context that you would like to apply in another? If you see an article that tests a hypothesis about a particular department, you could test the same hypothesis in another department.

The articles can also serve as general models for your essay. Note how the authors present their arguments and make their major points. You should also note some more technical points such as the use of charts, tables, and footnotes.

Alternatively, your paper could take the form of a case study. This book, like most textbooks, focuses on how things *should* work. Is there some incident that occurred recently that allows you to test whether the real world operates in this manner? For example, Chapter 10 suggests that regulatory agencies should be kept at arm's length from the partisan political fray. Is there a recent example where this principle was violated? Were the consequences beneficial or detrimental? You could examine some published case studies to see what others have done.

When you have selected a topic or had one assigned to you, your next task is to do research to determine what has already been written about the topic. It is dangerous to form your own conclusions before you have reviewed what experts in the field have said.

A good place to start your research is the bibliographies at the end of the chapters of this book or one of the other overview books mentioned, but these contain only the main sources. You will have to go considerably further than this. The *Canadian Public Administration Bibliography,* published by the Institute of Public Administration of Canada, is especially helpful in this regard. This bibliography was originally published in 1972; periodic supplements have been published since, the latest covering the period to 1985. It contains a complete listing of books and articles about public administration in Canada.

You should check the subject and/or keyword index of your library's card or computer catalogue for recent books. You should also peruse recent editions of the periodicals in the field. The main Canadian journal is *Canadian Public Administration,* published by the Institute of Public Administration of Canada. It is published four times per year and contains an annual index (as do most other journals). *Canadian Public Policy* is another valuable source of information about public policy formulation. The federal government publishes two periodicals that contain very good information on the latest management innovations in the federal government. *Optimum* is published by Consulting and Audit Canada and distributed by the Canada Communications Group, and *Manager's Magazine* is published by the Treasury Board Secretariat. There are analogous publications in some provinces that you can locate in your university library or in provincial government libraries. *Policy Options* is a magazine published by the Institute for Research on Public Policy that contains short articles that are less weighty, in an academic sense, than those in the above journals, but are more current.

In addition, there are journals that specialize in areas other than public administration, which contain some valuable articles. The *Canadian Tax Journal* is written primarily for tax lawyers and accountants, but it is also a valuable source of information about federal and provincial budgets, and it publishes the occasional article on the revenue or expenditure budget process. The journals of the learned societies such as the *Canadian Journal of Political Science,* the

Canadian Journal of Economics, and the *Canadian Review of Sociology and Anthropology* are all very useful in their own particular areas.

There are also many excellent journals published in other countries that can be helpful, particularly for theoretical or comparative papers. The main international journal is the *International Review of Administrative Sciences.* The main journal in the field in Britain is *Public Administration,* in Australia, the *Australian Journal of Public Administration. Public Administration Review* is the most widely read public-administration journal in the United States, but several others, such as the *American Journal of Public Administration, Administration & Society,* and the *Journal of Comparative Administration,* are also useful.

You can also communicate directly with government departments to obtain information on current policy. Most governments publish a directory that provides a brief description of the responsibilities of departments and agencies. This can direct you to the agency responsible for the field in which you are interested. These directories also provide some valuable addresses and telephone numbers. The federal government publishes the *Index to Federal Programs and Services* (Ottawa: Minister of Supply and Services Canada, annual publication); the Ontario government's equivalent publication is the *KWIK Index to Services of Your Ontario Government* (Toronto: Ministry of Government Services, annual publication).

You should not overlook popular magazines and newspapers as sources of topical information. Reports in these publications do not carry the same weight in an academic paper as articles from academic journals, but they are valuable sources of information on recent events. *Le Devoir* and *The Globe and Mail* both publish lengthy analysis articles on national issues. *The Citizen* (Ottawa) provides in-depth coverage of issues concerning the federal public service, and the newspapers in most provincial capitals contain similar coverage about provincial governments. Some of the most useful magazines are *Maclean's, L'Actualite,* and *Canadian Forum.*

There are a number of indexes that provide easy access to articles in these publications. Some of the most useful are *ABC Pol Sci, ABI/INFORM, Business Periodicals Index, Management Contents, PAIS Bulletin, International Political Science Abstracts, Canadian Periodical Index,* and *Canadian Business and Current Affairs.* Most of these indexes are issued in annual volumes with more frequent updates. Many are also available in CD-ROM (compact disk-read only memory) format on computers in your library. Computer searching is much easier and less tedious than searching through piles of books, updates, etc. Your librarian can assist you in choosing the appropriate index and beginning your search.

If you are interested in the case approach, you should be familiar with the many cases published in the Case Program in Canadian Public Administration, sponsored by the Institute of Public Administration of Canada. The cases cover almost all major areas of Canadian public administration. The Case Program is also the sales agent for cases developed by the Canadian Centre for Management Development. These cases deal with management issues in the federal government setting. Perusing the titles of these could give you some ideas for your own topic. Relevant cases are listed at the end of the chapters, and a free catalogue can be obtained by writing to the Institute (Suite 305, 150 Eglinton Avenue East, Toronto, Ontario M4P 1E8).

Now that you have selected a topic and have begun to find information, it's time to sit down and actually do the research and write the paper. One of the best books on all aspects of writing a paper is *Fit to Print: The Canadian Student's Guide to Essay Writing* by Joanne Buckley (Toronto: Harcourt, Brace and Company Canada, 1995). Some of the books that provide general information about preparing and organizing a paper are *How to Write a Research Paper Step by Step* by Phyllis Cash (New York: Monarch Press, 1977); *A Guide to Writing Essays and Research Papers* by Gordon Coggins (Toronto: Van Nostrand Reinhold Ltd., 1977); and *Making Sense: A Student's Guide to Writing and Style* by Margot Northey (Toronto: Oxford University Press, 1983). Some of the best books about writing style and grammar are *Canadian Style: A Guide to Writing and Editing* (Toronto: Dundurn Press and Department of the Secretary of State); *The Practical Stylist* by Sheridan Baker (New York: Harper & Row, 1981); and *The Elements of Style* by William Strunk and Elwyn B. White (New York: Macmillan, 1979). You might also need some advice about actual preparation of the paper—typing, charts, footnotes. The best source in this area is *A Manual for Writers of Term Papers, Theses, and Dissertations* by Kate L. Turabian (Chicago: University of Chicago Press, 1987).

Good luck!

Glossary

Note: The numbers in parentheses following each item refer to the page(s) on which further elaboration on that item can be found.

Access to Information Act. A statute designed to provide a right of access to government information for the public. Also referred to as the Freedom of Information Act. (513)

Accountability. See Administrative accountability.

Adjudication. In the context of employer-employee relations, the process by which an employee presents a grievance in relation to a collective agreement or arbitral award, or in relation to disciplinary action leading to discharge, suspension, or a financial penalty.

Administrative accountability. The obligation of public servants to answer for fulfilling responsibilities that flow from the authority given them. Similar in meaning to the concept of objective responsibility. (326, 370)

Administrative discretion. The element of choice or judgment left to individual public servants in their interpretation and application of laws, rules, regulations, policies, and procedures. (344)

Administrative ethics. Principles and standards of right conduct in public organizations. Normally used interchangeably with the term "administrative morality." (371)

Administrative law. The branch of public law concerned with relations between the government and individual citizens. It deals with the legal limitations on the actions of governmental officials and on the remedies that are available to anyone affected by a transgression of these limits. (448)

Advisory council. An organization composed of private citizens created by the government to provide an independent source of advice to a minister. It is established outside the normal departmental bureaucracy and does not ordinarily have responsibility for administering programs. (486)

Affirmative action. See Employment equity.

Alternative service delivery. The trend in recent years for governments to search for more innovative and efficient ways to deliver services than through traditional departments and agencies. (296)

Appropriation Act. The law passed annually by Parliament that allows the government to spend public funds. (633)

Arbitral award. See Arbitration.

Arbitration. In the context of collective bargaining, the procedure by which an individual or a board hears arguments from both the employer and the union sides of an interest dispute and makes a decision called an arbitral award, which is binding on both parties. (602)

Auditor General. The officer of Parliament who performs an annual audit of the Public Accounts and prepares an annual report to Parliament on the government's financial stewardship. (423)

Bargaining agent. An employee organization (a union) that has been certified, e.g., by the federal Public Service Staff Relations Board, as the organization responsible for bargaining on behalf of a particular bargaining unit. Examples include the Public Service Alliance of Canada and the Professional Institute of the Public Service of Canada. (600)

Bargaining unit. A group of two or more employees designated as constituting a unit of employees appropriate for collective bargaining. (600)

Blue Book. See Estimates.

Bureaucracy. A form of organization characterized by hierarchical structure, unity of command, hiring and promotion by merit, and specialization of labour.

Bureaucratic politics. An approach to the study of policy making that focuses on interactions among individuals, in the form of conflict, bargaining, compromise, and persuasion, as determinants of the actions of a government. (392)

Canada Health and Social Transfer. A single block fund covering federal transfers of money to the provinces for health, post-secondary education, and welfare. It combined the previous transfer programs known as the Canada Assistance Plan and Established Programs Financing. (466)

Captive agency theory. A theory that holds that regulatory agencies eventually become captive of, or controlled by, the interests they were established to regulate. (297)

Career public service. A public service composed of persons who have spent, or intend to spend, all or most of their working lives in government and who remain in office with a change of government because they are permanent employees, appointed on the basis of merit, rather than political appointees. (570)

Central agency. An agency that has a substantial amount of continuing legitimate authority to intervene in and direct the activity of departments. (213)

Centralization. A system of organization that involves minimal dispersal of operating and decision-making units outside the centre of power. (56)

Citizen participation. The direct involvement of individual citizens and citizens' groups in government decision making. (504)

Classical federalism. A concept according to which the powers of government are divided so that the general and regional governments are each, within a sphere, coordinate and independent. (462)

Classification standard. A definition of the category within which each occupational group falls, the groups within each occupational category, and the descriptions of benchmark positions to be used as guides for assessing jobs and rating them according to their level in the group. (563)

Collective agreement. An agreement in writing between the employer and the bargaining agent regarding terms and conditions of employment.

Collective bargaining. A method of determining wages, hours, and other conditions of employment through direct negotiations between the employer and the union.

Collective ministerial responsibility. The responsibility of ministers as a group (i.e., as members of the cabinet) for the policies and management of the government as a whole. (390, 425) See also Individual ministerial responsibility.

Comprehensive audit. A review of a program that considers its economy, efficiency, and effectiveness. (653)

Comprehensive rationality. A style of policy making based on a scientific assessment of alternative actions and conscious choice of the course of action that will yield the maximum benefit. (130)

Conciliation. A process by which an impartial party tries to resolve interest disputes in collective bargaining by seeking compromise or voluntary agreement between the two parties. Unlike arbitration, the recommendations of the conciliator (or mediator) are not binding on the parties. (603)

Conditional grants. Payments by the federal government to a provincial government (or by a provincial government to a municipal government) in which the receiving government undertakes programs according to conditions specified by the granting government. Often referred to as shared-cost programs. (465)

Conflict of interest. A situation in which a public employee has a private or personal interest sufficient to influence or appear to influence the objective exercise of his or her official duties. (376)

Contingency theory. A theory that suggests that there is no one ideal type of organizational structure. It argues that organizational structure should be contingent on such factors as predictability of the task performed, the technology employed, and the size of the organization. (80)

Control. That form of power in which A has authority to direct or command B to do something. Sometimes referred to as "authority of position" or "position power." (320)

Cooperative federalism. A term used to describe federal-provincial relations when the constitutional division of powers is preserved but federal and provincial ministers and public servants engage in consultation and coordination to reach joint decisions on matters of mutual concern. (463)

Coordination. The process by which two or more parties take one another into account for the purpose of bringing their decisions and/or activities into harmonious or reciprocal relation. (333)

Crown corporation. A corporation in the ordinary sense of the term, whose mandate relates to industrial, commercial, or financial activities but that also belong to the state. (225) See also Mixed enterprise and Public enterprise.

Decentralization. A system of organization that involves placing actual decision-making power in the hands of units outside the centre of power, either geographically or organizationally. (56)

Deconcentration. The physical dispersal of operating units with only limited delegation of decision-making authority. (56)

Deployment. The appointment of an employee to another position at the same level as his or her existing position, or to a higher or lower level, provided that there is no change in the employee's personnel classification. (565)

Deputy minister. The administrative head of a government department. Appointed by the prime minister or premier. Also referred to as the deputy head. (210)

Deregulation. The elimination of government regulatory control over an industry so that it can operate through the dictates of the private enterprise system. (282)

Double-image federalism. A term used to describe federal-provincial relations characterized by a combination of interaction between the central government and the provinces and a special relationship between French- and English-speaking Canadians.(464)

Economy. The acquisition of goods and services at the best possible price. (326) See also Effectiveness and Efficiency.

Effectiveness. A measure of the extent to which an activity achieves the organization's intended outcomes or objectives. To be distinguished from the related concept of efficiency. (327)

Efficiency. A measure of performance that may be expressed as a ratio between input and output. The use of administrative methods and resources that will achieve the greatest results for a specific objective at the least cost. To be distinguished from the related concept of effectiveness. (327)

Emergency federalism. A term used to describe federal-provincial relations during the two world wars and the Depression; these relations were characterized by a growth in federal power vis-à-vis the provinces. (463)

Emergent-process view. An approach to management that suggests that organizations grow and develop as a part of a broader environment, and that managers have only a limited amount of control over how the organization develops. (83)

Employment equity. An approach or program designed to identify and systematically remove employment policies, practices, and procedures that exclude or place at a disadvantage certain groups that have been historically underrepresented in the public service. (580) See also Representative bureaucracy.

Equalization. A program through which the federal government makes unconditional grants to provinces with a weak tax base. The program's purpose is to allow the so-called have-not provinces to provide adequate public services to their citizens without imposing excessively high taxes. (466)

Estimates. The series of documents containing the government's request for an annual appropriation and the necessary supporting documentation. When approved by Parliament, this becomes the Appropriation Act. (632)

Ethics. See Administrative ethics.

Evaluation. An in-depth analysis of a program carried out to determine its worth and to locate any needed administrative or policy changes. (180)

Executive federalism. A term used to describe federal-provincial relations characterized by the concentration and centralization of authority at the top of each participating government, the control and supervision of intergovernmental relations by politicians and officials with a wide range of functional interests, and the highly formalized and well-publicized proceedings of federal-provincial diplomacy. (463)

Executive Group. An occupational category in the federal public service composed of about 3500 senior public servants with responsibility for policy development; program formulation and delivery; the design and operation of management machinery; and the management of personnel, finances, and public affairs.

Expectancy theory. A theory that holds that people are motivated by their expectations about how their behaviour will help them satisfy their needs, desires, and goals. (104)

Expenditure Management System (EMS). The federal government's current budget process. It is a form of program budgeting that was designed to provide more information to Parliament and other decision makers. Its centre point is each department's Business Plan, an approach that ensures that the department is focusing on its main areas of responsibility. (629)

Federalism. A political system in which the powers of the state are formally divided between central and regional governments by a written Constitution but in which these governments are linked in a mutually interdependent political relationship. (462)

Feminine ethical perspective. Stresses the importance in organizations of nurturing inter-personal relationships and of caring, cooperation, and concern for others. Compare with the feminist ethical perspective.

Feminist ethical perspective. Stresses that the influence of feminine morality will not be felt unless there is a radical break from the hierarchical structures and competitive culture of male-dominated organizations. Compare with the feminine ethical perspective.

Financial Administration Act. The statute that governs the regime of financial accountability for federal departments and agencies. (643)

Freedom of information. See Access to Information Act.

Governor General. The representative of the Queen in Canada; functions as the head of state when the Queen is not in Canada. (201)

Governor General in Council. Refers to the governor general acting on the formal advice of the cabinet. (201)

Governor General's Warrants. An authorization for the government to spend in the absence of a parliamentary appropriation; used only for unforeseen expenditures when Parliament is not in session. (646)

Globalization. The movement from a world of distinct national economies to a global economy characterized by worldwide markets for investment, production, distribution, and consumption and by the economic power of multinational enterprises.

Hierarchy of needs. A concept developed by Abraham Maslow that suggests workers can be motivated by the satisfaction of a number of different needs ranging from basic shelter and food to self-actualization. As workers' lower-level needs are satisfied, they are motivated by desires to satisfy higher-level needs. (66)

Human relations school. An approach to management and motivation that emphasizes the dignity and needs of workers in the workplace. Usually associated with social psychologists such as Mayo, Roethlisberger, and Dickson. (63)

Human resource planning. The process through which a government strives to ensure that it has the appropriate quantity and quality of employees to carry out its responsibilities. (563)

Incrementalism. A style of policy making based on small, marginal changes from existing policies. (131)

Individual ministerial responsibility. The responsibility of the minister, as the political head of the department, to answer to the legislature and through the legislature to the public both for his or her personal acts and for those of departmental subordinates. (209, 390, 425) See also Collective ministerial responsibility.

Influence. That form of power in which B conforms to A's desires, values, or goals through suggestion, persuasion, emulation, or anticipation. A more general and pervasive form of power than control. Sometimes referred to as "authority of leadership" or "personal power." (321)

Institute of Public Administration of Canada. An association of public servants from all spheres of government and academics. Devoted to improving the study and practice of public administration in Canada. Publishes the journal *Canadian Public Administration*. (6)

Intergovernmental relations. The interactions between and among the federal, provincial, and municipal governments in the Canadian federal system. (462)

Interim supply. A limited appropriation of funds provided by Parliament at the beginning of the fiscal year until the full Estimates have been approved. (645)

Interstate federalism. The distribution of powers and financial resources between the federal and provincial governments as well as the relations between those two orders of government. (464)

Intrastate federalism. Arrangements whereby the interests of regional units—the interests either of the government or of the residents of these units—are channelled through and protected by the structures and operations of the central government. (464)

Job classification. The process by which jobs are assigned to an occupational group within an occupational category and to a level within that group. (563)

Job evaluation. The analysis of a job in terms of its duties, its physical and mental demands, the knowledge and skills it requires, and the conditions under which it is performed; the writing of a job description that explains the duties, working conditions, and other aspects of the job; and the assessment of these job characteristics against the classification standard established for the relevant occupational group. (563)

Line. The part of an organization directly involved in producing the organization's output. (52)

Line-item budgeting. A style of budgeting that emphasizes the object of expenditure (salaries, stationery) rather than the purpose of the expenditure. (621)

Lobbying. A legitimate means by which groups and individuals try to influence government decisions by direct contact with politicians or public servants. Usually associated with the activities of pressure groups or interest groups. (484)

Main Estimates. See Estimates.

Management information system (MIS). An organized method of collecting information about the internal operation and the external environment of an organization. It provides information for planning, control, and operation. (533)

Managing diversity. A comprehensive managerial process for developing an organizational environment in which all employees can realize their potential while pursuing the organization's objectives.

Memorandum to Cabinet. The key mechanism by which policy proposals are brought forward by ministers for consideration and approval by their cabinet colleagues. The formal means by which deputy ministers provide confidential policy advice to their ministers. (388)

Merit principle. A principle according to which (1) all citizens should have a reasonable opportunity to be considered for employment in the public service, and (2) selections must be based exclusively on qualification or fitness for the job. To be distinguished from the merit system. (347)

Merit system. The mechanism in use at any time by which the goals of the merit principle are achieved. An administrative device that can and should be adapted to changing circumstances. (347)

Mixed enterprise. A corporation in which the federal government has taken a direct equity position in common with other participants for the purposes of implementing a public policy or satisfying a public need. (226) See also Crown corporation and Public enterprise.

New public management (NPM). A style of management that borrows heavily from private sector principles and focuses on values like customer service, flexibility in delivery, entrepreneurship, and empowerment. (77)

Objective responsibility. The responsibility of a person or an organization to someone else, outside of self, for some thing or some kind of performance. Similar in meaning to accountability or answerability. (369)

Occupational category. A broad range of occupations of the same type, distinguished by the nature of the duties performed and the education required. Examples in the federal public service are the Executive Group and the Operational categories. (563)

Ombudsman. An official authorized by statute to investigate complaints from citizens about improper, unfair, or discriminatory treatment by public servants. Reports to the legislature and is independent of the political executive and the bureaucracy. (433)

Open systems approach. An approach to the study of organizations that emphasizes that organizations are a part of, and must interact with, their environment. (78) Contrast with a closed systems approach, which sees organizations as self-contained entities.

Operating department. An administrative unit comprising one or more organizational components over which a minister has direct management and control. (202)

Order in council. An official proclamation made by the governor general in council; usually a government regulation. (209)

Organization development. A participative approach to management that emphasizes team development and allows members of the organization to work together to identify and correct problems. (69)

Organizational humanism. See Human relations school.

Organizational socialization. The process through which individuals learn the expectations attached to the position they occupy in the organization and through which they selectively internalize as values some of the expectations of those with whom they interact. (330)

Participatory management. A style of management emphasizing the desirability of workers actually being involved in decision making. (69)

Partisan mutual adjustment. A process by which a large measure of coordination in government takes place without any deliberate or conscious attempt to coordinate. (334)

Patronage. The appointment of persons to government service or their advancement within the service on the grounds of contributions, financial or otherwise, to the governing party rather than of merit. (347)

Pay equity. A system that permits comparisons to be made between different jobs performed for the same employer. A shorthand term for equal pay for work of equal value. To be distinguished from equal pay for equal work, which requires that men and women be paid the same for doing the same job. (590)

Performance budgeting. A style of budgeting that relates expenditure to specific activities to determine unit costs of providing services. (624)

Performance evaluation. The process whereby information about the performance of employees over time is systematically collected and analyzed. Also referred to as "employee appraisal." (569)

Performance measurement. The process of comparing the level of a government service provided against some standard to see whether it meets that standard or is at least improving. (175)

Political neutrality. A constitutional doctrine or convention according to which public servants should not engage in activities that are likely to impair or appear to impair their impartiality or the impartiality of the public service. (339, 425)

Politics-administration dichotomy. The idea that a clear distinction can be made between the responsibilities of elected executives, who make policy decisions, and the responsibilities of public servants, who execute these decisions. (340)

Policy community. A cluster of interested groups (government organizations, interest groups, international agencies, interested companies and individuals, and journalists) organized around a particular policy. This group has a strong influence on the making of that policy. (138)

Policy network. The interconnections among actors in a policy community. (138)

Power. The capacity to secure the dominance of one's values or goals. There are two forms of power—control and influence. (320)

Pressure groups. Organizations composed of persons who have joined together to pursue a mutual interest by influencing government decisions and actions. Often referred to as interest groups. (484)

Prime Minister's Office (PMO). The central agency providing partisan policy advice to the prime minister. It is most concerned with relations between the prime minister and the media and the party. (215)

Privacy Act. A statute that gives individuals access to their personal information held by the government and that protects the privacy of individuals by limiting those who may see this personal information. Also sets out principles of fair information practices. (518)

Privative clauses. Statutory provisions designed to prevent judicial review of the decisions of administrative tribunals. (455)

Privatization. Turning over Crown corporations to the private sector by sale or other means. (245)

Privy Council Office (PCO). The central agency providing policy advice and administrative support to cabinet and its committees. (216)

Program budgeting. A style of budgeting that allocates funds by program and attempts to measure the impact of expenditures on the goals and objectives of programs. (625)

Program review. A technique that the federal and most provincial governments have used to reduce expenditures and to ensure that departments focus on their main responsibilities.

Every department is required to examine its activities by using a series of pointed questions about the value of its programs. (547)

Public Accounts. The series of documents containing the government's year-end financial statements. (437)

Public bureaucracy. The system of authority, people, offices, and methods that government uses to achieve its objectives. The means by which the practice of public administration is carried on. (23) See also Bureaucracy.

Public choice. The use of economic principles to analyze political activity. It suggests that people take political action to further their self-interest. (134)

Public enterprise. Crown corporations and mixed enterprise. (225)

Public interest group. A form of pressure group whose members try to influence government decisions in the name of the "public interest." Distinguished from special interest groups, which are primarily motivated by particular, selfish interests. (485)

Public participation. A broad range of direct and indirect forms of participation by members of the public in government decision making. Includes such forms of participation as membership in political parties, pressure groups, and advisory bodies. A broader concept than "citizen participation." (504)

Public policy. Whatever governments choose to do or not to do. (126)

Public Service Commission. An independent agency that serves Parliament as the guardian of the merit principle in human resource management. It is responsible for recruitment, staffing, and promotion in the public service. (435)

Quasi-federalism. A term used to describe the early decades of the Canadian federation during which the federal government dominated the provincial governments, in part by making frequent use of the federal constitutional powers to disallow and reserve provincial legislation. (462)

Recruitment. The process of identifying candidates for public service positions by such methods as inviting job applications from within and from outside the public service and using a human resource inventory system. (565)

Regulatory agency. A body that administers, fixes, establishes, controls, or regulates an economic, cultural, environmental, or social activity by regularized and established means in the public interest and in accordance with general policy guidelines specified by the government. (261)

Representative bureaucracy. The idea that the social composition of the bureaucracy should reflect that of the population as a whole. Also that larger numbers of persons from certain underrepresented groups (e.g., women, minority groups) should be brought into the public service. (575) See Employment equity.

Royal commission. A temporary organization constituted to investigate either specific incidents or general policy concerns and to report to government. It is usually disbanded after it delivers its report and therefore is not involved in the implementation of its recommendations. (144)

Scientific management. A management style that emphasizes tailoring the physical nature of work to the physical abilities of workers. Characterized by time-and-motion studies and precise work standards. Usually associated with Frederick W. Taylor. (44)

Selection. The process through which candidates for public service positions are screened by such means as application forms, written examinations, and interviews. (565)

Shared-cost programs. See Conditional grants.

Span of control. The number of subordinates reporting to a particular supervisor. (48)

Special operating agency. An organization structure that provides the unit with some autonomy from its department, but not as much autonomy as a Crown corporation has. (305)

Staff. The part of the organization that supports the line function but that is not directly involved in producing the organization's output (e.g., accounting or personnel). (53)

Statutory instruments. The rules, regulations, orders, etc., made by the executive under delegated legislative authority. (437)

Strategic planning. A disciplined effort to produce fundamental decisions and actions that shape and guide what an organization (or other entity) is, what it does, and why it does it.

Subjective responsibility. The responsibility a person feels toward others. Often described as personal or psychological responsibility. Similar in meaning to identification, loyalty, and conscience. (369)

Sunset legislation. Legislation that establishes an agency or program for a finite period and requires an assessment of the value of the agency or program before it is continued. (283)

Supplementary Estimates. A request for funds in addition to the original Estimates. Usually requested toward the end of the fiscal year. (646)

Task force. See Royal commission.

Tax expenditure. A tax reduction available to a taxpayer who does (or refrains from doing) something desired by government. (616)

Theory X-Theory Y. Developed by Douglas McGregor to describe different managers' views of workers. Theory X holds that workers are basically lazy and need to be closely watched. Theory Y holds that workers are highly motivated and will voluntarily work hard. (66)

Total Quality Management. A style of participative management popularized in the 1980s and early 1990s. It requires changing an organization's culture to focus on establishing and maintaining high standards of quality, especially with respect to meeting "customer" expectations. (72)

Transfer payments. See Conditional grants and Unconditional grants.

Treasury Board (TB). A cabinet committee consisting of the President of the Treasury Board, the Minister of Finance, and four other cabinet ministers. Responsible for preparation of the expenditure budget and for administrative management in departments. (217)

Treasury Board Secretariat (TSB). The central agency that assists the Treasury Board in carrying out its responsibilities. (217)

Unconditional grants. Payments by the federal government to a provincial government (or by a provincial government to a municipal government), which can be used for any purpose the receiving government desires. (466)

Unity of command. The bureaucratic principle that holds that all employees must report to one, and only one, supervisor in order to minimize confusion and misdirection. (42)

Values. Enduring beliefs that influence the choices made by individuals, groups, or organizations from among available means or ends. (325)

Visible minority. A person (other than an Aboriginal person) who is non-white in colour/race, regardless of place of birth. (588)

Vote (as a part of the Estimates). The basis on which Parliament appropriates funds to departments and agencies; usually, there is one vote for each program.

Whistle blowing. The overt or covert disclosure of confidential information to persons outside the organization about real or anticipated wrongdoing. (517)

Name Index

Abel, Albert, 20
Abizadeh, Sohrab, 140, 158
Agócs, Carol, 158
Al-Mashat, Mohammed, 424
Albo, Gregory, 289
Albrow, Martin, 24, 37
Alexandroff, Alan, 290, 291
Allison, Graham T., 136, 157, 403
Altshuler, Alan, 506, 522
Anderson, James R., 130, 156
Anderson, John, 612
Andrew, Caroline, 289
Appleby, Paul, 342, 361
Archibald, Kathleen, 593
Argyris, Chris, 100–02, 104, 117
Armit, Amelita, 551
Arnstein, Sherry R., 504, 522
Arsenault, Shelley, 551
Ashley, C.A., 252
Atkinson, Michael M., 157, 172, 190, 191, 638
Aucoin, Peter, 127, 146, 155, 156, 158, 160, 205, 220, 221, 253, 480, 500, 550
Austin, Nancy, 115
Axworthy, Thomas S., 221

Baar, Carl, 458
Bachrach, Samuel B., 321, 335
Baker, R.J.S., 360
Bakker, Isabella, 550
Bakvis, Herman, 205, 220, 221, 480, 499
Baldwin, Sidney, 20
Baltacioglu, C., 440, 443
Balzac, Honoré de, 25, 37
Barber, James, 37
Bardach, Eugene, 189
Barker, Robert G., 116
Barnard, Chester, 65, 83
Barnes, L.W.C.S., 612
Barnes, Maria Paulette, 191

Bashevkin, Sylvia, 160
Bassett, Glenn, 83
Baxter, Clive, 489, 499
Baxter-Moore, Nicolas J., 173, 190, 247, 255
Beaty, Jeremy, 483
Beauchesne, Arthur, 442
Beckhard, Richard, 84
Beer, Samuel H., 167, 190
Begadon, Stephen, 158
Behn, Robert D., 546, 551
Bell, Cecil H., Jr., 84
Bellamy, David J., 361
Bemelmans-Videc, M.L., 192
Bennett, Jim, 499
Bennis, Warren G., 44, 60
Berman, Paul, 168, 190
Bernier, Ivan, 251, 288, 289
Bernstein, Marilyn, 190
Bernstein, Marver H., 279, 290
Bertrand, Robert J., 638
Bibeau, Gilles, 593
Birch, A.H., 441
Bish, Robert L., 550
Black, Edwin R., 480
Blair, Cassandra, 443
Blais, André, 157, 550
Blake, Robert R., 84
Blau, Peter, 37
Boadway, Robin, 480
Boardman, Anthony E., 253
Bolduc, Roch, 20
Borcherding, Thomas A., 252
Borins, Sandford F., 78, 85, 117, 157, 251, 639
Botterell, Robert, 251
Bourgault, Jacques, 222, 362, 422, 551, 639
Bourgeois, Donald J., 458
Bourgon, Jocelyn, 4, 20, 313, 572
Bowen, Joseph L., 20
Bowman, Ann., 190
Boyatzis, Richard A., 116
Boychuk, Gerard, 157

Boyd, Melanie, 313
Braybrooke, David, 156
Breton, Albert, 134–35, 157
Brooks, Stephen, 156, 158, 188, 192, 250, 255, 288, 290
Brown, David, 667, 671
Brown, Lee, 253
Brown-John, C. Lloyd, 20, 288, 289, 639
Brownstone, Meyer, 159
Bryson, John M., 528–29, 548, 549
Bullock, John, 35
Burnham, James, 31, 37
Burrows, Barbara A., 191
Butler, Dan, 19, 21

Caiden, Gerald E., 442
Cairns, Alan C., 465, 479, 480, 481
Caldwell, Lynton, 20
Campbell, Colin, 221, 403, 421
Campbell, Kim, 205, 212, 395, 397
Cardoza, Andrew, 499
Carey, Ernestine Gilbreth, 60
Carroll, Barbara Wake, 56, 60, 118, 313
Cartwright, Dorwin, 116
Carty, R., 443
Cassidy, Michael, 362
Cassinelli, C.W., 384
Cernetig, Miro, 254, 636, 640
Chandler, Marsha A., 157, 191, 222, 229, 251, 403, 638
Chandler, William M., 222, 403
Chapman, Brian, 442
Charih, Mohamed, 79, 481, 499, 549, 671
Chrétien, Jean, 205, 206, 395, 398, 419, 468
Christie, Innis, 159, 160

Clark, Clarence M., 46
Clark, Ian, 221, 403, 551
Clark, Joe, 213, 357, 395, 396, 413
Clemens, Eric G., 313
Clokie, H. McDonald, 347, 361
Cohen, Michael D., 86
Coleman, William D., 37, 157, 158
Conger, Jay A., 118
Conner, R., 192
Connor, Patrick E., 117
Cooper, Terry L., 37
Corry, J.A., 288, 522
Courchene, Thomas J., 480
Courtney, John Childs, 145, 159, 160
Cox, Kevin, 254, 551
Crecine, John P., 640
Crépeau, P.-A., 480
Culbert, Samuel A., 84
Cutt, James, 639

D'Aquino, Thomas D., 443
Daglish, Brenda, 290
Dahl, Robert A., 156
Daigneault, Jean, 422, 638
Daniels, Arthur, 79, 481, 499
Davidson, Anneka M., 27, 37
Davidson, Jill E., 549
Dawson, Helen Jones, 499
Dawson, R. MacGregor, 11, 20, 48, 60, 572
de Balzac, Honoré, 25, 37
de Gournay, Vicent, 24
de Villars, Anne S., 457, 458, 459
Deaton, Rick, 158
Decter, Michael, 551
Demers, Maurice, 222, 639
Deming, W. Edwards, 72, 84
Denhardt, Robert B., 84, 157
Desjardins, Alice, 638
Desmarais, Paul, 148
Dewees, Donald N., 288
Diamant, Alfred, 38
Dickens, Charles, 25
Dickson, William J., 64, 83

Diefenbaker, John, 356
Dion, Stéphane, 157, 362, 422, 550
Dobell, Peter, 443
Dobell, Rodney, 192
Dobuzinskis, Laurent, 157
Doering, Ronald L., 313
Doern, G. Bruce, 155, 156, 158, 160, 172, 190, 192, 203–04, 220, 221, 222, 248, 251, 254, 255, 288, 443, 619, 638
Doerr, Audrey D., 160, 221, 408, 421
Doherty, A.G., 11
Donnelly, James H., Jr., 117
Dotson, Arch, 383
Dowdell, R.H., 361
Downs, Anthony, 157, 290, 332, 336, 384
Drohan, Madelaine, 314
Dror, Yehezkel, 132, 156
Drucker, Peter F., 69, 84
Drury, C.M., 639
Dunn, Christopher, 222, 403
Dunn, William N., 130, 156
Dunsire, Andrew, 94, 116, 550
Dussault, René, 458
Dvorin, Eugene P., 361, 384
Dwivedi, O.P., 190, 348, 361, 613
Dyck, Rand, 481
Dye, Thomas R., 37, 126–27, 155, 191, 551

Eager, Evelyn, 361
Eddy, William B., 84
Edwards, John, 573
Egger, Rowland, 384
Eggleston, Wilfred, 463
Eggleton, Art, 549
Enchin, Harvey, 289
Engels, Friedrich, 37
Estey, Willard, 149
Etzioni, Amitai, 83, 132, 133–34, 156, 335
Etzioni-Halevy, Eva, 33–34, 36, 37, 38

Falcone, David J., 140, 158
Faulkner, Hugh, 499, 500
Fayol, Henri, 93, 116
Feigenbaum, Armand V., 84, 85
Fenno, Richard F., Jr., 640
Ferguson, Kathy E., 27, 37
Ferris, Gerald R., 117
Fiedler, Fred E., 116
Filley, Alan C., 116
Finder, Herman, 366–68, 383
Finer, S.E., 431, 441, 442
Fink, Arlene, 191
Finkelman, Jacob, 605, 612, 613
Finkelstein, Neil R., 459
Finley, Lawrence K., 314
Flathman, Richard E., 384
Flemming, Jeanne M, 418, 422
Follett, Mary Parker, 63–64, 83
Ford, Henry, 100
Ford, Robin, 312, 313, 314
Fournier, Pierre, 252
Fox, Elliot M., 83
Franklin, Grace A., 166, 189, 191
Franks, C.E.S., 440, 443, 658
Fraser, Neil A., 352, 361
Freeman, Alan, 290
French, Richard D., 157, 221
French, Wendell L., 84
Friedman, Milton, 34–35, 38
Friedmann, K.A., 442
Friedrich, Carl J., 335, 366–68, 383, 384
Frum, David, 35
Fulford, Robert, 290

Gaebler, Ted, 297, 312, 313, 547
Gall, Gerald L., 458
Galt, Virginia, 550, 611
Garant, Patrice, 225, 244, 251, 252, 253, 254
Garvin, David A., 84
Gawthrop, Louis C., 361
Gerth, H.H., 60
Giacquinta, Joseph B., 190

Gibbon, Ann, 253
Gibson, Ann, 254
Gibson, Gordon, 478
Gibson, James L., 117
Gilbreth, Frank and Lillian, 45
Gilbreth, Frank B., Jr., 60
Gillen, David W., 255, 290
Gillespie, W. Irwin, 192
Gilligan, Carol, 27
Gilmour, Robert, 334, 336
Ginzberg, Eli, 549
Glazere, Nathan, 35
Goal, Vivek, 192
Goggin, Malcolm L., 190
Goldenberg, Shirley B., 612, 613
Golembiewski, Robert T., 76, 84, 85
Goodnow, Frank, 341
Goodsell, Charles T., 26, 37
Gordon, Marsha, 251
Gordon, Walter L., 618, 638
Gore, Carol, 36
Gow, Donald, 638, 639
Goyer, Jean-Pierre, 428
Gracey, D.P., 253
Graham, Katherine A., 20, 160, 508, 522
Graham, Ron, 255
Granatstein, J.L., 190
Gratias, F.X. Alan, 313
Gray, John A., 140, 158, 499
Green, Duncan, 254
Greenspon, Edward, 157, 220
Gross, Neal, 190
Grusec, Ted, 549
Gulick, Luther, 48–54, 60, 360
Gunderson, Morley, 594, 612

Hackman, J. Richard, 103, 104, 117
Haedrich, Richard L., 360
Halberstam, David, 92, 115
Hall, Michael H., 313
Hall, Richard H., 116
Halperin, Morton H., 403
Harder, Marvin A., 190

Harder, V. Peter, 313, 222, 639
Hardy, Cynthia, 550
Harmon, Michael M., 60, 83, 85, 368–69, 383
Harper, Tim, 157
Harrison, Kathryn, 156
Harrison, Peter, 572
Hartle, Douglas G., 135, 157, 185, 191, 285, 291, 384, 638, 639, 640
Hatton, Michael J., 253
Hayek, Friedrich A., 34
Heclo, Hugh, 321, 336, 639
Heeney, A.D.P., 598
Heffron, Florence, 66, 83, 84, 85, 86
Hehner, Eric, 345, 361
Heintzman, Ralph, 290
Henderson, George Fletcher, 158, 159
Herring, Pendleton, 360, 384
Herzberg, Frederick, 102–03, 104, 117
Hicks, Michael, 192
Hillel, David, 458, 459
Hines, Pamela G., 551
Hinings, Bob, 549
Hitler, Adolph, 30
Hoberg, George, 156
Hobson, A.R., 480
Hodgetts, J.E., 20, 21, 145, 159, 202–03, 220, 221, 252, 348, 360, 361, 442, 572, 611, 613
Holland, Denys C., 361, 443
Hood, Christopher, 550
Hornick, Joseph P., 191
House, Ernest R., 191
House, Robert J., 116
Howard, Ross, 288, 289
Howlett, Karen, 288, 290
Howlett, Michael, 157, 158
Howse, Robert, 313
Hubbard, Ruth, 314
Hudson, Joe, 192
Huffman, Kenneth J., 251
Hull, W.H.N., 290
Hurl, Lorna F., 314
Hurtubise, René, 638

Huse, Edgar F., 84
Hutchings, Jeffrey A., 360

Ilsley, J.L., 612
Ingram, Helen M., 190
Ip, Irene K., 480
Ivancevich, John M., 117

Jabes, Jak, 114, 118, 572
Jablonski, Joseph R., 84, 85
Jackson, Doreen, 190
Jackson, Robert J., 190
Jago, Arthur G., 116
Jenson, Jane, 149, 159
Jesus, 30
Johnson, A.W., 221, 413, 414, 421, 422, 657
Johnson, Andrew F., 422
Johnson, David, 268, 289
Johnston, John, 313
Jones, David Philip, 457, 458, 459
Jones, L.R., 550
Judek, Stanislaw, 593

Kahn, Robert L., 78–80, 85, 95, 116
Kanter, Rosabeth, 27, 37
Kanungo, Rabindra N., 118
Katz, Daniel, 78–80, 85, 95, 116
Katz, Robert L., 97, 116
Kennedy, John F., 30
Kennevan, Walter J., 549
Kernaghan, Kenneth, 118, 190, 252, 253, 288, 313, 336, 360, 361, 362, 383, 384, 403, 421, 422, 480, 481, 522, 549, 573, 612, 671
Kinaschuk, Kjerstine, 613
King, Suan, 550
Kingdon, John W., 156
Kiser, Kenneth J., 84, 85
Klein, Ralph, 242
Kosecoff, Jacqueline, 191
Koteen, Jack, 548
Kounin, Jacob S., 116
Krentz, Caroline, 192
Kristol, Irving, 35
Kroeger, Arthur, 156, 350, 362, 421

Kruhlak, Orest, 221
Kuper, Olivia, 336
Kuruvilla, P.K., 612
Kwavnick, David, 500

Labelle, Huguette, 36
Labreche, Juliane, 500
Laframboise, H.L., 190, 409, 413, 421, 422
Laidler, David, 550
Lajoie, Andrée, 251, 288, 289
Lalonde, Marc, 160, 221
Landau, Martin, 334, 336
Langford, John W., 251, 253, 360, 383, 384, 522, 549
Langhorn, Ken, 549
Langille, David, 289
Langton, Kenneth P., 336
Larson, Arthur D., 592
Laux, Jeanne Kirk, 230, 248, 252, 255
Lawler, Edward E., III, 104, 117
Lawler, Edward J., 321, 335
Lawton, P.J., 639
Laycock, David, 157
LeBlond, André, 639
Leighton, Barry N., 191
Lem, Gail, 254
Lesage, Jean, 599
Leslie, Peter, 480
Lester, James P., 190
Levin, Benjamin, 549
Levine, Charles H., 313, 550, 551
Lewin, Kurt, 84, 116
Leys, Wayne A.R., 344, 361
Lindblom, Charles E., 131–32, 156, 334, 336
Linden, Rick, 188
Lindquist, Evert A., 221, 222, 487, 499, 619, 638, 639
Lippitt, Ronald, 116
Lipset, S.M., 361, 500
Llambias, Henry J., 442
Lloyd, Trevor, 159
Loo, Robert, 549
Loreto, Richard A., 403
Love, Doug, 361

Lowi, Theodore, 369
Lussier, Gaetan, 549
Lyon, David, 549
Lyon, Vaughan, 221

MacAvoy, Paul W., 254
Macdonald, Bruce A., 549
MacDonald, Donald C, 289
MacDonald, Flora, 357
Macdonald, Roderick A., 288
Macdonald, V.N., 639
Macdonell, James J., 653, 654
MacKay, A. Wayne, 159
MacKay, R.A., 11
Macnaughton, Bruce, 19, 21, 135, 157
MacPherson, C.B., 480
MacPherson, James C., 481, 499, 500
Maillet, Lise, 159
Mallory, James R., 20, 362, 439, 442, 443, 462, 464, 480
Manchester, Lydia, 314
Manion, John L., 114, 118, 658
Mann, Dean E., 190
March, Artemis, 84
March, James G., 156, 403
Marini, Frank, 361, 383
Marriage, E., 37
Marshall, Geoffrey, 441
Marson, D. Brian, 116, 549, 639
Martin, Paul, 619
Martin, Robert, 638
Martin, Roscoe, 384
Marx, Karl, 28–29, 37
Maslove, Allan M., 192, 638
Maslow, Abraham H., 65–66, 83, 84
Mason, Edward S., 383
Matheson, W.A., 361, 403
Mausner, Bernard, 117
Mayer, Richard T., 60, 83, 85
Mayne, J., 192
Mayo, Elton, 64
Mazmanian, Daniel, 168–69, 190

McCaffery, Jerry L., 550
McCarthy, Shawn, 157
McCloskey, William, 572, 611
McDavid, James C., 313
McFarland, Janet, 288, 290
McGowan, John P., 361, 443
McGregor, Douglas, 66–67, 84
McInnes, Craig, 551
McInnes, Simon, 157, 442, 475, 481
McKee, Tom, 253
McKenna, Barrie, 253
McKenna, Frank, 207
McKichan, Alasdair J., 500
McLaren, Robert I., 49, 60
McLeod, Jack, 159
McLeod, T.H., 190, 361
McQueen, Jennifer, 8, 20, 549
Meier, Kenneth John, 577, 592
Menzies, Heather, 549
Mercer, Shawna L., 192
Merton, Robert K., 78, 403
Michelmann, Hans J., 361
Michels, Robert, 29
Mickleburgh, Rod, 159
Miles, Matthew B., 84
Miliband, Ralph, 33, 38
Millar, Perry S., 458
Mills, C. Wright, 31, 37, 60
Milne, A.G., 442
Mintzberg, Henry, 117, 312
Mitchell, Alanna, 21
Mitchell, Thomas H., 254
Mitzman, Arthur, 60
Molot, Maureen Appel, 230, 252
Monopoli, William, 499
Moodie, Graeme C., 441
Moore, W., 191
Morley, David, 500
Mosca, Gaetano, 29
Mosher, Frederick C., 369, 383, 384
Motherwell, Cathryn, 255
Mouton, Jane S., 84
Mouzelis, Nicos, 37
Muczyk, Jan P., 117
Mueller, Dennis C., 156

Mullan, David J., 289, 458
Müller-Clemm, Werner J., 191
Mullins, Willard A., 578, 592, 593
Mulroney, Brian, 145, 362, 395, 397, 468
Munro, Gary, 255
Murrell, Kenneth L., 118
Mylvaganam, Chandran, 314

Nachmias, David, 191, 192
Nadler, David A., 117
Nakamura, Robert T., 169, 190
Namiki, Nobuaki, 117
Neave, Edwin H., 290
Neilson, W.A.W., 481, 499, 500
Nemetz, Peter N., 290
Neu, Dean, 254
Nevitte, Neil, 550
Newall, Ted, 23
Newman, Peter C., 479
Newstead, R., 191
Nigol, Robert A., 172, 190
Nigro, Felix A., 116, 192
Nigro, Lloyd C., 192, 577, 592
Niskanen, William A., Jr., 157
Norrie, Kenneth, 480
Nossal, Kim Richard, 481
Novelle, Thierry J., 549

O'Connor, James, 158
O'Connor, Loretta J., 422
O'Toole, Laurence J., Jr., 190
Oake, George, 254
Oldham, Greg R., 103, 104, 117
Olive, David, 253
Olsen, Dennis, 578, 592
Olson, Mancur, 157
Osbaldeston, Gordon F., 220, 416, 422
Osborne, David, 297, 312, 313, 547
Ouchi, William G., 108, 117, 118

Ouellet, Lionel, 254
Oum, Tae H., 255, 290
Owen, Stephen, 442

Pacquet, Gilles, 313, 551
Pal, Leslie A., 156, 158, 191, 192
Palumbo, Dennis J., 190
Pammett, Jon H., 361
Panet, Philip de L., 314
Panitch, Leo, 38, 158, 289, 613
Paquet, Gilles, 156
Paquin, Michel, 549
Parsons, Talcott, 78
Partridge, John, 289
Pearson, Jean, 192
Pearson, Lester B., 214, 394, 395, 403, 585
Pelletier, Rejean, 289
Perrow, Charlesr, 26, 37, 83, 84
Perry, David B., 480
Peters, B. Guy, 156
Peters, Tom, 115
Pfiffner, John, 20, 335
Phidd, Richard W., 160, 172, 190, 220, 222
Phillips, Susan D., 159, 220, 499, 508, 522, 638
Picard, André, 159
Pigeon, Lise, 593
Plumptre, Timothy W., 188, 192, 657, 658
Podhoretz, Norman, 35
Pollard, Bruce G., 480
Ponak, Allen, 612, 613
Porter, John, 577–78, 592
Porter, Lyman, 104
Poulantzas, Nicos, 33, 38, 158
Pressman, Jeffrey L., 171, 190
Presthus, Robert, 20, 102, 117, 346, 361, 488, 499
Prichard, J. Robert S., 251, 254
Prince, Michael J., 422, 612, 638
Pross, A. Paul, 20, 138, 158, 159, 160, 499, 500
Punnett, R.M., 441

Pursley, Robert D., 90, 95, 115, 116

Rabin, Jack, 20
Rahnema, Saeed, 221
Rasmussen, Ken, 20
Rawson, Bruce, 362
Rayner, Jeremy, 158
Reed, Paul B., 313
Reid, Robert F., 458, 459
Reisel, Jerome, 84
Richardson, Ivan L., 20
Richter, Luther, 11
Ridler, Neil B., 550
Ripley, Randall B., 166, 189, 191
Rist, Ray, 181, 191
Ritchie, Ronald S., 158
Ritter, Richard, 639
Robb, Roberta Edgecombe, 594
Robbins, Sharon B., 118
Roberts, Alasdair, 658
Roberts, Julian, 192
Robertson, Gordon, 221, 344, 361, 479, 481
Robson, William, 20
Rock, Allan, 483
Roethlisberger, F.J., 64, 83
Rogers, Brian MacLeod, 459
Roman, Andrew J., 456, 459, 499
Rosch, Winn L., 550
Rose, Joseph B., 611
Rose, Richard, 141, 158
Rosenbloom, David H., 20
Rouillard, Lucie, 79
Rowat, Donald C., 20, 361, 442, 577–78, 592
Rubin, Irene S., 640
Rusk, James, 290
Russell, Linda, 550
Ryan, Alan G., 192

Sabatier, Paul, 168–69, 190
Sage, G. Arthur, 25, 37
Salter, Liora, 289
Sashkin, Marshall, 84, 85
Savas, E.E., 313
Savoie, Donald J., 77, 85, 219, 221, 421, 637, 640
Sayles, Leonard R., 117

Sayre, Wallace S., 360
Sayre, William, 20
Schick, Allen, 628, 639
Schick, Gregory K., 313
Schmuck, Richard A., 84
Schonberger, Richard J., 117
Schoonhoven, Claudia Bird, 86
Schubert, Glendon, 384
Schultz, Richard J., 157, 221, 261, 281, 288, 290, 291, 411, 421, 475, 481
Schwartz, Bryan, 160
Scoffield, Heathere, 550
Scott, Richard W., 37
Segsworth, R.V., 187, 191, 192
Seidle, F. Leslie, 312
Seidman, Harold, 334, 336
Self, Peter, 639
Selznick, Philip, 44, 60
Sethi, Amarjit S., 613
Sethi, S. Prakash, 117
Shane, Gary S., 117
Sharp, Mitchell, 339, 360, 412, 421, 422
Shepherd, Robert, 551
Sheriff, Peta E., 577, 592
Sherwood, Frank P., 335
Shields, James, 459
Shortt, A., 11
Siegel, David, 56, 60, 118, 157, 313, 360, 549
Simeon, Richard, 140, 158, 473, 481
Simmons, Robert H., 361, 384
Simon, Herbert, 54–55, 60, 132–33, 156, 330, 332, 336, 403
Simpson, J., 421
Sinclair, Sonja, 658
Sinclair, William F., 290
Skogstad, Grace, 156, 158
Slater, Philip E., 44, 60
Smails, R.G.H., 252
Smallwood, Frank, 169, 190
Smiley, Donald V., 463, 474, 478, 480, 481
Smith, B.C., 37

Smith, Brian, 441
Smith, Stuart L., 549
Smythe, Mary Ann, 500
Snell, James, 149
Snortland, Neil, 90, 95, 115, 116
Snyderman, Barbara Bloch, 117
Sorauf, Frank, 384
Splane, Richard, 498, 499
Sproule-Jones, Mark H., 156, 157
St. Hilaire, France, 480
Stanback, Thomas M., Jr., 549
Stanbury, William T., 254, 384, 499
Stanfield, Robert, 339, 478
Stanyer, Jeffrey, 441
Steel, Robert P., 117
Steeves, Jeffrey S., 361
Stein, Harold, 361
Steinfels, Peter, 38
Stevens, Douglas F., 253, 254
Stevens, Sinclair, 146
Stevenson, Garth, 255, 463, 480
Stewart, Arthur E., 156
Stewart, William H., 480
Stitch, Andrew, 288
Stogdill, Ralph M., 96, 97, 116
Storing, Herbert J., 384
Strang, Vicki, 192
Strauss, George, 117
Strick, John C., 288
Stritch, Andrew, 290
Subramaniam, V., 592
Surtees, Lawrence, 254
Sutherland, Sharon L., 21, 440, 442, 443, 658
Swanson, Carl L., 117
Swartz, D., 613
Swift, Allan, 253
Swimmer, Gene, 221, 551, 606, 608, 611, 612, 613, 658
Swinton, Katherine, 613
Szablowski, George J., 221, 403, 421

Tanguay, A. Brian, 253
Tapscott, Don, 671
Tawney, R.H., 335
Taylor, Alison, 254
Taylor, Frederick Winslow, 44–47, 60, 63, 80
Taylor, Malcolm, 20, 128, 156
Tellier, Paul, 573, 593
Teram, Eli, 551
Terry, John c., 221
Thomas, Paul G., 551
Thomas, R. Roosevelt, Jr., 594
Thompson, Mark, 606, 612, 613
Thompson, Victor, 25, 37
Todres, Elaine, 372, 383
Trebilcock, Michael J., 159, 174, 191, 220, 251, 290, 314
Tretheway, Michael W., 255, 290
Trudeau, Pierre Elliott, 145, 214, 394, 395, 396, 403, 426, 429, 468, 504, 522, 585
Tupper, Allan, 248, 251, 252, 253, 254, 255, 499
Turner, John, 395, 396, 399, 407

Urwick, Lyndall, 48–54, 60, 83

Vaison, Robert A., 612
Vallance, Ian C., 459
Van Horn, Carl E., 190
Van Loon, Richard J., 214, 221, 421, 640
Van Meter, Donald S., 190
Vandervort, Lucinda, 290, 291
Vaughan, Frederick, 149
Veilleux, Gerard, 219, 221
Vile, M.J.C., 479
Villard, H.S., 20
Vincent, Donovan, 159
Vining, Aidan R., 251, 253
Vocino, Thomas, 20
Vogt, Judith F., 118

Vroom, Victor H., 99–100, 104, 116, 117

Waddell, Christopher, 255
Wagar, Terry H., 551
Wagner, John A., III, 117
Waldo, Dwight, 361
Walker, Michael, 35
Walters, Carl, 360
Walters, Roy W., 117
Walton, Eugene, 115
Ward, W., 443
Warhust, John, 481
Waterfield, S., 564, 573
Watts, Ronald L., 480
Weber, Max, 30, 37, 41–44, 60, 335
Weiler, Paul C., 459
Wente, Margaret, 594
Whalen, Hugh, 159
Wheare, K.C., 462, 480
Whitaker, Reginald, 572, 611
White, Graham, 222, 403

White, L.D., 341
White, Ralph K., 116
Whittington, Michael S., 21, 140, 158, 289, 421, 550
Wichern, Phil H., 522
Wildavsky, Aaron B., 171, 190, 321, 336, 639, 640
Williams, Cynthia, 222, 639
Williams, Glen, 21, 158, 289, 550
Williams, J.D., 116
Williams, Walter, 185
Willis, John, 288, 448
Willoughby, W., 20, 341
Wilson, Jeremy, 138, 158
Wilson, V. Seymour, 20, 152, 158, 160, 172, 190, 204, 222, 252, 341, 432, 572, 578, 592, 593, 612
Wilson, Woodrow, 11, 341, 360
Winfield, Mark, 290
Winn, Conrad, 135, 157
Winsor, Hugh, 36

Wintrobe, Ronald, 135, 157
Woll, Peter, 20, 360
Woodside, Kenneth, 172, 174, 190, 191, 638
Woolstencroft, Timothy B., 480
Wright, Herbert F., 116

Yarrow, George, 254
Yetton, Philip W., 99–100, 116
Yogis, John A., 159, 160
York, Geoffrey, 611
Young, Bruce, 118
Young, Robert A., 638

Zander, Alvin, 116
Zawacki, Robert A., 84
Zeckhauser, Richard J., 254
Ziegler, Harmon, 37
Zussman, David, 114, 118, 192, 312, 313, 314, 422, 572

Subject Index

Abella Commission, 581
Aboriginal peoples, 583, 587–88
Abuse of power, 453
Accepting gifts, 376
Access to Information Act, 513–17
Accountability, 9–10, 326
   administrative, 370–71
   conclusions (summary), 668
   ministers, of, 426–32
   public servants, of, 437–41
Action research, 71
Action travail des femmes, 457
Adaptive implementation, 168
Administrative account-ability, 370–71
   See also Accountability
Administrative agencies. *See* Regulatory agencies
Administrative discretion, 344–46
Administrative ethics, 371–78
Administrative law, 448
Administrative responsi-bility, 365–70, 381–82
Advisory agencies, 285
Advisory bodies, 507–08
Advisory commissions, 145
Advisory councils, 486
Advocates, 379
Affirmative action, 580–81
Agreement on Internal Trade (AIT), 472
"Airplane", 515
Al-Mashat affair, 424, 429
Alternate dispute resolution process, 604
Alternative service delivery, 294–315, 544
   accountability, 311
   benefits of, 299–301
   caveats/criticisms, 310–12

citizen vs. customer, 298–99
colocation, 304
commercialization, 309–10
consumer satisfaction, 312
contracting out, 308–09
cooperation between departments, 301–02
creation of agencies, 302
Crown corporations, 305
definition, 296–98
labour relations, 311
new technology, 303
partnerships, 306–08
public interest, 312
restructuring with gov-ernments, 301
single window, 304–05
special operating agen-cies, 306
user charges, 303–04
Annual budget, 208
   See also Budgetary process
Anonymity, 354–55
Appropriation Act, 633, 645
Arbitration model, 610
ASD mechanisms. *See* Alternative service delivery
Assistant deputy ministers, 212
Attentive public, 138
Attest audit, 651
Audi alteram partem, 451
Auditor General, 435–36, 651–56
Authoritarian leadership style, 98
Authority of leadership, 321
Authority of position, 321
Auxiliary function, 53

Babel house, 94
Bargaining approach, 167

Bargaining model, 474
Blais v. Basford, 451
Blue Book, 632
Blue paper, 154
BOOT (build-own-operate-transfer), 307
Bounded rationality, 132–33
Briefings to parliamentary caucuses, 441
British Columbia Agents (B.C. Agents), 305
Broadcasting regulation, 278
Budget speech, 618
Budgetary process, 208, 615–42
   evaluation of, 637
   expenditure budget, 620–29
   expenditure manage-ment system, 629–33
   line-item budgeting, 621–24
   performance budgeting, 622, 624
   program budgeting, 622, 624–29
   revenue budget, 616–20
   spenders and guardians, 633–36
   strategies, 633–36
Bureaucracy, 23, 24
   See also Public bureau-cracy
Bureaucrat bashing, 545
Bureaucrat's values, 330
Bureaucratic entrepreneur approach, 167–68
Bureaucratic politics, 136–37, 392
Bureaucratic politics model, 475
Bureaucratic power, 339–60
   anonymity, 354–55
   permanence in office, 356–58
   political appointments, 347–49

political neutrality, and, 358–60
political partisanship, 349–51
politics-administration dichotomy, 340–47
public comment, 351–54
Business centres, 305
Business impact test (BIT), 274, 276

Cabinet, 201, 205, 213, 393
Cabinet approval, 400–03
Cabinet committees, 394–98
Cabinet memoranda, 401–02
Canada and Its Provinces (Shortt/Doherty), 11
Canada Assistance Plan (CAP), 465–66
Canada Customs and Revenue Agency, 302
Canada Gazette, 210, 269, 273, 646
Canada Health and Social Transfer (CHST), 466
Canadian Broadcasting Corporation (CBC), 224, 235
Canadian Centre for Management Development, 568
Canadian Charter of Rights and Freedoms, 455–57, 581
Canadian Council of Resource and Environment Ministers, 473
Canadian Food Inspection Agency (CFIA), 302
Canadian Human Rights Act, 560
Canadian Human Rights Commissioner, 435
Canadian Intergovernmental Conference Secretariat, 470
Canadian Journal of Program Evaluation, 181

Canadian Public Administration, 6, 11
CAP, 465–66
Capitalism and Freedom (Friedman), 34
Captive agency theory, 279–80
Care perspective, 27–28
Career public service, 570–72
Carpal tunnel syndrome, 538
Case for Bureaucracy, The (Goodsell), 26
CBC, 224, 235
Central agencies, 398–400
coordinating role, 203
defined, 213
Department of Finance, 219
government departments, and, 410–11
Prime Minister's Office, 215–16
Privy Council Office, 216–17
provincial governments, in, 219–20
rationale for, 212–13
roles/responsibilities, 213–15
Treasury Board, 217–19
Centralist intrastate federalism, 465
Certiorari, 454
Charismatic authority, 30
Charlottetown Agreement, 469
Charter of Rights and Freedoms, 455–57, 581
Cheaper by the Dozen, 45
Chief of staff, 418
Choice of governing instrument, 172–75
CIC, 239
Circular response, 63
Citizen participation, 504
Citizen's Code of Regulatory Fairness, 272–73
Civil Service Commission (CSC), 47

Civil Service of Canada (Dawson), 11
Classical elite theory, 29
Classical federalism, 462
Classical technocratic approach, 167–68
Classification standard, 563
Clerk of the Privy Council, 216
Codes of ethics, 374–78
Coercion theory, 172–73
COGO (company-owned-government-operated), 307
Collective bargaining, 311, 596–614
arbitration vs. conciliation-strike, 602–03, 607
bargaining units, 600, 605–07
demotions/terminations, 609
designation issue, 607–08
dispute resolution, 601–05, 607–08
evolution of, 597–99
exclusions from bargaining, 600, 606
future of, 610–11
government restrictions, 608–09
legal/administrative framework, 599–605
master agreement bargaining, 601
provinces, in, 609–10
scope of bargaining, 600, 606–07
Collective ministerial responsibility, 390, 425
Colocation, 304
Coloured papers, 153–55, 507
Commercialization, 309–10
Commissions. *See* Royal commissions
Committee of Senior Officials (COSO), 562
Committees to advise, 408
Committees to evaluate, 408
Committees to initiate, 408

Committees to monitor, 408

Committees to negotiate or arbitrate, 408

Communication, 90–95
  Canadian experience, 113–15
  implementation, and, 169–70
  kinds of, 90–94
  obstacles to, 94–95

Communications overload, 95

Community policing (Edmonton), 182–84

Compensation principle, 249

Competitiveness, 277

Compliance audit, 651

Comprehensive audit, 653–54

Comprehensive rationality, 130–31

Comptrollership volumes, 647

Computers, 532–39
  evolution of computer technology, 534–35
  jobs, and, 536–37
  mental/physical health concerns, 537–38
  privacy/security, 535–36
  special delivery, and, 535
  telework (home work), 538–41

Conceptual skills, 97–98

Conditional grants, 465

Confidentiality of records, 514–15

Conflict of interest, 376–77

Conflict of Interest and Post-Employment Code for the Public Service, 377

Congressional system of government, 202

Consensus Report on the Constitution, 469

Consolidated Revenue Fund, 650

Constitution Act of 1982, 468

Constitution Amendment, 1987, 468

Constitutional relations, 467–70

Consultant lobbyists, 495

Consultation, 508

Consulting and Audit Canada, 306

Consumers' Association of Canada, 284

Consumers' associations, 284

Contingency theory, 80–82

Contract failure, 310

Contracting out, 308–09, 544

Controlled strike, 604

Conventional interest arbitration, 604

Cooperation model, 474

Cooperative federalism, 463

Coordinating Committee of Deputy Ministers, 408

Coordination, 333–35, 391

Corporatism, 32

Correctional Investigator, 434–35

COSO, 562

Council of Maritime Premiers, 473–74

Courts, 446–48

Cover Your Ass, 25

Crown corporations
  accountability, 243
  accountability-autonomy conundrum, 233
  alternative service delivery, and, 305
  annual corporate plan, 235
  annual reports, 235–36, 243–44
  classification system, 232–33
  compensation principle, 249
  criticisms, 240–44

Crown Investments Corporation of Saskatchewan, 239
  directives, 236
  directors, 237–38
  establishment, 233–34
  federal, 226–28

Financial Administration Act, 232, 234
  funding, 236–37
  inefficiency, 240–41
  legislative committees, and, 238–39
  management of, 238
  mandate, 243
  ministerial responsibility, 234–35
  political control of, 233–39
  privatization, 245–49
  profits vs. public purpose, 242
  provincial, 228–29
  rationale for creation of, 229–32
  recent improvements, 244
  reform proposals, 244–49
  single window approach, 244–45
  structure/operation, 240

Crown Corporations and Other Interests of Canada, 244

Crown Investments Corporation (CIC) of Saskatchewan, 239

CRTC, 278

CSC, 47

Culture, 14

Cutbacks, 541–48

D'Avignon Committee, 559, 565

Damages, 455

Day of the Jackal, The, 95

Decentralization, 55–58

Decentralization by place, 57, 59

Decentralization by purpose, 58, 59

Decision letter, 402

Decision-making agencies, 285

Declaratory judgment, 455

Deconcentration, 57

Deficit problems, 17

Delegated legislation, 262, 449

Delivery mechanisms, 199–201
Democracy, 36
Democratic leadership style, 98–99
Demography, 15
Department, 202
See also Government departments
Department of Finance, 219
Department of Justice, 275
Department of Public Works and Government Services, 650–51
Department of Transport, 211–12
Departmental decentralization, 57
Departmental Performance Reports, 179, 632
Deployment, 565, 609
Deputy minister, 210–12, 392, 412–17, 419
Deregulation, 282–83
Descriptive models, 129
Direct regulation, 260
Disabled persons, 583, 589
Discretionary experimenter approach, 167–68
Discretionary powers, 344–46, 449
Dispersed discretions, 345, 449
Distortion, 95
Diversity in Leadership Program, 589
Doomsday hypothesis, 611
Double-image federalism, 464
Downloading, 546
Downsizing, 546
Downward communications, 91
Drag, 69
Dubin Commission, 147

E-filing of tax returns, 303
E-mail (electronic mail), 534
Economic regulation, 260
Economy, 15–16, 326

Edmonton neighbourhood foot patrol program, 182–84
Effectiveness, 327, 668–69
Efficiency, 8–9, 327, 668–69
Efficiency of the Federation Initiative, 472
Elite theorists, 29, 31–32
Emergency federalism, 463
Emergent process view, 82–83
Emerging issues, 665–67
Employee appraisal, 569
Employment equity, 580–84
Empowerment, 110–13
EMS, 629–33
Enhancing the Safety and Soundness of the Canadian Financial System, 154
Entropy, 80
Envelope system, 396
Environmental factors, 14–16
EPF, 466
Equal opportunity, 580
Equal pay for equal work, 590–91
Equal pay for work of equal value, 590
Equalization, 466
Equity, 329, 670
Errors of law, 453–54
Errors of procedure, 452
Essence of Decision (Allison), 136
Established programs financing (EPF), 466
Estimates, 632–33, 644–46
Ethics, 371–78
Evaluation
    current state of, 186–87
    definitions, 180–82
    evaluating, 187–89
    example (Edmonton neighbourhood foot patrol program), 182–84
    impediments to, 184–86
    uses of, 188–89
Evolution scenario, 663

Executive branch, 201–02, 209–10, 389–405
Executive-bureaucratic interaction, 390–92
Executive federalism, 463, 473
Expectancy theory, 104–07
Expenditure budget, 620–20
Expenditure management system (EMS), 629–33
External Advisory Committee on Senior Level Retention and Compensation, 562
External interactions, 322–25
Externalities, 266

Fact finding, 602
Fairness, 329, 452, 670
Federal Court of Appeal, 448
Federal Court of Canada, 447–48
Federal courts, 446–47
Federal Regulatory Plan, 273
Federal-provincial business centres, 305
Federal-provincial committees, 470
Federal-provincial constitutional relations, 467–70
Federal-provincial fiscal relations, 465–67
Federal-provincial independence, 281
Federal-Provincial Relations Office (FPRO), 472
Federal-Provincial Relations Secretariat, 472
Federalism, 462–64
Feedback, 91
Feminine perspective, 27–28
Feminist perspective, 28
Final offer selection, 604
Financial administration, 643–59
    assessment of existing system, 657

auditor general, 651–56
Department of Public
    Works and
    Government
    Services, 650–51
operating departments,
    649–50
overview (chart), 644
Parliament, 644–46
Public Accounts
    Committee, 656
Treasury Board, 646–49
Financial Administration
    Act, 232, 234, 560, 599,
    643
Financial restraint, 541–48
First-level outcomes, 105
First-line supervisor, 98
First Ministers' Conference,
    471
Fiscal relations, 465–67
Flattened tax revenues, 541
Flattening the hierarchy, 50
Flexiplace, 539
Formative evaluation,
    186–87
Francophones, 584–86
Free to Choose (Friedman), 34
Free Trade Agreement
    (FTA), 469
Freedom of information,
    512–17
Friedrich-Finer debate,
    366–68
Functions of the Executive, The
    (Barnard), 65
Future of public administra-
    tion, 663–71

Game theory, 636
    See also Spenders and
        guardians
Gang plank, 93, 116
"Garbage Can Model of
    Organizational Choice,
    A", 82
Geographic decentraliza-
    tion, 56
Geography, 14
Glassco Commission, 558,
    585, 586
Globalization, 16

GOCO (government-
    owned-company-oper-
    ated), 308
Governing instrument, 172
Government departments
    central agencies, and,
        410–11
    classification systems,
        203–07
    definition, 202–03
    executive, and, 209–10
    financial administration,
        and, 649–50
    interdepartmental rela-
        tions, 406–10
    legislature, and, 207–09
    management of, 419–21
    organization, 210–12
Government expenditure,
    17–18
Government Expenditure
    Plan, 632
Governmental politics,
    136–37
Governor general, 201
Governor General in
    Council, 201
Governor General's
    Warrants, 646
Green paper, 154

Habeas corpus, 454
Hackers, 536
Halloween paper, 154
Hawthorne effect, 65
Hawthorne experiments,
    64–65
Head of the Public Service,
    216
*Health Insurance and
    Canadian Public Policy:
    The Seven Decisions That
    Created the Canadian
    Health Insurance System
    and Their Outcomes*
    (Taylor), 128
Hepatitis C, 483
Hierarchy, 391
Hierarchy of needs, 65–66
Hiring freezes, 545
Home work, 538–41

Horizontal administrative
    coordinative depart-
    ments, 203
Horizontal job loading, 104
Horizontal policy coordina-
    tive departments, 203
    See also Central agencies
Horizontal relations, 406–10
Horizontality, 301
Hospitalization, 230
Hughes Royal Commission,
    147
Human relations school, 63
Human resource manage-
    ment, 554–74
    career public service,
        570–72
    history, 556–59
    job classification, 563
    legislative/organizational
        framework, 560–62
    merit, 555–56
    performance evaluation,
        569–70
    planning, 563–64
    staffing, 564–66
    training and develop-
        ment, 566–68
Human resource planning,
    563–64
Human Resources
    Development Council,
    562
Human skills, 97
Hygiene factors, 102–03
Ideal-type bureaucracy, 41
"If You're So Damned
    Smart, Why Don't You
    Run Government like a
    Business", 3
IMAA, 410
Impact evaluation, 183–84
Implementation, 166–75
    choice of governing
        instrument, 172–75
    conditions for effective,
        168–69
    difficulties, 169–72
In-house lobbyists (corpo-
    rate), 495
In-house lobbyists (organi-
    zations), 495

Increased ministerial authority and accountability (IMAA), 410
Incrementalism, 131–32
Individual ministerial responsibility, 209, 354, 390, 425–32
Individual privacy, 518–21, 535–36
Influence, 321
Information Commissioner, 435, 517
Information highway, 532–33
Injunction, 454
Inner cabinet, 213
Institutional framework, 320–25
Institutional groups, 485
Instructed delegate approach, 167
Instrumentality, 105
Integration, 64
Integrity, 329, 371, 670
   See also Ethics
Interdepartmental committees, 407–10
Interdepartmental relations, 406–10
Interdepartmental task forces, 409
Interest groups. See Pressure groups
Intergovernmental administrative relations, 461–82
   constitutional relations, 467–70
   federalism, 462–65
   fiscal relations, 465–67
   intergovernmental officials, 471, 476–79
   interprovincial administrative relations, 473–74
   models, 474–76
   regionalism, 464–65
   structures/processes/participants, 470–72
Intergovernmental affairs specialists, 471, 476–79
Intergovernmental officials, 471, 476–79

Intergovernmental relations, 462
Intergovernmental secretariats, 470
Interim Supply, 645
Internal interactions, 322–25
Interprovincial administrative relations, 473–74
Interstate federalism, 464
Intervener funding, 284
Intradepartmental relations, 411–21
Intragovernmental bargaining, 475–76
Intrastate federalism, 464–65
Investigatory commissions, 145
"Is Scientific Inquiry Compatible with Government Information Control?", 338
Issue-oriented groups, 485

Job classification, 563
Job enlargement, 103–04
Job enrichment, 104
Job evaluation, 563
Job redesign, 103–04
Job rotation, 103
Joint enterprises, 226
Joint regulatory mechanisms, 286
Judicial deference, 271
Judicial review
   appeal/review, 450
   Charter of Rights, 455–57
   classification of function, 450
   discretionary powers, 449
   focus on agencies, 448
   forms of relief, 454–55
   grounds for review, 450–54
   privative clauses, 455
   utility of, 457–58
Judiciary, 445–60

Krever Commission, 146

La Relève, 559
Labour relations. See Collective bargaining
Laissez-faire leadership style, 98
Lambert Commission, 147, 236, 369, 370, 415, 424, 425, 439
Language differences, 94
Lateral communication, 92–94
Leadership, 95–99
   Canadian experience, 113–15
   situational/contingency theories, 99–100
   styles, 98–99
   traits/skills, 97–98
Leaking of information, 518
Legal authority, 30
Legislative branch, 201, 207–09, 424–44
Legislative committees, 436–37, 507
Les Employés (Balzac), 25
Libertarian theory, 34–36
Lieutenant Governor in Council, 201
Lieutenant governors, 201
Limited strike model, 610
Line function, 52–54
Line-item budgeting, 621–24
Linkages between institutional/value frameworks, 331–33
Little Dorrit (Dickens), 25
Lobbying, 484
   See also Pressure groups
Lobbyists' Code of Conduct, 496
Lobbyists Registration Act, 495
M.P.A. degree, 13
Main Estimates, 632
Majority government, 208
Management by wandering around (MBWA), 92
Management information system (MIS), 533–34

See also Computers
Managing diversity, 590
Mandamus, 454
Manitoba Education and Training mission statement, 530
Margaret Johnson v. The Minister of Veterans Affairs, 445
Mario Duarte v. Her Majesty the Queen, 456–57
Market scenario, 664
Martineau v. Matsqui Institution Disciplinary Board, 454
Marxism, 28
See also Modern Marxist theory
Mass media, 509–12
Master agreement bargaining, 601
Master of Public Administration (M.P.A.) degree, 13
Maturity-immaturity theory, 100–02
MBWA, 92
McGrath Committee, 440
Media, 509–12
Meech Lake Accord, 468–69
Memoranda of understanding (MOUs), 410
Memorandum to Cabinet, 400–01
Merit, 555–56
Merit principle, 347, 555
Merit system, 347, 555
Mini-ombudsmen, 434–35
Ministerial assistants, 417–19
Ministerial responsibility
  anonymity, 354
  answerability of Ministers, 429–32
  collective, 390
  freedom of information, and, 513–14
  individual, 390
  political neutrality, and, 425–32
  resignation of Ministers, 426–29

Ministerial staff, 417–19
Ministers, 210
  answerability, 429–31
  delegation of duties to deputy, 414
  pressure to make changes, 211
  resignation of, 426–29
Ministry of State for Economic and Regional Development (MSERD), 395, 396, 399
Ministry of State for Social Development (MSSD), 395, 396, 399
Minority government, 208
Mirror committees, 407
Mixed-enterprise corporations, 7
Mixed enterprises, 226, 250
Mixed scanning, 133–34
Modern concepts of bureaucracy, 24
Modern elite theory, 31–32
Modern Marxist theory, 33–34
Money bills, 644
Moonlighting, 376
Motivation
  Canadian experience, 113–15
  empowerment, 110–13
  expectancy theory, 104–07
  Japanese management, 107–10
  job redesign, 103–04
  maturity-immaturity theory, 100–02
  motivation-hygiene theory, 102–03
  Theory Z, 107–10
Motivation-hygiene theory, 102–03
MOUs, 410

Nationalized industries, 229
Native peoples, 583, 587–88
Natural justice, 451–52
NavCanada, 310
Negative entropy, 80

Nemo judex in sua causa debet esse, 451
Neo-Marxism, 33–34, 142–43
Neo-Marxist approach (choosing governing instruments), 173
Neoconservatism, 35–36
Neutrality, 326, 667–68
  See also Political neutrality
New public management (NPM), 77–79, 343
New values, 329–30, 670
Nicholson v. Haldimand-Norfolk Police Commrs. Bd., 452
Noise, 95
Normative models, 129
North America Free Trade Agreement (NAFTA), 469
NPM, 77–79, 343

Objective responsibility, 369
Objectively responsible public servants, 381
Occupational category, 563
OD, 69–72
Office of the Auditor General (OAG), 435–36, 651–56
Official Languages Act, 560
Official Languages Commissioner, 434–35
Official Languages Program, 585
Official reticence, 351
Official Secrets Act, 351
Ombudsman, 433–34
One best way, 45, 47
Open systems theory, 78–80
Operating department. *See* Government departments
Operational performance measurement system (OPMS), 420
Optimistic hypothesis, 611
Orange paper, 154
Order in council, 209

Organization by process, 51–52, 59

Organization by purpose, 51–52, 59

Organization chart, 391

Organization development (OD), 69–72

Organization theory, 40–88
Canadian experience, 47–48, 76–78
centralization/decentralization, 55–58
contingency theory, 80–82
emergent process view, 82–83
humanistic response, 62–88
new public management, 77–79
open systems theory, 78–80
organization development, 69–72
organizational humanism, 63–68, 76
participatory management, 68–76
proverbs of administration, 54–55
scientific management, 44–47
scientific theory of organization, 48–54
total quality management, 72–74, 76–77
Weberian bureaucracy, 41–44

Organizational culture, 70

Organizational humanism, 63–68, 76

Organizational socialization, 330

Organized irresponsibility, 346

Other entities, 226

Outcome evaluation, 183

Outside employment, 376

Outsourcing, 308–09, 544

Padding the budget, 634

Parent corporations, 225

Parkinson's Law, 25

Parliamentary committees, 436–37

Parliamentary systems, 202

Participative leadership style, 98

Participatory management, 68–76

Partisan mutual adjustment, 334

Partnerships, 306–08

Patronage, 347–49

Pay equity, 590–92

PCO, 216–17, 275, 399

PEMS, 396

Performance budgeting, 622, 624

Performance evaluation, 569–70

Performance indicators, 176

Performance measurement, 175–80

Performance review, 569

Permanence in office, 356–58

Personal Information Index, 519, 521

Personal power, 321

Planning programming budgeting system (PPBS), 420

Pluralism, 30–31

PMO, 215–16, 399

Policy and expenditure management system (PEMS), 396

Policy communities, 137–38, 495

Policy development, 344

Policy formation, 344

Policy implementation, 344

Policy institutes, 486

Policy-making process, 125–64
bounded rationality, 132–33
coloured papers, 153–55
comprehensive rationality, 130–31

governmental/bureaucratic politics, 136–37
incrementalism, 131–32
Marxist analysis, 142–43
mixed scanning, 133–34
overview (charts), 126
policy communities, 137–38
public choice, 134–36
Royal commissions, 143–53
socio-economic determinants, 139–42

Policy networks, 138, 495

Political aides, 417

Political appointments, 347–49, 357–58

Political neutrality
bureaucratic power, and, 358–60
doctrine of, 339–40
freedom of information, and, 513–14
ministerial responsibility, and, 425–32
on the decline, 668
threats to, 571
value neutrality, distinguished, 326

Political parties, 496–98

Political partisanship, 349–51

Political regulation, 287

Political staff, 417

Political sterilization, 349

Political support, 9

Politicized public service, 357–58, 476

Politics of Public Spending in Canada (Savoie), 637

Politics-administration dichotomy, 340–47

Pollution, 283

Porter-Rowat debate, 577–78

POSDCORB, 52

Position power, 321

Post-audit, 651

Post-employment problem, 377

Power, 320

See also Bureaucratic power
Pre-audit procedures, 649
Prerogative remedies, 454
Pressure groups, 483–96
  definition/classification, 484–87
  functions, 487–88
  Lobbyists Registration Act, 495
  Lobbyists' Code of Conduct, 496
  political parties, and, 498
  recognition of, 491–92
  self-interest, 503–04
  tactics, 492–95
  targets, 488–91
Prime minister, 206, 393–94
Prime Minister's Office (PMO), 215–16, 399
Principles for the Evaluation of Program by Federal Departments and Agencies, 648
Privacy, 518–21, 535–36
Privacy Act, 518–19
Privacy Commissioner, 435, 519
Private administration, 7–11
Private sector model, 609
Private sector organizations, 7
Privative clauses, 455
Privatization, 245–49
Privy Council Office (PCO), 216–17, 275, 399
Procedural fairness, 452
Process evaluation, 183–84
Program budgeting, 622, 624–29
Program delivery alternatives. *See* Alternative service delivery
Program evaluation, 180
  See also Evaluation
Program review, 547–48
Program termination, 546
Programmed implementation, 168
Prohibition, 454
Promotion, 565

Proverbs of administration, 54–55
Provincial auditors, 436
Provincial commissions, 151
Provincial courts, 446–47
Provincial intrastate federalism, 465
Provincial legislatures, 201
Provincial privacy legislation, 521–22
Public Accounts, 650, 651
Public Accounts Committee (PAC), 437, 656
Public administration
  administrative science, as, 13
  definitions, 5–6
  environmental influences, 14–16
  future of, 663–71
  growth of, 16–19
  mission, 7
  political science, as, 12
  private administration, contrasted, 7–11
  public bureaucracy, contrasted, 6
  scope, 4–5
  study of, 11–14
Public bureaucracy, 23–39
  classical theories of bureaucracy, 28–30
  criticisms, 24–27
  democracy, and, 36
  evolution, 24
  feminist critique, 27–28
  modern theories of bureaucracy, 30–36
  praise, 26
  public administration, contrasted, 6
Public choice, 134–36, 174
Public comment, 351–54
Public corporations, 7
Public enterprises, 225–26
  See also Crown corporations
Public interest, 378–82
Public interest groups, 485, 504
Public opinion, 503–04
Public opinion surveys, 507

Public participation, 504–09
Public policy, 126–30
Public scrutiny, 10
Public Sector Compensation Restraint Act, 608
Public sector growth, 16–19
Public sector reforms, 19
Public service anonymity, 354–55
Public Service Commission, 435, 560–61
Public Service Employment Act, 560, 599
Public service ethics, 371–78
Public Service Rearrangement and Transfer of Duties Act, 206, 208
Public Service Staff Relations Act, 560, 599–601, 603
Public Service Staff Relations Board, 561
Public Service Superannuation Act, 560
Public support, 9

Quality circle, 109
Quasi-federalism, 462
Quasi-private sector model, 610
Quiet Revolution, 585
Quo warranto, 454

Recruitment, 565
Regionalism, 464
Regulation-making process, 272–75
Regulatory agencies, 258–93
  accountability-autonomy conundrum, 267, 285
  adjudication process, 275–76
  appeal, 270
  appointment of members, 268–69
  captive agency theory, 279–80

compliance, 278
consumer representatives, as, 279
consumers' associations, 284
criticisms, 276–82
definition, 259–61
deregulation, 282–83
enabling legislation, 268
federalism, and, 280–82
functions, 261–63
hearings, 276
intervener funding, 284
judicial control of, 270–71
judicial review, 448–58
legislative committees, and, 268
organizational structure, 271–72
policy directives, 286
policy statements/directives, 269–70
political control, 267–70
prior approval of decisions, 270
rationale for, 263–67
reform proposals, 282–87
regulation-making process, 272–75
Standing Joint Committee on Scrutiny of Regulations, 268, 437
sunset legislation, 283
Regulatory agency independence, 281
Regulatory functions, 4
Regulatory impact analysis statement (RIAS), 273–74
Reinventing Government (Osborne/Gaebler), 297, 547
Removing layers of management, 50
Renaissance scenario, 664
Repetitive strain injury (RSI), 538

Report on Plans and Priorities (RPP), 178–79, 632
Representative bureaucracy, 575–80
Representative cabinet, 213
Representativeness, 328–29, 669
Research activities, 4
Responsibility, 365–70, 381–82
Responsiveness, 328, 669
Restraint programs, 541–48
Results-based management, 176–78
Revenue budget, 616–20
RIAS, 273–74
Rightsizing, 546
Road to Serfdom, The (Hayek), 34
Roncarelli v. Duplessis, 453
Rowing, 297
Royal commissions, 143–53
academic research, 150
categories, 145
criticisms, 151–53
fact finding, 147
identifying innovative approaches, 147
interim reports, 151
low-cost way of showing concern, 148
objective policy analysis, 146–47
operation, 149–51
postponing an embarrassing problem, 148
provincial commissions, 151
public participation movements, and, 507
stimulating interaction with public, 148
when used, 145
Ruling Class, The (Mosca), 29

Satisficing, 133
Scenarios of the future, 663–64

Schedule I Crown corporations, 232
Schedule II Crown corporations, 232
Schedule III-Part I Crown corporations, 233
Schedule III-Part II Crown corporations, 232
Scientific management, 44–47
Scientific theory of organization, 48–54
Second-level outcomes, 105
Sectoral deputy minister committees, 407
Security of tenure, 356–58
Selection, 565
Senior managers, 98
Serial decision making, 131
Service delivery mechanisms, 199–201
Service functions, 4
Shared-cost programs, 465, 467
Silo approach to management/service delivery, 301
Singh v. Minister of Employment and Immigration, 456
Single window approach, 244, 304–05
Situational theories, 99–100
6 and 5 program, 608
SOAs, 306
Social regulation, 260
Social surveys, 507
Socialization, 330
Socio-economic determinants, 139–42
Soldiering, 45
Somalia affair, 319
Span of control, 48–50
Special committees, 436
Special interest groups, 485
Special Measures Initiatives Fund, 589
Special operating agencies (SOAs), 306
Specialized ombudsmen, 434–35

Spenders and guardians, 633–36
Spill-overs, 266
Staff function, 53–54
Staffing, 564–66
Standards of Conduct for Public Service Employees, 375
Standing committees, 436
Standing Joint Committee on Scrutiny of Regulations, 268, 437
Statesman type of public servant, 332
Statistical process control (SPC), 72
Statutory instruments, 437
Steering, 297
Strategic planning, 528–32
"Study of Administration, The" (Wilson), 11, 341
Subdelegate authority, 449
Subgovernment, 138
Subjective responsibility, 369
Subjectively responsible public servants, 381–82
Subordinate legislation, 449
Summative evaluation, 186–87
Sunset legislation, 283
Supplementary Estimates, 646
Supply management, 265
Supreme Court of Canada, 446
SWOT analysis, 531
Sympathetic observer effect, 65
Systemic barriers (discrimination), 582

Task forces, 143–44
    See also Royal commissions
Tax collection agency, 312
Tax collection agreement, 465
Tax expenditures, 616

TB. *See* Treasury Board (TB)
TBS, 217–18, 275, 328, 647
Team participation, 112
Technical skills, 97
Technocratic theory, 31
Technological change, 14
Technology of the obvious, 92
Telecommuting, 539
Telework, 538–41
Theory X, 66–67
Theory Y, 66–67
Theory Z, 107–10
Think tanks, 486–87
Three Es, 327, 653
Time-and-motion study, 45
Total quality management (TQM), 72–74, 76–77
TQM, 72–74, 76–77
Trade unions. *See* Collective bargaining
Traditional authority, 30
Training and development, 566–68
Transfer payments, 465–67, 542
Treasury Board (TB)
    efficiency/effectiveness, and, 328
    evaluations, and, 186
    financial management, and, 646–49
    overview, 217–19, 560
    senior officers, 212
Treasury Board Manual, 647
Treasury Board Secretariat (TBS), 217–18, 275, 328, 647
Treasury Board submission, 402
Turf wars, 299

Ultra vires, 268, 452–53
Unconditional grants, 466–67
Unions. *See* Collective bargaining
Unity of command, 42

Upward communications, 91
User charges/fees, 303–04, 544

Valence, 105
Value conflict, 332–33
Value framework, 325–30
Value neutrality, 326
Values, 327–30, 667–70
Valuing differences, 589–90
Vertical constituency departments, 204
Vertical job loading, 104
Vertical Solitude, The (Zussman/Jabes), 114
Visible minorities, 583, 588–89
Volunteers, 544
Vroom-Yetton normative model, 99–100

Wage roll backs, 545
Watchdog agencies, 433–36
Web sites, 534–35
Weberian bureaucracy, 41–44
Western Premiers' Conference, 473
When in Doubt: Mumble, 25
Whistle blowing, 517–18
White paper, 154
Wicked problems, 301
Women
    employment equity, 580–84
    pay equity, 590–92
    representation of, 583, 586–87
Work and Motivation (Vroom), 104
Workforce adjustment, 546
Workplace safety, 283
Workplace tension, 545–46
Workteams, 112

Zealots, 379

To the owner of this book

We hope that you have enjoyed *Public Administration in Canada: A Text,* fourth edition, and we would like to know as much about your experiences with this text as you would care to offer. Only through your comments and those of others can we learn how to make this a better text for future readers.

School _____ Your instructor's name _____

Course _____ Was the text required? _____ Recommended? _____

1. What did you like the most about *Public Administration in Canada?*

_____
_____
_____

2. How useful was this text for your course?

_____
_____
_____

3. Do you have any recommendations for ways to improve the next edition of this text?

_____
_____
_____

4. In the space below or in a separate letter, please write any other comments you have about the book. (For example, please feel free to comment on reading level, writing style, terminology, design features, and learning aids.)

_____
_____
_____
_____

Optional

Your name _____ Date _____

May ITP Nelson quote you, either in promotion for *Public Administration in Canada* or in future publishing ventures?

Yes _____ No _____

Thanks!

You can also send your comments to us via e-mail at
college_arts_hum@nelson.com

PLEASE TAPE SHUT. DO NOT STAPLE.

TAPE SHUT

TAPE SHUT

- - - - - - - - - - FOLD HERE - - - - - - - - - -

MAIL≫POSTE
Canada Post Corporation
Société canadienne des postes

Postage paid	Port payé
if mailed in Canada	si posté au Canada
Business Reply	**Réponse d'affaires**

0066102399   **01**

Nelson

0066102399-M1K5G4-BR01

TAPE SHUT

TAPE SHUT

```
ITP NELSON
MARKET AND PRODUCT DEVELOPMENT
PO BOX 60225 STN BRM B
TORONTO ON M7Y 2H1
```